Reading STREET

Grade 4, Unit 2

Work and Play

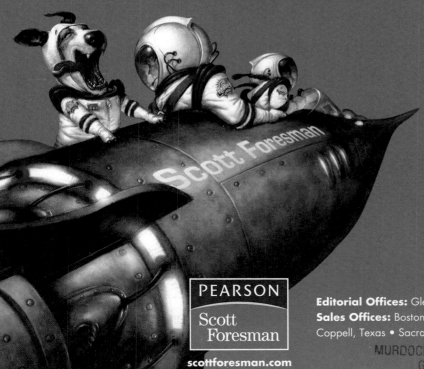

PEARSON

Scott Foresman

scottforesman.com

Editorial Offices: Glenview, Illinois • Parsippany, New Jersey • New York, New York
Sales Offices: Boston, Massachusetts • Duluth, Georgia • Glenview, Illinois
Coppell, Texas • Sacramento, California • Mesa, Arizona

We dedicate Reading Street to
Peter Jovanovich.

His wisdom, courage,
and passion for education
are an inspiration to us all.

This work is protected by United States copyright laws and is provided *solely for the use of teachers and administrators* in teaching courses and assessing student learning in their classes and schools. Dissemination or sale of any part of this work (including the World Wide Web) will destroy the integrity of the work and is *not* permitted.

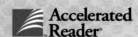
Cover Tim Jessell

About the Cover Artist

Tim Jessell draws and paints in Stillwater, Oklahoma. He and his wife are raising three great children, whom he coaches in many sports. When not playing catch or illustrating, Tim trains falcons for the sport of falconry. Occasionally, he can still be found making a racket behind his drum set, with kids dancing around.

ISBN-13: 978-0-328-24380-8

ISBN-10: 0-328-24380-9

Copyright © 2008 Pearson Education, Inc.

2 3 4 5 6 7 8 9 10 11 V063 16 15 14 13 12 11 10 09 08 07
CC:N1

Reading

STREET

Where the Love of Reading Begins

Reading Street Program Authors

Peter Afflerbach, Ph.D.
Professor, Department of
Curriculum and Instruction
University of Maryland at
College Park

Camille L.Z. Blachowicz, Ph.D.
Professor of Education
National-Louis University

Candy Dawson Boyd, Ph.D.
Professor, School of Education
Saint Mary's College of California

Wendy Cheyney, Ed.D.
Professor of Special Education
and Literacy, Florida
International University

Connie Juel, Ph.D.
Professor of Education, School of
Education, Stanford University

Edward J. Kame'enui, Ph.D.
Professor and Director, Institute for
the Development of Educational
Achievement, University of Oregon

Donald J. Leu, Ph.D.
John and Maria Neag Endowed
Chair in Literacy and Technology
University of Connecticut

Jeanne R. Paratore, Ed.D.
Associate Professor of Education
Department of Literacy
and Language Development
Boston University

P. David Pearson, Ph.D.
Professor and Dean,
Graduate School of Education
University of California, Berkeley

Sam L. Sebesta, Ed.D.
Professor Emeritus,
College of Education,
University of Washington, Seattle

Deborah Simmons, Ph.D.
Professor, College of Education
and Human Development
Texas A&M University
(Not pictured)

Sharon Vaughn, Ph.D.
H.E. Hartfelder/Southland
Corporation Regents Professor
University of Texas

Susan Watts-Taffe, Ph.D.
Independent Literacy Researcher
Cincinnati, Ohio

Karen Kring Wixson, Ph.D.
Professor of Education
University of Michigan

Components

Student Editions (1–6)

Teacher's Editions (PreK–6)

Assessment
Assessment Handbook (K–6)

Baseline Group Tests (K–6)

DIBELS™ Assessments (K–6)

ExamView® Test Generator CD-ROM (2–6)

Fresh Reads for Differentiated
Test Practice (1–6)

Online Success Tracker™ (K–6)*

Selection Tests Teacher's Manual (1–6)

Unit and End-of-Year
Benchmark Tests (K–6)

Leveled Readers
Concept Literacy Leveled Readers (K–1)

Independent Leveled Readers (K)

Kindergarten Student Readers (K)

Leveled Reader Teaching Guides (K–6)

Leveled Readers (1–6)

Listen to Me Readers (K)

Online Leveled Reader Database (K–6)*

Take-Home Leveled Readers (K–6)

Trade Books and Big Books
Big Books (PreK–2)

Read Aloud Trade Books (PreK–K)

Sing with Me Big Book (1–2)

Trade Book Library (1–6)

Decodable Readers
Decodable Readers (K–3)

Strategic Intervention
Decodable Readers (1–2)

Take-Home Decodable Readers (K–3)

Phonics and Word Study
Alphabet Cards in English and Spanish
(PreK–K)

Alphabet Chart in English and Spanish
(PreK–K)

Animal ABCs Activity Guide (K)

Finger Tracing Cards (PreK–K)

Patterns Book (PreK–K)

Phonics Activities CD-ROM (PreK–2)*

Phonics Activities Mats (K)

Phonics and Spelling Practice Book (1–3)

Phonics and Word-Building Board and Letters
(PreK–3)

Phonics Songs and Rhymes Audio CD (K–2)

Phonics Songs and Rhymes Flip Chart (K–2)

Picture Word Cards (PreK–K)

Plastic Letter Tiles (K)

Sound-Spelling Cards and Wall Charts (1–2)

Strategies for Word Analysis (4–6)

Word Study and Spelling Practice Book (4–6)

Language Arts
Daily Fix-It Transparencies (K–6)

Grammar & Writing Book and
Teacher's Annotated Edition, The (1–6)

Grammar and Writing Practice Book
and Teacher's Manual (1–6)

Grammar Transparencies (1–6)

Six-Trait Writing Posters (1–6)

Writing Kit (1–6)

Writing Rubrics and Anchor Papers (1–6)

Writing Transparencies (1–6)

Practice and Additional Resources
AlphaBuddy Bear Puppet (K)

Alphasaurus Annie Puppet (PreK)

Amazing Words Posters (K–2)

Centers Survival Kit (PreK–6)

Graphic Organizer Book (2–6)

Graphic Organizer Flip Chart (K–1)

High-Frequency Word Cards (K)

Kindergarten Review (1)

Practice Book and Teacher's Manual (K–6)

Read Aloud Anthology (PreK–2)

Readers' Theater Anthology (K–6)

Research into Practice (K–6)

Retelling Cards (K–6)

Scott Foresman Research Base (K–6)

Skill Transparencies (2–6)

Songs and Rhymes Flip Chart (PreK)

Talk with Me, Sing with Me Chart (PreK–K)

Tested Vocabulary Cards (1–6)

Vocabulary Transparencies (1–2)

Welcome to Reading Street (PreK–1)

ELL
ELL and Transition Handbook (PreK–6)

ELL Comprehensive Kit (1–6)

ELL Posters (K–6)

ELL Readers (1–6)

ELL Teaching Guides (1–6)

Ten Important Sentences (1–6)

Digital Components
AudioText CDs (PreK–6)

Background Building Audio CDs (3–6)

ExamView® Test Generator
CD-ROM (2–6)

Online Lesson Planner (K–6)

Online New Literacies Activities (1–6)*

Online Professional Development (1–6)

Online Story Sort (K–6)*

Online Student Editions (1–6)*

Online Success Tracker™ (K–6)*

Online Teacher's Editions (PreK–6)

Phonics Activities CD-ROM (PreK–2)*

Phonics Songs and Rhymes
Audio CD (K–2)

Sing with Me/Background Building
Audio CDs (PreK–2)

Songs and Rhymes Audio CD (PreK)

My Sidewalks Early Reading Intervention (K)

My Sidewalks Intensive Reading Intervention (Levels A–E)

Reading Street for the Guided Reading Teacher (1–6)

v

Unit 2
Work & Play

Unit Opener. 140a
Unit 2 Skills Overview 140c
Unit 2 Monitor Progress 140e
Grouping for AYP 140g
Theme Launch 140
Unit 2 Inquiry Project 141
Unit 2 Concept Development 141a

What Jo Did. 142a–161l
by Charles R. Smith Jr.
Poetry
**Fast Break/Allow Me
to Introduce Myself** 158

Coyote School News 162a–187l
by Joan Sandin
Social Studies in Reading
**How to Start
a School Newspaper** 186

**Grace and
the Time Machine** 188a–211l
From *Starring Grace* by Mary Hoffman
adapted for Story Theater by Donald Abramson
Social Studies in Reading
What's There to Do? 210

**Marven of the
Great North Woods** 212a–239l
by Kathryn Lasky
Reading Online
Logging Camps 236

**So You Want to
Be President?** 240a–259l
by Judith St. George
Social Studies in Reading
Our National Parks 258

Unit 2 Concept Wrap-Up 260a
Unit 2 Reading Poetry 260
Unit 2 Wrap-Up 264
Glossary. 265a
ELL Glossary 265g

Writing and Assessment WA1–WA18

Leveled Resources LR1–LR48

Differentiated Instruction . . . . . DI•1–DI•60

Teacher Resources TR1–TR25

Unit 3
Patterns in Nature

Unit Opener. 266a
Unit 3 Skills Overview 266c
Unit 3 Monitor Progress 266e
Grouping for AYP 266g
Theme Launch 266
Unit 3 Inquiry Project 267
Unit 3 Concept Development 267a

The Stranger 268a–291l
by Chris Van Allsburg
Science in Reading
Time for a Change 288

Adelina's Whales 292a–313l
by Richard Sobol
Science in Reading
Sea Animals on the Move 310

**How Night Came
from the Sea** 314a–337l
retold by Mary–Joan Gerson
Folk Literature
The Ant and the Bear 334

Eye of the Storm 338a–359l
by Stephen Kramer
Reading Online
Severe Weather Safety 356

The Great Kapok Tree 360a–383l
by Lynne Cherry
Science in Reading
Living in a World of Green 380

Unit 3 Concept Wrap-Up 384a
Unit 3 Reading Poetry 384
Unit 3 Wrap-Up 388
Glossary. 389a
ELL Glossary 389g

Writing and Assessment WA1–WA18

Leveled Resources LR1–LR48

Differentiated Instruction . . . . . . DI•1–DI•60

Teacher Resources TR1–TR25

Unit 4
Puzzles and Mysteries

Unit Opener 390a
Unit 4 Skills Overview 390c
Unit 4 Monitor Progress 390e
Grouping for AYP 390g
Theme Launch 390
Unit 4 Inquiry Project 391
Unit 4 Concept Development 391a

The Houdini Box 392a–415l
by Brian Selznick

Science in Reading
So You Want to Be an Illusionist . . 412

Encantado: Pink Dolphin of the Amazon 416a–439l
by Sy Montgomery

Science in Reading
Mysterious Animals 436

The King in the Kitchen 440a–465l
by Margaret E. Slattery

Poetry
A Man for All Seasonings/ A Confectioner/Expert 464

Seeker of Knowledge 466a–487l
by James Rumford

Reading Online
Word Puzzles 484

Encyclopedia Brown and the Case of the Slippery Salamander . . . 488a–507l
by Donald J. Sobol

Science in Reading
Young Detectives of Potterville Middle School 504

Unit 4 Concept Wrap–Up 508a
Unit 4 Reading Poetry 508
Unit 4 Wrap–Up 512
Glossary 513a
ELL Glossary 513g

Writing and Assessment WA1–WA18

Leveled Resources LR1–LR48

Differentiated Instruction . . . . DI•1–DI•60

Teacher Resources TR1–TR25

Unit 5
Adventures by Land, Air, and Water

Unit Opener 514a
Unit 5 Skills Overview 514c
Unit 5 Monitor Progress 514e
Grouping for AYP 514g
Theme Launch 514
Unit 5 Inquiry Project 515
Unit 5 Concept Development 515a

Sailing Home: A Story of a Childhood at Sea 516a–537l
by Gloria Rand

Social Studies in Reading
Sharing a Dream 536

Lost City: The Discovery of Machu Picchu 538a–559l
by Ted Lewin

Social Studies in Reading
Riding the Rails to Machu Picchu . . 556

Amelia and Eleanor Go for a Ride 560a–581l
by Pam Muñoz Ryan

Reading Online
Women Explorers 578

Antarctic Journal 582a–607l
by Jennifer Owings Dewey

Social Studies in Reading
Swimming Towards Ice 604

Moonwalk 608a–629l
by Ben Bova

Science in Reading
A Walk on the Moon 626

Unit 5 Concept Wrap–Up 630a
Unit 5 Reading Poetry 630
Unit 5 Wrap–Up 634
Glossary 635a
ELL Glossary 635g

Writing and Assessment WA1–WA18

Leveled Resources LR1–LR48

Differentiated Instruction . . . . DI•1–DI•60

Teacher Resources TR1–TR25

Unit 6
Reaching for Goals

Unit Opener 636a
Unit 6 Skills Overview 636c
Unit 6 Monitor Progress 636e
Grouping for AYP 636g
Theme Launch 636
Unit 6 Inquiry Project 637
Unit 6 Concept Development 637a

My Brother Martin 638a–659l
by Christine King Farris

Poetry
**Hopes and Dreams
of Young People** 658

Jim Thorpe's Bright Path 660a–685l
by Joseph Bruchac

Social Studies in Reading
**Special Olympics,
Spectacular Athletes** 682

**How Tía Lola
Came to ~~Visit~~ Stay** 686a–711l
by Julia Alvarez

Social Studies in Reading
The Difficult Art of Hitting 708

**To Fly: The Story of
the Wright Brothers** 712a–737l
by Wendie C. Old

Reading Online
Early Flying Machines 734

**The Man Who Went to
the Far Side of the Moon** . . . 738a–761l
by Bea Uusma Schyffert

Science in Reading
The Earth and the Moon 758

Unit 6 Concept Wrap–Up 762a
Unit 6 Reading Poetry 762
Unit 6 Wrap–Up 766
Glossary. 767a
ELL Glossary 767g

Writing and Assessment WA1–WA18

Leveled Resources LR1–LR48

Differentiated Instruction . . . . . DI•1–DI•60

Teacher Resources TR1–TR25

Unit 1
This Land Is
Your Land

Unit Opener 16a
Unit 1 Skills Overview 16c
Unit 1 Monitor Progress 16e
Grouping for AYP 16g
Theme Launch 16
Unit 1 Inquiry Project 17
Unit 1 Concept Development 17a

Because of Winn–Dixie 18a–39l
by Kate DiCamillo

Science in Reading
Fast Facts: Black Bears 36

Lewis and Clark and Me 40a–65l
by Laurie Myers

Social Studies in Reading
**They Traveled with
Lewis and Clark** 62

Grandfather's Journey 66a–87l
by Allen Say

Reading Online
A Look at Two Lands 84

The Horned Toad Prince 88a–111l
by Jackie Mims Hopkins

Science in Reading
**Horned Lizards and
Harvesting Ants** 108

**Letters Home
from Yosemite**. 112a–133l
by Lisa Halvorsen

Poetry
This Land Is Your Land 130

Unit 1 Concept Wrap–Up 134a
Unit 1 Reading Poetry 134
Unit 1 Wrap–Up 138
Genre/Author Studies 139a
Author/Illustrator Biographies 139c
Glossary. 139q
ELL Glossary 139w

Writing and Assessment WA1–WA18

Leveled Resources LR1–LR48

Differentiated Instruction . . . . . DI•1–DI•60

Teacher Resources TR1–TR25

Work & Play

What is the value of work and play?

What Jo Did

A basketball player shows surprising skill.

FICTION

connect to SOCIAL STUDIES

Paired Selection

"Fast Break" and "Allow Me to Introduce Myself"

POETRY

Coyote School News

Children in a country school publish a newspaper.

HISTORICAL FICTION

connect to SOCIAL STUDIES

Paired Selection

How to Start a School Newspaper

HOW-TO ARTICLE

Grace and the Time Machine

Friends use their imaginations to travel through time.

PLAY

connect to SOCIAL STUDIES

Paired Selection

What's There to Do?

EXPOSITORY NONFICTION

Marven of the Great North Woods

A boy keeps the books at a Minnesota logging camp.

BIOGRAPHY

connect to SOCIAL STUDIES

Paired Selection

Logging Camps

E-MAIL

So You Want to Be President?

Every President leaves a mark on history.

EXPOSITORY NONFICTION

connect to SOCIAL STUDIES

Paired Selection

Our National Parks

EXPOSITORY NONFICTION

Unit 2
Skills Overview

		WEEK 1 146–161 **What Jo Did/ Fast Break/ "Allow Me to Introduce Myself"** **FICTION** *How can we learn to appreciate the talents of others?*	**WEEK 2** 166–187 **Coyote School News/How to Start a School Newspaper** **HISTORICAL FICTION** *How can we work together to achieve a goal?*
Reading	**Comprehension**	**T** ◉ **Skill** Cause and Effect ◉ **Strategy** Prior Knowledge **T** REVIEW **Skill** Draw Conclusions	**T** ◉ **Skill** Draw Conclusions ◉ **Strategy** Prior Knowledge **T** REVIEW **Skill** Setting
	Vocabulary	**T** ◉ **Strategy** Word Structure	**T** ◉ **Strategy** Dictionary/Glossary
	Fluency	Rhythmic Patterns of Language	Emotion
Word Work	**Spelling and Phonics**	Adding -s and -es	Irregular Plurals
Oral Language	**Speaking/Listening/ Viewing**	Sportscast Analyze Media	Newscast Listen to a Newscast
Language Arts	**Grammar, Usage, and Mechanics**	**T** Common and Proper Nouns	**T** Regular Plural Nouns
	Weekly Writing	Poem Writing Trait: Word Choice	News Story Writing Trait: Focus/Ideas
	Unit Process Writing	How-to Report	How-to Report
	Research and Study Skills	Technology: Chart/Table	Newspaper/Newsletter
	Integrate Science and Social Studies Standards	Time for SOCIAL STUDIES U.S. History	Time for SOCIAL STUDIES U.S. History

◉ Target Skill   **T** Tested Skill

	WEEK 3	WEEK 4	WEEK 5
	192–211 **Grace and the Time Machine/ What's There to Do?** PLAY *What can we accomplish by using our imaginations?*	216–239 **Marven of the Great North Woods/ Logging Camps** BIOGRAPHY *What is the value of a job well done?*	244–259 **So You Want to Be President?/ Our National Parks** EXPOSITORY NONFICTION *What is the job of the President of the United States?*
	T 🔊 **Skill** Draw Conclusions 🔊 **Strategy** Answer Questions **T** REVIEW **Skill** Compare and Contrast	**T** 🔊 **Skill** Fact and Opinion 🔊 **Strategy** Monitor and Fix Up **T** REVIEW **Skill** Main Idea	**T** 🔊 **Skill** Main Idea 🔊 **Strategy** Summarize **T** REVIEW **Skill** Generalize
	T 🔊 **Strategy** Word Structure	**T** 🔊 **Strategy** Dictionary/Glossary	**T** 🔊 **Strategy** Dictionary/Glossary
	Characterization/Dialogue	Volume	Stress/Emphasis
	Words with *ar, or*	Consonant Pairs *ng, nk, ph, wh*	Words with *ear, ir, our, ur*
	Dramatization Analyze Media	Job Description Listen to a Description	Press Conference Analyze a Speech
	T Irregular Plural Nouns	**T** Singular Possessive Nouns	**T** Plural Possessive Nouns
	Play Scene Writing Trait: Organization/Paragraphs	Describe a Job Writing Trait: Focus/Ideas	Explanation Writing Trait: Organization/Paragraphs
	How-to Report	How-to Report	How-to Report
	Advertisement	Graph	Time Line

 Literature, Geography

 U.S. Geography, Citizenship, U.S. History

 U.S. History, U.S. Government, U.S. Geography

Unit 2
Monitor Progress

Predictors of Reading Success	WEEK 1	WEEK 2	WEEK 3	WEEK 4
Fluency (WCPM)	Rhythmic Patterns of Language 100–110 WCPM	Emotion 100–110 WCPM	Characterization/ Dialogue 100–110 WCPM	Volume 100–110 WCPM
Vocabulary/ Concept Development (assessed informally) (Vocabulary)	accept learn nervous	convince energetic offers	excursion invention research	business resourceful team trustworthy
Lesson Vocabulary	🐾 🎯 **Strategy** Word Structure fouled hoop jersey marveled rim speechless swatted unbelievable	🐾 🎯 **Strategy** Dictionary/ Glossary bawling coyote dudes roundup spurs	🐾 🎯 **Strategy** Word Structure aboard atlas awkward capable chant mechanical miracle reseats vehicle	🐾 🎯 **Strategy** Dictionary/ Glossary cord dismay grizzly immense payroll
Text Comprehension (Retelling)	🐾 🎯 **Skill** Cause and Effect 🎯 **Strategy** Prior Knowledge	🐾 🎯 **Skill** Draw Conclusions 🎯 **Strategy** Prior Knowledge	🐾 🎯 **Skill** Draw Conclusions 🎯 **Strategy** Answer Questions	🐾 🎯 **Skill** Fact and Opinion 🎯 **Strategy** Monitor and Fix Up

🎯 Target Skill   🐾 SuccessTracker/Unit 2 Benchmark Tested Skills

Make Data–Driven Decisions

Data Management	Classroom Management
• Assess	• Monitor Progress
• Diagnose	• Group
• Prescribe	• Differentiate Instruction
• Disaggregate	• Inform Parents

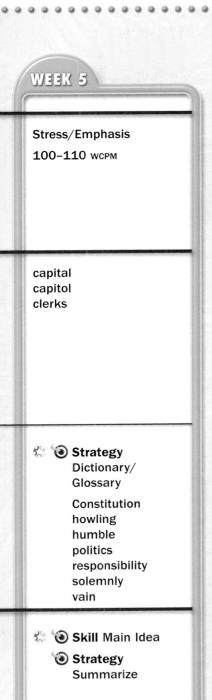

WEEK 5

Stress/Emphasis

100–110 WCPM

capital
capitol
clerks

Strategy
Dictionary/
Glossary

Constitution
howling
humble
politics
responsibility
solemnly
vain

Skill Main Idea

Strategy
Summarize

ONLINE CLASSROOM

Manage Data

- Assign the Unit 2 Benchmark Test for students to take online.
- SuccessTracker records results and generates reports by school, grade, classroom, or student.
- Use reports to disaggregate and aggregate Unit 2 skills and standards data to monitor progress.
- Based on class lists created to support the categories important for AYP (gender, ethnicity, migrant education, English proficiency, disabilities, economic status), reports let you track adequate yearly progress every six weeks.

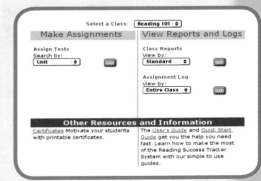

Group

- Use results from Unit 2 Benchmark Tests taken online through SuccessTracker to regroup students.
- Reports in SuccessTracker suggest appropriate groups for students based on test results.

Individualize Instruction

- Tests are correlated to Unit 2 tested skills and standards so that prescriptions for individual teaching and learning plans can be created.
- Individualized prescriptions target instruction and accelerate student progress toward learning outcome goals.
- Prescriptions include resources to reteach Unit 2 skills and standards.

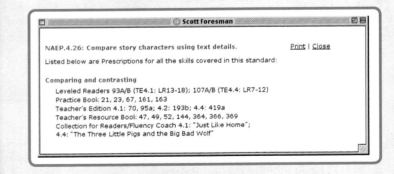

NAEP.4.26: Compare story characters using text details.   Print | Close

Listed below are Prescriptions for all the skills covered in this standard:

Comparing and contrasting
Leveled Readers 93A/B (TE4.1: LR13-18); 107A/B (TE4.4: LR7-12)
Practice Book: 21, 23, 67, 161, 163
Teacher's Edition 4.1: 70, 95a; 4.2: 193b; 4.4: 419a
Teacher's Resource Book: 47, 49, 52, 144, 364, 366, 369
Collection for Readers/Fluency Coach 4.1: "Just Like Home";
4.4: "The Three Little Pigs and the Big Bad Wolf"

Grouping for AYP

STEP 1

Diagnose and Differentiate

Diagnose

To make initial grouping decisions, use the Baseline Group Test or another initial placement test. Depending on children's ability levels, you may have more than one of each group.

Differentiate

If... student performance is **Below-Level** **then...** use the regular instruction and the daily Strategic Intervention, lessons on pp. DI·2–DI·50.

If... student performance is **On-Level** **then...** use the regular instruction for On-Level learners throughout each selection.

If... student performance is **Advanced** **then...** use the regular instruction and the daily instruction notes and activities for Advanced learners, pp. DI·3–DI·51.

Group Time

On-Level

- Explicit instructional routines teach core skills and strategies.
- Independent activities provide practice for core skills and extension and enrichment options.
- Leveled readers (LR1–LR45) provide additional reading and practice with core skills and vocabulary.

Strategic Intervention

- Daily Strategic Intervention lessons provide more intensive instruction, more scaffolding, more practice with critical skills, and more opportunities to respond.
- Reteach lessons (DI·52–DI·56) provide additional instructional opportunities with target skills.
- Leveled readers (LR1–LR45) build background for the selections and practice target skills and vocabulary.

Advanced

- Daily Advanced lessons provide compacted instruction for accelerated learning, options for investigative work, and challenging reading content.
- Leveled readers (LR1–LR45) provide additional reading tied to lesson concepts.

Additional opportunities to differentiate instruction:
- Reteach Lessons, pp. DI·52–DI·56
- Leveled Reader Instruction and Leveled Practice, LR1–LR45
- My Sidewalks on Scott Foresman Reading Street Intensive Reading Intervention Program

Monitor Progress

STEP 2

- **Guiding comprehension questions** and skill and strategy instruction during reading
- **Monitor Progress boxes** to check comprehension and vocabulary
- **Weekly Assessments** on Day 3 for comprehension, Day 4 for fluency, and Day 5 for vocabulary
- **Practice Book** pages at point of use
- **Weekly Selection Tests** or **Fresh Reads for Differentiated Test Practice**

Assess and Regroup

STEP 3

- **Days 3, 4, and 5 Assessments** Record results of weekly Days 3, 4, and 5 assessments in retelling, fluency, and vocabulary (pp. WA16–WA17) to track student progress.
- **Unit 2 Benchmark Test** Administer this test to check mastery of unit skills.
- Use weekly assessment information, Unit Benchmark Test performance, and the Unit 2 Assess and Regroup (p. WA18) to make regrouping decisions. See the time line below.

YOU ARE HERE
Begin Unit 2

SCOTT FORESMAN ASSESSMENT

Group Baseline Group Test

Regroup Units 1 and 2 (p. WA18)

Regroup Unit 3

Regroup Unit 4

Regroup Unit 5

END OF YEAR

| 1 | 5 | 10 | 15 | 20 | 25 | 30 |

OUTSIDE ASSESSMENT

Initial placement — Outside assessment for regrouping — Outside assessment for regrouping

Outside assessments (e.g., DIBELS) may recommend regrouping at other times during the year.

Summative Assessment

STEP 4

- **Benchmark Assessment** Use to measure a student's mastery of each unit's skills.
- **End-of-Year Benchmark Assessment** Use to measure a student's mastery of program skills covered in all six units.

Unit 2
Theme Launch

Discuss the Big Idea

As a class, discuss the Big Idea question, *What is the value of work and play?*

Explain that people's work and play experiences can have both personal and social benefits.

Ask students what they enjoy about working and playing with others and what qualities or strategies help them work and play well together.

A good example of teamwork and collaboration can be seen on a basketball court. Team members work together toward a common goal and gain satisfaction from doing their personal best.

Theme and Concept Connections

Weekly lesson concepts help students connect the reading selections and the unit theme. Theme-related activities throughout the week provide opportunities to explore the relationships among the selections, the lesson concepts, and the unit theme.

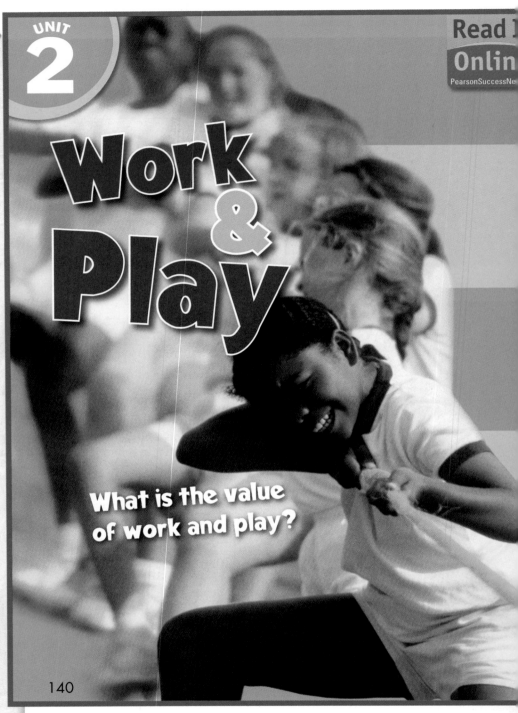

UNIT 2

Read
Onlin
PearsonSuccessNe

Work & Play

What is the value of work and play?

140

 ## CONNECTING CULTURES

Use the following selections to help students appreciate the value of individual talents and teamwork.

What Jo Did Have students discuss how the boys' perception of Jo changes during the story. They can also discuss what it would be like to have a talent that others admire.

Coyote School News Have students discuss the characters and their contributions to the class newspaper. They can also share their experiences of working together on a group project like a class newspaper.

What Jo Did

A basketball player shows surprising skill.
FICTION

connect to SOCIAL STUDIES

Paired Selection

"Fast Break" and "Allow Me to Introduce Myself"
POETRY

Coyote School News

Children in a country school publish a newspaper.
HISTORICAL FICTION

connect to SOCIAL STUDIES

Paired Selection

How to Start a School Newspaper
HOW-TO ARTICLE

Grace and the Time Machine

Friends use their imaginations to travel through time.
PLAY

connect to SOCIAL STUDIES

Paired Selection

What's There to Do?
EXPOSITORY NONFICTION

Marven of the Great North Woods

A boy keeps the books at a Minnesota logging camp.
BIOGRAPHY

connect to SOCIAL STUDIES

Paired Selection

Logging Camps
E-MAIL

So You Want to Be President?

Every President leaves a mark on history.
EXPOSITORY NONFICTION

connect to SOCIAL STUDIES

Paired Selection

Our National Parks
EXPOSITORY NONFICTION

141

Unit Inquiry Project

All in a Day's Work

In the unit inquiry project, students choose a job or career and research the skills needed to be successful at it. Students may use print or online resources as available.

The project assessment rubric can be found on p. 260a. Discuss the rubric's expectations before students begin the project. [Rubric] [4][3][2][1]

PROJECT TIMETABLE

WEEK	ACTIVITY/SKILL CONNECTION
1	**IDENTIFY QUESTIONS** Each student chooses a job and browses a few Web sites or print reference materials to develop an inquiry question about the skills needed to be successful at it.
2	**NAVIGATE/SEARCH** Students conduct effective information searches and look for text and images that can help them answer their questions.
3	**ANALYZE** Students explore Web sites or print materials. They analyze the information they have found to determine whether or not it will be useful to them. Students print or take notes on valid information.
4	**SYNTHESIZE** Students combine relevant information they've collected from different sources to develop answers to their inquiry questions from Week 1.
	ASSESSMENT OPTIONS
5	**COMMUNICATE** Students create classified ads for the jobs they researched. Students may also give brief presentations about the jobs and the skills needed to perform them.

CONCEPT DEVELOPMENT

Unit 2
Work and Play

CONCEPT QUESTION

What is the value of work and play?

Week 1

Expand the Concept
How can we learn to appreciate the talents of others?

Connect the Concept

Literature

Develop Language
accept, learn, nervous

Teach Content
Women's Rights
Title IX
Basketball Beginnings

Writing
Poem

Internet Inquiry
Biographies of Talented People

Time for SOCIAL STUDIES

Week 2

Expand the Concept
How can we work together to achieve a goal?

Connect the Concept

Literature

Develop Language
convince, energetic, offers

Teach Content
U.S. Expansion
Spanish Explorers
Hispanic Cowboys
History of Newspapers

Writing
News Story

Internet Inquiry
Achieving Goals

Time for SOCIAL STUDIES

Week 3

Expand the Concept
What can we accomplish by using our imaginations?

Connect the Concept

Literature

Develop Language
excusion, invention, research

Teach Content
Time Travel
The Gambia
Trinidad

Writing
Play Scene

Internet Inquiry
Using Our Imaginations

Time for SOCIAL STUDIES

Week 4

Expand the Concept
What is the value of a job well done?

Connect the Concept

Literature

Develop Language
business, resourceful, team, trustworthy

Teach Content
Minnesota
Citizenship
A Bookkeeper's Job
Child Labor Laws

Writing
Job Description

Internet Inquiry
Job Responsibilities

Time for SOCIAL STUDIES

Week 5

Expand the Concept
What is the job of the President of the United States?

Connect the Concept

Literature

Develop Language
capital, capitol, clerks

Teach Content
The Secret Service
The Executive Branch
FDR's New Deal
Mount Rushmore

Writing
Explanation

Internet Inquiry
The U.S. Presidency

Time for SOCIAL STUDIES

Oregon

Planning Guide for Common Curriculum Goals

What Jo Did

Reading Street Teacher's Edition pages	**Grade 4 Oregon Grade-Level Standards for English/Language Arts**
Oral Language **Speaking/Listening** Build Concept Vocabulary: 142l, 151, 155, 161c Read Aloud: 142m **Viewing** Analyze Media: 161d	**EL.04.RE.01** Read aloud grade-level narrative text and informational text fluently and accurately with effective pacing, intonation, and expression. **EL.04.RE.07** Understand, learn, and use new vocabulary that is introduced and taught directly through informational text, literary text, and instruction across the subject areas.
Word Work Adding -s and -es: 161i–161j	**EL.04.WR.15** Spell correctly: suffixes and prefixes (-ly, -ness, mis-, un-); syllables (word parts each containing a vowel sound, such as sur-prise or e-col-o-gy).
Reading **Comprehension** Cause and Effect: 142–143, 146–155, 161, 161b Prior Knowledge: 142–143, 146–155 **Vocabulary** Lesson Vocabulary: 144b, 151, 155 Word Structure: 144–145, 151, 161c **Fluency** Model Rhythmic Patterns of Language: 142l–142m, 161a **Self-Selected Reading:** LR1–9, TR16–17 **Literature** Genre—Realistic Fiction: 146 Reader Response: 156	**EL.04.RE.10** Develop vocabulary by listening to and discussing both familiar and conceptually challenging selections read aloud across the subject areas. **EL.04.RE.22** Make and confirm predictions about text by using prior knowledge and ideas presented in the text itself, including illustrations, titles, topic sentences, and important words. **EL.04.RE.26** Distinguish between cause-and-effect and between fact and opinion in expository text. **EL.04.LI.01** Listen to text and read text to make connections and respond to a wide variety of significant works of literature, including poetry, fiction, non-fiction, and drama, from a variety of cultures and time periods that enhance the study of other subjects.
Language Arts **Writing** Poems: 161g–161h **Six-Trait Writing** Word Choice: 157, 161g–161h **Grammar, Usage, and Mechanics** Common and Proper Nouns: 161e–161f **Research/Study** Technology—Chart/Table: 161l **Technology** New Literacies: 161k	**EL.04.RE.17** Locate information in titles, tables of contents, chapter headings, illustrations, captions, glossaries, indexes, graphs, charts, diagrams, and tables to aid understanding of grade-level text. **EL.04.WR.14** Create interesting sentences using a variety of sentence patterns by selecting words that describe, explain, or provide additional detail and connections.
Unit Skills **Writing** How-To Report: WA2–9 **Poetry:** 260–263 **Project/Wrap-Up:** 264–265	**EL.04.WR.25** Write informational reports: ask and then address a central question about an issue or event; include facts and details for focus; develop the topic with simple facts, details, examples, and explanations; use more than one source of information, including speakers, books, newspapers, other media sources, and online information.

This Week's Leveled Readers

Intensive Intervention

SCOTT FORESMAN

SiDEWALKS

Intensive Intervention for Tier 3 Students

Below-Level

Cheers for the Cheetahs
by Kim Whiting

Illustrated by Aleksey Ivanov

Fiction

EL.04.RE.09 Understand, learn, and use new vocabulary that is introduced and taught directly through informational text, literary text, and instruction across the subject areas.

EL.04.RE.26 Distinguish between cause-and-effect and between fact and opinion in expository text.

On-Level

Biography

Fabulous Female Athletes

Nonfiction

EL.04.RE.26 Distinguish between cause-and-effect and between fact and opinion in expository text.

EL.04.RE.28 Identify and analyze text that uses sequential or chronological order.

Advanced

EQUALITY IN AMERICAN SCHOOLS
by Lillian Forman

Nonfiction

EL.04.RE.24 Identify the main idea of a passage when it is not explicitly stated.

EL.04.RE.26 Distinguish between cause-and-effect and between fact and opinion in expository text.

Content-Area Content Standards and Benchmarks in This Lesson

Social Studies

SS.05.EC.02 Identify and give examples of the concepts of "trade-off" and "opportunity costs." (Previews Grade 5 Benchmark)

SS.05.SA.04 Identify characteristics of an event, issue, or problem, suggesting possible causes and results. (Previews Grade 5 Benchmark)

Science

SC.05.LS.01 Group or classify organisms based on a variety of characteristics. (Previews Grade 5 Benchmark)

SC.05.LS.03.01 Associate specific structures with their functions in the survival of the organism. (Previews Grade 5 Benchmark)

Oregon!

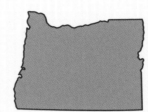

A FAMOUS OREGONIAN
Joseph Meek

Joseph Meek (1810–1875) was a U.S. marshal and a trapper who was born in Virginia but settled near Hillsboro in 1840. He was eager to form a government there, and in 1843 he was elected sheriff of a provisional government. As part of his job as sheriff, Meek also served as tax collector, and in 1845 he was the first census taker in the Oregon Territory. In 1848 Meek went to Washington, D.C., and argued successfully to make the Oregon Territory a federal territory.

Students can . . .
Read an encyclopedia entry about the U.S. Census and write a paragraph explaining how and when it is taken.

A SPECIAL OREGON PLACE
Jacksonville

Originally named for a gold prospector, Jacksonville is located in Jackson County in the southwestern part of the state. Jacksonville was founded in the 1850s as a mining camp when gold was found near Jackson Creek. The city's population declined in the 1920s as the gold mining industry diminished, but Jacksonville is still known as one of the most successfully preserved historic settlements in the state. The Jacksonville Museum displays a collection of Native American and pioneer artifacts and maintains some of the city's original buildings, including Beekman Bank, Beekman House, and two churches.

Students can . . .
Write a letter to teachers urging them to plan a field trip to the Jacksonville Museum.

OREGON FUN FACTS
Did You Know?

• The Minnesota Educational Computing Consortium (MECC) introduced Oregon Trail, a trailblazing educational electronic game, in 1974. Players lead a covered wagon to Oregon in 1848.

• Grant County was formed in 1864. Its name honors Gen. Ulysses S. Grant, who helped safeguard Oregon pioneers in the 1850s.

• Depoe Bay, which was once named Depot Bay, was named for a Siletz Native American man who worked at a U.S. Army depot and called himself Charlie Depot.

Students can . . .
Choose new names for themselves. Ask students to make an outline drawing of themselves, label it with their new name, and add phrases to the drawing explaining why they chose that name.

Unit 2
Work and Play

CONCEPT QUESTION
What is the value of work and play?

Week 1

How can we learn to appreciate the talents of others?

Week 2

How can we work together to achieve a goal?

Week 3

What can we accomplish by using our imaginations?

Week 4

What is the value of a job well done?

Week 5

What is the job of the President of the United States?

EXPAND THE CONCEPT
How can we learn to appreciate the talents of others?

Time for SOCIAL STUDIES

CONNECT THE CONCEPT

▶ **Build Background**

accept, learn, nervous

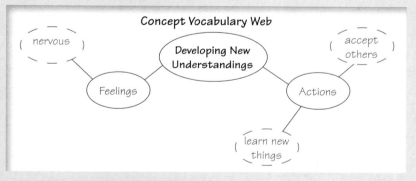

▶ **Social Studies Content**

Women's Rights, Title IX, Basketball Beginnings

▶ **Writing**

Poem

▶ **Internet Inquiry**

Biographies of Talented People

Preview Your Week

How can we learn to appreciate the talents of others?

What can **Jo do** that others cannot?

What Jo Did

text and images by Charles R. Smith Jr.

Genre **Fiction** often has characters and events that seem real. As you read, try to picture this story taking place where...

Student Edition pages 146–155

Audio CD

Genre Fiction
Vocabulary Strategy Word Structure
Comprehension Skill Cause and Effect
Comprehension Strategy Prior Knowledge

Paired Selection

Reading Across Texts
Compare the Story to the Poems

Genre
Poetry

Poetry

Genre
- Poetry is meant to appeal to the senses, emotions, or mind.
- Often poetry gives the reader a fresh, unexpected way of looking at things.
- In many poems the rhyme helps establish the rhythm, or regular beat of stressed syllables.
- Preview the poems. Notice how the author captures the reader's attention with varied text sizes and styles.

Link to Writing
The speaker uses rhyme to describe himself in both poems. Use this style to write a poem about yourself playing a sport or doing some other activity.

FAST BREAK

Fleet feet
streak
up the **concrete**
to pull a
sweet treat
for the crowd.
The outlet pass—
fast—
as the break
is on
and I'm
gone.
A scene from
The Flash
I *dash*
down**court**
to
meet the pass.
Eyes wide
arms out
a reverse *jam*
is coming
no doubt.
Sky-high
I *fly*
to bring the
silent **crowd**
back
to life.

by Charles R. Smith Jr.

Prior Knowledge What are some things you know about basketball?

158

Student Edition pages 158–161

Audio CD

Read It
ONLINE
PearsonSuccessNet.com

• Student Edition
• Leveled Readers

Leveled Readers

◎ **Skill** Cause and Effect
◎ **Strategy** Prior Knowledge
Lesson Vocabulary

Below-Level

On-Level

Advanced

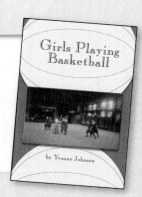

ELL Reader
· Concept Vocabulary
· Text Support
· Language Enrichment

Time for **SOCIAL STUDIES**

Integrate Social Studies Standards
• U.S. History

✓ Read

"What Jo Did," pp. 146–155

"Fast Break" and "Allow Me to Introduce Myself," pp. 158–161

Leveled Readers

Below-Level   **On-Level**   **Advanced**

• Support Concepts   • Develop Concepts   • Extend Concepts
                                          • Social Studies
                                            Extension Activity

ELL Reader

✓ Build Concept Vocabulary
Developing New
Understandings, pp. 142l–142m

✓ Teach Social Studies Concepts
Women's Rights, p. 149
Title IX, p. 153
Basketball Beginnings, p. 159

✓ Explore Social Studies Center
Research the Rules, p. 142k

Weekly Plan

READING

45–90 minutes

TARGET SKILLS OF THE WEEK

- **Comprehension Skill**
  Cause and Effect
- **Comprehension Strategy**
  Prior Knowledge
- **Vocabulary Strategy**
  Word Structure

LANGUAGE ARTS

30–60 minutes

Trait of the Week

Word Choice

DAY 1
PAGES 142l–144b, 161a, 161e–161k

Oral Language

QUESTION OF THE WEEK *How can we learn to appreciate the talents of others?*

Read Aloud: "The Circuit," 142m
Build Concepts, 142l

Comprehension/Vocabulary

Comprehension Skill/Strategy Lesson, 142–143
- Cause and Effect **T**
- Prior Knowledge

Build Background, 144a

Introduce Lesson Vocabulary, 144b
fouled, hoop, jersey, marveled, rim, speechless, swatted, unbelievable **T**

Read Leveled Readers

Grouping Options 142c–142g

Fluency

Model Rhythmic Patterns of Language, 142l–142m, 161a

Grammar, 161e
Introduce Common and Proper Nouns **T**

Writing Workshop, 161g
Introduce Poem
Model the Trait of the Week: Word Choice

Spelling, 161i
Pretest for Adding -s and -es

Internet Inquiry, 161k
Identify Questions

DAY 2
PAGES 144–151, 161a, 161e–161k

Oral Language

QUESTION OF THE DAY *Do you think Jo would have had a chance to show off her talent if she hadn't worn her hat?*

Comprehension/Vocabulary

Vocabulary Strategy Lesson, 144–145
- Word Structure **T**

Read "What Jo Did," 146–151

Grouping Options
142f–142g

- Cause and Effect **T**
- Prior Knowledge
- Word Structure **T**
- **REVIEW** Draw Conclusions **T**

Develop Vocabulary

Fluency

Echo Reading, 161a

Grammar, 161e
Develop Common and Proper Nouns **T**

Writing Workshop, 161g
Improve Writing with Figurative Language

Spelling, 161i
Teach the Generalization

Internet Inquiry, 161k
Navigate/Search

DAILY WRITING ACTIVITIES

Day 1 Write to Read, 142

Day 2 Words to Write, 145
Strategy Response Log, 146, 151

DAILY SOCIAL STUDIES CONNECTIONS

Day 1 Developing New Understandings Concept Web, 142l

Day 2 Time for Social Studies: Women's Rights, 149
Revisit the Developing New Understandings Concept Web, 151

DAILY SUCCESS PREDICTORS
for Adequate Yearly Progress

Monitor Progress and Corrective Feedback

Vocabulary — Check Vocabulary, *142l*

RESOURCES FOR THE WEEK

- Practice Book, *pp. 51–60*
- Word Study and Spelling Practice Book, *pp. 21–24*
- Grammar and Writing Practice Book, *pp. 21–24*

- Selection Test, *pp. 21–24*
- Fresh Reads for Differentiated Test Practice, *pp. 31–36*
- The Grammar and Writing Book, *pp. 80–85*

Grouping Options for Differentiated Instruction

Turn the page for the small group lesson plan.

DAY 3 — PAGES 152-157, 161a, 161e-161k

Oral Language

QUESTION OF THE DAY *What do the other basketball players think about Jo's talent?*

Comprehension/Vocabulary

Read "What Jo Did," 152–156

Grouping Options
142f–142g

- Prior Knowledge
- Draw Conclusions **T**
- Develop Vocabulary

Reader Response
Selection Test

Fluency

Model Rhythmic Patterns of Language, 161a

Grammar, 161f
Apply Common and Proper Nouns in Writing **T**

Writing Workshop, 157, 161h
Write Now
Prewrite and Draft

Spelling, 161j
Connect Spelling to Writing

Internet Inquiry, 161k
Analyze Sources

Day 3 Strategy Response Log, 154
Look Back and Write, 156

Day 3 Time for Social Studies: Title IX, 153
Revisit the Developing New Understandings
Concept Web, 155

DAY 4 — PAGES 158-161a, 161e-161k

Oral Language

QUESTION OF THE DAY *In what ways might the boys' attitudes toward girls in sports have changed after they played basketball with Jo?*

Comprehension/Vocabulary

Read "Fast Break," 158–161

Grouping Options
142f –142g

Poetry
Reading Across Texts

Fluency

Partner Reading, 161a

Grammar, 161f
Practice Common and Proper Pronouns for
Standardized Tests **T**

Writing Workshop, 161h
Draft, Revise, and Publish

Spelling, 161j
Provide a Strategy

Internet Inquiry, 161k
Synthesize Information

Day 4 Writing Across Texts, 161

Day 4 Time for Social Studies: Basketball
Beginnings, 159

DAY 5 — PAGES 161a-161l

Oral Language

QUESTION OF THE WEEK *To wrap up the week, revisit the Day 1 question.*

Build Concept Vocabulary, 161c

Fluency

Read Leveled Readers

Grouping Options 142f–142g

Assess Reading Rate, 161a

Comprehension/Vocabulary

- Reteach Cause and Effect, 161b **T**
- Short Story, 161b
- Review Word Structure, 161c **T**

Speaking and Viewing, 161d
Sportscast
Analyze Media

Grammar, 161f
Cumulative Review

Writing Workshop, 161h
Connect to Unit Writing

Spelling, 161j
Posttest for Adding -s and -es

Internet Inquiry, 161k
Communicate Results

Research/Study Skills, 161l
Chart/Table

Day 5 Short Story, 161b

Day 5 Revisit the Developing New Understandings
Concept Web, 161c

KEY ◉ = Target Skill **T** = Tested Skill

Check Retelling, *157*

Check Fluency wcpm, *161a*

Check Vocabulary, *161c*

Comprehension

Fluency

Vocabulary

SUCCESS PREDICTOR

Small Group Plan *for Differentiated Instruction*

Daily Plan
AT A GLANCE

Reading
Whole Group
- Oral Language
- Comprehension/Vocabulary

Group Time
Differentiated Instruction
Meet with small groups to provide:
- Skill Support
- Reading Support
- Fluency Practice

Read

This week's lessons for daily group time can be found behind the Differentiated Instruction (DI) tab on pp. DI·2–DI·11.

Whole Group
- Fluency

Language Arts
- Grammar
- Writing
- Spelling
- Research/Inquiry
- Speaking/Listening/Viewing

Use *My Sidewalks on Reading Street* for Tier III intensive reading intervention.

DAY 1

On-Level	Strategic Intervention	Advanced
Teacher-Led *Page DI·3*	**Teacher-Led** *Page DI·2*	**Teacher-Led** *Page DI·3*
• Develop Concept Vocabulary	• Reinforce Concepts	• **Read** Advanced Reader *Equality in American Schools*
• **Read** On-Level Reader *Fabulous Female Athletes*	• **Read** Below-Level Reader *Cheers for the Cheetahs*	• Independent Extension Activity

(i) Independent Activities
While you meet with small groups, have the rest of the class...
- Visit the Reading/Library Center
- Listen to the Background Building Audio
- Finish Write to Read, p. 142
- Complete Practice Book pp. 53–54
- Visit Cross-Curricular Centers

DAY 2

On-Level	Strategic Intervention	Advanced
Teacher-Led *Pages 148–151*	**Teacher-Led** *Page DI·4*	**Teacher-Led** *Page DI·5*
• **Read** "What Jo Did"	• Practice Lesson Vocabulary	• Extend Vocabulary
	• Read Multisyllabic Words	• **Read** "What Jo Did"
	• **Read** or Listen to "What Jo Did"	

(i) Independent Activities
While you meet with small groups, have the rest of the class...
- Visit the Reading/Library Center
- Listen to the AudioText for "What Jo Did"
- Finish Words to Write, p. 145
- Complete Practice Book pp. 55–56
- Write in their Strategy Response Logs, pp. 146, 151
- Visit Cross-Curricular Centers
- Work on inquiry projects

DAY 3

On-Level	Strategic Intervention	Advanced
Teacher-Led *Pages 152–155*	**Teacher-Led** *Page DI·6*	**Teacher-Led** *Page DI·7*
• **Read** "What Jo Did"	• Practice Cause and Effect and Prior Knowledge	• Extend Cause and Effect and Prior Knowledge
	• **Read** or Listen to "What Jo Did"	• **Read** "What Jo Did"

(i) Independent Activities
While you meet with small groups, have the rest of the class...
- Visit the Reading/Library Center
- Listen to the AudioText for "What Jo Did"
- Write in their Strategy Response Logs, p. 154
- Finish Look Back and Write, p. 156
- Complete Practice Book p. 57
- Visit Cross-Curricular Centers
- Work on inquiry projects

① Begin with whole class skill and strategy instruction.

② Meet with small groups to provide differentiated instruction.

③ Gather the whole class back together for fluency and language arts.

On-Level
Teacher-Led
Pages 158–161

- **Read** "Fast Break" and "Allow Me to Introduce Myself"

Strategic Intervention
Teacher-Led
Page DI · 8

- Practice Retelling
- **Read** or Listen to "Fast Break" and "Allow Me to Introduce Myself"

Advanced
Teacher-Led
Page DI · 9

- **Read** "Fast Break" and "Allow Me to Introduce Myself"
- Genre Study

DAY 4

ⓘ Independent Activities

While you meet with small groups, have the rest of the class...

- Visit the Reading/Library Center
- Listen to the AudioText for "Fast Break" and "Allow Me to Introduce Myself"
- Visit the Writing/Vocabulary Center
- Finish Writing Across Texts, p. 161
- Visit Cross-Curricular Centers
- Work on inquiry projects

On-Level
Teacher-Led
Page DI · 11

- **Reread** Leveled Reader *Fabulous Female Athletes*
- Retell *Fabulous Female Athletes*

Strategic Intervention
Teacher-Led
Page DI · 10

- **Reread** Leveled Reader *Cheers for the Cheetahs*
- Retell *Cheers for the Cheetahs*

Advanced
Teacher-Led
Page DI · 11

- **Reread** Leveled Reader *Equality in American Schools*
- Share Extension Activity

DAY 5

ⓘ Independent Activities

While you meet with small groups, have the rest of the class...

- Visit the Reading/Library Center
- Complete Practice Book pp. 58–60
- Visit Cross-Curricular Centers
- Work on inquiry projects

Grouping Place English language learners in the groups that correspond to their reading abilities in English.

Use the appropriate Leveled Reader or other text at students' instructional level.

TIP Send home the appropriate Multilingual Summary of the main selection on Day 1.

Take It to the NET™ ONLINE
PearsonSuccessNet.com

Susan Watts-Taffe
For activities to build vocabulary, see the article "The Place of Word Consciousness in a Research-based Vocabulary Program" by M. Graves and Scott Foresman author Susan Watts-Taffe.

TEACHER TALK

An **affix** is a prefix, suffix, or inflected ending attached to a base word.

Be sure to schedule time for students to work on the unit inquiry project "All in a Day's Work." This week students develop an inquiry question about the skills needed to be successful at a chosen job.

Looking Ahead

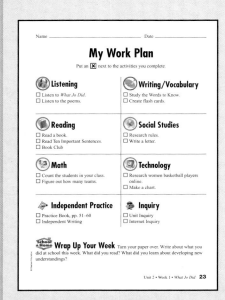

▲ **Group-Time Survival Guide** p. 23, Weekly Contract

☑ Customize Your Plan *by Strand*

ORAL LANGUAGE

Concept Development

How can we learn to appreciate the talents of others?

CONCEPT VOCABULARY
accept   learn   nervous

BUILD

☐ **Question of the Week** Introduce and discuss the question of the week. This week students will read a variety of texts and work on projects related to the concept *developing new understandings*. Post the question for students to refer to throughout the week. DAY 1 *142d*

☐ **Read Aloud** Read aloud "The Circuit." Then begin a web to build concepts and concept vocabulary related to this week's lesson and the unit theme, Work and Play. Introduce the concept words *accept, learn,* and *nervous* and have students place them on the web. Display the web for use throughout the week. DAY 1 *142l–142m*

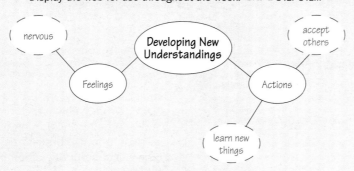

- nervous
- Developing New Understandings
- accept others
- Feelings
- Actions
- learn new things

DEVELOP

☐ **Question of the Day** Use the prompts from the Weekly Plan to engage students in conversations related to this week's reading and the unit theme. **EVERY DAY** *142d-142e*

☐ **Concept Vocabulary Web** Revisit the Developing New Understandings Concept Web and encourage students to add concept words from their reading and life experiences. **DAY 2** *151,* **DAY 3** *155*

CONNECT

☐ **Looking Back/Moving Forward** Revisit the Developing New Understandings Concept Web and discuss how it relates to this week's lesson and the unit theme. Then make connections to next week's lesson. **DAY 5** *161c*

CHECK

☐ **Concept Vocabulary Web** Use the Developing New Understandings Concept Web to check students' understanding of the concept vocabulary words *accept, learn,* and *nervous.* DAY 1 *142l,* **DAY 5** *161c*

VOCABULARY

 **STRATEGY WORD STRUCTURE**
Prefixes and suffixes have their own meanings. When you see an unfamiliar word, check to see if a prefix or suffix has been added to the base word. This will help you figure out the word's meaning.

LESSON VOCABULARY

fouled	rim
hoop	speechless
jersey	swatted
marveled	unbelievable

TEACH

☐ **Words to Know** Give students the opportunity to tell what they already know about this week's lesson vocabulary words. Then discuss word meaning. DAY 1 *144b*

☐ **Vocabulary Strategy Lesson** Use the vocabulary strategy lesson in the Student Edition to introduce and model this week's strategy, *word structure.* DAY 2 *144-145*

Vocabulary Strategy Lesson

PRACTICE/APPLY

☐ **Leveled Text** Read the lesson vocabulary in the context of leveled text. DAY 1 *LR1-LR9*

☐ **Words in Context** Read the lesson vocabulary and apply *word structure* in the context of "What Jo Did." DAY 2 *146-151,* DAY 3 *152-156*

Leveled Readers

☐ **Writing/Vocabulary Center** Make flash cards for the Words to Know from "What Jo Did." **ANY DAY** *142k*

Main Selection—Fiction

☐ **Homework** Practice Book pp. 54–55. DAY 1 *144b,* DAY 2 *145*

☐ **Word Play** Have students work in pairs to look up toponyms (names based on places) online or using an advanced dictionary to complete the chart. **ANY DAY** *161c*

ASSESS

☐ **Selection Test** Use the Selection Test to determine students' understanding of the lesson vocabulary words. **DAY 3**

RETEACH/REVIEW

☐ **Reteach Lesson** If necessary, use this lesson to reteach and review *word structure.* DAY 5 *161c*

COMPREHENSION

SKILL CAUSE AND EFFECT   An effect is what happens. A cause is why it happens.

STRATEGY PRIOR KNOWLEDGE   Prior knowledge is what the reader already knows about a subject. Good readers use their prior knowledge to help them understand what they read.

TEACH

☐ **Skill/Strategy Lesson** Use the skill/strategy lesson in the Student Edition to introduce and model *cause and effect* and *prior knowledge*. DAY 1 *142-143*

☐ **Extend Skills** Teach short story. **ANY DAY** *149*

Skill/Strategy Lesson

PRACTICE/APPLY

☐ **Leveled Text** Apply *cause and effect* and *prior knowledge* to read leveled text. DAY 1 *LR1-LR9*

☐ **Skills and Strategies in Context** Read "What Jo Did," using the Guiding Comprehension questions to apply *cause and effect* and *prior knowledge*. **DAY 2** *146-151*, **DAY 3** *152-156*

Leveled Readers

☐ **Skills and Strategies in Context** Read "Fast Break" and "Allow Me To Introduce Myself," guiding students as they apply *cause and effect* and *prior knowledge*. Then have students discuss and write across texts. **DAY 4** *158-161*

Main Selection—Fiction

☐ **Homework** Practice Book pp. 53, 57, 58. DAY 1 *143*, **DAY 3** *155*, **DAY 5** *161b*

Paired Selection—Poetry

☐ **Fresh Reads for Differentiated Test Practice** Have students practice *cause and effect* with a new passage. **DAY 3**

ASSESS

☐ **Selection Test** Determine students' understanding of the selection and their use of *cause and effect*. **DAY 3**

☐ **Retell** Have students retell "What Jo Did." **DAY 3** *156-157*

RETEACH/REVIEW

☐ **Reteach Lesson** If necessary, reteach and review *cause and effect*. **DAY 5** *161b*

FLUENCY

SKILL RHYTHMIC PATTERNS OF LANGUAGE   Rhythm is the patterns of sound in speech or writing. All writing has a rhythm. By varying your pitch, tone, and volume and using logical phrasing and pauses, you can read with a pleasing rhythm.

TEACH

☐ **Read Aloud** Model fluent reading by rereading "The Circuit." Focus on this week's fluency skill, rhythmic patterns of language. DAY 1 *142l-142m, 161a*

PRACTICE/APPLY

☐ **Echo Reading** Read aloud selected paragraphs from "What Jo Did," emphasizing the rhythmic patterns. Have the class practice by doing three echo readings of the paragraphs. **DAY 2** *161a*, **DAY 3** *161a*

☐ **Partner Reading** Have partners practice reading aloud, reading with a pleasing rhythm and offering each other feedback. As students reread, monitor their progress toward their individual fluency goals. **DAY 4** *161a*

☐ **Listening Center** Have students follow along with the AudioText for this week's selections. **ANY DAY** *142j*

☐ **Reading/Library Center** Have students reread a selection of their choice. **ANY DAY** *142j*

☐ **Fluency Coach** Have students use Fluency Coach to listen to fluent readings or practice reading on their own. **ANY DAY**

ASSESS

☐ **Check Fluency** WCPM Do a one-minute timed reading, paying special attention to this week's skill—rhythmic patterns of language. Provide feedback for each student. **DAY 5** *161a*

☑ Customize Your Plan *by Strand*

GRAMMAR

SKILL COMMON AND PROPER NOUNS Review that a noun is a word that names a person, place, or thing. A common noun names any person, place, or thing and a proper noun names a particular person, place, or thing. Proper nouns begin with capital letters.

TEACH

☐ **Grammar Transparency 6** Use Grammar Transparency 6 to teach common and proper nouns. DAY 1 *161e*

Grammar Transparency 6

PRACTICE/APPLY

☐ **Develop the Concept** Review the concept of common and proper nouns and provide guided practice. DAY 2 *161e*

☐ **Apply to Writing** Have students review something they have written and add common and proper nouns. DAY 3 *161f*

☐ **Test Preparation** Examine common errors in common and proper nouns to prepare for standardized tests. DAY 4 *161f*

☐ **Homework** Grammar and Writing Practice Book pp. 21–23. DAY 2 *161e*, DAY 3 *161f*, DAY 4 *161f*

ASSESS

☐ **Cumulative Review** Use Grammar and Writing Practice Book p. 24. DAY 5 *161f*

RETEACH/REVIEW

☐ **Daily Fix-It** Have students find and correct errors in grammar, spelling, and punctuation. EVERY DAY *161e-161f*

☐ **The Grammar and Writing Book** Use pp. 80–83 of The Grammar and Writing Book to extend instruction for common and proper nouns. ANY DAY

The Grammar and Writing Book

WRITING

Trait of the Week

WORD CHOICE Good writers choose their words carefully. Strong verbs, specific nouns, and vivid adjectives help writers elaborate on their ideas. Well-chosen words make writing clear and lively.

TEACH

☐ **Writing Transparency 6A** Use the model to introduce and discuss the Trait of the Week. DAY 1 *161g*

☐ **Writing Transparency 6B** Use the transparency to show students how figurative language can improve their writing. DAY 2 *161g*

Writing Transparency 6A **Writing Transparency 6B**

PRACTICE/APPLY

☐ **Write Now** Examine the model on Student Edition p. 157. Then have students write their own poem. DAY 3 *157, 161h*, DAY 4 *161h*

> **Prompt** In "What Jo Did," the author describes an exciting basketball game. Think about something that you love to do. Now write a poem about what it feels like when you are doing this activity.

Write Now p. 157

☐ **Writing/Vocabulary Center** Make flash cards for the Words to Know from "What Jo Did." ANY DAY *142k*

ASSESS

☐ **Writing Trait Rubric** Use the rubric to evaluate students' writing. DAY 4 *161h*

RETEACH/REVIEW

☐ **The Grammar and Writing Book** Use pp. 80–85 of The Grammar and Writing Book to extend instruction for common and proper nouns, figurative language, and poetry. ANY DAY

The Grammar and Writing Book

SPELLING

GENERALIZATION ADDING -S AND -ES Add -s to words ending in a *vowel and y* and to most words: *monkeys, friends.* Change *y* to *i* and add -es to words ending in a *consonant and y: supplies.* Add -es to words ending in *sh, ch, s, ss, x: taxes.* Words that end in -s, -es, or -ies are often plural.

TEACH

❑ **Pretest** Give the pretest for words to which -s and -es are added. Guide students in self-correcting their pretests and correcting any misspellings. **DAY 1** *161i*

❑ **Think and Practice** Connect spelling to the phonics generalization for adding -s and -es. **DAY 2** *161i*

PRACTICE/APPLY

❑ **Connect to Writing** Have students use spelling words to write two-line rhymes. Then review frequently misspelled words: *friends, a lot, because.* **DAY 3** *161j*

❑ **Homework** Word Study and Spelling Practice Book pp. 21–24. **EVERY DAY**

RETEACH/REVIEW

❑ **Review** Review spelling words to prepare for the posttest. Then provide students with a spelling strategy—problem parts. **DAY 4** *161j*

ASSESS

❑ **Posttest** Use dictation sentences to give the posttest for words to which -s and -es are added. **DAY 5** *161j*

Spelling Words

1. monkeys	8. companies	15. counties
2. friends	9. costumes	16. teammates*
3. plays	10. sandwiches	17. memories
4. supplies	11. hobbies	18. bunches
5. taxes	12. daisies	19. batteries
6. holidays	13. delays	20. donkeys
7. months	14. scratches	

Challenge Words

21. eyelashes	23. trophies	25. inventories
22. ambulances	24. secretaries	

*Word from the selection

RESEARCH AND INQUIRY

❑ **Internet Inquiry** Have students conduct an Internet inquiry on the biographies of talented people. **EVERY DAY** *161k*

❑ **Chart/Table** Discuss with students the purpose of using a chart or table, what kind of information can be placed in them and demonstrate how to create a table using a word processing software program. **DAY 5** *161l*

❑ **Unit Inquiry** Allow time for students to develop an inquiry question about skills needed to be successful at a chosen job. **ANY DAY** *141*

SPEAKING AND VIEWING

❑ **Sportscast** Have students create and present a sportscast of a short action sequence. Provide a sportscast for the students to view and then have students write scripts and practice their sportscast. **DAY 5** *161d*

❑ **Analyze Media** Provide students with a taped segment of a sports event to view and analyze. Prior to viewing, point out specific areas you want students to focus on such as the camera positions. After viewing, have small groups discuss and answer questions. **DAY 5** *161d*

Resources for Differentiated Instruction

LEVELED READERS

▶ **Comprehension**
- ◉ **Skill** Cause and Effect
- ◉ **Strategy** Prior Knowledge

▶ **Lesson Vocabulary**
- ◉ Word Structure

fouled	speechless
jersey	hoop
rim	marveled
swatted	unbelievable

▶ **Social Studies Standards**
- • U.S. History

Leveled Reader Database

ONLINE

PearsonSuccessNet.com

Use the Online Database of over 600 books to
- • Download and print additional copies of this week's leveled readers.
- • Listen to the readers being read online.
- • Search for more titles focused on this week's skills, topic, and content.

On-Level

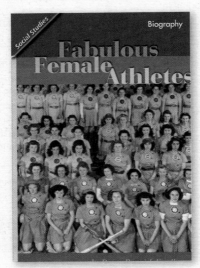

On-Level Reader

Cause and Effect

- • A **cause** is why something happens. An **effect** is what happens.
- • Sometimes there is more than one cause of an effect, and sometimes there are multiple effects of a cause.

Directions Answer the questions on the lines provided. **Possible answers given.**

1. Why was the All-American Girls Professional Baseball League started? What was the cause?
   Men were away at war, and people wanted to see baseball games.

2. What were the two causes that ended this baseball league?
   Men came home from the war; people didn't want to see women playing anymore.

3. How was Wilma Rudolf able to conquer her illness? How does what she did help you understand how she was able to win in the Olympics?
   Wilma Rudolf refused to give up. She worked with doctors. She was determined, and this helped her to win in the Olympics.

4. Choose one female athlete in the story and describe the changes she brought about in women's sports. Billy Jean King got the U.S. Open to award equal prizes to men and women; Althea Gibson made it easier for African American women to compete in sports; Wilma Rudolf made it easier for women to compete in track events.

5. Because brave women fought for the right to compete in sports, women athletes today have three main benefits. Can you name them?
   They earn better pay; they can compete in events that were previously just for men; they get better training.

◉ **On-Level Practice** TE p. LR5

Vocabulary

Directions Using your vocabulary words, put the correct word in each blank below.

Check the Words You Know
- amateur
- fouled
- hoop
- jersey
- marveled
- rim
- speechless
- swatted
- unbelievable

1–5. Nancy got up early and pulled on her bright yellow **jersey** Today was the big game, and she was scared. She was not a good player, and many of her friends thought it was **unbelievable** that she had been chosen to play.

"Don't worry," her best friend Kim told her. "You're an **amateur** No one expects you to play like a professional."

When Nancy got on the court, the ball came right toward her! She grabbed it and made a **rim** shot! Nancy was so **speechless** she couldn't say a word!

Directions The words below are spelled incorrectly. Write the correct spelling for each. Then write the definition of each word.

6. foled **fouled**
   Definition: **made an unfair play**

7. swated **swatted**
   Definition: **hit sharply or violently**

8. marvelled **marveled**
   Definition: **filled with wonder**

9. hop **hoop**
   Definition: **ring; round, flat band**

On-Level Practice TE p. LR6

Strategic Intervention

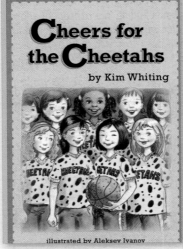

Below-Level Reader

Cause and Effect

- • A **cause** is why something happens. An **effect** is what happens.
- • Sometimes there is more than one cause of an effect, and sometimes there are multiple effects of a cause.

Directions Answer the questions on the lines provided. **Possible answers given.**

1. Why did Mr. Giddings give the boys more gym time? What was the cause of his actions?
   He thought boys were better at sports than girls because he always watched the boys and saw how good they were.

2. Although Hannah was not the best player, she did something important for the team that no one else could do. What was this?
   She wrote a letter.

3. What did Hannah and her teammates risk by speaking out for themselves? What was the benefit of speaking out?
   The principal and the coach could get mad. The benefit was that they were able to prove themselves.

4. Based on what you know after having read the story, how do you think the coach will act differently from now on? Why?
   The coach will probably be more likely to give all girls a chance at sports now because he has seen that they can play well.

5. What lesson do you think this story teaches about standing up for yourself?
   It is important to speak up for yourself. Hannah and her team did, and they got a chance to play that they would not have had otherwise.

◉ **Below-Level Practice** TE p. LR2

Vocabulary

Directions Draw a line from the vocabulary word to its correct definition.

Check the Words You Know
- fouled
- hoop
- jersey
- marveled
- unbelievable
- speechless
- swatted

1. swatted — a. not able to be believed
2. fouled — b. made an error in the game
3. hoop — c. wondered
4. jersey — d. a ring; a round, flat band
5. marveled — e. the edge
6. rim — f. unable to speak
7. speechless — g. a shirt
8. unbelievable — h. hit sharply or violently

Directions Unscramble the vocabulary words and then write a definition for each one.

9. ludefo **fouled**
   Definition: **Answers will vary.**

10. poho **hoop**
    Definition:

11. yjrese **jersey**
    Definition:

12. mir **rim**
    Definition:

13. eulvalenebib **unbelievable**
    Definition:

Below-Level Practice TE p. LR3

Advanced

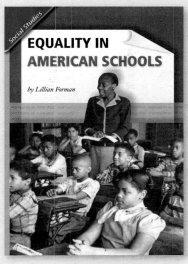

Advanced Reader

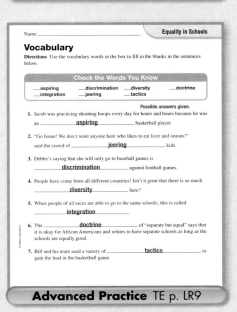

Advanced Practice TE p. LR8

Advanced Practice TE p. LR9

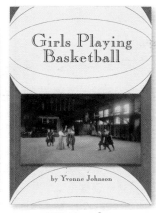

ELL Reader

ELL Poster 6

Teacher's Edition Notes

ELL notes throughout this lesson support instruction and reference additional resources at point of use.

Teaching Guide
pp. 36–42, 222–223

- Multilingual summaries of the main selection
- Comprehension lesson
- Vocabulary strategies and word cards
- ELL Reader 4.2.1 lesson

ELL and Transition Handbook

Ten Important Sentences

- Key ideas from every selection in the Student Edition
- Activities to build sentence power

More Reading

Readers' Theater Anthology

- Fluency practice
- Five scripts to build fluency
- Poetry for oral interpretation

Leveled Trade Books

Below-Level

Advanced

On-Level

- Extended reading tied to the unit concept
- Lessons in the Trade Book Library Teaching Guide

Homework

- Family Times Newsletter
- ELL Multilingual Selection Summaries

Take-Home Books

- Leveled Readers

Cross-Curricular Centers

Listen to the *Selections*

MATERIALS `SINGLES`
CD player, headphones, AudioText CD, student book

LISTEN TO LITERATURE Listen to "What Jo Did," "Fast Break," and "Allow Me to Introduce Myself" as you follow or read along in your book. Listen for cause-effect relationships in "What Jo Did."

If there is anything you don't understand, you can listen again to any section.

Read It *Again!*

MATERIALS `SINGLES` `PAIRS` `GROUPS`
Collection of books for self-selected reading, reading logs, student book

Select a book you have already read. Record the title of the book in your reading log. You may want to read with a partner.

Choose from the following:

- **Leveled Readers**
- **ELL Readers**
- **Books or Stories Written by Classmates**
- **Books from the Library**
- **"What Jo Did"**

TEN IMPORTANT SENTENCES Read the Ten Important Sentences for "What Jo Did." Then locate the sentences in the student book.

BOOK CLUB Read other books about playing sports. Get together with a group and discuss which sports you enjoy reading about.

Find the Quotient

MATERIALS `SINGLES` `PAIRS` `GROUPS`
Writing and art materials, graph paper, student book

Find out how many teams your class makes.

1. **Count the total number of students in your reading class.**
2. **Use the table below to see how many players make up a team for different sports.**
3. **Figure out how many complete teams your class could make for each sport. For example, if your class has 21 students, you could make 4 complete basketball teams.**
4. **Fill in the last column of the table to show the number of complete teams your class could make for each sport.**

EARLY FINISHERS Draw a bar graph showing the number of players on each team for different sports.

Type of Sport	Number of Players on a Team	Number of Teams Your Class Makes
Relay Team	4	
Basketball	5	
Ice Hockey	6	
Baseball	9	
Football or Soccer	11	

Scott Foresman Reading Street Centers Survival Kit
Use the "What Jo Did" materials from the Reading Street
Centers Survival Kit to organize this week's centers.

Writing/ Vocabulary

Create Flash Cards

MATERIALS
Writing and art materials, index cards, student book

SINGLES
PAIRS
GROUPS

Make flash cards of the Words to Know from "What Jo Did."

1. Look at p. 144 for a list of Words to Know for the story.
2. Write each word on a separate index card.
3. On the back of the card, write a definition for each word.
4. Draw a picture to illustrate the definition.
5. Show your flash card definitions and pictures to a partner and have him or her guess the Word to Know.

EARLY FINISHERS Write a short story using four or five words from the list. Use one vocabulary word per sentence.

—shirt made of soft, knitted cloth

Social Studies

Research the Rules

MATERIALS
Writing materials, library books on different sports, encyclopedia, art materials

SINGLES

Write a letter about a rule change you want to see in your favorite sport.

1. Using your classroom resources, come up with ideas for a rule change you would like to see in your favorite sport, such as a four-point field goal in football or just two strikes for an out in baseball.
2. Write a letter to the commissioner of your sport asking for the change. Include how your change would make the game better. Give reasons to support your idea.

EARLY FINISHERS Draw a picture to show the sport before and after your rules change.

The Office of the
Commissioner of Baseball
245 Park Avenue, 31st floor
New York, NY 10167

Dear Commissioner of Baseball,
I would like to see the rules change in baseball by having…

Technology

Research the Players

MATERIALS
Internet access, writing materials, library books about basketball

SINGLES
PAIRS

Search the Internet to find information on the pioneers of women's basketball.

1. Use your classroom resouces to find names of early women basketball players.
2. Using a student-friendly search engine, type in the names of the female players to begin your search.
3. Choose a Web site to begin gathering information.
4. Make a chart of female basketball players. Include when, where, and for which teams they played. List any awards or honors they won.
5. Write at least one sentence describing how these women changed the game for players today.

EARLY FINISHERS Make a time line to show when your players were active in the sport.

Search Engine

Nancy Lieberman

Player	Nancy Lieberman
When Played	1976 Olympics, 1976-1980 college, 1986-1988, 1997 pro
Awards/ Honors	Olympic Silver Medal
Teams	U.S. Women's Olympic Team; Old Dominion University; Dallas Diamonds

ALL CENTERS

Build Concepts

OBJECTIVES

- Build vocabulary by finding words related to the lesson concept.
- Listen for cause-effect relationships.

Concept Vocabulary

accept to receive with approval

learn to become able by study

nervous easily excited or upset; restless; uneasy

Monitor Progress

Check Vocabulary

If...	then... review the
students are unable to place words on the web,	lesson concept. Place the words on the web and provide additional words for practice, such as *believe* and *help*.

SUCCESS PREDICTOR

DAY 1 Grouping Options

Reading

Whole Group

Introduce and discuss the Question of the Week. Then use pp. 142l–144b.

Group Time

Differentiated Instruction

Read this week's Leveled Readers. See pp. 142f–142g for the small group lesson plan.

Whole Group

Use p. 161a.

Language Arts

Use pp. 161e–161k.

FLUENCY

MODEL RHYTHMIC PATTERNS OF LANGUAGE As you read "The Circuit," model fluent reading, modulating your voice in a natural pattern of tones and stresses. Point out that dialogue should sound like the way people speak everyday. You may want to read a few sentences using a robotic monotone or atypical rhythm and discuss the impact on meaning.

LISTENING COMPREHENSION

After reading "The Circuit," use the following questions to assess listening comprehension.

1. **Why is the narrator so nervous the first day at school?** *(Possible responses: He doesn't know anyone. Others are looking at him. English isn't his first language, and he didn't want to read aloud.)* **Cause and Effect**

2. **Why do you think the narrator practices reading in the restroom?** *(Possible response: He wants to practice by himself before having to read in front of the class.)* **Cause and Effect**

BUILD CONCEPT VOCABULARY

Start a web to build concepts and vocabulary related to this week's lesson and the unit theme.

- Draw the Developing New Understandings Concept Web.
- Read the sentence with the word *nervous* again. Ask students to pronounce *nervous* and discuss its meaning.
- Place *nervous* in an oval attached to *Feelings*. Explain that *nervous* is one type of feeling people often have in new situations. Read the sentences in which *accept* and *learn* appear. Have students pronounce the words, place them on the Web, and give reasons.
- Brainstorm additional words and categories for the Web. Keep the Web on display and add words throughout the week.

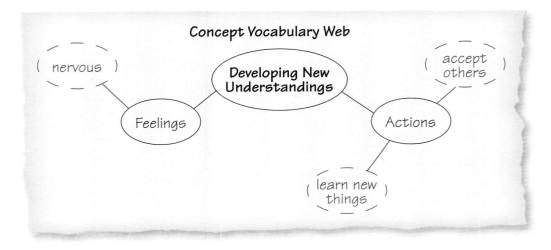

Concept Vocabulary Web

THE CIRCUIT

by Francisco Jiménez

The first day in a new school can be challenging—especially when English is your second language. But, as this young boy finds, sometimes all it takes is for one person to accept and believe in you.

Mr. Lema, the sixth-grade teacher, greeted me and assigned me a desk. He then introduced me to the class. I was so nervous and scared at that moment when everyone's eyes were on me that I wished I were with Papá and Roberto picking cotton. After taking roll, Mr. Lema gave the class the assignment for the first hour. "The first thing we have to do this morning is finish reading the story we began yesterday," he said enthusiastically. He walked up to me, handed me an English book, and asked me to read. "We are on page 125," he said politely. When I heard this, I felt my blood rush to my head; I felt dizzy. "Would you like to read?" he asked hesitantly. I opened the book to page 125. My mouth was dry. My eyes began to water. I could not begin. "You can read later," Mr. Lema said understandingly.

During recess I went into the restroom and opened my English book to page 125. I began to read in a low voice, pretending I was in class. There were many words I did not know. I closed the book and headed back to the classroom.

Mr. Lema was sitting at his desk correcting papers. When I entered he looked up at me and smiled. I felt better. I walked up to him and asked if he could help me with the new words. "Gladly," he said.

The rest of the month I spent my lunch hours working on English with Mr. Lema, my best friend at school.

One Friday, during lunch hour, Mr. Lema asked me to take a walk with him to the music room. "Do you like music?" he asked me as we entered the building. "Yes, I like *corridos*," I answered. He then picked up a trumpet, blew on it, and handed it to me. The sound gave me goose bumps. I knew that sound. I had heard it in many *corridos*. "How would you like to learn how to play it?" he asked. He must have read my face because before I could answer, he added, "I'll teach you how to play it during our lunch hours."

That day I could hardly wait to tell Papá and Mamá the great news. As I got off the bus, my little brothers and sister ran up to meet me. They were yelling and screaming. I thought they were happy to see me, but when I opened the door to our shack, I saw that everything we owned was neatly packed in cardboard boxes.

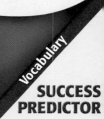

SKILLS ⟷ STRATEGIES IN CONTEXT

Cause and Effect Prior Knowledge

OBJECTIVES

 Determine cause-effect relationships.

 Use prior knowledge to determine cause-effect relationships.

Skills Trace
Cause and Effect

Introduce/Teach	**TE: 4.2 142–143; 4.3 268–269; 4.6 638–639**
Practice	TE: 149, 275, 281, 645, 653 PB: 53, 57, 58, 103, 107, 108, 253, 257, 258
Reteach/Review	TE: 4.1 49; 4.2 161b, DI·52; 4.3 291b, 323, 347, DI·52; 4.6 659b, DI·52 PB: 16, 126, 136
Test	Selection Test: 21–24, 41–44, 101–104; Benchmark Test: Unit 3

INTRODUCE

Hold out a ball and let it drop to the floor. Ask what happened. *(The ball fell.)* Then ask why it happened. *(Gravity pulled it to the ground.)* Explain an effect is *what* happens (the ball fell). The cause is what made it happen (gravity).

Have students read the information on p. 142. Explain the following:

- Words like *because* and *so* are clues to causes and effects in texts. Words that follow *because* often state the cause. Words that follow *so* often state the effect.
- Sometimes you have to use what you already know to figure out a cause-effect relationship.

Use Skill Transparency 6 to teach cause-effect relationships and prior knowledge.

What Jo Did

Comprehension

Skill
Cause and Effect

Strategy
Prior Knowledge

 **Cause and Effect**

- An effect is *what* happens. A cause is *why* it happens.
- Clue words such as *because, so,* and *cause* sometimes signal a cause-effect relationship. Sometimes you must figure out for yourself that one thing causes another.

Cause	→	Effect

Strategy: Prior Knowledge

Good readers use what they know, their prior knowledge, to help them understand what they read. As they read new information, they try to connect it to what they already know. They think about whether they have ever seen or experienced what they are reading about. This helps them understand the new information. Using what you already know can help you understand causes and effects.

Write to Read

1. Read "Up, Up, and Down." Make a graphic organizer like the one above to describe two cause-effect relationships.

2. Write a sentence about each cause-effect relationship. Use a clue word to show the relationship.

142

Strategic Intervention

 Cause and Effect Explain that whenever students want to find an effect, they should ask themselves: *What happened?* To find the cause, they should ask: *Why did it happen?* To help students develop the cause-effect organizer on p. 142, begin by reading the second sentence in paragraph 2 on p. 143. Ask students what happened. Then ask them: *What made it happen?* Point out that the word *because* is a clue word that a cause is being stated.

ELL

Access Content

Beginning/Intermediate For a Picture It! lesson on cause and effect, see the ELL Teaching Guide, pp. 36–37.

Advanced Sometimes when people release balloons in the air, they say "Up, up, and away!" Have students tell how this expression relates to the title on p. 143.

Up, Up, and Down

Did you ever see basketball players leap high into the air to shoot a ball into a basket? Or even higher still to block a shot? How do they jump so high?

The trick is to beat the Earth's gravity. Because of this force, a person is pulled to the ground. To move away from this force, you need energy.

Think of a spring, or better yet, think of a spring in a pogo stick. Your weight on the stick presses the spring down. That stores energy in the spring. When that energy is released, it is enough to lift the stick and you off the ground.

In a similar way, you can build up energy in your legs. If you stand straight and then try to jump up, you can't. You may be able to lift off the ground an inch or so, but that's all. That's why you bend at the knees before jumping up. When you bend, it's as if you are putting a "spring" in your legs. Release that spring, and up you go.

Of course, the energy is not nearly enough to overcome Earth's gravity. That's why the Earth will always pull you back down again.

1 **Skill** There is a cause-effect relationship in this paragraph. Look for a clue word.

2 **Strategy** Think of what you know about gravity. What effect does this force have on you?

3 **Skill** Look for cause-effect relationships in this paragraph. What causes energy to be stored? What effect does releasing it have?

4 **Strategy** Have you ever seen or played on a pogo stick? If not, just think of what you know about jumping off the ground as you read the next paragraph.

143

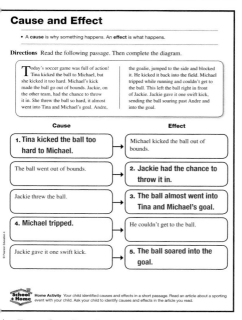

Available as **Skill Transparency** 6

Cause and Effect

• A **cause** is why something happens. An **effect** is what happens.

Directions Read the following passage. Then complete the diagram.

Today's soccer game was full of action! Tina kicked the ball to Michael, but she kicked it too hard. Michael's kick made the ball go out of bounds. Jackie, on the other team, had the chance to throw it in. She threw the ball so hard, it almost went into Tina and Michael's goal. Andre, the goalie, jumped to the side and blocked it. He kicked it back into the field. Michael tripped while running and couldn't get to the ball. This left the ball right in front of Jackie. Jackie gave it one swift kick, sending the ball soaring past Andre and into the goal.

Cause	Effect
1. Tina kicked the ball too hard to Michael.	Michael kicked the ball out of bounds.
The ball went out of bounds.	2. Jackie had the chance to throw it in.
Jackie threw the ball.	3. The ball almost went into Tina and Michael's goal.
4. Michael tripped.	He couldn't get to the ball.
Jackie gave it one swift kick.	5. The ball soared into the goal.

Home Activity Your child identified causes and effects in a short passage. Read an article about a sporting event with your child. Ask your child to identify causes and effects in the article you read.

▲ **Practice Book** p. 53

TEACH

1 **SKILL** Use paragraph 2 to model how to find a cause-effect relationship.

Think Aloud **MODEL** To find the effect, I ask myself: *What happens?* What happens is that the person is pulled to the ground. To find the cause, I ask: *Why does it happen?* The first two sentences talk about gravity. The word *because* is a clue word. It is because of gravity that a person is pulled to the ground, so gravity is the cause.

2 **STRATEGY** Discuss what you already know to model using prior knowledge.

Think Aloud **MODEL** I know that gravity is what pulls things down. That's why my body stays on the ground when I walk. People float in space because there is no gravity there. So I can use what I already know about gravity to figure out that gravity is the cause of people being pulled to the ground.

PRACTICE AND ASSESS

3 **SKILL** Cause: Your weight presses the spring down. Effect: The spring lifts the stick and you off the ground.

4 **STRATEGY** Students' responses should reflect understanding of how gravity and muscles work when students jump.

WRITE Have students complete steps 1 and 2 of the Write to Read activity. You might consider using this as a whole-class activity.

Monitor Progress
Cause and Effect

If... students are unable to complete **Write to Read** on p. 142,	then... use Practice Book p. 53 to provide additional practice.

ONLINE

Students can go online and use a student-friendly search engine to find out more about basketball rules, favorite teams, or players. Have them use *playing basketball* or the name of a specific team or player as keywords for their search.

ELL

Build Background Use ELL Poster 6 to build background and vocabulary for the lesson concept of developing new understandings.

▲ **ELL Poster** 6

Build Background

ACTIVATE PRIOR KNOWLEDGE

BEGIN A FOUR-COLUMN CHART about basketball.

- Display a four-column chart with the heads *Basketball Terms, Basketball Equipment, Special Skills,* and *Important Rules.* Give students a few minutes to list as many things as they can in each category. Record students' responses in the chart. Add ideas of your own, if needed.
- You may wish to invite volunteers to demonstrate an imaginary game to help students less familiar with this sport.
- Tell students that, as they read, they should look for new information about basketball and what it takes to be a good player.

Basketball Terms	Basketball Equipment	Special Skills	Important Rules
jump shot	basketball	can jump high	must dribble ball as you move
foul	hoop	can run fast	
	backboard	can get ball in hoop	

▲ **Graphic Organizer** 27

BACKGROUND BUILDING AUDIO This week's audio explores the WNBA. After students listen, discuss what they found out about the challenges female players faced.

Background Building Audio

Introduce Vocabulary

CATEGORIES CHART

Create a three-column chart that students can use to classify their lesson vocabulary words.

Basketball Words	Action Words	Describing Words
rim	swatted	unbelievable
fouled	fouled	

▲ **Graphic Organizer** 26

Display the lesson vocabulary words. Have students tell what they know about the words. Ask them to think about word meaning, check their glossary if needed, and write each word in one or more columns of the chart. **Activate Prior Knowledge**

Discuss other meanings of words from the *Basketball Words* column. Explain that sports is one area in which jargon, or specialized vocabulary, is common. **Specialized Vocabulary**

Students may create different categories for lesson vocabulary words at the end of the week or add additional words to the categories above.

Have students use these steps for reading multisyllabic words. (See the Multisyllabic Word Routine on p. DI·1.)

1. **Look for Meaningful Word Parts** (base words, endings, prefixes, suffixes, roots) Think about the meaning of each part. Use the parts to read the word. Model: I see *–less* at the end of *speechless*. The word speech means "talk." The suffix *–less* means "without" or "not." So *speechless* means "without talk."

2. **Chunk Words with No Recognizable Parts** Say each chunk slowly. Then say the chunks fast to make a word. Model: *jer, sey—jersey*.

By the end of the week, students should know the lesson vocabulary words. Have them classify as many words as they can in the three-column chart.

Lesson Vocabulary

WORDS TO KNOW

T fouled in sports, made an unfair play against

T hoop a ring or round, flat band

T jersey a shirt that is pulled over the head, made of a soft, knitted cloth

T marveled was filled with wonder; was astonished

T rim an edge, border, or margin on or around anything

T speechless not able to talk

T swatted hit sharply or violently

T unbelievable incredible; hard to think of as true or real

MORE WORDS TO KNOW

backboard in basketball, the flat, elevated surface of wood, glass, or plastic on which the basket on a basketball court is fastened

dribbling moving a ball by bouncing it

dunk to shoot a basketball by leaping, so that the hands are above the rim, and throwing the ball down through the netting

T = Tested Word

Vocabulary

Directions Choose the word from the box that best matches each definition. Write the word on the line shown to the left.

speechless   1. not able to speak

swatted   2. hit sharply away

marveled   3. was filled with wonder

hoop   4. a ring or round band

unbelievable   5. incredible

Check the Words You Know
__fouled
__hoop
__jersey
__marveled
__rim
__speechless
__swatted
__unbelievable

Directions Choose the word from the box that best matches each clue. Write the word on the line.

jersey   6. You might wear this while playing a sport.

rim   7. This is part of a basketball hoop.

fouled   8. This is when someone made an unfair play in a sport.

speechless   9. This is what you are when you don't have anything to say.

unbelievable   10. This is something you thought was not possible.

Write a News Report

On a separate sheet of paper, write a news report about a sporting event. Use as many vocabulary words as you can. **News reports should include words from the vocabulary list and details describing a sporting event.**

School + Home Home Activity Your child identified and used vocabulary words from *What Jo Did*. Work with your child to make a crossword puzzle with the words and to write original clues for it.

▲ **Practice Book** p. 54

Vocabulary Strategy

OBJECTIVE

⊙ Use word structure to determine word meaning.

INTRODUCE

Discuss the strategy for word structure by using the steps on p. 144.

TEACH

- Have students read "At the Game," paying attention to how vocabulary words are used.
- Model using word structure to determine the meaning of *unbelievable.*

Think Aloud **MODEL** The prefix *un-* means "not" and the suffix *-able* means "able to." So if I put these meanings together with the base word *believe,* the word means "not able to believe" or "not believable."

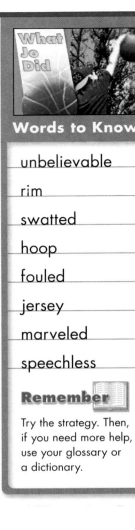

Words to Know

- unbelievable
- rim
- swatted
- hoop
- fouled
- jersey
- marveled
- speechless

Remember

Try the strategy. Then, if you need more help, use your glossary or a dictionary.

Vocabulary Strategy
for Prefixes and Suffixes

Word Structure Prefixes and suffixes have their own meanings. When they are added to words, they change the meaning of the original word, the base word. The prefix *un-* means "the opposite of ____" or "not ____," as in *unhappy.* The suffix *-able* means "able to be ___ed," as in *enjoyable.* The suffix *-less* means "without ____," as in *painless.* You can use prefixes and suffixes to help you figure out the meanings of words.

1. Look at an unfamiliar word to see if it has a base word you know.

2. Check to see if the prefix *un-* or the suffix *-able* or *-less* has been added to the base word.

3. Think about how the prefix or suffix changes the meaning of the base word.

4. Try the meaning in the sentence.

As you read "At the Game," look for words with the prefix *un-* or the suffix *-able* or *-less.* Use the prefix and suffixes to help you figure out the meanings of the words.

144

DAY 2 Grouping Options

Reading

Whole Group Discuss the Question of the Day. Then use pp. 144–147.

Group Time **Differentiated Instruction**
Read "What Jo Did." See pp. 142f–142g for the small group lesson plan.

Whole Group Use p. 161a.

Language Arts
Use pp. 161e–161k.

Strategic Intervention

⊙ **Word Structure** Follow the steps on p. 144. Write the meaning of each suffix, prefix, and base word and then put them together.

ELL

Access Content Use ELL Poster 6 to preteach vocabulary. Choose from the following to meet language proficiency levels.

Beginning Provide a photograph of a basketball action shot. Have students point out the vocabulary words pictured.

Intermediate Have students work in pairs. One partner writes the vocabulary words on a set of cards while the other partner writes the definitions on another set of cards. Have them use the cards to test each other.

Advanced Teach the lesson on pp. 144–145. Have students rephrase the sentences containing vocabulary words.

Resources for home-language words may include parents, bilingual staff members, bilingual dictionaries, or online translation sources.

At the Game

"Hello again, sports fans. This is Bud Sherman, WXXT Channel 6, coming to you from the Grandview Center, where the third-place Tigers are battling the second-place Lions in the first round of the HSBA playoffs. Tiger forward Matt Roberts has had a flawless game, scoring 28 points so far. Lion center Darren Jones has been unbelievable under the basket.

"Now Roberts moves in and throws the ball. He's looking for another three-pointer. The ball hits the rim. Maxwell tries a shot, but it's swatted away by Jones.

Grundig has the ball and he's heading for the Tigers' hoop. Oh, my, he's been fouled by Lee, who grabbed Grundig's jersey and arm. I imagine Coach Simmons is unhappy. That's Lee's fourth foul in this half. Grundig, a reliable free-thrower, makes both points. Pfizer throws in to Barton, who passes to—Roberts! You know, I have always marveled at the way Roberts moves around the court, but his performance tonight just leaves me speechless. Roberts shoots from 30 feet out—and he scores! The Tigers win, 87–84."

Words to Write

Imagine that you are playing basketball with a friend. Describe the action. Use words from the Words to Know list.

145

Connect to Phonics

Word Study/Decoding Point out that a prefix or a suffix changes the meaning of the base word. Model identifying the suffix and base word using *flawless* on p. 145, paragraph 1. Have students suggest other words they know with *un-*, *-able*, and *-less*. Have students identify the prefix or suffix and base in each word. Then have them identify the meaning of each word with and without the prefix or suffix.

PRACTICE AND ASSESS

- Have students determine the meaning of *speechless* using their knowledge of suffixes.
- Have students figure out the meanings of the remaining words and tell the strategies they used.
- If you began a categories chart (p. 144b), have students reassess their charts.
- Have students complete Practice Book p. 55.

WRITE Writing could also include vocabulary words that give the reaction of the players as a result of the action.

Monitor Progress

Word Structure

If... students need more practice with the lesson vocabulary,	then... use Tested Vocabulary Cards.

Vocabulary • Word Structure

- **Prefixes** and **suffixes** have their own meanings and are added to base words. They change the meanings of base words.
- The prefix *un-* means "the opposite of _____" or "not _____." The suffix *-able* means "able to be _____ed." The suffix *-less* means "without _____."

Directions Read the following passage about a basketball game. Look for the prefix *un-* and the suffixes *-able* and *-less* as you read. Then answer the questions below.

It was the most unforgettable basketball game I ever saw. When the referee said a foul had been made against our star player, I was speechless. The fans for our team were unable to stop yelling. It was useless to try to quiet them. They couldn't believe we were so lucky. We had played an unbelievable game and we were tied with a few seconds to go. It was up to our guard at the free-throw line. As I uncovered my eyes, I saw the effortless shot soar through the hoop like a bird. We won!

1. What does *unbelievable* mean? What are its prefix and suffix?

not able to be believed; prefix *un-*, suffix *-able*

2. What does *useless* mean? Does it have a prefix or suffix?

without use; It has the suffix *-less.*

3. How are *speechless* and *effortless* alike? What does each word mean?

Each has the suffix *-less;* They mean "without speech" and "without effort."

4. What does *unforgettable* mean? What are its prefix and suffix?

not able to be forgotten; prefix *un-*, suffix *-able*

5. Write a sentence using two words that have a prefix or a suffix. Tell the meaning of those words.

Students' answers should include at least two words with a prefix or suffix and those words' meanings.

Home Activity Your child identified and used prefixes and suffixes to understand words in a passage. With your child, make a list of words associated with a favorite sport or activity. Ask your child how the meanings change when you add a prefix, a suffix, or both.

▲ **Practice Book** p. 55

Prereading Strategies

GENRE STUDY

Fiction

"What Jo Did" is fiction. Explain that fiction tells stories about events that are possible, but not necessarily probable. "What Jo Did" is a short story–a piece of fiction that focuses on one or only a few characters and a single event.

PREVIEW AND PREDICT

Have students preview the title and illustrations and predict what they think the story is about. Point out the spelling of *Jo* in the title and have them make predictions about the story's main character. Encourage students to use lesson vocabulary words as they talk about their predictions.

Activate Prior Knowledge Have students list what they know about the skills of a good basketball player. Students will review and revise their lists in the Strategy Response Log activity on p. 151.

What Jo Did

text and images by Charles R. Smith Jr.

 Genre   **Fiction** often has characters and events that seem real. As you read, try to picture this story taking place where you live, with people you know.

146

ELL

Access Content Lead a picture walk to reinforce basketball-related vocabulary, such as *basketball* (p. 148), *rim* (p. 148), *hoop* (p. 150), and *dunk* (p. 151).

Consider having students read the selection summary in English or in students' home languages. See the Multilingual Summaries in the ELL Teaching Guide, pp. 40–42.

What can Jo do that others cannot?

SET PURPOSE

Read the first page of the story aloud to students. Have them recall the preview discussion and tell what they hope to find out about Jo as they read the story.

Remind students to look for cause and effect relationships as they read.

STRATEGY RECALL

Students have now used these before-reading strategies:

- preview the selection to be aware of its genre, features, and possible content;
- activate prior knowledge about that content and what to expect of that genre;
- make predictions;
- set a purpose for reading.

Remind students to be aware of and flexibly use the during-reading strategies they have learned:

- link prior knowledge to new information;
- summarize text they have read so far;
- ask clarifying questions;
- answer questions they or others pose;
- check their predictions and either refine them or make new predictions;
- recognize the text structure the author is using, and use that knowledge to make predictions and increase comprehension;
- visualize what the author is describing;
- monitor their comprehension and use fix-up strategies.

After reading, students will use these strategies:

- summarize or retell the text;
- answer questions they or others pose;
- reflect to make new information become part of their prior knowledge.

 **AudioText**

Guiding Comprehension

1 🎯 **Cause and Effect • Literal**

Why do Joanna's parents hang the basketball rim up so high?

They don't know how high a basketball rim should be, so they decide to hang it the height of their roof.

Monitor Progress
🎯 **Cause and Effect**

If... students are unable to determine the cause,	**then...** use the skill and strategy instruction on p. 149.

2 **Draw Conclusions • Critical**

Text to Self **Think about when Jo meets the boys. Does this situation remind you of a time you tried something new? Would you act like Jo does?**

Possible response: Jo feels nervous playing basketball with others, so she lets the boys think she is a boy. If I were Jo, I might not tell the boys about being a girl or that I hadn't played before. Student responses will vary about first-time experiences.

Tech Files
ONLINE

Students can search the Internet to find out more about the rules, court dimensions, and history of basketball. Have them use a student-friendly search engine and keywords such as *basketball*, *women and basketball*, and *Basketball Hall of Fame*. Be sure to follow classroom rules for Internet use.

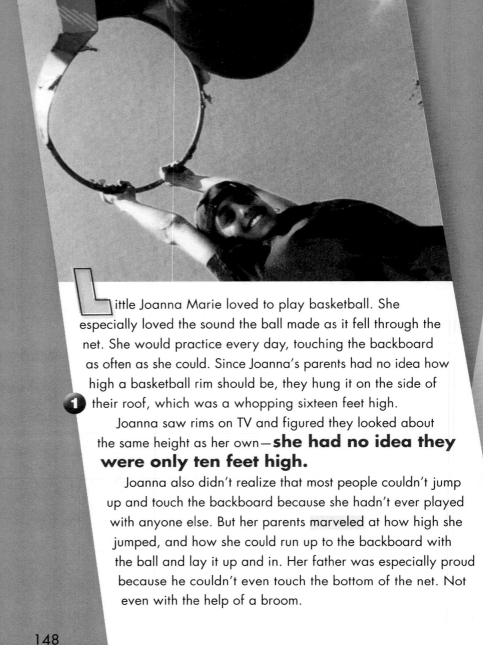

Little Joanna Marie loved to play basketball. She especially loved the sound the ball made as it fell through the net. She would practice every day, touching the backboard as often as she could. Since Joanna's parents had no idea how high a basketball rim should be, they hung it on the side of **1** their roof, which was a whopping sixteen feet high.

Joanna saw rims on TV and figured they looked about the same height as her own—**she had no idea they were only ten feet high.**

Joanna also didn't realize that most people couldn't jump up and touch the backboard because she hadn't ever played with anyone else. But her parents marveled at how high she jumped, and how she could run up to the backboard with the ball and lay it up and in. Her father was especially proud because he couldn't even touch the bottom of the net. Not even with the help of a broom.

148

ELL

Access Content Point out the names *Jo* and *Joe* in the last two paragraphs on p. 149. Explain that *Jo* is short for *Joanna*, a girl's name. *Joe* is short for *Joseph*, a boy's name. Ask students why Joanna says her name is Jo.

ne day Joanna, her hair bundled up under her baseball cap, was dribbling her basketball on the way to the store to get some sugar for her mother. Her mother said that she didn't have to hurry home, as long as she was in by dark. As Joanna moved down the street, a basketball came rolling out of nowhere and bumped her high-tops.

"I'm sorry, man, I didn't mean to hit you with the ball like that," said a young boy dressed in sneakers, shorts, and a Bulls tank top as he picked up the ball.

"Oh, that's okay. I wasn't even paying attention," Joanna said.

"Hey, we need one more to play a game. You in?" he asked her.

"Sure, why not?" she responded.

As Joanna approached the other boys, she remembered that she had her hat on.

They probably think I'm a boy, she thought. Might as well enjoy the ride.

The boys picked teams, and since Joanna was smaller than everyone else, she got picked last. It didn't bother her, though, because she had never played with anyone before and was just happy to be there.

"Hey, kid, what's your name?" asked a freckle-faced kid with red hair.

"Ahhh . . . Jo. My name is Jo," Joanna said nervously. ❷

"All right, Joe, you pick up T.J. over there, see. Make sure he doesn't score a basket. He can jump pretty high, ya know!"

Women's Rights

In the early history of the United States, women had few educational or job opportunities. They did not have the same rights as men regarding property ownership, public speaking, or voting. Frustrated by such inequalities, a group of men and women met in Seneca Falls, New York, in 1848 to address women's rights. As a result, sixty-eight women and thirty-two men signed The Declaration of Sentiments. This document, modeled after the Declaration of Independence, declared that "...all men and women are created equal," and demanded women be given "...all the rights and privileges which belong to them as citizens of the United States." The efforts of these men and women eventually led to improved rights for women, including the right to vote guaranteed by the Nineteenth Amendment in 1920.

Time for SOCIAL STUDIES

⟳ SKILLS ⟷ STRATEGIES IN CONTEXT

Cause and Effect

TEACH

- Remind students that a cause is *why* something happens and an effect is *what* happens.
- Clue words such as *because, since, so,* and *cause* signal a cause and effect relationship.
- Model understanding of the cause and effect relationship on p. 148, paragraph 1.

Think Aloud **MODEL** To find out why Joanna's parents hung the rim so high, I look for a cause. The word *since* is a clue that the first part of the sentence shows a cause: Joanna's parents don't know how high the rim should be hung. That explains why they hung it sixteen feet high.

PRACTICE AND ASSESS

Have students read p. 148, paragraph 3, and tell why Joanna's father is especially proud of her. *(She can jump higher than he could reach with a broom.)*

EXTEND SKILLS
Short Story

Tell students that "What Jo Did" is a short story, a fictional narrative that focuses on a few characters and describes a single event. A short story is shorter than a novel but has the same elements.

Guiding Comprehension

3  **Vocabulary • Word Structure**

Have students explain the meanings of the prefix and suffix for *unbelievable* on p. 151, paragraph 3. Then have them tell the meaning of the word.

Un- means "not" and *-able* means "able to," so *unbelievable* means "not able to believe something."

Monitor Progress

Word Structure

If... students have difficulty using prefixes and suffixes to determine meaning,	**then...** use the vocabulary instruction on p. 151.

---

4 **Character • Inferential**

What does Joanna think might happen if she removes her hat?

Possible response: The boys will find out that she is a girl, and they might not want to keep playing basketball with her.

5 **Cause and Effect • Inferential**

What happens because Jo blocks some of the boys' shots?

Possible responses: The boys become impressed by Jo's skills. They start passing the ball to keep it away from her. They wonder if she is able to dunk the ball.

J o moved around, not really touching the ball at first, just trying to get a feel for playing with other people. She had never even passed the ball or received a pass herself. Playing with others took getting used to, but in no time she was passing the ball. The only thing that puzzled her was why the hoop was so low.

Even though the boys passed the ball around a lot, T.J. didn't really touch it much, and when he did, he didn't take a shot. Finally, he was wide open for a jump shot when Jo came out of nowhere, jumped high into the air, **and swatted his shot into the next court.**

150

ELL

Understanding Idioms To explain the idiom *get used to*, restate "Playing with others took getting used to," (p. 150, paragraph 1) as "Jo needed to feel comfortable playing with others." Ask students to share new experiences they had to get used to (or feel comfortable with).

"**W**OW, did you see that?"

Did you see how high he jumped?" the freckle-faced kid said, his mouth wide open.

"I've never seen anybody jump that high. Not even Michael Jordan," said the kid with the Bulls jersey on.

"Unbelievable."

"Where'd you learn to do that?"

"Oh, my goodness!!!"

"Poor T.J."

"Hey—I got fouled, and besides, it wasn't that high," said T.J., but his face was so red that he couldn't hide his embarrassment.

"Uh, uh . . . it's just something I picked up. I practice a lot with my dad," Jo added, surprised at how big a deal the boys made of her block.

"Man! You must have some dad," one of the boys said. The game continued, and Jo was passed the ball more often. Her teammates encouraged her to shoot more, and when she did, they were amazed how the ball arced in the air like a rainbow before falling straight through the hoop, without touching the rim. As the game progressed, Jo felt hot, but she knew she couldn't take her hat off, or else she'd be found out. **4**

Whenever a boy got the ball and Jo came over to play defense, he quickly passed the ball away. Jo blocked a few more shots, which created more *ooooohs* and *aaaaaaahs,* and **5** one of the boys on her team asked her if she could dunk the ball.

"Dunk? What's that?" Jo asked. This was a word she had never heard before.

151

Develop Vocabulary

PRACTICE LESSON VOCABULARY

Students orally respond *yes* or *no* to each question and provide a reason for each answer. Possible responses are given.

1. Would you react if someone *swatted* something at you? *(Yes; that person would be hitting something quickly toward me.)*

2. Does a glass have a *rim*? *(Yes; it has an edge that is shaped like a circle.)*

3. Would a *hoop* fit snugly around a desk? *(No; a hoop is a circular shape, and a desk is rectangular.)*

BUILD CONCEPT VOCABULARY

Review previous concept words with students. Ask if students have come across any words today in their reading or elsewhere that they would like to add to the Developing New Understandings Concept Web, such as *surprised* or *encouraged*.

VOCABULARY STRATEGY

Word Structure

TEACH

- Prefixes and suffixes have their own meanings and can change the meaning of a base word.

- *Un-* means "the opposite of" or "not"; *-able* means "able to be"; *-less* means "without."

- Model using prefixes and suffixes to determine the meaning of *unbelievable.*

Think Aloud **MODEL** To figure out the meaning of *unbelievable,* I look at its parts. I see the prefix *un-* at the beginning, the base word *believe* in the middle, and the suffix *-able* at the end. I can use the meanings of these word parts to figure out that *unbelievable* means "not able to be believed."

PRACTICE AND ASSESS

Have students use prefixes and suffixes to determine the meaning of *enjoyable, unfair, unforgettable, hopeless,* and *scoreless.* To assess, have them use one of these words in a sentence about a basketball game.

Strategy Response Log

Monitor Comprehension Have students review the lists they made about the skills good basketball players need. (See p. 146.) Have them revise or add to their lists based on what they have read.

If you want to teach this story in two sessions, stop here.

Guiding Comprehension

If you are teaching this story in two days, discuss cause and effect relationships read thus far and review the vocabulary.

6 **Draw Conclusions • Inferential**
Why do you think the freckle-faced boy wants to see Jo dunk the ball?

Possible response: He wants to see if she can make a tough shot like a dunk.

Monitor Progress

REVIEW Draw Conclusions

If... students have difficulty drawing conclusions,	**then...** use the skill and strategy instruction on p. 153.

---

7 **Author's Craft • Critical**
Question the Author **Why do you think the text on p. 153 is slanted?**

Possible response: It reflects Jo going up high to the rim and then coming down.

8 **Draw Conclusions • Inferential**
What causes the boys' mouths to hang open?

Possible response: Jo to dunked the ball.

DAY 3 Grouping Options

Reading
Whole Group Discuss the Question of the Day.

Group Time Differentiated Instruction
Read "What Jo Did." See pp. 142f–142g for the small group lesson plan.

Whole Group Discuss the Reader Response questions on page 156. Then use p. 161a.

Language Arts
Use pp. 161e–161k.

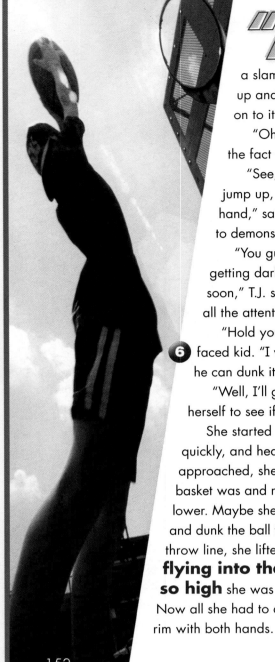

"**A dunk.** You know— a slam, a jam, to throw it down. You jump up and put the ball in the rim while holding on to it."

"Ohhhh . . . that," she said, trying to hide the fact that she had never heard of it before.

"See, what you do is, you dribble the ball, jump up, and put the ball in the rim with your hand," said a kid with a Lakers jersey on, trying to demonstrate on the ground as best he could.

"You guys, can we finish this game? It's getting dark and my mom wants me home soon," T.J. said, still upset that Jo was getting all the attention and that his shot was blocked.

"Hold your horses, T.J.," said the freckle-**6** faced kid. "I wanna see Joe dunk. I'll bet that he can dunk it better than Michael can."

"Well, I'll give it a shot," Jo said, curious herself to see if she could "dunk."

She started at half-court, dribbling the ball quickly, and headed straight for the rim. As she approached, she remembered how high her basket was and realized that this one was much lower. Maybe she *could* jump a little farther out and dunk the ball through. As she got to the free throw line, she lifted her left leg up and went **flying into the air, till she was so high** she was looking down on the hoop. Now all she had to do was put the ball in the rim with both hands.

152

ELL

Build Background If students are unfamiliar with the game of basketball or the terms *dunk* and *dribble* (p. 152, paragraphs 1 and 3), have volunteers pantomime the movements.

She was up there for a while before she felt her hands on the rim, the ball going through, and her feet touching the ground. **7**

When she landed, all of the boys' mouths were hanging open, **8** and for a moment they were speechless.

153

Title IX

Today, it's common to see girls like Jo playing sports. This happened as a result of Title IX, a 1972 law passed by the U.S. Congress banning gender discrimination in schools receiving Federal money. Title IX requires schools to give boys and girls equal opportunities to participate in school classes and programs, including sports. Because of this law, boys and girls can now participate in classes that traditionally might have excluded them. Since the passing of Title IX, the number of women earning college degrees and playing sports has greatly increased. However, Title IX has caused controversy over how schools' resources are used. Under Title IX, schools must provide money, staffing, facilities, and other resources to boys' and girls' programs in proportion to the number of girls and boys enrolled in a school. In some cases, schools that are not able or willing to improve or expand resources for programs involving girls have had to make cuts to other programs.

SKILLS ←→ STRATEGIES IN CONTEXT

Draw Conclusions REVIEW

TEACH

- Remind students that when they draw conclusions they use story details and what they already know to form opinions or make decisions about characters and events.

- Model drawing conclusions using p. 152, paragraph 5.

Think Aloud **MODEL** I think the boy wants to see Jo dunk the ball because he wants to see if she can really make this kind of a shot. He knows Jo can jump high. I know not many people can dunk a ball, so I'd be curious to see someone do it.

PRACTICE AND ASSESS

- Ask students how they think Jo feels after she makes the dunk. Have them support their conclusions. (*Possible response: She probably feels surprised and proud. She wasn't sure she could make the shot. It's the first time she tried to dunk the ball.*)

- To assess, use Practice Book p. 56.

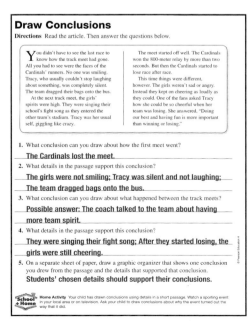

Draw Conclusions

Directions Read the article. Then answer the questions below.

You didn't have to see the last race to know how the track meet had gone. All you had to see were the faces of the Cardinals' runners. No one was smiling. Tracy, who usually couldn't stop laughing about something, was completely silent. The team dragged their bags onto the bus.

At the next track meet, the girls' spirits were high. They were singing their school's fight song as they entered the other team's stadium. Tracy was her usual self, giggling like crazy.

The meet started off well. The Cardinals won the 800-meter relay by more than two seconds. But then the Cardinals started to lose race after race.

This time things were different, however. The girls weren't sad or angry. Instead they kept cheering as loudly as they could. One of the fans asked Tracy how she could be so cheerful when her team was losing. She answered, "Doing our best and having fun is more important than winning or losing."

1. What conclusion can you draw about how the first meet went?
   The Cardinals lost the meet.
2. What details in the passage support this conclusion?
   The girls were not smiling; Tracy was silent and not laughing; The team dragged bags onto the bus.
3. What conclusion can you draw about what happened between the track meets?
   Possible answer: The coach talked to the team about having more team spirit.
4. What details in the passage support this conclusion?
   They were singing their fight song; After they started losing, the girls were still cheering.
5. On a separate sheet of paper, draw a graphic organizer that shows one conclusion you drew from the passage and the details that supported that conclusion.
   Students' chosen details should support their conclusions.

School + Home **Home Activity** Your child has drawn conclusions using details in a short passage. Watch a sporting event in your local area or on television. Ask your child to draw conclusions about why the event turned out the way that it did.

▲ **Practice Book** p. 56

What Jo Did **153**

Guiding Comprehension

9 **Plot • Inferential**

How do the boys find out Jo is a girl?

When she dunks the ball, her hat falls off.

10 **Draw Conclusions • Critical**

Why is "Jumpin' Jo" a good nickname for Jo?

Possible responses: Both names begin with *J*, so they sound good together. Jo can jump really well, so it's a positive nickname that emphasizes her playing skills.

11 ⦿ **Prior Knowledge • Critical**

Text to World **Does Jo's experience with these boys remind you of girls and boys you know? Explain why or why not.**

Possible response: Yes, I play sports with boys, and most of them don't care if I'm a girl as long as I'm a good player.

Strategy Response Log

Summarize When students finish reading the selection, provide this prompt: Imagine a friend has asked you for a good story about sports. Write your friend a summary of "What Jo Did" in four or five sentences.

"No way."

"It can't be!"

"Am I seeing right?"

"That's impossible."

"How did she . . . ?"

Then:

As the boys stared at her, Jo looked down at the ground and saw her hat lying there.

She froze.

154

ELL

Activate Prior Knowledge Discuss nicknames. Ask why the boys gave Jo a nickname (p. 155, paragraph 5). Invite students to share any nicknames they have and tell how they got these nicknames. You might distinguish between positive nicknames people enjoy having and the idea of "calling someone names" that are insulting.

"S o, like . . . you're a girl?" said the kid with the **9** Lakers jersey.

"Ahhhh . . . yeah . . . you could say that," Jo answered slowly.

"I can't believe it, you guys, we've been playing basketball with a girl," T.J. said with disgust.

"Hey, she may be a girl, but I'd play on her team anytime." The kid with the Bulls jersey approached Jo and gave her a high five.

After that, they congratulated Jo and introduced themselves. They even came up with a nickname for her: Jumpin' Jo. In the **10** end, T.J. walked up to her and apologized.

"Sorry, Jo," he whispered. "I just never played against a girl before. Especially a girl as good as you. I've never seen anyone who can jump like that! You should come and play with us again sometime.

But next time, leave the hat at home." **11**

155

Develop Vocabulary

PRACTICE LESSON VOCABULARY

Students orally respond *yes* or *no* to each question and provide a reason for each answer. Possible responses are given.

1. Would an alien coming out of a spaceship be *unbelievable*? *(Yes; that is something you could not believe would happen.)*

2. When you get *fouled* by someone, did the other player act fairly? *(No; you get fouled when someone makes an unfair play.)*

3. Can you bounce a *jersey*? *(No; you wear a jersey.)*

4. Would your friends have *marveled* if you jumped 16 feet high? *(Yes; they would be astonished if I jumped that high.)*

BUILD CONCEPT VOCABULARY

Review previous concept words with students. Ask if they have come across any words today that they would like to add to the Developing New Understandings Concept Web, such as *introduced* or *apologized*.

STRATEGY SELF-CHECK

Prior Knowledge

Discuss what happens when the boys discover Jo is a girl and why they react as they do. Students can use prior knowledge about girls and boys playing sports together to help them understand cause and effect relationships in the story. Use Practice Book p. 57.

SELF-CHECK

Students can ask themselves these questions to assess understanding of the story.

- Can I describe *what* happens at the end of the story and tell *why* it happens?
- How does my prior knowledge help me understand cause and effect relationships in the story?

Monitor Progress	
Cause and Effect	
If... students have difficulty using prior knowledge to understand cause-effect relationships,	**then...** use the Reteach lesson on p. 161b.

Cause and Effect

- A **cause** is why something happens. An **effect** is what happens.
- Clue words such as *because, so,* and *since* sometimes signal a cause-effect relationship. Sometimes you must figure out for yourself that one thing causes another.

Directions Read the following passage. Then answer the questions below.

Ana's brothers said she couldn't play baseball with them because she was younger than they were. This made Ana angry. She knew she was good at throwing, and she also had a strong swing. "They're just worried about what their friends will say," thought Ana. She took a seat behind the dugout to watch the game. During the first inning, Ana's brother Jose jammed his finger while trying to catch a fast grounder. He had to leave the game to get some ice. This was Ana's chance. She volunteered to take his place. Everado, her other brother, stared her down with an irritated look. "Of course you can play," said one of the other players. "Do you have your mitt?" asked another. Ana did, and she ran onto the field with a smile on her face.

1. At the beginning of the passage, what was the cause of Ana not being able to play?

   Ana was younger than her brothers, and they were afraid of what their friends would say.

2. What was the effect of this event?

   Ana got angry.

3. What was the cause of Jose's jammed finger?

   He was trying to catch a fast grounder.

4. What was the effect of this event?

   Ana was able to join the game.

5. Have you ever been told you could not do something you knew you were able to do? How did it make you feel? Compare your situation with Ana's.

   Students' answers should describe their situations and compare their own feelings with Ana's.

School + Home Home Activity Your child identified causes and effects in a short passage. Have your child write a short story about a sporting event or other event. Ask your child to underline the causes and effects of the events in the story.

▲ **Practice Book** p. 57

Reader Response

Open for Discussion Personal Response

Think Aloud **MODEL** I'd start by saying something like, "Guess what just happened!" Then I'd tell about how I played basketball with a group of boys and that they were amazed by how well I played.

Comprehension Check Critical Response

1. Responses will vary. Words: *backboards, jam, net, basket, jumpshot.* **Author's Purpose**

2. Joanna blocks his shot. T.J. feels embarrassed, claims he was fouled, and says Joanna's jump wasn't that high. ⊙ *Cause/Effect*

3. Responses will vary but should describe a personal experience like Joanna's. ⊙ *Prior Knowledge*

4. Words: *unbelievable, speechless, marveled.* Phrases should indicate understanding of Joanna's performance. ⊙ *Vocabulary*

Look Back and Write For test practice, assign a 10–15 minute time limit. For assessment, see the Scoring Rubric at the right.

Retell

Have students retell "What Jo Did."

Monitor Progress
Check Retelling Rubric 4 3 2 1

| If... students have difficulty retelling the story, | then... use the Retelling Cards and the Scoring Rubric for Retelling on p. 157 to assist fluent retelling. SUCCESS PREDICTOR |

Assessment Go through the illustrations with students, verifying they know character names and English words for items pictured. For more ideas on assessing students' retellings, see the ELL and Transition Handbook.

Reader Response

Open for Discussion Suppose that Joanna went home and told her parents about the game. Tell what she told, play by play.

1. The author uses basketball terms such as *dunk*. Why? Identify five more basketball terms in the story and tell why they are there. **Think Like an Author**

2. What does Joanna do to T.J.'s jump shot? Why does he react the way he does? **Cause and Effect**

3. Have you ever surprised someone with a skill or talent the person didn't know you had? How did that person react? **Prior Knowledge**

4. Three words on the Words to Know list describe people's reactions to Joanna's basketball talent. Write them, along with other words and phrases from the story that people used when they saw her play. **Vocabulary**

Look Back and Write When the boys discovered that Jo was really Joanna, were they pleased? Reread pages 153–155. Describe how the boys reacted.

Meet author **and** photographer **Charles R. Smith Jr. on page 771.**

156

Scoring Rubric | Look Back and Write

Top-Score Response A top-score response uses details from pages 153 through 155 to describe how the boys reacted when they discovered that Jo was really Joanna.

Example of a Top-Score Response When the boys first discovered that Jo was a girl, they were very surprised. They couldn't believe their eyes. However, they soon congratulated Jo on her great game. One kid gave her a high five. They all said they would play basketball with her anytime. T.J. even apologized for being rude..

For additional rubrics, see p. WA10.

Write Now

Poem

Prompt

In "What Jo Did," the author describes an exciting basketball game.
Think about something that you love to do. Now write a poem about what it feels like when you are doing this activity.

Student Model

Lines are grouped to form stanzas.

> The Performer
> The music starts.
> The curtain parts.
> It's just me.
>
> My feet ring.
> My arms sing.
>
> A jump! A bend!
> A turn! The end.
> It's just me, dancing.
>
> The applause is like rain,
> Soft at first, and then
> THUNDERING!

Writer chooses words for rhyme.

Writer uses figurative, imaginative language and format.

Use the model to help you write your own poem.

157

Write Now

Look at the Prompt Explain that each sentence in the prompt has a purpose.

- Sentence 1 presents a topic.
- Sentence 2 suggests students think about the topic.
- Sentence 3 tells what to write—a poem.

Strategies to Develop Word Choice

Have students

- draw an illustration of their activity.
- search for interesting words in books or magazines.
- read their poems aloud to a partner to listen for rhythm and rhyme.

NO: I kick the ball during soccer.
YES: My feet are power.
　　　The ball flies.　　Goal!

For additional suggestions and rubric, see pp. 161g–161h.

Writer's Checklist

☑ **Focus** Do sentences stick to a favorite activity?
☑ **Organization** Are lines grouped to form stanzas?
☑ **Support** Do details tell your feelings?
☑ **Conventions** Are proper nouns and *I* capitalized?

Scoring Rubric　Narrative Retelling

Rubric 4 3 2 1	4	3	2	1
Connections	Makes connections and generalizes beyond the text	Makes connections to other events, stories, or experiences	Makes a limited connection to another event, story, or experience	Makes no connection to another event, story, or experience
Author's Purpose	Elaborates on author's purpose	Tells author's purpose with some clarity	Makes some connection to author's purpose	Makes no connection to author's purpose
Characters	Describes the main character(s) and any character development	Identifies the main character(s) and gives some information about them	Inaccurately identifies some characters or gives little information about them	Inaccurately identifies the characters or gives no information about them
Setting	Describes the time and location	Identifies the time and location	Omits details of time or location	Is unable to identify time or location
Plot	Describes the problem, goal, events, and ending using rich detail	Tells the problem, goal, events, and ending with some errors that do not affect meaning	Tells parts of the problem, goal, events, and ending with gaps that affect meaning	Retelling has no sense of story

Retelling Plan

☑ **This week assess Strategic Intervention students.**
☐ **Week 2** Assess Advanced students.
☐ **Week 3** Assess Strategic Intervention students.
☐ **Week 4** Assess On-Level students.
☐ **Week 5** Assess any students you have not yet checked during this unit.

Use the Retelling Chart on p. TR16 to record retelling.

Selection Test To assess with "What Jo Did," use Selection Tests, pp. 21–24.

Fresh Reads for Differentiated Test Practice For weekly leveled practice, use pp. 31–36.

SUCCESS PREDICTOR

Poetry

OBJECTIVES

- Examine features of poetry.
- Practice a test-taking strategy.
- Compare and contrast across texts.

PREVIEW

Have students look at the titles, text, and illustrations on pp. 158–161 and tell what they think these poems will be about. Then ask:

- **Why do you think some words are in larger and darker print?** *(Possible responses: The poet wants readers to pay attention to these words. These words should be stressed when the poem is read aloud.)*

Link to Writing

Have students list vivid action words used in the poems. *(streak, dash, fly)* Then have them use this list to describe a sport or activity they like to do. Ask them to brainstorm rhymes for these action words.

Genre

- **Poetry is meant to appeal to the senses, emotions, or mind.**

- **Often poetry gives the reader a fresh, unexpected way of looking at things.**

- **In many poems the rhyme helps establish the rhythm, or regular beat of stressed syllables.**

- **Preview the poems. Notice how the author captures the reader's attention with varied text sizes and styles.**

Link to Writing

The speaker uses rhyme to describe himself in both poems. Use this style to write a poem about yourself playing a sport or doing some other activity.

FAST BREAK

by Charles R. Smith Jr.

Prior Knowledge What are some things you know about basketball?

158

DAY 4 Grouping Options

Reading
Whole Group Discuss the Question of the Day.

Group Time Differentiated Instruction
Read poetry. See pp. 142f–142g for the small group lesson plan.

Whole Group Use p. 161a.

Language Arts
Use pp. 161e–161k.

Fleet feet
streak
up the concrete
to pull a
sweet treat
for the crowd.
The outlet *pass*—
fast—
as the break
is on
and I'm
gone.
A scene from
The Flash
I *dash*
down**court**
to
meet the pass.
Eyes wide
arms out
a reverse *jam*
is coming
no doubt.
Sky-high
I *fly*
to bring the
silent **crowd**
back
to life.

159

POETRY

Use the sidebar on p. 158 to guide discussion.

- Explain that poetry is made up of words in lines that have rhythm and sometimes rhyme. It often is highly imaginative and emotional, expressing deep feelings and thoughts.

- Tell students poetry can have a variety of formats. Here the poet uses rhyme and very short lines to set a fast-paced rhythm, but he doesn't use a specific rhyme pattern.

- Discuss with students rhyme, rhythm, and other techniques the poet uses in the two poems to express his passion for basketball.

 **AudioText**

Prior Knowledge

Responses may vary. Prompt students by asking them to describe any experiences they have had playing or watching basketball.

Basketball Beginnings

Time for SOCIAL STUDIES

In December 1891, James Naismith hung two empty peach baskets in a gym, wrote down thirteen rules, and tossed a soccer ball to students at a YMCA in Springfield, Massachusetts. The game of basketball was born. In its early years, basketball was much rougher than today. Also, wire cages enclosed the court to keep the ball in play. Naismith not only invented the world's most widely played indoor sport; he was also a doctor, educator, minister, and World War I veteran. He died in 1939, three years after basketball became an official Olympic sport.

ELL

Build Background Use the photographs to explain unfamiliar basketball terms. Point out some of the names the speaker is called in "Allow Me to Introduce Myself," and discuss how nicknames sometimes describe a person's special talents or skills.

Strategies for Poetry

USE RHYME Rhyme doesn't always occur at the end of lines or stanzas. In some poems, internal rhymes or the absence of rhyme can speed up or cause a change in a poem's rhythm. Provide the following strategy.

Use the Strategy

1. Read test questions to find out what is asked about a poem's rhyme or rhythm. Then locate rhymes in the poem.

2. Say the lines of poetry silently in your mind and quietly tap out the rhythm as you read.

3. Make sure you can describe the poem's use of rhyme and rhythm and give examples. Do the rhymes follow a pattern? Is the rhythm fast or slow, regular or irregular?

GUIDED PRACTICE Have students discuss how they would use the strategy to answer the following question.

How does rhyme affect the rhythm in the first six lines of "Fast Break"? Use an example from the poem in your answer.

INDEPENDENT PRACTICE After students answer the following test question, discuss the process they used to find information.

How does rhyme make your voice rise and fall when you read the first eight lines of "Allow Me to Introduce Myself"? Use two examples from the poem in your answer.

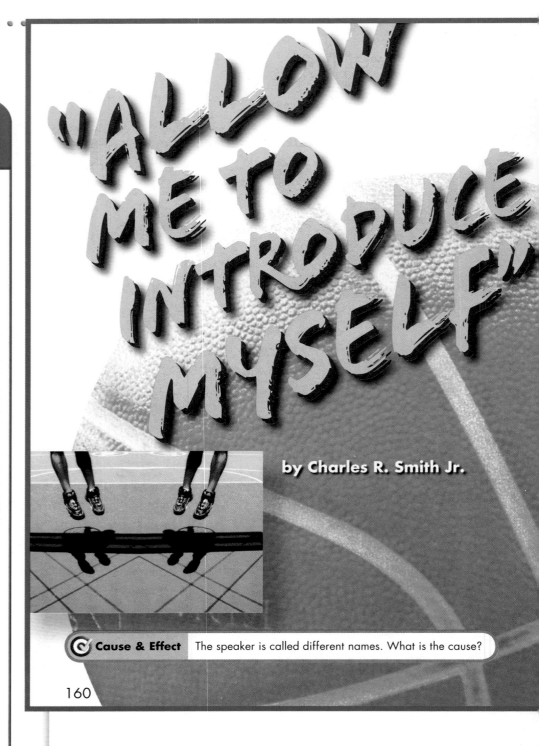

"ALLOW ME TO INTRODUCE MYSELF"

by Charles R. Smith Jr.

 Cause & Effect The speaker is called different names. What is the cause?

160

ELL

Guided Practice Write the Guided Practice question on the board. Read aloud the poems and have students follow along. Read the poems again, having students clap out the rhythm as you read.

They call me
the show
stopper
the dime
dropper
    the
    spin-move-to-the-left
    reverse jam **poppa.**
The high
flier
on the high
wire.
    The intense
    rim-rattlin'
    noise
    amplifier.
The net-**shaker**
back
board **breaker**
creator
of the funky dunk
hip-**shaker.**
    The Man
    Sir Slam
    The Legend
    I be.
That's just
a few of the
names
they call **me.**

Reading Across Texts

The story "What Jo Did" and the poems "Fast Break" and "'Allow Me to Introduce Myself'" are all by Charles R. Smith Jr. How are they alike and different?

Writing Across Texts Write some paragraphs comparing the three selections by Charles R. Smith Jr.

161

CONNECT TEXT TO TEXT

Reading Across Texts

Discuss similarities and differences among the story "What Jo Did" and the poems. Have students consider how Jo and the speaker of each poem feel about their basketball skills or how the writer uses humor and everyday language in all three selections.

Writing Across Texts Before they write, students can organize their thinking by creating a three-column chart and recording details about each selection. Prompt them to look for similarities and differences in topic, language, and emotional content.

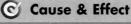

 Cause & Effect

Possible response: The speaker is called different names depending on the skill he displays—jumping, making a spectacular shot, slam-dunking the ball, or making an unusual move.

Fluency Assessment Plan

☑ **This week assess Advanced students.**

☐ **Week 2** Assess Strategic Intervention students.

☐ **Week 3** Assess On-Level students.

☐ **Week 4** Assess Strategic Intervention students.

☐ **Week 5** Assess any students you have not yet checked during this unit.

Set individual goals for students to enable them to reach the year-end goal.

• Current Goal: 100–110 WCPM
• Year-End Goal: 130 WCPM

Measuring a student's oral reading speed—words per minute—provides a low-stress informal assessment of fluency. Such an assessment should not take the place of more formal measures of words correct per minute.

To develop fluent readers, use Fluency Coach.

DAY 5   Grouping Options

Reading
Whole Group
Revisit the Question of the Week.

Group Time
Differentiated Instruction
Reread this week's Leveled Readers. See pp. 142f–142g for the small group lesson plan.

Whole Group
Use p. 161b–161c.

Language Arts
Use pp. 161d–161l.

RHYTHMIC PATTERNS OF LANGUAGE
Fluency

DAY 1

Model Reread aloud "The Circuit" on p. 142m. Have students note your rhythmic pattern, which stresses important and emotionally charged words and makes dialogue sound like everyday conversation. Explain that you also change the pace of the words and the tone of your voice to match the context. Model as you read.

DAY 2

Echo Reading Read aloud p. 150. Have students notice how your voice moves in a natural rhythm, stressing some words and word parts more than others. Have students practice as a class doing three echo readings of p. 150.

DAY 3

Model Read aloud p. 152, the last paragraph. Have students notice how some words, like *could* and *high,* are high points in the rhythmic pattern of language. Practice as a class by doing three echo readings.

DAY 4

Partner Reading Partners practice reading aloud the last paragraph on p. 152 three times. Students should read with natural rhythmic cadence and offer each other feedback.

Monitor Progress   **Check Fluency** WCPM

As students reread, monitor their progress toward their individual fluency goals. Current Goal: 100–110 words correct per minute. End-of-Year Goal: 130 words correct per minute.

If... students cannot read fluently at a rate of 100–110 words correct per minute,
then... make sure students practice with text at their independent level. Provide additional fluency practice, pairing nonfluent readers with fluent readers.

If... students already read at 130 words correct per minute,
then... they do not need to reread three times.

SUCCESS PREDICTOR

DAY 5

Assessment
Individual Reading Rate Use the Fluency Assessment Plan and do a one-minute timed reading of either selection from this week to assess students in Week 1. Pay special attention to this week's skill, the rhythmic patterns of language. Provide corrective feedback for each student.

RETEACH

Cause and Effect

TEACH

Review the definitions of *cause* and *effect* on p. 142. Students can complete Practice Book p. 58 on their own, or they can complete it as a class. As they fill in the boxes under *Effect*, they should ask themselves *what* happened. As they fill in the box under *Cause*, they should ask *why* it happened. Remind them to look for clue words. The word *so* is a clue: what follows is an effect. The word *because* is a clue: what follows is a cause.

ASSESS

Have partners reread p. 151 and identify a cause-effect relationship. *(Possible response: Jo felt hot [effect] because she was playing so hard [cause].)*

For additional instruction on cause and effect, see DI•52.

EXTEND SKILLS

Short Story

TEACH

A short story is fiction that focuses on one main character or a limited number of characters. It describes a single event or a closely related series of events.

- A short story usually contains all the story elements: setting, plot, theme, characterization.
- A short story could be science fiction, realistic fiction, fantasy, or some other fiction genre.

Ask students if "What Jo Did" is a short story. What makes them think so? Discuss how "What Jo Did" is different from a novel students have read.

ASSESS

Have students name another short story they have read. Ask them to validate classifying the story as a short story by writing answers to these questions:

1. **What is the theme of this story?**
2. **What single event or related series of events does it describe?**
3. **Who is this story about?**

OBJECTIVES

- Identify cause-and-effect relationships.
- Identify elements of a short story.

Skills Trace
Cause and Effect

Introduce/Teach	TE: 4.2 142–143; 4.3 268–269; 4.6 638–639
Practice	TE: 149, 275, 281, 645, 653 PB: 53, 57, 58, 103, 107, 108, 253, 257, 258
Reteach/Review	**TE: 4.1 49; 4.2 161b, DI•52; 4.3 291b, 323, 347, DI•52; 4.6 659b, DI•52 PB: 16, 126, 136**
Test	Selection Test: 21–24, 41–44, 101–104; Benchmark Test: Unit 3

Access Content Reteach the skill by reviewing the Picture It! lesson on cause and effect in the ELL Teaching Guide, pp. 36–37.

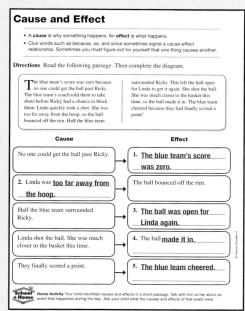

Cause and Effect

- A **cause** is why something happens. An **effect** is what happens.
- Clue words such as *because*, *so*, and *since* sometimes signal a cause-effect relationship. Sometimes you must figure out for yourself that one thing causes another.

Directions Read the following passage. Then complete the diagram.

The blue team's score was zero because no one could get the ball past Ricky. The blue team's coach told them to take shots before Ricky had a chance to block them. Linda quickly took a shot. She was too far away from the hoop, so the ball bounced off the rim. Half the blue team surrounded Ricky. This left the ball open for Linda to get it again. She shot the ball. She was much closer to the basket this time, so the ball made it in. The blue team cheered because they had finally scored a point!

Cause	Effect
No one could get the ball past Ricky.	1. The blue team's score was zero.
2. Linda was **too far away from the hoop.**	The ball bounced off the rim.
Half the blue team surrounded Ricky.	3. The ball was open for Linda again.
Linda shot the ball. She was much closer to the basket this time.	4. The ball made it in.
They finally scored a point.	5. The blue team cheered.

Home Activity Your child identified causes and effects in a short passage. Talk with him or her about an event that happened during the day. Ask your child what the causes and effects of that event were.

▲ **Practice Book** p. 58

Vocabulary and Word Study

Word Structure

PREFIXES AND SUFFIXES Remind students that they can use prefixes and suffixes to figure out word meanings. Review the meanings of *un-* ("not") and *-able* ("able to be"). Model how to divide *unbreakable* and use word structure to determine its meaning. Then give students other words that include the prefix *un-* and the suffix *-able* and have them create a chart like the one shown below.

Word	Prefix/Base Word/Suffix	Word Meaning
unbreakable	un/break/able	not able to be broken
unforgivable		
unacceptable		
unreliable		

Toponyms

Explain that the word *jersey* comes from Jersey, a British island that was famous for its knitted fabric hundreds of years ago. Have pairs use an advanced dictionary or search online to look up the following toponyms (names based on places) and complete the chart.

Word	Where It Came From
jersey	Jersey, England, where people were famous for knitting
limerick	
cheddar	
hamburger	
lima bean	
cologne	

New Understandings

LOOKING BACK Remind students of the question of the week: *How can we learn to appreciate the talents of others?* Discuss how this week's Concept Web of vocabulary words relates to the theme of appreciating and understanding others. Ask students if they have any words or categories to add. Discuss if words and categories are appropriately related to the concept.

MOVING FORWARD Preview the title of the next selection, *Coyote School News.* Ask students which Concept Web words might apply to the new selection based on the title alone. Put a star next to these words on the Web.

Display the Concept Web and revisit the vocabulary words as you read the next selection to check predictions.

Monitor Progress

Check Vocabulary

If... students suggest words or categories that are not related to the concept,	**then...** review the words and categories on the Concept Web and discuss how they relate to the lesson concept.

SUCCESS PREDICTOR

Speaking and Viewing

SPEAKING

Sportscast

SET-UP Have students create a sportscast of a short action sequence after watching a sports event. Explain most sportscasts are delivered live and are designed to help listeners understand action that happens quickly.

PLANNING Watch a school event or a TV sportscast with the sound turned off. Have students use a tape recorder or take notes to record their impressions of the action. They should draft and then polish their scripts after they practice saying them aloud.

DELIVERY Provide time for students to rehearse and deliver their sportscasts. Share these suggestions:

- Speed up your delivery for fast-paced action.
- Use tone of voice to express excitement and enthusiasm, but try not to shout.
- Use descriptive words that give listeners a vivid and clear picture of what's happening.
- Remember, it is OK if you are not telling about the action *as it happens.* Most sportscasters' descriptions are a few seconds behind the action.

Listening Tips

- As you listen, picture the action in your mind.
- If you miss a sentence or two, don't worry. Keep your attention on what's being said now.

VIEWING

Analyze Media

Have students watch a 10-minute taped segment of a sports event you have recorded. Before viewing, remind students to notice camera positions and how they change to record the action. After viewing, have small groups discuss these questions:

1. **How do the cameras capture action in a game?** *(Possible response: There is more than one camera to let viewers see events from different angles.)*

2. **Why does the camera zoom in close on certain plays?** *(Possible response: to show details of the action)*

3. **What are the advantages of watching a game on TV? What are the disadvantages?** *(Advantages: You see action up close from different angles, and important plays are repeated. You can see players' expressions. Disadvantages: TV sportscasts often show commercials whenever the action stops. You can't choose what to look at as you watch.)*

Support Vocabulary Use the following to review and extend vocabulary and to explore lesson concepts further:
- ELL Poster 6, Days 3–5 instruction
- Vocabulary Activities and Word Cards in ELL Teaching Guide, pp. 38–39

Assessment For information on assessing students' speaking, listening, and viewing, see the ELL and Transition Handbook.

SUCCESS PREDICTOR

Vocabulary

Grammar Common and Proper Nouns

Monitor Progress

Grammar

If... students have difficulty identifying common and proper nouns,	then... provide additional instruction and practice in The Grammar and Writing Book pp. 80–83.

DAILY FIX-IT

This week use Daily Fix-It Transparency 6.

Spiral REVIEW

Grammar Support See the Grammar Transition lessons in the ELL and Transition Handbook.

▲ **The Grammar and Writing Book**
For more instruction and practice, use pp. 80–83.

DAY 1 Teach and Model

DAILY FIX-IT

1. Her teamates think shes a great player. *(teammates; she's)*

2. We went to New york. To see the game. *(York to)*

READING-GRAMMAR CONNECTION

Write the following sentence from "What Jo Did" on the board:

Little Joanna Marie loved to play basketball.

Point out that the underlined words are nouns, or words that name a person, place, or thing. Explain that a **common noun,** such as *basketball,* names any person, place, or thing, while a **proper noun,** such as *Joanna Marie,* names a particular person, place, animal, or thing.

Display Grammar Transparency 6. Read aloud the definitions and example sentences. Work through the items.

Common and Proper Nouns

A noun is a word that names a person, place, or thing.
A **common noun** names any person, place, or thing.
A **proper noun** names a particular person, place, or thing. Proper nouns begin with capital letters.
  Common Nouns The game will be next week.
  Proper Nouns Amy is free to play on Saturday.
Some proper nouns have more than one word, such as *Boston Red Sox.* Some include titles that tell what a person is or does, such as *Ms. Gomez* or *Professor Chu.*

Directions One of the underlined words in each sentence is a noun. Write the noun. Then write *C* if it is a common noun and *P* if it is a proper noun.
1. I enjoy basketball. — **basketball C**
2. Mr. Summers says that I could make the team. — **Mr. Summers P**
3. I'm going to practice all month. — **month C**
4. By December I should be ready for the first meeting. — **December P**
5. We will get together in the gym at Springfield Middle School.
   Springfield Middle School P

Directions Underline the two nouns in each sentence. Then write each noun under the correct heading in the chart.
6. The nearest court is in Grove Street Park.
7. Go down Elm Street and turn left at the library.
8. Look for Rico and me in the playground.
9. We play basketball there every Saturday.
10. I have to go to City Hall after our game.

Common Nouns	Proper Nouns
court	Grove Street
library	Park
playground	Elm Street
basketball	Rico
game	Saturday
	City Hall

Unit 2 What Jo Did Grammar **6**

▲ **Grammar Transparency** 6

DAY 2 Develop the Concept

DAILY FIX-IT

3. Collecting basketball jerseys are one of my hobbys. *(is; hobbies)*

4. Do you have a Michael jordan jersey! *(Jordan jersey?)*

GUIDED PRACTICE

Review the concept of common and proper nouns.

- A **common noun** names any person, place, or thing. A proper noun names a particular person, place, or thing.

- **Proper nouns** begin with capital letters.

- Proper nouns, such as the titles of books, magazines, newspapers, works of art, musical compositions, and the names of organizations, may consist of two or more words.

HOMEWORK Grammar and Writing Practice Book p. 21. Work through the first two items with the class.

Common and Proper Nouns

- A noun is a word that names a person, place, or thing.
- A **common noun** names any person, place, or thing.
- A **proper noun** names a particular person, place, or thing. Proper nouns begin with capital letters.
  Common Nouns That girl plays basketball at our school.
  Proper Nouns Sandy will play for Centerville on Friday.
Some proper nouns have more than one word, such as *Boston Celtics.* Some include titles that tell what a person is or does, such as *Aunt Rosa* or *Captain Edwards.*

Directions One of the underlined words in each sentence is a noun. Circle the noun. Write *C* if it is a common noun and *P* if it is a proper noun.
1. Dr. James Naismith invented the game of basketball. — **C**
2. He worked at the YMCA Training School in Springfield, Massachusetts. — **P**
3. Naismith wanted to find a game to play inside during the winter. — **C**

Directions Underline the three nouns in each sentence. Then write each noun under the correct heading in the chart.
4. The first game of basketball was played in Massachusetts.
5. Soon people all over the world were playing the sport.
6. In 1936, basketball was played at the Olympic Games in Berlin.
7. Today, many cities compete every winter in the National Basketball Association.
8. I watch our team at the stadium every weekend.

Common Nouns			Proper Nouns
game	sport	team	Massachusetts
basketball	basketball	weekend	Olympic Games
people	cities	stadium	Berlin
world	winter		National Basketball Association

Home Activity Your child learned about common and proper nouns. Have your child name people, places, or things around the house and say whether the names are common or proper nouns.

▲ **Grammar and Writing Practice Book** p. 21

DAY 3 — Apply to Writing

DAILY FIX-IT

5. The game was played at our Gym last friday. *(gym; Friday)*

6. What a exciting finish that was. *(an; was!)*

USE EXACT NOUNS

Point out that using exact common nouns *(collie* instead of *dog; beef stew* instead of *food)* and exact proper nouns *(Ms. Lopez* instead of *our teacher)* can help make writing vivid and clear.

- Have students review something they have written to see if they can make it more vivid by replacing general nouns with exact common nouns or proper nouns.

HOMEWORK Grammar and Writing Practice Book p. 22.

Common and Proper Nouns

Directions Replace the underlined word in each sentence with a noun from the box that gives a more exact description. Write the new sentence. Write *C* if the word you chose is a common noun. Write *P* if it is a proper noun.

| pizza | roar | fans | December | Mr. Ames |

1. He is our basketball coach.
   Mr. Ames is our basketball coach. P
2. I joined the team last month.
   I joined the team last December. P
3. After each game, the coach takes us out for food.
   After each game, the coach takes us out for pizza. C
4. Many people come to our games.
   Many fans come to our games. C
5. I love hearing the sound of the crowd when we score.
   I love hearing the roar of the crowd when we score. C

Directions Write several sentences about your school. Mention some of the people you meet there. Identify the common nouns you used and underline them once. Underline the proper nouns twice. **Possible answer:**

My <u>school</u> is <u>Burbank Elementary</u> on <u>Main Street</u>. The <u>principal</u> is <u>Ms. Bond</u>, and my <u>teacher</u> is <u>Mr. Vasquez</u>. My favorite <u>day</u> is <u>Friday</u> because the <u>weekend</u> comes next.

Home Activity Your child learned how to use common and proper nouns in writing. Have your child write a sentence or two describing a place in your community. Ask your child to identify the common and proper nouns in the sentences.

▲ **Grammar and Writing Practice Book** p. 22

DAY 4 — Test Preparation

DAILY FIX-IT

7. If you wanna play on the team. You must practice. *(want to; team, you)*

8. Sam practiced every day but he didn't make the team? *(day,; team.)*

STANDARDIZED TEST PREP

Test Tip

Capitalize nouns when they give the title of a particular place, not when they simply describe the place.

Small letters: We went to <u>the big city</u>.

Capital letters: We went to <u>New York City</u>.

Small letters: I love playing in <u>that park</u>.

Capital letters: I love playing in <u>Cabot Park</u>.

HOMEWORK Grammar and Writing Practice Book p. 23.

Common and Proper Nouns

Directions Mark the letter of the word that is a common noun.

1. Dr. Naismith wrote thirteen rules for basketball.
   A Dr. Naismith
   B wrote
   C thirteen
   D rules
2. The ball could be thrown in any direction.
   A ball
   B could
   C thrown
   D any
3. A player must not run with the ball.
   A player
   B must
   C not
   D with

Directions Mark the letter of the word or words that are a proper noun.

7. The inventor of basketball was born in Canada.
   A The
   B basketball
   C born
   D Canada
8. James Naismith attended a one-room school.
   A James Naismith
   B attended
   C one-room
   D school
4. Boston and Chicago have had great teams.
   A Boston
   B Chicago
   C great
   D teams
5. Not all basketball players are Americans.
   A Not
   B players
   C are
   D Americans
6. Basketball is a popular sport in Asia.
   A is
   B popular
   C sport
   D with
9. He went to college in Montreal, Canada.
   A He
   B college
   C in
   D Canada
10. While living in Massachusetts, he invented the game.
    A While
    B living
    C Massachusetts
    D game

Home Activity Your child prepared for taking tests on common and proper nouns. Read a paragraph to your child from a book, magazine, or newspaper. Ask your child to identify nouns and to explain whether they are common or proper.

▲ **Grammar and Writing Practice Book** p. 23

DAY 5 — Cumulative Review

DAILY FIX-IT

9. Basketball is a fastest game then baseball. *(faster; than)*

10. You can watch the game if its not on to late. *(it's; too)*

ADDITIONAL PRACTICE

Assign pp. 80–83 in The Grammar and Writing Book.

EXTRA PRACTICE Grammar and Writing Practice Book p. 127.

TEST PREPARATION Grammar and Writing Practice Book pp. 153–154.

ASSESSMENT

CUMULATIVE REVIEW Grammar and Writing Practice Book p. 24.

Common and Proper Nouns

Directions Circle *C* if the underlined word is a common noun. Circle *P* if the underlined word is a proper noun.

1. There's a girl at <u>Central High</u> who is a basketball star.   C   **P**
2. She plays center on the all-state team for <u>Maryland</u>.   C   **P**
3. She averages 24 points a <u>game</u>.   **C**   P
4. Her name is <u>Toyana Jumper</u>.   C   **P**
5. That's a great <u>name</u> for a basketball player!   **C**   P

Directions Underline the three nouns in each sentence. They may be common or proper.

6. The <u>book</u> we are reading is about a <u>girl</u> called <u>Jo</u>.
7. She plays <u>basketball</u> with a <u>group</u> of <u>boys</u>.
8. <u>Jo</u> wore a <u>hat</u> over her long <u>hair</u>.
9. She flew through the <u>air</u> and dunked the <u>ball</u> into the <u>hoop</u>.
10. <u>T. J.</u> told <u>Jo</u> that he had never played with a <u>girl</u> before.

Directions Write one sentence about a place you like to visit and another sentence about a person you know. Include common and proper nouns in each sentence. Underline the common nouns once and the proper nouns twice. **Possible answers:**

11. Place
    My <u>family</u> goes to <u>New York City</u> every summer.

12. Person
    <u>Aunt Sal</u> is the funniest <u>person</u> in the <u>world</u>.

Home Activity Your child reviewed common and proper nouns. Ask your child to name things, places, animals, or people he or she passes on the way to school each day. Have your child tell you whether these names are common or proper.

▲ **Grammar and Writing Practice Book** p. 24

Writing Workshop   Poem

OBJECTIVES

- Identify qualities of a poem.
- Write a poem using figurative language.
- Focus on word choice.
- Use a rubric.

Genre Poem
Writer's Craft Figurative Language
Writing Trait Word Choice

 **E L L**

Word Choice Pair an English learner with a proficient English speaker to discuss pictures in books or magazines. Have them list colorful words from the discussion to use in writing, such as *friendly, picnic, caterpillar, broken, snowstorm,* and *furry.*

Writing Traits

FOCUS/IDEAS The narrator pictures herself "flying" through the air toward the basket. Her purpose is to describe the game's beauty and excitement.

ORGANIZATION/PARAGRAPHS The poem's lines are divided by ideas into groups, or stanzas.

VOICE The narrator speaks directly to the reader in an excited, imaginative voice.

WORD CHOICE The writer chooses words for rhyme *(bird/word)* and for figurative language *(like a hawk/for a fish).*

SENTENCES The writer uses sentences of varied lengths and types, just as she would in writing prose.

CONVENTIONS Correct punctuation helps the reader understand the poem.

READING-WRITING CONNECTION

- "What Jo Did" uses exact words to describe a basketball game's excitement.
- Choose your words carefully to create figurative language.
- Students will write a **poem,** using carefully chosen words and language.

MODEL WORD CHOICE Display Writing Transparency 6A. Then discuss the model and the writing trait of word choice.

Think Aloud I can see that the writer has put a lot of thought into the words in this poem. Some words are chosen for their sounds, such as *bird* and *word, fish* and *swish.* Other words, such as *wingsspread,* seem chosen for the way they look. A specific word such as *hawk* helps me see a basketball player's action.

WRITER'S CRAFT
Figurative Language

Display Writing Transparency 6B. Read the directions and work together to identify examples of figurative language.

Think Aloud **FIGURATIVE LANGUAGE** Tomorrow we will be writing a poem about a favorite activity. I am going to write about rollerblading. To make my poem effective, I can use figurative language, such as metaphor, simile, and hyperbole. For example, I might say, "I'm faster than light, like a shooting star in the night."

GUIDED WRITING Write *simile, metaphor, personification,* and *hyperbole* on the board. Invite students to come up with examples of their own. Write their ideas on the board under the appropriate heading.

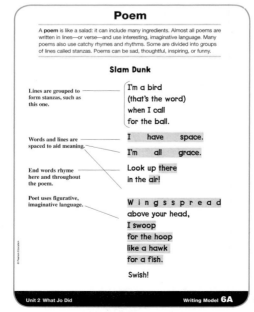

▲ **Writing Transparency** 6A

Poem

A **poem** is like a salad: it can include many ingredients. Almost all poems are written in lines—or verse—and use interesting, imaginative language. Many poems also use catchy rhymes and rhythms. Some are divided into groups of lines called stanzas. Poems can be sad, thoughtful, inspiring, or funny.

Slam Dunk

Lines are grouped to form stanzas, such as this one.
> I'm a bird
> (that's the word)
> when I call
> for the ball.

Words and lines are spaced to aid meaning.
> I   have   space.
> I'm   all   grace.

End words rhyme here and throughout the poem.
> Look up there
> in the air!

Poet uses figurative, imaginative language.
> W i n g s s p r e a d
> above your head,
> I swoop
> for the hoop
> like a hawk
> for a fish.
>
> Swish!

Unit 2 What Jo Did   Writing Model 6A

Figurative Language

Good writers do not always speak directly. Sometimes they say what they mean indirectly, by using **figurative language.** One type of figurative language—or figure of speech—is a **simile,** which uses the word *like* or *as* to compare two unlike things. A **metaphor** also compares two unlike things but without using *like* or *as.* A third figure of speech is **personification,** in which the writer gives an animal, object, or idea human characteristics. **Hyperbole** is a form of exaggeration, used by an author to make a point.

Simile	That player is tall as a tree.
Metaphor	The game was a war from beginning to end.
Personification	The sun smiled on us when we left the gym.
Hyperbole	I could have slept for a year after that game.

Directions Identify the figure of speech in each sentence.

1. The basket was a mile away. **hyperbole**
2. I charged down the court like an angry bull. **simile**
3. The ball jumped into my hands. **personification**
4. Suddenly I was an eagle. **metaphor**
5. That was the game of the century. **hyperbole**
6. I slept like a log that night. **simile**

Directions Write several sentences describing a summer day at the pool or beach. Use at least two figures of speech. **Possible answer:** The waves are laughing. The sun is my best friend. A fresh breeze strokes my hair. I could be happy here forever because this is like a dream.

Unit 2 What Jo Did   Writer's Craft 6B

▲ **Writing Transparency** 6B

DAY 3 Prewrite and Draft

READ THE WRITING PROMPT

on page 157 in the Student Edition.

In "What Jo Did," the author describes an exciting basketball game.

Think about something that you love to do.

Now write a poem about what it feels like when you are doing this activity.

Writing Test Tips

- Try to show, not tell, the reader how this activity makes you feel. You might ask yourself, "What animal am I like when I do this?"
- Listen to the sound of the words you use. Poetry is like music, with the words as notes.
- Think of the shape of the poem on the page. Do you want long lines or short lines? Do you want to divide the poem into stanzas or have one long column?

GETTING STARTED Students can do any of the following:

- Create a concept web around the name of their favorite activity.
- Decide whether they want their poem to have a specific rhythm or rhyme scheme.
- Close their eyes and imagine the activity. Then write down a list of details.

DAY 4 Draft and Revise

EDITING/REVISING CHECKLIST

☑ Do I use figurative language?

☑ Do I use exact nouns?

☑ Are proper nouns capitalized?

☑ Are the plurals of nouns with -s and -es spelled correctly?

See *The Grammar and Writing Book,* pp. 80–85.

Revising Tips

Word Choice

- Support exact word choice by selecting words that bring a sound or rhythm to your poem.
- Make sure nouns are specific and verbs are strong.
- Use figurative language to describe your feelings.

PUBLISHING Have students copy their poems on paper and draw a picture or find a photograph to illustrate it. Some students may wish to revise their work later for publication in a local or national contest, internet web site, newspaper, or school display.

ASSESSMENT Use the scoring rubric to evaluate students' work.

DAY 5 Connect to Unit Writing

How-to Report	
Week 1	Poem 161g–161h
Week 2	News Story 187g–187h
Week 3	Play Scene 211g–211h
Week 4	Describe a Job 239g–239h
Week 5	Explanation 259g–259h

PREVIEW THE UNIT PROMPT

Think of something that you know how to do well. Write a clear, step-by-step description of how to do this task or activity. Make your report interesting to read and easy to understand.

APPLY

- A how-to report explains the steps for making or doing something.
- Figurative language is not just for poetry. It can make any writing— including a how-to report—more interesting.

Writing Trait Rubric

	4	3	2	1
Word Choice	Word choice strong and exact; figurative language	Word choice adequate; some figurative language	Word choice weak; few examples of figurative language	Dull and/or inaccurate word choices throughout; no figurative language
	Poem engaging with strong word choices	Poem generally engaging	Poem weakened by lack of exact language	Poem weak and/or confusing with ineffective language

Spelling & Phonics — Adding -s and -es

DAY 1 — Pretest and Sort

DAY 2 — Think and Practice

OBJECTIVE

- Spell plural words by adding -s or -es.

Generalization

Connect to Phonics Add -s to words ending in a *vowel and y* and to most words: *monkeys, friends.* Change *y* to *i* and add -es to words ending in a *consonant and y: supplies.* Add -es to words ending in *sh, ch, s, ss, x: taxes.* Words that end in -s, -es, or -ies are often plural.

Spelling Words

1. monkeys	11. hobbies
2. friends	12. daisies
3. plays	13. delays
4. supplies	14. scratches
5. taxes	15. counties
6. holidays	16. teammates*
7. months	17. memories
8. companies	18. bunches
9. costumes	19. batteries
10. sandwiches	20. donkeys

Challenge Words

21. eyelashes	24. secretaries
22. ambulances	25. inventories
23. trophies	

*Word from the selection

Spelling/Phonics Support See the ELL and Transition Handbook for spelling support.

PRETEST

Use the Dictation Sentences from Day 5 to administer the pretest. Read the word, read the sentence, and then read the word again. Guide students in self-correcting their pretests and correcting any misspellings.

Monitor Progress

Spelling

If... students misspell more than 5 pretest words,	then... use words 1–10 for Strategic Intervention.
If... students misspell 1–5 pretest words,	then... use words 1–20 for On-Level practice.
If... students correctly spell all pretest words,	then... use words 1–25 for Advanced Learners.

HOMEWORK Spelling Practice Book, p. 21.

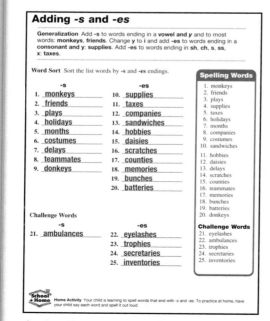

▲ **Spelling Practice Book** p. 21

TEACH

Plural nouns, which name more than one person, place, or thing, can be formed in different ways. Write *county* on the board. Underline *ty.* Explain that when a word ends in a *consonant plus y,* the *y* is changed to *i* before adding -es to make it plural. Then write *counties* and underline *-ies.* Write *donkey, month,* and *scratch,* and model how to make each word plural.

county / counties

WORD WEBS Have students make word webs for each ending. Have them write -s, -es, or -ies in the center circle of a web and then write the appropriate list words in smaller circles around the center circles.

HOMEWORK Spelling Practice Book, p. 22.

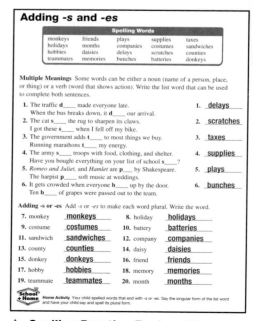

▲ **Spelling Practice Book** p. 22

DAY 3 Connect to Writing

WRITE RHYMES

Ask students to use at least five spelling words to write two-line rhymes. The rhyming words do not need to be the list words, and students may use one or more than one list word in each rhyme.

Frequently Misspelled Words

friends   *a lot*

because

These words may seem easy to spell, but they are often misspelled by fourth-graders. Alert students to these frequently misspelled words. Point out the vowels *ie* in friends. Point out that *a lot* is two words. Point out the vowels *au* and *e* in *because*.

HOMEWORK Spelling Practice Book, p. 23.

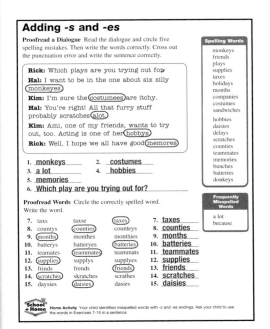

▲ **Spelling Practice Book** p. 23

DAY 4 Review

REVIEW ADDING -s AND -es

Have students write the singular form of each list word. Then have them exchange papers with a partner and have the partner write the plural form of each word.

Spelling Strategy Problem Parts

We all have words that are hard for us to spell.

Step 1: Ask yourself: Which part of the word gives me a problem?

Step 2: Underline your problem part.

Step 3: Picture the word. Focus on the problem part.

HOMEWORK Spelling Practice Book, p. 24.

▲ **Spelling Practice Book** p. 24

DAY 5 Posttest

DICTATION SENTENCES

1. I like to watch monkeys at the zoo.
2. Good friends help each other.
3. Our class will put on two plays.
4. Please take out your art supplies.
5. Our taxes help pay for the park.
6. What are your favorite holidays?
7. How many months are in a year?
8. Big companies hire many people.
9. It's fun to dress up in costumes.
10. We made sandwiches for lunch.
11. What hobbies do you enjoy in your spare time?
12. Dad planted daisies in the yard.
13. There were many delays at the airport.
14. The fallen branch left scratches on the car.
15. How many counties does your state have?
16. Jen's teammates cheered when she scored a goal.
17. That song brings back good memories.
18. We picked bunches of grapes.
19. How many batteries does the game need?
20. The donkeys enjoy pulling carts.

CHALLENGE

21. The baby has thick eyelashes.
22. Two ambulances raced to the accident.
23. Our math team won two trophies.
24. The secretaries learned the new computer program quickly.
25. The stores' inventories were lost in the fire.

OBJECTIVES

- Formulate an inquiry question that is connected to this week's lesson focus.
- Effectively and efficiently find, evaluate, and communicate information related to an inquiry question using electronic sources.

New Literacies

Day 1	Identify Questions
Day 2	Navigate/Search
Day 3	Analyze
Day 4	Synthesize
Day 5	Communicate

NEW LITERACIES

Internet Inquiry Activity

EXPLORE BIOGRAPHIES OF TALENTED PEOPLE

Use the following 5-day plan to help students conduct this week's Internet inquiry activity on appreciating the talents of others. Remind students to follow classroom rules when using the Internet.

DAY 1

Identify Questions Discuss the lesson focus question: *How can we learn to appreciate the talents of others?* As a group, brainstorm the names of talented people and explore their accomplishments. Have students work individually, in pairs, or in small groups to choose a person or group and write an inquiry question they want to answer. For example, they may want to find out about a particular basketball star or a sports team.

DAY 2

Navigate/Search Help students determine keywords related to their inquiry questions. Remind them to double-check the spelling of keywords. Point out that when they research a person with a common name, they may need to match facts across sites to be sure they have found the correct biographical information. Have students record URLs of a few sites or, if allowed, bookmark them.

DAY 3

Analyze Have students explore Web sites they identified on Day 2. Tell them to scan each site for information that helps answer their inquiry questions. Students should also analyze information for credibility and reliability. Point out, for example, that fan sites are probably biased. Remind them that if they discover contradictions in facts, they should try to verify the correct information using two or more sources. Students can print out and highlight relevant information, if allowed, or take notes.

DAY 4

Synthesize Have students synthesize information from Day 3. Remind them that when they synthesize, they combine relevant ideas and information from different sources to develop answers to their inquiry questions.

DAY 5

Communicate Have students share their inquiry results. They can use a word processing program to create a short biography. They can print or draw a picture to illustrate the biography.

RESEARCH/STUDY SKILLS
Chart/Table

TEACH

Ask students how they might report basketball statistics for a research report. Discuss how they could create a chart or table using word processing software. Show a table created on a computer and explain these features.

- A **chart** shows information visually. Lists, diagrams, and tables are all kinds of charts.

- A **table** is a special kind of chart that shows information in rows and columns. **Rows** list information horizontally, or across. **Columns** list information vertically, or up and down.

- A single box in a table is often called a **cell.**

- Most charts or tables have a **title** that tells what the chart or table shows.

Demonstrate how to create a table using word processing software. Give pairs basketball statistics. (To find data, search the Internet for *basketball statistics*.) Have pairs create a table to display the data. Then discuss these questions:

1. **How did you decide how many columns and rows to create?**

2. **Was it easy to add or delete columns and rows?**

3. **How is creating a table on a computer like drawing a table on paper? How is it different?**

ASSESS

As students work, first check that they are able to conceptualize an appropriate table for their data. (If necessary, have them draw the table on paper.) Then check that they are able to use the software to create and revise a table. Data should be entered correctly and organized logically.

For more practice or to assess students, use Practice Book pp. 59–60.

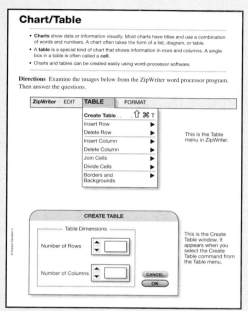

▲ **Practice Book** p. 59

▲ **Practice Book** p. 60

Assessment Checkpoints *for the Week*

Selection Assessment

Use pp. 21–24 of Selection Tests to check:

 Selection Understanding

 Comprehension Skill *Cause and Effect*

Selection Vocabulary

fouled	*rim*
hoop	*speechless*
jersey	*swatted*
marveled	*unbelievable*

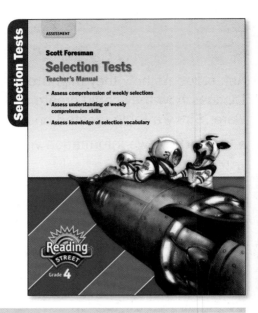

Leveled Assessment

On-Level

Strategic Intervention

Advanced

Use pp. 31–36 of Fresh Reads for Differentiated Test Practice to check:

 Comprehension Skill *Cause and Effect*

REVIEW Comprehension Skill
Draw Conclusions

Fluency *Words Correct Per Minute*

Managing Assessment

Use Assessment Handbook for:

 Observation Checklists

 Record-Keeping Forms

 Portfolio Assessment

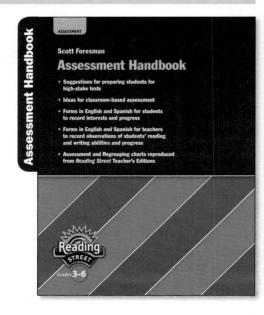

Oregon
Planning Guide for Common Curriculum Goals
Coyote School News

Reading Street Teacher's Edition pages	Grade 4 Oregon Grade-Level Standards for English/Language Arts
Oral Language **Speaking/Listening** Build Concept Vocabulary: 162l, 175, 183, 187c Read Aloud: 162m	**EL.04.RE.01** Read aloud grade-level narrative text and informational text fluently and accurately with effective pacing, intonation, and expression. **EL.04.RE.09** Understand, learn, and use new vocabulary that is introduced and taught directly through informational text, literary text, and instruction across the subject areas.
Word Work Irregular Plurals: 187i–187j	**EL.04.WR.15** Spell correctly: suffixes and prefixes (-ly, -ness, mis-, un-); syllables (word parts each containing a vowel sound, such as sur-prise or e-col-o-gy).
Reading **Comprehension** Draw Conclusions: 162–163, 166–183, 187b Prior Knowledge: 162–163, 166–183 **Vocabulary** Lesson Vocabulary: 164b, 175, 183, 186 Dictionary/Glossary: 164–165, 173, 177, 187c **Fluency** Model Emotion: 162l–162m, 187a **Self-Selected Reading:** LR10–18, TR16–17 **Literature** Genre—Historical Fiction: 166 Reader Response: 184	**EL.04.RE.10** Develop vocabulary by listening to and discussing both familiar and conceptually challenging selections read aloud across the subject areas. **EL.04.RE.17** Locate information in titles, tables of contents, chapter headings, illustrations, captions, glossaries, indexes, graphs, charts, diagrams, and tables to aid understanding of grade-level text. **EL.04.RE.22** Make and confirm predictions about text by using prior knowledge and ideas presented in the text itself, including illustrations, titles, topic sentences, and important words. **EL.04.LI.08** Draw inferences or conclusions about a text based on explicitly stated information.
Language Arts **Writing** News Story: 187g–187h **Six-Trait Writing** Focus/Ideas: 185, 187g–187h **Grammar, Usage, and Mechanics** Regular Plural Nouns: 187e–187f **Research/Study** Newspaper/Newsletter: 187l **Technology** New Literacies: 187k	**EL.04.WR.24** Write informational reports: ask and then address a central question about an issue or event; include facts and details for focus; develop the topic with simple facts, details, examples, and explanations. **EL.04.WR.31** Understand the organization of almanacs, newspapers, and periodicals and how to use those print materials.
Unit Skills **Writing** How-To Report: WA2–9 **Poetry:** 260–263 **Project/Wrap-Up:** 264–265	**EL.04.WR.25** Write informational reports: ask and then address a central question about an issue or event; include facts and details for focus; develop the topic with simple facts, details, examples, and explanations; use more than one source of information, including speakers, books, newspapers, other media sources, and online information.

This Week's Leveled Readers

Intensive Intervention

SCOTT FORESMAN
SiDEWALKS

Intensive Intervention for Tier 3 Students

Below-Level

Home on the Range
by Cynthia Swain

Nonfiction

EL.04.RE.06 Match reading to purpose—location of information, full comprehension, and personal enjoyment.

EL.04.LI.08 Draw inferences or conclusions about a text based on explicitly stated information.

On-Level

ON A RANCH
✕ ✕ ✕
by Patty North

Nonfiction

EL.04.LI.03 Identify and/or summarize sequence of events, main ideas, and supporting details in literary selections.

EL.04.LI.08 Draw inferences or conclusions about a text based on explicitly stated information.

Advanced

The Life of César Chávez
by Gretchen McBride

Nonfiction

EL.04.RE.04 Make connections to text, within text, and among texts across the subject areas.

EL.04.LI.08 Draw inferences or conclusions about a text based on explicitly stated information.

Content-Area Content Standards and Benchmarks in This Lesson

Science

SC.05.LS.01.01 Classify a variety of living things into groups using various characteristics. (Previews Grade 5 Benchmark)

SC.05.LS.05 Describe the relationship between characteristics of specific habitats and the organisms that live there. (Previews Grade 5 Benchmark)

SC.05.LS.05.02 Identify the producers, consumers, and decomposers in a given habitat. (Previews Grade 5 Benchmark)

Social Studies

SS.05.GE.04.01 Identify and locate major landforms, bodies of water, vegetation, and climate found in regions of the United States. (Previews Grade 5 Benchmark)

SS.05.GE.05 Identify patterns of migration and cultural interaction in the United States. (Previews Grade 5 Benchmark)

Oregon!

A FAMOUS OREGONIAN
Dave Kingman

Oregon native Dave Kingman (1948–) has had a turbulent professional baseball career, but he is probably best remembered for his many home runs. Although he became a well-known baseball personality, Kingman made it clear that he did not like the attention, and this attitude formed his reputation as a difficult teammate. Kingman played on as many as seven teams, including the San Francisco Giants and New York Mets. He had a career record of 442 home runs.

Students can . . .
List a professional baseball player whose number of home runs is higher and someone whose number is lower than Dave Kingman's. Have students write the players' names with Kingman's in an equation using "greater than" and "less than" symbols.

A SPECIAL OREGON PLACE
Oregon State University

Located in Corvallis, Oregon State University has colleges of forestry, agricultural science, atmospheric and oceanic science, and veterinary medicine, among many others. The university has branches throughout the state, including its Cascades Campus in Bend and the Hatfield Marine Science Center in Newport. Linus Pauling, the winner of two Nobel Prizes, attended Oregon State University, and the school's Linus Pauling Institute is named for this famous alumnus. In athletics the Oregon State Beavers participate in many NCAA sports, including basketball, golf, football, and soccer.

Students can . . .
Find Oregon State University's Web site. Ask students to list ten reasons why a young person might choose to attend the university.

OREGON FUN FACTS
Did You Know?

• The Oregon Audubon Society conducted a poll of schoolchildren in 1927 that led to designating the western meadowlark the state bird.

• Three national monuments lie in Oregon: the John Day Fossil Beds, the Newberry National Volcanic Monument, and the Oregon Caves.

• At Coos Bay, visitors can see piles of wood chips destined to become paper being loaded onto factory ships for transport to Asia.

Students can . . .
Learn how paper is made from wood. Ask students to make a flow chart that shows the steps involved in making paper from wood particles.

Unit 2
Work and Play

CONCEPT QUESTION
What is the value of work and play?

Week 1
How can we learn to appreciate the talents of others?

Week 2
How can we work together to achieve a goal?

Week 3
What can we accomplish by using our imaginations?

Week 4
What is the value of a job well done?

Week 5
What is the job of the President of the United States?

Week 2

EXPAND THE CONCEPT
How can we work together to achieve a goal?

CONNECT THE CONCEPT

▶ **Build Background**
convince, energetic, offers

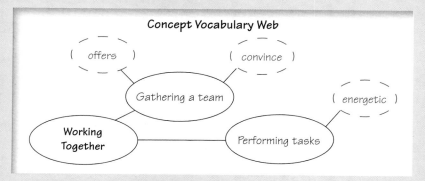

Concept Vocabulary Web

offers — convince — Gathering a team — energetic — Working Together — Performing tasks

▶ **Social Studies Content**
U.S. Expansion, Spanish Explorers, Hispanic Cowboys, History of Newspapers

▶ **Writing**
News Story

▶ **Internet Inquiry**
Achieving Goals

Preview Your Week

How can we work together to achieve a goal?

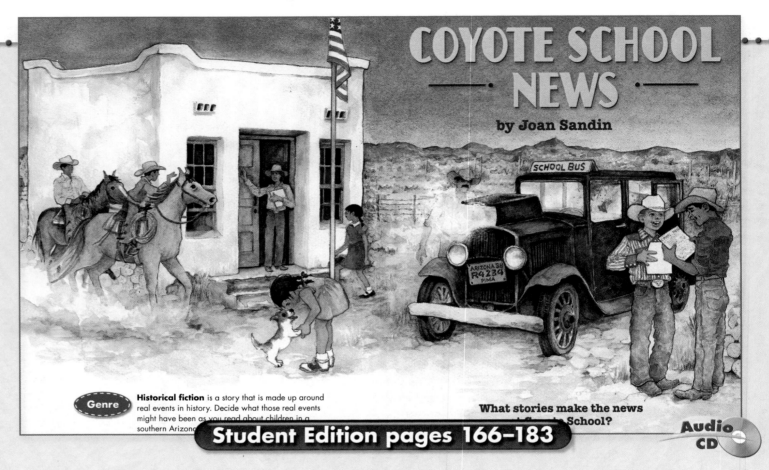

COYOTE SCHOOL NEWS

by Joan Sandin

Genre Historical fiction is a story that is made up around real events in history. Decide what those real events might have been as you read about children in a southern Arizona...

What stories make the news at Coyote School?

Student Edition pages 166–183

Audio CD

Genre Historical Fiction
◉ **Vocabulary Strategy** Dictionary/Glossary
◉ **Comprehension Skill** Draw Conclusions
◉ **Comprehension Strategy** Prior Knowledge

Paired Selection

Reading Across Texts
Identify Types of Writing in Coyote News

Genre
How-to Article

Text Features
Bold-faced Type
Checkmarks

Social Studies in Reading

How-to Article

Genre
- A how-to article gives step-by-step directions for making or doing something.
- It often includes a list of materials to gather or things to think about before you begin.

Text Features
- Bold-faced type sets off the steps and calls attention to newspaper jobs and kinds of newspaper articles.
- Checkmarks make the text seem like a list that is easy to follow.

Link to Social Studies
Look through a community newspaper. Make a list of the kinds of articles it contains. Share what you learn with your class.

How to Start a School Newspaper

by Lisa Klobuchar

Starting your own school paper can be fun! You get to share news and say what you think about it. But starting a paper takes planning and teamwork. Here's how to do it.

First, pick your team. You'll need to fill these jobs:

✓ The **editor** decides what stories writers will work on. Everybody comes up with ideas, but the editor has the final say.

✓ The **writers** write the stories. They talk to people and dig up facts.

✓ The **copyeditor** checks the writers' work. He or she fixes spelling and other mistakes.

✓ The **photo editor** chooses pictures to go with the stories.

✓ The **designer** decides where the stories and pictures will go on the page. The final result is called a layout.

✓ The **staff adviser** is the adult who guides you. The adviser answers your questions...

Next, figure out what to write about. Find out what your classmates want to read about. Ask around, or place an idea box outside your classroom. Here are just a few kinds of writing to put in your paper:

✓ **News** stories tell about what is going on in your school, your town, or even around the world. They must be factual, or true.

✓ In **sports** stories, you can tell when games will be played at your school. You can describe the sports action and list scores, or you can profile a player.

✓ **Arts and entertainment** stories may tell about special school events or introduce readers to a poem, short story, piece of artwork, or movie.

✓ In an **advice column**, students can ask questions about anything, and "Dear So-and-So" will answer them.

Finally, start writing! It feels wonderful to share your ideas and stories with your classmates. And there's no better way to do that than to start a school newspaper.

Reading Across Texts
This article identifies several kinds of writing that can go into a school newspaper. Which kinds of writing appear in *Coyote News*?

Writing Across Texts Make a list of the stories or features in one issue of *Coyote News*. Tell what kind of writing each is.

◉ **Prior Knowledge** What do you already know about newspaper workers?

186

Student Edition pages 186–187

Audio CD

Read It
ONLINE
PearsonSuccessNet.com
• Student Edition
• Leveled Readers

Leveled Readers

◉ **Skill** Draw Conclusions
◉ **Strategy** Prior Knowledge
Lesson Vocabulary

Below-Level

On-Level

Advanced

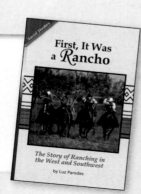

ELL Reader

· Concept Vocabulary
· Text Support
· Language Enrichment

Time for
SOCIAL STUDIES

Integrate Social Studies Standards

• U.S. History

✓ **Read**

Coyote School News,
pp. 166–183

"How to Start a School Newspaper," pp. 186–187

Leveled Readers

Below-Level   **On-Level**   **Advanced**

• Support Concepts   • Develop Concepts   • Extend Concepts
                                          • Social Studies
                                            Extension Activity

ELL Reader

✓ **Build**
Concept Vocabulary
Working Together,
pp. 162l–162m

✓ **Teach**
Social Studies Concepts
U.S. Expansion, p. 169
Spanish Explorers, p. 173
Hispanic Cowboys, p. 179
History of Newspapers, p. 187

✓ **Explore**
Social Studies Center
Compare Schools, p. 162k

Weekly Plan

READING

45–90 minutes

TARGET SKILLS OF THE WEEK

Comprehension Skill
Draw Conclusions

Comprehension Strategy
Prior Knowledge

Vocabulary Strategy
Dictionary/Glossary

LANGUAGE ARTS

30–60 minutes

Trait of the Week

Focus/Ideas

DAY 1
PAGES 162l–164b, 187a, 187e–187k

Oral Language

QUESTION OF THE WEEK   *How can we work together to achieve a goal?*

Read Aloud: "A Big-City Dream," 162m
Build Concepts, 162l

Comprehension/Vocabulary

Comprehension Skill/Strategy Lesson, 162–163
　Draw Conclusions **T**
　Prior Knowledge
Build Background, 164a
Introduce Lesson Vocabulary, 164b
bawling, coyote, dudes, roundup, spurs **T**

Read Leveled Readers

Grouping Options 162f–162g

Fluency

Model Emotion, 162l–162m, 187a

Grammar, 187e
Introduce Regular Plural Nouns **T**

Writing Workshop, 187g
Introduce News Story
Model the Trait of the Week: Focus/Ideas

Spelling, 187i
Pretest for Irregular Plurals

Internet Inquiry, 187k
Identify Questions

DAY 2
PAGES 164–175, 187a, 187e–187k

Oral Language

QUESTION OF THE DAY   *What work must be done on a ranch?*

Comprehension/Vocabulary

Vocabulary Strategy Lesson, 164–165
　Dictionary/Glossary **T**

Read *Coyote School News,* 166–175

Grouping Options
162f–162g

　Draw Conclusions **T**
　Prior Knowledge
　Dictionary/Glossary **T**
　REVIEW Setting **T**
Develop Vocabulary

Fluency

Choral Reading, 187a

Grammar, 187e
Develop Regular Plural Nouns **T**

Writing Workshop, 187g
Improve Writing with Include Necessary Information

Spelling, 187i
Teach the Generalization

Internet Inquiry, 187k
Navigate/Search

DAILY WRITING ACTIVITIES

Day 1 Write to Read, 162

Day 2 Words to Write, 165
Strategy Response Log, 166, 175

DAILY SOCIAL STUDIES CONNECTIONS

Day 1 Working Together Concept Web, 162l

Day 2 Time for Social Studies: U.S. Expansion, 169;
Spanish Explorers, 173
Revisit the Working Together Concept Web, 175

DAILY SUCCESS PREDICTORS

for Adequate Yearly Progress

Monitor Progress and Corrective Feedback

Check Vocabulary, *162l*

Vocabulary

RESOURCES FOR THE WEEK

- Practice Book, *pp. 61–70*
- Word Study and Spelling Practice Book, *pp. 25–28*
- Grammar and Writing Practice Book, *pp. 25–28*
- Selection Test, *pp. 25–28*
- Fresh Reads for Differentiated Test Practice, *pp. 37–42*
- The Grammar and Writing Book, *pp. 86–91*

Grouping Options for Differentiated Instruction

Turn the page for the small group lesson plan.

DAY 3 — PAGES 176–185, 187a, 187e–187k

Oral Language

QUESTION OF THE DAY *How do all the children contribute to* Coyote News?

Comprehension/Vocabulary

Read *Coyote School News, 176–184*

Grouping Options 162f–162g

- Draw Conclusions **T**
- Prior Knowledge
- Dictionary/ Glossary **T**

Develop Vocabulary

Reader Response
Selection Test

Fluency

Model Emotion, 187a

Grammar, 187f
Apply Regular Plural Nouns in Writing **T**

Writing Workshop, 185, 187h
Write Now
Prewrite and Draft

Spelling, 187j
Connect Spelling to Writing

Internet Inquiry, 187k
Analyze Sources

Day 3 Strategy Response Log, 182
Look Back and Write, 184

Day 3 Time for Social Studies: Hispanic Cowboys, 179
Revisit the Working Together Concept Web, 183

DAY 4 — PAGES 186–187a, 187e–187k

Oral Language

QUESTION OF THE DAY *How is teamwork necessary in Monchi's life, both in and out of the Coyote School?*

Comprehension/Vocabulary

Read "How to Start a School Newspaper," 186–187

Grouping Options 162f –162g

How-to Article/ Text Features

Reading Across Texts

Content-Area Vocabulary

Fluency

Partner Reading, 187a

Grammar, 187f
Practice Regular Plural Nouns for Standardized Tests **T**

Writing Workshop, 187h
Draft, Revise, and Publish

Spelling, 187j
Provide a Strategy

Internet Inquiry, 187k
Synthesize Information

Day 4 Writing Across Texts, 187

Day 4 Time for Social Studies: History of Newspapers, 187

DAY 5 — PAGES 187a–187l

Oral Language

QUESTION OF THE WEEK *To wrap up the week, revisit the Day 1 question.*

Build Concept Vocabulary, 187c

Fluency

Read Leveled Readers

Grouping Options 162f–162g

Assess Reading Rate, 187a

Comprehension/Vocabulary

- Reteach Draw Conclusions, 187b **T**

Narrative Writing, 187b

- Review Dictionary/Glossary, 187c **T**

Speaking and Listening, 187d
Newscast
Listen to a Newscast

Grammar, 187f
Cumulative Review

Writing Workshop, 187h
Connect to Unit Writing

Spelling, 187j
Posttest for Irregular Plurals

Internet Inquiry, 187k
Communicate Results

Research/Study Skills, 187l
Newspaper/Newsletter

Day 5 Narrative Writing, 187b

Day 5 Revisit the Working Together Concept Web, 187c

KEY = Target Skill **T** = Tested Skill

Comprehension Check Retelling, *184*

Fluency Check Fluency wcpm, *187a*

Vocabulary Check Vocabulary, *187c*

SUCCESS PREDICTOR

Small Group Plan for Differentiated Instruction

Daily Plan AT A GLANCE

Reading
Whole Group
- Oral Language
- Comprehension/Vocabulary

Group Time
Differentiated Instruction

Meet with small groups to provide:
- Skill Support
- Reading Support
- Fluency Practice

Read

This week's lessons for daily group time can be found behind the Differentiated Instruction (DI) tab on pp. DI·12–DI·21.

Whole Group
- Fluency

Language Arts
- Grammar
- Writing
- Spelling
- Research/Inquiry
- Speaking/Listening/Viewing

Use *My Sidewalks on Reading Street* for Tier III intensive reading intervention.

DAY 1

On-Level
Teacher-Led
Page DI·13
- Develop Concept Vocabulary
- **Read** On-Level Reader *On a Ranch*

Strategic Intervention
Teacher-Led
Page DI·12
- Reinforce Concepts
- **Read** Below-Level Reader *Home on the Range*

Advanced
Teacher-Led
Page DI·13
- **Read** Advanced Reader *The Life of César Chávez*
- Independent Extension Activity

(i) Independent Activities
While you meet with small groups, have the rest of the class...

- Visit the Reading/Library Center
- Listen to the Background Building Audio
- Finish Write to Read, p. 162
- Complete Practice Book pp. 63–64
- Visit Cross-Curricular Centers

DAY 2

On-Level
Teacher-Led
Pages 168–175
- **Read** *Coyote School News*

Strategic Intervention
Teacher-Led
Page DI·14
- Practice Lesson Vocabulary
- Read Multisyllabic Words
- **Read** or Listen to *Coyote School News*

Advanced
Teacher-Led
Page DI·15
- Extend Vocabulary
- **Read** *Coyote School News*

(i) Independent Activities
While you meet with small groups, have the rest of the class...

- Visit the Reading/Library Center
- Listen to the AudioText for *Coyote School News*
- Finish Words to Write, p. 165
- Complete Practice Book pp. 65–66
- Write in their Strategy Response Logs, pp. 166, 175
- Visit Cross-Curricular Centers
- Work on inquiry projects

DAY 3

On-Level
Teacher-Led
Pages 176–183
- **Read** *Coyote School News*

Strategic Intervention
Teacher-Led
Page DI·16
- Practice Draw Conclusions and Prior Knowledge
- **Read** or Listen to *Coyote School News*

Advanced
Teacher-Led
Page DI·17
- Extend Draw Conclusions and Prior Knowledge
- **Read** *Coyote School News*

(i) Independent Activities
While you meet with small groups, have the rest of the class...

- Visit the Reading/Library Center
- Listen to the AudioText for *Coyote School News*
- Write in their Strategy Response Logs, p. 182
- Finish Look Back and Write, p. 184
- Complete Practice Book p. 67
- Visit Cross-Curricular Centers
- Work on inquiry projects

DAY 4

On-Level
Teacher-Led
Pages 186–187
- **Read** "How to Start a School Newspaper"

Strategic Intervention
Teacher-Led
Page DI · 18
- Practice Retelling
- **Read** or Listen to "How to Start a School Newspaper"

Advanced
Teacher-Led
Page DI · 19
- **Read** "How to Start a School Newspaper"
- Genre Study

Independent Activities

While you meet with small groups, have the rest of the class...

- Visit the Reading/Library Center
- Listen to the AudioText for "How to Start a School Newspaper"
- Visit the Writing/Vocabulary Center
- Finish Writing Across Texts, p. 187
- Visit Cross-Curricular Centers
- Work on inquiry projects

DAY 5

On-Level
Teacher-Led
Page DI · 21
- **Reread** Leveled Reader *On a Ranch*
- Retell *On a Ranch*

Strategic Intervention
Teacher-Led
Page DI · 20
- **Reread** Leveled Reader *Home on the Range*
- Retell *Home on the Range*

Advanced
Teacher-Led
Page DI · 21
- **Reread** Leveled Reader *The Life of César Chávez*
- Share Extension Activity

Independent Activities

While you meet with small groups, have the rest of the class...

- Visit the Reading/Library Center
- Complete Practice Book pp. 68–70
- Visit Cross-Curricular Centers
- Work on inquiry projects

ELL

Grouping Place English language learners in the groups that correspond to their reading abilities in English.

Use the appropriate Leveled Reader or other text at students' instructional level.

TiP Send home the appropriate Multilingual Summary of the main selection on Day 1.

Take It to the NET™ ONLINE
PearsonSuccessNet.com

Sharon Vaughn
For ideas and activities for English language learners, see the article "Storybook Reading" by P. Hickman, S. Pollard-Durodola, and Scott Foresman author S. Vaughn.

TEACHER TALK

Fluency is the ability to read words and connected text rapidly, accurately, and smoothly. Fluency may be measured in words correct per minute.

Be sure to schedule time for students to work on the unit inquiry project "All in a Day's Work." This week students conduct information searches for text and images to help them answer their questions.

Looking Ahead

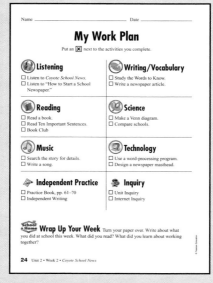

Name _____ **Date** _____

My Work Plan
Put an ☒ next to the activities you complete.

Listening
- ☐ Listen to *Coyote School News*.
- ☐ Listen to "How to Start a School Newspaper."

Writing/Vocabulary
- ☐ Study the Words to Know.
- ☐ Write a newspaper article.

Reading
- ☐ Read a book.
- ☐ Read Ten Important Sentences.
- ☐ Book Club

Science
- ☐ Make a Venn diagram.
- ☐ Compare schools.

Music
- ☐ Search the story for details.
- ☐ Write a song.

Technology
- ☐ Use a word-processing program.
- ☐ Design a newspaper masthead.

Independent Practice
- ☐ Practice Book, pp. 61–70
- ☐ Independent Writing

Inquiry
- ☐ Unit Inquiry
- ☐ Internet Inquiry

Wrap Up Your Week Turn your paper over. Write about what you did at school this week. What did you read? What did you learn about working together?

24   Unit 2 • Week 2 • *Coyote School News*

▲ **Group-Time Survival Guide**
p. 24, Weekly Contract

☑ Customize Your Plan *by Strand*

SOCIAL STUDIES

Concept Development

How can we work together to achieve a goal?

CONCEPT VOCABULARY
convince   energetic   offers

BUILD

❏ **Question of the Week** Introduce and discuss the question of the week. This week students will read a variety of texts and work on projects related to the concept *working together*. Post the question for students to refer to throughout the week. DAY 1 *162d*

❏ **Read Aloud** Read aloud "A Big-City Dream." Then begin a web to build concepts and concept vocabulary related to this week's lesson and the unit theme, Work and Play. Introduce the concept words *convince, energetic,* and *offers* and have students place them on the web. Display the web for use throughout the week. DAY 1 *162l–162m*

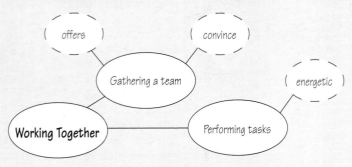

DEVELOP

❏ **Question of the Day** Use the prompts from the Weekly Plan to engage students in conversations related to this week's reading and the unit theme. **EVERY DAY** *162d–162e*

❏ **Concept Vocabulary Web** Revisit the Working Together Concept Web and encourage students to add concept words from their reading and life experiences. **DAY 2** *175,* **DAY 3** *183*

CONNECT

❏ **Looking Back/Moving Forward** Revisit the Working Together Concept Web and discuss how it relates to this week's lesson and the unit theme. Then make connections to next week's lesson. **DAY 5** *187c*

CHECK

❏ **Concept Vocabulary Web** Use the Working Together Concept Web to check students' understanding of the concept vocabulary words *convince, energetic,* and *offers*. DAY 1 *162l,* **DAY 5** *187c*

 **STRATEGY DICTIONARY/ GLOSSARY** When you come across a word whose meaning you don't know, and the words around it don't help, you can use a dictionary or glossary to find the meaning.

LESSON VOCABULARY

*bawling   roundup
coyote   spurs
dudes*

TEACH

❏ **Words to Know** Give students the opportunity to tell what they already know about this week's lesson vocabulary words. Then discuss word meaning. DAY 1 *164b*

❏ **Vocabulary Strategy Lesson** Use the vocabulary strategy lesson in the Student Edition to introduce and model this week's strategy, *dictionary/ glossary.* **DAY 2** *164–165*

Vocabulary Strategy Lesson

PRACTICE/APPLY

❏ **Leveled Text** Read the lesson vocabulary in the context of leveled text. DAY 1 *LR10–LR18*

❏ **Words in Context** Read the lesson vocabulary and apply *dictionary/ glossary* in the context of *Coyote School News.* **DAY 2** *166–175,* **DAY 3** *176–184*

Leveled Readers

❏ **Writing/Vocabulary Center** Write a newspaper article about your classroom or school. **ANY DAY** *162k*

Main Selection—Fiction

❏ **Homework** Practice Book pp. 64–65. DAY 1 *164b,* **DAY 2** *165*

❏ **Word Play** Have students work in small groups to locate all the compound words in *Coyote School News.* To make the activity more challenging set a time limit and have teams illustrate their favorite compound word. **ANY DAY** *187c*

ASSESS

❏ **Selection Test** Use the Selection Test to determine students' understanding of the lesson vocabulary words. **DAY 3**

RETEACH/REVIEW

❏ **Reteach Lesson** If necessary, use this lesson to reteach and review *dictionary/glossary.* DAY 5 *187c*

COMPREHENSION

👁 **SKILL DRAW CONCLUSIONS** Drawing conclusions is forming an opinion based on what you already know or on the facts and details in the text.

👁 **STRATEGY PRIOR KNOWLEDGE** Prior knowledge is what the reader already knows about a subject. Good readers use their prior knowledge to help them understand what they read.

TEACH

☐ **Skill/Strategy Lesson** Use the skill/ strategy lesson in the Student Edition to introduce and model *draw conclusions* and *prior knowledge*. **DAY 1** *162-163*

Skill/Strategy Lesson

☐ **Extend Skills** Teach narrative writing. **ANY DAY** *187b*

PRACTICE/APPLY

☐ **Leveled Text** Apply *draw conclusions* and *prior knowledge* to read leveled text. **DAY 1** *LR10-LR18*

☐ **Skills and Strategies in Context** Read *Coyote School News*, using the Guiding Comprehension questions to apply *draw conclusions* and *prior knowledge*. **DAY 2** *166-175*, **DAY 3** *176-184*

Leveled Readers

☐ **Skills and Strategies in Context** Read "How to Start a School Newspaper," guiding students as they apply *draw conclusions* and *prior knowledge*. Then have students discuss and write across texts. **DAY 4** *186-187*

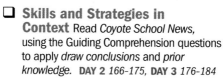

Main Selection—Fiction

☐ **Homework** Practice Book pp. 63, 67, 68. **DAY 1** *163*, **DAY 3** *183*, **DAY 5** *187b*

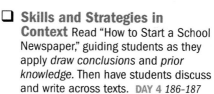

Paired Selection—Nonfiction

☐ **Fresh Reads for Differentiated Test Practice** Have students practice *draw conclusions* with a new passage. **DAY 3**

ASSESS

☐ **Selection Test** Determine students' understanding of the selection and their use of *draw conclusions*. **DAY 3**

☐ **Retell** Have students retell *Coyote School News*. **DAY 3** *184-185*

RETEACH/REVIEW

☐ **Reteach Lesson** If necessary, reteach and review *draw conclusions*. **DAY 5** *187b*

FLUENCY

SKILL EMOTION Reading with emotion is the ability to change pace, tone, pitch, or volume to make the reading more expressive and lively to the listeners.

TEACH

☐ **Read Aloud** Model fluent reading by rereading "A Big-City Dream." Focus on this week's fluency skill, emotion. **DAY 1** *162l-162m, 187a*

PRACTICE/APPLY

☐ **Choral Reading** Read aloud selected paragraphs from *Coyote School News*, emphasizing the changing pace, tone, pitch, or volume in your voice. Then practice as a class by doing three choral readings of the paragraphs. **DAY 2** *187a*, **DAY 3** *187a*

☐ **Partner Reading** Have partners practice reading with emotion and offering each other feedback. As students reread, monitor their progress toward their individual fluency goals. **DAY 4** *187a*

☐ **Listening Center** Have students follow along with the AudioText for this week's selections. **ANY DAY** *162j*

☐ **Reading/Library Center** Have students reread a selection of their choice. **ANY DAY** *162j*

☐ **Fluency Coach** Have students use Fluency Coach to listen to fluent readings or practice reading on their own. **ANY DAY**

ASSESS

☐ **Check Fluency** WCPM Do a one-minute timed reading, paying special attention to this week's skill—emotion. Provide feedback for each student. **DAY 5** *187a*

☑ Customize Your Plan *by Strand*

GRAMMAR

SKILL REGULAR PLURAL NOUNS Plural nouns name more than one person, place, or thing. Plural nouns are often formed by adding *-s, -es*.

TEACH

❑ **Grammar Transparency 7** Use Grammar Transparency 7 to teach regular plural nouns.
DAY 1 *187e*

Grammar Transparency 7

PRACTICE/APPLY

❑ **Develop the Concept** Review the concept of regular plural nouns and provide guided practice. DAY 2 *187e*

❑ **Apply to Writing** Have students review something they have written and add regular plural nouns. DAY 3 *187f*

❑ **Test Preparation** Examine common errors in regular plural nouns to prepare for standardized tests. DAY 4 *187f*

❑ **Homework** Grammar and Writing Practice Book pp. 25–27.
DAY 2 *187e*, DAY 3 *187f*, DAY 4 *187f*

ASSESS

❑ **Cumulative Review** Use Grammar and Writing Practice Book p. 28. DAY 5 *187f*

RETEACH/REVIEW

❑ **Daily Fix-It** Have students find and correct errors in grammar, spelling, and punctuation. **EVERY DAY** *187e-187f*

❑ **The Grammar and Writing Book** Use pp. 86–89 of The Grammar and Writing Book to extend instruction for regular plural nouns. **ANY DAY**

The Grammar and Writing Book

WRITING

Trait of the Week

FOCUS/IDEAS Good writers focus on a main idea and develop this idea with strong supporting details. Having a purpose, to inform, to persuade, or to entertain, helps keep focus on the main idea.

TEACH

❑ **Writing Transparency 7A** Use the model to introduce and discuss the Trait of the Week. DAY 1 *187g*

❑ **Writing Transparency 7B** Use the transparency to show students how including necessary information can improve their writing. DAY 2 *187g*

Writing Transparency 7A   **Writing Transparency 7B**

PRACTICE/APPLY

❑ **Write Now** Examine the model on Student Edition p. 185. Then have students write their own news story. DAY 3 *185, 187h*, DAY 4 *187h*

> **Prompt** *Coyote School News* includes several news stories written by students. Think about something that has happened recently in your school or community. Now write a news story about that event.

Write Now p. 185

❑ **Writing/Vocabulary Center** Write a newspaper article about your classroom or school. **ANY DAY** *162k*

ASSESS

❑ **Writing Trait Rubric** Use the rubric to evaluate students' writing. DAY 4 *187h*

RETEACH/REVIEW

❑ **The Grammar and Writing Book** Use pp. 86–91 of The Grammar and Writing Book to extend instruction for regular plural nouns, include necessary information, and news story. **ANY DAY**

The Grammar and Writing Book

❶ Use assessment data to determine your instructional focus.

❷ Preview this week's instruction by strand.

❸ Choose instructional activities that meet the needs of your classroom.

SPELLING

GENERALIZATION IRREGULAR PLURALS Some plurals are formed by adding -s or -es: roof<u>s</u>, potato<u>es</u>. Sometimes the spelling of the singular form changes: *loaves*. Some words do not change at all: *moose*. Regular plurals follow the rules. Irregular plurals do not. Some words may be both singular and plural.

TEACH

❑ **Pretest** Give the pretest for words with irregular plurals. Guide students in self-correcting their pretests and correcting any misspellings. DAY 1 *187i*

❑ **Think and Practice** Connect spelling to the phonics generalization for irregular plurals. DAY 2 *187i*

PRACTICE/APPLY

❑ **Connect to Writing** Have students use spelling words to write one-sentence news bulletins. Then review frequently misspelled words: *they, said, went.* DAY 3 *187j*

❑ **Homework** Word Study and Spelling Practice Book pp. 25–28. **EVERY DAY**

RETEACH/REVIEW

❑ **Review** Review spelling words to prepare for the posttest. Then provide students with a spelling strategy—memory tricks. DAY 4 *187j*

ASSESS

❑ **Posttest** Use dictation sentences to give the posttest for words with irregular plurals. DAY 5 *187j*

Spelling Words

1. videos	8. roofs	15. patios
2. teeth	9. halves	16. banjos
3. potatoes	10. moose	17. tornadoes
4. themselves	11. radios	18. tomatoes
5. lives	12. sheep	19. hoofs
6. leaves	13. cuffs	20. loaves
7. cliffs	14. beliefs	

Challenge Words

21. portfolios	23. handkerchiefs	25. lassoes
22. embargoes	24. calves	

*Word from the selection

RESEARCH AND INQUIRY

❑ **Internet Inquiry** Have students conduct an Internet inquiry on achieving goals. **EVERY DAY** *187k*

❑ **Newspaper/Newsletter** Review the features of a newspaper or newsletter and discuss how students can use these resources to find information. **DAY 5** *187l*

❑ **Unit Inquiry** Allow time for students to conduct information searches for text and images to help them answer their questions. **ANY DAY** *141*

SPEAKING AND LISTENING

❑ **Newscast** Have students create and present a TV newscast using the information from the news story they wrote. **DAY 5** *187d*

❑ **Listen to a Newscast** Provide students with a pre-recorded radio newscast to listen to and analyze. Prior to listening, ask them to listen carefully for the main idea of each news story and then follow up with class discussion. **DAY 5** *187d*

Resources for
Differentiated Instruction

LEVELED READERS

▶ **Comprehension**
- ⚙ **Skill** Draw Conclusions
- ⚙ **Strategy** Prior Knowledge

▶ **Lesson Vocabulary**
- ⚙ Dictionary/Glossary

bawling   coyote   dudes   roundup   spurs

▶ **Social Studies Standards**
- • U.S. History

Leveled Reader Database
ONLINE
PearsonSuccessNet.com

Use the Online Database of over 600 books to
- Download and print additional copies of this week's leveled readers.
- Listen to the readers being read online.
- Search for more titles focused on this week's skills, topic, and content.

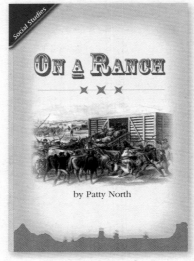

On a Ranch
★★★
by Patty North

On-Level Reader

Name _____ On a Ranch

Draw Conclusions
- Drawing conclusions means making a decision or forming an opinion that makes sense after you think about facts or details.

Directions Look back at *On a Ranch*. Take your time and think about the story. Then follow these three steps.

1. First, write down what you already know about life on a ranch.
   Answers will vary.

2. Next, write down three different details that support what you wrote in step 1.
   Answers will vary.

3. Finally, think about any conclusions you can draw about life on a ranch. Try to write about a conclusion that means something to you personally.
   Answers will vary.

⚙ **On-Level Practice** TE p. LR14

Name _____ On a Ranch

Vocabulary
Directions Some of the letters of each vocabulary word have been left out. Fill in the missing letters to make a word. Write a sentence using each vocabulary word.

Check the Words You Know
__bawling __coyote __dudes __roundup __spurs

1. _ a w _ _ n g   bawling
Your sentence: **Sentences will vary.**

2. _ _ y _ t e   coyote
Your sentence: _____

3. _ _ d e _   dudes
Your sentence: _____

4. _ _ u n d _ _   roundup
Your sentence: _____

5. _ p _ s   spurs
Your sentence: _____

On-Level Practice TE p. LR15

Home on the Range
by Cynthia Swain

Below-Level Reader

Name _____ Home on the Range

Draw Conclusions
- To draw a conclusion means to make a decision or form an opinion that makes sense after you think about facts or details.

Directions Below are three conclusions about *Home on the Range*. Go back to the book and find supporting details for each conclusion.

1. **Conclusion:** The U.S. government needed to force ranchers to graze their cattle in different areas.
Supporting Details: Cattle eat and trample plants. Cattle make waterways dirty. Cattle destroy plant growth, which threatens local plants and the animals that depend on them for food.

2. **Conclusion:** Guests can have a lot of fun at dude ranches.
Supporting Details: Guests learn how to rope cattle. They can take tennis or yoga. They are given comfortable quarters and good food.

3. **Conclusion:** Ranching life is hard.
Supporting Details: Ranchers must be up before dawn; they aren't done until eight at night; ranching is still done in winter.

4. After reading *Home on the Range*, what conclusions can you draw about how you would like living on a ranch?
Answers will vary.

⚙ **Below-Level Practice** TE p. LR11

Name _____ Home on the Range

Vocabulary
Directions Underline the sentence in which the word is used correctly. Then write a sentence of your own.

Check the Words You Know
__bawling __coyote __dudes __roundup __spurs

The coyote was bawling for its mother.
The bawling coyote was so quiet we didn't even know it was there.
1. Your sentence: **Sentences will vary.**

Wild coyotes live high in the mountains.
My sister had a coyote in her lunchbox.
2. Your sentence: _____

We had a delicious dinner of rice and dudes last night.
Sometimes they call guys "dudes."
3. Your sentence: _____

Please roundup all the beds and then wash the dishes.
At the roundup, all the cattle were put into pens.
4. Your sentence: _____

The cowboy never used his spurs on his horses.
The spurs were not enough to pay for the food.
5. Your sentence: _____

Below-Level Practice TE p. LR12

Advanced

Advanced Reader

Name _____   The Life of César Chávez

Draw Conclusions

To **draw a conclusion** is to make a decision or form an opinion that makes sense after you think about facts or details.

Directions You've just read about how César Chávez fought injustice and helped his people. Based on what you have read, what conclusions can you draw about what works in solving injustices and what doesn't? Give supporting details for your answers.

1. _Answers will vary._

_____
_____
_____
_____

Directions Imagine there is an injustice in the school. Students are not allowed to eat their lunches at the same time, and because of this, many are going hungry. In the past, students were able to talk to the principal, who would listen to them and try to help. Students have also found that when they work together, they can often get things done faster. What conclusions can you draw about what might work to solve this problem and why?

2. _Answers will vary._

_____
_____
_____
_____

Advanced Practice TE p. LR17

Name _____   The Life of César Chávez

Vocabulary

Directions Unscramble each word, match it to its definition, and then make up a sentence of your own.

Check the Words You Know
__boycotts   __discrimination   __fast
__grueling   __predetermined   __strikes

1. cottsyob _boycotts_   4. kesirts _strikes_

2. satf _fast_   5. deterdenimepre _predetermined_

3. crimdisination _discrimination_   6. elurging _grueling_

7. refusals to buy or use a product or service _boycotts_

Your sentence: _Sentences will vary._

8. an act of showing an unfair difference in treatment _discrimination_

Your sentence: _____

9. to go without food _fast_

Your sentence: _____

10. very tiring _grueling_

Your sentence: _____

11. determined or decided beforehand _predetermined_

Your sentence: _____

Advanced Practice TE p. LR18

ELL

ELL Reader

ELL Poster 7

Teacher's Edition Notes

ELL notes throughout this lesson support instruction and reference additional resources at point of use.

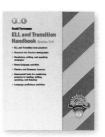

Teaching Guide pp. 43–49, 224–225
- Multilingual summaries of the main selection
- Comprehension lesson
- Vocabulary strategies and word cards
- ELL Reader 4.2.2 lesson

ELL and Transition Handbook

Ten Important Sentences
- Key ideas from every selection in the Student Edition
- Activities to build sentence power

More Reading

Readers' Theater Anthology
- Fluency practice
- Five scripts to build fluency
- Poetry for oral interpretation

Leveled Trade Books

Below-Level

On-Level

- Extended reading tied to the unit concept
- Lessons in the Trade Book Library Teaching Guide

School + Home

Homework
- Family Times Newsletter
- ELL Multilingual Selection Summaries

Take-Home Books
- Leveled Readers

Cross-Curricular Centers

 Reading/Library

Music

Listen to the Selections

MATERIALS `SINGLES`
CD player, headphones, AudioText CD, student book

LISTEN TO LITERATURE Listen to *Coyote School News* and "How to Start a School Newspaper" as you follow or read along in your book. Listen to draw conclusions about *Coyote School News*.

If there is anything you don't understand, you can listen again to any section.

Read It AGAIN!

MATERIALS `SINGLES` `PAIRS` `GROUPS`
Collection of books for self-selected reading, reading logs, student book, local newspapers

Select a book you have already read. Record the title of the book in your reading log. You may want to read with a partner.

Choose from the following:

- **Leveled Readers**
- **ELL Readers**
- **Books or Stories Written by Classmates**
- **Books from the Library**
- *Coyote School News*

TEN IMPORTANT SENTENCES Read the Ten Important Sentences for *Coyote School News*. Then locate the sentences in your student book.

BOOK CLUB Read parts of your local newspapers. Discuss with a group which parts you like and did not like. Give reasons for your opinions.

Write a Song

MATERIALS `SINGLES`
Writing materials, student book, audiotape recorder

Write a campfire song about an event from *Coyote School News*.

1. **Look back through the story to find details for your song.**
2. **Think about songs people sing while sitting around a campfire. Pick a melody you know and write at least one verse to go with that melody.**
3. **Include vivid details about the story's characters, setting, and plot in your song.**

EARLY FINISHERS Practice singing your song quietly. Record your song.

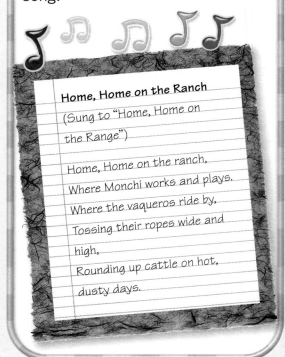

Home, Home on the Ranch
(Sung to "Home, Home on the Range")

Home, Home on the ranch,
Where Monchi works and plays.
Where the vaqueros ride by,
Tossing their ropes wide and high,
Rounding up cattle on hot, dusty days.

Scott Foresman Reading Street Centers Survival Kit

Use the *Coyote School News* materials from the Reading Street Centers Survival Kit to organize this week's centers.

Writing/Vocabulary

Write for a Newspaper

MATERIALS **SINGLES** **PAIRS**
Writing and art materials, student book

Write a newspaper article about your classroom or school.

1. Read one of the *Coyote News* issues in the student book on pp. 173, 178, or 181.
2. Think about an event that recently happened in your classroom or school or an upcoming event at your school such as a book fair.
3. Interview a classmate about the event. Ask what he or she thinks about the event.
4. Write a short newspaper article describing the event. Use the articles in the *Coyote News* issues as a model. Include quotations from your interview. Remember to give your article a title.

EARLY FINISHERS Draw a picture for your story.

New Classroom Pet

Mrs. Foster's 4th grade students are excited about a new addition to the classroom: a goldfish! "We all help take care of Bubbles," said Christie, a student in the class.

Social Studies

Compare Schools

MATERIALS **GROUPS**
Graphic Organizer 18, writing materials, student book

Create a Venn diagram showing how your school and Coyote School are alike and different.

1. Make a Venn diagram and label the left circle *My School* and label the right circle *Coyote School.*
2. In the right circle, list details about Coyote School. Use your book to find details. In the left circle list details about your school, such as number of students and location.
3. In the space where the two circles overlap, show how the schools are alike.

EARLY FINISHERS Create a list of awards you could have in your classroom. Use ideas from the story and your Venn diagram.

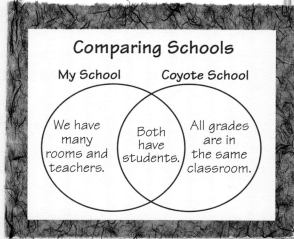

Comparing Schools

My School   Coyote School

We have many rooms and teachers. | Both have students. | All grades are in the same classroom.

Technology

Design a Masthead

MATERIALS **SINGLES**
Word processing program, printer, student book, newspapers

Design a masthead for your school newspaper.

1. Open the word processing program on the computer.
2. Look at the top of a *Coyote News* issue in the student book on pp. 173, 178 or 181, or a newspaper.
3. Think of a good name for your school newspaper. Type the name into your document. Use an interesting font type (the way the text looks) or font size (the size of the text).
4. Type the date, issue number, school name, and location below it. Use a smaller font size for this information.
5. Add art to the masthead or draw it by hand after you print.
6. Follow classroom rules about printing from a computer.

EARLY FINISHERS Draft story ideas for your newspaper.

Issue Number 3   October 10

Tompkins County Times

News, Sports, and Fun written by the Students in Tompkins County, New York.

ALL CENTERS

Concept Vocabulary

convince to make someone feel sure; to persuade by argument or proof

energetic full of energy; vigorous

offers holds out to be taken; is willing if another approves

Monitor Progress

Check Vocabulary

If...	then... review the
students are unable to place words on the web,	lesson concept. Place the words on the web and provide additional words for practice, such as *proud* and *contrib-uted.*

SUCCESS PREDICTOR

DAY 1 **Grouping Options**

Reading

Whole Group
Introduce and discuss the Question of the Week. Then use pp. 162l–164b.

Group Time
Differentiated Instruction
Read this week's Leveled Readers. See pp. 162f–162g for the small group lesson plan.

Whole Group
Use p. 187a.

Language Arts
Use pp. 187e–187k.

Build Concepts

FLUENCY

MODEL EMOTION As you read "A Big-City Dream," model reading expressively to convey Luz's emotions. Quicken your pace and raise your voice to show excitement and use lower tones and slower cadence to show discouragement.

LISTENING COMPREHENSION

After reading "A Big-City Dream," use the following questions to assess listening comprehension.

1. **At the beginning of the story, how does Luz feel about her plan for creating a garden?** (Possible response: She tries to be confident, but she is worried she won't get the clean-up done in time.) **Draw Conclusions**

2. **What kind of person is Luz? How do you know?** (Possible response: She is hard-working, enthusiastic, and persistent. Even though the work is very hard, she remains enthusiastic about the project and doesn't give up.) **Draw Conclusions**

BUILD CONCEPT VOCABULARY

Start a web to build concepts and vocabulary related to this week's lesson and the unit theme.

- Draw the Working Together Concept Web.
- Read the sentence with the word *offers* again. Ask students to pronounce *offers* and discuss its meaning.
- Place *offers* in an oval attached to *Gathering a team*. Discuss how *offers* is related to this concept. Read the sentences in which *convince* and *energetic* appear. Have students pronounce the words, place them on the Web, and provide reasons.
- Brainstorm additional words and categories for the Web. Keep the Web on display and add words throughout the week.

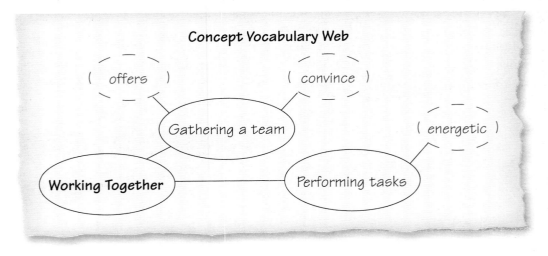

Concept Vocabulary Web

A Big-City Dream

by Ellen Schecter

Luz dreams of turning an empty lot in her neighborhood into a vegetable and flower garden.

After what feels like a million hours, I'm still picking up cans and bottles. Papi is still raking trash out of corners. And Ms. Kline and Mrs. Chapman are still shoveling junk into bags.

Lots of people walk past. Most of them don't even notice what we're doing. And nobody offers to help.

I count eighteen huge garbage bags piled up at the curb. I've got blisters on my hands, sunburn on my nose, and aches in strange muscles I never knew I had. But the lot still looks like a junk heap.

I've never been so tired in my whole life. But I'm afraid to say one word of complaint. Otherwise, Ms. Kline will think I can't do this. And I'm trying so hard to convince her!

Now I count twenty-eight bags stuffed with garbage. Most of the small junk is gone. Papi and Ms. Kline drag the bedsprings and other big stuff out to the curb where the garbage truck can pick it up Monday morning.

I look around the lot. You can actually see the ground! And there's the red tulip, standing straight up in the middle. No old newspapers hide it now. It waves in the wind like a brave red flag that says, "You can do it! You can!" But we still have a long way to go.

"Well, Luz, you certainly are energetic." Ms. Kline stretches her back. "But you've still got to get more people to help." She frowns at me.

I try to smile. "Don't worry, Ms. Kline, we'll do it. I'll get lots of people to help. You'll see."

I only hope I'm right.

That night I realize I only have six days to get the lot cleaned up and come up with the rest of the Dream Garden Group. Otherwise, Ms. Kline will take back the key and lock up the lot for good. I know I'll have to spend every spare minute either working on the garden or trying to convince other people to help me.

On Sunday, Mami forbids me to go anywhere near the garden. Instead, I have to get all dressed up and go to Mass.

On Monday, I rush home after school, change into my grungy clothes, grab my gloves and key, and go to work. Whenever somebody I know walks by, I invite them to come in, look around, maybe even give me a hand. But Mrs. Chapman and Papi are my only helpers. We fill two more bags with cans and bottles before it's supper and homework.

Luz eventually finishes the cleanup and with the help of others plants the most beautiful garden the neighborhood has seen. Now everyone believes in her Dream Garden.

SUCCESS PREDICTOR

SKILLS ⟷ STRATEGIES IN CONTEXT

Draw Conclusions
Prior Knowledge

OBJECTIVES

◎ Draw conclusions from facts and details.

◎ Use prior knowledge to draw conclusions.

Skills Trace

◎ Draw Conclusions	
Introduce/Teach	TE: 4.2 162–163, 188–189; 4.5 608–609
Practice	TE: 169, 179, 181, 195, 203, 205, 615, 619 PB: 63, 67, 68, 73, 77, 78, 243, 247, 248
Reteach/Review	TE: 4.2 153, 187b, 211b, DI·53, DI·54; 4.5 569, 591, 629b, DI·56 PB: 56, 226, 236
Test	Selection Test: 25–28, 29–32, 97–100; Benchmark Test: Units 2, 5

INTRODUCE

Present this scenario: *Suppose you go to the bus stop. Usually there are lots of kids there, but today you are the only one. You wait and wait for the school bus, but it doesn't come. Then one of your friends rides by on his bike.* Ask students what conclusion they can draw from these details. *(Possible responses: School is closed today. You missed the bus.)*

Have students read the information on p. 162. Explain the following:

- When you read, think about facts and details in the text to draw conclusions.

- Think about what the text reminds you of from your own life, the world, or another text. This prior knowledge also will help you draw conclusions.

Use Skill Transparency 7 to teach draw conclusions and prior knowledge.

Comprehension

Skill
Draw Conclusions

Strategy
Prior Knowledge

 Draw Conclusions

- Drawing a conclusion while you read or after you read is forming an opinion based on what you already know or on the facts and details in a text.

- Check an author's conclusions or your own conclusions by asking: Is this the only logical choice? Are the facts accurate?

Facts and Details
Facts and Details	→	Conclusion
Facts and Details

Strategy: Prior Knowledge

Active readers bring what they already know to a piece of text to help them understand new information. As you read, think about what you know from your own life, from the world around you, and from other things you've read. Use that knowledge to help you draw conclusions.

Write to Read

1. Make a graphic organizer like the one above to help you find facts and details in "Home, Home on the Range."

2. Would you like to live on a ranch? Use your graphic organizer to draw a conclusion. Write a paragraph with your reasons.

162

Strategic Intervention

◎ **Draw Conclusions** Have students share what they know about ranches and cattle. Have each group list facts from the text and their own experience to help them draw conclusions about why ranches need to be large and how cattle get food during the winter.

ELL

Access Content

Beginning/Intermediate For a Picture It! lesson on drawing conclusions, see the ELL Teaching Guide, pp. 43–44.

Advanced Before reading "Home, Home on the Range," ask students if they know the song of the same name.

HOME, HOME ON THE RANGE

A *ranch* is a particular kind of farm where cattle or sheep are raised. Most ranches in the United States are located in the West, in wide open country called the *range*, and most ranches are enormous, consisting of several thousand acres.

Cattle and sheep need a lot of room to roam and graze. In addition, they must be able to get to streams and ponds for fresh drinking water.

Ranchers today still use horses to get around as cowboys did in the days of the Old West. But they also use vehicles, such as trucks, jeeps, and even helicopters. This is especially important in the winter. When snow covers the ground, the livestock can't graze, so ranchers have to bring hay to them.

The children of ranchers have to get around too. Because ranches are so large and far apart, most ranch children have to ride a bus a long way to school.

Would you like to live on a ranch?

1 **Skill** Draw a conclusion as to why ranches have to be so large. Call on your prior knowledge about cattle and sheep.

2 **Strategy** Do you have prior knowledge of what the words *roam* and *graze* mean? If not, can you draw a conclusion about what they mean from the context?

3 **Skill** Think back to what you know about cattle and how they eat. Then draw a conclusion about how they get food in the winter.

4 **Strategy** Based on what you have seen, read, or experienced, what would this be like?

163

Available as **Skill Transparency** 7

TEACH

1 **SKILL** Model using prior knowledge to draw a conclusion.

Think Aloud **MODEL** I've read about cattle before, and I've seen sheep at a farm. I know these animals may spend an entire day eating grass in a field. I think ranches have to be large so that there is enough grass for the cattle and sheep to eat.

2 **STRATEGY** Model drawing conclusions about word meanings.

Think Aloud **MODEL** I learned from another story that *roam* means "to wander." I don't know what *graze* means. The article talks about cattle and sheep needing a lot of room to graze. I know that cattle and sheep need plenty of grass to eat. I think *graze* may mean "to feed on growing grass."

PRACTICE AND ASSESS

3 **SKILL** In the winter, cattle can't eat grass because land may be frozen or covered with snow. The ranchers must bring hay to the cattle on trucks or even by helicopter.

4 **STRATEGY** Responses will vary but should include student's prior knowledge of what a long bus ride is like.

WRITE Have students complete steps 1 and 2 of the Write to Read activity. You might consider using this as a whole-class activity.

Monitor Progress

🔾 Draw Conclusions

If... students are unable to complete **Write to Read** on p. 162,	**then...** use Practice Book p. 63 to provide additional practice.

Draw Conclusions

- **Drawing a conclusion** is forming an opinion based on what you already know or on the facts and details in a text.
- Check an author's conclusions or your own conclusions by asking: Is this the only logical choice? Are the facts accurate?

Directions Read the following passage. Then complete the diagram below by finding facts and details to support a conclusion.

A cowboy's job changed with the seasons. In the fall, the cowboys brought cattle roaming on the open land to the ranch. They branded the cattle, so they could keep track of them. Then during the winter months, the cowboys fed the cattle and raised them.

When spring arrived, the ranchers chose the cattle they wished to sell. Next, the cowboys would take the cattle on a long journey to a busy town so that others could buy the cattle. After the cowboys sold the cattle, they rested a little while before they started the process all over again.

Possible answers given.

Facts and Details		**Conclusion**
1. Fall: bring cattle to ranch and brand them	→	4. The cowboys' jobs changed with the seasons.
Facts and Details 2. Winter: take care of cattle	→	
Facts and Details 3. Spring: sell cattle	→	

5. How would you decide if the facts and details are accurate?
I could read a nonfiction book about the lives of cowboys.

School + Home **Home Activity** Your child read a short passage and drew a conclusion using facts or details. Tell your child about a job you once had. Have your child draw a conclusion about that job based on the facts and details you provide.

Tech Files ONLINE

Students can search the Internet to find out more about life on a ranch or Hispanic culture. Have them use a student-friendly search engine and keywords such as *ranches, cowboys,* and *Hispanic Americans.*

ELL

Build Background Use ELL Poster 7 to build background and vocabulary for the lesson concept of Hispanic American culture and history.

▲ **ELL Poster** 7

Build Background

ACTIVATE PRIOR KNOWLEDGE

MAKE A WEB about life on a ranch.

- Show a word web with the topic *Life on a Ranch* in a large center oval and the category *Work* in a medium-sized oval.

- Have students tell what they know about working on a ranch. Encourage them to think about any books, movies, or TV shows that have been set in the Southwest. Record their ideas in small ovals near *Work.*

- Have students suggest other categories that tell about life on a ranch. Record categories in medium-sized ovals, and have students provide details for each category.

- Tell students that, as they read, they should look for new information about life on a ranch to add to their webs.

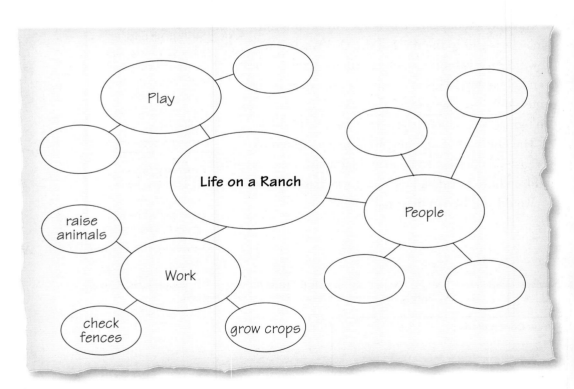

▲ **Graphic Organizer** 16

BACKGROUND BUILDING AUDIO This week's audio explores life on a cattle ranch. After students listen, discuss what students find most interesting about the job of a rancher.

Background Building Audio

Introduce Vocabulary

QUESTION AND ANSWER

Ask questions about lesson vocabulary words in the context of cattle ranching.

Display the lesson vocabulary words and discuss meanings. Ask questions like those below, and direct students to use lesson vocabulary words in their responses. **Activate Prior Knowledge**

- What do calves sound like when they are *bawling?*
- What do ranchers hear at night when a *coyote* is nearby?
- Why would a *dude* want to visit a ranch?
- What happens during a *roundup* on a ranch?
- To what does a cowhand attach a pair of *spurs?*

Explain that the word *coyote* comes from a Spanish word that is based on a Native American word for the animal. Tell students that as they read the story, they can look for other Spanish words that English speakers also use. **Word Origins**

At the end of the week have students use lesson vocabulary words to write their own questions and answers.

Use Multisyllabic Word Routine on p. DI·1 to help students read multisyllabic words.

Lesson Vocabulary

WORDS TO KNOW

T bawling crying out in a noisy way

T coyote a small, wolflike mammal living in many parts of North America

T dudes people raised in the city, especially easterners who vacation on a ranch

T roundup the act of driving or bringing cattle together from long distances

T spurs metal points or pointed wheels, worn on a rider's boot heels for urging a horse on

---

MORE WORDS TO KNOW

mesquite any of several trees or bushes common in southwestern United States and Mexico, which often grow in dense clumps or thickets

promoted raised in rank, condition, or importance

T = Tested Word

Vocabulary

Directions Choose the word from the box that best matches each definition. Write the word on the line.

dudes	**1.** people who were raised in the city but vacation on a ranch	**Check the Words You Know**
spurs	**2.** metal points worn on a horse rider's boot heel	
coyote	**3.** small, wolf-like animal	___bawling
		___coyote
roundup	**4.** the act of driving or bringing cattle together from long distances	___dudes
		___roundup
bawling	**5.** shouting or crying out in a noisy way	___spurs

Directions Choose the word from the box that best completes each sentence. Write the word on the line shown to the left.

bawling — **6.** Juan heard a calf ____ in the middle of the night.

spurs — **7.** He got dressed, put on his ____, and ran to his horse.

coyote — **8.** A hungry-looking ____ had frightened the herd.

roundup — **9.** Juan had to quickly do a ____ to get the cattle to safety.

dudes — **10.** There was so much noise, the ____ visiting the ranch came outside to see what was going on.

Write a Pep Talk

On a separate sheet of paper, write a pep talk a cowboy would give other cowboys before going on a long journey to do a cattle roundup. Use as many vocabulary words as you can.

Pep talks should include words from the vocabulary list and details about what to expect during a roundup.

School + Home Home Activity Your child identified and used vocabulary words from *Coyote School News*. With your child, create a word search using the words from this selection.

▲ **Practice Book** p. 64

Vocabulary Strategy

INTRODUCE

Discuss the strategy for using a dictionary or glossary by following the steps on p. 164.

TEACH

- Have students think about unfamiliar words as they read "At a Guest Ranch."
- Model looking up *bawling* in the glossary.

Think Aloud

MODEL I read that the "calves were *bawling*." The context doesn't help me, so I look for the base word *bawl* in the glossary. I start with the guide words at the top of the page and search alphabetically. I try out the pronunciation and read the definition. Now I know the calves were "crying out in a noisy way."

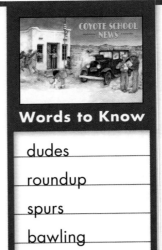

Words to Know

dudes
roundup
spurs
bawling
coyote

Vocabulary Strategy
for Unfamiliar Words

Dictionary/Glossary When you are reading, you may come across a word you don't know. If you can't use the context, or words and sentences around the word, to figure out the word's meaning, you can use a dictionary or glossary to help you.

1. Check the back of your book for a glossary. If there is no glossary, look up the word in a dictionary.

2. Find the entry for the word. The entries are in alphabetical order.

3. Read the pronunciation to yourself. Saying the word may help you recognize it.

4. Read all the meanings given for the word.

5. Choose the one that makes sense in the sentence.

As you read "At a Guest Ranch," use a dictionary or glossary to find the meanings of the vocabulary words. Which meaning makes sense?

164

DAY 2   Grouping Options

Reading
Whole Group Discuss the Question of the Day. Then use pp. 164–167.

Group Time Differentiated Instruction
Read *Coyote School News.* See pp. 162f–162g for the small group lesson plan.

Whole Group Use p. 187a.

Language Arts
Use pp.187e–187k.

Strategic Intervention

◉ **Dictionary/Glossary** Have students look up each lesson vocabulary word in the glossary and discuss definitions. Point out the two meanings for *dude.* Ask students which clues in the text on p. 165 help them decide which meaning of *dude* is correct for this context.

Access Content Use ELL Poster 7 to preteach vocabulary. Choose from the following to meet language proficiency levels.

Beginning Point out the context clues that give the meaning of the word *dude* (p. 165, paragraph 1).

Intermediate Have students create word cards and include picture clues.

Advanced Teach the lesson on pp. 164–165. Use the vocabulary words to create a story, with each student contributing a sentence.

Resources for home-language words may include parents, bilingual staff members, bilingual dictionaries, or online translation sources.

AT A GUEST RANCH

Howdy, pardner! That may sound corny, but it's appropriate because my family and I are at a ranch that lets people pay to stay there. This gives them a chance to see what ranch life is like. Guests are called dudes. That's what the cowhands called people from back East. Some dude ranches are just for entertaining visitors, excuse me, dudes. Some are real cattle or sheep ranches that take in a few dudes on the side.

Our ranch, the Double K near Bozeman, Montana, is a working cattle ranch. We went with the cowhands on a roundup. It was exciting to watch. With just a touch of his spurs, a cowhand moves his horse into the herd

and cuts out one cow. It was hot, dusty, and noisy too. The cattle were mooing, and the calves were bawling.

We also rode out on a trail and camped out under the stars. Dinner from a chuckwagon, a bedroll by the campfire, and a coyote howling in the distance— I felt as if I were in a Western movie!

Words to Write

Imagine that you have gone to stay at a dude ranch. Write a journal entry describing a day at the ranch. Use words from the Words to Know list.

165

PRACTICE AND ASSESS

- Have students determine the meanings of the remaining words and explain how they used a dictionary or glossary to find the meanings.
- Ask students to match the symbols in the two pronunciations for *coyote* to the key in the glossary. Have them pronounce *coyote* both ways.
- If you introduced the question-and-answer activity (p. 164b), have students use the vocabulary words to write their own questions and answers.
- Have students complete Practice Book p. 65.

WRITE Writing should include several vocabulary words as well as words about ranch animals and jobs.

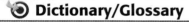

Monitor Progress

🎯 Dictionary/Glossary

If... students need more practice with the lesson vocabulary,	**then**... use Tested Vocabulary Cards.

Vocabulary • Dictionary/Glossary

- **Dictionaries** and **glossaries** provide alphabetical lists of words and their meanings.
- Sometimes looking at the words around an unfamiliar word can't help you figure out the word's meaning. If this happens, use a dictionary or glossary to find the meaning.

Directions Read the following passage. Then answer the questions below.

At the crack of dawn, my uncle went around to the tents to wake up the dudes at the ranch. Today they were going on a roundup and needed to get everything ready before they left. The dudes sat down for breakfast and then got dressed for the trip. Some of them had never ridden a horse before, so putting on their chaps and spurs took a lot of time. They heard some cattle bawling far in the distance. Before long, the group headed out into the open plains.

Possible answers given.
1. How would you define *dudes* by looking at the words that are near it?

   <u>**Dudes** are people at a ranch.</u>

2. Look up *dudes* in a glossary or dictionary. How is the meaning that you looked up different from the meaning you thought it had by looking at the words near it?

   <u>**From the glossary, I learned that** *dudes* **are people from the city**</u>
   <u>**who take a vacation at a ranch.**</u>

3. How would you define *bawling* by looking at the words that are near it?

   <u>**Bawling** is making a noise that can be heard from far away.</u>

4. Look up *bawling* in a glossary or dictionary. How is the meaning that you looked up different from the meaning you thought it had by looking at the words near it?

   <u>**From the dictionary, I learned that** *bawling* **is loud crying.**</u>

5. Look up *roundup* in a glossary or dictionary. What part of speech is it?

   <u>**Roundup** is a noun.</u>

 Home Activity Your child read a short passage and used a dictionary or glossary to understand unfamiliar words. Have a conversation about your day with your child. When your child hears an unfamiliar word, help your child to find the word's meaning in a dictionary.

▲ **Practice Book** p. 65

Prereading Strategies

GENRE STUDY

Historical Fiction

Coyote School News is historical fiction. It combines imagination and facts to tell a fictional story with characters placed in a factually historical setting.

PREVIEW AND PREDICT

Have students preview the title and illustrations and discuss when and where they think the story takes place and what the story will be about. Encourage students to use lesson vocabulary words as they talk about what they expect to read.

Activate Prior Knowledge Have students write what they know about cowboys, ranching, the Southwest, and the 1930s in their strategy response logs. Students will revise or add ideas in the Strategy Response Log activity on p. 175.

Genre **Historical fiction** is a story that is made up around real events in history. Decide what those real events might have been as you read about children in a southern Arizona country school in 1938–1939.

166

ELL

Access Content The question on p. 167 contains the journalism jargon "make the news." Restate as "What stories deserve to be printed in the Coyote School newspaper?"

Consider having students read the selection summary in English or in students' home languages. See the Multilingual Summaries in the ELL Teaching Guide, pp. 47–49.

COYOTE SCHOOL NEWS

by Joan Sandin

SCHOOL BUS

ARIZONA 38
R4234
PIMA

What stories make the news at Coyote School?

167

SET PURPOSE

Discuss the illustrations on pp. 166–167, and have students talk about where the characters are and what they are doing. Have them discuss what they will find out as they read the story.

Remind students to use what they already know and details from the story to help them draw conclusions as they read.

STRATEGY RECALL

Students have now used these before-reading strategies:

- preview the selection to be aware of its genre, features, and possible content;
- activate prior knowledge about that content and what to expect of that genre;
- make predictions;
- set a purpose for reading.

Remind students that, as they read, they should monitor their own comprehension. If they realize something does not make sense, they can regain their comprehension by using fix-up strategies they have learned, such as:

- use phonics and word structure to decode new words;
- use context clues or a dictionary to figure out meanings of new words;
- adjust their reading rate—slow down for difficult text, speed up for easy or familiar text, or skim and scan just for specific information;
- reread parts of the text;
- read on (continue to read for clarification);
- use text features such as headings, subheadings, charts, illustrations, and so on as visual aids to comprehension;
- make a graphic organizer or a semantic organizer to aid comprehension;
- use reference sources, such as an encyclopedia, dictionary, thesaurus, or synonym finder;
- use another person, such as a teacher, a peer, a librarian, or an outside expert, as a resource.

After reading, students will use these strategies:

- summarize or retell the text;
- answer questions they or others pose;
- reflect to make new information become part of their prior knowledge.

Audio CD AudioText

Guiding Comprehension

1 **Point of View • Inferential**

Who is the narrator in *Coyote School News*?

Ramón Ernesto Ramírez, or Monchi

2 ◉ **Draw Conclusions • Inferential**

What language or languages does Monchi speak? How do you know?

Spanish and English; Possible response: He uses English in the story and also uses Spanish words like *americano*. The ranch where he lives used to be part of Mexico, where people speak Spanish.

Monitor Progress

◉ Draw Conclusions

If... students are unable to determine the languages Monchi speaks,	**then...** use the skill and strategy instruction on p. 169.

---

3 **Simile • Inferential**

Reread p. 169, paragraph 5. What does the phrase *squeezed together like sardines in a can* tell you about the bus ride to Coyote School?

Possible response: The children are sitting very close together on the bus.

Rancho San Isidro

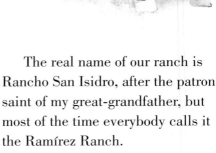

1 **M**y name is Ramón Ernesto Ramírez, but everybody calls me Monchi. I live on a ranch that my great-grandfather built a long time ago when this land was part of Mexico. That was before the United States bought it and moved the line in 1854. My father has a joke about that. He says my great-grandfather **2** was an *americano,* not because he crossed the line, but because the line crossed him.

In my family we are six kids: me, my big brother Junior, my big sister Natalia, my little tattletale brother Victor, my little sister Loli, and the baby Pili. My *tío* Chaco lives with us too. He is the youngest brother of my father.

The real name of our ranch is Rancho San Isidro, after the patron saint of my great-grandfather, but most of the time everybody calls it the Ramírez Ranch.

On our ranch we have chickens and pigs and cattle and horses. The boys in the Ramírez family know

168

Fluency Spanish-speaking students can demonstrate their fluency by reading the Spanish vocabulary. Point out the italicized Spanish words in the story and model how to use the pronunciation guides in the footnotes found on p. 169.

how to ride and rope. We are a family of *vaqueros*. In the fall and spring we have roundup on our ranch. Many people come to help with the cattle and the horses. Those are the most exciting days of the year, even more exciting than Christmas.

The things I don't like about our ranch are always having to get the wood for the fire, and the long and bumpy ride to school.

My tío Chaco drives the school bus.

"It's not fair," I tell him. "We have to get up earlier than all the other kids at Coyote School, and we get home the latest too."

"Don't forget," says my tío, "you get first choice of seats."

Ha, ha. By the time the last kid gets in we are all squeezed together like sardines in a can. And the bus is shaking and bumping like it has a flat tire.

"I wish President Roosevelt would do something about these roads," I tell my tío.

"Hey, you know how to write English," he says. "Write him a letter."

"Maybe I will," I say.

americano (*AH-mair-ee-CAHN*-oh)— American
tío (TEE-oh)—uncle
rancho (RAHN-choe)—ranch
san (sahn)—saint
vaqueros (bah-CARE-rose)—cowboys

169

SKILLS ↔ STRATEGIES IN CONTEXT

Draw Conclusions

TEACH

- Remind students that a conclusion is a decision they reach or an opinion they have about what they have read.
- Students should use facts and details from the story and what they already know to help them draw logical conclusions.
- Model how to draw a conclusion about which languages Monchi speaks.

Think Aloud **MODEL** First, I'll think about the facts that are given. Monchi tells the story in English and speaks English to others. Monchi mentions that Rancho San Isidro used to be part of Mexico. I know that people speak Spanish in Mexico. He also uses Spanish words, such as *americano,* in the story. I put all of this together to draw the conclusion that Monchi speaks English and Spanish. This makes sense based on the facts and details in the story.

PRACTICE AND ASSESS

Ask students to reread p. 169 and tell what they think the roads are like near the Coyote School. *(The roads are rough and bumpy.)* Have them point out story details they used to draw their conclusions. *(Monchi doesn't like the long, bumpy ride to school. The bus shakes and bumps like it has a flat tire.)*

U.S. Expansion

Time for SOCIAL STUDIES

Monchi's great-grandfather became an *americano* when Rancho San Isidro became a part of the United States through the Gadsden Purchase of 1854. In this agreement, the United States bought close to 30,000 square miles of land from Mexico for $10,000,000. This land is now part of southern Arizona and New Mexico. The purchase was prompted in part by supporters of a southern cross-country railroad that would pass through the land. The Mexican heritage of this region still influences the culture today.

Guiding Comprehension

④ Setting • Inferential

What is the setting of *Coyote School News*? Tell how you know.

Possible responses: It is set in the past in the southwestern United States near Mexico. The pictures show an old-fashioned car and a one-room schoolhouse. The map shows where Monchi's ranch is, and he mentions that Rosie and Miss Byers live on ranches.

Monitor Progress	
REVIEW Setting	
If... students have difficulty identifying the setting,	**then...** use the skill and strategy instruction on p. 171.

⑤ Cause and Effect • Literal

Why do the students like Miss Byers?

Possible response: They like her because she is young, nice, and fair. She lives on a ranch and has fun ideas for school.

Coyote School

"*Mira, mira,* Monchi," Natalia says, pinching my cheek. "There's your little *novia.*"

She means Rosie. I like Rosie, but I hate it when Natalia teases me. Rosie lives at Coyote Ranch, close enough to school that she can walk. Always she waits by the road so she can race the bus.

"*¡Ándale! ¡Ándale!* Hurry up!" we yell at my tío Chaco, but every time he lets her win.

Rosie wasn't first today anyway. Lalo and Frankie were. Their horses are standing in the shade of the big mesquite tree.

Yap! Yap! Yap! Always Chipito barks when he sees us, and Miss Byers says, "Hush, Chipito!" Then she smiles and waves at us.

Miss Byers is new this year. Her ranch is a hundred miles from here, in Rattlesnake Canyon, so five days of the week she and Chipito live in the little room behind the school. All of us like Miss Byers, even the big kids, because she is young and nice and fair. We like that she lives on a ranch, and we like her swell ideas: **⑤**

1. Baseball at recess,
2. The Perfect Attendance Award,
3. *Coyote News.*

—————✧—————

mira (MEER-ah)—look
novia (NOVE-ee-ah)—girlfriend
ándale (AHN-dah-lay)—come on; hurry up

Access Content Point out the newspaper titles on p. 171. Discuss what they show about the newspapers' content. Have students make a list of possible names for a newspaper at their school. Encourage them to think about their school setting when coming up with names.

Coyote News

All week we have been working on our first *Coyote News*. Natalia made up the name, and Joey drew the coyote. First we looked at some other newspapers: the *Arizona Daily Star*, *Western Livestock Journal,* and *Little Cowpuncher*. That one we liked best because all the stories and pictures were done by kids.

"Monchi," said Loli, "put me cute."

"What?" I said. Sometimes it's not easy to understand my little sister's English.

"Miss Byers says you have to help me put words to my story," she said.

"Okay," I told her. "But I have my own story to do, so hurry up and learn to write."

171

SKILLS ◆▶ STRATEGIES IN CONTEXT

Setting REVIEW

TEACH

- Remind students the setting of a story is the time and place in which the story occurs.
- Text and illustrations will provide clues to the setting of a story.
- Model how to identify the story's setting.

Think Aloud **MODEL** The illustrations show an old-fashioned car and a one-room school-house. Monchi talks about President Roosevelt who was president in the 1930s and 1940s. These are clues that the story takes place in the past. The map on p. 168 shows Monchi's ranch is in the Southwest in what looks like Arizona. So the setting is long ago near some ranches in Arizona.

PRACTICE AND ASSESS

- Have students describe other picture details that provide clues about the setting. *(Possible responses: The American flag shows the story is set in United States. There are mountains in the background.)*
- To assess, use Practice Book p. 66.

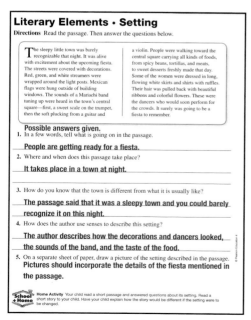

▲ **Practice Book** p. 66

Guiding Comprehension

6  **Vocabulary • Dictionary/Glossary**

Use a dictionary to find the meaning of *mimeograph* on p. 172, paragraph 4.

A machine for making copies of written or typewritten materials by means of stencils.

Monitor Progress	
 **Dictionary/Glossary**	
If... students have difficulty using a dictionary to determine the meaning of *mimeograph*,	**then...** use the vocabulary strategy instruction on p. 173.

7 **Compare and Contrast • Critical**

Text To Text **How is the *Coyote News* like your school newspaper or another newspaper you have read? How is it different?**

Responses will vary, but students should be able to cite features of each that show they can compare and contrast.

Tech Files
ONLINE

Many word processing programs include reference tools, such as dictionaries, thesauruses, and spelling or grammar checkers. Students can use these features when they write to make sure they are using words properly.

Loli's story was *muy tonta*, but one thing was good. She remembered how to write all the words I spelled for her.

Even if Victor is my brother I have to say he is a big tattletale—*chismoso*. When Gilbert was writing his story for *Coyote News*, Victor told on him for writing in Spanish. But Miss Byers did not get mad at Gilbert. She smiled at him! And then she said Spanish is a beautiful language that people around here have been speaking for hundreds of years, and that we should be proud we can speak it too!

Ha ha, Victor, you big chismoso!

When we finished our stories and pictures, Miss Byers cut a stencil for the mimeograph. Then **6** she printed copies of *Coyote News* for us to take home, and we hung them up on the ceiling to dry the ink. My tío Chaco said it looked like laundry day at Coyote School.

muy (MOO-ee)—very
tonta (TONE-tah)—silly
chismoso (cheese-MOE-soe)—tattletale
señor (sin-YORE)—Mr.
grandote (grahn-DOE-tay)—great big, huge

ELL

Extend Language Point out phrases constructed with Spanish syntax, such as "the bus of Mr. Ramírez" and "the dog of the teacher" (p. 173, third and fifth news stories). Encourage students to restate these phrases using singular possessives. *(Mr. Ramírez's bus; the teacher's dog)*

Issue Number One

September 15, 1938

7

COYOTE NEWS

I am new!

Stories and Pictures by the Students of Coyote School, Pima County, Arizona

Something New at Coyote School
Coyote News was the idea of our teacher, but we write the stories and draw the pictures. The big kids help the little kids...Rosie Garcia, Grade 3

About Coyote School
This year we have 12 kids and all the grades except Grade 5...Billy Mills, Grade 3

We Ride Our Horses to School
The road to Rancho del Cerro is a very big problem for the bus of Mr. Ramirez. For that reason Lalo and I ride our horses to school--16 miles all the days. The year past it was 2,352 miles. We had to put new shoes on the horses 5 times...Frankie Lopez, Grade 6

Andale Andale We want to go home

by Lalo Lopez

The Perfect Attendance
Miss Byers will give a prize to anybody who comes to school all the days, no matter what. The prize is called The Perfect Attendance Award and it is a silver dollar! For me perfect attendance is not easy, but oh boy, I would like to win that silver dollar............Monchi Ramirez, Grade 4

Yap! Yap!

by Cynthia

Chipito
The dog of the teacher is called Chipito. He is very cute. He likes Loli best.....story by Loli Ramirez, Grade 1 with help by Monchi Ramirez, Grade 4

Señor Grandote
Our bus driver ran over a big rattlesnake. We took the skin and gave it to our teacher. She measured him with the yardstick. He was 5 feet and 7 inches! She hung him on the wall next to President Roosevelt. We kids call him Señor Grandote because in Spanish it means Mr. Huge.................Gilbert Perez, Grade 6

Señor Grandote
by Joey Brown

173

Spanish Explorers

Time for **SOCIAL STUDIES**

Monchi and the other students at Coyote School speak and write Spanish because their ancestors settled the land after Spanish explorers searched the American Southwest for legendary cities of gold in the sixteenth century. Though the explorers did not find riches, they eventually settled and claimed the land for Spain. Juan de Oñate was a Spanish explorer who settled New Mexico. He explored much of the American Southwest in a futile search for the legendary gold. The colonization of this region by Spain still affects the culture of the American Southwest.

VOCABULARY STRATEGY

Dictionary/ Glossary

TEACH

- Discuss the purpose and organization of a dictionary.
- If a word has more than one meaning, students should try each meaning in context to find the one that makes sense.
- Read p. 172, paragraph 4. Model using a dictionary to find the meaning of *mimeograph*.

Think Aloud **MODEL** First, I look at the guide words at the top of the dictionary pages to help me find the page that has *mimeograph* on it. Then, I use alphabetical order and look through the words on that page until I find *mimeograph*. The dictionary gives two meanings. The first meaning says it is a machine for making copies of written or typewritten materials by means of stencils. That makes sense for this sentence.

PRACTICE AND ASSESS

Have students use a dictionary to determine the meaning of *stencil* on p. 172, paragraph 4. To choose the correct meaning, have them first decide if the word is used as a noun or a verb. *(Noun; a thin sheet of metal, paper, or cardboard with letters or designs cut through it.)*

Guiding Comprehension

8 Cause and Effect • Inferential

Why does Monchi go to Tucson?

He hurts his wrist and needs a doctor to examine it.

9  Draw Conclusions • Critical

How do Monchi's feelings about his trip to Tucson change over the course of this story?

Possible response: At first, he doesn't want to go to Tucson. Then, he's happy to stay because his aunt cooks his favorite foods, takes him to a movie, buys him ice cream, and shows him shops with interesting things.

Tech Files
ONLINE

Students can find out more about chile peppers and silver jewelry by using a student-friendly search engine. Be sure to follow classroom rules for Internet use.

Chiles

Every day I am asking my father when we will have roundup. He says I am making him *loco* with my nagging and that first we have to pick *todos los chiles*.

All of us kids are tired of picking the chiles. It doesn't matter that we get home late from school, we still have to do it. And then, before the chiles dry out, we have to string them to make the *sartas*.

Last night we were taking about 600 pounds of the chiles to my tío Enrique's ranch. I was in the back of the truck when it hit a big rock. All the heavy sacks fell on me. Oh boy, it hurt so much! But I did not tell my father. He had told me not to ride in the back of the truck, and I was afraid he would be mad.

My hand was still hurting this morning when Miss Byers did Fingernail Inspection.

"Monchi," she said, "what happened to your wrist? It's all black-and-blue and swollen."

"The chiles fell on him," Victor told her. "My father told him not to ride in the back."

"¡Chismoso!" I hissed at him.

Miss Byers called my tío Chaco over, and they had a long talk.

"Back in the bus, *mi'jo*," my tío said. "I have to take you to Tucson."

174

ELL

Access Content If students are unfamiliar with the word *buckle* (p. 175, last paragraph), direct them to an any belt buckles worn by students or to p. 183 where a belt buckle is illustrated.

"Tucson!" I said. "Why?"

8 "You got to see the doctor," he said. So we drove all the way to Tucson to my *tía* Lena's house. At first my aunt was surprised and happy to see us, but then my *tío* told her why we were there.

"Monchi!" my *tía* said. "*¡Pobrecito!*" Then she told my *tío* Chaco to go back with the bus and she would take care of me.

My *tía* took me to a doctor. He moved my hand around. It hurt when he did that.

"I'm afraid the wrist is broken," he told my *tía*. "I need to set it and put it in a cast."

So I got a cast of plaster on my arm, and I had to stay in Tucson. But for me that was no problem! My *tía* felt very sorry for me. She cooked

my favorite foods, and I got to pick the stations on her radio. That night Miss Byers called on the telephone to ask about me. She said she would come early Monday morning to drive me to school.

On Sunday my *tía* took me to the Tarzan picture show at the Fox Theater. It was swell! After the show we got ice cream and walked around downtown to look in the windows of the stores. I saw many things I **9** liked. The best was a silver buckle with a hole to put a silver dollar. *¡Ay caramba!* I wish I had a buckle like that.

loco (LOW-coe)—crazy
todos (TOE-dose)—all
los (lohs)—the
chiles (CHEE-less)—chile peppers
sartas (SAR-tahs)—strings of chile peppers
mi'jo (MEE-hoe)—my son, sonny
tía (TEE-ah)—aunt
pobrecito (pobe-ray-SEE-toe)—
    poor little thing
¡ay caramba! (EYE car-RAHM-bah)—
    oh boy!

175

Develop Vocabulary

PRACTICE LESSON VOCABULARY

Students orally respond *yes* or *no* to each question and provide a reason for each answer. Possible reasons are given.

1. At *roundup*, do the vaqueros drive the cattle apart? *(No; vaqueros bring the cattle together at roundup.)*

2. Do you think a *coyote* howls? *(Yes; because a coyote is like a wolf and wolves howl.)*

BUILD CONCEPT VOCABULARY

Review previous concept words with students. Ask if students have come across any words today in their reading or elsewhere that they would like to add to the Working Together Concept Web, such as *help* or *energetic*.

↩ **STRATEGY SELF-CHECK**

Prior Knowledge

Explain to students they can use prior knowledge—what they know from their own experiences, books, movies, or TV shows—to help them draw conclusions.

Read the first sentence on p. 174, and ask students to tell how Monchi feels about round-up and why. Remind students to review what they've read and to think about special events they enjoy. *(Possible responses: Monchi looks forward to roundup. It's a big celebration and many people visit. He says it is more exciting than Christmas.)*

SELF-CHECK

Students can ask themselves these questions to assess their ability to use the skill and strategy.

• Was I able to draw logical conclusions about Monchi's feelings?

• How did my prior knowledge help me draw conclusions?

Monitor Progress	
↩ **Draw Conclusions**	
If... students have difficulty using prior knowledge to draw conclusions,	**then**... revisit the skill lesson on pp. 162–163. Reteach as necessary.

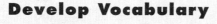

Strategy Response Log

Monitor Comprehension Have students review what they previously wrote about cowboys, ranching, the Southwest, and the 1930s. (See p. 166.) Have them revise or add ideas based on what they have read.

If you want to teach this story in two sessions, stop here.

Guiding Comprehension

If you are teaching the story in two days, discuss conclusions drawn so far and review the vocabulary.

10 **Onomatopoeia • Inferential**
What word describes the sound of the stick hitting the piñata?
BAM

11 🔊 **Vocabulary • Dictionary/Glossary**
Use your book's glossary to determine the meaning of *spurs* on p. 177, paragraph 4.
Spurs are metal points or pointed wheels worn on a rider's boot heels for urging a horse on.

Monitor Progress

🔊 Dictionary/Glossary

If... students have difficulty using the glossary to determine the meaning of *spurs*,	then... use the vocabulary strategy instruction on p. 177.

DAY 3 **Grouping Options**

Reading
Whole Group Discuss the Question of the Day.

Group Time **Differentiated Instruction**
Read *Coyote School News.* See pp. 162f–162g for the small group lesson plan.

Whole Group Discuss the Reader Response questions on page 184. Then use p. 187a.

Language Arts
Use pp. 187e–187k.

Nochebuena

For *Nochebuena* we are many people. Some are family I see only at Christmas and roundup and weddings and funerals. The day before Nochebuena my cousins from Sonora arrived. Now we could make the *piñata!*

First we cut the strips of red, white, and green paper. Then we paste them on a big *olla.* When the piñata is ready, we give it to my mother to fill with the *dulces* she hides in her secret places.

On Nochebuena, Junior and my tío Chaco hung the piñata between two big mesquite trees and we kids lined up to hit it, the littlest ones first. My mother tied a *mascada* over my little brother Pili's eyes and my tía Lena turned him around and around. She gave him the stick and pointed him toward the piñata. My tío Chaco and Junior made it easy for him. They did not jerk on the rope when he swung.

"*¡Dale! ¡Dale!*" we were yelling, but Pili never came close. None of the little kids could hit it. Then it was Loli's turn.

BAM. **10**

176

Access Content Explain that *go to the Mass at Amado* (p. 177, paragraph 3) means the family is going to a church. On Christmas Eve, many Catholics and other Christians attend late-night church services.

Some peanuts fell out. Gilbert and I dived to get them. One by one, the other kids tried and missed. Then it was Natalia's turn. She took a good swing and—*BAM*.

The piñata broke open, and all the kids were in the dirt, screaming and laughing and picking up gum and nuts and oranges and candies.

Just before midnight we got into my tío Chaco's bus and my father's pickup to go to the Mass at Amado. When we got home my mother and my tías put out *tamales* and *menudo* and *tortillas* and cakes and coffee and other drinks. We had music and

dancing. Nobody told us we had to go to bed.

Sometime in the night Santa Claus came and gave us our presents. Junior got a pair of spurs, Victor got a big red top, and Loli got a little toy dog that looks like Chipito. But I got the best present. It was a silver-dollar buckle, the one I had seen with my tía Lena in Tucson. It doesn't have a dollar yet, only a hole, but when I win the Perfect Attendance I will put my silver dollar in that hole.

Nochebuena (NO-chay-BUAY-nah)—
    Christmas Eve
piñata (peen-YAH-tah)—clay pot *(olla)*
    filled with treats
olla (OY-yah)—clay pot
dulces (DOOL-sehss)—sweets, candy
mascada (mas-KAH-dah)—scarf
¡dale! (DAH-lay)—hit it!
tamales (tah-MAH-less)—steamed
    filled dough
menudo (men-OO-doe)—tripe soup
tortillas (tor-TEE-yahs)—flat Mexican bread

177

VOCABULARY STRATEGY

Dictionary/ Glossary

TEACH

- Remind students that a glossary is a short dictionary found at the back of some books. Like a dictionary, it includes guide words, entry words, and definitions.

- Read p. 177, paragraph 4. Model how to use the student book's glossary to find the meaning of *spurs*.

Think Aloud | **MODEL** First, I will look at the guide words at the top of the pages to help me find the page containing *spurs*. The entry words are in dark type and alphabetical order. I scan them quickly to find *spurs*. The glossary shows the singular form of *spur* and says it is "a metal point or pointed wheel worn on a rider's boot heel for urging a horse on."

PRACTICE AND ASSESS

Have students use the glossary to find the meaning of Words to Know or More Words to Know from this story or other selections.

EXTEND SKILLS

Onomatopoeia

Tell students that onomatopoeia is when a word sounds like its meaning. An onomatopoeia helps reinforce meaning, dramatize events, and add liveliness to text. Have students find examples of onomatopoeia on these pages and p. 170. *(BAM, Yap!)* Challenge them to think of additional examples.

Guiding Comprehension

12 **Dialect • Critical**

Why do you think President Roosevelt pronounces "war" differently from the students at Coyote School?

Possible response: He is from a different part of the country.

13 🔵 **Draw Conclusions • Inferential**

Why does Junior think roundup is more important than Perfect Attendance?

Possible response: It is a part of the family's tradition. They are a family of cowboys, and roundup is more important to cowboys than Perfect Attendance.

Monitor Progress

🔵 Draw Conclusions

If... students are unable to determine why Junior thinks roundup is more important,	**then...** use the skill and strategy instruction on p. 179.

Issue Number Five   January 12, 1939

COYOTE 🦊 NEWS
Happy New Year!

Stories and Pictures by the Students of Coyote School, Pima County, Arizona

Miss Byers' Radio
Miss Byers brought her new radio to school. It has a big battery, so it doesn't matter that Coyote School has no electricity. We got to hear President Roosevelt's speech to the Congress. He told them to be prepared for war. Then he said, "Happy New Year."........Monchi Ramirez, Grade 4

Our President

Our President's Voice
12 None of us kids had heard the President's voice before. When he said "war" it sounded like "waw." We were all laughing because we never heard anybody who talked like that, but Billy said some of the dudes do............Rosie Garcia, Grade 3

waw

by Joey Brown

Some Noisy Children
When the President was talking, Loli was noisy. Miss Byers gave her peanuts to make her quiet. I was quiet without the peanuts...Victor, Grade 2

Yap!
By Frankie López

Music on the Radio
We got to listen to the music on Miss Byers' radio. She has many stations, but I liked best to hear the one with the rancheras..........Gilbert Perez, Grade 6

No Earrings for Christmas
Santa Claus didn't bring me any earrings. Loli says it's because he knows that I don't have any holes in my ears like she does......Cynthia Brown, Grade 2

The Perfect Attendance Report
Miss Byers says Santa Claus must have given some of our kids the flu and chicken pox for Christmas. The only kids who still have perfect attendance are Natalia, Monchi, Victor, and me.........Billy Mills, Grade 3

La Fiesta de los Vaqueros Rodeo Parade
We are so excited because Miss Byers just told us something wonderful. Our school gets to be in the Tucson Rodeo Parade!...Natalia Ramirez, Grade 8

178

Build Background Identify the war mentioned on p. 178 as World War II, which was fought in Europe, Africa, and Asia from 1939 to 1945.

Roundup!

The vaqueros were hollering, "¡Ándale! ¡Ándale!" They were cutting through the cattle on their horses, swinging their lassoes in the air to rope out the steers. My tío Chaco threw his saddle up on his horse, Canelo, and joined them. We kids clapped and whistled. Sometimes we helped my father or my tíos. We brought them rope or a fresh horse or something to drink.

That night we boys got to eat with the vaqueros and sit by the fire and listen to them play their guitars and sing their *rancheras*. We got to hear their exciting stories and their bragging and their bad words. When my father came over to Junior and me I thought he was going to tell us to go in to bed, but instead he said, "Tomorrow I want you boys to help with the branding." Junior had helped since he was eleven, but it was the first time my father had ever asked me.

"Tomorrow I have school," I said.

"School!" said Junior. "Monchi, don't you understand? You get to help with the branding!"

"He doesn't want to lose the Perfect Attendance," said Victor.

"The Perfect Attendance!" said Junior. "Monchi, you are crazier than a goat. You are a Ramírez. We are a family of vaqueros. Roundup is more important than the Perfect Attendance."

I knew Junior was right, but I touched the empty hole of my silver-dollar buckle and I sighed. *Adiós,* Perfect Attendance.

rancheras (rahn-CHAIR-ahs)—Mexican folk songs
fiesta (fee-ESS-tah)—party, celebration
de (day)—of
adiós (ah-DYOHSS)—good-bye

Time for SOCIAL STUDIES

Hispanic Cowboys

Hispanic cowboys, known as *vaqueros,* have a long history as expert cattlemen. They began the open-range system of raising cattle in the Southwest long before the first American pioneers arrived around 1820. Vaqueros had a great influence on the cattle industry in the United States. American pioneers adapted the vaqueros' herding techniques and their tools, such as saddles, spurs, lariats (ropes), and branding irons.

◉ SKILLS ◆▶ STRATEGIES IN CONTEXT

Draw Conclusions

TEACH

Model for students how to draw a conclusion about why Junior thinks that roundup is more important than Perfect Attendance.

Think Aloud **MODEL** I'll use story details to help me draw conclusions. Junior says Ramírez is a family of *vaqueros.* We know vaqueros take part in roundup, and it is an important event at the ranch. Junior's words also tell me that he thinks it's a big deal that Monchi will be allowed to help with the branding. I can conclude that Junior believes family tradition is more important than a school award.

PRACTICE AND ASSESS

Ask students how Monchi feels about missing school for roundup. *(He is disappointed to miss school, but also excited about roundup.)*

EXTEND SKILLS

Dialect

Explain that dialect is a form of speech that is typical of a particular class or region. Words from a certain dialect may be pronounced differently than standard language. Point out that President Roosevelt was from New York, and some people from that region pronounce *war* like "waw." Have students identify examples of dialect from their region.

Guiding Comprehension

14 **Simile • Inferential**

Reread p. 180, paragraph 2. Monchi compares the calves to what? In what way are they alike?

He compares them to giant babies. They are alike because both the calves and babies cry.

15 **Draw Conclusions • Critical**

If Monchi had to make the choice between the Perfect Attendance Award or roundup again, which would he choose? Why?

Possible response: Roundup. Monchi is sad he won't win Perfect Attendance and the silver dollar for his belt buckle, but he's glad he went to roundup. It was exciting, and he got to do new things, such as helping to brand the cattle.

Monitor Progress

Draw Conclusions

If... students are unable to state or report their conclusion about Monchi,	then... use the skill and strategy instruction on p. 181.

---

16 **Personification • Inferential**

Look at the drawing of the calf on p. 181. What is one way this art makes the calf seem like a human?

Possible responses: The calf is talking, and calves can't talk. The face on the calf looks sad; it makes it seem like he feels sorry for stepping on Miss Byers's foot.

For two exciting days Junior and I helped with the roundup. First the vaqueros lassoed the calves and wrestled them down to the ground. Then Junior and I held them while my father and my tío Enrique branded them and cut the ears and gave them the shot.

14 *¡Qué barullo!* The red-hot irons were smoking, and the burned hair was stinking. The calves were fighting and bawling like giant babies. They were much heavier than Junior and me. It was hard work and dangerous to hold them down. I got dust in my eyes and in my nose, but I didn't care.

After the work of the roundup was over, we made the fiesta! First was a race for the kids. We had to ride as fast as we could to the chuck wagon, take an orange, and ride back again. Junior won on Pinto. He got a big jar of candies and gave some to all of us. Last came Victor and his little *burro.* All that day we had races and roping contests.

That night we had a big *barbacoa.* The kids got cold soda pops. When the music started, all the vaqueros wanted to dance with Natalia. The one they call Chapo asked her to be his *novia,* but Natalia told him she doesn't want to get married. She wants to go to high school.

Monday morning when we left for school, the vaqueros were packing their bedrolls. We waved and hollered from our bus, "*¡Adiós! ¡Adiós! ¡Hasta la vista!*"

---

qué (kaye)—what, how
barullo (bah-ROO-yoe)—noise, racket
burro (BOOR-row)—donkey
barbacoa (bar-bah-KOH-ah)—barbecue
hasta la vista (AH-stah lah VEE-stah)— see you

180

ELL

Activate Prior Knowledge Have students tell about any races, contests, or awards they have attempted to win and how they felt when they did or didn't win. Have them compare their feelings to the characters' feelings.

Issue Number Nine   ¡Hasta la vista!   May 10, 1939

COYOTE NEWS

Stories and Pictures by the Students of Coyote School, Pima County, Arizona

Adios Coyote School!   Lalo Natalia   _Good-bye, everybody! Thank you, Miss Byers!_

by Lalo Lopez

Eduardo (Lalo) and Natalia Graduate!

Lalo and I have passed the Eighth Grade Standard Achievement Test! I am happy to graduate and I am excited about high school, but I will miss my teacher and all the kids at my dear Coyote School...Natalia Ramirez, Grade 8

I Lose the Perfect Attendance

I was absent from school to help with the roundup. It was very exciting, but now it is over and I am feeling sad. The vaqueros are gone and I will not get a silver dollar for my buckle....Monchi Ramirez, Grade 4

The Perfect Attendance Report

The only one who still has perfect attendance is Victor. Even Miss Byers has been absent, because when it was roundup on her ranch a big calf stepped on her foot. We had Miss Elias for 3 days. Miss Byers had to pay her 5 dollars a day to take her place.....Gilbert Perez, Grade 6

Please forgive me, Miss Byers   300 pounds

BY Rosie Garcia

A Visit to the Boston Beans

Mr. and Mrs. Bean invited my family to visit them this summer in Boston. Boston is Back East. It is even bigger than Tucson. No other kid at Coyote School has ever gone that far away!.............Billy Mills, Grade 3

Earrings

My daddy is getting married. Joey and I will get a new mother and 4 new brothers. Laura is nice and she can cook, but the best part is she has pierced ears and now I will get to have them too!....Cynthia Brown, Grade 2

Last Issue for the School Year

This is the last issue before the summer vacation. I am saving all my Coyote News newspapers so that someday I can show my children all the swell and exciting things we did at Coyote School...........Rosie Garcia, Grade 3

15

16

181

SKILLS ◄► STRATEGIES IN CONTEXT

Draw Conclusions Prior Knowledge

TEACH

- Remind students that they can use their own experiences and knowledge to help them draw conclusions about what they read.
- Model how to use prior knowledge to help draw a conclusion about whether or not Monchi would choose school over roundup if he had to choose again.

Think Aloud **MODEL** If I think about Monchi's feelings about roundup and Perfect Attendance, and what I know about Monchi, I can form my own opinion about what I think he'd do. Monchi had fun and got to try new things at roundup. Even though he really wanted to win Perfect Attendance, he feels it's more important that he go to round-up. I think he would make the same choice again.

PRACTICE AND ASSESS

Ask students to think of a time they had to choose between two things to do. Have them describe what they did and why. Then have them use what they know about Monchi to conclude what they think he would do in the same situation.

Guiding Comprehension

17 **Draw Conclusions • Inferential**

Why isn't Monchi happy for Victor when he wins Perfect Attendance?

Monchi wanted to win the award himself.

18 **Character • Critical**

Based on what you read about Monchi, how might you describe him?

Possible responses: Monchi is hardworking, and he helps people. He cares about school and his family, and he likes to have fun.

19 **Plot • Critical**

Text To Text **How is Monchi rewarded for his hard work at the end of the story? Name another story you have read where a character's hard work paid off in the end.**

He is given a silver dollar as a reward for his work on the school newspaper. Stories will vary, but should involve a character who gets rewarded for work done.

Summarize When students finish reading the selection, provide this prompt: Write a summary of what happened in the story. Write it like a short newspaper article.

The Last Day of School

On the last day of school Miss Byers gave us a fiesta with cupcakes and candies and Cracker Jacks and soda pops. We got to listen to Mexican music on her radio. I didn't have to dance with Natalia. I got to dance with Rosie.

Then Miss Byers turned off the radio and stood in the front of the room between President Roosevelt and Señor Grandote. She called Natalia and Lalo up to the front and told them how proud we were that they were graduates of Coyote School, and how much we would miss them. We all clapped and whistled.

Next, Miss Byers gave Edelia a paper and said, "Please read what it says, Edelia."

Edelia read: "Edelia Ortiz has been promoted to Grade Two." Miss Byers had to help her to read "promoted," but we all clapped and cheered anyway. Edelia looked very happy and proud.

Then Miss Byers asked Victor to come to the front of the room, and I knew what that meant. I didn't want to listen when she said how good it was that he had not missed a day of school, and I didn't want to look when she gave him the silver dollar. I knew I should be

182

ELL

Extend Language Point out the exclamation marks on p. 183, and explain that these marks are used to express strong feelings. Read aloud declarative and exclamatory sentences from the story so students can hear the differences in expression. In Spanish, an inverted exclamation or question mark is used at the beginning of a sentence to signal what type of sentence it is.

"Go up to the front," Natalia said and gave me a push.

Miss Byers smiled and shook my hand. "Congratulations, Monchi," she said, and then she gave me the award.

¡Ay caramba! The *Coyote News* Writing Award was a shiny silver dollar!

"Oh thank you, Miss Byers!" I said. "*¡Gracias!*" I was so surprised and happy. I pushed the silver dollar into the round hole on my buckle. It fit perfectly!

"*¡Muy hermosa!*" Miss Byers said.

She was right. It was very beautiful. **19**

gracias (GRAHS-see-ahs)—thank you
hermosa (air-MOE-sah)—beautiful

happy that Victor won the Perfect Attendance, but I was not. **17**

"And now, boys and girls," Miss Byers said, "it's time for the next award."

"What next award?" we asked.

"The *Coyote News* Writing Award for the student who has contributed most to *Coyote News* by writing his own stories and by helping others write theirs. The winner of the *Coyote News* Writing Award is Ramón Ernesto Ramírez."

"Me?" I said.

All the kids were clapping and whistling. I just sat there. **18**

183

Develop Vocabulary

PRACTICE LESSON VOCABULARY

Students orally respond to each question and provide a reason for each.

1. Are *dudes* more likely to talk like someone from the West or someone from the East? *(someone from the East; dudes are city people usually from the East.)*

2. Who is more likely to be *bawling,* a horse or a baby? *(a baby; babies can cry very loudly.)*

3. How is a vaquero likely to get a horse to move by using *spurs*? *(A rider can poke a horse with the sharp spurs on his or her boots.)*

BUILD CONCEPT VOCABULARY

Review previous concept words with students. Ask if students have come across any words today in their reading or elsewhere that they would like to add to the Working Together Concept Web such as *contributed* or *congratulations.*

 STRATEGY SELF-CHECK

Prior Knowledge

Ask students what lesson they think Monchi learns from his experiences. *(Possible response: Sometimes good things happen to you when you don't expect it.)* Remind students to use story details and prior knowledge to draw conclusions about Monchi. Use Practice Book p. 67 for more practice.

SELF-CHECK

Students can ask themselves these questions to assess their understanding of the story.

- Was I able to identify a lesson that Monchi learns?
- Did I use story details and my own experiences to help me draw my conclusion?

Monitor Progress
Draw Conclusions

If... students have difficulty using prior knowledge to draw conclusions,	then... use the Reteach lesson on p. 187b.

Draw Conclusions

- **Drawing a conclusion** is forming an opinion based on what you already know or on the facts and details in a text.
- Check an author's conclusions or your own conclusions by asking: Is this the only logical choice? Are the facts accurate?

Directions Read the following passage. Then answer the questions below.

It took quite a bit of teamwork for the first issue of the Wide Valley School Newspaper to come out successfully. The editor, Sally Jo, did a good job of making sure everything ran smoothly. Candice read through the reporters' articles to correct any errors. Brian then took Candice's edited articles and entered them into the classroom computer. Then Taylor arranged the articles and added graphics. Finally, Ms. Jackson had the newspaper printed.

Possible answers given.

1. Draw a conclusion about how much time it took to put together the paper's first issue.

   It took a lot of time to put it together.

2. What details support this conclusion?

   The descriptions of the students' and their teacher's jobs in creating the first issue suggest a lot of work.

3. What do you think was Sally Jo's main duty as editor?

   She made sure people were doing their jobs.

4. Draw a conclusion about the teamwork it takes to put together a newspaper.

   People have to work well with each other to be able to put together a newspaper.

5. Describe any prior knowledge that helped you draw these conclusions.

   Working with a team on a project is like working on a newspaper.

School + Home Home Activity Your child read a short passage and drew conclusions using facts and details. Read an article with your child. Have your child draw a conclusion from the article and explain to you how prior knowledge helped him or her to do so.

▲ **Practice Book** p. 67

Reader Response

Open for Discussion Personal Response

Think Aloud

MODEL I would include stories about the roundup and the Perfect Attendance Award because I think those are the most important and interesting.

Comprehension Check Critical Response

1. Possible response: Monchi helps Loli write her story. He really wants to win the Perfect Attendance Award. He says "Me?" when he wins the Writing Award. **Author's Purpose**

2. Responses should include details that support the conclusion that members of Monchi's family care about and help each other. ⊚ **Draw Conclusions**

3. Responses should include details about Coyote School and explanations of why the students were surprised. ⊚ **Prior Knowledge**

4. Responses should be three logical and appropriate rules that include Words to Know. ⊚ **Vocabulary**

Look Back and Write For test practice, assign a 10–15 minute time limit. For assessment, see the Scoring Rubric at the right.

Retell

Have students retell *Coyote School News*.

Monitor Progress

Check Retelling Rubric 4 3 2 1

If... students have difficulty retelling the story,	then... use the Retelling Cards and Scoring Rubric for Retelling on p. 185 to assist fluent retelling.

SUCCESS PREDICTOR

ELL

Check Retelling As students retell, focus on comprehension, overlooking mistakes in English such as inconsistent verb tenses. For more ideas on assessing students' retellings, see the ELL and Transition Handbook.

Reader Response

Open for Discussion Plan a super issue of *Coyote News*. What words will describe life at the Ramírez Ranch and Coyote School? What stories, articles, poems, and drawings will you include?

1. The author helps you get to know Monchi through his words and actions. Find examples of how Monchi's words and actions help you get to know him. **Think Like an Author**

2. How do the members of Monchi's family feel about one another? How do they feel about being a family? Support your answer with details from the story. **Draw Conclusions**

3. What surprised you about Coyote School? Why? **Prior Knowledge**

4. Pretend you are a vaquero on the Ramírez Ranch. Make up at least three Ramírez Ranch Rules you would have to follow. Use a Words to Know word in each rule. **Vocabulary**

Look Back and Write Monchi did not receive the Perfect Attendance Award. Read page 183 again. Write about the award Monchi did get and why he got it.

Meet author and illustrator Joan Sandin on page 775.

184

Scoring Rubric   Look Back and Write

Top-Score Response A top-score response will use information from page 183 to explain that Monchi got the *Coyote News* Writing Award for his contribution to the newspaper.

Example of a Top-Score Response Monchi did not get the Perfect Attendance Award. Instead he got the *Coyote News* Writing Award. This award went to the student who had done the most for the school newspaper by writing stories and helping other students write stories. The prize was a silver dollar.

For additional rubrics, see p. WA10.

Write Now
News Story

Prompt

Coyote School News includes several news stories written by students.

Think about something that has happened recently in your school or community.

Now write a news story about that event.

Writing Trait

Your news story should **focus** on one event. Use supporting details that make your **ideas** clear and interesting.

Student Model

Introductory paragraph focuses on who, what, when, where, and why of the event.

The Union Street Community Garden celebrated its first Spring Festival on Saturday. Hundreds of people from the neighborhood gathered to eat, drink, listen to music, and enjoy the beautiful garden. The lilacs, tulips, and budding trees were a beautiful setting.

Writer provides details to describe the scene.

Several kids from the neighborhood ran a bake sale. They made cookies, brownies, and cupcakes. They also sold lemonade. The money earned was donated to the garden's flower fund. Local musicians also shared their talent. There was a guitarist who sang children's songs, followed by a string quartet.

A direct quote creates interest.

"I think they should do this every year," said Jamie North, a fourth grader who lives on the block. Organizers are already making plans for next year's festival.

Use the model to help you write your own news story.

185

Write Now

Look at the Prompt Have students identify and discuss key words and phrases in the prompt. (school or community, news story about that event)

Strategies to Develop Focus/Ideas

Have students

- take out details that don't focus on the main idea of the event.
- state the who, what, where, when and why of the story in the first few sentences.
- anticipate and answer questions the reader might have about the event.

NO: There was a concert.

YES: Over fifty musicians participated in last night's Middle School orchestra concert.

For additional suggestions and rubric, see pp. 187g–187h.

Hints for Better Writing

- Carefully read the prompt.
- Use a graphic organizer to plan your writing.
- Support your ideas with information and details.
- Use words that help readers understand.
- Proofread and edit your work.

Scoring Rubric | Narrative Retelling

Rubric 4 3 2 1	4	3	2	1
Connections	Makes connections and generalizes beyond the text	Makes connections to other events, stories, or experiences	Makes a limited connection to another event, story, or experience	Makes no connection to another event, story, or experience
Author's Purpose	Elaborates on author's purpose	Tells author's purpose with some clarity	Makes some connection to author's purpose	Makes no connection to author's purpose
Characters	Describes the main character(s) and any character development	Identifies the main character(s) and gives some information about them	Inaccurately identifies some characters or gives little information about them	Inaccurately identifies the characters or gives no information about them
Setting	Describes the time and location	Identifies the time and location	Omits details of time or location	Is unable to identify time or location
Plot	Describes the problem, goal, events, and ending using rich detail	Tells the problem, goal, events, and ending with some errors that do not affect meaning	Tells parts of the problem, goal, events, and ending with gaps that affect meaning	Retelling has no sense of story

Retelling Plan

- ☑ **Week 1** Assess Strategic Intervention ✓ students.
- ☑ **This week assess Advanced students.**
- ☑ **Week 3** Assess Strategic Intervention ✓ students.
- ☐ **Week 4** Assess On-Level students.
- ☐ **Week 5** Assess any students you have not yet checked during this unit.

Use the Retelling Chart on p. TR16 to record retelling.

Selection Test To assess with *Coyote School News*, use Selection Tests, pp. 25–28.

Fresh Reads for Differentiated Test Practice For weekly leveled practice, use pp. 37–42.

SUCCESS PREDICTOR

Social Studies in Reading

PREVIEW/USE TEXT FEATURES

As students preview, have them identify *first, next,* and *finally* and bold-faced words. Ask:

- **What is the purpose of using the words *first, next,* and *finally* and bold-faced type in this how-to article?** (They show steps in the process; bold-faced type helps to find information.)

Link to Social Studies

Encourage students to start by looking at a newspaper's section titles and table of contents to help them identify article types.

HOW-TO ARTICLE

Use the sidebar on p. 186 to guide discussion. Explain that a how-to article is nonfiction with directions that tell how to do something. Discuss how numbered steps or key words like *first, next,* and *finally* help.

DAY 4 Grouping Options

Reading
Whole Group Discuss the Question of the Day.

Group Time Differentiated Instruction
Read "How to Start a School Newspaper." See pp. 162f–162g for the small group lesson plan.

Whole Group Use p. 187a.

Language Arts
Use pp. 187e–187k.

Social Studies in Reading

How-to Article

Genre

- **A how-to article gives step-by-step directions for making or doing something.**
- **It often includes a list of materials to gather or things to think about before you begin.**

Text Features

- **Bold-faced type sets off the steps and calls attention to newspaper jobs and kinds of newspaper articles.**
- **Checkmarks make the text seem like a list that is easy to follow.**

Link to Social Studies

Look through a community newspaper. Make a list of the kinds of articles it contains. Share what you learn with your class.

Starting your own school paper can be fun! You get to share news and say what you think about it. But starting a paper takes planning and teamwork. Here's how to do it.

First, pick your team. You'll need to fill these jobs:

✓ The **editor** decides what stories writers will work on. Everybody comes up with ideas, but the editor has the final say.

✓ The **writers** write the stories. They talk to people and dig up facts.

✓ The **copyeditor** checks the writers' work. He or she fixes spelling and other mistakes.

✓ The **photo editor** chooses pictures to go with the stories.

✓ The **designer** decides where the stories and pictures will go on the page. The final result is called a layout.

✓ The **staff adviser** is the adult who guides you. The adviser answers your questions and steers your paper in the right direction.

186

Content-Area Vocabulary · Social Studies

layout	a plan or design for an advertisement, book, etc.
profile	a short description of someone's abilities, personality, or career

 **AudioText**

How to Start a School Newspaper

by Lisa Klobuchar

Next, figure out what to write about. Find out what your classmates want to read about. Ask around, or place an idea box outside your classroom. Here are just a few kinds of writing to put in your paper:

✓ **News** stories tell about what is going on in your school, your town, or even around the world. They must be factual, or true.

✓ In **sports** stories, you can tell when games will be played at your school. You can describe the sports action and list scores, or you can profile a player.

✓ **Arts and entertainment** stories may tell about special school events or introduce readers to a poem, short story, piece of artwork, or movie.

✓ In an **advice column,** students can ask questions about anything, and "Dear So-and-So" will answer them.

Finally, start writing! It feels wonderful to share your ideas and stories with your classmates. And there's no better way to do that than to start a school newspaper.

Reading Across Texts

This article identifies several kinds of writing that can go into a school newspaper. Which kinds of writing appear in *Coyote News?*

Writing Across Texts Make a list of the stories or features in one issue of *Coyote News.* Tell what kind of writing each is.

Prior Knowledge What do you already know about newspaper workers?

187

Strategies for Nonfiction

USE BOLD-FACED WORDS Bold-faced words are important words. Students can use them to answer test questions. Provide the following strategy.

Use the Strategy

1. Scan the article for bold-faced words that match key words in the test question.
2. When you find a match, read that part of the article to look for the answer to the question.

GUIDED PRACTICE Discuss how to use the strategy to answer the following question.

What does the editor of a school paper do?

INDEPENDENT PRACTICE Discuss the process they used to find the information in the following question.

Why would you find movie information in the arts and entertainment section?

Prior Knowledge

Response may vary, but should include accurate information about newspaper workers.

CONNECT TEXT TO TEXT

Reading Across Texts

Have students list the four types of stories named in the how-to article. Skim the newspaper stories in *Coyote School News* and place a check on the list for each type of story they find.

Writing Across Texts Have students use their lists to identify the types of writing found in one issue of *Coyote News.*

History of Newspapers

Time for SOCIAL STUDIES

The first official newspaper in the United States, *The Boston News-Letter,* was published in Boston, Massachusetts, in 1704. The American colonies were under British rule, and the newspaper's content was controlled by British authorities. Eventually, independent newspapers emerged. They played an important role, calling for political change around the time of the American Revolution. The First Amendment to the U.S. Constitution guarantees the right to a free press. This means U.S. newspapers can publish criticisms of the government without fear of criminal punishment or censorship.

Fluency Assessment Plan

☑ **Week 1** Assess Advanced students.

☑ **This week assess Strategic Intervention students.**

☐ **Week 3** Assess On-Level students.

☐ **Week 4** Assess Strategic Intervention students.

☐ **Week 5** Assess any students you have not yet checked during this unit.

Set individual goals for students to enable them to reach the year-end goal.

• Current Goal: 100–110 WCPM

• Year-End Goal: 130 WCPM

Provide opportunities for students to read aloud from their books as they follow an audio recording of the text. As students gain fluency with the text, they can read and reread it independently.

 To develop fluent readers, use Fluency Coach.

DAY 5 — Grouping Options

Reading
Whole Group
Revisit the Question of the Week.

Group Time
Differentiated Instruction
Reread this week's Leveled Readers. See pp. 162f–162g for the small group lesson plan.

Whole Group
Use p. 187b–187c.

Language Arts
Use pp. 187d–187l.

EMOTION
Fluency

 DAY 1

Model Reread aloud "A Big-City Dream" on p. 162m. Explain that you will express Luz's emotions by changing your pacing and tone of voice. Point out reading with emotion makes dialogue more interesting. Model as you read.

DAY 2

Choral Reading Read aloud p. 172, paragraphs 2–3. Have students notice how your pitch and your tone changes to express Monchi's feelings about Victor and Miss Byers. Practice as a class by doing three choral readings.

DAY 3

Model Read aloud p. 183, paragraphs 3–9 (begin with "The winner of …") Have students notice how your voice changes to express Monchi's surprise and then sense of pride. Practice as a class by doing three choral readings.

DAY 4

Partner Reading Partners practice reading aloud p. 183, paragraphs 3–9, three times. Students should read with emotion and offer each other feedback.

Monitor Progress | Check Fluency WCPM

As students reread, monitor their progress toward their individual fluency goals. Current Goal: 100–110 words correct per minute. End-of-Year Goal: 130 words correct per minute.

If… students cannot read fluently at a rate of 100–110 words correct per minute,

then… make sure students practice with text at their independent level. Provide additional fluency practice, pairing nonfluent readers with fluent readers.

If… students already read at 130 words correct per minute,

then… they do not need to reread three times.

SUCCESS PREDICTOR

DAY 5

Assessment
Individual Reading Rate Use Fluency Assessment Plan and do a one-minute timed reading of either selection from this week to assess students in Week 2. Pay special attention to this week's skill, emotion. Provide corrective feedback for each student.

RETEACH

⊙ Draw Conclusions

TEACH

Review the definition of *draw conclusions* on p. 162. Students can complete Practice Book p. 68 on their own, or you can complete it as a class. Point out the phrases in the facts and details boxes on the Practice Book page. Students must use information from the passage to turn each phrase into a complete sentence and then use these facts and details to draw a conclusion.

ASSESS

Have pairs read p. 172, paragraphs 2–3, and draw a conclusion about how Monchi feels about his brother, Victor. *(Monchi thinks Victor is a tattletale and he doesn't like that part of him.)* Ask students to point out facts and details that support their conclusion.

For additional instruction on draw conclusions, see DI·53.

EXTEND SKILLS

Narrative Writing

TEACH

Narrative writing recalls an event or series of events through the storyteller, or narrator.

- Narrative writing describes events in detail as seen through the eyes of the storyteller.
- Think about the storyteller's point of view when reading narrative writing.

Have students read p. 174, starting at paragraph 3. Help them identify the narrator and describe the event he is recounting.

ASSESS

Have students read p. 180, paragraphs 3–4. Ask: **What is the narrator describing in this passage?** *(a fiesta after the roundup)* Then have students write about a special event in their lives. Check that students write in the first person and that events are in chronological order.

OBJECTIVES

- ⊙ Use facts and details to draw conclusions.
- Understand narrative writing.

Skills Trace	
⊙ Draw Conclusions	
Introduce/Teach	TE: 4.2 162–163, 188–189; 4.5 608–609
Practice	TE: 169, 179, 181, 195, 203, 205, 615, 619 PB: 63, 67, 68, 73, 77, 78, 243, 247, 248
► Reteach/Review	**TE: 4.2 153, 187b, 211b, DI•53, DI•54; 4.5 569, 591, 629b, DI•56 PB: 56, 226, 236**
Test	Selection Test: 25–28, 29–32, 97–100; Benchmark Test: Units 2, 5

ELL

Access Content Reteach the skill by reviewing the Picture It! lesson on draw conclusions in the ELL Teaching Guide, pp. 43–44.

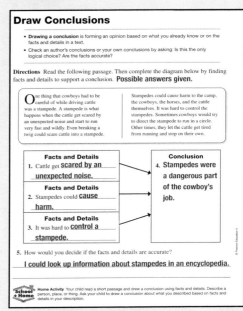

▲ **Practice Book** p. 68

Vocabulary and Word Study

VOCABULARY STRATEGY

Dictionary/ Glossary

UNFAMILIAR WORDS Remind students that the dark, or bold, words defined in a dictionary or glossary are called entry words. Point out that when looking up the meaning of an unfamiliar word, its entry word may not match exactly the word in the selection. Entry words are often base words without endings, prefixes, or suffixes. Ask students to use a dictionary to define the following words from *Coyote School News*. Have them list the entry word and meaning for each word.

Word in Story	Entry Word and Meaning
promoted	promote: to raise in rank
nagging	
wrestled	
branded	
perfectly	

Compound Words

Point out that *roundup* is a compound word, a word made up of two smaller words. Have students scan *Coyote School News* to find other examples of compound words. You can organize students into small groups and set a time limit. Have each team see how many compound words they can generate. Display students' lists and have them illustrate their favorite compound words.

Some Compound Words

roundup	baseball	downtown
grandfather	newspapers	bedrolls
tattletale	livestock	cupcakes
rattlesnake		

BUILD CONCEPT VOCABULARY

Working Together

LOOKING BACK Remind students of the question of the week: *How can we work together to achieve a goal?* Discuss how this week's Concept Web of vocabulary words relates to the theme of working together. Ask students if they have any words or categories to add. Discuss if words and categories are appropriately related to the concept.

MOVING FORWARD Preview the title of the next selection, *Grace and the Time Machine*. Ask students which Concept Web words might apply to the new selection based on the title alone. Put a star next to these words on the Web.

Display the Concept Web and revisit the vocabulary words as you read the next selection to check predictions.

Monitor Progress

Check Vocabulary

If... students suggest words or categories that are not related to the concept,	**then**... review the words and categories on the Concept Web and discuss how they relate to the lesson concept.

SUCCESS PREDICTOR

Speaking and Listening

SPEAKING

Newscast

SET-UP Have students use information from the news story they wrote in this week's Writing Workshop to create and present a TV newscast for the class. Have students revise and then "report" their stories in a TV newscast format with one to three news anchors.

PLANNING Ask students to think about how TV reporters tell news stories. View and discuss a TV newscast, or if possible, invite a local TV reporter to be interviewed by students. Students' questions should focus on how news stories are best prepared and delivered.

SHARE THESE SUGGESTIONS:

- TV news stories are usually brief, so include only the most important ideas and details.
- Use language that will capture viewers' attention.
- Observe the transitions reporters use to move from one story to the next. Include similar transitions in your newscast.

DELIVERY Good newscasters know their material well before they deliver it on air. Students can use prompt cards or refer to news scripts, but should avoid simply reading their stories aloud.

LISTENING

Listen to a Newscast

Have students listen to a newscast presented by classmates or to a pre-recorded radio newscast. Ask them to listen carefully for the main idea of each news story. Students can answer these questions orally or in writing:

1. **How was this newscast like others you have heard?** *(Possible response: This newscast was like others I've heard, delivered in a polished, matter-of-fact way.)*

2. **What was the most important idea in each story? Which details supported that idea?** *(Responses should include the main idea and supporting details for each news story.)*

3. **Did the speakers report facts or opinions? How do you know?** *(Possible response: The speakers reported mostly facts; I know because their statements can be proved true or false.)*

Support Vocabulary Use the following to review and extend vocabulary and to explore lesson concepts further:
- ELL Poster 7, Days 3–5 instruction
- Vocabulary Activities and Word Cards in ELL Teaching Guide, pp. 45–46

Assessment For information on assessing students' speaking and listening, see the ELL and Transition Handbook.

Vocabulary

SUCCESS PREDICTOR

Grammar **Regular Plural Nouns**

Monitor Progress

Grammar

If... students have difficulty identifying regular plural nouns,	**then...** provide additional instruction and practice in The Grammar and Writing Book pp. 86–89.

DAILY FIX-IT

This week use Daily Fix-It Transparency 7.

Spiral REVIEW

ELL

Grammar Support See the Grammar Transition lessons in the ELL and Transition Handbook.

▲ **The Grammar and Writing Book**
For more instruction and practice, use pp. 86–89.

DAY 1 Teach and Model

DAILY FIX-IT

1. Tornadoes sometimes sweep, through the western states? *(sweep through; states.)*

2. They can blow. The rooves off houses. *(blow the roofs)*

READING-GRAMMAR CONNECTION

Write the following sentence on the board:

Many of the <u>kids</u> on the <u>ranches</u> rode <u>ponies</u>.

Point out that the underlined words are **plural nouns.** They name more than one person, place, or thing. Explain that some nouns form their plural by adding an -s. Others form plurals by adding -es or -ies.

Display Grammar Transparency 7. Read aloud the definitions and example sentences. Work through the items.

Regular Plural Nouns

Singular nouns name one person, place, or thing.
Plural nouns name more than one person, place, or thing.
Add -s to form the plural of most nouns.
  school/schools   dog/dogs   cow/cows
Add -es to form the plural of nouns that end in ch, sh, s, ss, or x.
  ranch/ranches   bush/bushes   bus/buses   cross/crosses   fox/foxes
To form the plural of nouns that end in a consonant followed by a y,
change the y to i and add -es.
  family/families   party/parties   pony/ponies

Directions Write the plural noun in each sentence.

1. The students had a long bus ride to school.   **students**
2. They squeezed together like sardines in a can.   **sardines**
3. Several families from the area rode the bus.   **families**
4. They lived on ranches and went to the same school.   **ranches**
5. There were no big cities nearby.   **cities**

Directions Write each singular noun as a plural noun.

6. chicken   **chickens**
7. story   **stories**
8. newspaper   **newspapers**
9. box   **boxes**
10. baby   **babies**
11. recess   **recesses**
12. teacher   **teachers**
13. dish   **dishes**
14. bench   **benches**

Unit 2 Coyote School News   Grammar **7**

▲ **Grammar Transparency** 7

DAY 2 Develop the Concept

DAILY FIX-IT

3. We saw cows, horsies, sheeps, chickens, and pigs on the ranch. *(horses, sheep)*

4. There were to many cows two count. *(too; to)*

GUIDED PRACTICE

Review the concept of regular plural nouns.

- A **plural noun** names more than one person, place, or thing.
- Add *-s* to form the plural of most nouns. Add *-es* to form the plural of nouns ending in *ch, sh, s, ss,* or *x.*
- When a noun ends in a consonant followed by *y,* form its plural by changing the *y* to *i* and adding *-es.*

HOMEWORK Grammar and Writing Practice Book p. 25. Work through the first two items with the class.

Regular Plural Nouns

- Singular nouns name one person, place, or thing. **Plural nouns** name more than one person, place, or thing.
- Add *-s* to form the plural of most nouns.
  bird/birds   snake/snakes   monkey/monkeys
- Add *-es* to form the plural of nouns that end in *ch, sh, s, ss,* or *x.*
  finch/finches   dish/dishes   gas/gases   dress/dresses   box/boxes
- To form the plural of nouns that end in a consonant followed by a *y,* change the *y* to *i* and add *-es.*
  butterfly/butterflies   puppy/puppies

Directions Underline the plural noun in each sentence.

1. Texas has many cattle <u>ranches</u>.
2. A cowboy rides after <u>cows</u>.
3. A cowboy can throw a rope within <u>inches</u> of his target.
4. Wild <u>ponies</u> also live in the Southwest.
5. Many <u>movies</u> have been made about the Old West.

Directions Write the singular form of each noun.

6. outlaws   **outlaw**
7. stories   **story**
8. patches   **patch**
9. foxes   **fox**
10. saddles   **saddle**
11. coyotes   **coyote**
12. losses   **loss**

Home Activity Your child learned about regular plural nouns. Point to objects around the house. Ask your child to say the nouns and their plural forms and to explain how the plurals were formed.

▲ **Grammar and Writing Practice Book** p. 25

DAY 3 — Apply to Writing

5. It was fun watching the horses look after there babys. *(their babies)*

6. The foals have long thin legs, they run after their motheres. *(legs. They; mothers)*

SPELL PLURALS CORRECTLY

Point out that good writers are careful to spell words correctly. Review with students the rules for spelling regular plural nouns. Have them pay particular attention to nouns ending in a consonant followed by a *y*.

• Have students review something they have written to see if they can improve it by correcting the spelling of plural nouns.

HOMEWORK Grammar and Writing Practice Book p. 26.

Regular Plural Nouns

Directions Use the plural form of the underlined noun. Add a word from the box to describe the noun. Write the new sentence.

| yellow | noisy | wooden | interesting | bumpy |

1. Those ___ chicken woke us up. **Possible answers:**
   Those noisy chickens woke us up.

2. He drove his truck along the ___ road.
   He drove his truck along the bumpy roads.

3. They wrote ___ story for the newspaper.
   They wrote interesting stories for the newspaper.

4. The students sat on rows of hard ___ bench.
   The students sat on rows of hard wooden benches.

5. They went home in bright ___ bus.
   They went home in bright yellow buses.

Directions Write a short description of horses that you have seen in books, in movies, or on television. Use at least three different plural nouns. Underline the plural nouns you use.

Possible answer: Horses are very fast animals. Cowboys ride them to round up cows. Some horses are brown or black, and some are white with spots or patches. Their babies are called foals. Small horses are called ponies.

Home Activity Your child learned how to use regular plural nouns in writing. Ask your child to write a sentence about his or her day using at least one plural noun.

▲ **Grammar and Writing Practice Book** p. 26

DAY 4 — Test Preparation

7. If I get the chance. Im going to work on a ranch. *(chance, I'm)*

8. Its hard work but I know I'd enjoy it. *(It's; work, but)*

STANDARDIZED TEST PREP

Test Tip

Do not use apostrophes (') to form plural nouns. Only contractions and possessive nouns use apostrophes.

NO: The mother cow's are feeding their baby's.

YES: The mother cows are feeding their babies.

HOMEWORK Grammar and Writing Practice Book p. 27.

Regular Plural Nouns

Directions Mark the letter of the correct plural form that completes each sentence.

1. *Vaqueros* means ___ in Spanish.
   A cowboys'
   B cowboys
   C cowboyes
   D cowboy's

2. They were skilled ___.
   A rideres
   B riders'
   C riderz
   D riders

3. They worked on the ___ of the Southwest.
   A ranchies
   B ranch'es
   C ranches
   D ranchus

4. Often they were far from their ___.
   A familys
   B families
   C familyes
   D familease

Directions Mark the letter of the ending that will form the plural of the singular noun in the phrases below.

5. wild bunch
   A -s
   B -ess
   C -ies
   D -es

6. near miss
   A -es
   B -e's
   C -es's
   D -s

7. leather saddle
   A -'s
   B -s
   C -ies
   D -es

8. fine lady
   A -'s
   B -ies
   C -s
   D -es

9. whirling rope
   A -s'
   B -es
   C -s
   D -ies

10. red-hot brand
    A -s
    B -z
    C -es
    D -ez

Home Activity Your child prepared for taking tests on regular plural nouns. Read a brief passage to your child from a book, magazine, or newspaper. Ask him or her to identify any plural nouns in the passage and to say how they were formed.

▲ **Grammar and Writing Practice Book** p. 27

DAY 5 — Cumulative Review

9. What great rider those *vaqueros* are? *(riders; are!)*

10. They can rode all day and never get tired, I'd like to do that. *(ride; tired.)*

ADDITIONAL PRACTICE

Assign pp. 86–89 in The Grammar and Writing Book.

EXTRA PRACTICE Grammar and Writing Practice Book p. 128.

TEST PREPARATION Grammar and Writing Practice Book pp. 153–154.

ASSESSMENT

CUMULATIVE REVIEW Grammar and Writing Practice Book p. 28.

Regular Plural Nouns

Directions Circle the plural noun in each sentence.

1. Our newspaper has an editor and five (writers).

2. Our teacher prints (copies) for us each month.

3. She puts a star next to (articles) she really likes.

4. I write (stories) about football.

5. All the (classes) read our newspaper.

Directions Write the plural form of the underlined noun or nouns in each sentence.

6. School newspaper is one of my favorite activity.   activities

7. We write the news and the headline.   headlines

8. Newspapers are printed by printing press.   presses

9. Paper that come out every day are called daily.   Papers; dailies

10. We store our old papers in big box.   boxes

Directions Write a sentence about each of the following places. Include two plural nouns in each sentence. **Possible answers:**

11. a ranch   We saw cows and horses on the ranch.

12. a school   There are more girls than boys in our school.

Home Activity Your child reviewed regular plural nouns. Ask your child to pretend that he or she is teaching a second-grade class about plural nouns. Have your child show you how he or she would explain the concept.

▲ **Grammar and Writing Practice Book** p. 28

Writing Workshop News Story

OBJECTIVES

- Identify qualities of a news story.
- Write a news story including necessary information.
- Focus on focus/ideas
- Use a rubric.

Genre News Story
Writer's Craft Include Necessary Information
Writing Trait Focus/Ideas

ELL

Focus/Ideas Talk with English learners about what they plan to write. Record ideas and help them generate language for support. Help them tighten their focus by eliminating unrelated details. See more writing support in the ELL and Transition Handbook.

Writing Traits

FOCUS/IDEAS The writer has a clear main idea and purpose. All necessary information is included.

ORGANIZATION/PARAGRAPHS Necessary information is told in the first paragraph. Interesting details follow later.

VOICE The writer reports clearly and factually about the event.

WORD CHOICE The writer uses exact nouns *(tennis balls),* names *(Ms. Carol Brown),* and details *($72).*

SENTENCES The writer uses declarative sentences of varied lengths, including direct quotations.

CONVENTIONS There is excellent control and accuracy.

READING-WRITING CONNECTION

- *Coyote School News* includes examples of news stories. Each story focuses on a specific idea.
- News stories must also include all of the necessary information.
- Students will write a **news story** focusing on an event and giving all of the necessary information.

MODEL FOCUS/IDEAS Discuss Writing Transparency 7A. Then discuss the model and the writing trait of focus/ideas.

Think Aloud All of the information in this news story is focused on one event. The opening sentence gets the reader's attention. Then the writer presents all of the information you need, including who was there, what happened, where and when it took place, and why the students "soaked" the teacher.

News Story

A **news story** gives readers information about recent events, from around the world to around your school. Whatever the subject, news stories focus on the facts. They answer the questions *who, what, where, when,* and *why*—known as the 5 Ws. They may also answer the question *how.* Writers of news stories should never give their opinions.

Teacher in the Tank

Necessary information is in first paragraph. → Students at Millbrook Elementary School got a chance to soak a teacher last Friday afternoon. As part of the all-school field day, fourth grade teacher Ms. Carol Brown sat on a platform above a tank of water. Students paid 50 cents to throw three tennis balls at a target below Ms. Brown's chair. Those hitting the bull's eye sent Ms. Brown for a sudden swim.

Details come later in story. → Ms. Brown plunged into the tub 37 times. "Fortunately, it was a warm day," she said.

Quotations add interest to story. → Fifth-grader Laurie Snell held the record, dunking Ms. Brown five times. "I spent a lot of money, but it was worth it," Laurie said. The event raised $72 for the school.

Unit 2 Coyote School News   Writing Model **7A**

▲ **Writing Transparency** 7A

WRITER'S CRAFT
Include Necessary Information

Display Writing Transparency 7B. Read the directions and work together to identify necessary information.

Think Aloud **INCLUDE NECESSARY INFORMATION** Tomorrow we will be writing a news story about a school or community event. I'm going to write about last week's Art Fair. It's important that I include all of the necessary information that a reader might need to know. I should describe who was at the fair, what happened, where and when the fair took place, and why the event was held. I can also talk about why the event is important for the community.

GUIDED WRITING Give students extra practice in finding necessary information by reading and discussing the opening paragraphs of actual news stories.

Include Necessary Information

Writers of news stories must be careful to **include necessary information** in their reports. The basic rule for a news reporter is to answer the questions *who, what, where, when,* and *why* when telling about an event.

Directions Each sentence gives information about an event. Circle the word that describes the information given.

1. There was an assembly.
   who   (what)   where   when   why

2. It took place at 1 P.M. on Friday, December 12.
   who   what   where   (when)   why

3. The assembly was called because some students won a poetry contest.
   who   what   where   when   (why)

4. Students in grades 3–5 attended.
   (who)   what   where   when   why

5. The assembly took place in the auditorium.
   who   what   (where)   when   why

Directions Write a short report about a real or imaginary event at your school. Make sure to include necessary information in your report. **Possible answer:**
The school band gave a concert on Sunday afternoon at 3 o'clock in the cafeteria. The concert raised $125 for new band uniforms.

Unit 2 Coyote School News   Writer's Craft **7B**

▲ **Writing Transparency** 7B

DAY 3 Prewrite and Draft

READ THE WRITING PROMPT

on page 185 in the Student Edition.

Coyote School News *includes several news stories written by students.*

Think about something that has happened recently in your school or community.

Now write a news story about that event.

Writing Test Tips

- Provide necessary information in the first paragraph of your story.
- Include interesting, colorful details to make your story interesting.
- Make sure that you focus on the event you are describing. Remember that you are writing to inform your readers. Details should support your main idea.

GETTING STARTED Students can do any of the following:

- Make a chart with columns headed *Who, What, When, Where,* and *Why.*
- Vary their writing with quotations from people involved in the event.
- Think of details that will catch their reader's attention.

DAY 4 Draft and Revise

EDITING/REVISING CHECKLIST

☑ Do I include necessary information?

☑ Do details add support to the main idea?

☑ Are words clear and exact?

☑ Are regular plural nouns spelled correctly?

See *The Grammar and Writing Book,* pp. 86–91.

Revising Tips

Focus/Ideas

- Check that your main idea is clear to the reader.
- Make sure that you have kept to your purpose—to inform your reader.
- Delete details that do not support your main idea.

PUBLISHING Print students' news stories in a class newspaper using newsletter software, post them on a class web site, or enter them in a contest. Some students may wish to revise their work later.

ASSESSMENT Use the scoring rubric to evaluate students' work.

DAY 5 Connect to Unit Writing

How-to Report

Week 1	Poem 161g–161h
Week 2	News Story 187g–187h
Week 3	Play Scene 211g–211h
Week 4	Describe a Job 239g–239h
Week 5	Explanation 259g–259h

PREVIEW THE UNIT PROMPT

Think of something that you know how to do well. Write a clear, step-by-step description of how to do this task or activity. Make your report interesting to read and easy to understand.

APPLY

- A how-to report explains the steps for making or doing something.
- The writer of a how-to report must be sure to include all necessary information.

Writing Trait Rubric

	4	3	2	1
Focus/Ideas	Ideas well-focused; thorough description of event	Ideas somewhat focused; description of event	Weak focus; description of event unclear	No focus; description of event unclear
	News story clear and informative	News story generally clear and informative	News story vague; some information missing	News story unclear; important information missing

Spelling & Phonics **Irregular Plurals**

OBJECTIVE

- Spell irregular plurals.

Generalization

Connect to Phonics Some plurals are formed by adding *-s* or *-es*: *roofs, potatoes*. Sometimes the spelling of the singular form changes: *loaves*. Some words do not change at all: *moose*. Regular plurals follow the rules. Irregular plurals do not. Sometimes the singular form changes. Some words may be either singular or plural.

Spelling Words

1. videos	11. radios
2. teeth	12. sheep
3. potatoes	13. cuffs
4. themselves	14. beliefs
5. lives	15. patios
6. leaves	16. banjos
7. cliffs	17. tornadoes
8. roofs	18. tomatoes
9. halves	19. hoofs
10. moose	20. loaves

Challenge Words

21. portfolios	24. calves
22. embargoes	25. lassoes
23. handkerchiefs	

ELL

Spelling/Phonics Support See the ELL and Transition Handbook for spelling support.

DAY 1 — Pretest and Sort

PRETEST

Use the Dictation Sentences from Day 5 to administer the pretest. Read the word, read the sentence, and then read the word again. Guide students in self-correcting their pretests and correcting any misspellings.

Monitor Progress

Spelling

If...	then...
If... students misspell more than 5 pretest words,	**then...** use words 1–10 for Strategic Intervention.
If... students misspell 1–5 pretest words,	**then...** use words 1–20 for On-Level practice.
If... students correctly spell all pretest words,	**then...** use words 1–25 for Advanced Learners.

HOMEWORK Spelling Practice Book, p. 25.

▲ **Spelling Practice Book** p. 25

DAY 2 — Think and Practice

TEACH

Plural nouns are sometimes irregular. Write *tooth* and use the singular word in a sentence. Then write *teeth* and use *teeth* in a sentence. Underline *ee*. Explain that *teeth* is an irregular plural because the spelling of the singular form changed. Write *half* and *sheep* and model the plural form of each word.

> tooth / t<u>ee</u>th

USE THE DICTIONARY Explain that the plurals of words that end in *o* may be formed by adding *-s* or *-es*. Model how to find the plural form in a dictionary. Have students look up the plural forms of other words such as *stereo, hero, piano, studio, echo,* and *mosquito*.

HOMEWORK Spelling Practice Book, p. 26.

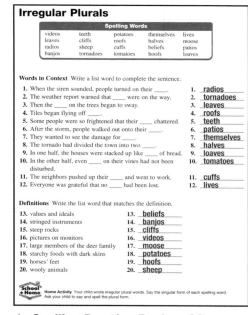

▲ **Spelling Practice Book** p. 26

DAY 3 Connect to Writing

WRITE NEWS BULLETINS

Ask students to use at least five spelling words to write one-sentence news bulletins that could appear as a crawl at the bottom of the screen during a television show.

Frequently Misspelled Words

they   *went*

said

These words may seem easy to spell, but they are often misspelled by fourth-graders. Alert students to these frequently misspelled words. Point out that the long *a* sound in *they* is spelled *ey*, and the short *e* sound in *said* is spelled *ai*. Show that the initial sound in *went* is spelled differently than the initial sound in *when*.

HOMEWORK Spelling Practice Book, p. 27.

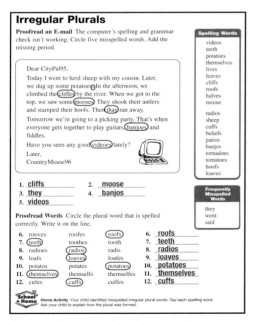

▲ **Spelling Practice Book** p. 27

DAY 4 Review

REVIEW IRREGULAR PLURALS

Have students write sentences with incorrect list words, such as *tooths* or *mooses,* and then trade sentences with a partner. Have the partner cross out the incorrect word and write the correct word above it.

Spelling Strategy Memory Tricks

Some words seem so tricky to spell that we need to outsmart them with tricks of our own.

Step 1: Mark the letters that give you a problem.

Step 2: Find words you know with the same letters.

Step 3: Use your problem words and the word you know in a phrase or sentence.

Example:

Hard word: tomato**es**

Memory trick: He plants tomato**es** wherever he g**oes**.

HOMEWORK Spelling Practice Book, p. 28.

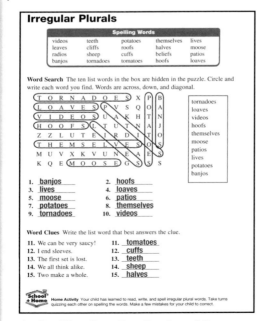

▲ **Spelling Practice Book** p. 28

DAY 5 Posttest

DICTATION SENTENCES

1. We rent videos every weekend.

2. Brush your teeth at bedtime.

3. Dad ate all the baked potatoes.

4. They hurt themselves when they fell.

5. They say a cat has nine lives.

6. In fall, leaves change color.

7. Steep cliffs are hard to climb.

8. Snow covered the roofs of the houses.

9. Let's break the cookie into halves and share it.

10. Two moose walked out of the woods.

11. Please turn your radios down.

12. The farmer fed all the sheep.

13. The cuffs of my shirt are white.

14. Many old beliefs were wrong.

15. Many people like to eat on their patios.

16. Al and Ann played their banjos.

17. Most tornadoes cause damage.

18. The tomatoes are ripe.

19. The horse's hoofs were muddy.

20. We bought two loaves of bread.

CHALLENGE

21. Artists put their work in portfolios.

22. The government set embargoes on goods from other countries.

23. I bought lace handkerchiefs as a gift for Grandma.

24. The calves grazed in the field.

25. The cowboy can twirl two lassoes at once.

OBJECTIVES

- Formulate an inquiry question that is connected to this week's lesson focus.
- Effectively and efficiently find, evaluate, and communicate information related to an inquiry question using electronic sources.

New Literacies

Day 1	**Identify Questions**
Day 2	**Navigate/Search**
Day 3	**Analyze**
Day 4	**Synthesize**
Day 5	**Communicate**

NEW LITERACIES

Internet Inquiry Activity

EXPLORE ACHIEVING GOALS

Use the following 5-day plan to help students conduct this week's Internet inquiry activity on achieving goals. Remind students to follow classroom rules when using the Internet.

DAY 1

Identify Questions Discuss the lesson focus question: *How can we work together to achieve a goal?* Have students brainstorm groups or organizations where people work together to achieve goals. Sports teams, NASA scientists, and volunteer organizations like Habitat for Humanity are some examples. Have individuals, pairs, or small groups write an inquiry question about a group or organization of their choice.

DAY 2

Navigate/Search Have students use a student-friendly search engine to conduct a simple Internet search and identify a few sites to explore. Demonstrate how searches produce a list of entries, each containing the name or title of a Web site, a brief description of its contents, and the site's URL. The URL is an Internet address of a specific Web site. Show students how to locate a Web page by clicking on a link in the search engine results or by typing the URL directly into the Address box and clicking "Go."

DAY 3

Analyze Have students explore the Web sites they identified on Day 2. Tell them to scan each site for information that helps answer their inquiry questions. Have them take notes and record the addresses of sites they used.

DAY 4

Synthesize Ask students to synthesize information from Day 3 by combining ideas and information from different sources to answer their inquiry questions.

DAY 5

Communicate Have students write a summary of their inquiry results to share with the class. They can use a word processing program to type up their summary and give it a title. Have students read aloud their summaries in small groups.

RESEARCH/STUDY SKILLS
Newspaper/Newsletter

TEACH

Ask students to name a newspaper and share what they know about how it is organized. Show examples of a newspaper and a newsletter and discuss similarities and differences between these publications. Review these terms:

- A **newspaper** is a daily or weekly publication containing world and local news and other features.

- Newspapers are divided into **sections**. Each section focuses on a subject, such as local news, arts, or sports.

- A newspaper has an **index** on or near the front page.

- Newspapers include **editorial pages** that express opinions on current events.

- A **newsletter** is a brief publication from a group that contains news of interest to the group's members.

- Newspaper and newsletter articles are identified with **headlines** and may also include **illustrations** or **photographs** with **captions.**

Provide copies of newspapers and newsletters for students. Have them scan the publications. Then discuss questions such as these:

1. **In which section of the newspaper would you find information about new homes being built in your town?** (Local news or Real Estate section.)

2. **What is the quickest way to find the score of a football game?** (Use the index to locate the sports section.)

3. **What is the purpose of the newsletter? Which group of people most likely read it?** (Responses will vary depending on the newsletter.)

This newsletter is for ranchers.

THE RANCHER'S QUARTERLY
A Publication of the Southwest Rancher's Group

No. 15 | January 15, 2007

Winter Care of Cattle
Cattle need extra care and attention during the winter months...

Rancher's Group Meets in Tucson
Over 300 rancher's met in Tucson on December 2 to...

The headline tells what the article is about.

ASSESS

Ask students to point out important features of the newspaper or newsletter they studied. Make sure they can identify the parts and purpose of each publication, use a newspaper index, and describe topics of individual articles.

For more practice or to assess students, use Practice Book pp. 69–70.

Assessment Checkpoints *for the Week*

Selection Assessment

Use pp. 25–28 of Selection Tests to check:

 Selection Understanding

  Comprehension Skill *Draw Conclusions*

 Selection Vocabulary
bawling
coyote
dudes
roundup
spurs

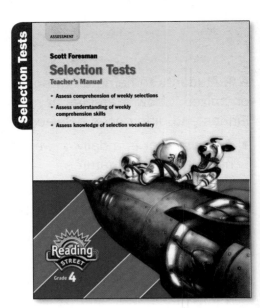

ASSESSMENT
Scott Foresman
Selection Tests
Teacher's Manual

- Assess comprehension of weekly selections
- Assess understanding of weekly comprehension skills
- Assess knowledge of selection vocabulary

Reading STREET
Grade 4

Leveled Assessment

On-Level
Strategic Intervention
Advanced

Use pp. 37–42 of Fresh Reads for Differentiated Test Practice to check:

  Comprehension Skill *Draw Conclusions*

 REVIEW **Comprehension Skill** *Setting*

 Fluency *Words Correct Per Minute*

ASSESSMENT Teacher's Manual
Scott Foresman
Fresh Reads
for Differentiated Test Practice

Leveled passages—strategic intervention, on-level, and advanced—for

- Fluency checks
- Practice and application of weekly comprehension skills
- Answer key for all practice pages

Reading STREET
Grade 4

Managing Assessment

Use Assessment Handbook for:

 Observation Checklists

 Record-Keeping Forms

 Portfolio Assessment

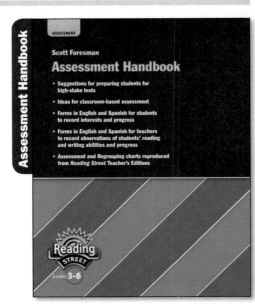

ASSESSMENT
Scott Foresman
Assessment Handbook

- Suggestions for preparing students for high-stake tests
- Ideas for classroom-based assessment
- Forms in English and Spanish for students to record interests and progress
- Forms in English and Spanish for teachers to record observations of students' reading and writing abilities and progress
- Assessment and Regrouping charts reproduced from *Reading Street* Teacher's Editions

Reading STREET
Grades 3–6

Oregon

Planning Guide for Common Curriculum Goals

Grace and the Time Machine

Reading Street Teacher's Edition pages	Grade 4 Oregon Grade-Level Standards for English/Language Arts
Oral Language **Speaking/Listening** Build Concept Vocabulary: 188l, 201, 207, 211c Read Aloud: 188m **Viewing** Analyze Media: 211d	**EL.04.RE.01** Read aloud grade-level narrative text and informational text fluently and accurately with effective pacing, intonation, and expression. **EL.04.RE.09** Understand, learn, and use new vocabulary that is introduced and taught directly through informational text, literary text, and instruction across the subject areas.
Word Work Words with *ar, or*: 211i–211j	**EL.04.WR.15** Spell correctly: syllables (word parts each containing a vowel sound, such as *sur-prise* or *e-col-o-gy*).
Reading **Comprehension** Draw Conclusions: 188–189, 192–207, 211b Prior Knowledge: 188–189, 192–207 **Vocabulary** Lesson Vocabulary: 190b, 201, 207, 210 Word Structure: 190–191, 199, 211c **Fluency** Characterization/Dialogue: 188l–188m, 211a **Self-Selected Reading:** LR19–27, TR16–17 **Literature** Genre—Play: 192 Reader Response: 208	**EL.04.RE.10** Develop vocabulary by listening to and discussing both familiar and conceptually challenging selections read aloud across the subject areas. **EL.04.RE.22** Make and confirm predictions about text by using prior knowledge and ideas presented in the text itself, including illustrations, titles, topic sentences, and important words. **EL.04.LI.01** Listen to text and read text to make connections and respond to a wide variety of significant works of literature, including poetry, fiction, non-fiction, and drama, from a variety of cultures and time periods that enhance the study of other subjects. **EL.04.LI.08** Draw inferences or conclusions about a text based on explicitly stated information.
Language Arts **Writing** Play Scene: 211g–211h **Six-Trait Writing** Organization/Paragraphs: 209, 211g–211h **Grammar, Usage, and Mechanics** Irregular Plural Nouns: 211e–211f **Research/Study** Advertisement: 211l **Technology** New Literacies: 211k	**EL.04.WR.14** Create interesting sentences using a variety of sentence patterns by selecting words that describe, explain, or provide additional detail and connections. **EL.04.WR.15** Spell correctly: syllables (word parts each containing a vowel sound, such as *sur-prise* or *e-col-o-gy*).
Unit Skills **Writing** How-To Report: WA2–9 **Poetry:** 260–263 **Project/Wrap-Up:** 264–265	**EL.04.WR.25** Write informational reports: ask and then address a central question about an issue or event; include facts and details for focus; develop the topic with simple facts, details, examples, and explanations; use more than one source of information, including speakers, books, newspapers, other media sources, and online information.

This Week's Leveled Readers

Below-Level

Nonfiction

EL.04.RE.17 Locate information in titles, tables of contents, chapter headings, illustrations, captions, glossaries, indexes, graphs, charts, diagrams, and tables to aid understanding of grade-level text.

EL.04.LI.08 Draw inferences or conclusions about a text based on explicitly stated information.

On-Level

Nonfiction

EL.04.RE.10 Develop vocabulary by listening to and discussing both familiar and conceptually challenging selections read aloud across the subject areas.

EL.04.LI.08 Draw inferences or conclusions about a text based on explicitly stated information.

Advanced

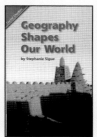

Nonfiction

EL.04.RE.05 Demonstrate listening comprehension of more complex text through class and/or small group interpretive discussions across the subject areas.

EL.04.LI.08 Draw inferences or conclusions about a text based on explicitly stated information.

Content-Area Content Standards and Benchmarks in This Lesson

Science

SC.05.PS.06.03 Identify examples of energy transfer in the environment. (Previews Grade 5 Benchmark)

SC.05.LS.01.01 Classify a variety of living things into groups using various characteristics. (Previews Grade 5 Benchmark)

SC.05.LS.03.01 Associate specific structures with their functions in the survival of the organism. (Previews Grade 5 Benchmark)

SC.05.LS.05 Describe the relationship between characteristics of specific habitats and the organisms that live there. (Previews Grade 5 Benchmark)

SC.05.LS.05.04 Explain the relationship between animal behavior and species survival. (Previews Grade 5 Benchmark)

Social Studies

SS.05.HS.01 Interpret data and chronological relationships presented in timelines and narratives. (Previews Grade 5 Benchmark)

SS.05.HS.03 Understand how history can be organized using themes, geography, or chronology. (Previews Grade 5 Benchmark)

Oregon!

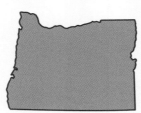

A FAMOUS OREGONIAN
Homer Davenport

Homer Davenport (1867–1912) was born in a small pioneer cabin near Silverton. He came to be a famous and respected political cartoonist. Davenport's interest in drawing, with which he said he "wasted his time," began at an early age. William Randolph Hearst brought Davenport to New York, where the artist had a great deal of freedom to comment on behavior and justice through his drawing. His cartoons showed his strong negative feelings about the corporate giants of his time.

Students can . . .
Study a few political cartoons in pairs and sketch one. Have students exchange cartoons and ask their partners to present the cartoon and its meaning.

A SPECIAL OREGON PLACE
McLoughlin House National Historic Site

After spending twenty years as a powerful businessman at Fort Vancouver, John McLoughlin made a new career of helping to establish communities in the Oregon Territory. In 1846 McLoughlin moved his family into a home in Oregon City, where he served as mayor in the 1850s. After his death the home was saved from demolition and moved to its current location in Oregon City to be part of the Fort Vancouver National Historic Site. It was restored and opened to the public as a tribute to the man known as the father of Oregon, whose efforts and support helped make the state what it is today.

Students can . . .
Find a photograph of McLoughlin House and label its features with the help of a reference book about architecture.

OREGON FUN FACTS
Did You Know?

- "Drive a nail in the land and it comes up green," said Oregon pioneers about the land's fertility.

- Amtrak train routes link Portland with Eugene; Seattle, Washington; Vancouver, Canada; and Los Angeles and San Francisco in California.

- Pioneers who reached the end of the Oregon Trail had a choice of floating their wagons down the Columbia River or crossing the Cascade Mountains via the Barlow Road.

Students can . . .
Suppose they are on the Oregon Trail. Ask students to write journal entries, including what they encountered on their journey. Ask them to discuss what they learned from their successes or failures.

Unit 2
Work and Play

CONCEPT QUESTION
What is the value of work and play?

Week 1
How can we learn to appreciate the talents of others?

Week 2
How can we work together to achieve a goal?

Week 3
What can we accomplish by using our imaginations?

Week 4
What is the value of a job well done?

Week 5
What is the job of the President of the United States?

EXPAND THE CONCEPT
What can we accomplish by using our imaginations?

CONNECT THE CONCEPT

▶ **Build Background**

excursion, invention, research

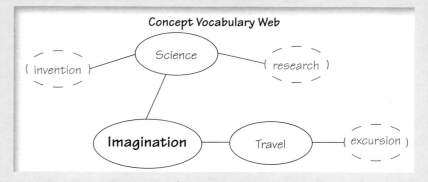

Concept Vocabulary Web

▶ **Social Studies Content**
Time Travel, The Gambia, Trinidad

▶ **Writing**
Play Scene

▶ **Internet Inquiry**
Using Our Imaginations

Grace and the Time Machine 188a

Preview Your Week

What can we accomplish by using our imaginations?

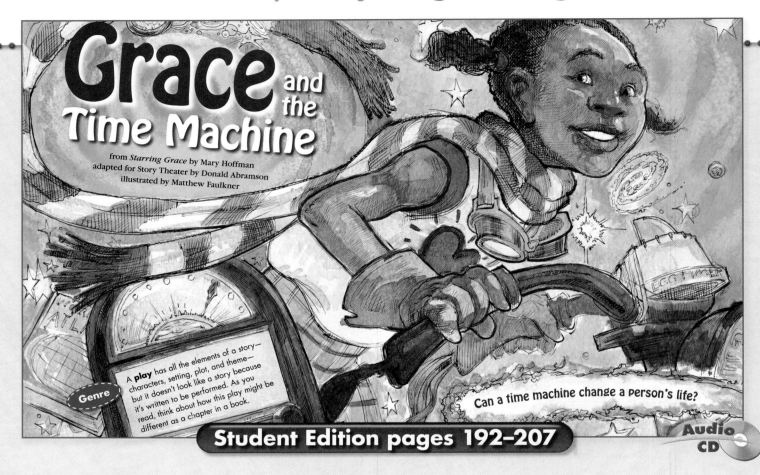

Grace and the Time Machine

from *Starring Grace* by Mary Hoffman
adapted for Story Theater by Donald Abramson
illustrated by Matthew Faulkner

Genre

A **play** has all the elements of a story—characters, setting, plot, and theme—but it doesn't look like a story because it's written to be performed. As you read, think about how this play might be different as a chapter in a book.

Can a time machine change a person's life?

Student Edition pages 192–207

Audio CD

Genre	Play
◉ **Vocabulary Strategy**	Word Structure
◉ **Comprehension Skill**	Draw Conclusions
◉ **Comprehension Strategy**	Answer Questions

Paired Selection

SOCIAL STUDIES

Reading Across Texts

Suggest Activities for Grace and Her Friends

Genre

Expository Nonfiction

Text Features

Subheads

Art

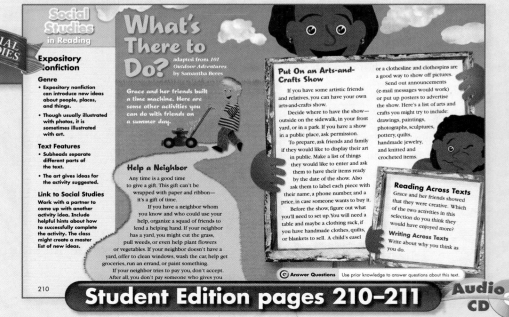

Social Studies in Reading

Expository Nonfiction

Genre
- Expository nonfiction can introduce new ideas about people, places, and things.
- Though usually illustrated with photos, it is sometimes illustrated with art.

Text Features
- Subheads separate different parts of the text.
- The art gives ideas for the activity suggested.

Link to Social Studies
Work with a partner to come up with another activity idea. Include helpful hints about how to successfully complete the activity. The class might create a master list of new ideas.

What's There to Do?
adapted from *101 Outdoor Adventures* by Samantha Beres

Grace and her friends built a time machine. Here are some other activities you can do with friends on a summer day.

Help a Neighbor

Any time is a good time to give a gift. This gift can't be wrapped with paper and ribbon—it's a gift of time.

If you have a neighbor whom you know and who could use your help, organize a squad of friends to lend a helping hand. If your neighbor has a yard, you might cut the grass, pull weeds, or even help plant flowers or vegetables. If your neighbor doesn't have a yard, offer to clean windows, wash the car, help get groceries, run an errand, or paint something. If your neighbor tries to pay you, don't accept. After all, you don't pay someone who gives you

Put On an Arts-and-Crafts Show

If you have some artistic friends and relatives, you can have your own arts-and-crafts show.

Decide where to have the show—outside on the sidewalk, in your front yard, or in a park. If you have a show in a public place, ask permission.

To prepare, ask friends and family if they would like to display their art in public. Make a list of things they would like to enter and ask them to have their items ready by the date of the show. Also ask them to label each piece with their name, a phone number, and a price, in case someone wants to buy it.

Before the show, figure out what you'll need to set up. You will need a table and maybe a clothing rack, if you have handmade clothes, quilts, or blankets to sell. A child's easel

or a clothesline and clothespins are a good way to show off pictures.

Send out announcements (e-mail messages would work) or put up posters to advertise the show. Here's a list of arts and crafts you might try to include: drawings, paintings, photographs, sculptures, pottery, quilts, handmade jewelry, and knitted and crocheted items.

Reading Across Texts
Grace and her friends showed that they were creative. Which of the two activities in this selection do you think they would have enjoyed more?

Writing Across Texts
Write about why you think as you do.

210

◉ **Answer Questions** Use prior knowledge to answer questions about this text.

Student Edition pages 210–211

Audio CD

Read It
ONLINE
PearsonSuccessNet.com
• Student Edition
• Leveled Readers

Leveled Readers

⊙ **Skill** Draw Conclusions

⊙ **Strategy** Answer Questions

Lesson Vocabulary

Below-Level

On-Level

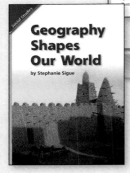

Advanced

ELL Reader
· Concept Vocabulary
· Text Support
· Language Enrichment

Integrate Social Studies Standards

• Literature
• Geography

✓ Read

Grace and the Time Machine, pp. 192–207

"What's There to Do?"
pp. 210–211

Leveled Readers

  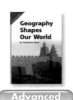

Below-Level · Support Concepts

On-Level · Develop Concepts

Advanced · Extend Concepts

ELL Reader

✓ Build Concept Vocabulary

Imagination, pp. 188l–188m

✓ Teach Social Studies Concepts

Time Travel, p. 199
The Gambia, p. 203
Trinidad, p. 205

✓ Explore Social Studies Center

Travel the World, p. 188k

Weekly Plan

READING

45–90 minutes

TARGET SKILLS OF THE WEEK

- **Comprehension Skill**
  Draw Conclusions
- **Comprehension Strategy**
  Answer Questions
- **Vocabulary Strategy**
  Word Structure

LANGUAGE ARTS

30–60 minutes

Trait of the Week

Organization/Paragraphs

DAY 1
PAGES 188l–190b, 211a, 211e–211k

Oral Language

QUESTION OF THE WEEK *What can we accomplish by using our imaginations?*

Read Aloud: "Journal of a Teenage Genius," 188m
Build Concepts, 188l

Comprehension/Vocabulary

Comprehension Skill/Strategy Lesson, 188–189
- Draw Conclusions **T**
- Answer Questions

Build Background, 190a

Introduce Lesson Vocabulary, 190b
aboard, atlas, awkward, capable, chant, mechanical, miracle, reseats, vehicle **T**

Read Leveled Readers

Grouping Options 188f–188g

Fluency

Model Characterization/Dialogue, 188l–188m, 211a

Grammar, 211e
Introduce Irregular Plural Nouns **T**

Writing Workshop, 211g
Introduce Play Scene

Model the Trait of the Week: Organization/Paragraphs

Spelling, 211i
Pretest for Words with *ar, or*

Internet Inquiry, 211k
Identify Questions

Day 1 Write to Read, 188

Day 1 Imagination Concept Web, 188l

DAY 2
PAGES 190–201, 211a, 211e–211k

Oral Language

QUESTION OF THE DAY *What happens when Grace and her friends use their imaginations?*

Comprehension/Vocabulary

Vocabulary Strategy Lesson, 190–191
- Word Structure **T**

Read *Grace and the Time Machine,* 192–201

Grouping Options 188f–188g

- Draw Conclusions **T**
- Answer Questions
- Word Structure **T**
- **REVIEW** Compare and Contrast **T**

Develop Vocabulary

Fluency

Echo Reading, 211a

Grammar, 211e
Develop Irregular Plural Nouns **T**

Writing Workshop, 211g
Improve Writing with Visual Details

Spelling, 211i
Teach the Generalization

Internet Inquiry, 211k
Navigate/Search

Day 2 Words to Write, 191
Strategy Response Log, 192, 201

Day 2 Time for Social Studies: Travel the World, 188k
Time for Science: Time Travel, 199
Revisit the Imagination Concept Web, 201

DAILY WRITING ACTIVITIES

DAILY SOCIAL STUDIES CONNECTIONS

DAILY SUCCESS PREDICTORS
for Adequate Yearly Progress

Monitor Progress and Corrective Feedback

Vocabulary   Check Vocabulary, *188l*

RESOURCES FOR THE WEEK

- Practice Book, *pp. 71–80*
- Word Study and Spelling Practice Book, *pp. 29–32*
- Grammar and Writing Practice Book, *pp. 29–32*
- Selection Test, *pp. 29–32*
- Fresh Reads for Differentiated Test Practice, *pp. 43–48*
- The Grammar and Writing Book, *pp. 92–97*

Grouping Options for Differentiated Instruction

Turn the page for the small group lesson plan.

DAY 3 PAGES 202–209, 211a, 211e–211k

Oral Language

QUESTION OF THE DAY *How did using her imagination affect Mrs. Myerson?*

Comprehension/Vocabulary

Read *Grace and the Time Machine,* 202–208

Grouping Options 188f–188g

- Draw Conclusions **T**
- Answer Questions
  Develop Vocabulary

Reader Response
Selection Test

Fluency

Model Characterization/Dialogue, 211a

Grammar, 211f
Apply Irregular Plural Nouns in Writing **T**

Writing Workshop, 209, 211h
Write Now
Prewrite and Draft

Spelling, 211j
Connect Spelling to Writing

Internet Inquiry, 211k
Analyze Sources

Day 3 Strategy Response Log, 206
Look Back and Write, 208

Day 3 Time for Social Studies: The Gambia, 203; Trinidad, 205
Revisit the Imagination Concept Web, 207

DAY 4 PAGES 210–211a, 211e–211k

Oral Language

QUESTION OF THE DAY *When would it be valuable for you to use your imagination?*

Comprehension/Vocabulary

Read *"What's There to Do?"* 210–211

Grouping Options 188f –188g

Expository Nonfiction/
Text Features

Reading Across Texts

Content-Area Vocabulary

Fluency

Partner Reading, 211a

Grammar, 211f
Practice Irregular Plural Nouns for Standardized Tests **T**

Writing Workshop, 211h
Draft, Revise, and Publish

Spelling, 211j
Provide a Strategy

Internet Inquiry, 211k
Synthesize Information

Day 4 Writing Across Texts, 211

Day 4 Time for Social Studies: Travel the World, 188k

DAY 5 PAGES 211a–211l

Oral Language

QUESTION OF THE WEEK *To wrap up the week, revisit the Day 1 question.*
Build Concept Vocabulary, 211c

Fluency

Read Leveled Readers

Grouping Options 188f–188g

Assess Reading Rate, 211a

Comprehension/Vocabulary

- Reteach Draw Conclusions, 211b **T**
Flashback, 211b
- Review Word Structure, 211c **T**

Speaking and Viewing, 211d
Dramatization
Analyze Media

Grammar, 211f
Cumulative Review

Writing Workshop, 211h
Connect to Unit Writing

Spelling, 211j
Posttest for Words with *ar, or*

Internet Inquiry, 211k
Communicate Results

Research/Study Skills, 211l
Advertisement

Day 5 Flashback, 211b

Day 5 Revisit the Imagination Concept Web, 211c

KEY ◉ = Target Skill **T** = Tested Skill

Comprehension	Check Retelling, *208*
Fluency	Check Fluency WCPM, *211a*
Vocabulary	Check Vocabulary, *211c*

SUCCESS PREDICTOR

Small Group Plan *for Differentiated Instruction*

Daily Plan
AT A GLANCE

Reading
Whole Group
- Oral Language
- Comprehension/Vocabulary

Group Time
Differentiated Instruction

Meet with small groups to provide:
- Skill Support
- Reading Support
- Fluency Practice

Read

This week's lessons for daily group time can be found behind the Differentiated Instruction (DI) tab on pp. DI·22–DI·31.

Whole Group
- Fluency

Language Arts
- Grammar
- Writing
- Spelling
- Research/Inquiry
- Speaking/Listening/Viewing

Use *My Sidewalks on Reading Street* for Tier III intensive reading intervention.

DAY 1

On-Level
Teacher-Led
Page DI·23
- Develop Concept Vocabulary
- **Read** On-Level Reader *To Market, To Market*

Strategic Intervention
Teacher-Led
Page DI·22
- Reinforce Concepts
- **Read** Below-Level Reader *A World Tour of Cultures*

Advanced
Teacher-Led
Page DI·23
- **Read** Advanced Reader *Geography Shapes Our World*
- Independent Extension Activity

(*i*) Independent Activities
While you meet with small groups, have the rest of the class...

- Visit the Reading/Library Center
- Listen to the Background Building Audio
- Finish Write to Read, p. 188
- Complete Practice Book pp. 73–74
- Visit Cross-Curricular Centers

DAY 2

On-Level
Teacher-Led
Pages 194–201
- **Read** *Grace and the Time Machine*

Strategic Intervention
Teacher-Led
Page DI·24
- Practice Lesson Vocabulary
- Read Multisyllabic Words
- **Read** or Listen to *Grace and the Time Machine*

Advanced
Teacher-Led
Page DI·25
- Extend Vocabulary
- **Read** *Grace and the Time Machine*

(*i*) Independent Activities
While you meet with small groups, have the rest of the class...

- Visit the Reading/Library Center
- Listen to the AudioText for *Grace and the Time Machine*
- Finish Words to Write, p. 191
- Complete Practice Book pp. 75–76
- Write in their Strategy Response Logs, pp. 192, 201
- Visit Cross-Curricular Centers
- Work on inquiry projects

DAY 3

On-Level
Teacher-Led
Pages 202–207
- **Read** *Grace and the Time Machine*

Strategic Intervention
Teacher-Led
Page DI·26
- Practice Draw Conclusions and Answer Questions
- **Read** or Listen to *Grace and the Time Machine*

Advanced
Teacher-Led
Page DI·27
- Extend Draw Conclusions and Answer Questions
- **Read** *Grace and the Time Machine*

(*i*) Independent Activities
While you meet with small groups, have the rest of the class...

- Visit the Reading/Library Center
- Listen to the AudioText for *Grace and the Time Machine*
- Write in their Strategy Response Logs, p. 206
- Finish Look Back and Write, p. 208
- Complete Practice Book p. 77
- Visit Cross-Curricular Centers
- Work on inquiry projects

① Begin with whole class skill and strategy instruction.

② Meet with small groups to provide differentiated instruction.

③ Gather the whole class back together for fluency and language arts.

DAY 4

On-Level	Strategic Intervention	Advanced
Teacher-Led *Pages 210–211*	**Teacher-Led** *Page DI · 28*	**Teacher-Led** *Page DI · 29*
• **Read** "What's There to Do?"	• Practice Retelling • **Read** or Listen to "What's There to Do?"	• **Read** "What's There to Do?" • Genre Study

ⓘ Independent Activities

While you meet with small groups, have the rest of the class...

- Visit the Reading/Library Center
- Listen to the AudioText for "What's There to Do?"
- Visit the Writing/Vocabulary Center
- Finish Writing Across Texts, p. 211
- Visit Cross-Curricular Centers
- Work on inquiry projects

DAY 5

On-Level	Strategic Intervention	Advanced
Teacher-Led *Page DI · 31*	**Teacher-Led** *Page DI · 30*	**Teacher-Led** *Page DI · 31*
• **Reread** Leveled Reader *To Market, To Market* • Retell *To Market, To Market*	• **Reread** Leveled Reader *A World Tour of Cultures* • Retell *A World Tour of Cultures*	• **Reread** Leveled Reader *Geography Shapes Our World* • Share Extension Activity

ⓘ Independent Activities

While you meet with small groups, have the rest of the class...

- Visit the Reading/Library Center
- Complete Practice Book pp. 78–80
- Visit Cross-Curricular Centers
- Work on inquiry projects

Grouping Place English language learners in the groups that correspond to their reading abilities in English.

Use the appropriate Leveled Reader or other text at students' instructional level.

TiP Send home the appropriate Multilingual Summary of the main selection on Day 1.

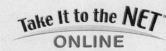

Take It to the NET ONLINE
PearsonSuccessNet.com

Karen Wixson
For ideas on teaching reading strategies, see the article "Becoming a Strategic Reader" by S. G. Paris, M. Y. Lipson, and Scott Foresman author Karen Wixson.

TEACHER TALK

Repeated reading is a method for building fluency in which a student reads a short passage repeatedly until reaching a predetermined level of fluency.

Looking Ahead

Be sure to schedule time for students to work on the unit inquiry project "All in a Day's Work." This week students analyze the information they have found from Web sites or print materials.

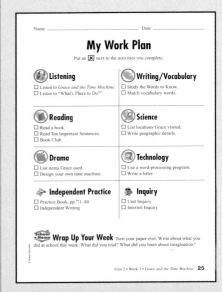

▲ **Group-Time Survival Guide** p. 25, Weekly Contract

☑ Customize Your Plan *by Strand*

ORAL LANGUAGE

SOCIAL STUDIES

Concept Development

What can we accomplish by using our imaginations?

CONCEPT VOCABULARY
excursion   invention   research

BUILD

❑ **Question of the Week** Introduce and discuss the question of the week. This week students will read a variety of texts and work on projects related to the concept *imagination*. Post the question for students to refer to throughout the week. **DAY 1** *188d*

❑ **Read Aloud** Read aloud "Journal of a Teenage Genius." Then begin a web to build concepts and concept vocabulary related to this week's lesson and the unit theme, Work and Play. Introduce the concept words *excursion, invention,* and *research* and have students place them on the web. Display the web for use throughout the week. **DAY 1** *188l-188m*

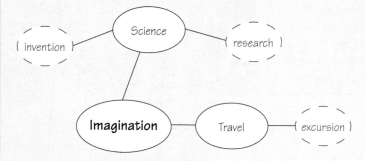

DEVELOP

❑ **Question of the Day** Use the prompts from the Weekly Plan to engage students in conversations related to this week's reading and the unit theme. **EVERY DAY** *188d-188e*

❑ **Concept Vocabulary Web** Revisit the Imagination Concept Web and encourage students to add concept words from their reading and life experiences. **DAY 2** *201,* **DAY 3** *207*

CONNECT

❑ **Looking Back/Moving Forward** Revisit the Imagination Concept Web and discuss how it relates to this week's lesson and the unit theme. Then make connections to next week's lesson. **DAY 5** *211c*

CHECK

❑ **Concept Vocabulary Web** Use the Imagination Concept Web to check students' understanding of the concept vocabulary words *excursion, invention,* and *research.* **DAY 1** *188l,* **DAY 5** *211c*

VOCABULARY

🔊 **STRATEGY WORD STRUCTURE**
When you are reading and see an unfamiliar word, look to see if it has a prefix at the beginning. The meaning of the prefix will help you understand the meaning of the word.

LESSON VOCABULARY

aboard	mechanical
atlas	miracle
awkward	reseats
capable	vehicle
chant	

TEACH

❑ **Words to Know** Give students the opportunity to tell what they already know about this week's lesson vocabulary words. Then discuss word meaning. **DAY 1** *190b*

❑ **Vocabulary Strategy Lesson** Use the vocabulary strategy lesson in the Student Edition to introduce and model this week's strategy, *word structure.* **DAY 2** *190-191*

Vocabulary Strategy Lesson

PRACTICE/APPLY

❑ **Leveled Text** Read the lesson vocabulary in the context of leveled text **DAY 1** *LR19-LR27*

❑ **Words in Context** Read the lesson vocabulary and apply *word structure* in the context of *Grace and the Time Machine.* **DAY 2** *192-201,* **DAY 3** *202-208*

Leveled Readers

❑ **Writing/Vocabulary Center** Match vocabulary words to definitions. **ANY DAY** *188k*

Main Selection—Drama

❑ **Homework** Practice Book pp. 74–75. **DAY 1** *190b,* **DAY 2** *191*

❑ **Word Play** Have students research *Atlas* and other figures from Greek and Roman mythology. **ANY DAY** *211c*

ASSESS

❑ **Selection Test** Use the Selection Test to determine students' understanding of the lesson vocabulary words. **DAY 3**

RETEACH/REVIEW

❑ **Reteach Lesson** If necessary, use this lesson to reteach and review *word structure.* **DAY 5** *211c*

COMPREHENSION

◉ SKILL DRAW CONCLUSIONS Drawing conclusions is forming an opinion based on what you already know or on the facts and details in the text.

◉ STRATEGY ANSWER QUESTIONS Answering questions can help support conclusions drawn during reading. Answers to the questions may be in the text, but often students will need to combine details from the text with their prior knowledge to draw conclusions.

TEACH

☐ **Skill/Strategy Lesson** Use the skill/strategy lesson in the Student Edition to introduce and model *draw conclusions* and *answer questions.* **DAY 1** *188-189*

Skill/Strategy Lesson

☐ **Extend Skills** Teach Flashback. **ANY DAY** *211b*

PRACTICE/APPLY

☐ **Leveled Text** Apply *draw conclusions* and *answer questions* to read leveled text. **DAY 1** *LR19-LR27*

Leveled Readers

☐ **Skills and Strategies in Context** Read *Grace and the Time Machine,* using the Guiding Comprehension questions to apply *draw conclusions* and *answer questions.* **DAY 2** *192-201,* **DAY 3** *202-208*

Main Selection—Drama

☐ **Skills and Strategies in Context** Read "What's There to Do?" guiding students as they apply *draw conclusions* and *answer questions.* Then have students discuss and write across texts. **DAY 4** *210-211*

Paired Selection—Nonfiction

☐ **Homework** Practice Book pp. 73, 77, 78. **DAY 1** *189,* **DAY 3** *207,* **DAY 5** *211b*

☐ **Fresh Reads for Differentiated Test Practice** Have students practice *draw conclusions* with a new passage. **DAY 3**

ASSESS

☐ **Selection Test** Determine students' understanding of the selection and their use of *draw conclusions.* **DAY 3**

☐ **Retell** Have students retell *Grace and the Time Machine.* **DAY 3** *208-209*

RETEACH/REVIEW

☐ **Reteach Lesson** If necessary, reteach and review *draw conclusions.* **DAY 5** *211b*

FLUENCY

SKILL CHARACTERIZATION/DIALOGUE Choosing the tone, pitch, or volume of your voice to go with a character makes the dialogue more interesting and like a real-life conversation.

TEACH

☐ **Read Aloud** Model fluent reading by rereading "Journal of a Teenage Genius." Focus on this week's fluency skill, characterization/dialogue. **DAY 1** *188l-188m, 211a*

PRACTICE/APPLY

☐ **Echo Reading** Read aloud selected paragraphs from *Grace and the Time Machine,* emphasizing expression and emotion in the dialogue. Have the class practice by doing echo readings of the selected paragraphs. **DAY 2** *211a,* **DAY 3** *211a*

☐ **Partner Reading** Have partners practice reading with adding expression and emotion. Have partners offer each other feedback. As students reread, monitor their progress toward their individual fluency goals. **DAY 4** *211a*

☐ **Listening Center** Have students follow along with the AudioText for this week's selections. **ANY DAY** *188j*

☐ **Reading/Library Center** Have students reread a selection of their choice. **ANY DAY** *188j*

☐ **Fluency Coach** Have students use Fluency Coach to listen to fluent readings or practice reading on their own. **ANY DAY**

ASSESS

☐ **Check Fluency** WCPM Do a one-minute timed reading, paying special attention to this week's skill—characterization/dialogue. Provide feedback for each student. **DAY 5** *211a*

☑ Customize Your Plan *by Strand*

GRAMMAR

SKILL IRREGULAR PLURAL NOUNS A plural noun names more than one person, place, or thing. Most nouns add *-s* to form the plural. An irregular plural noun has a special form for the plural.

TEACH

☐ **Grammar Transparency 8** Use Grammar Transparency 8 to teach irregular plural nouns. DAY 1 *211e*

Grammar Transparency 8

PRACTICE/APPLY

☐ **Develop the Concept** Review the concept of irregular plural nouns and provide guided practice. **DAY 2** *211e*

☐ **Apply to Writing** Have students review something they have written and apply irregular plural nouns. **DAY 3** *211f*

☐ **Test Preparation** Examine common errors in irregular plural nouns to prepare for standardized tests. **DAY 4** *211f*

☐ **Homework** Grammar and Writing Practice Book pp. 29–31. **DAY 2** *211e*, **DAY 3** *211f*, **DAY 4** *211f*

ASSESS

☐ **Cumulative Review** Use Grammar and Writing Practice Book p. 32. **DAY 5** *211f*

RETEACH/REVIEW

☐ **Daily Fix-It** Have students find and correct errors in grammar, spelling, and punctuation. **EVERY DAY** *211e–211f*

☐ **The Grammar and Writing Book** Use pp. 92–95 of The Grammar and Writing Book to extend instruction for irregular plural nouns. **ANY DAY**

The Grammar and Writing Book

WRITING

Trait of the Week

ORGANIZATION/PARAGRAPHS Good writers organize their writing. They write in an order that will help readers understand what they have to say and show connections among their ideas.

TEACH

☐ **Writing Transparency 8A** Use the model to introduce and discuss the Trait of the Week. **DAY 1** *211g*

☐ **Writing Transparency 8B** Use the transparency to show students how visual details can improve their writing. **DAY 2** *211g*

Writing Transparency 8A **Writing Transparency 8B**

PRACTICE/APPLY

☐ **Write Now** Examine the model on Student Edition p. 209. Then have students write their own play scene. **DAY 3** *209, 211h*, **DAY 4** *211h*

> **Prompt** *Grace and the Time Machine* is a play in one scene. Think about several characters having a conversation. Now write a play scene, including what is said as well as stage directions.

Write Now p. 209

☐ **Writing/Vocabulary Center** Match vocabulary words to definitions. **ANY DAY** *188k*

ASSESS

☐ **Writing Trait Rubric** Use the rubric to evaluate students' writing. **DAY 4** *211h*

RETEACH/REVIEW

☐ **The Grammar and Writing Book** Use pp. 92–97 of The Grammar and Writing Book to extend instruction for irregular plural nouns, visual details, and a play scene. **ANY DAY**

The Grammar and Writing Book

SPELLING

GENERALIZATION WORDS WITH AR, OR   The vowel sound in *arm* is often spelled *ar*: *start*. The vowel sound in *for* is often spelled *or*: *morning*. The vowels *a* and *o* have a slightly different sound when they are followed by *r*. Vowels followed by *r* are called r-controlled vowels.

TEACH

☐ **Pretest** Give the pretest for words with *ar* and *or*. Guide students in self-correcting their pretests and correcting any misspellings. **DAY 1** *211i*

☐ **Think and Practice** Connect spelling to the phonics generalization for adding *ar* and *or*.   **DAY 2** *211i*

PRACTICE/APPLY

☐ **Connect to Writing** Have students use spelling words to write a short dialogue between two characters. Then review frequently misspelled words: *favorite, morning*.   **DAY 3** *211j*

☐ **Homework** Word Study and Spelling Practice Book pp. 29–32. **EVERY DAY**

RETEACH/REVIEW

☐ **Review** Review spelling words to prepare for the posttest. Then provide students with a spelling strategy—pronouncing for spelling.   **DAY 4** *211j*

ASSESS

☐ **Posttest** Use dictation sentences to give the posttest for words with *ar* and *or*.   **DAY 5** *211j*

Spelling Words

1. morning*	8. argue	15. sport
2. forest	9. backyard	16. force
3. garbage	10. start*	17. forward*
4. form	11. partner	18. sharp*
5. alarm	12. storm	19. garden*
6. corner	13. Florida	20. Arkansas
7. story	14. apartment	

Challenge Words

21. departure	23. informative	25. carnation
22. margarine	24. snorkel	

*Word from the selection

RESEARCH AND INQUIRY

☐ **Internet Inquiry** Have students conduct an Internet inquiry on the power of using our imaginations.   **EVERY DAY** *211k*

☐ **Advertisement** Review what an advertisement is and its purpose. Have students look through newspapers and magazines to identify advertisements and what product or service they are trying to sell. **DAY 5** *211l*

☐ **Unit Inquiry** Allow time for students to analyze the information they found from the Web sites or printed materials.   **ANY DAY** *141*

SPEAKING AND VIEWING

☐ **Dramatization** Have students work in groups to improvise a short scene from *Grace and the Time Machine*.   **DAY 5** *211d*

☐ **Analyze Media** Have students view a short scene from a recorded stage play or improvisation and follow up with a class discussion. **DAY 5** *211d*

Resources for Differentiated Instruction

LEVELED READERS

► **Comprehension**
  ⊙ **Skill** Draw Conclusions
  ⊙ **Strategy** Answer Questions

► **Lesson Vocabulary**
  ⊙ Word Structure

aboard · atlas · awkward · capable · chant · mechanical · reseats · miracle · vehicle

► **Social Studies Standards**
  • Literature
  • Geography

Leveled Reader Database ONLINE

PearsonSuccessNet.com

Use the Online Database of over 600 books to

• Download and print additional copies of this week's leveled readers.

• Listen to the readers being read online.

• Search for more titles focused on this week's skills, topic, and content.

On-Level Reader

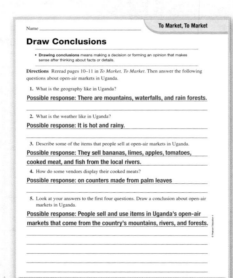

To Market, To Market
by Marianne Lenihan
illustrated by Reggie Holladay

On-Level Reader

Name _____ To Market, To Market

Draw Conclusions

• **Drawing conclusions** means making a decision or forming an opinion that makes sense after thinking about facts or details.

Directions Reread pages 10–11 in *To Market, To Market*. Then answer the following questions about open-air markets in Uganda.

1. What is the geography like in Uganda?
Possible response: There are mountains, waterfalls, and rain forests.

2. What is the weather like in Uganda?
Possible response: It is hot and rainy.

3. Describe some of the items that people sell at open-air markets in Uganda.
Possible response: They sell bananas, limes, apples, tomatoes, cooked meat, and fish from the local rivers.

4. How do some vendors display their cooked meats?
Possible response: on counters made from palm leaves

5. Look at your answers to the first four questions. Draw a conclusion about open-air markets in Uganda.
Possible response: People sell and use items in Uganda's open-air markets that come from the country's mountains, rivers, and forests.

⊙ **On-Level Practice** TE p. LR23

Name _____ To Market, To Market

Vocabulary

Directions Use each of the following words in a sentence about open-air markets.

Check the Words You Know		
__aboard	__atlas	__awkward
__capable	__chant	__mechanical
__miracle	__reseats	__vehicle

Possible responses given.

1. capable
Sentences will vary.

2. awkward

3. chant

4. vehicle

5. mechanical

6. atlas

7. miracle

Directions Use your knowledge of prefixes to answer the following questions.
Possible responses given.

8. The word *ashore* means "on the shore or on land." What does the prefix *a-* mean? Use your understanding of this prefix to define the word *aboard*.
"on" or "in"; on a ship, airplane, or train

9. The word *rejoins* means "gets together again." What does the prefix *re-* mean? Use your understanding of this prefix to define the word *reseats*.
again; takes a seat again

10. Use either *aboard* or *reseats* in a sentence.
Sentences will vary.

On-Level Practice TE p. LR24

Below-Level Reader

Social Studies
A World Tour of Cultures
by Sharon Franklin

Below-Level Reader

Name _____ A World Tour of Cultures

Draw Conclusions

• To **draw a conclusion** means to make a decision or form an opinion that makes sense after you think about facts or details.

Directions Read the following passage. Complete the chart by listing facts from the passage. Then draw a conclusion by making a decision that makes sense about the facts. **Possible responses given.**

Paper was invented in China about A.D. 105. At first, it was made from bamboo, hemp, or mulberry plants. Only the rich could afford it. It took another 800 years before all Chinese could afford paper.	Paper is an important part of Chinese culture. During the spring New Year Festival in central China, people hang red paper cuttings to decorate their homes. This is thought to bring good luck.

1. Fact: **Paper was invented in China about A.D. 105.**

2. Fact: **At first, paper was made from bamboo, hemp, or mulberry plants, and only the rich could afford it.**

3. Fact: **People hang red paper cuttings for good luck during the New Year Festival in central China.**

↓

4. Conclusion: In the Chinese culture, **paper has been important for many years.**

Directions Answer the following question about the passage.
5. Why do you think some Chinese people think that paper brings good luck?
Answers will vary.

⊙ **Below-Level Practice** TE p. LR20

Name _____ A World Tour of Cultures

Vocabulary

Directions Choose the word from the box that best completes each sentence. Write the word on the line.

Check the Words You Know				
__aboard	__atlas	__awkward	__capable	__chanted
__mechanical	__miracle	__reseats	__vehicle	

1. The hat perched on her head at an **awkward** angle.

2. I used an **atlas** to find the country of Niger on the continent of Africa.

3. The people danced and **chanted** to celebrate the new year.

4. A tractor is an important **vehicle** to a farmer.

5. It was a **miracle** that the falling rocks did not land on the house at the bottom of the cliff.

6. Some people in India use elephants for difficult jobs because they are **capable** of pushing and pulling heavy objects.

7. The travelers **aboard** the ship were excited about sailing to a new land.

8. **Mechanical** tools have replaced hand-operated tools in many industries around the world.

Directions The word *reseat* means "to sit back down again." Think about the meaning of the prefix *re-* and use it to define the following words.

9. revisit **Possible response: to visit something again**

10. rebuild **Possible response: to build something again**

Below-Level Practice TE p. LR21

Advanced

Social Studies

Geography Shapes Our World

by Stephanie Sigue

Advanced Reader

Name _____ **Geography Shapes World**

Draw Conclusions

- To **draw a conclusion** means to make a decision or form an opinion that makes sense after you think about facts and details.

Directions Complete the following table with facts or details about each place from the selection *Geography Shapes Our World.* Use them to draw a conclusion about each culture.

Possible responses given.

Facts About the Geography of Mali	Conclusion About the Culture of Mali
1. The Niger River flows through villages.	3. People eat fish from the river.
2. There are fish in the river.	

Facts About the Geography of Brazil	Conclusion About the Culture of Brazil
4. There are beaches.	6. People use the water for vacations and food such as fish.
5. People hunt and fish along the Amazon River.	

Facts About the Geography of Jamaica	Conclusion About the Culture of Jamaica
7. There are colorful flowers and a bright blue sky.	9. Jamaica's music, reggae, is loud and bright.
8. The land inspires their music.	

10. Draw a conclusion about how geography can affect the culture of a people.
Geography can affect what types of food people eat in a culture.

Advanced Practice TE p. LR26

Name _____ **Geography Shapes World**

Vocabulary

Directions Write the word from the box that is a synonym or near synonym for each of the following words.

Check the Words You Know

climate	continents	geography
industry	irrigate	native
plantation	products	typhoons

1. business   industry
2. goods   products
3. weather   climate
4. farm   plantation
5. storms   typhoons

Directions Write a definition for each of the following words. Possible responses given.

6. continents   seven large landmasses of Earth

7. geography   the study of Earth, its people, resources, climate, and physical features

8. irrigate   to supply water to crops by artificial means

9. native   a person, an animal, or a plant that originally lived or grew in a certain place

10. products   things that are manufactured or made by a natural process

11. typhoons   violent storms occurring in the western Pacific Ocean

12. climate   the kind of weather a place has over time

Advanced Practice TE p. LR27

ELL

Social Studies

Hello, Good-bye, and Other Customs

by Anthony James

ELL Reader

ELL Poster 8

Teacher's Edition Notes

ELL notes throughout this lesson support instruction and reference additional resources at point of use.

Teaching Guide pp. 50–56, 226–227

- Multilingual summaries of the main selection
- Comprehension lesson
- Vocabulary strategies and word cards
- ELL Reader 4.2.3 lesson

ELL and Transition Handbook

Ten Important Sentences

- Key ideas from every selection in the Student Edition
- Activities to build sentence power

More Reading

Readers' Theater Anthology

- Fluency practice
- Five scripts to build fluency
- Poetry for oral interpretation

Leveled Trade Books

Below-Level

Advanced

On-Level

- Extended reading tied to the unit concept
- Lessons in the Trade Book Library Teaching Guide

School + Home

Homework

- Family Times Newsletter
- ELL Multilingual Selection Summaries

Take-Home Books

- Leveled Readers

Family Times

Cross-Curricular Centers

Listening

Listen to the Selections

MATERIALS SINGLES
CD player, headphones,
AudioText CD, student book

LISTEN TO LITERATURE Listen to *Grace and the Time Machine* and "What's There to Do?" as you follow or read along in your book. Listen to draw conclusions about *Grace and the Time Machine*.

If there is anything you don't understand, you can listen again to any section.

Reading/Library

Read It Again!

MATERIALS SINGLES PAIRS GROUPS
Collection of books for self-selected reading, reading logs, student book

Select a book you have already read. Record the title of the book in your reading log. You may want to read with a partner.

Choose from the following:

- **Leveled Readers**
- **ELL Readers**
- **Books or Stories Written by Classmates**
- **Books from the Library**
- *Grace and the Time Machine*

TEN IMPORTANT SENTENCES Read the Ten Important Sentences for *Grace and the Time Machine*. Then locate the sentences in the student book.

BOOK CLUB Read books about inventors and their inventions. Brainstorm with a group about things you would like to invent.

Classroom Library

Drama

Design a Time Machine

MATERIALS SINGLES PAIRS GROUPS
Writing and art materials, student book

Draw your own design for the time machine.

1. Imagine you can travel like Grace and her friends. Look at p. 197 in your student book to find details about the time machine.
2. Make a list of items Grace and her friends use to build the time machine.
3. Design your own time machine from items around your house or neighborhood. Then draw your own design for the time machine. Be sure to include all the items on your list.

EARLY FINISHERS Choose a time or place to visit and list souvenirs of that time or place on your picture. *Drama*

beach umbrella
kitchen timer
alarm clocks and radio dials
atlas hanging from string
bike
pinwheels
rake

Writing/ Vocabulary

Match-Up Vocabulary

MATERIALS   `PAIRS`
Writing materials, index cards

Match vocabulary words to definitions.

1. **Look at the Words to Know on p. 190 in the student book. Write each word on an index card.**
2. **On another set of index cards, write the meaning for each word.**
3. **Mix up all the cards and spread them face down on a table.**
4. **Take turns selecting two cards. If you match a word to its meaning, keep the pair. If the cards don't match, put them back face down.**
5. **Keep playing until you've matched all words to their meanings.**

EARLY FINISHERS Replace the definitions with synonyms, antonyms, or pictures. Play the game again.

vehicle

a device used for carrying people or things.

 Social Studies

Travel the World

MATERIALS   `GROUPS`
World map, writing and art materials, student book, travel catalog

Use a world map to find out more about the real-life places Grace and her friends visit in their time machine.

1. **Review the play and make a list of the specific locations Grace and her friends visit in West Africa, the West Indies, and Germany.**
2. **Find each place on a world map.**
3. **Write interesting geographic details about each place. For example, tell if it is in the mountains or near a desert.**

EARLY FINISHERS Use the catalog and details from the story and the map to make a list of items you would need if you traveled to one of the locations. Illustrate and describe the needed items.

Places Visited– Geographical Details
1. The Gambia–It's surrounded on 3 sides by Senegal.
2. Trinidad–It's a very small island.
3. Heidelberg–It's a city in southern Germany.

 Technology

Write a Letter

MATERIALS   `SINGLES`
Word processing program, printer, art materials

Imagine you have traveled to the future in a time machine. Write a letter to a friend describing your trip.

1. **Open a word processing program on your computer.**
2. **Explain in your letter what year you are visiting and describe some things you think you might see or do in the future.**
3. **Proofread your letter before printing it out. Follow classroom rules for printing.**

EARLY FINISHERS Draw a picture and write a paragraph describing how people will send messages in the future.

1 Sky Tower, 300th FL
City of the Future, TN 37700
November 2, 2027

Dear Tim,
    I just traveled into the future on a time machine! In 2027, people drive cars that fly through the sky! I played a game of basketball using shoes that let me jump 20 feet high.

ALL CENTERS 🕐

Build Concepts

Concept Vocabulary

excursion a short trip taken for interest or pleasure

invention something made for the first time

research hunting for facts or truth

Monitor Progress

Check Vocabulary

If...	then... review the
students are unable to place words on the web,	lesson concept. Place the words on the web and provide additional words for practice, such as *genius* and *fictional*.

SUCCESS PREDICTOR

DAY 1 Grouping Options

Reading

Whole Group
Introduce and discuss the Question of the Week. Then use pp. 188l–190b.

Group Time
Differentiated Instruction
Read this week's Leveled Readers. See pp. 188f–188g for the small group lesson plan.

Whole Group
Use p. 211a.

Language Arts
Use pp. 211e–211k.

FLUENCY

MODEL CHARACTERIZATION/DIALOGUE As you read "Journal of a Teenage Genius," model using your voice to express each character's personality and making the dialogue sound like a real-life conversation.

LISTENING COMPREHENSION

After reading "Journal of a Teenage Genius," use the following questions to assess listening comprehension.

1. **What do the characters' reactions about the time machine tell you about them?** *(Possible response: The narrator focuses on what the machine can do and is more impulsive than Loretta. Loretta focuses on the machine's limitations and is more practical than the narrator.)* **Draw Conclusions**

2. **Could the narrator have invented the time machine? How do you know?** *(No, because the narrator doesn't know exactly how the machine works or its origins.)* **Draw Conclusions**

BUILD CONCEPT VOCABULARY

Start a web to build concepts and vocabulary related to this week's lesson and the unit theme.

- Draw the Imagination Concept Web.
- Read the sentence with the word *invention* again. Ask students to pronounce *invention* and discuss its meaning.
- Place *invention* in an oval attached to *Science*. Discuss how *invention* is related to this concept. Read the sentences in which *research* and *excursion* appear. Have students pronounce the words, place them on the Web, and provide reasons.
- Brainstorm additional words and categories for the Web. Keep the Web on display and add words throughout the week.

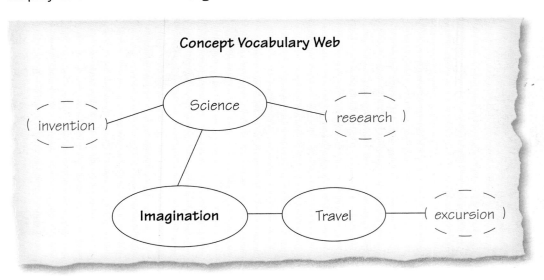

Concept Vocabulary Web

Journal of a Teenage Genius

by Helen V. Griffith

Friday, September 30
11:00 P.M.

I've done it, I think. Sorry not to keep you up-to-date on a daily basis, avid readers, but thinking and experimenting has taken every available minute, except for a few short breaks to eat, sleep, and feed the mice.

My schoolwork has suffered, but now that I'm finished with my time machine work, I can easily catch up with (and surpass) the class. Just one of the advantages of being a genius.

A week of intensive lunch periods (the only time I've been able to talk to Loretta) has given me a somewhat better understanding of the capabilities of the time machine, although getting information from Loretta is like pulling teeth.

She's so used to having a time machine around the house, she sees it in the same light as a dishwasher.

I tried to wake her up. "Aside from some of my own work, it's the most remarkable invention I've ever seen," I told her, and she said, "It has its limitations."

I know I expressed some slight criticism myself, fellow scientists, but the fact remains that this is not an achievement to be taken lightly.

"It sends you through time," I reminded her, "and you complain of limitations."

"What do you call this?" she asked. "When you go on a trip, you land exactly where you leave from. That means if you leave from this room, you land in the same place in the same room, or if you want to go back to the days before the house was built, you'll land in a swamp or an Indian camp or a dinosaur wallow—whatever was in this spot at the time you go back to."

"A little research before the trip would protect the traveler from surprises," I said.

"A lot of research," she said. "You can't just jump in and push buttons."

Was this an allusion to my unexpected excursion to her Aunt Maggie's?

"I did not jump in and push buttons," I said stiffly, but she was already making her next point.

"And not being able to dial a particular day is very inconvenient," she complained.

I suppose she's right. Marvelous as the machine is, it does have limitations.

My biggest surprise was finding that the machine goes back in time only—not forward. I found it hard to absorb this new concept into my understanding of the vehicle—all the time machines I've ever known have gone either way. Of course, all the time machines I've ever known have been fictional. When I commented, Loretta said, "They felt no good could come of visiting the future."

Loretta obviously knows more about the origin of the machine than she admits. Why won't she tell me?

Activate Prior Knowledge

Before students listen to the Read Aloud, have them share stories, TV shows, or movies they know involving time machines.

Set Purpose

Read aloud the title and have students predict what the selection will be about.

Have students listen to draw conclusions about the two main characters and their thoughts about a time machine invention.

Creative Response

Have students imagine they are directing a play of "Journal of a Teenage Genius." Have them draw a picture of the narrator and list acting notes telling how the person playing the narrator would talk, move, and dress. Students can present their drawings and ideas to the class. **Drama**

Access Content Before reading, share this summary: A teenager writes a journal entry describing a time machine and telling what a friend thinks about it.

Homework Send home this week's Family Times newsletter.

SKILLS ⟷ STRATEGIES IN CONTEXT

Draw Conclusions
Answer Questions

OBJECTIVES

⦿ Draw conclusions about what happens in a story.

⦿ Answer questions about conclusions with facts and details.

Skills Trace
⦿ Draw Conclusions

Introduce/Teach	TE: 4.2 162–163, 188–189; 4.5 608–609
Practice	TE: 169, 179, 181, 195, 203, 205, 615, 619 PB: 63, 67, 68, 73, 77, 78, 243, 247, 248
Reteach/Review	TE: 4.2 153, 187b, 211b, DI·53, DI·54; 4.5 569, 591, 629b, DI·56 PB: 56, 226, 236
Test	Selection Test: 25–28, 29–32, 97–100; Benchmark Test: Units 2, 5

INTRODUCE

Ask students where they would think a fire truck was going if it raced past with its siren howling. Have them explain their reasoning. *(The truck was going to a fire. We know fire trucks turn on their sirens and drive quickly when they are going to fires.)* Tell them their response is an example of drawing a conclusion.

Have students read the information on p. 188. Explain the following:

- You draw a conclusion by using facts, details, and logical thinking.
- Answers to questions may be found in the book or in your mind.

Use Skill Transparency 8 to teach draw conclusions and answer questions.

Comprehension

| **Skill** Draw Conclusions |
| **Strategy** Answer Questions |

Draw Conclusions

- Facts and details are the small pieces of information in an article or story.
- Facts and details "add up" to a conclusion— a decision or opinion the author or the reader forms that must make sense.

$$\boxed{\text{Facts and Details}} + \boxed{\text{Facts and Details}} = \boxed{\text{Conclusion}}$$

Strategy: Answer Questions

Good readers can support their conclusions with facts and details. If you are asked questions about conclusions you draw, you should answer them using the facts and details. Some answers are in the text in one place. Others are in the text but in different places. Some answers combine the text with what you already know. Some answers you just know or can find out.

Write to Read

1. Read "Time Traveler." Make a graphic organizer like the one above to record strange details about Peter's experience.

2. Write a paragraph about how you can conclude that Peter went back in time.

188

Strategic Intervention

⦿ **Draw Conclusions** To help students draw conclusions about "Time Traveler," read the story aloud, stopping occasionally to note strange or unusual details. Assist students in recording these details in a graphic organizer like the one shown on p. 188 in the student edition.

ELL

Access Content

Beginning/Intermediate For a Picture It! lesson on drawing conclusions, see the ELL Teaching Guide, pp. 50–51.

Advanced Before reading the story, have students explain the concept of time travel.

Time Traveler

A storm was approaching, but Peter crawled through the strange little hole in the fence anyway. The last thing he expected to see was a man dressed in peculiar clothes holding a kite.

Surprised, Peter yelled, "Are you going to fly that kite? It could be dangerous! It looks like a storm's coming!"

"Why, my boy, I'm conducting an experiment. I'm trying to demonstrate that lightning is electricity. If I'm correct, when lightning strikes the kite, it will travel down the string. I just don't know how to keep it from giving me a shock."

"That's easy!" said Peter. "We learned about electricity in science. You need to redirect the electricity."

"What genius! I'll tie this key to the kite string," said the man.

"Well, it worked for Ben Franklin, didn't it?" said Peter.

The man was astonished. "My boy, how did you come to know my name?"

Before Peter could reply, he heard his mother calling him as if from very, very far away. "I have to go now," he said. Peter scurried back through the hole in the fence. But when he turned around to wish the strange man good luck, the hole had vanished.

1 Skill This story seems to be a fantasy. How might you conclude this?

2 Strategy Who is this strange man? (Hint: Think of the type of story and use your prior knowledge.)

3 Strategy Would Peter's mother believe him if he told her his story? Why or why not? (Hint: Think about the hole and the strangeness of what happened.)

4 Skill What conclusion does this story draw about how Ben Franklin came up with his famous experiment?

189

Available as **Skill Transparency** 8

Draw Conclusions

- **Drawing a conclusion** is forming an opinion based on what you already know or on the facts and details in a text. Facts and details are the small pieces of information in an article or story.
- Facts and details "add up" to a conclusion. Conclusions formed by the author or the reader must make sense.

Directions Read the following passage. Then complete the diagram and answer the question.

> Traveling can teach you many things. It can teach you about land features, such as deserts, mountains, and mesas, and the differences between them. Traveling can teach you about a new climate, whether it's hot and humid or cold and windy, and how the people deal with the climate from day to day.
>
> Visiting a new city or country also can tell you much about the people who live there. You can hear the language they speak, eat the foods they eat, dress in the clothes they dress in, and appreciate the art they make.

Possible answers given.

Fact or Detail 1. Traveling can teach you about land features.	Fact or Detail 2. Traveling can teach you about climate.	Fact or Detail 3. Traveling can teach you about people.	Conclusion 4. You can learn about the world's land and people by traveling.
+	+	=	

5. What do you think would happen if people did not travel?

People would not know how other people lived and wouldn't be
open to new ideas.

 Home Activity Your child drew a conclusion using facts or details in a passage. Talk to your child about any traveling you have done in your life, such as visiting another city, state, or country. Ask your child to draw a conclusion about your travel experiences.

▲ **Practice Book** p. 73

TEACH

1 SKILL Use the title and illustration to model how to draw a conclusion.

 MODEL I know from the title that the story is about a time traveler. Time travel is not possible, so this story is probably a fantasy. The art shows a boy in modern clothes and a man in colonial clothes. This is another clue that the story may be about time travel, which is fantasy.

2 STRATEGY Model using details and prior knowledge to answer questions.

 MODEL The man sounds familiar. He is flying a kite for an experiment. Is he Ben Franklin? I remember reading that Franklin discovered electricity in an experiment with a kite. Since this is a story about time travel, the boy must be traveling back in time to when Franklin was alive.

PRACTICE AND ASSESS

3 STRATEGY Probably not, because it is unbelievable that a modern boy could have met Ben Franklin.

4 SKILL Peter told him to redirect the electricity, so he tied the key to the string. The story implies that it was Peter's suggestion that led to Franklin's discovery.

WRITE Have students complete steps 1 and 2 of the Write to Read activity. You might consider using this as a whole-class activity.

Monitor Progress

◯ Draw Conclusions

If... students are unable to complete **Write to Read** on p. 188,	**then...** use Practice Book p. 73 to provide additional practice.

Grace and the Time Machine **189**

Tech Files ONLINE

Students can explore the possibility of time travel by going online and using a student-friendly search engine. Have them use the keywords *time travel*.

ELL

Build Background Use ELL Poster 8 to build background and vocabulary for the lesson concept of world cultures.

▲ **ELL Poster** 8

Build Background

ACTIVATE PRIOR KNOWLEDGE

BEGIN A DISCUSSION about time travel.

- Prompt students with questions such as the following:

  Do you think time travel is possible?

  If you could make a trip to a different time, would you rather travel to the past or the future? Why?

  What would be the benefit of time travel?

  Why could traveling through different times be dangerous?

- Create a T-chart about the benefits and dangers of time travel. Record students' ideas in appropriate columns of the T-chart.

- Tell students that the play they will read is about time travel. Have them look for new ideas about time travel to add to the T-chart.

Benefits	Dangers
1. You could find out what will happen in the future.	1. You might change the past in a way that changes the present for the worse.
2. You could change something in the past to stop a bad thing from happening.	2. You might get stuck in a different time.

▲ **Graphic Organizer** 25

BACKGROUND BUILDING AUDIO This week's audio explores time travel. After students listen, discuss what they learned and what surprised them about time travel.

Background Building Audio

Introduce Vocabulary

WORD RATING CHART

Create word rating charts using the categories *Know, Have Seen,* and *Don't Know.*

Word Rating Chart

Word	Know	Have Seen	Don't Know
aboard		✓	
atlas	✓		
awkward	✓		
capable			✓
chant			
mechanical			
miracle			
reseats			
vehicle			

▲ **Graphic Organizer** 5

Read each word to students and have them rate their knowledge of the word by placing a checkmark in one of the three columns: *Know* (know and can use); *Have Seen* (have seen or heard the word; don't know meaning); *Don't Know* (don't know the word). ***Activate Prior Knowledge***

Display or read aloud this sentence: *The mechanic moved in a mechanical way and fixed the broken mechanism in the machine.* Ask students to restate the sentence in their own words and to name the words they think are related. *(mechanic, mechanical, mechanism, machine)* ***Related Words***

By the end of the week students should know lesson vocabulary words. Have them revise their charts and demonstrate their understanding by using each word in a sentence.

Use Multisyllabic Word Routine on p. DI·1 to help students read multisyllabic words.

Lesson Vocabulary

WORDS TO KNOW

T aboard on board; in or on a ship, train, bus, airplane, etc.

T atlas book of maps

T awkward not graceful or skillful in movement or shape; not easily managed

T capable having fitness, power, or ability; able; efficient; competent

T chant to call over and over again

T mechanical like a machine; automatic; without expression

T miracle a wonderful happening that is contrary to, or independent of, the known laws of nature

T reseats sits again

T vehicle device for carrying people or things, such as a car, bus, airplane, etc.

MORE WORDS TO KNOW

contraption device or gadget

pantomime to express by gestures

T = Tested Word

Vocabulary

Directions Choose the word from the box that best completes each sentence. Write the word on the line.

awkward _____ 1. At first, it felt ____ to be in a new country.

vehicle _____ 2. We rode in a special ____ to tour the city and its rivers.

capable _____ 3. My sister is ____ of getting around by herself.

atlas _____ 4. Sharon opened the ____ to see where we were.

chant _____ 5. We listened to the tribe ____ as they danced.

Check the Words You Know

___aboard
___atlas
___awkward
___capable
___chant
___mechanical
___miracle
___reseats
___vehicle

Directions Choose the word from the box that best matches each clue. Write the word in the puzzle.

Across
6. like a machine
9. on or in a car or train
10. book of maps

Down
7. seats again
8. a wonder

Write an E-mail Message

On a separate sheet of paper write an e-mail message to a friend about an imaginary trip you took to another country. Use as many vocabulary words as you can.

E-mail messages should include words from the vocabulary list and details about a trip to another country.

Home Activity Your child identified and used vocabulary words from *Grace and the Time Machine.* With your child, make up a story about living in another part of the world. Use as many of the vocabulary words as you can.

▲ **Practice Book** p. 74

Vocabulary Strategy

⊙ Use word structure to determine word meaning.

INTRODUCE

Discuss the strategy for word structure by using the steps on p. 190.

TEACH

- Have students read "Riding into History," paying attention to how vocabulary is used.
- Model using word structure to determine the meaning of *reseats*.

MODEL When I read the word *reseats,* I notice it has the prefix *re-* in it. I cover *re-* and see the word *seats.* I know what it means to seat yourself, and I know *re-* means "again." So the word *reseats* must mean "to take a seat again."

Words to Know

| mechanical |
| miracle |
| aboard |
| awkward |
| capable |
| reseats |
| chant |
| vehicle |
| atlas |

Remember

Try the strategy. Then, if you need more help, use your glossary or a dictionary.

Vocabulary Strategy
for Prefixes

Word Structure Sometimes when you are reading, you come to a word you do not know. See if the word has a prefix. Prefixes are letters added to the beginning of a word that change its meaning. For example, the prefix *re-* means "again." If you *retie* a knot, you tie it again. The prefix *a-* means "on, in, or at." If you are *abed,* you are in bed.

1. Cover the prefix.

2. Look at the base word. See if you know what it means.

3. Add the meaning of the prefix.

4. Check to see if this meaning makes sense in the sentence.

As you read "Riding into History," look for words that begin with the prefix *re-* or *a-.* Use the prefixes to help you figure out the meanings of the words.

190

DAY 2 Grouping Options

Reading
Whole Group Discuss the Question of the Day. Then use pp. 190–193.

Group Time Differentiated Instruction
Read *Grace and the Time Machine.* See pp. 188f–188g for the small group lesson plan.

Whole Group Use p. 211a.

Language Arts
Use pp. 211e–211k.

Strategic Intervention

⊙ **Word Structure** Using the steps on p. 190, have students think of words they know with *re-,* such as *rewind, rewrite, repay,* and *retake.* Write the meaning of the prefix and the base word for each word.

ELL

Access Content Use ELL Poster 8 to preteach vocabulary. Choose from the following to meet language proficiency levels.

Beginning Find words that are cognates in their home languages.

Intermediate If you began a Word Rating Chart (p. 190b), have students use words they rated as *Have Seen* in sentences.

Advanced Teach the lesson on pp. 190–191. Have students quiz each other on definitions of the vocabulary words.

Resources for home-language words may include parents, bilingual staff members, bilingual dictionaries, or online translation sources.

RIDING INTO HISTORY

Inventions have made travel better, safer, and faster in the past 200 years. When each new invention appeared, it seemed like a mechanical miracle. Take the train, for example. The first steam locomotives offered rides in the 1820s. Early riders felt a thrill when they heard "All aboard!" Their hearts raced as they sat on hard, awkward benches and held on for dear life. After all, the train was capable of wild speeds of up to 20 miles per hour!

Put yourself on such a train. Black smoke streams back and coats your hat and gloves. One traveler stands and points at a horse and buggy racing the train. Then he happily reseats himself and waits for the next adventure. Wheels click and engines puff. The sound is like a chant, a travel song with strong rhythm.

In another 150 years, every kind of vehicle will take to the roads. All sizes and shapes of airplanes will fly into the sky. They will bring the farthest countries in the atlas within reach. What is next in transportation? Maybe space buses will take us to the moon!

Words to Write

Pretend you took a ride in one of the first automobiles. Write a letter describing your wild ride. Use words from the Words to Know list.

191

PRACTICE AND ASSESS

- Have students determine the meaning of *aboard* using their knowledge of prefixes.
- Have students figure out the meanings of the remaining words and tell if they used context or a glossary or dictionary.
- If you began a Word Rating Chart (p. 190b), have students reassess their ratings.
- Have students complete Practice Book p. 75.

WRITE Writing should include vocabulary words and describe how the ride feels, how it looks, and how people judge the ride.

Monitor Progress

⊙ Word Structure

If... students need more practice with the lesson vocabulary,	**then...** use Tested Vocabulary Cards.

Vocabulary • Word Structure

- A **prefix** is a syllable added at the beginning of a base word to change its meaning.
- The prefix *re-* means *to do over* or *again*.

Directions Read the following passage. Then answer the questions below.

I love to retell how much fun it was to ride the train while traveling abroad with my family. We carried an atlas to keep track of how many miles we'd crossed. It was amazing how quickly we moved from city to city! There were no mechanical problems with the train, so nothing slowed down our trip.

The best thing about the train trip my family took was the lunch breaks. At these times, everyone got off the train to have a picnic in a beautiful meadow or to walk around a tiny village. Then the conductor reseated us, and when everything was reorganized, ZOOM! We were off to explore more of the country.

1. What is the prefix in the word *retell*? What does the word mean?
   re-; The word means "to tell again."

2. What does the word *reseated* mean?
   It means "seated again."

3. Why did the conductor need to *reseat* the passengers?
   The conductor reseats them because they are getting back on the train.

4. If you *reorganized* your bedroom, what did you do?
   You organized it again.

5. Write a sentence using a word with the prefix *re-*.
   Possible answer: I retook my school photograph.

Home Activity Your child identified the prefix *re-* to understand the meanings of new words. Have a conversation with your child and try to use as many words that begin with *re-* as you can. Count how many you can use in one sentence.

▲ **Practice Book** p. 75

Grace and the Time Machine

Prereading Strategies

GENRE STUDY

Play

Grace and the Time Machine is a play. Explain that readers learn about characters and events in a play by focusing on the dialogue and stage directions. In this play, the setting changes frequently, and extra attention is needed to figure out when and where the action takes place.

PREVIEW AND PREDICT

Have students preview the play title, list of characters, and illustrations. Have students predict what they think will happen in the play. Encourage students to use lesson vocabulary as they talk about their predictions.

Strategy Response Log

Ask Questions Have students write two questions they have about the play in their strategy response logs. Students will answer their questions in the Strategy Response Log activity on p. 201.

Grace and the Time Machine

from *Starring Grace* by Mary Hoffman
adapted for Story Theater by Donald Abramson
illustrated by Matthew Faulkner

Genre

A **play** has all the elements of a story—characters, setting, plot, and theme—but it doesn't look like a story because it's written to be performed. As you read, think about how this play might be different as a chapter in a book.

192

ELL

Build Background Lead a picture walk so students see the different time periods the characters are cast in. Then ask students to imagine what a time machine would be used for.

Consider having students read the selection summary in English or in students' home languages. See the Multilingual Summaries in the ELL Teaching Guide, pp. 54–56.

Can a time machine change a person's life?

193

SET PURPOSE

Point out the list of characters on the top of p. 194 and read the opening stage directions in italics aloud to students. Have them consider their preview discussion and state why they want to read the play.

Remind students to think about what they read and what they know to draw conclusions about characters and events in the play.

STRATEGY RECALL

Students have now used these before-reading strategies:

• preview the selection to be aware of its genre, features, and possible content;
• activate prior knowledge about that content and what to expect of that genre;
• make predictions;
• set a purpose for reading.

Remind students to be aware of and flexibly use the during-reading strategies they have learned:

• link prior knowledge to new information;
• summarize text they have read so far;
• ask clarifying questions;
• answer questions they or others pose;
• check their predictions and either refine them or make new predictions;
• recognize the text structure the author is using, and use that knowledge to make predictions and increase comprehension;
• visualize what the author is describing;
• monitor their comprehension and use fix-up strategies.

After reading, students will use these strategies:

• summarize or retell the text;
• answer questions they or others pose;
• reflect to make new information become part of their prior knowledge.

Audio CD **AudioText**

Guiding Comprehension

1 **Setting • Literal**

What is the setting for the opening scene in the play?

The setting is in the kitchen and the backyard of Grace's house. The time is a summer morning.

2 **Draw Conclusions • Inferential**

What is Nana's role in the household when Ava is at work?

Possible responses: Nana watches Grace while her mother works. Nana is Grace's baby-sitter.

Monitor Progress

Draw Conclusions

If... students are unable to conclude that Nana is baby-sitting Grace,	then... use the skill and strategy instruction on p. 195.

Characters

AVA Grace's Mother

MRS. MYERSON

MARIA

NANA Grace's Grandmother

GRACE

RAJ

AIMEE

KESTER

ACTOR 1   ACTRESS 1   ACTOR 2   ACTRESS 2

1 *The scene is the kitchen and backyard of the house that GRACE shares with her mother, AVA, and her grandmother, NANA. The time is during summer vacation.*

AVA: Grace, I'm off to work at the hospital now.

GRACE: Okay, Ma.

AVA: And what have you got lined up for today?

GRACE: Oh, you know. The kids are coming over. Aimee and Kester and Raj and Maria. I guess we'll find something to do.

AVA: Well, try not to leave the house in a shambles.

GRACE: We won't, Ma.

AVA: And you will help your grandmother? I know she gets around pretty well on her crutches, but it's still awkward for her to do things with that cast on her ankle.

194

ELL

Extend Language Many terms of endearment exist for family members. Grandmothers can be called *Nana*, *Grandma*, or *Grammy*. Mothers can be called *Ma*, *Mommy*, or *Mom*. Have students share the terms they use to address special people.

GRACE: Oh, I will, Ma. I bring her the phone or her book—

AVA: Good girl. Nana is in capable hands, then.

NANA *(walking with crutches and favoring one leg):* Nana's in fine hands, thank you. Morning, Ava. Morning, Grace.

AVA: Good morning, Mom. I'd get you some breakfast, but I'm already late.

NANA: Grace can do it. She's been real helpful since I tripped over that silly cat and broke my ankle. You go to work.

AVA: Okay. Bye!

GRACE: Bye, Ma. What can I get for you, Nana?

NANA: Well, Grace, you can bring me a cup of coffee, if you will.

GRACE: Oh, sure.

NANA: Thank you, Honey.

AIMEE *(calling from the yard):* Hello, Grace!

GRACE: It's Aimee. I'm in the kitchen, Aimee! Come on in!

AIMEE *(entering the kitchen):* Hi, Grace. Good morning, Nana.

NANA: Hello, Aimee.

AIMEE: I just saw Kester and Raj. They're on their way over.

GRACE: Good!

KESTER *(calling from the yard):* Hey, Grace!

GRACE: There they are! Are you okay, Nana?

NANA: I'm fine, Grace. I'll just sit here and drink my coffee. Go on out. But take that dangerous cat with you, so I don't fall over him again.

GRACE: Okay. Come on, Paw-Paw.

ACTRESS 1 *(as a cat):* Meowerow!

NANA: I'll call you if I need you.

Grace and Aimee move into the yard.

SKILLS ⟷ STRATEGIES IN CONTEXT

Draw Conclusions

TEACH

- Remind students that small pieces of information can help them draw a conclusion about characters or events. Using what they know about life also can help them draw conclusions.

- Model how to draw conclusions after reading pp. 194–195.

Think Aloud **MODEL** The text tells me that Grace is helping Nana while her mother is at work, but the text doesn't say who is in charge of the children as they play. I know that sometimes grandparents supervise grandchildren while parents are at work, so I can draw the conclusion that this is what Nana is doing. There are no other adults at Grace's house, so it probably is Nana's job to be in charge.

PRACTICE AND ASSESS

Have students use their own experiences to draw conclusions about Grace and back up their answers with evidence in the text. Ask which of the following sentences best describes Grace. *(Choice c)*

a) She is careless because she doesn't keep the cat out of the way.

b) She likes to cook because she makes Nana coffee.

c) She is helpful because she helps Nana with things that Nana can't do on crutches.

Guiding Comprehension

3 **Generalize • Inferential**

How are all the children's invention ideas alike?

They all think of things that don't exist but would be helpful.

4 **Cause and Effect • Inferential**

Why do the children agree to make a time machine?

Each of them thinks of a way he or she could use the time machine for something useful.

5 **REVIEW** **Compare and Contrast • Critical**

Text to Self **Can you share a time when you played with your friends and did something similar to making a time machine?**

Possible response: Inventing the time machine might remind students of a time they played a make-believe game.

Monitor Progress	
REVIEW **Compare and Contrast**	
If... students are unable to compare and contrast their own experiences with the play,	**then...** use the skill and strategy instruction on p. 197.

GRACE: Hi, Kester, Raj. What's up?

RAJ: Hi, Grace. Look—remember we were talking about inventing something? Well, all we have to do is think of something that no one else has thought of.

KESTER: Oh, is that all? That should be easy, then!

MARIA: Hi, guys. What's easy?

GRACE: Hi, Maria.

AIMEE: Good morning.

KESTER: Hey, Maria.

RAJ: We're talking about inventing stuff.

GRACE: Listen, let's try to think hard of something we wish existed, but doesn't.

3 Something useful.

MARIA: I know. Grass that doesn't need cutting. I'm tired of cutting Mrs. Myerson's back lawn every Saturday.

KESTER: Skateboards with brakes.

RAJ: I told you, that's what feet are for.

GRACE: What do you want to invent, Raj?

RAJ: A machine that would read books for you. I have too much trouble doing it on my own!

MARIA: I don't think that would be any fun!

AIMEE: What about you, Grace?

GRACE: Oh, I don't know. What about a time machine?

A Time Machine!

196

Access Content As you read the names of the objects gathered to make the time machine (p. 197), have students point to the picture of each item.

KESTER: Hey, that's cheating. You said something useful!

MARIA: That would be useful. You could go forward in time and find out the questions for a math test.

KESTER: Hmmm. Or go back and change things.

AIMEE: Yes, you could go back and pick up your cat, Paw-Paw, so that he didn't trip Nana.

RAJ: So she wouldn't fall and break her ankle.

GRACE: Well, that'd be great.

MARIA: Yeah, I think a time machine would be the best invention of all.

KESTER: That'd be so cool!

MARIA: So, what do we need?

KESTER: Well, let's see what we can find.

They arrange five chairs in the center of the stage and then pantomime adding things to them.

GRACE: We can start with my bike!

AIMEE: Here's an old radio. It's got a dial.

KESTER: Here are a couple of alarm clocks.

GRACE: And here's Nana's kitchen timer, so we know how long we're gone.

RAJ: I'll tape it to your handlebars.

MARIA: Here's a garden rake.

AIMEE: And some garden spinners.

MARIA: Hey, what about this beach umbrella?

KESTER: What's the umbrella for?

MARIA: Well, it looks fancy.

GRACE: And here—I want to bring my atlas, so we can choose places as well as times.

5

Compare and Contrast REVIEW

TEACH

Remind students they should make comparisons between the text and their own lives as they read. It is often helpful to ask, "What does this remind me of?"

Think Aloud **MODEL** The children in this play are pulling together things to make their time machine. When I was young, I did things like that too. I remember one day my brother and I made a fort out of blankets. Another time we made a huge castle in the snow after a snowstorm. I never made a time machine, but I did play other "pretend" games.

PRACTICE AND ASSESS

• Have partners work together to discuss how Nana's life might be the same or different if the children could go back in time and prevent the accident. Have them record their ideas in a compare and contrast chart.

• To assess, use Practice Book p. 76.

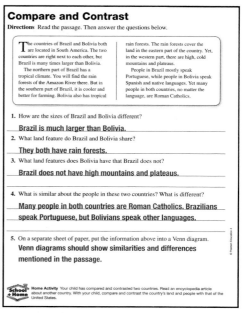

▲ **Practice Book** p. 76

Guiding Comprehension

6 🎯 **Vocabulary • Word Structure**

How can your knowledge of prefixes help you know the meaning of *aboard*?

The prefix *a-* can mean "on." This helps me figure out that *aboard* means "on board."

Monitor Progress

🎯 Word Structure

If... students are unable to tell how the prefix *a-* helps them define *aboard*,	**then...** use the vocabulary instruction on p. 199.

7 **Compare and Contrast • Critical**

How would a world of robots compare to a world of humans?

Possible response: In a world of robots there probably would be no war, crime, or hunger. Since robots don't have feelings, there probably wouldn't be friends, love, or joy either.

8 🎯 **Draw Conclusions • Inferential**

Why do you think Grace suddenly decides they should go?

Possible response: The robots say they got rid of humans a hundred years ago. Perhaps they will try to "get rid" of Grace and her friends too.

RAJ: Well, that's it, I guess.

AIMEE: It really does look like a mad inventor's been here.

KESTER: But who's going to drive this thing?

AIMEE: It was Grace's idea.

GRACE: Okay, I'll go first, but we can all take turns.

RAJ: That's good.

6 **GRACE:** So—all aboard! Where should we go first?

KESTER: I know! Let's go to the future and see what it's like.

GRACE: How far into the future?

KESTER: What do you think? Five hundred years?

GRACE: Okay. We'll just set this clock dial for five hundred years and set the timer. Hold on, everybody—here we go!

They make time-machine noises. Meanwhile, ACTORS *and* ACTRESSES 1 *and 2 come forward and walk about stiffly. Their voices sound very mechanical.*

198

Understanding Idioms Help students use context to figure out that the phrase *check out these people* (p. 199, line 3) means "look at these people." Ask students to tell other meanings of the idiom *check out.*

Encourage students to record English idioms and their meanings in language journals, word lists, or computer files of English vocabulary.

GRACE: And he-e-ere we are!

AIMEE: Well, it doesn't look much different.

MARIA: But check out these people. They look different.

KESTER: Hello—uh, future people.

ACTOR AND ACTRESS 1 *(speaking together):* Hello.

KESTER: What shall we say? Um—is it nice here in the future?

ACTOR AND ACTRESS 2 *(together):* Oh, yes. It is very nice.

MARIA: Tell us about it.

ACTOR AND ACTRESS 1: We have no wars.

ACTOR AND ACTRESS 2: We have no crime.

ACTOR AND ACTRESS 1: No one is ever hungry.

AIMEE: That sounds great.

KESTER: Yeah, but excuse me for asking.
You're robots, aren't you?

ACTOR AND ACTRESS 2: Yes, we are robots. **7**

AIMEE: Oh, but where are the humans then?

ACTOR AND ACTRESS 1: There are no humans.

ACTOR AND ACTRESS 2: We got rid of humans
a hundred years ago.

ACTOR AND ACTRESS 1: It is much better this way.

GRACE: Uh—guys! D'you think we'd better go?

KESTER: Yeah. Come on! **8**

199

Word Structure

TEACH

Remind students that they can use their knowledge of prefixes to figure out an unknown word. Read p. 198, line 8, and model how to use prefixes to determine the meaning of *aboard*.

Think Aloud **MODEL** When I read the word *aboard*, I'm not sure what it means. I remember that *a-* can sometimes be a prefix, so I cover the letter *a* and read the rest of the word: *board*. I know that the prefix *a-* can mean "on," "in," or "at." I try each meaning with *board* and "on" makes sense in the context of the sentence. *Aboard* means "on board."

PRACTICE AND ASSESS

Have students use their knowledge of prefixes to write the meaning of *afoot, afire,* or *ashore* and use it in a sentence. To assess, make sure students understand how to consider the meaning of the base word before adding the prefix to it.

Time Travel

TIME FOR **Science**

Novelists and scientists have been fascinated with time travel for years. Some people want to go into the past to stop bad things from happening. Others worry that any change in the past could change the present in unknown ways. The novel *The Time Machine* by H. G. Wells is a classic science fiction story of time travel. Scientists disagree on whether time travel is possible. Scientist Stephen Hawking says it's impossible, but astronomer Carl Sagan believed it might be possible, especially travel into the future.

Guiding Comprehension

9 **Graphic Sources • Critical**

How does the art add to your understanding of the story?

Possible response: The art gives us an idea of the setting—when and where the action takes place. On this page, it shows what dinosaurs look like.

10 **Draw Conclusions • Inferential**

Why do the children make a quick getaway from the past?

They are afraid of being eaten by the tyrannosaurus.

11 **Answer Questions • Critical**

Is the answer to the previous question in the text or do you use information you already have to answer it? Explain.

The text says that the tyrannosaurus has lots of long, sharp teeth. You have to combine this information with what you already know (the tyrannosaurus was a dangerous, carnivorous dinosaur) to draw the conclusion that the children are afraid of being eaten.

Tech Files
ONLINE

Students can search an online encyclopedia or use a student-friendly Internet search engine to learn more about dinosaurs. Have them use the keywords *dinosaurs, triceratops, stegosaurus,* or *tyrannosaurus.* Be sure to follow classroom rules for Internet use.

GRACE: Raj can drive now.

RAJ: Okay.

MARIA: Where do you want to go, Raj?

RAJ *(busily setting dials):* Well, the future's kind of scary. What about the past?

AIMEE: How far past?

RAJ: Oh—millions of years! Here we go!

They make time-machine noises. ACTORS *and* ACTRESSES 1 *and* 2 *are now dinosaurs. They prowl around and roar.*

RAJ: And we're here! Now remember, everybody. You can't make any changes here. Otherwise you might change the future.

MARIA: I know—and then we'd never exist.

KESTER: Just look at those trees. They're like ferns—as big as palm trees.

ACTOR 1: Ro-o-oar!

AIMEE: Look, what's that?

MARIA: It's a dinosaur!

RAJ: With those two huge horns and that bony frill, that's got to be a triceratops.

ACTRESS 2: Ro-o-oar!

KESTER: There's another one.

RAJ: I think that's a stegosaurus.

AIMEE: How can you tell?

RAJ: It's got those rows of bony plates all down its back.

GRACE: These guys are really big.

MARIA: Yeah. Aren't you glad they're plant eaters?

200

ELL

Access Content In the sentence "This is a different story" (p. 201, line 2), the word *story* is used in a less common context. Have students restate the sentence. *(Possible response: "This dinosaur is different.")*

ACTOR 2: Ro-o-oar!

RAJ: Uh-oh. This is a different story. **9**

KESTER: Walking on its hind legs—two little
  front legs—

GRACE: A huge head with powerful jaws—

AIMEE: And lots of long—sharp—teeth!

MARIA: Even I can tell what kind this is!

ALL TOGETHER: Tyrannosaurus!

ACTOR 2: Ro-o-o-o-oar!!!

*They scream and run
back to the time machine.* **10**

GRACE: Time for a quick getaway! **11**

AIMEE: I'll drive now. Where do
  you want to go?

GRACE: How about West Africa?

RAJ: That's not time travel.

201

Develop Vocabulary

PRACTICE LESSON VOCABULARY

Students orally respond to each question.

1. **If you bumped into a wastebasket, would you feel *awkward* or
   graceful?** *(awkward)*

2. **To find a country in Asia, would you use an almanac or an *atlas*?**
   (an atlas)

3. **If someone acts in a *mechanical* manner, do they show a lot of
   emotion or no emotion?** *(no emotion)*

BUILD CONCEPT VOCABULARY

Review previous concept words with students. Ask if students have come
across any words today in their reading that they would like to add to the
Imagination Concept Web, such as *future, time travel,* or *pantomime.*

⊙ STRATEGY SELF-CHECK

Answer Questions

Have students review the strategies they can
use to answer questions that ask them to draw
conclusions. Remind them that answers may be
in the text, but they often will need to combine
details from the text with their own prior knowledge to draw conclusions.

Ask students to write a paragraph about why
the children suddenly left the past and how they
came to these conclusions. Have them check
that the paragraph includes details from the play
and their own ideas.

SELF-CHECK

Students can ask themselves these questions
to assess their ability to use the skill and
strategy.

• Was I able to find text details to help me
  answer questions about this play?

• Did I use what I already know to help me draw
  conclusions to answer questions?

Monitor Progress	
⊙ **Draw Conclusions**	
If... students have difficulty answering questions that require drawing conclusions,	**then**... revisit the skill lesson on pp. 188–189. Reteach as necessary.

Strategy Response Log

Answer Questions Have students review the questions
they wrote before reading the play. (See p. 192.) Ask:
*Have your questions been answered? If so, write the
answers. Then write a question about the rest of the play.*

***If you want to teach this story in two sessions,
stop here.***

Guiding Comprehension

If you are teaching the play in two days, discuss the conclusions that students have drawn so far and review the vocabulary.

12 ● **Draw Conclusions • Inferential**

Why does Nana want to ride on the time machine?

Possible response: She sees the children are having fun and wants to join in.

Monitor Progress
● **Draw Conclusions**

If... students have difficulty drawing conclusions,	then... use the skill and strategy instruction on p. 203.

13 Realism and Fantasy • Inferential

What part of this play is realistic and what part is fantasy?

The beginning of the play where the children make the time machine is realistic. The make-believe trips to other places and times are fantasy.

DAY 3 Grouping Options

Reading

Whole Group Discuss the Question of the Day.

Group Time Differentiated Instruction
Read *Grace and the Time Machine.* See pp. 188f–188g for the small group lesson plan.

Whole Group Discuss the Reader Response questions on page 208. Then use p. 211a.

Language Arts
Use pp. 211e–211k.

GRACE: All right then, make it last year when Nana and I went to The Gambia.

AIMEE: Okay. I've set the dials for last year.

RAJ: Here we go again!

They make time-machine noises. ACTORS *and* ACTRESSES 1 *and 2 start walking about, their voices overlapping as they chant the goods they are selling.*

ACTOR 1: Mangos here! Papayas here!

ACTRESS 1: Fresh passion fruit! Fresh jack fruit!

ACTOR 2: Milk, milk, sweet fresh milk! Fresh from the goat!

ACTRESS 2: Smell my fresh bread! Fresh bread!

GRACE: It's the open-air market, right in the middle of town.

KESTER: And the women all walk around carrying baskets and trays and everything on their heads.

202

E L L

Context Clues Help students use context to figure out that a *wee, bitty island* (p. 203, fifth line from bottom) is a small island. The word *just* also suggests the size of the island.

AIMEE: Look at this. The money has pictures of crocodiles!

MARIA: This is more exciting than shopping at home.

RAJ: Grace, you were so lucky to really visit here.

GRACE: And there was one special food we had. I've never tasted anything like it. It was—um—um—

NANA *(coming into the yard):* Benachin.

GRACE: Benachin, yes!

NANA: You ate enough of it!

KESTER: What's benachin, Nana?

NANA: Oh, there's all kinds. We had some with beef, cabbage, and eggplant all cooked together in one big pot.

GRACE: What are you doing out, Nana? Do you need something?

NANA: No. I was taking a nap. The dinosaurs woke me up.

AIMEE: Sorry!

NANA: It's all right, Aimee. Looks like fun.

MARIA: It is. Let's give Nana a turn!

RAJ: Yeah! Come on, Nana!

NANA: Well now, I haven't ridden in a time machine for a good long while. *(They help her sit in the machine.)* **12**

KESTER: Choose a place. Here, here's the atlas.

NANA: No question. Trinidad, where I was born. Here it is, see?

KESTER: It's an island!

NANA: It's just a wee, bitty island in the West Indies. But there's nowhere else in the world quite like it.

MARIA: And when would you like it to be?

NANA: Oh, when I was a little girl about your age. Let's say sixty years ago. **13**

The Gambia

Time for **SOCIAL STUDIES**

The Gambia is the smallest country in Africa. It is located on the western coast of Africa and is surrounded by Senegal. The Gambia River runs east to west through The Gambia, dividing the country in half. There are more than 1.5 million people in The Gambia, most of whom are farmers. Although it is a relatively poor country, there is a strong sense of community in The Gambia. Everyone looks out for others, especially for those who are poor, old, or sick. Music is important in Gambian culture, and recently many young Gambians have become rap singers.

⊙ SKILLS ↔ STRATEGIES IN CONTEXT

Draw Conclusions

TEACH

Remind students to use details from the play to help them draw conclusions. Model using details from p. 203 to draw conclusions about why Nana wants to try the time machine.

Think Aloud **MODEL** I think that Nana wants to try the time machine because she sees how much fun the children are having. She says "Looks like fun." She says she hasn't been in a time machine for a long time, which makes me think she once played this game as a child. All these clues from the text help me decide that she thinks it would be fun to try the time machine.

PRACTICE AND ASSESS

Ask students to work in groups to draw conclusions about what The Gambia is like. Have them make a list of details from the text and their own knowledge about Africa to support their conclusions. *(For example, they could conclude that The Gambia is a warm place since tropical fruits like papaya and mangos are sold there.)* To assess, make sure students draw reasonable conclusions and can support them with details from the text and their own experiences.

Guiding Comprehension

DURING READING

14 **Imagery • Inferential**

Which details help you imagine what Trinidad is like?

The purple flowers growing on the house, a path down to the beach, and the sound of the sea help me imagine Trinidad.

15 **Cause and Effect • Inferential**

Why doesn't Mrs. Myerson leave her house?

Because of her experiences during World War II, she doesn't trust people.

16 **Draw Conclusions • Inferential**

Why does Mrs. Myerson decide to try the time machine?

Possible response: Nana says that the children seem to be bringing her back to life. Maybe she is less fearful of children than adults.

Monitor Progress	
Draw Conclusions	
If… students have difficulty finding details in the text to support conclusions,	**then…** use the skill and strategy instruction on p. 205.

KESTER: I'll set the dials. All set? Let's go.

They make time-machine noises. ACTORS *and* ACTRESSES 1 *and* 2 *make a continual* shhhhh *noise, the sound of the sea, with occasional seagull screeches.*

GRACE: Nana, you are now in Trinidad.

14 **NANA:** Oh, how wonderful! There's the house where I grew up. See the purple bougainvillea growing up the side of it? And over there is the path down to the beach where the fishermen catch crabs in their pots. You can hear the sound of the sea from here. I bet my brother Maxie is down there playing in the sand. And listen! I can hear my mother calling me—Lucie—Lucie!

MRS. MYERSON *(overlapping with* NANA*):* Lucie! Lucie!

GRACE: The time machine! It works!

RAJ: No, look. It's Mrs. Myerson, over the back fence.

NANA: Hello, Gerda.

MRS. MYERSON: Whatever is that? What are you doing?

NANA: It's a wonderful machine that can take you back to when you were small.

KESTER: Or into the future. But I wouldn't advise that.

RAJ: Would you like a turn, Mrs. Myerson?

NANA *(quietly, to the children):* Now, children, you know Mrs. Myerson doesn't leave her house.

MRS. MYERSON: Well, but I could never climb this fence the way you children do.

GRACE: We could come and walk you around.

MRS. MYERSON: No, thank you. I'll be all right. Just give me a minute.

204

ELL

Understanding Idioms The word *off* has multiple meanings, the most common being in the context of "on/off," quite the contrast to the phrase "And we're off!" (p. 205, last line), which means "We're going!" Ask students why Maria says "We're off!" Where are they off to?

NANA *(getting out of the machine):* I must say I'm amazed. For as long as I've known her, Gerda Myerson has kept to herself.

MARIA: But what's wrong with her?

NANA: She had some very bad experiences during World War II. Her whole family was killed, and she was imprisoned for a long time. She survived, but usually she finds it hard to trust people. So she keeps her house all locked up. But you children seem to be bringing her back to life. **16**

MRS. MYERSON: Well, here I am.

RAJ: Right this way, Mrs. Myerson.

KESTER: Please have a comfortable seat in our time machine. *(He helps her sit in the machine.)*

AIMEE: Now you must tell us where you would like to go.

MRS. MYERSON: Oh—Germany. My home in Heidelberg.

GRACE: And when?

MRS. MYERSON: Oh yes, before all that trouble. 1925.

MARIA *(dialing the timer):* I will be your captain for this voyage. Please remain in your seat while the vehicle is in motion. And we're off!

205

Trinidad

Time for SOCIAL STUDIES

Trinidad is a warm, tropical Caribbean island. It is part of a country called The Republic of Trinidad and Tobago. Trinidad is located in the Caribbean Sea, northeast of Venezuela. Trinidad and Tobago is one of the wealthiest countries in the Caribbean. Oil is a major export of the country, and it produces more oil and gas than any other Caribbean country.

⟲ SKILLS ⟷ STRATEGIES IN CONTEXT

Draw Conclusions Answer Questions

TEACH

Students often must answer questions that require them to draw conclusions from the text. Remind them to look for answers in the text, but also to think about what they already know. Read p. 204 and model how to answer questions that require drawing conclusions.

Think Aloud **MODEL** I wonder why Mrs. Myerson is coming over to use the time machine. Nana says that the children are bringing Mrs. Myerson back to life, so that must mean that she is beginning to trust them. I know from my own experience that sometimes people find it easier to trust children than adults. Maybe that is true for Mrs. Myerson too.

PRACTICE AND ASSESS

Have students answer more questions that require them to draw conclusions. Ask: *What is it like to live in Trinidad? Why does Kester say he doesn't advise traveling to the future? Why does Mrs. Myerson want to travel to 1925?* To assess, ask them how they know their conclusions are reasonable.

Guiding Comprehension

17 Author's Craft • Critical
Question the Author **What is the function of Actors 1 and 2 and Actresses 1 and 2 throughout the play?**

Possible response: They play the other characters the children come across during their travels. They give more information about the setting.

18 Answer Questions • Critical
Do you think the time machine really took the children to different times and places? What details help you answer this question?

Possible response: No; they were pretending. One detail that makes me conclude this is that Grace says, at the end, "It was just as if she really did travel back in time."

19 Compare and Contrast • Critical
Text to Text **What other book does *Grace and the Time Machine* remind you of?**

Responses will vary, but students should name a book or story with a time-travel or science fiction theme.

Strategy Response Log

Summarize When students finish reading the play, provide this prompt: Imagine a friend loves time travel stories. Write a summary of *Grace and the Time Machine* telling the main events in four or five sentences.

---

17 *They all make time-machine noises. When they stop, we can hear ACTORS and ACTRESSES 1 and 2 laughing and making noises of children playing in the distance.*

MRS. MYERSON: It's my grandparents' house in Heidelberg. With the big backyard. *(She gets up.)*

ACTRESS 1: Mutti, Papa—Look at me!

ACTOR 1: You be careful now, Lili!

MRS. MYERSON: They are all here. My mother and father. My cousins Franz and Fritz and little Lili.

ACTRESS 2: Here, Blackie! Come on, boy!

MRS. MYERSON: My dear sister Hilde, and the dogs—so many dogs! It is a lovely summer day.

ACTOR 2: Lili, over here! Gotcha!

ACTRESS 1 *(screaming):* Fritz! Don't! You'll get me all wet!

MRS. MYERSON: We are playing in the brook at the bottom of the backyard. Fritz is catching minnows and splashing Cousin Lili.

ACTRESS 1: Fritz, you're a meanie!

MRS. MYERSON: I'm wearing a dress—white, with a blue sash. Such a pretty dress!

ACTOR 2: Gerda—look out!

MRS. MYERSON: Ha ha! Fritz, you can't splash me! There is Hilde, picking flowers for the dinner table.

ACTRESS 2: Lilies and roses, I love them. Aren't they beautiful, Cousin Franz?

ACTOR 1: They are beautiful, Cousin Hilde. And they have a heavenly scent. *(sniffing deeply)* Ahhh!

MRS. MYERSON: I can smell them now. Ahhh—

AIMEE: Mrs. Myerson, are you all right?

ELL

Extend Language Sometimes words are spelled the way they are pronounced. *Gotcha!* (p. 206, line 13) is really "I got you!" said quickly and playfully. Other examples that students may encounter are *gonna* (going to) and *gimme* (give me).

RAJ: You're not crying, are you?

MRS. MYERSON: No, no. Well—yes.

KESTER: What's wrong?

MRS. MYERSON: Nothing. There is nothing wrong. Thank you, children. It is a wonderful machine.

NANA: I think maybe it's time to come back to the present and have a good strong cup of tea.

MRS. MYERSON: Oh, yes. That would be nice. But first—Maria, you have to bring me back. *(She reseats herself in the machine.)*

MARIA *(adjusting the dials):* Right away. Here we go.

They all make time-machine noises. Ava enters and watches.

AVA: Grace, what's going on here? What is this contraption?

GRACE: Hi, Ma! It's a time machine, see?

NANA: It's a miracle. Not only did Gerda Myerson walk here from her house—she told us all about her childhood. She remembered how happy she was.

MRS. MYERSON *(getting up and joining them):* I'm ready now, Lucie. Hello, Ava.

AVA: It's nice to see you, Gerda.

NANA: Yes. Let's go in then.

(NANA and MRS. MYERSON go inside.)

GRACE: It was just as if she really did travel back in time, Ma. **18**

AVA: Then your machine works, Grace. What a wonderful invention! **19**

207

Develop Vocabulary

PRACTICE LESSON VOCABULARY

As a class, complete the following sentences orally. Possible responses are given.

1. A fan *reseats* himself at a ballgame after (*catching a foul ball*).

2. Spectators might *chant* a cheer to (*encourage their team to win*).

3. It would be a *miracle* if your *vehicle* suddenly (*flew*).

4. An eight-year-old is *capable* of (*playing soccer well*).

BUILD CONCEPT VOCABULARY

Review previous concept words with students. Ask if students have come across any words today in their reading they would like to add to The Imagination Concept Web, such as *contraption* or *voyage*.

⊙ STRATEGY SELF-CHECK

Answer Questions

Have students draw conclusions about the time machine. Does it really travel to different times and places? How do they know? Students can complete a draw conclusions diagram like the one on p. 188 to answer questions about the time machine. Use Practice Book p. 77 for more practice.

SELF-CHECK

Students can ask themselves these questions to assess their understanding of the play.

* Did I make decisions and form opinions about what happened in the play?

* Did I use facts and details from the play and my own knowledge to help me draw conclusions and answer questions about the play?

Draw Conclusions

* **Drawing a conclusion** is forming an opinion based on what you already know or on the facts and details in a text. Facts and details are the small pieces of information in an article or story.
* Facts and details "add up" to a conclusion. Conclusions formed by the author or the reader must make sense.

Directions Read the following passage. Then answer the questions below.

If you ever travel to Trinidad, you might hear a calypso song. This special kind of song is an important part of the culture of Trinidad. Calypso songs make fun of an event in society or in politics that everyone in the area knows about. The song might be sung with Spanish, African, and Creole words. The calypso singer can sing the words to a popular melody or a made-up one. The musical instruments that back up the singer play an offbeat rhythm. These instruments might include a guitar, a shak-shak, which is like a maraca, a stringed instrument called a cuatro, a bamboo instrument called a tamboo-bamboo, and steel drums.

Possible answers given.
1. Draw a conclusion about the purpose of the calypso song.

   It lets people share their opinions about current events.

2. What detail(s) supports this conclusion?

   People make fun of events in society or politics that everyone knows about in calypso songs.

3. In a few of your own words, describe calypso music.

   Fun and lively

4. What detail(s) supports this description?

   It is sung to a popular tune; the instruments play off-beat; the types of instruments used make the music fun.

5. Describe an event where you might hear calypso music.

   You might hear it at a party or a parade.

School + Home Home Activity Your child drew conclusions using facts or details in a passage. While reading an article or short story with your child, stop periodically and ask him/her to draw conclusions about the paragraphs you have just finished.

▲ **Practice Book** p. 77

Reader Response

Open for Discussion Personal Response

Think Aloud

MODEL The actors in this play act out being in different times and places. It's almost like being there.

Comprehension Check Critical Response

1. Possible noises: time machine; background noises of places the characters visit. Possible movements: Nana walking with crutches; construction of the machine; the robots; dinosaurs. **Author's Purpose**

2. Possible response: She experienced terrible things during World War II, so it's hard for her to trust others. She's excited to go back to the time before the war because that was a happier time. **Draw Conclusions**

3. It allows them to revisit a time when they were young. They get to experience good times from their past. **Answer Questions**

4. Responses should show an understanding of the meaning of *capable*. **Vocabulary**

Look Back and Write For test practice, assign a 10–15 minute time limit. For assessment, see the Scoring Rubric at the right.

Retell

Have students retell *Grace and the Time Machine*.

Monitor Progress
Check Retelling Rubric 4 3 2 1

If... students have difficulty retelling the play,	**then...** use the Retelling Cards and Scoring Rubric for Retelling on p. 209 to assist fluent retelling.

SUCCESS PREDICTOR

ELL

Assessment As students retell, focus on comprehension, overlooking mistakes in English such as inconsistent verb tenses. For more ideas on assessing students' retellings, see the ELL and Transition Handbook.

Reader Response

Open for Discussion In a way, a play is a time machine. It can take you to surprising times and places. Explain how that happens in this play.

1. What noises and movements are needed to make this play work on the stage? Think Like an Author

2. Draw conclusions about Mrs. Myerson. Why does she keep to herself? Why is she excited to travel back in time? Draw Conclusions

3. What does the time machine allow Nana and Mrs. Myerson to do? Why is this nice for them? Answer Questions

4. When Grace's mother says that Nana is in *capable* hands, she means that Grace is able to take care of Nana. What else does Grace do to show that she is capable? Vocabulary

TEST PRACTICE

Look Back and Write Reread the ending of the play. Then write the reason that Ava says, "Then your machine works, Grace."

Meet author Mary Hoffman on page 770.

208

Scoring Rubric | Look Back and Write

Top-Score Response A top-score response uses information from the play's ending to explain why Ava says that Grace's time machine works.

Example of a Top-Score Response Grace's time machine was just pretend, but her mother Ava said that it really worked. The machine got shy Mrs. Myerson to leave her house and join in with the neighbors. It also got Mrs. Myerson to talk about her happy childhood. The machine was magical in its own special way.

For additional rubrics, see p. WA10.

Write Now

Play Scene

Prompt

Grace and the Time Machine is a play in one scene.

Think about several characters having a conversation.

Now write a play scene, including what is said as well as stage directions.

Student Model

Characters are listed at the beginning.

> **Characters:** Alex, a ten-year-old boy; his mom; Rex, a dog
>
> **Setting:** An animal shelter in Miami, Florida
>
> **ALEX** (*points excitedly*): Look at this golden retriever. Isn't he beautiful?
>
> **MOM** (*reads sign on cage*): Rex was found on May 8 in Gil Park. He's trained and well behaved.
>
> **REX** (*softly to Alex*): Hey, please take me home. I'll never run away, again, I promise.
>
> **ALEX** (*shocked, whispers*): Was that you, Rex?
>
> **REX:** Yes, I can talk. I'm a math whiz too.
>
> **ALEX:** I like this dog. Can we take him, Mom?
>
> **MOM:** Yes, I think he'll be a good pet. Can you manage a pet and still keep your grades up?
>
> **ALEX** (*gives Rex a thumbs-up*): No problem, Mom!
> (**REX** *says Thanks but only Alex can hear.*)

Stage directions reveal Alex's feelings.

The scene is organized with an ending that suggests Alex and Rex will be an unusual twosome.

Use the model to help you write your own play scene.

209

Write Now

Look at the Prompt Explain that each sentence in the prompt has a purpose.

- Sentence 1 presents a topic.
- Sentence 2 suggests students think about the topic.
- Sentence 3 tells what to write—a play scene.

Strategies to Develop Organization/Paragraphs

Have students

- read their scenes aloud. Does the conversation unfold logically?
- Write stage directions that create an emotion, such as fear.

The street is dark and deserted, except for one man. He walks quickly and glances nervously behind him.

For additional suggestions and rubric, see pp. 211g–211h.

Writer's Checklist

☑ **Focus** Do sentences stick to the conversation?

☑ **Organization** Do stage directions explain the action?

☑ **Support** Do details give information about the characters?

☑ **Conventions** Are stage directions set apart in special type?

Scoring Rubric — Narrative Retelling

Rubric 4 3 2 1	4	3	2	1
Connections	Makes connections and generalizes beyond the text	Makes connections to other events, stories, or experiences	Makes a limited connection to another event, story, or experience	Makes no connection to another event, story, or experience
Author's Purpose	Elaborates on author's purpose	Tells author's purpose with some clarity	Makes some connection to author's purpose	Makes no connection to author's purpose
Characters	Describes the main character(s) and any character development	Identifies the main character(s) and gives some information about them	Inaccurately identifies some characters or gives little information about them	Inaccurately identifies the characters or gives no information about them
Setting	Describes the time and location	Identifies the time and location	Omits details of time or location	Is unable to identify time or location
Plot	Describes the problem, goal, events, and ending using rich detail	Tells the problem, goal, events, and ending with some errors that do not affect meaning	Tells parts of the problem, goal, events, and ending with gaps that affect meaning	Retelling has no sense of story

Retelling Plan

☑ **Week 1** Assess Strategic Intervention students.

☑ **Week 2** Assess Advanced students.

☑ **This week assess Strategic Intervention students.**

☐ **Week 4** Assess On-Level students.

☐ **Week 5** Assess any students you have not yet checked during this unit.

Use the Retelling Chart on p. TR16 to record retelling.

Selection Test To assess with *Grace and the Time Machine*, use Selection Tests, pp. 29–32.

Fresh Reads for Differentiated Test Practice For weekly leveled practice use, pp. 43–48.

SUCCESS PREDICTOR

Social Studies in Reading

PREVIEW/USE TEXT FEATURES

After students preview "What's There to Do?", ask:

- **How do the subheads help you figure out what ideas the article will include?** (*Each subhead lists an idea for something to do.*)

Link to Social Studies

Have pairs discuss good deeds they have done or could do for neighbors, family, or friends.

EXPOSITORY NONFICTION

Use the sidebar on p. 210 to guide discussion. Point out that expository nonfiction can explain an idea. Students can use text structure and text features to understand the selection better. The ideas here are organized by type of activity. Discuss how the title, introduction, subheads, and artwork show what the selection covers.

DAY 4 Grouping Options

Reading
Whole Group Discuss the Question of the Day.

Group Time Differentiated Instruction
Read "What's There to Do?" See pp. 188f–188g for the small group lesson plan.

Whole Group Use p. 211a.

Language Arts
Use pp. 211e–211k.

Social Studies in Reading

What's There to Do?

adapted from *101 Outdoor Adventures*
by Samantha Beres

Expository Nonfiction

Genre

- Expository nonfiction can introduce new ideas about people, places, and things.
- Though usually illustrated with photos, it is sometimes illustrated with art.

Text Features

- Subheads separate parts of the text.
- The art gives ideas for the activity suggested.

Link to Social Studies

Work with a partner to come up with another activity idea. Include helpful hints about how to successfully complete the activity. The class might create a master list of new ideas.

Grace and her friends built a time machine. Here are some other activities you can do with friends on a summer day.

Help a Neighbor

Any time is a good time to give a gift. This gift can't be wrapped with paper and ribbon— it's a gift of time.

If you have a neighbor whom you know and who could use your help, organize a squad of friends to lend a helping hand. If your neighbor has a yard, you might cut the grass, pull weeds, or even help plant flowers or vegetables. If your neighbor doesn't have a yard, offer to clean windows, wash the car, help get groceries, run an errand, or paint something. If your neighbor tries to pay you, don't accept. After all, you don't pay someone who gives you a birthday gift, do you?

210

Content-Area Vocabulary | Social Studies

artistic	skilled in any of the fine arts, such as sculpture, music, or literature
crochet	needlework or knitting created by looping thread or yarn into links with a single hooked needle
squad	any small group of persons working together

 AudioText

Put On an Arts-and-Crafts Show

If you have some artistic friends and relatives, you can have your own arts-and-crafts show.

Decide where to have the show—outside on the sidewalk, in your front yard, or in a park. If you have a show in a public place, ask permission.

To prepare, ask friends and family if they would like to display their art in public. Make a list of things they would like to enter and ask them to have their items ready by the date of the show. Also ask them to label each piece with their name, a phone number, and a price, in case someone wants to buy it.

Before the show, figure out what you'll need to set up. You will need a table and maybe a clothing rack, if you have handmade clothes, quilts, or blankets to sell. A child's easel or a clothesline and clothespins are a good way to show off pictures.

Send out announcements (e-mail messages would work) or put up posters to advertise the show. Here's a list of arts and crafts you might try to include: drawings, paintings, photographs, sculptures, pottery, quilts, handmade jewelry, and knitted and crocheted items.

Reading Across Texts

Grace and her friends showed that they were creative. Which of the two activities in this selection do you think they would have enjoyed more?

Writing Across Texts

Write about why you think as you do.

Answer Questions Use prior knowledge to answer questions about this text.

211

Strategies for Nonfiction

USE SUBHEADS A subhead identifies the specific topic, or idea, covered in a selection. Subheads can be used to find information to answer test questions.

Use the Strategy

1. Read the test question and locate a keyword or phrase.
2. Scan the subheads for information that matches the keyword from the question.

GUIDED PRACTICE Discuss how to use the strategy to answer the following question.

What are two ways this article suggests you could help a neighbor?

INDEPENDENT PRACTICE Discuss the process used to find information in the following question.

According to the author, how can you advertise an arts-and-crafts show?

Answer Questions

Prior knowledge means using experiences and information students already know to answer questions when reading. Some answers require prior knowledge and details from the selection.

CONNECT TEXT TO TEXT

Reading Across Texts

Discuss different ways to be creative, using students' experiences and the activities in this article. Then have students decide which two activities from the article Grace and her friends would enjoy most.

Writing Across Texts Students can use notes from their discussion to explain and support their thinking.

Fluency Assessment Plan

- ☑ **Week 1** Assess Advanced students.
- ☑ **Week 2** Assess Strategic Intervention students.
- ☑ **This week assess On-Level students.**
- ☐ **Week 4** Assess Strategic Intervention students.
- ☐ **Week 5** Assess any students you have not yet checked during this unit.

Set individual goals for students to enable them to reach the year-end goal.

- Current Goal: 100–110 WCPM
- Year-End Goal: 130 WCPM

Fluency, particularly for English learners reading texts in English, develops gradually and through much practice. Focus on each student's improvement rather than solely monitoring the number of words correct per minute.

To develop fluent readers, use Fluency Coach.

DAY 5   Grouping Options

Reading
Whole Group
Revisit the Question of the Week.

Group Time
Differentiated Instruction
Reread this week's Leveled Readers. See pp. 188f–188g for the small group lesson plan.

Whole Group
Use p. 211b–211c.

Language Arts
Use pp. 211d–211l.

CHARACTERIZATION/DIALOGUE

Fluency

DAY 1

Model Reread aloud "Journal of a Teenage Genius" on p. 188m. Explain how you use what you know about the characters to choose a voice for each one and make the dialogue more interesting. Model for students as you read.

DAY 2

Echo Reading Read aloud p. 196, starting at Grace's third speech. Point out how characters' voices sound more animated when they discover new ideas. Have students practice by echo reading p. 196 three times.

DAY 3

Model Read aloud p. 206, starting at Mrs. Meyerson's third speech. Have students note how your voice changes for each character and expresses the character's feelings. Practice as a class by doing three echo readings.

DAY 4

Partner Reading Partners practice reading aloud the dialogue on p. 206, three times. They should express characters' feelings, make dialogue sound realistic, and give each other feedback.

Monitor Progress   **Check Fluency WCPM**

As students reread, monitor their progress toward their individual fluency goals. Current Goal: 100–110 words correct per minute. End-of-Year Goal: 130 words correct per minute.

If... students cannot read fluently at a rate of 100–110 words correct per minute,
then... make sure students practice with text at their independent level. Provide additional fluency practice, pairing nonfluent readers with fluent readers.

If... students already read at 130 words correct per minute,
then... they do not need to reread three times.

SUCCESS PREDICTOR

DAY 5

Assessment

Individual Reading Rate Use the Fluency Assessment Plan and do a one-minute timed reading of either selection from this week to assess students in Week 3. Pay special attention to this week's skill, characterization/dialogue. Provide corrective feedback for each student.

RETEACH

◎ Draw Conclusions

TEACH

Review the definition of *draw conclusions* on p. 188. Students can complete Practice Book p. 78 on their own, or they can complete it as a class. As they write conclusions, remind students they can use facts from their prior experiences.

ASSESS

Have students review the end of the story. Ask if they agree with the conclusion that Mrs. Myerson's life was changed by the time machine. They should support their answer with story details. *(Possible response: Yes, because it got her to leave her yard and helped her remember happier times.)*

For additional instruction on draw conclusions, see DI·54.

EXTEND SKILLS

Flashback

TEACH

A flashback interrupts the story to tell about an event that happened earlier.

- A flashback briefly "pauses" the present-time events of the story.
- A flashback helps explain something that is happening now in the story.

Ask students to find a flashback on pp. 202–203. Have them tell what event is described in the flashback. *(Grace's visit to The Gambia.)*

ASSESS

Have students work in small groups to find an example of a flashback on p. 206 and then write answers to these questions:

1. **Where and when does this scene take place?** *(It takes place in Heidelberg when Mrs. Myerson was a young girl.)*
2. **What happens in this scene?** *(Mrs. Myerson plays in the brook, and her cousin Fritz splashes her cousin Lili.)*
3. **How does it help us understand Mrs. Myerson?** *(It shows she once had a happy family life.)*

OBJECTIVES

- ◎ Use facts and details to draw conclusions.
- ● Identify flashbacks in literature.

Skills Trace
◎ Draw Conclusions

Introduce/Teach	TE: 4.2 162–163, 188–189; 4.5 608–609
Practice	TE: 169, 179, 181, 195, 203, 205, 615, 619 PB. 63, 67, 68, 73, 77, 78, 243, 247, 248
▶ Reteach/Review	**TE: 4.2 153, 187b, 211b, DI•53, DI•54; 4.5 569, 591, 629b, DI•56 PB: 56, 226, 236**
Test	Selection Test: 25–28, 29–32, 97–100; Benchmark Test: Units 2, 5

Access Content Reteach the skill by reviewing the Picture It! lesson on draw conclusions in the ELL Teaching Guide, pp. 50–51.

Draw Conclusions

- **Drawing a conclusion** is forming an opinion based on what you already know or on the facts and details in a text. Facts and details are the small pieces of information in an article or story.
- Facts and details "add up" to a conclusion. Conclusions formed by the author or the reader must make sense.

Directions Read the following passage. Then complete the diagram and answer the question.

> When I got off the boat and stepped onto the island, I was amazed by what I saw. The sand was white and soft, almost like powder. It felt so soothing on my tired feet. There were palm trees that stretched up into the sky. Large flowers of every color surrounded the bases of the trees. Butterflies with spots and stripes fluttered in the light of the summer sun. A small path led through the trees to an open-air market, where travelers were greeted by friendly faces, delicious-smelling foods, and sweet island music.

Fact or Detail		Fact or Detail		Fact or Detail		Conclusion
1. The sand was **white and soft, like powder.**	+	2. There were palm **trees and flowers.**	+	3. Butterflies **fluttered in the summer sun.**	=	4. The island was a _____ place. **Possible answer: beautiful**

5. What conclusion could you draw about the people of this island?
   Possible answer: The people of the island are friendly and like to have visitors.

 Home Activity Your child drew a conclusion using facts or details in a passage. Describe to your child your idea of a perfect island. Have your child draw conclusions from your description.

▲ **Practice Book** p. 78

Vocabulary and Word Study

VOCABULARY STRATEGY

Word Structure

PREFIXES Remind students that the prefix *re-* means "again." Have students review *Grace and the Time Machine* to find five verbs that can be turned into new words by adding the prefix *re-*. Have them record their work in a chart like the one below.

Word in Play	Add Prefix re-	Sentence with New Word
think	rethink	I'll rethink my plan to make it better.
work		
read		
visit		
set		
play		
told		

Words from Mythology

The lesson vocabulary word *atlas* comes from Atlas, a figure from Greek mythology who carried the heavens on his shoulders. Have small groups use reference sources to find out more about Atlas and other figures from Greek and Roman mythology. Have each group identify at least one English word with a connection to mythology and share information about it.

BUILD CONCEPT VOCABULARY

Imagination

LOOKING BACK Remind students of the question of the week: *What can we accomplish using our imaginations?* Discuss how this week's Concept Web of vocabulary words relates to the theme of imagination. Ask students if they have any words or categories to add. Discuss whether words and categories are appropriately related to the concept.

MOVING FORWARD Preview the title of the next selection, *Marven of the Great North Woods.* Ask students which Concept Web words might apply to the new selection based on the title alone. Put a star next to these words on the web.

Display the Concept Web and revisit the vocabulary words as you read the next selection to check predictions.

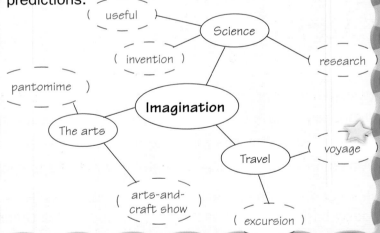

Monitor Progress

Check Vocabulary

If... students suggest words or categories that are not related to the concept,	**then...** review the words and categories on the Concept Web and discuss how they relate to the lesson concept.

SUCCESS PREDICTOR

Speaking and Viewing

SPEAKING

Dramatization

SET-UP Have groups improvise a short scene involving the characters in *Grace and the Time Machine* the day after the play ends. Groups should assign these parts: Grace, Aimee, Kester, Maria, Raj. A narrator may be named to fill in the story between lines of dialogue.

PLANNING Have students brainstorm what might happen in the scene and agree on a situation to portray, such as traveling to another time and place or creating a new invention. Remind students that in many dramatic scenes, characters try to solve a problem or achieve a goal.

PRESENTATION Provide time for students to act out their scene. Share these suggestions:

- Act like the character did in the play.
- Use natural language, speaking as people do in real life.
- Use body language, tone of voice, and facial expressions to show a character's feelings.

Listening Tips

- Focus on each actor as he or she speaks.
- Listen for the problem a character has or what a character wants to do or achieve.
- As you listen, pay attention to the actors' tone of voice, facial expressions, and movements to identify feelings not stated in words.

VIEWING

Analyze Media

Have the class watch a short scene from a recorded stage play or improvisation. Discuss the scene with the class. Ask:

1. **How did each character use his or her voice, body, or facial expressions to show emotion?**
2. **How did the actors use movement to show what was happening in the scene?**
3. **What did you enjoy about the scene? What changes could make the scene more effective?**

Responses will vary but should be based on observed details.

Support Vocabulary Use the following to review and extend vocabulary and to explore lesson concepts further:
- ELL Poster 8, Days 3–5 instruction
- Vocabulary Activities and Word Cards in ELL Teaching Guide, pp. 52–53

Assessment For information on assessing students' speaking, listening, and viewing, see the ELL and Transition Handbook.

Grammar Irregular Plural Nouns

OBJECTIVES

- Define and identify irregular plural nouns.
- Use irregular plural nouns correctly in writing.
- Become familiar with irregular plural noun assessment on high-stakes tests.

Monitor Progress

Grammar

If... students have difficulty identifying irregular plural nouns,	then... provide additional instruction and practice in The Grammar and Writing Book pp. 92–95.

DAILY FIX-IT

This week use Daily Fix-It Transparency 8.

Spiral REVIEW

ELL

Grammar Support See the Grammar Transition lessons in the ELL and Transition Handbook.

▲ **The Grammar and Writing Book**
For more instruction and practice, use pp. 92–95.

DAY 1 Teach and Model

DAILY FIX-IT

1. We built a time machine. In our base ment. *(machine in; basement)*

2. It can goes forword or backward in time. *(go forward)*

READING-GRAMMAR CONNECTION

Write the following sentence on the board:

> The <u>children</u> made a time machine.

Point out that the word *children* is a plural noun. Because it does not form its plural by adding *-s, -es, or -ies,* it is called an **irregular plural noun.**

Display Grammar Transparency 8. Read aloud the definitions and sample sentences. Work through the items.

Irregular Plural Nouns

A plural noun names more than one person, place, or thing. Most nouns add -s to form the plural. An **irregular plural noun** has a special form for the plural.

Singular Nouns The <u>child</u> learned about the <u>life</u> of the <u>woman</u>.
Irregular Plural Nouns The <u>children</u> learned about the <u>lives</u> of the <u>women</u>.

Some nouns and their irregular plural forms are calf/calves, child/children, deer/deer, foot/feet, goose/geese, life/lives, man/men, moose/moose, mouse/mice, sheep/sheep, shelf/shelves, and woman/women.

Directions Write *S* if the underlined noun is singular. Write *P* if it is plural.

1. The <u>children</u> made a time machine. **P**
2. They built it from things they found on <u>shelves</u> in the kitchen. **P**
3. One <u>woman</u> asked them to take her back to Germany. **S**
4. Grace learned about the <u>lives</u> of Nana and Mrs. Myerson. **P**
5. Nana could put no weight on her broken <u>foot</u>. **S**

Directions Write the plural form of each underlined singular noun.

6. Long ago Great-Grandpa lived on a dairy farm with <u>cow</u> and <u>calf</u>.
   cows, calves
7. Other farmers nearby kept <u>sheep</u> and <u>goose</u>.
   sheep, geese
8. They all had cat to kill the <u>mouse</u> in their barn.
   cats, mice, barns
9. The woods around them were full of <u>moose</u> and <u>deer</u>.
   moose, deer
10. Many of the <u>man</u> on the <u>farm</u> moved to the city to find <u>job</u>.
    men, farms, jobs

Unit 2 Grace and the Time Machine Grammar **8**

▲ **Grammar Transparency** 8

DAY 2 Develop the Concept

DAILY FIX-IT

3. Our time machine took us back in time, we lands in an ancient forest. *(time. We landed)*

4. We saw wolfes and mooses among the trees. *(wolves and moose)*

GUIDED PRACTICE

Review the concept of irregular plural nouns.

- A plural noun names more than one person, place, or thing. Most nouns add *-s* to form the plural.

- An **irregular plural noun** has a special form for the plural. Some nouns and their irregular plural forms are *child/children, deer/deer, foot/feet, goose/geese, leaf/leaves, life/lives, man/men, mouse/mice, ox/oxen.*

HOMEWORK Grammar and Writing Practice Book p. 29. Work through the first two items with the class.

Irregular Plural Nouns

A plural noun names more than one person, place, or thing. Most nouns add -s to form the plural. An **irregular plural noun** has a special form for the plural.

Singular Nouns The <u>man</u> photographed a <u>wolf</u> chasing a <u>moose</u>.
Irregular Plural Nouns Two <u>men</u> photographed some <u>wolves</u> chasing some <u>moose</u>.

Some nouns and their irregular plural forms are child/children, deer/deer, foot/feet, leaf/leaves, life/lives, loaf/loaves, man/men, moose/moose, mouse/mice, sheep/sheep, tooth/teeth, wolf/wolves, and wife/wives.

Directions Write the irregular plural noun in each sentence.

1. A time machine could show us what our lives were like long ago. **lives**
2. Before there were cars or trains, we were on our feet a lot more. **feet**
3. Many men worked in the fields or hunted in the forests. **men**
4. Their wives spent hard days cooking and cleaning. **wives**
5. I wonder if children were happy then. **children**

Directions If the noun is plural, write *P*. If it is singular, write its plural form. If the noun could be either singular or plural, write *S/P*.

6. loaves **P**
7. sheep **S/P**
8. wolf **wolves**
9. leaves **P**
10. deer **S/P**
11. tooth **teeth**
12. mouse **mice**

Home Activity Your child learned about irregular plural nouns. Say the words tooth, wife, and sheep and have your child say and spell the plural form of each word.

▲ **Grammar and Writing Practice Book** p. 29

DAY 3 Apply to Writing

DAILY FIX-IT

5. Did you see men and woman on your visit to the distant past. *(women; past?)*

6. There were no human beings but there was huge animals. *(beings, but; were)*

USE IRREGULAR PLURALS

Point out that many common nouns have irregular plurals. Explain to students that learning to spell irregular plural nouns correctly will make their writing easy to read and understand.

• Have students review something they have written to see if they can improve it by correcting the spelling of irregular plural nouns.

HOMEWORK Grammar and Writing Practice Book p. 30.

Irregular Plural Nouns

Directions Write sentences using the plural forms of the given nouns.

1. wolf, tooth **Possible answers:**
A pack of wolves tore at the meat with their teeth.

2. man, wife The men and their wives went to a movie.

3. mouse, loaf Mice have been eating those loaves of bread.

4. child, foot Did the children hurt their feet on the rocks?

5. moose, leaf Moose ran through the leaves.

Directions Write about what you would like to see if you traveled back in time or into the future in a time machine. Use at least two irregular plural nouns and underline them.

Possible answer: I would visit the future to see if <u>men</u> and <u>women</u> were still alive. Maybe there would be only animals such as <u>mice</u> or <u>moose</u>.

School-Home CONNECTION **Home Activity** Your child learned how to use irregular plural nouns in writing. Have your child write a note or an e-mail to a family member about life long ago. Have your child use at least two irregular plural nouns.

▲ **Grammar and Writing Practice Book** p. 30

DAY 4 Test Preparation

DAILY FIX-IT

7. Next we'l take our time machine. To visit the future. *(we'll; machine to)*

8. What will citys of the future look like! *(cities; like?)*

STANDARDIZED TEST PREP

Test Tip

Remember that there are no consistent patterns for spelling irregular plural nouns. The plural forms must be learned.

Example: When one goose joins another goose, we have two <u>geese</u>. When one moose joins another moose, we have two <u>moose</u>.

HOMEWORK Grammar and Writing Practice Book p. 31.

Irregular Plural Nouns

Directions Mark the letter of the correct plural form for each underlined word.

1. <u>Life</u> were different long ago.
A Lifes
B Live's
C Lives
D Live

2. <u>Woman</u> worked at home.
A Women
B Womans
C Womens'
D Woman

3. The <u>man</u> went out and worked.
A mans
B mens
C man
D men

4. Their <u>wife</u> did the housework.
A wifes
B wives
C wive
D wivies

Directions Mark the letter of the word that correctly completes each sentence.

5. Not all ___ went to school.
A woman
B children
C childrens
D womens

6. Women spun yarn from the wool of ___.
A mooses
B sheeps
C sheeps
D sheep

7. They made ___ of bread in their kitchens.
A loaves
B loaf's
C loafes
D loaf

8. Sometimes they saw ___ in the forest.
A mooses
B wolves
C moosies
D wolfs

School-Home CONNECTION **Home Activity** Your child prepared for taking tests on irregular plural nouns. Have a discussion with your child about the families in your neighborhood. Ask him or her to use the singular and plural forms of man, woman, and child.

▲ **Grammar and Writing Practice Book** p. 31

DAY 5 Cumulative Review

DAILY FIX-IT

9. Its fun to going back and forth in time *(It's fun going; time.)*

10. You must come with us on a trip, you'll loved it. *(trip. You'll love)*

ADDITIONAL PRACTICE

Assign pp. 92–95 in The Grammar and Writing Book.

EXTRA PRACTICE Grammar and Writing Practice Book p. 129.

TEST PREPARATION Grammar and Writing Practice Book pp. 153–154.

ASSESSMENT

CUMULATIVE REVIEW Grammar and Writing Practice Book p. 32.

Irregular Plural Nouns

Directions Underline the singular nouns and circle the plural nouns in the sentences.

1. Long ago wolves ran through forests where our city is now.
2. Then men and women from Europe arrived on these shores.
3. They brought cows, horses, chickens, and geese to this country.
4. They built a town with houses and schools for their children.
5. They worked hard to improve their lives.

Directions Write C if the underlined plural noun is correct. If it is not correct, write the correct form.

6. How did they brush their <u>teeths</u> in the old days? teeth
7. I love those old-fashioned crusty <u>loaves</u>. C
8. <u>Mices</u> were everywhere years ago. Mice
9. Many <u>deers</u> roamed the land. deer
10. Clothes were made mostly from the wool of <u>sheep</u>. C

Directions Write one or two sentences about animals. Use at least two irregular plural nouns. **Possible answers:**

The words *moose* and *mouse* sound the same, but they mean very different things. Moose are huge, and mice are tiny.

School-Home CONNECTION **Home Activity** Your child reviewed irregular plural nouns. Look at an article from a newspaper or magazine. Have your child point out three or four irregular plural nouns.

▲ **Grammar and Writing Practice Book** p. 32

Writing Workshop Play Scene

OBJECTIVES

- Identify qualities of a play scene.
- Write a play scene including visual details.
- Focus on organization/paragraphs.
- Use a rubric.

Genre Play Scene
Writer's Craft Visual Details
Writing Trait Organization/Paragraphs

E L L

Organization/Paragraphs Make sure English learners can decode words in the prompt. Work with students to complete a cloze sentence that addresses the prompt and could be used to launch writing. [e.g., "_____ make great pets because _____."]

Writing Traits

FOCUS/IDEAS The writer has a clear story to tell. Stage directions describe important visual details.

ORGANIZATION/PARAGRAPHS The conversation between Sam and Edy flows naturally. Stage directions show when nonspoken action takes place.

VOICE The writer captures the language and personality of two children.

WORD CHOICE The writer uses vivid descriptions (*a long green tentacle*) and lively, realistic dialogue (*Zap it!*).

SENTENCES The writer uses a variety of kinds and lengths of sentences, including interjections and appropriate fragments.

CONVENTIONS There is excellent control and accuracy.

DAY 1 Model the Trait

READING-WRITING CONNECTION

- *Grace and the Time Machine* is organized as a play in one scene.
- Stage directions provide visual details that help the story flow naturally.
- Students will write a **play scene** that is organized to include visual details.

MODEL ORGANIZATION/PARAGRAPHS

Display Writing Transparency 8A. Then discuss the model and the writing trait of organization/paragraphs.

Think Aloud When I read this play scene, I see that it is organized so that the conversation flows smoothly. The names of the characters are listed at the top. Then each character's name appears before his or her line. Stage directions tell me how to visualize unspoken actions and feelings.

Play Scene/Skit

A **play scene** or **skit** is a brief story told in dialogue—the words that the characters actually say. A play is meant to be performed before an audience, but a reader can imagine what is happening by reading the lines and the author's descriptions of the action, known as the stage directions.

Real Life

Characters are listed at the beginning.

Characters: Sam; Edy, Sam's sister
Sam's dark bedroom. Sam and Edy are in front of the television, operating the video game controls. A window is behind them.

Dialogue is lively and realistic.

Sam: This is so awesome. Look at that.
Edy: Watch out! It's after you! Zap it!
Sam *(working frantically)*: Gotcha!
The window fills with a green light.
Sam: Oh, man! Here's another one!
Edy: Let me get this one. Come on, boy.

Stage directions give visual details.

A long, green tentacle slowly enters the room through the window. It waves in the air, as if taking in information.
Sam *(his eyes on the screen):* Nice one!
Edy: Ha! So long, space aliens.
The tentacle withdraws. The light fades.
Sam: That was cool. I wish things were like that in real life.

Unit 2 *Grace and the Time Machine*   Writing Model **8A**

▲ **Writing Transparency** 8A

DAY 2 Improve Writing

WRITER'S CRAFT
Visual Details

Display Writing Transparency 8B. Read the directions and work together to identify strong visual details.

Think Aloud **VISUAL DETAILS** Tomorrow we will be writing a play scene about two characters having a conversation. I'm going to write about my two best friends trying to decide which game to play. My scene should include visual details so that the reader can see actions and feelings that might be unspoken. For example, I can add stage directions to explain the characters' body language.

GUIDED WRITING Give students extra practice in supplying visual details by having them write a description of a villain or hero from fiction.

Visual Details

Good writing helps the reader "see" what is happening. Writers provide **visual details** with exact and vivid nouns, adjectives, verbs, and figures of speech.

Weak A dinosaur came quickly out of the forest.
Strong A tyrannosaurus burst from a tangle of creepers and lunged at us.

Directions Read the paragraph. Then find items in the box that give stronger visual details than the underlined words. Write your answers on the numbered lines.

| blue-green glow | oozed | monstrous |
| a ghastly mask of terror | slimy | dash |

1. The <u>wet</u> creature crawled across the field toward the houses. 2. Its body gave off a <u>light</u>. 3. When it <u>moved</u> over the grass, it left a sticky trail. 4. Two or three people who had not found shelter tried to <u>run</u> to the forest. 5. One man's face was <u>scared</u> as he stumbled. 6. The <u>big</u> shape had terrified the entire village.

1. slimy
2. blue-green glow
3. oozed
4. dash
5. a ghastly mask of terror
6. monstrous

Directions Think of two or three characters for a play. Write strong visual details to describe them. **Possible answer:**
Andy: a tall skinny boy who wears glasses; Ms. Soames, Andy's teacher: a woman with fluffy gray hair; Julia, Andy's friend: a short, dark-haired girl who loves math

Unit 2 *Grace and the Time Machine*   Writer's Craft **8B**

▲ **Writing Transparency** 8B

DAY 3 Prewrite and Draft

READ THE WRITING PROMPT

on page 209 in the Student Edition.

Grace and the Time Machine is a play in one scene.

Think about several characters having a conversation.

Now write a play scene, including what is said as well as stage directions.

Writing Test Tips

- Make your characters' speech—or dialogue—sound the way people really talk.
- Describe important actions occurring on stage using adverbs and prepositions (walks *quickly through* the door).
- Organize your writing carefully. Always begin with a description of the scene.

GETTING STARTED Students can do any of the following:

- Create a chart about each character with the headings *Name, Age, Appearance,* and *Personality.*
- Draw a sketch to help visualize the scene.
- Write a two- or three-sentence summary of what the scene is about.

DAY 4 Draft and Revise

EDITING/REVISING CHECKLIST

☑ Do I include visual details?

☑ Are irregular plural nouns spelled correctly?

☑ Does the dialogue sound the way people really speak?

☑ Are words with *ar* and *or* spelled correctly?

See *The Grammar and Writing Book,* pp. 92–97.

Revising Tips

Organization/ Paragraphs

- Describe the scene clearly at the beginning.
- Check that each character's name appears before he or she speaks.
- Read the dialogue aloud to see if the characters respond naturally to each other.

PUBLISHING Print students' plays in script form, with characters' names in bold type and stage directions in italic type. Some students may wish to revise their work later.

ASSESSMENT Use the scoring rubric to evaluate students' work.

DAY 5 Connect to Unit Writing

How-to Report	
Week 1	Poem 161g–161h
Week 2	News Story 187g–187h
Week 3	Play Scene 211g–211h
Week 4	Describe a Job 239g–239h
Week 5	Explanation 259g–259h

PREVIEW THE UNIT PROMPT

Think of something that you know how to do well. Write a clear, step-by-step description of how to do this task or activity. Make your report interesting to read and easy to understand.

APPLY

- A how-to report explains the steps for making or doing something.
- The writer of a how-to report must often include visual details when explaining how to perform an action.

Writing Trait Rubric

	4	3	2	1
Organization/ Paragraphs	Conversation presented in clear order; includes visual details	Conversation presented in order; some visual details	Conversation confusing at times; few visual details	No organization to conversation; no visual details
	Play scene flows naturally	Play scene generally flows naturally	Play scene lacks natural flow	Play scene confusing; lacks format

Spelling & Phonics **Words with *ar*, *or***

- Spell words with *ar* and *or*.

Generalization

Connect to Phonics The vowel sound in *arm* is often spelled *ar*: *start*. The vowel sound in *for* is often spelled *or*: *morning*. The vowels *a* and *o* have a slightly different sound when they are followed by *r*. Vowels followed by *r* are called r-controlled vowels.

Spelling Words

1. morning*	11. partner
2. forest	12. storm
3. garbage	13. Florida
4. form	14. apartment
5. alarm	15. sport
6. corner	16. force
7. story	17. forward*
8. argue	18. sharp*
9. backyard	19. garden*
10. start*	20. Arkansas

Challenge Words

21. departure	24. snorkel
22. margarine	25. carnation
23. informative	

*Word from the selection

Spelling/Phonics Support See the ELL and Transition Handbook for spelling support.

DAY 1 Pretest and Sort

PRETEST

Use the Dictation Sentences from Day 5 to administer the pretest. Read the word, read the sentence, and then read the word again. Guide students in self-correcting their pretests and correcting any misspellings.

Monitor Progress

Spelling

If... students misspell more than 5 pretest words,	then... use words 1–10 for Strategic Intervention.
If... students misspell 1–5 pretest words,	then... use words 1–20 for On-Level practice.
If... students correctly spell all pretest words,	then... use words 1–25 for Advanced Learners.

HOMEWORK Spelling Practice Book, p. 29.

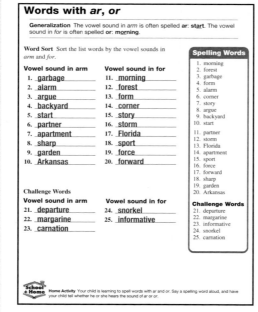

▲ **Spelling Practice Book** p. 29

DAY 2 Think and Practice

TEACH

Vowels that are followed by *r* are called r-controlled vowels because the *r* changes the vowel sound. Write and say *spot*. Then write and say *sport*. Underline *or* and say the sound the letters stand for. Repeat with the words *start* and *stat*, which mean "quickly" and "a short word for *statistic*." Lead students in saying *or* and *ar*.

sport

MISSING LETTERS Have students copy the list words, replacing *ar* and *or* with two blank lines. Then have them close their books and fill in *ar* or *or* to complete each word correctly.

HOMEWORK Spelling Practice Book, p. 30.

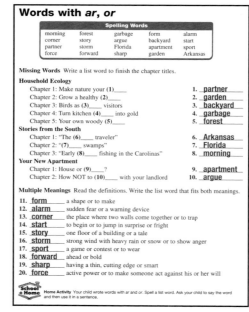

▲ **Spelling Practice Book** p. 30

DAY 3 Connect to Writing

WRITE DIALOGUE

Model how to indicate the speaker in a script by writing the character's name and a colon. Ask students to use at least five spelling words to write a short dialogue between two characters.

Frequently Misspelled Words

favorite   morning

These words may seem easy to spell, but they are often misspelled by fourth-graders. Alert students to these frequently misspelled words. Have students say *fa-vor-ite* to hear the *or* sound. Have students clearly pronounce the *ing* sound in *morning*.

HOMEWORK Spelling Practice Book, p. 31.

Words with ar, or

Proofread a Travel Brochure Check the brochure before it goes to the printer. Circle six misspelled words. Write the words correctly. Then correct the sentence fragment.

All aboard! Daily sightseeing trains leave Tallahassee at 6 A.M. in the (morening) Start your day right. With some delicious (Florida) orange juice. Enjoy the view from the top (storry) of our observation car. Have lunch in everyone's (favarit) tearoom in Theodore, Alabama, and tour the (graden) There's just time to hike in the forest around the Buffalo River before our last stop at Little Rock, (Arkansaw)

Spelling Words: morning, forest, garbage, form, alarm, corner, story, argue, backyard, start, partner, storm, Florida, apartment, sport, force, forward, sharp, garden, Arkansas

1. morning   2. Florida
3. story   4. favorite
5. garden   6. Arkansas
7. Start your day right with some delicious Florida orange juice.

Missing Letters Chose *ar* or *or* to complete each word. Then write the word.

8. __gue   8. argue
9. ap__tment   9. apartment
10. sh__p   10. sharp
11. p__tner   11. partner
12. g__bage   12. garbage
13. f__ward   13. forward
14. sp__t   14. sport
15. st__m   15. storm
16. f__ce   16. force
17. g__den   17. garden
18. al__m   18. alarm

Frequently Misspelled Words: favorite, morning

Home Activity Your child identified misspelled words with ar or or. Say list words and spell them incorrectly. Have your child correct his mistakes.

▲ **Spelling Practice Book** p. 31

DAY 4 Review

REVIEW WORDS WITH *ar, or*

Have students play Tic-Tac-Toe with a partner. Instead of writing *X* or *O*, students should write *ar* words or *or* words.

Spelling Strategy
Pronouncing for Spelling

We spell some words wrong because we say them wrong.

Step 1: Say the word correctly. Listen to the sound of each letter.

Step 2: Say the word again as you write it.

HOMEWORK Spelling Practice Book, p. 32.

Words with ar, or

Spelling Words: morning, forest, garbage, form, alarm, corner, story, argue, Florida, backyard, start, partner, storm, Florida, apartment, sport, force, forward, sharp, garden, Arkansas

Crossword Puzzle Use the clues to finish the puzzle. Words are list words.

Across
2. A.M.
5. home
6. quarrel
7. strength
9. heavy rain
10. pointed

Down
1. angle
3. trash
4. garden
8. woods

Word Scramble Unscramble the list words. Write the word on the line.

11. wordarf   11. forward
12. npeartr   12. partner
13. mlara   13. alarm
14. oridfla   14. Florida

Home Activity Your child has learned to read, write, and spell words with ar and or. Use list words to play Hangman with your child.

▲ **Spelling Practice Book** p. 32

DAY 5 Posttest

DICTATION SENTENCES

1. Breakfast is a good way to begin the morning.
2. Many animals live in the forest.
3. You'll have less garbage if you recycle.
4. Fill in the form to apply for the job.
5. We jumped when the alarm rang.
6. Write your name in the upper left corner.
7. Dad told us a bedtime story.
8. Even friends sometimes argue.
9. We swam in their backyard pool.
10. Let's start the race.
11. Choose a partner for the game.
12. The power went out during the storm.
13. Florida has sandy beaches.
14. We moved to a new apartment.
15. What sport do you like to play?
16. The force of the wind bent the trees.
17. Step forward when I say your name.
18. The can has a sharp edge.
19. Mom planted roses in the garden.
20. My friend lives in Arkansas.

CHALLENGE

21. The plane's departure was delayed.
22. Do you want margarine on your bread?
23. The speech was very informative.
24. The diver uses a snorkel to breathe underwater.
25. The groom wore a carnation in his lapel.

OBJECTIVES

- Formulate an inquiry question that is connected to this week's lesson focus.
- Effectively and efficiently find, evaluate, and communicate information related to an inquiry question using electronic sources.

New Literacies	
Day 1	**Identify Questions**
Day 2	**Navigate/Search**
Day 3	**Analyze**
Day 4	**Synthesize**
Day 5	**Communicate**

NEW LITERACIES

Internet Inquiry Activity

EXPLORE USING OUR IMAGINATIONS

Use the following 5-day plan to help students conduct this week's Internet inquiry activity on the power of our imagination to accomplish things. Remind students to follow classroom rules when using the Internet.

DAY 1

Identify Questions Discuss the lesson focus question: *What can we accomplish when we use our imaginations?* Create a list of categories students can investigate further, such as writers, artists, filmmakers, great thinkers, futurists, innovators, and inventors. Some students may wish to focus their searches on a particular person. Have them work individually, in pairs, or in small groups to write an inquiry question they want to answer.

DAY 2

Navigate/Search Have students determine keywords related to their inquiry questions. Students may need to narrow their inquiry questions, depending on the initial information they find. Discuss how to use a Web site's related links to find additional information. Remind students when searching to scan sites to see if they contain relevant information. Have them record URLs of helpful sites or, if allowed, bookmark them for later analysis.

DAY 3

Analyze Have students explore the Web sites they identified on Day 2. Tell them to review each site carefully to locate information that helps answer their inquiry questions and analyze information for credibility and reliability. Remind students to think critically about sources. For example, some commercial sites pick up text from other sites, so finding the same text in two locations does not necessarily make it more credible. Students can print out and highlight relevant information, if allowed, or take notes about it.

DAY 4

Synthesize Have students synthesize information from Day 3. Remind them to create a logical organization that combines information from different sources and focuses on a few important points.

DAY 5

Communicate Have students share their inquiry results. They can use a word processing program to create a short report and then present it to the class. Remind them to practice their presentations at home.

RESEARCH/STUDY SKILLS
Advertisement

TEACH

Ask students where they might find information about traveling to places like France or Japan. Remind them that newspapers often show advertisements for trips. Display a few travel ads and explain their parts.

- A **photograph** or **illustration** shows the product or service that is being sold, in this case a place to visit.

- A **headline** is the eye-catcher. This is usually in large type and is the most important idea about the product.

- **Information** about the product or service explains why we should visit. The text tries to make the product or service as appealing as possible.

- A **company name** tells who makes the product or provides the service. It may also include information about the **cost** of the product or service.

Advertisements may use **loaded words,** such as *best, greatest,* and *fun-packed* to persuade readers to buy or do something. It is important to distinguish **statements of fact** from loaded words in an ad.

Give pairs a magazine or newspaper ad and have them identify its parts. Ask them to look for loaded words and facts. Then, discuss these questions:

1. What is your ad trying to persuade you to do or buy?

2. What statements of fact and loaded words can you find in the ad?

Responses will vary but should be based on specific details from the ad.

Headline ——

Illustration

Company name

ASSESS

Check that pairs recognize the persuasive elements in the ads they analyze. Have them circle loaded words and underline statements of fact in the ads.

For more practice or to assess students, use Practice Book pp. 79–80.

Advertisement

- All **advertisements** sell a product or service. Advertisers want their product or service to appear at its best or most appealing.
- There are four parts to an advertisement: a photo or other picture of what is being sold, a headline in large type that "yells" about the product, information about the product, and who makes the product or service.

Directions Use this advertisement to answer the questions below.

The Sunny Fun Cruise will give your family the trip of a lifetime! The Sunny Fun Cruise ship sails to such locations as Jamaica, the Bahamas, and the Florida Keys. Your family will love the ride aboard this beautiful ship that has five refreshing swimming pools, three fine-dining restaurants, and two state-of-the-art game rooms. At any of the ship's ports you can enjoy water activities like snorkeling, shopping, and touring the local town. Contact the Sunny Fun Travel Company today to book a family vacation everyone will love!

1. What is this advertisement trying to sell?
   It is trying to sell a family cruise.
2. What is the headline in this advertisement?
   The Sunny Fun Cruise will give your family the trip of a lifetime!
3. Who wants you to book this cruise?
   Sunny Fun Travel Company
4. How does the ad appeal to families?
   It talks about things families would be interested in, such as swimming, games, and activities you can do at the ports.
5. In what kind of magazine would you see an ad like this?
   Possible answer: In a magazine about travel.

▲ **Practice Book** p. 79

Directions Use the advertisement below to answer the questions.

Ever wanted to go back in time? Now you can! With the Time Machine 3000 you can be swept away to the past or the future! Using the Time Machine 3000 is as easy as setting your watch. Simply set the day, date, and year you wish to travel to, hit the "Go" button, and you're off to a place you've been before or one you've never seen! The Time Machine 3000 is a product of the famous Gail Scientific Research Group—the same company that brought you the Teleporter 2000. Imagine the places you could go and the things you could do with the Time Machine 3000! Buy it today!

6. How does the headline grab your attention?
   It says they've found a way to go back in time.
7. Why does the ad include a picture of the Time Machine 3000?
   Possible answer: So you know it is a real product.
8. Why does the ad tell you that using the machine *is as easy as setting your watch?*
   The ad wants you to think it is easy to use so you will buy it.
9. Why do you think the ad told you that the Gail Scientific Research Group was the same company that brought you the Teleporter 2000?
   You will trust that the product is good and that it works.
10. Based on this ad, would you buy the Time Machine 3000? Why or why not?
    Possible answer: No; it doesn't explain how it would actually work.

 Home Activity Your child learned to identify the parts of an advertisement. Look through a newspaper or magazine with your child. Ask your child to indicate the different parts of the advertisements that appear in the periodical.

▲ **Practice Book** p. 80

Assessment Checkpoints *for the Week*

Selection Assessment

Use pp. 29–32 of Selection Tests to check:

☑ **Selection Understanding**

☑ **Comprehension Skill** *Draw Conclusions*

☑ **Selection Vocabulary**

aboard	mechanical
atlas	miracle
awkward	reseats
capable	vehicle
chant	

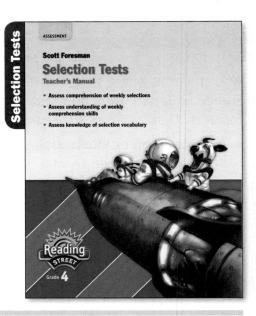

ASSESSMENT
Selection Tests
Scott Foresman
Selection Tests
Teacher's Manual
• Assess comprehension of weekly selections
• Assess understanding of weekly comprehension skills
• Assess knowledge of selection vocabulary
Reading STREET
Grade 4

Leveled Assessment

On-Level
Strategic Intervention
Advanced

Use pp. 43–48 of Fresh Reads for Differentiated Test Practice to check:

☑ **Comprehension Skill** *Draw Conclusions*

☑ **REVIEW Comprehension Skill** *Compare and Contrast*

☑ **Fluency** *Words Correct Per Minute*

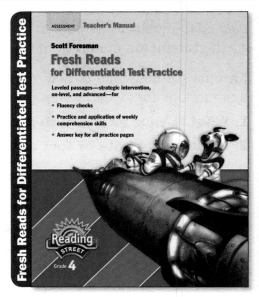

ASSESSMENT   Teacher's Manual
Scott Foresman
Fresh Reads
for Differentiated Test Practice
Leveled passages—strategic intervention, on-level, and advanced—for
• Fluency checks
• Practice and application of weekly comprehension skills
• Answer key for all practice pages
Reading STREET
Grade 4

Managing Assessment

Use Assessment Handbook for:

☑ **Observation Checklists**

☑ **Record-Keeping Forms**

☑ **Portfolio Assessment**

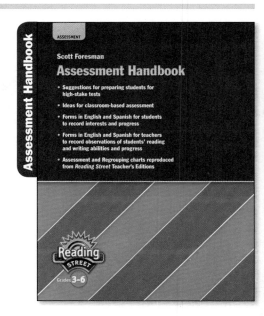

ASSESSMENT
Scott Foresman
Assessment Handbook
• Suggestions for preparing students for high-stake tests
• Ideas for classroom-based assessment
• Forms in English and Spanish for students to record interests and progress
• Forms in English and Spanish for teachers to record observations of students' reading and writing abilities and progress
• Assessment and Regrouping charts reproduced from *Reading Street* Teacher's Editions
Reading STREET
Grades 3–6

Oregon

Planning Guide for Common Curriculum Goals

Marven of the Great North Woods

Reading Street Teacher's Edition pages	Grade 4 Oregon Grade-Level Standards for English/Language Arts

Oral Language

Speaking/Listening Build Concept Vocabulary: 212l, 223, 231, 239c
Read Aloud: 212m

EL.04.RE.01 Read aloud grade-level narrative text and informational text fluently and accurately with effective pacing, intonation, and expression.

EL.04.RE.10 Understand, learn, and use new vocabulary that is introduced and taught directly through informational text, literary text, and instruction across the subject areas.

Word Work

Consonant Pairs *ng, nk, ph, wh*: 239i–239j

EL.04.WR.15 Spell correctly: syllables (word parts each containing a vowel sound, such as *sur-prise* or *e-col-o-gy*).

Reading

Comprehension Fact and Opinion: 212–213, 216–231, 236–239, 239b
Monitor and Fix Up: 212–213, 216–231
Vocabulary Lesson Vocabulary: 214b, 223, 231
Dictionary/Glossary: 214–215, 221, 239c
Fluency Model Volume: 212l–212m, 239a
Self-Selected Reading: LR28–36, TR16–17
Literature Genre—Biography: 216
Reader Response: 233

EL.04.RE.07 Understand and draw upon a variety of comprehension strategies as needed— rereading, self-correcting, summarizing, class and group discussions, generating and responding to essential questions, making predictions, and comparing information from several sources.

EL.04.RE.17 Locate information in titles, tables of contents, chapter headings, illustrations, captions, glossaries, indexes, graphs, charts, diagrams, and tables to aid understanding of grade-level text.

EL.04.RE.20 Identify and/or summarize sequence of events, main ideas, facts, supporting details, and opinions in informational and practical selections.

Language Arts

Writing Describe a Job: 239g–239h
Six-Trait Writing Focus/Ideas: 234–235, 239g–239h
Grammar, Usage, and Mechanics Singular Possesive Nouns: 239e–239f
Research/Study Graph: 239l
Technology New Literacies: 239k

EL.04.RE.17 Locate information in titles, tables of contents, chapter headings, illustrations, captions, glossaries, indexes, graphs, charts, diagrams, and tables to aid understanding of grade-level text.

EL.04.WR.12 Use words that describe, explain, or provide additional details and connections.

Unit Skills

Writing How-To Report: WA2–9
Poetry: 260–263
Project/Wrap-Up: 264–265

EL.04.WR.25 Write informational reports: ask and then address a central question about an issue or event; include facts and details for focus; develop the topic with simple facts, details, examples, and explanations; use more than one source of information, including speakers, books, newspapers, other media sources, and online information.

This Week's Leveled Readers

Intensive Intervention
SCOTT FORESMAN
SiDEWALKS
Intensive Intervention for Tier 3 Students

Nonfiction

Below-Level

EL.04.RE.19 Use structural features found in informational text (e.g., headings and sub-headings) to strengthen comprehension.
EL.04.RE.20 Identify and/or summarize sequence of events, main ideas, facts, supporting details, and opinions in informational and practical selections.

Fiction

On-Level

EL.04.RE.20 Identify and/or summarize sequence of events, main ideas, facts, supporting details, and opinions in informational and practical selections.
EL.04.LI.05 Make and confirm predictions about text using ideas presented in the text itself.

Nonfiction

Advanced

EL.04.RE.20 Identify and/or summarize sequence of events, main ideas, facts, supporting details, and opinions in informational and practical selections.
EL.04.RE.21 Identify key facts and information after reading two passages or articles on the same topic.

Content-Area Content Standards and Benchmarks in This Lesson

Science

SC.05.PS.03.01 Recognize and describe the motion of an object in terms of one or more forces acting on it. (Previews Grade 5 Benchmark)

SC.05.LS.01.01 Classify a variety of living things into groups using various characteristics. (Previews Grade 5 Benchmark)

SC.05.LS.05 Describe the relationship between characteristics of specific habitats and the organisms that live there. (Previews Grade 5 Benchmark)

SC.05.LS.06 Describe how adaptations help a species survive. (Previews Grade 5 Benchmark)

Social Studies

SS.05.EC.06.01 Recognize that people earn income by exchanging their labor for wages and salaries. (Previews Grade 5 Benchmark)

SS.05.GE.04 Identify physical and human characteristics of regions in the United States and the processes that have shaped them. (Previews Grade 5 Benchmark)

Oregon!

A FAMOUS OREGONIAN
Linus Carl Pauling

Linus Carl Pauling (1901–1994) was a Portland-born chemist who studied the application of quantum mechanics to molecular structures. Pauling was a double Nobel Prize winner, earning the 1954 Nobel Prize in chemistry and the 1962 Nobel Peace Prize. He also wrote a highly successful textbook, *The Nature of the Chemical Bond, and the Structure of Molecules and Crystals,* which he created from lectures he had given. It was one of the most influential textbooks of the twentieth century.

Students can . . .
Read an encyclopedia entry about the Nobel Prize. Ask students to list categories in which the prize is awarded and what the recipients receive.

A SPECIAL OREGON PLACE
Hells Canyon

Hells Canyon is the deepest river gorge in North America and the main attraction of Hells Canyon National Recreation Area. It is a ten-mile-wide natural wonder. Sandbars surround the Snake River, which flows through the canyon. The lower slopes of the canyon are steep and desertlike, and the peaks of Idaho's Seven Devils Mountains rise eight thousand feet around it. Wildlife such as cougars, bears, elk, and bighorn sheep live in the canyon. Visitors can view Native American artifacts, as well as evidence of the first settlers and 1860s gold miners at various sites.

Students can . . .
Create a computer slide presentation that includes facts about Hells Canyon.

OREGON FUN FACTS
Did You Know?

- Native Americans in the Northwest used cedar trees to produce canoes, cloth, fishing lines, eating utensils, and bows and arrows.

- William Holmes House is the oldest American home in Oregon City. It was the site of the 1849 inaugural address of Joseph Lane, the territory's first governor.

- Malheur National Forest, known as Oregon's "outback," is a vast, sparsely populated expanse of buttes, gorges, lakes, and deserts.

Students can . . .
Research the Australian outback. Ask students to create a Venn diagram comparing it to Oregon's Malheur National Forest.

Unit 2
Work and Play

CONCEPT QUESTION
What is the value of work and play?

Week 1
How can we learn to appreciate the talents of others?

Week 2
How can we work together to achieve a goal?

Week 3
What can we accomplish by using our imaginations?

Week 4
What is the value of a job well done?

Week 5
What is the job of the President of the United States?

Week 4

EXPAND THE CONCEPT
What is the value of a job well done?

CONNECT THE CONCEPT

▶ **Build Background**
business, resourceful, team, trustworthy

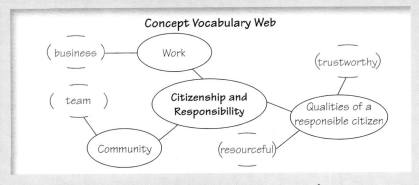

Concept Vocabulary Web

▶ **Social Studies Content**
Minnesota, Citizenship, A Bookkeeper's Job, Child Labor Laws

▶ **Writing**
Job Description

▶ **Internet Inquiry**
Job Responsibilities

Marven of the North Woods **212a**

Preview Your Week

What is the value of a job well done?

Marven
of the Great North Woods

by Kathryn Lasky illustrated by Kevin Hawkes

Genre A **biography** is the story of a real person's life as told by someone else. As you read this biography, try to imagine yourself in Marven's place.

Is the great north woods a great place for Marven?

Student Edition pages 216–232

Audio CD

Genre	Biography
Vocabulary Strategy	Dictionary/Glossary
Comprehension Skill	Fact and Opinion
Comprehension Strategy	Monitor and Fix Up

Paired Selection

Reading Across Texts

List Details About a Lumberjack's Life

Genre

E-mail

Text Features

The "To:" Box
The "Subject:" Box
The Message

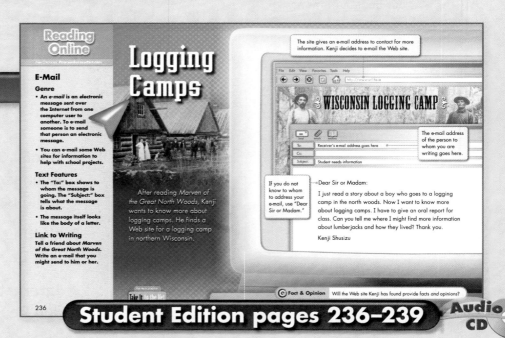

Reading Online

E-Mail

Genre
- An *e-mail* is an electronic message sent over the Internet from one computer user to another. To e-mail someone is to send that person an electronic message.
- You can e-mail some Web sites for information to help with school projects.

Text Features
- The "To:" box shows to whom the message is going. The "Subject:" box tells what the message is about.
- The message itself looks like the body of a letter.

Link to Writing
Tell a friend about *Marven of the Great North Woods*. Write an e-mail that you might send to him or her.

Logging Camps

After reading *Marven of the Great North Woods*, Kenji wants to know more about logging camps. He finds a Web site for a logging camp in northern Wisconsin.

The site gives an e-mail address to contact for more information. Kenji decides to e-mail the Web site.

WISCONSIN LOGGING CAMP

File Edit View Favorites Tools Help

To:	Receiver's e-mail address goes here
Cc:	
Subject:	Student needs information

The e-mail address of the person to whom you are writing goes here.

If you do not know to whom to address your e-mail, use "Dear Sir or Madam."

Dear Sir or Madam:

I just read a story about a boy who goes to a logging camp in the north woods. Now I want to know more about logging camps. I have to give an oral report for class. Can you tell me where I might find more information about lumberjacks and how they lived? Thank you.

Kenji Shusizu

Fact & Opinion Will the Web site Kenji has found provide facts and opinions?

Student Edition pages 236–239

Audio CD

Read It
ONLINE
PearsonSuccessNet.com
• Student Edition
• Leveled Readers

Leveled Readers

◉ **Skill** Fact and Opinion

◉ **Strategy** Monitor and Fix Up

Lesson Vocabulary

Below-Level

On-Level

Advanced

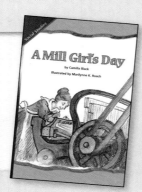

ELL Reader

· Concept Vocabulary
· Text Support
· Language Enrichment

A Mill Girl's Day
by Camilla Black
Illustrated by Marilynne K. Roach

Integrate Social Studies Standards

• U.S. Geography
• Citizenship
• U.S. History

✓ Read

Marven of the Great North Woods, pp. 216–232

"Logging Camps," pp. 236–239

Leveled Readers

Below-Level   On-Level   Advanced

• Support Concepts
• Develop Concepts
• Extend Concepts
• Social Studies Extension Activity

ELL Reader

✓ Build Concept Vocabulary

Citizenship and Responsibility, pp. 212l–212m

✓ Teach Social Studies Concepts

Minnesota, p. 219
Citizenship, p. 225
A Bookkeeper's Job, p. 227
Child Labor Laws, p. 229

✓ Explore Social Studies Center

Make a Job List, p. 212k

Marven of the Great North Woods

Weekly Plan

READING

45–90 minutes

TARGET SKILLS OF THE WEEK

- **Comprehension Skill**
  Fact and Opinion
- **Comprehension Strategy**
  Monitor and Fix Up
- **Vocabulary Strategy**
  Dictionary/Glossary

DAY 1 — PAGES 212l–214b, 239a, 239e–239k

Oral Language

QUESTION OF THE WEEK *What is the value of a job well done?*

Read Aloud: "Counting on Johnny," 212m
Build Concepts, 212l

Comprehension/Vocabulary

Comprehension Skill/Strategy Lesson, 212–213
- Fact and Opinion **T**
- Monitor and Fix Up

Build Background, 214a

Introduce Lesson Vocabulary, 214b
cord, dismay, grizzly (bear), immense, payroll **T**

Read Leveled Readers

Grouping Options 212f–212g

Fluency

Model Volume, 212l–212m, 239a

DAY 2 — PAGES 214–223, 239a, 239e–239k

Oral Language

QUESTION OF THE DAY *What were working conditions like for Marven at the logging camp?*

Comprehension/Vocabulary

Vocabulary Strategy Lesson, 214–215
- Dictionary/Glossary **T**

Read *Marven of the Great North Woods,* 216–223

Grouping Options 212f–212g

- Fact and Opinion **T**
- Monitor and Fix Up
- Dictionary/Glossary **T**
- **REVIEW** Main Idea **T**

  Develop Vocabulary

Fluency

Echo Reading, 239a

LANGUAGE ARTS

30–60 minutes

Trait of the Week

Focus/Ideas

DAY 1 (Language Arts)

Grammar, 239e
Introduce Singular Possessive Nouns **T**

Writing Workshop, 239g
Introduce Describe a Job
Model the Trait of the Week: Focus/Ideas

Spelling, 239i
Pretest for Consonant Pairs *ng, nk, ph, wh*

Internet Inquiry, 239k
Identify Questions

DAY 2 (Language Arts)

Grammar, 239e
Develop Singular Possessive Nouns **T**

Writing Workshop, 239g
Improve Writing with Time-Order Words

Spelling, 239i
Teach the Generalization

Internet Inquiry, 239k
Navigate/Search

DAILY WRITING ACTIVITIES

Day 1 Write to Read, 212

Day 2 Words to Write, 215
Strategy Response Log, 216, 223

DAILY SOCIAL STUDIES CONNECTIONS

Day 1 Citizenship and Responsibility Concept Web, 212l

Day 2 Time for Social Studies: Minnesota, 219
Revisit the Citizenship and Responsibility Concept Web, 223

DAILY SUCCESS PREDICTORS

for Adequate Yearly Progress

Monitor Progress and Corrective Feedback

Vocabulary — Check Vocabulary, *212l*

RESOURCES FOR THE WEEK

- Practice Book, *pp. 81–90*
- Word Study and Spelling Practice Book, *pp. 33–36*
- Grammar and Writing Practice Book, *pp. 33–36*
- Selection Test, *pp. 33–36*
- Fresh Reads for Differentiated Test Practice, *pp. 49–54*
- The Grammar and Writing Book, *pp. 98–103*

Grouping Options for Differentiated Instruction

Turn the page for the small group lesson plan.

DAY 3
PAGES 224–235, 239a, 239e–239k

Oral Language

QUESTION OF THE DAY *How do Marven and the lumberjacks make sure their jobs are done well?*

Comprehension/Vocabulary

Read *Marven of the Great North Woods,* 224–233

Grouping Options 212f–212g

- 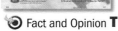 Fact and Opinion **T**
- Monitor and Fix Up
- Dictionary/Glossary **T**
- Main Idea **T**

Develop Vocabulary

Reader Response
Selection Test

Fluency

Model Volume, 239a

Grammar, 239f
Apply Singular Possessive Nouns in Writing **T**

Writing Workshop, 234, 239h
Write Now
Prewrite and Draft

Spelling, 239j
Connect Spelling to Writing

Internet Inquiry, 239k
Analyze Sources

Day 3 Strategy Response Log, 230
Look Back and Write, 233

Day 3 Time for Social Studies: Citizenship, 225;
A Bookkeeper's Job, 227; Child Labor Laws, 229
Revisit the Citizenship and Responsibility
Concept Web, 231

DAY 4
PAGES 236–239a, 239e–239k

Oral Language

QUESTION OF THE DAY *How does a person show qualities of citizenship and responsibility?*

Comprehension/Vocabulary

Read "Logging Camps," 236–239

Grouping Options 212f –212g

E-Mail/Text Features
Reading Across Texts

Fluency

Partner Reading, 239a

Grammar, 239f
Practice Singular Possessive Nouns for
Standardized Tests **T**

Writing Workshop, 239h
Draft, Revise, and Publish

Spelling, 239j
Provide a Strategy

Internet Inquiry, 239k
Synthesize Information

Day 4 Writing Across Texts, 239

Day 4 Time for Social Studies: Make a Job List,
212k

DAY 5
PAGES 239a–239l

Oral Language

QUESTION OF THE WEEK *To wrap up the week, revisit the Day 1 question.*

Build Concept Vocabulary, 239c

Fluency

Read Leveled Readers

Grouping Options 212f–212g

Assess Reading Rate, 239a

Comprehension/Vocabulary

- Reteach Fact and Opinion, 239b **T**

Narrative Writing, 239b

- Review Dictionary/Glossary, 239c **T**

Speaking and Listening, 239d
Job Description
Listen to a Description

Grammar, 239f
Cumulative Review

Writing Workshop, 239h
Connect to Unit Writing

Spelling, 239j
Posttest for Consonant Pairs *ng, nk, ph, wh*

Internet Inquiry, 239k
Communicate Results

Research/Study Skills, 239l
Graphs

Day 5 Narrative Writing, 239b

Day 5 Revisit the Citizenship and Responsibility
Concept Web, 239c

KEY ◉ = Target Skill **T** = Tested Skill

Comprehension Check Retelling, *233*

Fluency Check Fluency WCPM, *239a*

Vocabulary Check Vocabulary, *239c*

SUCCESS PREDICTOR

Small Group Plan *for Differentiated Instruction*

Daily Plan
AT A GLANCE

Reading
Whole Group
- Oral Language
- Comprehension/Vocabulary

Group Time
Differentiated Instruction
Meet with small groups to provide:
- Skill Support
- Reading Support
- Fluency Practice

Read

This week's lessons for daily group time can be found behind the Differentiated Instruction (DI) tab on pp. DI·32–DI·41.

Whole Group
- Fluency

Language Arts
- Grammar
- Writing
- Spelling
- Research/Inquiry
- Speaking/Listening/Viewing

Use *My Sidewalks on Reading Street* for Tier III intensive reading intervention.

DAY 1

On-Level	Strategic Intervention	Advanced
Teacher-Led *Page DI·33*	**Teacher-Led** *Page DI·32*	**Teacher-Led** *Page DI·33*
• Develop Concept Vocabulary • **Read** On-Level Reader *After School Excitement*	• Reinforce Concepts • **Read** Below-Level Reader *Lumberjacks*	• **Read** Advanced Reader *Danger! Children at Work* • Independent Extension Activity

(i) Independent Activities
While you meet with small groups, have the rest of the class...

- Visit the Reading/Library Center
- Listen to the Background Building Audio
- Finish Write to Read, p. 212
- Complete Practice Book pp. 83–84
- Visit Cross-Curricular Centers

DAY 2

On-Level	Strategic Intervention	Advanced
Teacher-Led *Pages 218–223*	**Teacher-Led** *Page DI·34*	**Teacher-Led** *Page DI·35*
• **Read** *Marven of the Great North Woods*	• Practice Lesson Vocabulary • Read Multisyllabic Words • **Read** or Listen to *Marven of the Great North Woods*	• Extend Vocabulary • **Read** *Marven of the Great North Woods*

(i) Independent Activities
While you meet with small groups, have the rest of the class...

- Visit the Reading/Library Center
- Listen to the AudioText for *Marven of the Great North Woods*
- Finish Words to Write, p. 215
- Complete Practice Book pp. 85–86
- Write in their Strategy Response Logs, pp. 216, 223
- Visit Cross-Curricular Centers
- Work on inquiry projects

DAY 3

On-Level	Strategic Intervention	Advanced
Teacher-Led *Pages 224–231*	**Teacher-Led** *Page DI·36*	**Teacher-Led** *Page DI·37*
• **Read** *Marven of the Great North Woods*	• Practice Fact and Opinion and Monitor and Fix Up • **Read** or Listen to *Marven of the Great North Woods*	• Extend Fact and Opinion and Monitor and Fix Up • **Read** *Marven of the Great North Woods*

(i) Independent Activities
While you meet with small groups, have the rest of the class...

- Visit the Reading/Library Center
- Listen to the AudioText for *Marven of the Great North Woods*
- Write in their Strategy Response Logs, p. 230
- Finish Look Back and Write, p. 233
- Complete Practice Book p. 87
- Visit Cross-Curricular Centers
- Work on inquiry projects

① Begin with whole class skill and strategy instruction.

② Meet with small groups to provide differentiated instruction.

③ Gather the whole class back together for fluency and language arts.

On-Level

Teacher-Led
Pages 236–239

- **Read** "Logging Camps"

Strategic Intervention

Teacher-Led
Page DI · 38

- Practice Retelling
- **Read** or Listen to "Logging Camps"

Advanced

Teacher-Led
Page DI · 39

- **Read** "Logging Camps"
- Genre Study

DAY 4

ⓘ Independent Activities

While you meet with small groups, have the rest of the class...

- Visit the Reading/Library Center
- Listen to the AudioText for "Logging Camps"
- Visit the Writing/Vocabulary Center
- Finish Writing Across Texts, p. 239
- Visit Cross-Curricular Centers
- Work on inquiry projects

On-Level

Teacher-Led
Page DI · 41

- **Reread** Leveled Reader *After School Excitement*
- Retell *After School Excitement*

Strategic Intervention

Teacher-Led
Page DI · 40

- **Reread** Leveled Reader *Lumberjacks*
- Retell *Lumberjacks*

Advanced

Teacher-Led
Page DI · 41

- **Reread** Leveled Reader *Danger! Children at Work*
- Share Extension Activity

DAY 5

ⓘ Independent Activities

While you meet with small groups, have the rest of the class...

- Visit the Reading/Library Center
- Complete Practice Book pp. 88–90
- Visit Cross-Curricular Centers
- Work on inquiry projects

Grouping Place English language learners in the groups that correspond to their reading abilities in English.

Use the appropriate Leveled Reader or other text at students' instructional level.

TiP Send home the appropriate Multilingual Summary of the main selection on Day 1.

Take It to the NET™ ONLINE
PearsonSuccessNet.com

Peter Afflerbach
For analysis of think-aloud studies and what they show about comprehension strategies, see a summary of the book *Verbal Protocols of Reading* by M. Pressley and Scott Foresman author Peter Afflerbach.

TEACHER TALK

Keywords are one or more words a researcher uses to explore a topic in an encyclopedia, index, or search engine.

Be sure to schedule time for students to work on the unit inquiry project "All in a Day's Work." This week students combine the information they have collected to answer their inquiry questions.

Looking Ahead

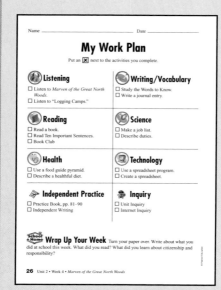

▲ **Group-Time Survival Guide** p. 26, Weekly Contract

☑ Customize Your Plan *by Strand*

ORAL LANGUAGE

SOCIAL STUDIES

Concept Development

What is the value of a job well done?

CONCEPT VOCABULARY

business   resourceful   team   trustworthy

BUILD

❑ **Question of the Week** Introduce and discuss the question of the week. This week students will read a variety of texts and work on projects related to the concept *citizenship and responsibility.* Post the question for students to refer to throughout the week. **DAY 1** *212d*

❑ **Read Aloud** Read aloud "Counting on Johnny." Then begin a web to build concepts and concept vocabulary related to this week's lesson and the unit theme, Work and Play. Introduce the concept words *business, resourceful, team,* and *trustworthy* and have students place them on the web. Display the web for use throughout the week. **DAY 1** *212l–212m*

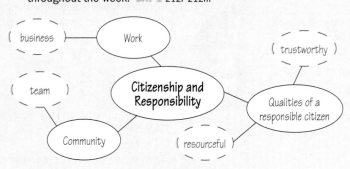

DEVELOP

❑ **Question of the Day** Use the prompts from the Weekly Plan to engage students in conversations related to this week's reading and the unit theme. **EVERY DAY** *212d–212e*

❑ **Concept Vocabulary Web** Revisit the Citizenship and Responsibility Concept Web and encourage students to add concept words from their reading and life experiences. **DAY 2** *223,* **DAY 3** *231*

CONNECT

❑ **Looking Back/Moving Forward** Revisit the Citizenship and Responsibility Concept Web and discuss how it relates to this week's lesson and the unit theme. Then make connections to next week's lesson. **DAY 5** *239c*

CHECK

❑ **Concept Vocabulary Web** Use the Citizenship and Responsibility Concept Web to check students' understanding of the concept vocabulary words *business, resourceful, team,* and *trustworthy.* **DAY 1** *212l,* **DAY 5** *239c*

VOCABULARY

◉ **STRATEGY DICTIONARY/ GLOSSARY** When you come across a word whose meaning you don't know, and the context, or words around it don't help, you can use a dictionary or glossary to find the meaning.

LESSON VOCABULARY

cord
dismay
grizzly (bear)
immense
payroll

TEACH

❑ **Words to Know** Give students the opportunity to tell what they already know about this week's lesson vocabulary words. Then discuss word meaning. **DAY 1** *214b*

❑ **Vocabulary Strategy Lesson** Use the vocabulary strategy lesson in the Student Edition to introduce and model this week's strategy, *dictionary/glossary.* **DAY 2** *214–215*

Vocabulary Strategy Lesson

PRACTICE/APPLY

❑ **Leveled Text** Read the lesson vocabulary in the context of leveled text. **DAY 1** *LR28–LR36*

❑ **Words in Context** Read the lesson vocabulary and apply *dictionary/glossary* in the context of *Marven of the Great North Woods.* **DAY 2** *216–223,* **DAY 3** *224–233*

Leveled Readers

Main Selection—Nonfiction

❑ **Writing/Vocabulary Center** Write a journal entry as if you are Marven. **DAY 4** *212k,* **DAY 5** *212k*

❑ **Homework** Practice Book pp. 84–85. **DAY 1** *214b,* **DAY 2** *215*

❑ **Word Play** Have students brainstorm lists of homophones and then select one homophone to use in drawing a cartoon showing the silly confusion that might arise from careless use of homophones. **ANY DAY** *239c*

ASSESS

❑ **Selection Test** Use the Selection Test to determine students' understanding of the lesson vocabulary words. **DAY 3**

RETEACH/REVIEW

❑ **Reteach Lesson** If necessary, use this lesson to reteach and review *dictionary/glossary.* **DAY 5** *239c*

COMPREHENSION

🎯 **SKILL FACT AND OPINION** A statement of fact can be proven true or false. To check if it is a fact you can look in a reference book, ask an expert, or use your own knowledge and experience. A statement of opinion cannot be proved true or false. It is a belief or a judgment.

🎯 **STRATEGY MONITOR AND FIX UP** When reading, you may realize you've forgotten what you just read or you did not understand what you read. When this happens, go back through the text and skim. Skimming the text is also a good strategy to use in locating facts and opinions.

TEACH

☐ **Skill/Strategy Lesson** Use the skill/strategy lesson in the Student Edition to introduce and model *fact and opinion* and *monitor and fix up*. **DAY 1** *212-213*

☐ **Extend Skills** Teach narrative writing. **ANY DAY** *239b*

Skill/Strategy Lesson

PRACTICE/APPLY

☐ **Leveled Text** Apply *fact and opinion* and *monitor and fix up* to read leveled text. **DAY 1** *LR28–LR36*

☐ **Skills and Strategies in Context** Read *Marven of the Great North Woods,* using the Guiding Comprehension questions to apply *fact and opinion* and *monitor and fix up*. **DAY 2** *216-223,* **DAY 3** *224-233*

Leveled Readers

☐ **Skills and Strategies in Context** Read "Logging Camps," guiding students as they apply *fact and opinion* and *monitor and fix up*. Then have students discuss and write across texts. **DAY 4** *236-239*

☐ **Homework** Practice Book pp. 83, 87, 88. **DAY 1** *213,* **DAY 3** *232,* **DAY 5** *239b*

Main Selection—Nonfiction

☐ **Fresh Reads for Differentiated Test Practice** Have students practice *fact and opinion* with a new passage. **DAY 3**

Paired Selection—Nonfiction

ASSESS

☐ **Selection Test** Determine students' understanding of the selection and their use of *fact and opinion*. **DAY 3**

☐ **Retell** Have students retell *Marven of the Great North Woods*. **DAY 3** *233-234*

RETEACH/REVIEW

☐ **Reteach Lesson** If necessary, reteach and review *fact and opinion*. **DAY 5** *239b*

FLUENCY

SKILL VOLUME Lowering and raising your voice during reading will make the story interesting and lively, as well as create the mood of the story.

TEACH

☐ **Read Aloud** Model fluent reading by rereading "Counting on Johnny." Focus on this week's fluency skill, volume. **DAY 1** *212l–212m, 239a*

PRACTICE/APPLY

☐ **Echo Reading** Read aloud-selected paragraphs from *Marven of the Great North Woods,* adjusting the volume in your voice. Then practice as a class by doing three echo readings of the paragraphs. **DAY 2** *239a,* **DAY 3** *239a*

☐ **Partner Reading** Have partners practice reading aloud, reading while lowering and raising the volume of their voice and offering each other feedback. As students reread, monitor their progress toward their individual fluency goals. **DAY 4** *239a*

☐ **Listening Center** Have students follow along with the AudioText for this week's selections. **ANY DAY** *212j*

☐ **Reading/Library Center** Have students reread a selection of their choice. **ANY DAY** *212j*

☐ **Fluency Coach** Have students use Fluency Coach to listen to fluent readings or practice reading on their own. **ANY DAY**

ASSESS

☐ **Check Fluency** wcpm Do a one-minute timed reading, paying special attention to this week's skill—volume. Provide feedback for each student. **DAY 5** *239a*

☑ Customize Your Plan *by Strand*

GRAMMAR

SINGULAR POSSESSIVE NOUNS A possessive noun shows ownership. A singular possessive noun shows that one person, place, or thing has or owns something. Add an apostrophe and the letter -s to a singular noun to make it possessive.

TEACH

☐ **Grammar Transparency 9** Use Grammar Transparency 9 to teach singular possessive nouns. DAY 1 *239e*

Grammar Transparency 9

PRACTICE/APPLY

☐ **Develop the Concept** Review the concept of singular possessive nouns and provide guided practice. **DAY 2** *239e*

☐ **Apply to Writing** Have students review something they have written and add to it some singular possessive nouns. **DAY 3** *239f*

☐ **Test Preparation** Examine common errors in singular possessive nouns to prepare for standardized tests. **DAY 4** *239f*

☐ **Homework** Grammar and Writing Practice Book pp., 33–35. **DAY 2** *239e*, **DAY 3** *239f*, **DAY 4** *239f*

ASSESS

☐ **Cumulative Review** Use Grammar and Writing Practice Book p. 36. **DAY 5** *239f*

RETEACH/REVIEW

☐ **Daily Fix-It** Have students find and correct errors in grammar, spelling, and punctuation. **EVERY DAY** *239e–239f*

☐ **The Grammar and Writing Book** Use pp. 98–101 of The Grammar and Writing Book to extend instruction for singular possessive nouns. **ANY DAY**

The Grammar and Writing Book

WRITING

Trait of the Week

FOCUS/IDEAS Good writers focus on a main idea and develop this idea with strong supporting details. Having a purpose, to inform, to persuade, or to entertain, helps keep focus on the main idea.

TEACH

☐ **Writing Transparency 9A** Use the model to introduce and discuss the Trait of the Week. DAY 1 *239g*

☐ **Writing Transparency 9B** Use the transparency to show students how time-order words can improve their writing. DAY 2 *239g*

Writing Transparency 9A **Writing Transparency 9B**

PRACTICE/APPLY

☐ **Write Now** Examine the model on Student Edition pp. 234–235. Then have students write their own job description. **DAY 3** *234, 239h,* **DAY 4** *239h*

> **Prompt** *Marven of the Great North Woods* describes a boy's job at a logging camp. Think about a job you might ask a friend to do. Now describe the job, explaining everything your friend will need to know.

Write Now p. 234

☐ **Writing/Vocabulary Center** Write a journal entry as if you are Marven. DAY 4 *212k,* **DAY 5** *212k*

ASSESS

☐ **Writing Trait Rubric** Use the rubric to evaluate students' writing. DAY 4 *239h*

RETEACH/REVIEW

☐ **The Grammar and Writing Book** Use pp. 98–103 of The Grammar and Writing Book to extend instruction for singular possessive nouns, time-order words, and job description. **ANY DAY**

The Grammar and Writing Book

❶ Use assessment data to determine your instructional focus.

❷ Preview this week's instruction by strand.

❸ Choose instructional activities that meet the needs of your classroom.

SPELLING

GENERALIZATION CONSONANT PAIRS *NG, NK, PH, WH*   Some words have two consonants that blend together: *among, think*. Some words have two consonants that are said as one sound: *graph, wheel*. The sound of each letter is heard in a consonant blend. In a consonant digraph, the consonant pair stands for a new sound.

TEACH

☐ **Pretest** Give the pretest for words with consonant pairs *ng, nk, ph, wh*. Guide students in self-correcting their pretests and correcting any misspellings. **DAY 1** *239i*

☐ **Think and Practice** Connect spelling to the phonics generalization for consonant pairs *ng, nk, ph, wh*. **DAY 2** *239i*

PRACTICE/APPLY

☐ **Connect to Writing** Have students use spelling words to write a newspaper want ad for a specific job. Then review frequently misspelled words: *where, when*. **DAY 3** *239j*

☐ **Homework** Word Study and Spelling Practice Book pp. 33–36. **EVERY DAY**

RETEACH/REVIEW

☐ **Review** Review spelling words to prepare for the posttest. Then provide students with a spelling strategy—problem parts. **DAY 4** *239j*

ASSESS

☐ **Posttest** Use dictation sentences to give the posttest for words with consonant pairs *ng, nk, ph, wh*. **DAY 5** *239j*

Spelling Words

1. Thanksgiving	8. nephew	15. wharf
2. among*	9. belong*	16. trunk
3. think	10. whiskers	17. strong
4. blank	11. whisper*	18. blink
5. graph	12. elephant	19. chunk
6. young*	13. white*	20. skunk
7. wheel	14. shrink	

Challenge Words

21. strengthen	23. phantom	25. whatever
22. bankrupt	24. whimsical	

*Word from the selection

RESEARCH AND INQUIRY

☐ **Internet Inquiry** Have students conduct an Internet inquiry on different job responsibilities. **EVERY DAY** *239k*

☐ **Graphs** Review terms related to types of graphs and discuss how students can use the different types of graphs to show information. **DAY 5** *239l*

☐ **Unit Inquiry** Allow time for students to combine the information they have collected to answer their inquiry questions. **ANY DAY** *141*

SPEAKING AND LISTENING

☐ **Job Description** With students working in small groups, have them prepare a presentation for a Career Day. Have groups choose a business or organization to represent and a job. The presentation should include the responsibilities of the job, the qualifications needed, and why it is a rewarding career. **DAY 5** *239d*

☐ **Listen to a Description** Invite local business people, professionals, or parents to be guest speakers informing students about their real-life jobs. Have students listen for facts and opinions to determine each speaker's point of view about his or her job. **DAY 5** *239d*

Resources for
Differentiated Instruction

LEVELED READERS

▶ **Comprehension**
  - ◎ **Skill** Fact and Opinion
  - ◎ **Strategy** Monitor and Fix Up

▶ **Lesson Vocabulary**
  - ◎ **Dictionary/Glossary**

cord | dismay | grizzly | payroll | immense

▶ **Social Studies Standards**
  - U.S. Geography
  - Citizenship
  - U.S. History

Leveled Reader Database
ONLINE
PearsonSuccessNet.com

Use the Online Database of over 600 books to

- Download and print additional copies of this week's leveled readers.
- Listen to the readers being read online.
- Search for more titles focused on this week's skills, topic, and content.

On-Level Reader

Fact and Opinion — On-Level Practice worksheet for *After School Excitement*

On-Level Practice TE p. LR32

Vocabulary — On-Level Practice worksheet for *After School Excitement*

On-Level Practice TE p. LR33

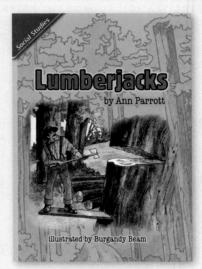

Below-Level Reader

Fact and Opinion — Below-Level Practice worksheet for *Lumberjacks*

Below-Level Practice TE p. LR29

Vocabulary — Below-Level Practice worksheet for *Lumberjacks*

Below-Level Practice TE p. LR30

Advanced

Advanced Reader

Advanced Practice TE p. LR35

Advanced Practice TE p. LR36

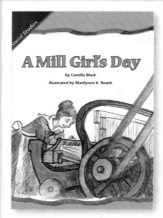

ELL Reader

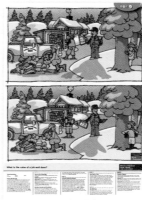

ELL Poster 9

Teacher's Edition Notes
ELL notes throughout this lesson support instruction and reference additional resources at point of use.

Teaching Guide pp. 57–63, 228–229
- Multilingual summaries of the main selection
- Comprehension lesson
- Vocabulary strategies and word cards
- ELL Reader 4.2.4 lesson

ELL and Transition Handbook

Ten Important Sentences
- Key ideas from every selection in the Student Edition
- Activities to build sentence power

More Reading

Readers' Theater Anthology
- Fluency practice
- Five scripts to build fluency
- Poetry for oral interpretation

Leveled Trade Books

- Extended reading tied to the unit concept
- Lessons in the Trade Book Library Teaching Guide

School + Home

Homework
- Family Times Newsletter
- ELL Multilingual Selection Summaries

Take-Home Books
- Leveled Readers

Cross-Curricular Centers

 **Listening**

Listen to the Selections

MATERIALS `SINGLES`
CD player, headphones, AudioText CD, student book

LISTEN TO LITERATURE Listen to *Marven of the Great North Woods* and "Logging Camps" as you follow or read along in your book. Listen for facts and opinions in *Marven of the Great North Woods*.

If there is anything you don't understand, you can listen again to any section.

 Reading/Library

Read It Again!

MATERIALS `SINGLES` `PAIRS` `GROUPS`
Collection of books for self-selected reading, reading logs, student book

Select a book you have already read. Record the title of the book in your reading log. You may want to read with a partner.

Choose from the following:

- **Leveled Readers**
- **ELL Readers**
- **Books or Stories Written by Classmates**
- **Books from the Library**
- ***Marven of the Great North Woods***

TEN IMPORTANT SENTENCES Read the Ten Important Sentences for *Marven of the Great North Woods*. Then locate the sentences in the student book.

BOOK CLUB Read other books by Kathryn Lasky listed on p. 776 of the student book. In a group, discuss which ones you liked best.

 Health

Describe a Healthy Diet

MATERIALS `GROUPS`
Food guide pyramid, writing materials, student book

Use a food guide pyramid to discuss a lumberjack's breakfast.

1. As a group, read p. 224 in the student book and list the food items the lumberjacks eat for breakfast.
2. Identify the food group for each of the food items. For example, "bacon" belongs in the meat group.
3. Discuss whether you think the lumberjacks' breakfast is a healthy way to eat. Give reasons to support your opinions.

EARLY FINISHERS List healthful foods the lumberjacks could eat. Think about the kind of work they do and the long hours they work.

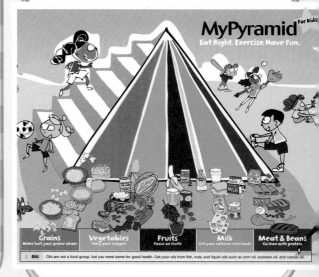

Scott Foresman Reading Street Centers Survival Kit

Use the *Marven* materials from the Reading Street
Centers Survival Kit to organize this week's centers.

Writing/ Vocabulary

Write a Journal Entry

MATERIALS
Writing materials,
student book

`SINGLES`
`PAIRS`

Write a journal entry as if you are Marven.

1. **Read pp. 221–227 of the story and note details about Marven's first day of work.**
2. **Imagine you are Marven, and write a journal entry describing your day.**
3. **Use details from the story and your imagination to tell about Marven's experiences. Write as if you are Marven, using the pronouns *I* and *me*.**

EARLY FINISHERS With a partner, discuss how you would act out Marven waking up Jean Louis. Ask your teacher if you and your partner can act out this scene for the class at a later time. *Drama*

Marven's Journal

Day 1
Today was my first day at the lumber camp. The bells rang very early, and it was so cold! My first job was to wake up the lumberjacks in the bunkhouse. Thankfully, everyone got up on his own except for one man—Jean Louis. Of course he looked the scariest of all the lumberjacks.

Social Studies

Make a Job List

MATERIALS
Writing and art materials

`GROUPS`

Brainstorm a list of jobs that can be done in the classroom.

1. Look around your classroom and think about the different jobs that can be done by students.
2. Make a list of these jobs. Include details about specific duties for each job. Tell why the job is important and how it helps the class.
3. Discuss your list with your teacher.

EARLY FINISHERS Create a chart that could be used to rate how well each job is done. For example, your chart might show four rows with descriptions for *excellent, good, fair,* or *poor* work.

Classroom Jobs

Collect homework papers: Ask everyone for their homework. Put the papers in Mr. Bartol's "homework" box. This job is important because our grades are based on our homework.

Straighten bookshelves: Put any books left out into neat rows on shelves. This job helps keep the classroom tidy and makes it easy to find books you want.

Technology

Create a Spreadsheet

MATERIALS
Spreadsheet program, printer,
student book, graph paper or
graphing program

`SINGLES`

Create an imaginary payroll spreadsheet for lumberjacks.

1. **Open the spreadsheet program on the computer.**
2. **Read pp. 224 and 227 to find out about cord chits (how the lumberjacks are paid) and Marven's bookkeeping system.**
3. **Create a spreadsheet with four columns like the one shown below. Make up names for the lumberjacks and the number of cords each one cuts for each pay period. The last column should find the total number of cords cut for the two pay periods.**
4. **Follow classroom rules for printing.**

EARLY FINISHERS Use graph paper or a graphing program to make a bar graph showing the total amount each lumberjack cut after two pay periods.

Name	Pay Period 1	Pay Period 2	Total
Jean Louis	7	6	13
Guy	4	5	9
Pierre	4	6	10
Marc	5	4	9

OBJECTIVES

- Build vocabulary by finding words related to the lesson concept.
- Listen for statements of fact and opinion.

Concept Vocabulary

business a place that makes or sells goods and services

resourceful good at thinking of ways to do things; quick-witted

team people working or acting together

trustworthy able to be depended on

Monitor Progress

Check Vocabulary

If...	then... review the
students are unable to place words on the web,	lesson concept. Place the words on the web and provide additional words for practice, such as *company* and *hard-working.*

SUCCESS PREDICTOR

DAY 1 Grouping Options

Reading

Whole Group
Introduce and discuss the Question of the Week. Then use pp. 212l–214b.

Group Time
Differentiated Instruction
 this week's Leveled Readers. See pp. 212f–212g for the small group lesson plan.

Whole Group
Use p. 239a.

Language Arts
Use pp. 239e–239k.

Build Concepts

FLUENCY

MODEL VOLUME As you read "Counting on Johnny" aloud, model varying your volume to produce a lively, fluent reading. For example, speak quietly when Paul says he is tired. Speak more loudly when reading the *Loggers Wanted* sign or to emphasize Paul's grumbling and exaggerations.

LISTENING COMPREHENSION

After reading "Counting on Johnny," use the following questions to assess listening comprehension.

1. **Is the statement "starting your own business isn't easy" a statement of fact or opinion? How do you know?** *(Opinion; it cannot be proven true or false.)* **Fact and Opinion**

2. **Why do you think the author included exaggerations such as "bunk beds stacked ten high"?** *(Possible response: For humor; to illustrate the large number of beds Paul needs)* **Exaggeration/Author's Purpose**

BUILD CONCEPT VOCABULARY

Start a web to build concepts and vocabulary related to this week's lesson and the unit theme.

- Draw the Citizenship and Responsibility Web.

- Read the sentence with the word *resourceful* again. Ask students to pronounce *resourceful* and discuss its meaning.

- Place *resourceful* in an oval attached to *Qualities of a responsible citizen.* Explain how *resourceful* relates to this concept. Read the sentences in which *business, trustworthy,* and *team* appear. Have students pronounce the words, place them on the Web, and provide reasons.

- Brainstorm additional words and categories for the Web. Keep the Web on display and add words throughout the week.

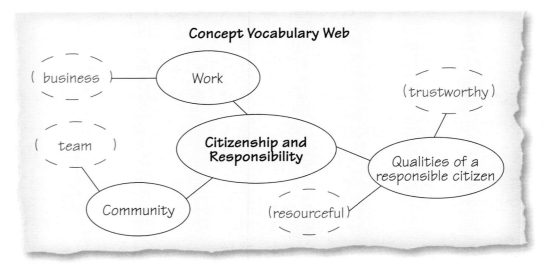

Concept Vocabulary Web

COUNTING ON JOHNNY

BY ROBERT KAUSAL

 One night Paul Bunyan, with his faithful ox Babe at his side, sat under a starry Minnesota sky and sighed, "I'm so tired, Babe."

In over thirty years of working alone, Paul had cleared timber from Maine to Arizona, straightened winding rivers, and by golly, he even dug the Grand Canyon! "Yep," he exclaimed, "I think it's about time I started my own logging company."

The following day Paul marched through the timberlands posting help wanted signs.

Hundreds of thousands of loggers swarmed to Big Onion the next day. After eliminating all of the loggers who were under ten feet tall and who couldn't pop buttons off their shirts with one breath, Paul was left with one thousand of the toughest lumberjacks this side of the Mississippi.

> **LOGGERS WANTED**
> Must be hardworking, tall, and strong. Excellent salary and benefits. If interested contact Paul Bunyan Big Onion, Minnesota

Of course, as many people know, starting your own business isn't easy. Where would the lumberjacks sleep? How would he feed them? And what would they drink? These were just a few of the problems that Paul faced.

Paul, however, was quite savvy and resourceful. He built a super-duper, colossal-sized logging camp equipped with bunk beds stacked ten high, and a griddle for flapjacks so big you could skate on it. As for drinking water, he dug a couple of small ponds—now known as the Great Lakes.

Finally, the Big Onion Lumber Company was in business. Everything was running along smoothly until Paul realized that he wasn't very good at keeping track of his bills: food bills, grain bills, medical bills. And let's not forget about payroll. The fellers could get real disagreeable and troublesome if they weren't paid on time. "Babe," Paul grumbled while chewing on a pencil the size of a spruce, "I need to find me an experienced bookkeeper who's trustworthy and can handle a twenty-foot-long fountain pen."

After posting another help wanted sign, Paul interviewed a man named Johnny Inkslinger. Johnny had been working at a bank, but eventually he lost interest. He was, however, so good at saving money that if you gave him a penny for his thoughts, you'd get change, and he'd take off his glasses when he wasn't looking at anything. Paul hired Johnny on the spot.

So began the Big Onion Lumber Company. And, even though Paul was just as tired now as when he worked alone, and certainly many of his problems did not end here, he came to enjoy working as a team with his fellow lumberjacks clearing trees from Minnesota to the West coast.

SKILLS ⟷ STRATEGIES IN CONTEXT

Fact and Opinion
Monitor/Fix Up

OBJECTIVES

⊙ Identify statements of fact and opinion.

⊙ Use a fix-up strategy to monitor comprehension of facts and opinions.

Skills Trace

⊙ **Fact and Opinion**

Introduce/Teach	TE: 4.2 212–213; 4.3 292–293; 4.6 660–661
Practice	TE: 219, 227, 229, 299, 303, 667, 675 PB: 83, 87, 88, 113, 117, 118, 263, 267, 268
Reteach/Review	TE: 4.1 125; 4.2 239b, DI·55; 4.3 313b, DI·53; 4.6 651, 685b, 747, DI·53 PB: 46, 256, 296
Test	Selection Test: 33–36, 45–48, 105–108; Benchmark Test: Unit 6

INTRODUCE

Read the following statements and have students identify them as statements of fact or opinion: *I work as a fourth-grade teacher at your school.* (fact) *Being a teacher is fun and challenging work.* (opinion) *Many teachers at this school have master's degrees.* (fact)

Have students read the information on p. 212. Explain the following:

- A statement of fact can be proven true or false, but a statement of opinion cannot.

- You can skim or scan text to look for facts or to find clue words that indicate statements of opinion.

Use Skill Transparency 9 to teach fact and opinion and monitor and fix up.

Comprehension

Skill
Fact and Opinion

Strategy
Monitor and Fix Up

Fact and Opinion

- A statement of fact can be proved true or false by looking in a reference book, asking an expert, or using your own knowledge and experience.

- A statement of opinion cannot be proved true or false. It is a belief or judgment. It often contains a word of judgment, such as *best, should,* or *beautiful.* It may begin with the words *In my opinion* or *I believe.*

Statement	Fact? How Can It Be Checked?	Opinion? What Are Clue Words?

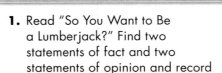 Strategy: Monitor and Fix Up

If you don't quite remember something you have read, you can skim the text to help you remember. You can use this same strategy to locate facts and opinions. To locate facts, scan for factual details, such as dates. To locate opinions, scan for opinion clue words.

Write to Read ✏

1. Read "So You Want to Be a Lumberjack?" Find two statements of fact and two statements of opinion and record them in a graphic organizer.

2. Would you want to be a lumberjack? Make a graphic organizer. Then explain why or why not. Include at least two opinions and two facts.

212

Strategic Intervention

⊙ **Fact and Opinion** Have students brainstorm clue words that may signal opinions and write them on the board. Have students copy the words as a reference when deciding if a statement is fact or opinion.

ELL

Access Content

Beginning/Intermediate For a Picture It! lesson on fact and opinion, see the ELL Teaching Guide, pp. 57–58.

Advanced Before reading "So You Want to Be a Lumberjack?" have students describe what they already know about lumberjacks.

So You Want to Be a Lumberjack?

At one time a vast forest covered much of the northern United States. This great north woods supplied lumber for homes and other buildings. Cutting down the forest trees for lumber was the job of lumberjacks.

The life of a lumberjack, or jack, was one few people would want today. Lumberjacks didn't live at home. They lived in lumber camps in the forest. They had to get up at 5 o'clock in the morning and work outside 11 hours a day, 6 days a week, in all kinds of weather–rain, snow, cold, even steamy heat.

All the jacks slept in a bunkhouse, where bunks were nailed up the walls. In my opinion, those beds must have been very uncomfortable. There was just enough room to crawl into a bunk and turn over without bumping into the bunk above.

If you love food, however, you might have enjoyed being a lumberjack. Large, hearty meals were prepared by the camp cook and served in a big dining room.

Probably the best time of day for a lumberjack was the evening. Then lumberjacks would play card games and tell stories–many of them tall tales about Paul Bunyan, the biggest lumberjack of them all.

1 Skill Look for a clue word in this paragraph that signals an opinion.

2 Strategy You could scan this paragraph to find evidence that facts have been given.

3 Strategy If you didn't catch the statement of opinion in this paragraph, you could scan now for clue words.

4 Skill There are several facts and one opinion in this last paragraph.

213

Available as **Skill Transparency** 9

TEACH

1 SKILL Model looking for clue words that indicate statements of opinion.

Think Aloud **MODEL** I'll scan this paragraph for clue words that signal an opinion. I'm looking for words that express judgment. The word *want* in the phrase "few people would want" expresses judgment, so it signals a statement of opinion.

2 STRATEGY Scan the paragraph to find statements of fact.

Think Aloud **MODEL** I know that specific information, such as dates and times, usually indicate that facts have been given. When I scan the second paragraph, I see phrases with times: "5 o'clock in the morning," "11 hours a day," and "6 days a week." These details are evidence of statements of fact.

PRACTICE AND ASSESS

3 STRATEGY Clue words: *In my opinion*

4 SKILL Opinion: The best time of day for a lumberjack was the evening. Facts: In the evenings, lumberjacks would play card games and tell stories. They told tall tales about Paul Bunyan.

WRITE Have students complete steps 1 and 2 of the Write to Read activity. You might consider using this as a whole-class activity.

Fact and Opinion

- A **statement of fact** can be proved true or false. You can look in a reference book, ask an expert, or use your own knowledge and experience.
- A **statement of opinion** cannot be proved true or false. It is a belief or a judgment. It often contains a word of judgment, such as *best*, *should*, or *beautiful*. It may begin with the words *in my opinion* or *I believe*.

Directions Read the following passage. Then complete the table. Read each statement and answer the questions at the top of each column.

I am a forester. My job is to take care of forests. Sometimes I recommend cutting trees to keep the forest healthy. If this happens, the loggers' work must follow laws that protect the environment, so the loggers should know these laws. There are other times when I suggest not cutting down trees. I disagree with people who think we should never cut down any trees. I believe we should preserve forests for the future as we use forest resources today.

Statement	Does it state a fact or an opinion?	If an opinion, what are the clue words? If a fact, how could you prove it?
I am a forester.	Fact	Check the person's job.
My job is to take care of forests.	1. Fact	2. Look up what a forester does.
I disagree with people who think we should never cut down any trees.	3. Opinion	4. *disagree, should never*

5. Find one sentence that contains both a statement of fact and a statement of opinion.

If this happens, the loggers' work must follow laws that protect the environment, so the loggers should know these laws.

Home Activity Your child identified statements of fact and statements of opinion in a short paragraph. Listen to or watch a news program with your child. Ask your child to tell you when he or she hears the news announcer expressing an opinion. Ask your child to explain why it is an opinion rather than a fact.

▲ **Practice Book** p. 83

Monitor Progress

Fact and Opinion

If... students are unable to complete **Write to Read** on p. 212,	**then...** use Practice Book p. 83 to provide additional practice.

Tech Files ONLINE

Students can search the Internet to find out more about lumbering in the past and today. Have them use a student-friendly search engine and the keywords *lumbering, logging,* and *timber.*

ELL

Build Background Use ELL Poster 9 to build background and vocabulary for the lesson concept of responsibility.

▲ **ELL Poster** 9

Build Background

ACTIVATE PRIOR KNOWLEDGE

BEGIN A VENN DIAGRAM about lumbering, or logging, in the past and today.

- Have students name things made out of wood, such as houses, furniture, and pencils. Ask them how manufacturers get wood to make these things. Guide the discussion toward lumbering.

- Have students think about lumbering in the past and lumbering today. Encourage them to consider the people, tasks, tools, transportation, environmental issues, and economics involved in lumbering. Have students tell what is the same and different about lumbering then and now. Record their responses in a Venn diagram. Add a few details of your own.

- Tell students, as they read, to look for new information about lumbering to add to the Venn diagram.

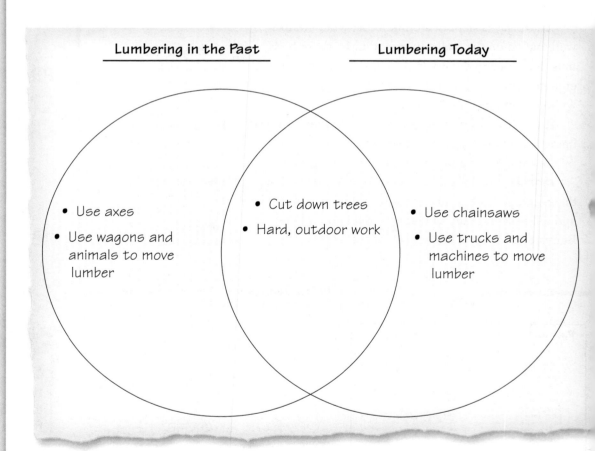

Lumbering in the Past — **Lumbering Today**

- Use axes
- Use wagons and animals to move lumber

- Cut down trees
- Hard, outdoor work

- Use chainsaws
- Use trucks and machines to move lumber

▲ **Graphic Organizer** 18

BACKGROUND BUILDING AUDIO This week's audio explores logging in the 1900s. After students listen, discuss what they found out and what surprised them most about logging in the 1900s.

Background Building Audio

Introduce Vocabulary

PICTURE CAPTIONS CHART

Create a four-column chart showing pictures with captions of lesson vocabulary words.

Word	Definition	Picture	Caption
cord	a measure of wood		a <u>cord</u> of wood
dismay			
immense			
grizzly			
payroll			

▲ **Graphic Organizer** 27

Have students list the five Words to Know in the left column of the chart. Discuss what students already know about these words. Guide students in using the glossary to find the definition of *cord* that fits with the topic of chopping wood. Then have them draw a picture and write a caption to the right of each word. ***Activate Prior Knowledge***

Ask students which Word to Know is made of two smaller words. *(payroll)* Explain that one meaning of *roll* is "a list of names." Ask how the meanings of the two words are combined in the compound word *payroll*. Tell students to notice other compound words in the selection and think about how meanings are combined. ***Compound Words***

By the end of the week, students should know the lesson vocabulary words, and can add to their definitions, pictures, or captions.

Use Multisyllabic Word Routine on p. DI·1 to help students read multisyllabic words.

Lesson Vocabulary

WORDS TO KNOW

T cord measure of quantity for cut wood, equal to 128 cubic feet. A pile of wood 4 feet wide, 4 feet high, and 8 feet long is a cord.

T dismay sudden helpless fear of what is about to happen or what has happened

T grizzly (bear) a large, gray or brownish bear of western North America

T immense very large; huge; vast

T payroll list of persons to be paid and the amount that each one is to receive

MORE WORDS TO KNOW

lumberjack person whose work is cutting down trees and sending the logs to the sawmill; woodsman; logger

silhouettes dark images outlined against a lighter background

T = Tested Word

Vocabulary

Directions Choose the word from the box that best matches each definition. Write the word on the line.

immense — 1. very big; huge; vast

cord — 2. a pile of cut wood measuring 128 cubic feet

dismay — 3. a sudden, helpless fear about what is about to happen

grizzly — 4. large, fierce North American bear

payroll — 5. a list of people to be paid and the amount each one is to receive

Check the Words You Know
___cord
___dismay
___grizzly
___immense
___payroll

Directions Choose the word from the box that best completes each sentence. Write the word on the line shown to the left.

grizzly — 6. Anil named his dog "Bear" because it reminded him of the _____ bear he'd seen in a picture.

dismay — 7. Charlotte looked with _____ at the flat tire on her bicycle.

payroll — 8. Mr. Ramos told me that I need to be on the _____ in order to be paid.

cord — 9. We will need at least a _____ of firewood to keep warm this winter.

immense — 10. Marta could not move the _____ rock from the trail.

Write a Journal Entry
On a separate piece of paper write a journal entry about a day you spent in a forest chopping firewood. Use as many vocabulary words as you can. Entries should include words from the vocabulary list and details about cutting wood in a forest.

Home Activity Your child identified and used vocabulary words from *Marven of the Great North Woods*. Read a selection with your child. List any unfamiliar words and try to figure out the meaning of each word by using other words that appear near it. Use a dictionary when necessary.

▲ **Practice Book** p. 84

Vocabulary Strategy

⊙ Use a dictionary or glossary to determine word meaning.

INTRODUCE

Discuss the strategy for using a dictionary or glossary by following the steps on p. 214.

TEACH

- Have students think about unfamiliar words as they read "Summer in the Woods."
- Model looking up *dismay* in the glossary.

MODEL I read that "to his *dismay*," the brother faces a bear. To locate a definition for *dismay*, I use the guide words at the top of each page to find entry words beginning with *d-i*. I find *dismay* and check my pronunciation. The word means "sudden, helpless fear at what is about to happen or what has happened." It makes sense that the brother feels "sudden, helpless fear" at the sight of a bear.

Words to Know

- payroll
- cord
- immense
- dismay
- grizzly

Vocabulary Strategy
for Unfamiliar Words

Dictionary/Glossary When you are reading, you may come across a word you don't know. If you can't use the context, or words and sentences around the unknown word, to figure out its meaning, you can use a dictionary or glossary for help.

1. Look in the back of your book for a glossary. If there is no glossary, look up the word in a dictionary.

2. Find the entry for the word. The entries are in alphabetical order.

3. Read the pronunciation. Saying the word softly to yourself may help you recognize it.

4. Read all the meanings given for the word.

5. Choose the meaning that makes the best sense in the sentence.

As you read "Summer in the Woods," use a dictionary or glossary to find the meanings of the vocabulary words.

214

DAY 2 Grouping Options

Reading
Whole Group Discuss the Question of the Day. Then use pp. 214–217.

Group Time Differentiated Instruction
Read *Marven of the Great North Woods.* See pp. 212f–212g for the small group lesson plan.

Whole Group Use p. 239a.

Language Arts
Use pp. 239e–239k.

 Strategic Intervention

⊙ **Dictionary/Glossary** Explain the purpose of example sentences in a glossary. Have partners find the example sentences for *dismay* and *immense* in the glossary and restate them in their own words.

ELL

Access Content Use ELL Poster 9 to preteach vocabulary. Choose from the following to meet language proficiency levels.

Beginning Use the Multilingual Lesson Vocabulary list that begins on p. 272 of the ELL Teaching Guide, as well as other home-language resources, to provide translations of the tested words.

Intermediate Have students find visuals for vocabulary words online.

Advanced Teach the lesson on pp. 214–215. Students can expand their picture captions chart (p. 214b) by writing complete sentences.

Resources for home-language words may include parents, bilingual staff members, bilingual dictionaries, or online translation sources.

Summer in the Woods

My older brother spent a summer in the deep woods and mountains of Montana. No, he was not camping with the scouts. He was on the payroll of a fishing resort, though. It sounds easy, but believe me, he earned that money.

In letters home, he told about the cozy cabins with their neat stacks of firewood outside. Part of his job each day was to load a cord of wood into a wagon and resupply each cabin. All around the pines stretched as far as he could see. They rose so high, they blocked out the sky. Some were so immense, he said they must be hundreds of years old.

There was excitement too. One day, to his dismay, he found himself facing a fat grizzly bear over a stack of wood. He was so frightened, he froze and couldn't make a sound. Lucky for him, the bear wasn't hungry and strolled away.

Words to Write

Write about an adventure you might have in the woods. Use some words from the Words to Know list.

215

PRACTICE AND ASSESS

- Explain that not every unfamiliar word needs to be looked up in a dictionary. Readers can read on to determine if the word's meaning is essential to understanding.
- Have students determine the meanings of the remaining words and tell if they used context clues, word structure, or a glossary or dictionary to find the meanings.
- If you used the picture captions chart (p. 214b), students may add details to their captions to explain more about the vocabulary words.
- Have students complete Practice Book p. 85.

WRITE Writing should include several vocabulary words as well as words that describe the woods.

Monitor Progress

Dictionary/Glossary

If... students need more practice with the lesson vocabulary,	then... use Tested Vocabulary Cards.

Vocabulary • Dictionary/Glossary

- **Dictionaries** and **glossaries** provide alphabetical lists of words and their meanings.
- Sometimes looking at the words around an unfamiliar word can't help you figure out the word's meaning. If this happens, use a dictionary or glossary to find the meaning.

Directions Read the following story. Then answer the questions below.

When Stella heard the low, growling sound, she hid quietly behind the cord of cut wood. She remembered the story about the grizzly bear who roamed the nearby woods. The bear was immense. A moment later, her Uncle Seth called out, "Stella, why are you hiding behind that pile of wood?" Stella could not hide the dismay in her voice. "I heard the bear growling," Stella answered in a fearful whisper. Stella's uncle laughed. "Didn't you know we have a new dog on the payroll? His bark sounds more like a growl than a regular bark!"

Possible answers given.

1. Which words around the word *cord* can help you figure out its meaning?
   hid behind, cut wood

2. What is the meaning of *immense*? How did you determine its meaning?
   very big, huge, vast; I used a dictionary.

3. What words around the word *dismay* help you figure out its meaning?
   could not hide, fearful whisper

4. What is the meaning of the word *grizzly?* How did you determine its meaning?
   a kind of bear; I used a dictionary.

5. Use a dictionary or glossary to find the definition for one of the words you couldn't use nearby words to understand. Write down the definition.
   Payroll: a list of people to be paid and the amount each one is to receive

Home Activity Your child identified unfamiliar words that could be defined using a dictionary or glossary. Work with your child to identify unfamiliar words in a newspaper or magazine article. Ask your child if he or she needs to use a dictionary to find the meaning of the words. If so, ask your child to look up at least one definition in a dictionary or glossary.

▲ **Practice Book** p. 85

Prereading Strategies

- Distinguish between statements of fact and opinion to improve comprehension.
- Monitor reading and use fix-up strategies to distinguish between statements of fact and opinion.

GENRE STUDY

Biography

Marven of the Great North Woods is a biography of Marven Lasky, the author's father. Explain that a biography is the story of a person's life as told by another person. It may tell about the person's whole life or just one part.

PREVIEW AND PREDICT

Have students preview the title and illustrations and discuss the topics or ideas they think this selection will cover. Encourage students to use lesson vocabulary words as they talk about what they expect to read.

Strategy Response Log

Graphic Organizer Have students write what they know and what they want to know in a KWL chart. Students will add to their KWL charts in the Strategy Response Log activity on p. 223.

Marven of the Great North Woods

by Kathryn Lasky   illustrated by Kevin Hawkes

Genre A **biography** is the story of a real person's life as told by someone else. As you read this biography, try to imagine yourself in Marven's place.

216

ELL

Build Background Say the title of the biography. Then lead a picture walk, pointing out details about ten-year-old Marven, the subject of the biography, and the setting, the north woods of Minnesota in 1918.

Consider having students read the selection summary in English or in students' home languages. See the Multilingual Summaries in the ELL Teaching Guide, pp. 61–63.

Is the great north woods a great place for Marven?

217

SET PURPOSE

Read the first page of the selection aloud to students. Have them consider the preview discussion and tell what they hope to find out about Marven Lasky as they read.

Remind students to distinguish between statements of fact and opinion as they read.

STRATEGY RECALL

Students have now used these before-reading strategies:

- preview the selection to be aware of its genre, features, and possible content;
- activate prior knowledge about that content and what to expect of that genre;
- make predictions;
- set a purpose for reading.

Remind students that, as they read, they should monitor their own comprehension. If they realize something does not make sense, they can regain their comprehension by using fix-up strategies they have learned, such as:

- use phonics and word structure to decode new words;
- use context clues or a dictionary to figure out meanings of new words;
- adjust their reading rate—slow down for difficult text, speed up for easy or familiar text, or skim and scan just for specific information;
- reread parts of the text;
- read on (continue to read for clarification);
- use text features such as headings, subheadings, charts, illustrations, and so on as visual aids to comprehension;
- make a graphic organizer or a semantic organizer to aid comprehension;
- use reference sources, such as an encyclopedia, dictionary, thesaurus, or synonym finder;
- use another person, such as a teacher, a peer, a librarian, or an outside expert, as a resource.

After reading, students will use these strategies:

- summarize or retell the text;
- answer questions they or others pose;
- reflect to make new information become part of their prior knowledge.

 AudioText

Guiding Comprehension

1 🎯 **Fact and Opinion • Inferential**

On p. 218, paragraph 2, the author writes, "It seemed for a moment as if the horses were keeping time to the music." Is this a statement of fact or opinion? How do you know?

Possible response: It is a statement of opinion. It cannot be proved true or false. It uses *seemed,* which is a judgment word.

Monitor Progress

🎯 **Fact and Opinion**

If... students have difficulty distinguishing between statements of fact and opinion,	**then...** use the skill and strategy instruction on p. 219.

---

2 **Draw Conclusions • Critical**

Text to Self **Think of a time you went to a new place or tried something new. If you were Marven, how would you feel as Mr. Murray showed you around the camp?**

Possible response: I'd feel nervous because I wouldn't know anyone, and I wouldn't know what was expected of me.

Ten-year-old Marven Lasky has left his parents and sisters and has traveled to the north woods to work there as a bookkeeper. Mr. Murray, who manages the lumber camp, shows Marven around the camp.

As they entered the camp, the longest shadows Marven had ever seen stretched across the snow, and he realized with a start that the shadows were the lumberjacks walking in the moonlight. He could smell hay and manure and saw the silhouettes of horses stomping in a snowy corral. From a nearby log building he heard the lively squeaks of a fiddle. **1** It seemed for a moment as if the horses were keeping time to the music. Mr. Murray must have thought the same. "You want to watch the horses dance, or the jacks?" He laughed. "Come along, we'll take a look."

When they entered the building, the long shadows from the yard suddenly sprung to life. Marven stared. Immense men with long beards and wild hair were jumping around to the fiddler's tunes like a pack of frantic grizzly bears. They were the biggest and wildest men Marven had ever seen.

Marven could have watched the dancing all night, but Mr. Murray said, "Come on, Marven. We start early in the **2** morning. I'll show you where you'll be living."

218

ELL

Access Content Point out that "jacks" (p. 218, paragraph 2) is short for "lumberjacks." A synonym for lumberjack is "logger." Both are names for a person who cuts down trees. Have students list other jobs that may have two or more names.

○ SKILLS ↔ STRATEGIES IN CONTEXT

Fact and Opinion

TEACH

- Remind students that a statement of fact can be proved true or false, but a statement of opinion is a judgment or belief that cannot be proved true or false.

- Point out that distinguishing between statements of fact and opinion helps students evaluate what they read.

- Model distinguishing between statements of fact and opinion using p. 218, paragraph 2, sentence 4.

Think Aloud **MODEL** When I read this statement, I notice the words *seemed as if*. These are judgment words that tell about a person's opinion. This statement tells what the horses' movement looks like. It isn't something I can prove true or false by looking in a reference book or asking an expert, so this sentence must be a statement of opinion. It isn't wrong to say the horses looked like they're moving to the music, but it isn't a fact.

PRACTICE AND ASSESS

Write a statement on the board. Discuss with students any clue words that identify the statement as fact or opinion. Read aloud five statements from pp. 218 and 220. Have pairs identify each statement as *fact* or *opinion* and give reasons for their answers.

Time for SOCIAL STUDIES

Minnesota

The lumber camp young Marven Lasky worked in was located in the Midwest region of the United States, in the forests of northern Minnesota. The great, or big, woods in the selection refers to a belt of hardwood forests extending from southeast Minnesota north to the Canadian border. These woods contain oak, maple, and basswood. Other parts of the state are covered with needle-leaf forests of spruce, fir, and pines. Lumber continues to be a major industry in the region. Minnesota has long, cold winters and warm, short summers. The Dakota Sioux and the Ojibwa were early inhabitants of the area. Early European settlers during the mid-1600s were Canadians of French, English, and Scottish descent. In the late 1800s, many German, Swedish, and Norwegian immigrants settled in the state.

Guiding Comprehension

3  Vocabulary • Dictionary/Glossary

Have students use a glossary to find the meaning of *payroll*.

Meaning: a list of persons to be paid and the amount that each one is to receive.

Monitor Progress	
Dictionary/Glossary	
If... students have difficulty using a glossary to find the meaning of *payroll*,	**then...** use the vocabulary strategy instruction on p. 221.

4 **Draw Conclusions • Critical**

Which job do you think would be more difficult for a ten-year-old: keeping a payroll or waking the lumberjacks? Explain.

Possible responses: Waking the lumberjacks is more difficult because they are so much bigger than a ten-year-old; keeping a payroll is more difficult because most ten-year-olds wouldn't know what a payroll is.

Tech Files ONLINE

Students can search an online encyclopedia or the Internet to find out more about Jewish customs. Have them use the keywords *Jewish customs* or *Judaism*. To help students find age-appropriate information on the Internet, suggest they use a student-friendly search engine. Be sure to follow classroom rules for Internet use.

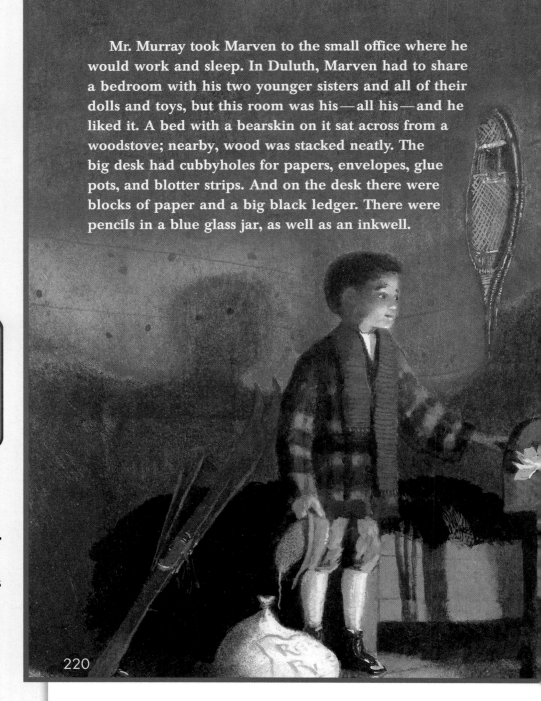

Mr. Murray took Marven to the small office where he would work and sleep. In Duluth, Marven had to share a bedroom with his two younger sisters and all of their dolls and toys, but this room was his—all his—and he liked it. A bed with a bearskin on it sat across from a woodstove; nearby, wood was stacked neatly. The big desk had cubbyholes for papers, envelopes, glue pots, and blotter strips. And on the desk there were blocks of paper and a big black ledger. There were pencils in a blue glass jar, as well as an inkwell.

220

ELL

Access Content Many words on pp. 220 and 221 indicate the time period of the selection: *woodstove, glue pots, blotter strips, inkwell, fountain pen.* Help students understand the purpose of these items by showing pictures of them and their modern-day counterparts.

Marven hoped that somewhere there was a very good pen—a fountain pen.

"In addition to keeping the payroll," Mr. Murray said, **3** "you have another job. The first bell in the morning is at four o'clock; second bell at four-fifteen. Third bell is at four-twenty. By four-twenty-five, if any jack is still in the sack, he's *en retard,* 'late.' So you, son, are the fourth bell. Starting tomorrow, you go into the bunkhouse and wake *les en retards.*"

"How?"

"You tap them on the shoulder, give 'em a shake, scream in their ear if you have to."

Then Mr. Murray said good night, and Marven was alone again.

It seemed to Marven he had just crawled under the bearskin when he heard the first bell. The fire was out and the room was cold and dark. He lit the kerosene lamp and pulled on his double-thick long underwear, two pairs of socks, two pairs of knickers, and two sweaters. Then he put on his cut-down overcoat.

After the second bell, Marven heard the jacks heading toward the eating hall. It was nearly time for his first job.

He ran through the cold morning darkness to the bunkhouse, peeked in, and counted five huge lumps in the shadows. Five jacks in the sacks. Marven waited just inside the door.

At the third bell, Marven was relieved to see two jacks climb out of bed. He thought there must be a *broche,* a Hebrew blessing, for something like this. His father knew all sorts of *broches*—blessings for seeing the sunrise, blessings for the first blossom of spring. Was there a *broche* for a rising lumberjack? If he said a *broche,* maybe the other three would get up on their own. **4**

221

VOCABULARY STRATEGY

Dictionary/ Glossary

TEACH

- Point out the glossary at the back of the student book, and remind students about its key parts: guide words, entry words, pronunciation information, parts-of-speech labels, definitions, and other forms of the entry words.

- Model using the glossary to find the meaning of *payroll.*

 Think Aloud **MODEL** I know words in a glossary are organized in alphabetical order. Since *payroll* begins with *p,* I'll open to the middle of the glossary. I can use the guide words at the top of the glossary to help me find the correct page. I'll quickly skim the page to find *payroll,* and then find the meaning that makes sense for the sentence on p. 221. A *payroll* is "a list of persons to be paid and the amount that each one is to receive."

PRACTICE AND ASSESS

Have students use the glossary to find the meaning of *lumberjack.* To assess, have them use *lumberjack* in a sentence.

Guiding Comprehension

5 **Author's Craft • Critical**

Question the Author **What words does the author use to describe Jean Louis? What is the author trying to tell you about Jean Louis?**

Students should identify visual details such as *granite boulder; beard; long, shaggy hair; thick, black eyebrows; hard blue squint of one eye.* Possible response: The author is trying to show how big and scary Jean Louis looks to Marven.

6 **Cause and Effect • Inferential**

What causes Jean Louis to open one eye?

Marven said "Lève-toi" to Jean Louis.

One lump stirred, then another. They grunted, rolled, and climbed out from under the covers. Their huge shadows slid across the ceiling.

One jack was still in the sack. Marven took a deep breath, walked bravely over to the bed, reached out, and tapped the jack's shoulder. It was like poking a granite boulder. The

5 jack's beard ran right into his long, shaggy hair; Marven couldn't even find an ear to shout into. He cupped his hands around his mouth and leaned forward.

"Up!"

The jack grunted and muttered something in French.

"Get up," Marven pleaded.

Another jack pulled on his boots, boomed, *"Lève-toi!* Jean Louis. *Lève-toi,"* and shuffled out the door.

6 *"Lève-toi!* Jean Louis. *Lève-toi,"* Marven repeated.

Jean Louis opened one eye. It glittered like a blue star beneath his thick black eyebrow. He squinted, as if trying to make out the shape in front of him, then blinked and sat up.

"Bonjour," Marven whispered.

"Qui es tu? Quel est ton nom?"

"I don't speak French—just *bonjour, derrière,* and *lève-toi."*

"That's all? No more?" The man opened his eyes wide now. "So what is your name?"

"Marven."

"Ah . . . Marven," Jean Louis repeated as if tasting the sound of his name.

"Will you get up?" Marven asked anxiously.

Jean Louis growled and fixed him in the hard blue squint of one eye.

"Please." Marven stood straight and tried not to tremble.

222

Understanding Idioms The phrase *trying to make out the shape in front of him* (p. 222, paragraph 8) contains the idiom *to make out.* Restate the sentence as "He squinted because he wanted to know who was in front of him."

Encourage students to record English idioms and their meanings in language journals, word lists, or computer files of English vocabulary.

223

STRATEGY SELF-CHECK

Monitor and Fix Up

Remind students that if they don't understand or remember what they have read, they may need to reread part of the selection more carefully or scan it to locate specific information.

Have students monitor their understanding of the text and use fix-up strategies as needed to identify statements of fact and opinion about Marven, the lumberjacks, and the camp.

SELF-CHECK

Students can ask themselves these questions to assess their ability to use the skill and strategy.

- Was I able to identify statements of fact and opinion in the selection?
- What strategies did I use to help me find statements of fact and opinion?

Monitor Progress	
Fact and Opinion	
If… students have difficulty monitoring their reading and using fix-up strategies to locate statements of fact and opinion,	**then…** revisit the skill lesson on pp. 212–213. Reteach as necessary.

Strategy Response Log

Update Graphic Organizer Review the KWL chart that students began (See p. 216). Have them record answers to their questions in the L column. Encourage them to record any new questions they have in the W column.

Develop Vocabulary

PRACTICE LESSON VOCABULARY

Students orally respond with an answer choice to each question and provide a reason for each answer. Possible reasons are given.

1. Which of these is *immense:* a mouse or a mountain? *(A mountain is immense because it is big.)*

2. Which of these is a *grizzly:* a bear or an ant? *(A grizzly is a kind of bear.)*

3. Which of these is a list: a paycheck or a *payroll?* *(A payroll is a list of people to be paid and the amount each is to be paid.)*

BUILD CONCEPT VOCABULARY

Review previous concept words with students. Ask if students have come across any words today in their reading or elsewhere that they would like to add to the Citizenship and Responsibility Concept Web, such as *ledger, bookkeeper,* or *manages.*

If you want to teach this selection in two sessions, stop here.

Guiding Comprehension

If you are teaching this selection in two days, discuss statements of fact and opinion read so far and review the vocabulary.

7 **Main Idea • Inferential**

Read p. 224, paragraph 3. Name the main idea and one supporting detail.

Main idea: Marven can't eat some of the food because it's not kosher. Possible supporting details: can't eat dairy and meat together; can eat flapjacks and oatmeal and milk together.

Monitor Progress

REVIEW Main Idea

If... students have difficulty identifying the main idea of the paragraph and a supporting detail,	**then...** use the skill and strategy instruction on p. 225.

---

8 **Fact and Opinion • Inferential**

What facts have you learned about lumberjacks and Marven's work in the camp?

Responses should include factual information about Marven's jobs as a bookkeeper and waking the lumberjacks.

DAY 3 **Grouping Options**

Reading
Whole Group Discuss the Question of the Day.

Group Time Differentiated Instruction
Read *Marven of the Great North Woods.* See pp. 212f–212g for the small group lesson plan.

Whole Group Discuss the Reader Response questions on page 233. Then use p. 239a.

Language Arts
Use pp. 239e–239k.

Jean Louis grunted and swung his feet from beneath the covers. They were as big as skillets, and one of his huge toenails was bruised black and blue. Marven tried not to stare.

Marven and Jean Louis were the last to arrive at the breakfast table. The only sounds were those of chewing and the clink of forks and knives against the plates. At each place were three stacks of flapjacks, one big steak, eight strips of bacon, and a bowl of oatmeal. In the middle of the table were bowls of potatoes and beans with molasses, platters with pies and cakes, and blue jugs filled with tea, coffee, and milk.

7 Marven stared at the food in dismay. *It's not kosher,* he thought. In Marven's house it was against ancient Jewish law to eat dairy products and meat together. And never, ever, did a Jew eat bacon. Marven came to a quick decision. One day he would eat the flapjacks and oatmeal with milk. The next day he would eat the steak and the oatmeal without milk. And never the bacon.

After breakfast, as they did every morning, the jacks went to the toolhouse to get their saws and axes. Then, wearing snowshoes and pulling huge sleds piled with equipment, they made their way into the great woods, where they would work all day.

Marven went directly to his office after breakfast. Mr. Murray was already there, setting out Marven's work. A fresh pot of ink was thawing in a bowl of hot water on the woodstove. There were two boxes on the desk filled with

8 scraps of paper.

"Cord chits," Mr. Murray said. "The jacks are paid according to the numbers of cords they cut in a pay period—two weeks. You figure it out. I'm no good as a bookkeeper

224

ELL

Context Clues Have students tell what a *cord chit* is. Point out the context clues "scraps of paper" and "number of cords they cut in a pay period" that students can use to determine that a cord chit is a scrap of paper that shows how many cords of wood a lumberjack has cut.

225

Main Idea REVIEW

TEACH

- Remind students that a main idea is the most important idea about a topic. Supporting details tell more about the main idea.
- Model identifying the main idea and some supporting details in p. 224, paragraph 3.

 Think Aloud **MODEL** The most important idea in this paragraph is that Marven can't eat foods if they aren't kosher. That's the main idea. Supporting details in the paragraph tell me more about the main idea by explaining what is and isn't kosher. Marven doesn't eat meat and dairy together, and he never eats pork.

PRACTICE AND ASSESS

- Have students read p. 224, paragraph 4, and record its main idea and supporting details using a main idea chart.
- To assess, use Practice Book p. 86.

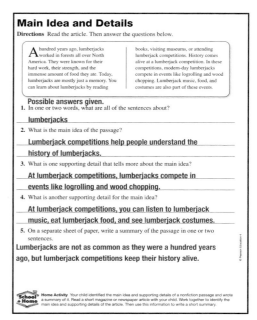

▲ **Practice Book** p. 86

Citizenship

Time for **SOCIAL STUDIES**

Good citizenship involves respect for oneself and respect for the rights, beliefs, and property of others. Students can learn and practice good citizenship at home, school, and in their everyday interactions with others. It requires students to be reliable, honest, truthful, and to respect themselves in order to earn the respect of others. It also includes respecting authority and communicating and behaving in a civil manner so conflicts can be avoided or resolved peacefully. Good citizenship requires taking personal responsibility and caring for others in need. Groups depend on their members to demonstrate characteristics of good citizenship in order to operate in an orderly, civil, and peaceful manner.

Guiding Comprehension

9 🎯 **Fact and Opinion • Inferential**

Have students distinguish between statements of fact and opinion on p. 227, paragraph 1.

The first sentence is a statement of opinion. The other sentences in the paragraph are statements of fact.

Monitor Progress

🎯 Fact and Opinion

If... students have difficulty distinguishing between statements of fact and opinion,	**then...** use the skill and strategy instruction on p. 227.

---

10 **Steps in a Process • Literal**

Describe the steps Marven took to organize the chits.

First, he listed the jack's names in alphabetical order with their symbols. Then he listed the pay periods, dated each chit, and made a chart.

11 **Character • Critical**

If Marven gave you his word that he would do something, would you trust him? Why?

Possible responses: Yes, I'd trust Marven to keep his word. He follows his family's beliefs about eating kosher. He does the work Mr. Murray asks him to do.

and have enough other things to do around here. Each chit should have the jack's name—or, if he can't write, his symbol."

"His symbol?" Marven asked weakly.

"Yes. Jean Louis's is a thumbprint. Here's one!" He held up a small piece of paper with a thumbprint on it the size of a baby's fist. Marven blinked.

226

Context Clues Help students use context clues to figure out the meaning of *triplees* on p. 227, paragraph 1. If a doublee has two names on a chit, how many does a triplee have? Isolate the root words, *double* and *triple*, plus the suffix *-ee*, which in this case indicates "possessing a particular quality."

It was all very confusing. Sometimes two names were on **9** one chit. These were called doublees; there were even some triplees. This meant more calculations. And sometimes chits were in the wrong pay-period box.

Marven sat staring at the scraps. "There is no system!" he muttered. Where to begin? His mother always made a list when she had many things to do. So first Marven listed the jacks' names alphabetically and noted the proper symbol for those who could not write. Then he listed the dates of a single pay period, coded each chit with the dates, and, with a ruler, made a chart. By the end of the morning, Marven had a system and knew the name or symbol for each man. There were many chits with the huge thumbprint of Jean Louis. **10**

Every day Marven worked until midday, when he went into the cookhouse and ate baked beans and two kinds of pie with Mr. Murray and the cook. After lunch he returned to his office and worked until the jacks returned from the forest for supper.

By Friday of the second week, Marven had learned his job so well that he finished early. He had not been on his skis since he had arrived at camp. Every day the routine was simply meals and work, and Marven kept to his office and away from the lumberjacks as much as he could. But today he wanted to explore, so he put on his skis and followed the sled paths into the woods. **11**

He glided forward, his skis making soft whisking sounds in the snow. This certainly was different from city skiing in Duluth, where he would dodge the ragman's cart or the milkman's wagon, where the sky was notched with chimney pots belching smoke, where the snow turned sooty as soon as it fell.

227

A Bookkeeper's Job

Time for SOCIAL STUDIES

Being a company's bookkeeper is an important job with many responsibilities. Bookkeepers keep track of the money that comes into or is paid out by a company. They create and update balance sheets, which show the company's current profits or losses. Business owners use a bookkeeper's records to make decisions about the company, including how much to pay their employees and how much to spend on new equipment. Banks use these records to make decisions about whether to give the company a loan. Investors use the records to decide if they should buy part of the company. The government may use these records to check whether the company has paid the correct amount of taxes.

SKILLS ↔ STRATEGIES IN CONTEXT

Fact and Opinion Monitor and Fix Up

TEACH

Remind students that they can locate statements of fact by scanning for details that can be proven true or false. To locate opinions, they can scan for judgment words. Model monitoring reading and using fix-up strategies to distinguish between statements of fact and opinion using p. 227, paragraph 1.

Think Aloud **MODEL** I'm not sure which statements are facts or opinions, so I'll scan the paragraph and look for clue words. The word *confusing* in the first sentence is a judgment word, so I know this sentence is statement of opinion. When I scan the other sentences, I see the names used for different types of chits and information about what was on the chits and how they were organized. I could prove these statements true or false by using reference sources or asking someone who worked at the camp, so these are statements of fact.

PRACTICE AND ASSESS

Have students read the third paragraph on p. 227 and decide if each sentence in the paragraph is a statement of fact or a statement of opinion. *(Both are statements of fact.)*

Guiding Comprehension

12 **Tone • Critical**

Read p. 228, paragraph 1. What is the tone, the feeling the author conveys, of this paragraph?

Possible response: The tone is one of awe at the beauty of nature.

13 **Fact and Opinion • Critical**

Think about how you can prove a statement of fact is true or false. How can you prove whether events in this biography really happened?

Possible responses: See if Marven or any of the lumberjacks left written records that tell about this time at the logging camp. Look at historical sources about the logging camp. Interview family members of people who were at the camp.

Monitor Progress

Fact and Opinion

If... students have difficulty describing ways to prove factual events,	**then...** use the skill and strategy instruction on p. 229.

ONLINE

Students can use a student-friendly search engine to find out more about grizzly bear behaviors. Have them use the keywords *grizzly bears* for their search. Remind students to read descriptions of links given to help them narrow the focus of their research. Be sure to follow classroom rules for Internet use.

12 Here in the great north woods all was still and white. Beads of ice glistened on bare branches like jewels. The frosted needles of pine and spruce pricked the eggshell sky, and a ghostly moon began to climb over the treetops.

Marven came upon a frozen lake covered with snow, which lay in a circle of tall trees like a bowl of sugar. He skimmed out across it on his skis, his cheeks stinging in the cold air, and stopped in the middle to listen to the quietness.

And then Marven heard a deep, low growl. At the edge of the lake a shower of snow fell from a pine. A grizzly bear? Marven gripped his ski poles. A grizzly awake in the winter! What would he do if a bear came after him? Where could he hide? Could he out-ski a grizzly?

Marven began to tremble, but he knew that he must remain still, very still. Maybe, Marven thought desperately, the grizzly would think he was a small tree growing in the middle of the lake. He tried very hard to look like a tree. But concentrating on being a tree was difficult because Marven kept thinking of the bundle on the train platform— his mother, his father, his two big sisters, his two little sisters. He belonged in Duluth with them, not in the middle of the

228

ELL

Access Content Students may be unfamiliar with the idea of *needles of pine and spruce* (p. 228, paragraph 1). Explain that pine and spruce are trees with thin, pointy leaves that look like sewing needles.

great north woods with a grizzly. The hot tears streaming down his cheeks turned cold, then froze.

When another tree showered snow, Marven, startled, shot out across the lake. As he reached the shore, a huge shadow slid from behind the trees. The breath froze in Marven's throat.

In the thick purple shadows, he saw a blue twinkle.

"Aaah! Marven!" Jean Louis held a glistening ax in one hand. He looked taller than ever. "I mark the tree for cutting next season." He stepped closer to the trunk and swung the ax hard. Snow showered at Marven's feet. **13**

229

Child Labor Laws

Time for SOCIAL STUDIES

In the early 1900s, when Marven went to work, children across the United States worked very long hours in dangerous jobs. Photographer Lewis Hine documented child labor in canning factories, coal mines, farm fields, and other places. Many Americans were outraged when they saw Hine's photos. They worked to pass laws protecting child workers. After a long struggle, the reformers succeeded. The Fair Labor Standards Act of 1938 made it illegal to hire children to do dangerous jobs or to work long hours when school is in session. The U.S. Labor Department fines employers who break child labor laws.

Fact and Opinion

TEACH

• Point out that the author uses both statements of fact and opinion to describe her father's childhood. Explain that good readers distinguish between statements of fact and opinion to help them evaluate what they read.

• Model how students could prove that the selection's events really happened.

Think Aloud **MODEL** This selection tells about events that happened to a real person, but the author uses both statements of fact and opinion, which makes me wonder if all parts of the selection are true. One way to prove if something in the selection is true would be to see if Marven, Jean Louis, or one of the lumberjacks wrote any diaries or letters that tell about this time at the logging camp. I might be able to find old newspapers or company records about the logging camp or talk to family members of the men who worked at the camp.

PRACTICE AND ASSESS

Have partners use a T-chart to record two statements of fact and two statements of opinion from what they have read thus far. Underneath each statement, have them tell how they know that it is a fact or an opinion.

Guiding Comprehension

14 🔊 **Vocabulary • Dictionary/Glossary**
Read p. 231, paragraph 4, sentence 1. Have students use a dictionary to determine an appropriate meaning of *drifting* for this sentence.

Meaning: Carried along on a current of air.

Monitor Progress

🔊 Dictionary/Glossary

If... students have difficulty using a dictionary to determine the meaning of *drifting* in context,	**then...** use the vocabulary strategy instruction on p. 231.

---

15 **Compare and Contrast • Critical**
Text To Text **How is this selection like other biographies you have read? How is it different?**

Possible response: It tells about a real person like other biographies I've read, but it seems more like fiction than nonfiction. It uses dialogue and gives opinions about what Marven thinks and feels. Other biographies I've read use more statements of fact.

Strategy Response Log

Summarize When students finish reading the selection, provide this prompt: Suppose your neighbor asked you what *Marven of the Great North Woods* is about. Summarize its main events in four or five sentences.

230

ELL

Extend Language Point out that the word *skied* (p. 231, paragraph 4) is special because it is pronounced with a long *e* sound. Words with a similar structure, such as *spied, lied, tried,* and *tied,* are pronounced with a long *i* sound.

"Ah, *mon petit*, you cry!" Jean Louis took off his glove and rubbed his huge thumb down Marven's cheek. "You miss your mama? Your papa?" Marven nodded silently.

"Jean Louis," he whispered. The huge lumberjack bent closer. "I thought you were a grizzly bear!"

"You what!" Jean Louis gasped. "You think I was a grizzly!" And Jean Louis began to laugh, and as he roared, more snow fell from the tree, for his laugh was as powerful as his ax.

As they made their way back to the sled paths, Marven heard a French song drifting through the woods. The other **14** jacks came down the path, their saws and axes slung across their shoulders, and Marven and Jean Louis joined them. Evening shadows fell through the trees, and as Marven skied alongside the huge men, he hummed the tune they were singing. **15**

231

VOCABULARY STRATEGY

Dictionary/ Glossary

TEACH

- Ask students to describe the steps they use to find the meaning of a word in a dictionary. Remind them that some words have multiple meanings, and they need to choose the meaning that makes sense for the context in which the word appears.

- Model using a dictionary to determine the meaning for *drifting* as it is used on p. 231.

 **MODEL** Since *drifting* begins with the letter *d,* and *d* is at the beginning of the alphabet, I'll turn to the beginning part of the dictionary. Now I'll use the guide words at the top to find the page where *drifting* should be. I don't see the word *drifting,* but I see the base word *drift.* The dictionary shows many meanings for *drift.* I know in the sentence *drifting* tells about a song moving through the woods. The meaning that makes the most sense for this context is "to carry or be carried along by currents of air or water." The sound of the song is carried through the woods by the air.

PRACTICE AND ASSESS

Have students use a dictionary to find the correct meaning of an unfamiliar word on p. 231, such as *slung* or *hummed.*

Develop Vocabulary

PRACTICE LESSON VOCABULARY

Students orally respond *yes* or *no* to each question and provide a reason for each answer. Possible reasons are given.

1. Do people frown when they feel *dismay?* *(Yes; when people feel dismay they are disappointed, so they might frown.)*

2. Can you wind a *cord* of wood around a tree? *(No; a cord of wood is a stack of logs 4 feet wide, 4 feet high, and 8 feet long.)*

BUILD CONCEPT VOCABULARY

Review previous concept words with students. Ask if students have come across any words today in their reading or elsewhere that they would like to add to the Citizenship and Responsibility Concept Web, such as *system* or *worked.*

☉ STRATEGY SELF-CHECK

Monitor and Fix Up

Have students monitor their comprehension of p. 232 by distinguishing between statements of fact and opinion. Remind them to use fix-up strategies such as scanning for dates, names, and judgment words. Use Practice Book p. 87.

SELF-CHECK

Students can ask themselves these questions to assess their understanding of the selection.

- Was I able to distinguish between statements of fact and opinion?
- Did I scan for details that show facts and judgment words that show opinions?

Monitor Progress
☉ Fact and Opinion

If... students have difficulty using fix-up strategies to distinguish between statements of fact and opinion,	**then...** use the Reteach lesson on p. 239b.

Fact and Opinion

- A **statement of fact** can be proved true or false. You can look in a reference book, ask an expert, or use your own knowledge and experience.
- A **statement of opinion** cannot be proved true or false. It is a belief or a judgment. It often contains a word of judgment, such as *best*, *should*, or *beautiful*. It may begin with the words *in my opinion* or *I believe*.

Directions Read the following passage. Then answer the questions below.

> Logging is the most dangerous occupation in the United States. Logging is a job that combines dangerous tools with a dangerous environment. Chainsaws are very frightening to use. Everyone should agree about how dangerous it is to be around a sliding and rolling log weighing more than a ton.
>
> Every year, loggers are injured by the equipment they use and by the trees they cut down. Loggers are injured almost twice as often as workers in other industries. To protect loggers, the United States has created many logging-safety laws.

Possible answers given.

1. Is the third sentence a fact or an opinion? How can you tell?

   Opinion; Not everybody might be frightened of using chainsaws.

2. Is the fourth sentence a fact or an opinion? How can you tell?

   Opinion; Some people might see a logger's job as dangerous.

3. Is the sixth sentence a fact or an opinion? How can you tell?

   Fact; I could look up statistics on loggers and injuries.

4. Is the seventh sentence a fact or an opinion? How can you tell?

   Fact; I could look up information on logging-safety laws.

5. Why do you think someone would want to have the dangerous job of being a logger? Use at least one fact and one opinion to support your answer.

   Loggers do interesting work. Cutting down trees is cool, and they see many kinds of animals in the forest.

School + Home **Home Activity** Your child identified statements of fact and opinion in a short paragraph. Read a letter to the editor from the newspaper with your child. Ask your child to tell you when he or she reads an opinion. Ask your child to explain why it is an opinion rather than a fact.

▲ **Practice Book** p. 87

A Note from the Author

Marven Lasky was born in 1907 in Duluth, Minnesota. He was the first child born in America to Ida and Joseph Lasky, who had emigrated from Tsarist Russia to escape the persecution of Jews. The story of their escape in 1900 was told in my novel *The Night Journey*.

Marven at age ten

In 1918, an influenza epidemic swept through the United States. The disease was the worst in the cities, among large populations. Old people and young children were the most vulnerable. Ida and Joseph believed that they might save at least one of their children if they could arrange for that child to go far from the city. Marven was not chosen because he was loved most; Joseph and Ida loved all of their children. Girls in that era, however, were never permitted to travel far from home by themselves— and the last place a girl would ever be sent was to a logging camp. Marven, therefore, was sent by himself on a train to a logging camp in the great north woods of Minnesota.

The last time Marven Lasky, my father, skied was at age eighty-three in Aspen, Colorado. He died at age ninety-one.

He always had a good head for figures.

Marven in his late sixties

232

Access Content To help students understand the historical sequence of events described on p. 232, sketch a time line on the board and work with students to restate key events in their own words. For example, *1900—Marven's parents escape from Russia and move to the United States.*

Reader Response

Open for Discussion Put yourself in Marven's place. What could you do to enjoy living in the lumber camp? How could you keep from getting too homesick?

1. The author describes the lumberjacks as "biggest and wildest" (page 218). Does she prove her point? Explain.
   Think Like an Author

2. That statement on page 218 ("They were the biggest and wildest men Marven had ever seen") seems to be a statement of opinion. Why is it really a statement of fact?
   Fact and Opinion

3. Marven has a problem about what to eat at breakfast (page 224). What would you do to understand why he has this problem? **Monitor and Fix Up**

4. Put yourself in Marven's place. Design a postcard and write a message Marven might have sent his parents from the logging camp. Use words from the Words to Know list and the selection. **Vocabulary**

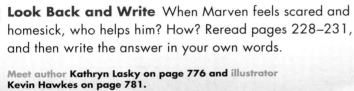

Look Back and Write When Marven feels scared and homesick, who helps him? How? Reread pages 228–231, and then write the answer in your own words.

Meet author **Kathryn Lasky** on **page 776** and **illustrator Kevin Hawkes** on **page 781.**

Reader Response

Reader Response

Open for Discussion Personal Response

MODEL I would go skiing as much as possible. I would try to learn French so that I could talk to the lumberjacks.

Comprehension Check Critical Response

1. Yes. She tells us the men are immense and have long beards. She compares them to a pack of frantic grizzly bears. ***Author's Purpose***

2. It is a statement of fact because it can be proved or disproved that Marven had seen bigger or wilder men. ***Fact/Opinion***

3. Possible response: I would reread the text to figure out what it means to be kosher, or I would look up the term *kosher* in a dictionary. ***Monitor and Fix Up***

4. Responses will vary but should use Words to Know written from Marven's point of view to describe the lumberjacks, woods, meals, or Marven's job. ***Vocabulary***

Look Back and Write For test practice, assign a 10–15 minute time limit. For assessment, see the Scoring Rubric below.

Retell

Have students retell *Marven of the Great North Woods.*

Monitor Progress
Check Retelling Rubric 4 3 2 1

If... students have difficulty retelling the selection,	then... use the Retelling Cards and Scoring Rubric for Retelling on p. 234 to assist fluent retelling.

SUCCESS PREDICTOR

Check Retelling Have students use the selection illustrations to guide their retellings. Let students listen to other retellings before attempting their own. For more ideas on assessing retellings, see the ELL and Transition Handbook.

Scoring Rubric | Look Back and Write

Top-Score Response A top-score response will use information from pages 228 through 231 to explain how Jean Louis helped Marven.

Example of a Top-Score Response Marven felt homesick and alone in the great north woods. He heard a noise that he thought was a grizzly bear. This made him even more sad and scared. However, the noise was only Jean Louis. Jean Louis wiped the tears from Marven's face. Then he laughed with Marven and brought him down the path to join the other lumberjacks.

For additional rubrics, see p. WA10.

Retelling

SUCCESS PREDICTOR

Write Now

Look at the Prompt Have students identify and discuss key words and phrases in the prompt. *(job, describe)*

Strategies to Develop Focus/Ideas

Have students

- eliminate details that do not help the reader understand the job. After each sentence, have students ask themselves if the sentence relates to the main idea.
- imagine they are receiving the job description. What other essential information would they need?

NO: My dog likes dry food. My friend's cat is seventeen years old.

YES: Each morning, give Willie one cup of dry food and clean water.

For additional suggestions and rubric, see pp. 239g–239h.

Write Now
Job Description

Prompt

Marven of the Great North Woods describes a boy's job at a logging camp.

Think about a job you might ask a friend to do.

Now describe the job, explaining everything your friend will need to know.

Write Now

Writing Trait

Your description shoul **focus** on the job and give the important job information.

Student Model

Writer provides a clear _focus_ by stating the job.

Here is everything you need to know to take care of my plants.

In the living room, there is a small potted palm You don't need to give the tree a lot of water. Ha a cup every other day is fine. But this tree likes to have its leaves sprayed with water every day. There is a spray bottle next to the sink.

Writer includes important details.

In my bedroom window, there is a flowerbox filled with flowers. These flowers need water ever day. But water them slowly. If you put in too muc water, it will leak onto the windowsill.

Each paragraph describes a separate task.

Finally, I have a small pot of herbs in the kitche window. I turn the pot every day so that all sides

234

Scoring Rubric | Narrative Retelling

Rubric 4 3 2 1	4	3	2	1
Connections	Makes connections and generalizes beyond the text	Makes connections to other events, stories, or experiences	Makes a limited connection to another event, story, or experience	Makes no connection to another event, story, or experience
Author's Purpose	Elaborates on author's purpose	Tells author's purpose with some clarity	Makes some connection to author's purpose	Makes no connection to author's purpose
Characters	Describes the main character(s) and any character development	Identifies the main character(s) and gives some information about them	Inaccurately identifies some characters or gives little information about them	Inaccurately identifies the characters or gives no information about them
Setting	Describes the time and location	Identifies the time and location	Omits details of time or location	Is unable to identify time or location
Plot	Describes the problem, goal, events, and ending using rich detail	Tells the problem, goal, events, and ending with some errors that do not affect meaning	Tells parts of the problem, goal, events, and ending with gaps that affect meaning	Retelling has no sense of story

Retelling Plan

☑ **Week 1** Assess Strategic Intervention students.

☑ **Week 2** Assess Advanced students.

☑ **Week 3** Assess Strategic Intervention students.

☑ **This week assess On-Level students.**

☐ **Week 5** Assess any students you have not yet checked during this unit.

Use the Retelling Chart on p. TR17 to record retelling.

Selection Test To assess with *Marven of the Great North Woods*, use Selection Tests, pp. 33–36.

Fresh Reads for Differentiated Test Practice For weekly leveled practice, use pp. 49–54.

get the sun. Give them water only when the leaves start to droop. Let me know if you have any questions.

Use the model to help you write your own job description.

Hints for Writing with a Focus

- Stick to the topic. If a sentence is unrelated or loosely related to the topic, drop it or connect it more closely.
- Avoid unnecessary words. For example, substitute *because* for *due to the fact that* or *on account of*.
- Choose a topic you can work with. For example, "Flying an Airplane" is too big a topic for a brief job description.
- Choose precise words to make your ideas clear.
- Make sure the details you choose focus on your topic or main idea.

Hints for Better Writing

- Carefully read the prompt.
- Use a graphic organizer to plan your writing.
- Support your ideas with information and details.
- Use words that help readers understand.
- Proofread and edit your work.

235

Reading Online

- Examine the features of e-mail.
- Compare and contrast across texts.

PREVIEW/USE TEXT FEATURES

Have students preview "Logging Camps," paying special attention to the sender and subject of each e-mail. Then ask:

- **Why does Kenji's e-mail message on p. 237 begin with "Dear Sir or Madam"?** *(Kenji isn't sure if he is writing to a man or a woman. This greeting followed by a colon is a polite way to begin a business e-mail or letter.)*
- **Who replied to Kenji's e-mail on p. 238? How do you know?** *(Kris Jensen; the sender's name is listed next to the "From:" line at the top of the message.)*

The Technology Tools box defines e-mail features.

Link to Writing

Remind students that e-mails written to friends can be less formal than business e-mails. Point out that the subject should tell the main idea of the e-mail. Ask why "Hi!" is not a helpful subject.

DAY 4 Grouping Options

Reading
Whole Group Discuss the Question of the Day.

Group Time Differentiated Instruction
Read "Logging Camps." See pp. 212f–212g for the small group lesson plan.

Whole Group Use p. 239a.

Language Arts
Use pp. 239e–239k.

Reading Online

New Literacies: PearsonSuccessNet.com

Logging Camps

E-Mail

Genre

- An *e-mail* is an electronic message sent over the Internet from one computer user to another. To e-mail someone is to send that person an electronic message.
- You can e-mail some Web sites for information to help with school projects.

Text Features

- The "To:" box shows to whom the message is going. The "Subject:" box tells what the message is about.
- The message itself looks like the body of a letter.

Link to Writing

Tell a friend about *Marven of the Great North Woods*. Write an e-mail that you might send to him or her.

After reading *Marven of the Great North Woods*, Kenji wants to know more about logging camps. He finds a Web site for a logging camp in northern Wisconsin.

For more practice
Take It to the Net
PearsonSuccessNet.com

236

TECHNOLOGY TOOLS

e-mail

To: The e-mail address of the person to whom you are writing goes here. Type the receiver's address or, if using your home computer, choose an address from your personal address book.

Cc: You can send a copy of the e-mail to several people by adding other receivers' addresses here.

Subject: In a few words, tell the receiver what you are writing about.

Address On your home computer, click *Address* to get a screen that shows your personal address book, which contains a list of e-mail addresses of your pen pals.

Attach Click *Attach* to add a file (such as a word processing document or a picture) to your e-mail.

Send Click *Send* to send your message. This is the last thing you do.

The site gives an e-mail address to contact for more information. Kenji decides to e-mail the Web site.

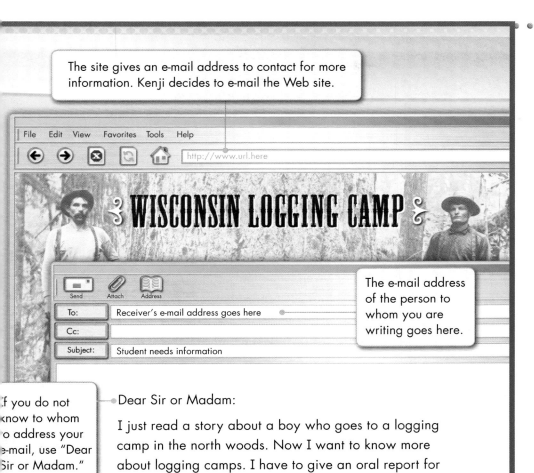

File   Edit   View   Favorites   Tools   Help

http://www.url.here

WISCONSIN LOGGING CAMP

Send   Attach   Address

The e-mail address of the person to whom you are writing goes here.

To:	Receiver's e-mail address goes here
Cc:	
Subject:	Student needs information

If you do not know to whom to address your e-mail, use "Dear Sir or Madam."

Dear Sir or Madam:

I just read a story about a boy who goes to a logging camp in the north woods. Now I want to know more about logging camps. I have to give an oral report for class. Can you tell me where I might find more information about lumberjacks and how they lived? Thank you.

Kenji Shusizu

Fact & Opinion   Will the Web site Kenji has found provide facts *and* opinions?

237

WEB-IQUETTE

e-mail

Tell students that while e-mail is a quick and efficient way to exchange information, there are rules of etiquette they should follow:

- Remember your audience. There is a big difference between writing a quick e-mail to a friend and writing to an adult to ask for information for school.
- If you receive an e-mail from a friend or trusted adult, reply promptly.
- Do not open, read, or respond to e-mail from addresses you don't recognize.

NEW LITERACIES: E-mail

Use the sidebar on p. 236 to guide discussion.

- *E-mail* is short for "electronic mail"— messages sent over the Internet from one computer user to another. E-mail usually arrives very quickly at its destination. Point out that many Web sites include contact links. Clicking on a contact link on a Web site causes an e-mail form to appear on the screen with an address automatically entered in the *To:* box.
- Remind students that e-mail can be a friendly note or a more formal letter. Here, Kenji has written a business letter, asking for more information.
- Discuss different reasons for sending e-mails and how the purpose of the e-mail impacts the structure and language of the message.

Audio CD   **AudioText**

Fact & Opinion

Remind students that statements of fact can be proven, but statements of opinion express someone's beliefs or judgments. Most Web sites would likely include both statements of fact and opinion.

ELL

Activate Prior Knowledge Invite students to share their experiences with e-mail. Then preview the selection, helping students identify the sequence of events Kenji followed and the order of the Web sites and e-mails.

Marven of the Great North Woods   **237**

Strategies for Navigation

USE FOLDERS Explain that students can use folders in their e-mail accounts to sort and save e-mails they send and receive. Point out that electronic folders can be used to organize e-mails in the same way people use paper folders at home, school, or work. Electronic folders can be labeled, or named, in different ways, such as by topic. Sorting and saving e-mails in folders makes them easy to find.

Use the Strategy

1. The next time you are using your e-mail account, look for information on how to create, name, and use folders.

2. When you send or receive an e-mail, decide if you want to save it. If you do, save or drag it into a folder. If not, delete it.

3. Make sure your e-mails are sorted and filed into logical categories. That will make them easier to find.

PRACTICE Think about the ways you use folders when e-mailing at home and at school.

- Make a list of folder names you can use to organize e-mails logically. Think about whether it will work best to organize messages by topic, sender's name, or date.

- The next time you access your e-mail account, try filing some e-mails in folders. If you have trouble creating or using folders, consult the *Help* menu or ask someone for assistance.

The next day Kenji receives this reply.

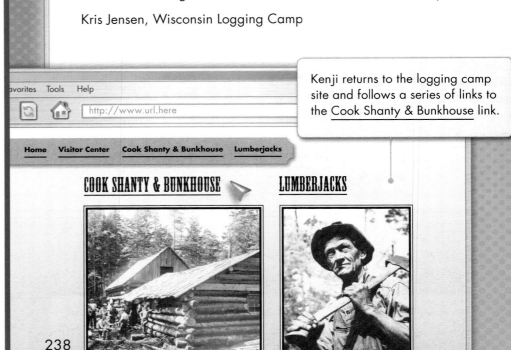

From: Jensen, Kris
To: Shusizu, Kenji
Sent: Tuesday, November 1, 200_, 11:15 AM
cc:
Subject: Re: Student needs information

Hi Kenji,

Our Web site has several links that can help you learn about logging in this area. For information about how lumberjacks lived, follow the Cook Shanty & Bunkhouse link.

Thanks for visiting us. Let us know if we can be of further help.

Kris Jensen, Wisconsin Logging Camp

> Kenji returns to the logging camp site and follows a series of links to the Cook Shanty & Bunkhouse link.

Home   Visitor Center   Cook Shanty & Bunkhouse   Lumberjacks

COOK SHANTY & BUNKHOUSE   LUMBERJACKS

238

Guided Practice If time allows, have students log onto the Internet. Show them how to create a new folder and file an e-mail message in it. Help students make connections between the steps they are doing and related vocabulary terms.

When Kenji clicks on the link, he finds this description of daily life in a camp.

| Home | Visitor Center | Cook Shanty & Bunkhouse | Lumberjacks |

COOK SHANTY & BUNKHOUSE

The cook shanty was where lumberjacks ate. The cooks were up before dawn to set the table and cook a breakfast of pancakes, salt pork, and coffee. The lumberjacks sat at long, oilcloth-covered tables. Talk was limited to requests for food.

The wanigan served as the camp store. Lumberjacks could buy clothing, shoes, blankets, tobacco, and some tools.

The bunkhouse was the crowded home for the lumberjacks during the logging season. Sleeping on bunk beds on mattresses of burlap, hay, straw, or branches, they found it difficult to keep the bedbugs or body lice away.

Reading Across Texts

What have you learned about life in a logging camp? Look at the information above and in *Marven* for details about how lumberjacks lived. List some of these details.

Writing Across Texts Use your list to write a description of life in a logging camp. Would you like to be a logger? Why or why not?

Monitor & Fix Up   How could you find out what *wanigan* means?

239

CONNECT TEXT-TO-TEXT

Reading Across Texts
Suggest students review both texts and record information about life in a logging camp on a word web.

Writing Across Texts Students can use the ideas in their webs to write their descriptions. Remind them to support their opinions with details from the text.

Monitor and Fix-up

Have students scan p. 239 for the word *wanigan* and reread nearby text looking for context clues. A wanigan is a type of shelter used for sleeping, eating, or storage. In this context, it held items for a camp store. If students have difficulty using context clues, suggest they consult an online or print dictionary.

Fluency Assessment Plan

- ☑ **Week 1** Assess Advanced students.
- ☑ **Week 2** Assess Strategic Intervention students.
- ☑ **Week 3** Assess On-Level students.
- ☑ **This week assess Strategic Intervention students.**
- ☐ **Week 5** Assess any students you have not yet checked during this unit.

Set individual goals for students to enable them to reach the year-end goal.

- Current Goal: 100–110 WCPM
- Year-End Goal: 130 WCPM

Build students' fluency by encouraging them to repeatedly read aloud passages from familiar and favorite selections, including books that reflect their cultures.

To develop fluent readers, use Fluency Coach.

DAY 5   Grouping Options

Reading
Whole Group
Revisit the Question of the Week.

Group Time
Differentiated Instruction
Reread this week's Leveled Readers. See pp. 212f–212g for the small group lesson plan.

Whole Group
Use p. 239b–239c.

Language Arts
Use pp. 239d–239l.

VOLUME

Fluency

DAY 1

Model Reread aloud "Counting on Johnny" on p. 212m. Explain that good readers speak loudly enough to be sure everyone can hear them, but they vary the volume to make the story interesting and lively. Model as you read.

DAY 2

Echo Reading Read aloud p. 222, paragraphs 1–7. Have students notice to how you vary your volume to reflect the booming lumberjack and Jean Louis's mutterings. Practice as a class by doing three echo readings of this passage.

DAY 3

Model Read aloud p. 231, paragraphs 1–3. Have students notice how you lower and raise your voice when you see clue words such as _whispered_ and _gasped._ Practice as a class by doing three echo readings of this passage.

DAY 4

Partner Reading Partners practice reading aloud p. 231, paragraphs 1–3, three times. Students should vary their volume appropriately and offer each other feedback.

Monitor Progress   Check Fluency WCPM

As students reread, monitor their progress toward their individual fluency goals. Current Goal: 100–110 words correct per minute. End-of-Year Goal: 130 words correct per minute.

If... students cannot read fluently at a rate of 100–110 words correct per minute,
then... make sure students practice with text at their independent level. Provide additional fluency practice, pairing nonfluent readers with fluent readers.

If... students already read at 130 words correct per minute,
then... they do not need to reread three times.

SUCCESS PREDICTOR

DAY 5

Assessment
Individual Reading Rate Use the Fluency Assessment Plan and do a one-minute timed reading of either selection from this week to assess students in Week 4. Pay special attention to this week's skill, volume. Provide corrective feedback for each student.

RETEACH

🎯 Fact and Opinion

TEACH

Review the definitions of *statement of fact* and *statement of opinion* on p. 212. Students can complete Practice Book p. 88 on their own or as a class. Discuss the graphic organizer on the Practice Book page and make sure students understand they must draw lines to complete it. Encourage them to look for clue words and phrases in statements that may indicate opinions.

ASSESS

Have partners identify one statement of fact and one statement of opinion in the last paragraph on p. 228. *(Facts: Marven began to tremble. Tears streamed down his cheeks. Possible opinions: He must remain still. Concentrating on being a tree was difficult. He belonged in Duluth.)*

For additional instruction on fact and opinion, see DI·55.

EXTEND SKILLS

Narrative Writing

TEACH

When a storyteller describes an event or series of events, the text is called narrative writing. The storyteller may be called the narrator of the story. Narrative writing can be fiction or nonfiction.

- In a biography, such as *Marven of the Great North Woods,* the narrator describes a series of real-life events in another person's life.

- It is important to remember that a story is told from the narrator's point of view, and others may view the events differently.

Have students read p. 218. Discuss who the narrator is and the events the narrator describes.

ASSESS

Have pairs read p. 222 and rewrite it as if Jean Louis was the narrator. Ask:

1. **Does your narrative show how Jean Louis views the event?**
2. **Have you told what happened in an interesting, lively way?**

OBJECTIVES

- 🎯 Identify statements of fact and opinion.
- ● Understand narrative writing.

Skills Trace

🎯 Fact and Opinion

Introduce/Teach	TE: 4.2 212–213; 4.3 292–293; 4.6 660–661
Practice	TE: 219, 227, 229, 299, 303, 667, 675 PB: 83, 87, 88, 113, 117, 118, 263, 267, 268
▶ Reteach/Review	**TE: 4.1 125; 4.2 239b, DI•55; 4.3 313b, DI•53; 4.6 651, 685b, 747, DI•53 PB: 46, 256, 296**
Test	Selection Test: 33–36, 45–48, 105–108; Benchmark Test: Unit 6

Access Content Reteach the skill by reviewing the Picture It! lesson on fact and opinion in the ELL Teaching Guide, pp. 57–58.

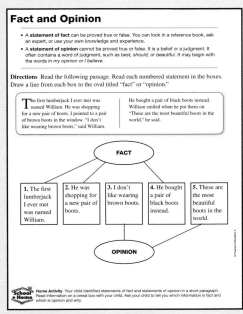

Fact and Opinion

- A **statement of fact** can be proved true or false. You can look in a reference book, ask an expert, or use your own knowledge and experience.
- A **statement of opinion** cannot be proved true or false. It is a belief or a judgment. It often contains a word of judgment, such as *best, should,* or *beautiful.* It may begin with the words *in my opinion* or *I believe.*

Directions Read the following passage. Read each numbered statement in the boxes. Draw a line from each box to the oval titled "fact" or "opinion."

The first lumberjack I ever met was named William. He was shopping for a new pair of boots. I pointed to a pair of brown boots in the window. "I don't like wearing brown boots," said William.

He bought a pair of black boots instead. William smiled when he put them on. "These are the most beautiful boots in the world," he said.

FACT

| 1. The first lumberjack I ever met was named William. | 2. He was shopping for a new pair of boots. | 3. I don't like wearing brown boots. | 4. He bought a pair of black boots instead. | 5. These are the most beautiful boots in the world. |

OPINION

Home Activity Your child identified statements of fact and statements of opinion in a short paragraph. Read information on a cereal box with your child. Ask your child to tell you which information is fact and which is opinion and why.

▲ **Practice Book** p. 88

Vocabulary and Word Study

VOCABULARY STRATEGY
Dictionary/Glossary

UNFAMILIAR WORDS Point out the pronunciation key on the right-hand pages of the student glossary. Remind students that when they look up a word in a glossary or a dictionary, they can also find out how to pronounce it. For practice, have students choose two or three glossary words and carefully copy the pronunciations shown in parentheses. They can exchange pronunciations with a partner and use the glossary's key to identify each other's words. Remind them to check the meanings of any unfamiliar words.

(lum′ bər jak′)
lumberjack

Homophones

Write the lesson vocabulary word *cord* on the board and the homphone *chord* next to it. Explain that homophones are words that sound alike but have different spellings and meanings. Brainstorm other examples with students. Challenge them to draw a cartoon showing a silly confusion that might arise from a careless use of homophones. For example, have them illustrate one of these sentences: *The lumberjack had a shaggy head of hare. Jean Louis ate a thick stake.*

Some Homophones

cord/chord	steak/stake
hair/hare	night/knight
wood/would	blue/blew
bear/bare	see/sea

BUILD CONCEPT VOCABULARY
Responsibility

LOOKING BACK Remind students of the question of the week: *What is the value of a job well done?* Discuss how this week's Concept Web of vocabulary words relates to the theme of citizenship and responsibility. Ask student if they have any words or categories to add. Discuss if words are appropriately related to the lesson concept.

MOVING FORWARD Preview the title of the next selection, *So You Want to Be President?* Ask students which Concept Web words might apply to the new selection based on the title alone. Put a star next to these words on the Web.

Display the Concept Web and revisit the vocabulary words as you read the next selection to check predictions.

Monitor Progress
Check Vocabulary

If… students suggest words or categories that are not related to the concept,	**then…** review the words and categories on the Concept Web and discuss how they relate to the lesson concept.

SUCCESS PREDICTOR

Speaking and Listening

SPEAKING

Job Description

SET-UP Have students work in small groups to give a career day presentation. They will role-play being representatives from a local business or service organization and describe the jobs of the business or organization.

TEAM PRESENTATION Have groups choose a business or organization to represent and a job. They will describe the responsibilities of the job, any special skills or talents it requires, and give anecdotes or statistics that support this job as being rewarding. Have each group outline its presentation and decide on the information each speaker will present.

AUDIENCE Career day presentations provide accurate information about a job, while making it sound as interesting and rewarding as possible. Encourage the audience to ask questions after each presentation.

Delivery Tips
- If you are feeling nervous, take deep, slow breaths.
- Concentrate on speaking slowly and clearly.
- Remember to speak in complete sentences.
- Use note cards to help you remember what to say.
- Stay in your role when presenting and answering questions.

LISTENING

Listen to a Description

Have students listen to job descriptions presented by classmates or invite professionals to tell about their real-life jobs. Encourage students to listen for facts and opinions to determine each speaker's point of view about the job. Tell them to decide whether the job presented is one they would be interested in having one day. Have students answer the following questions orally or in writing.

1. **What did you want or expect to hear about the job?** *(Possible response: I wanted to know how many hours I'd have to work and how interesting the job would be.)*

2. **Given your purpose, which speaker's words were most important to you? Why?** *(Possible response: I listened most carefully to the speaker's description of job duties to help me decide if the job is one I'd like to have some day.)*

3. **Do you think you would be interested in having this job one day? Why or why not?** *(Responses will vary but should include valid reasons why the students would or would not want to have the job described.)*

Support Vocabulary Use the following to review and extend vocabulary and to explore lesson concepts further:
- ELL Poster 9, Days 3–5 instruction
- Vocabulary Activities and Word Cards in ELL Teaching Guide, pp. 59–60

Assessment For information on assessing students' speaking and listening, see the ELL and Transition Handbook.

Grammar **Singular Possessive Nouns**

OBJECTIVES

- Define and identify singular possessive nouns.
- Use singular possessive nouns correctly in writing.
- Become familiar with singular possessive nouns on high-stakes tests.

Monitor Progress

Grammar	
If... students have difficulty identifying singular possessive nouns,	**then...** provide additional instruction and practice in The Grammar and Writing Book pp. 98–101.

DAILY FIX-IT

This week use Daily Fix-It Transparency 9.

Spiral REVIEW

Grammar Support See the Grammar Transition lessons in the ELL and Transition Handbook.

▲ **The Grammar and Writing Book**
For more instruction and practice, use pp. 98–101.

DAY 1 Teach and Model

DAILY FIX-IT

1. Marven felt very small amung the enormous lumberjack's. *(among; lumberjacks)*

2. What a huge amount of food they eated for breakfast? *(ate; breakfast!)*

READING-GRAMMAR CONNECTION

Write the following sentence on the board:

> *Marven's bed was in the office.*

Point to the word *Marven's* and explain that this is a **singular possessive noun**. The apostrophe (') and *-s* at the end show ownership or possession—the bed belongs to Marven.

Display Grammar Transparency 9. Read aloud the definitions and sample sentences. Work through the items.

Singular Possessive Nouns

A **possessive noun** shows ownership. A **singular possessive noun** shows that one person, place, or thing has or owns something. Add an apostrophe (') and the letter *s* to a singular noun to make it possessive.

Singular Nouns	Marven worked in the same office as his boss.
Singular Possessive Nouns	Marven's workplace was his boss's office.

Directions Write the possessive form of each underlined singular noun.

1. lumberjack ax — **lumberjack's**
2. forest trees — **forest's**
3. boy job — **boy's**
4. Mr. Murray plan — **Mr. Murray's**
5. bear dinner — **bear's**
6. camp location — **camp's**
7. lake water — **lake's**
8. Minnesota winters — **Minnesota's**
9. building entrance — **building's**
10. ax blade — **ax's**

Directions Write the possessive form of each underlined noun.

11. Marven life changed at the logging camp. — **Marven's**
12. His first day work was difficult. — **day's**
13. A bookkeeper job was a challenge for a young boy. — **bookkeeper's**
14. Marven learned each man signature or symbol. — **man's**
15. Jean-Louis symbol was his thumbprint. — **Jean-Louis's**

Unit 2 Marven of the Great North Woods   Grammar **9**

▲ **Grammar Transparency** 9

DAY 2 Develop the Concept

DAILY FIX-IT

3. Marven slid smoothly. Over the wite carpet of snow. *(smoothly over; white)*

4. He thought Jean Louis was a grizzly bear but he laughed when he found out her mistake. *(bear,; his)*

GUIDED PRACTICE

Review the concept of singular possessive nouns.

- A possessive noun shows ownership or possession.
- A singular noun that shows ownership is called a **singular possessive noun.**
- To form a singular possessive noun, add an apostrophe and *-s.*

HOMEWORK Grammar and Writing Practice Book p. 33. Work through the first two items with the class.

Singular Possessive Nouns

A **possessive noun** shows ownership. A **singular possessive noun** shows that one person, place, or thing has or owns something. Add an apostrophe (') and the letter *s* to a singular noun to make it possessive.

Singular Nouns	This country had forests that were a valuable resource.
Irregular Plural Nouns	This country's forests were a valuable resource.

Directions Write the possessive form of each underlined noun.

1. Minnesota forests were once full of white pines.
   Minnesota's
2. The white pine wood was soft and easy to cut.
   pine's
3. This lumber helped build the Midwest cities.
   Midwest's
4. The nation need for lumber was enormous.
   nation's
5. A lumberjack work was long and hard.
   lumberjack's
6. At first, a nearby river provided a logging camp source of power.
   camp's
7. Later, steam power speeded up a sawmill rate of work.
   sawmill's
8. Sadly, the state supply of big trees could not last forever.
   state's

Home Activity Your child learned about singular possessive nouns. Ask your child to write the names of family members as possessive nouns and to use them in sentences.

▲ **Grammar and Writing Practice Book** p. 33

DAY 3 Apply to Writing

DAILY FIX-IT

5. Marven made a list of each mans name. And recorded his signature. *(man's name and)*

6. Marven and mr. Murray enjoyed the cooks beans and pies at lunch. *(Mr.; cook's)*

REDUCE WORDINESS

Point out that possessive nouns can make writing smoother and less wordy. Explain that *Marven's bed* is shorter and sounds more natural than the *bed of Marven*.

• Have students review something they have written to see if they can replace prepositional phrases with singular possessive nouns.

HOMEWORK Grammar and Writing Practice Book p. 34.

Singular Possessive Nouns

Directions Make each sentence less wordy by replacing the underlined words with a possessive noun phrase. Write the new sentences.

1. <u>The need of America</u> for lumber was great 100 years ago. **America's need for lumber was great 100 years ago.**

2. <u>The forests of Minnesota</u> supplied much of this material. **Minnesota's forests supplied much of this material.**

3. <u>The rivers of the state</u> played an important part in the logging industry. **The state's rivers played an important part in the logging industry.**

4. Lumberjacks braved <u>the cruel weather of winter</u>. **Lumberjacks braved winter's cruel weather.**

5. <u>The appetite of a lumberjack</u> was enormous. **A lumberjack's appetite was enormous.**

Directions Write about a time (real or imaginary) that you spent in the country. Use at least two singular possessive nouns and underline them.

Possible answers:

Last summer my family went to Lake Sebago. It is one of Maine's biggest lakes. My dad told my brother and me not to go out alone in the woods. He said we might end up being a bear's breakfast!

Home Activity Your child learned how to use singular possessive nouns in writing. Ask your child to write a journal entry about the day's activities. Have him or her use at least two singular possessive nouns.

▲ **Grammar and Writing Practice Book** p. 34

DAY 4 Test Preparation

DAILY FIX-IT

7. When the men returned from a days work they ate supper. *(day's work, they)*

8. If Marven finished his work early. He could go out skiing? *(early, he; skiing.)*

STANDARDIZED TEST PREP

Test Tip

Add an apostrophe with a singular possessive noun. Do not add an apostrophe with a plural noun. Ask yourself: *Do I mean more than one of this noun, or do I mean something belongs to this noun?*

Example: The universe has many suns. *(more than one sun)*

The sun's rays melted the snow. *(rays belong to the sun)*

HOMEWORK Grammar and Writing Practice Book p. 35.

Singular Possessive Nouns

Directions Mark the letter of the word that completes each sentence.

1. A ___ job was to cut down trees.
   A lumberjacks
   (B) lumberjack's
   C lumberjack
   D lumberjacks'

2. A ___ long journey started in the forest.
   (A) log's
   B loges
   C log
   D logies

3. Cut logs floated on the ___ current.
   A rivers
   B river
   (C) river's
   D riveres

4. ___ trees floated south to Iowa.
   A Minnesotan'
   (B) Minnesota's
   C Minnesota
   D Minnesotas

5. The ___ end was at a sawmill.
   A journeys
   B journies
   C journey
   (D) journey's

6. The logs became wood for ___ cities.
   A American'
   B Americas
   C America
   (D) America's

7. In time, ___ supply of trees ran out.
   (A) nature's
   B natures'
   C nature
   D natural'

8. The ___ great north woods were gone.
   A Midwests
   B Midwest
   (C) Midwest's
   D Midwestern'

Home Activity Your child prepared for taking tests on singular possessive nouns. Name two or three familiar objects in the house. Have your child write the possessive forms of these nouns and use them in sentences.

▲ **Grammar and Writing Practice Book** p. 35

DAY 5 Cumulative Review

DAILY FIX-IT

9. Do you think that Marven saw any moose or wolfes in the forest. *(wolves; forest?)*

10. Marvens work was hard, he did it well. *(Marven's; hard, but [or hard. He])*

ADDITIONAL PRACTICE

Assign pp. 98–101 in The Grammar and Writing Book.

EXTRA PRACTICE Grammar and Writing Practice Book p. 130.

TEST PREPARATION Grammar and Writing Practice Book pp. 153–154.

ASSESSMENT

CUMULATIVE REVIEW Grammar and Writing Practice Book p. 36.

Singular Possessive Nouns

Directions Write the possessive form of each underlined noun.

1. wood grain   **wood's**
2. river bank   **river's**
3. winter cold   **winter's**
4. bed pillow   **bed's**
5. desk drawer   **desk's**
6. snow wetness   **snow's**
7. horse saddle   **horse's**
8. fiddle music   **fiddle's**
9. kitchen warmth   **kitchen's**
10. saw handle   **saw's**

Directions Write a singular possessive noun to complete each sentence.

11. A ___ job is very hard.   **Possible answers:** **lumberjack's**
12. Some people earn $200 for one ___ work.   **day's**
13. A ___ day is spent at school.   **student's**
14. A ___ place of work is often a hospital.   **nurse's**
15. A ___ job is very important.   **president's**

Home Activity Your child reviewed singular possessive nouns. Look at a newspaper or magazine article with your child. Have him or her identify singular possessive nouns.

▲ **Grammar and Writing Practice Book** p. 36

Writing Workshop Describe a Job

ELL

Focus/Ideas Talk with English learners about what they plan to write. Record ideas and help them generate language for support. Help them tighten their focus by eliminating unrelated details. See more writing support in the ELL and Transition Handbook.

Writing Traits

FOCUS/IDEAS The writer has a clear main idea—how to take care of the dog—and purpose—to inform the caregiver.

ORGANIZATION/PARAGRAPHS Paragraphs clearly divide the job into separate tasks.

VOICE The writer's tone is instructive and precise.

WORD CHOICE The writer uses exact language (*two scoops, chewy rubber rabbit*) to make her message clear.

SENTENCES The writer uses straightforward imperative and declarative sentences.

CONVENTIONS There is excellent control and accuracy.

DAY 1 Model the Trait

READING-WRITING CONNECTION

- *Marven of the Great North Woods* focuses on a boy's job at a logging camp.
- Time-order words can help describe a job effectively.
- Students will **describe a job** using time-order words.

MODEL FOCUS/IDEAS Discuss Writing Transparency 9A. Then discuss the model and the writing trait of focus/ideas.

 Think Aloud All of the information in this description is focused on how to take care of the writer's dog, Fifi. The writer presents everything you would need to know in order to complete this job, including how to feed and walk the dog. All of the questions I might have as a reader are answered. There is also no information that is unnecessary to doing the job.

Describe a Job

A *job description* tells the person who is going to do the job exactly what he or she should do. Because it includes important information, a job description must be well-organized and clearly written.

Taking Care of Fifi

Each paragraph describes a separate task.

Give Fifi breakfast no later than 8 A.M. She gets one scoop of dry cereal and two spoonfuls from a can in the refrigerator. Put her in the backyard for a few minutes after breakfast.

Writer includes important details.

At midday, Fifi needs a good walk. Her leash is hanging up in the hall. Don't take her to the park because the other dogs frighten her.

Time-order words make instructions clear.

Come back again at six to give Fifi her supper. She gets two scoops of dry cereal. Then take her out for another walk.

Finally, put Fifi to bed. Remember that she likes to sleep with the chewy rubber rabbit. Say good night to her and tell her I'll be back soon.

* Unit 2 Marven of the Great North Woods   Writing Model **9A**

▲ **Writing Transparency 9A**

DAY 2 Improve Writing

WRITER'S CRAFT
Time-Order Words

Display Writing Transparency 9B. Read the directions and work together to use time-order words.

TIME-ORDER WORDS

Think Aloud Tomorrow we will be writing a job description. I am going to tell a friend how to take care of my garden. I can use time-order words to explain when to do what. I should tell my friend which activities to do *first, second, next,* and *last.*

GUIDED WRITING Some students may need more help with using time-order words. Work with them to describe the events of a typical day using time-order words.

Time-Order Words

Writers use **time-order words** to describe the order in which to do something or to tell readers exactly when events took place. Words such as *first, then, next,* and *finally* can make a process clear and a story understandable.

Confusing Use a ladle to drop mixed-up milk, flour, and eggs into a hot pan.

Clear First mix milk, flour, and eggs. Then heat the pan. Finally, ladle the mixture into the pan.

Directions Write a time-order word from the box to show the order of the events in Marven's day.

[Next   Then   Second   Finally   First]

1. ____ Marven had to wake up the lumberjacks.   **First**
2. ____ he had his breakfast.   **Second**
3. ____ he spent the morning working with Mr. Murray.   **Next** *or* **Then**
4. ____ he had his lunch.   **Then** *or* **Next**
5. ____ if he finished work in time, he could go skiing.   **Finally**

Directions Rewrite the instructions in the correct order, using time-order words. Add your own concluding sentence.

Call everyone to breakfast. Clear the table and wash the dishes. Set the table and prepare the pancakes. Serve everyone pancakes. **Possible answer: First, set the table and prepare the pancakes. Then call everyone to breakfast. Next, serve everyone pancakes. Finally, clear the table and wash the dishes. It's hard work, but you'll get used to it.**

Unit 2 Marven of the Great North Woods   Writer's Craft **9B**

▲ **Writing Transparency 9B**

DAY 3 — Prewrite and Draft

READ THE WRITING PROMPT

on page 234 in the Student Edition.

Marven of the Great North Woods *describes a boy's job at a logging camp.*

Think about a job you might ask a friend to do.

Now describe the job, explaining everything your friend will need to know.

Writing Test Tips

- Think of the most important parts of the job and be sure to include them.
- Describe the job in the order the steps must be done, using time-order words where necessary.
- Make sure that the task you are describing is absolutely clear.

GETTING STARTED Students can do any of the following:

- Divide the job into parts. Then number the parts according to the order in which they should be done.
- Visualize themselves doing the job.
- Make of list of equipment necessary to complete the job.

DAY 4 — Draft and Revise

EDITING/REVISING CHECKLIST

☑ Do I include time-order words?

☑ Are singular possessive nouns correctly written?

☑ Is the description organized in the order the work must be done?

☑ Are words with the consonant pairs *ng, nk, ph,* and *wh* spelled correctly?

See *The Grammar and Writing Book,* pp. 98–103.

Revising Tips

Focus/Ideas

- Check that the main task is completely clear to the reader.
- Be sure to include only necessary details.
- Have a reader describe the job back to you in his or her own words. Check for accuracy.

PUBLISHING Post students' job descriptions under the title "Help Wanted" on a bulletin board. Some students may wish to revise their work later.

ASSESSMENT Use the scoring rubric to evaluate students' work.

DAY 5 — Connect to Unit Writing

How-to Report	
Week 1	Poem 161g–161h
Week 2	News Story 187g–187h
Week 3	Play Scene 211g–211h
Week 4	Describe a Job 239g–239h
Week 5	Explanation 259g–259h

PREVIEW THE UNIT PROMPT

Think of something that you know how to do well. Write a clear, step-by-step description of how to do this task or activity. Make your report interesting to read and easy to understand.

APPLY

- A how-to report explains the steps for making or doing something.
- The writer of a how-to report should include time-order words to make the sequence of actions clear.

Writing Trait Rubric

	4	3	2	1
Focus/Ideas	Description well-focused; uses time-order words	Description somewhat focused; some time-order words	Weak focus; few time-order words	No focus; no time-order words
	Job thoroughly described	Job generally described	Job vague; some information missing	Job unclear; important information missing

Spelling & Phonics Consonant Pairs *ng, nk, ph, wh*

Spelling Words

1. Thanksgiving	11. whisper*
2. among*	12. elephant
3. think	13. white*
4. blank	14. shrink
5. graph	15. wharf
6. young*	16. trunk
7. wheel	17. strong
8. nephew	18. blink
9. belong*	19. chunk
10. whiskers	20. skunk

Challenge Words

21. strengthen	24. whimsical
22. bankrupt	25. whatever
23. phantom	

*Word from the selection

Spelling/Phonics Support See the ELL and Transition Handbook for spelling support.

DAY 1 Pretest and Sort

PRETEST

Use the Dictation Sentences from Day 5 to administer the pretest. Read the word, read the sentence, and then read the word again. Guide students in self-correcting their pretests and correcting any misspellings.

Monitor Progress

Spelling

If...	then...
If... students misspell more than 5 pretest words,	**then...** use words 1–10 for Strategic Intervention.
If... students misspell 1–5 pretest words,	**then...** use words 1–20 for On-Level practice.
If... students correctly spell all pretest words,	**then...** use words 1–25 for Advanced Learners.

HOMEWORK Spelling Practice Book, p. 33.

Consonant Pairs *ng, nk, ph, wh*

Generalization Some words have two consonants that blend together: **among, think.** Some words have two consonants that are said as one sound: **graph, wheel.**

Word Sort Sort the list words by their consonant pair.

ng and nk
1. Thanksgiving

ng
2. young
3. among
4. belong
5. strong

nk
6. think
7. blank
8. shrink
9. trunk
10. blink
11. chunk
12. skunk

ph
13. graph
14. nephew
15. elephant

wh
16. wheel
17. whiskers
18. whisper
19. white
20. wharf

Challenge Words

ng
21. strengthen

nk
22. bankrupt

ph
23. phantom

wh
24. whimsical
25. whatever

Spelling Words
1. Thanksgiving
2. among
3. think
4. blank
5. graph
6. young
7. wheel
8. nephew
9. belong
10. whiskers
11. whisper
12. elephant
13. white
14. shrink
15. wharf
16. trunk
17. strong
18. blink
19. chunk
20. skunk

Challenge Words
21. strengthen
22. bankrupt
23. phantom
24. whimsical
25. whatever

Home Activity Your child is learning to spell words with ng, nk, ph, and wh. Ask your child to circle list words that have two consonants that stand for one sound in each list word.

▲ **Spelling Practice Book** p. 33

DAY 2 Think and Practice

TEACH

In some consonant pairs, both sounds can be heard. In others, the two consonants stand for one sound. Write *wheel.* Underline the consonant pair. Point to each phoneme as you say *wh-ee-l* and explain that the consonant pair *wh* stands for one sound. Write *think* and help students find the consonant pair in which each sound can be heard.

wheel

HOW MANY SOUNDS? Have students take turns reading the list words with a partner. Have the partners listen for /w/ and /f/ and tell which consonant pair stands for each sound.

HOMEWORK Spelling Practice Book, p. 34.

Consonant Pairs *ng, nk, ph, wh*

Spelling Words

Thanksgiving	among	think	blank	graph
young	wheel	nephew	belong	whiskers
whisper	elephant	white	shrink	wharf
trunk	strong	blink	chunk	skunk

Context Clues Write a list word to complete each saying.

1. The ____ never forgets. — 1. elephant
2. The squeaky ____ gets the oil. — 2. wheel
3. He vanished in the ____ of an eye. — 3. blink
4. Its fleece was ____ as snow. — 4. white
5. The wet dog was as smelly as a ____. — 5. skunk
6. I ____ therefore I am. — 6. think
7. The weightlifter is as ____ as an ox. — 7. strong
8. I ate until I felt as stuffed as a ____ turkey. — 8. Thanksgiving

Classifying Write the list word that fits into each group.

9. shout, talk, ____ — 9. whisper
10. between, in, ____ — 10. among
11. empty, unused, ____ — 11. blank
12. childlike, immature, ____ — 12. young
13. chart, map, ____ — 13. graph
14. reduce, decrease, ____ — 14. shrink
15. briefcase, suitcase, ____ — 15. trunk
16. piece, slab, ____ — 16. chunk
17. uncle, grandfather, ____ — 17. nephew
18. join, fit, ____ — 18. belong
19. pier, dock, ____ — 19. wharf
20. beard, mustache, ____ — 20. whiskers

Home Activity Your child spelled words with ng, nk, ph, and wh. Say a list word and have your child spell the word and use it in a sentence.

▲ **Spelling Practice Book** p. 34

DAY 3 Connect to Writing

WRITE A WANT AD

Ask students to use at least five spelling words to write a newspaper want ad for a specific job.

Frequently Misspelled Words

where *when*

These words may seem easy to spell, but they are often misspelled by fourth-graders. Alert students to these frequently misspelled words. Point out that both words begin with the consonant pair *wh.*

HOMEWORK Spelling Practice Book, p. 35.

Consonant Pairs *ng, nk, ph, wh*

Proofread a Poster Andy made a poster for the team fundraiser. Circle six words that are spelled incorrectly. Write the words correctly. Correct the run-on sentence. Write it.

	Spelling Words
Come to the white elefant sale!	Thanksgiving
Wen Friday after Thanksgivin	among
Where: Kennedy School Gym	think
Why: To buy sports equipment for youg boys'	blank
and girls' sports teams	graph
	young
One person's junk is another person's	wheel
treasure, so bring a chunk of change to	nephew
spend. Your children, nieces, and nefew	belong
will benefit. Everyone is welcome!	whiskers
We need some stronge people to help with	
set up come early.	whisper
	elephant
	white
	shrink
	wharf
	trunk
	strong
	blink
	chunk
	skunk

1. elephant   2. When
3. Thanksgiving   4. young
5. nephews   6. strong
7. We need some strong people to help set up. Come early.

	Frequently Misspelled Words
	where
	when

Proofread Words Write the underlined words correctly. Then follow the directions. What you see may surprise you.

8. Draw a large red dot in the middle of a sheet of graf paper.   8. graph
9. Stare at the dot for 30 seconds. Don't blin!   9. blink
10. Then stare at a blanc wall for 15 seconds.   10. blank
11. A wite wall works best.   11. white
12. What color dot do you thik you will see?   12. think

Home Activity Your child identified misspelled words with *ng, nk, ph,* or *wh.* Ask your child to spell the words he or she did not write when answering the questions on this page.

▲ **Spelling Practice Book** p. 35

DAY 4 Review

REVIEW WORDS WITH CONSONANT PAIRS *ng, nk, ph, wh*

Distribute graph paper and have students use at least ten list words to make a word search puzzle. Have students solve each other's puzzles.

Spelling Strategy Problem Parts

We all have words that are hard for us to spell.

Step 1: Ask yourself: Which part of the word gives me a problem?

Step 2: Underline the problem part.

Step 3: Picture the word. Focus on the problem part.

HOMEWORK Spelling Practice Book, p. 36.

Consonant Pairs *ng, nk, ph, wh*

Double Puzzle Unscramble the list words and write the letters on the lines. Then write the numbered letters to answer the question.

What do many people watch on television on a holiday morning in November?

		Thanksgiving
1. magno	a m o n g	among
2. hktin	t h i n k	think
3. lbnak	b l a n k	blank
4. ragph	g r a p h	graph
5. nuyog	y o u n g	young
6. ewhel	w h e e l	wheel
7. penhwe	n e p h e w	nephew
8. shwisrke	w h i s k e r s	belong
9. wephirs	w h i s p e r	whiskers
10. teanhelp	e l e p h a n t	whisper
11. eithw	w h i t e	elephant
12. hiksrn	s h r i n k	white
13. frhaw	w h a r f	shrink
14. nrtuk	t r u n k	wharf
15. tosgnr	s t r o n g	trunk
16. kuhnc	c h u n k	strong
		blink
		chunk
		skunk

T H A N K S G I V I N G
D A Y   P A R A D E

Home Activity Your child has learned to read, write, and spell words with *ng, nk, ph,* and *wh.* Write the words, leaving out the consonant pairs. Have your child fill in the missing letters.

▲ **Spelling Practice Book** p. 36

DAY 5 Posttest

DICTATION SENTENCES

1. We ate turkey on <u>Thanksgiving</u>.
2. Tiny plants are growing <u>among</u> the rocks.
3. I'll have to <u>think</u> about it.
4. Write your name in the <u>blank</u>.
5. The <u>graph</u> shows how much our town has <u>grown</u>.
6. A <u>young</u> seal is called a pup.
7. The <u>wheel</u> fell off the wagon.
8. Mom's <u>nephew</u> lives next door.
9. Do you <u>belong</u> to any clubs?
10. The cat licked his <u>whiskers</u>.
11. She wants to <u>whisper</u> the secret to me.
12. An <u>elephant</u> is huge and gray.
13. The sky filled with fluffy, <u>white</u> clouds.
14. Will this shirt <u>shrink</u> if I wash it?
15. We tied our boat to the <u>wharf</u>.
16. Tina packed her <u>trunk</u> for the trip.
17. An ant is small but <u>strong</u>.
18. It was over in the <u>blink</u> of an eye.
19. A <u>chunk</u> of ice fell off the building.
20. A <u>skunk</u> lives under the porch.

CHALLENGE

21. Exercise will <u>strengthen</u> your muscles.
22. The business closed because the owner went <u>bankrupt</u>.
23. People say a <u>phantom</u> haunts the woods.
24. Chad's idea was <u>whimsical</u> and funny.
25. You may do <u>whatever</u> you like.

New Literacies	
Day 1	**Identify Questions**
Day 2	**Navigate/Search**
Day 3	**Analyze**
Day 4	**Synthesize**
Day 5	**Communicate**

NEW LITERACIES
Internet Inquiry Activity

EXPLORE JOB RESPONSIBILITIES

Use the following 5-day plan to help students conduct this week's Internet inquiry activity on different job responsibilities. Remind students to follow classroom rules when using the Internet.

DAY 1

Identify Questions Discuss the focus question: *What is the value of a job well done?* Ask students to brainstorm important jobs they would like to explore. Have individuals, pairs, or small groups write an inquiry question about the responsibilities associated with a specific job.

DAY 2

Navigate/Search Have students begin a simple Internet search. Ask them if they know the meanings of endings of URLs such as *.com, .org, .gov,* and *.edu. (commercial, organization, government agency, educational institution)* Discuss how these endings can help them determine the reliability and accuracy of the information on a Web site. For example, a government site is likely to be reliable and contain up-to-date, factual information. Point out some education sites may be created by students and may not be as reliable.

DAY 3

Analyze Have students explore the Web sites they identified on Day 2. Tell them to review each site for information that helps answer their inquiry question and take notes.

DAY 4

Synthesize As students synthesize information from Day 3, show them how to cite the Web sites they use as sources. When citing a Web site, tell students to include the URL exactly as it as shown on the page they are referencing and to name the individual, company, organization, school, or government agency that produced the page. They should include the date they accessed the page, as well as any additional information such as the title, author, and copyright date of an article reproduced on the Web site.

DAY 5

Communicate Have students share their inquiry results. Suggest they use bullets or numbering in a word processing program to list job duties. Have them include a statement explaining the results when the job is done well.

RESEARCH/STUDY SKILLS
Graph

OBJECTIVES
- Review terms related to types of graphs.
- Use graphs to locate information.

TEACH

Ask students where they have seen graphs. Students may mention textbooks, newspapers, or magazines. Show a graph from a classroom text and use it to review these terms:

- A **graph** shows data, or information, in visual form. The **title** and **labels** tell what information the graph shows and compares.
- A **bar graph** uses vertical or horizontal bars to compare data.
- A **circle graph** is a circle that shows how a whole is divided into parts.
- A **line graph** contains lines that connect a series of points. Line graphs often show changes over time.
- A **picture graph**, or **pictograph**, uses pictures to represent amounts.

Provide groups with examples of different types of graphs. Have each group show its graph to the class, telling what kind it is and what it shows. Discuss these questions:

1. **How do you know what information the graph shows?** *(The title and labels tell you what the graph is about.)*
2. **How are the graphs alike and different?** *(They all show information in a visual way, but different types of graphs compare things in different ways.)*

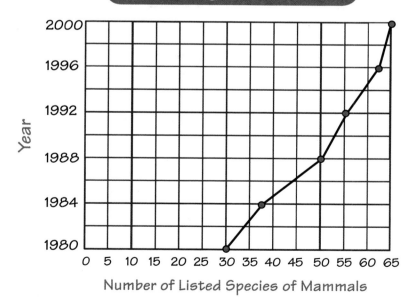

ASSESS

After groups describe their graphs, ask specific questions about the data in their graphs. For example, ask: *Does the line graph show an increase, a decrease, or no change over time?*

For more practice or to assess students, use Practice Book pp. 89–90.

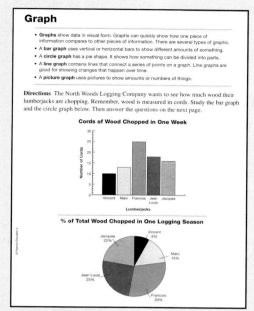

▲ **Practice Book** p. 89

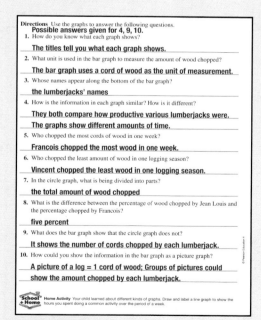

▲ **Practice Book** p. 90

Assessment Checkpoints *for the Week*

Selection Assessment

Use pp. 33–36 of Selection Tests to check:

 Selection Understanding

 Comprehension Skill *Fact and Opinion*

☑ **Selection Vocabulary**
cord
dismay
grizzly
immense
payroll

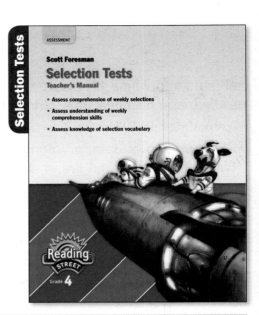

Leveled Assessment

Use pp. 49–54 of **Fresh Reads for Differentiated Test Practice** to check:

  Comprehension Skill *Fact and Opinion*

 REVIEW **Comprehension Skill** *Main Idea*

☑ **Fluency** *Words Correct Per Minute*

Managing Assessment

Use Assessment Handbook for:

 Observation Checklists

 Record-Keeping Forms

☑ **Portfolio Assessment**

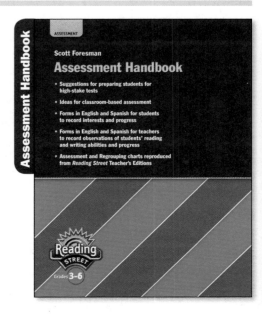

Oregon

Planning Guide for Common Curriculum Goals

So You Want to Be President?

Reading Street Teacher's Edition pages	Grade 4 Oregon Grade-Level Standards for English/Language Arts
Oral Language **Speaking/Listening** Build Concept Vocabulary: 240l, 251, 255, 259c Read Aloud: 240m **Viewing** Analyze a Speech: 259d	**EL.04.RE.01** Read aloud grade-level narrative text and informational text fluently and accurately with effective pacing, intonation, and expression. **EL.04.RE.09** Understand, learn, and use new vocabulary that is introduced and taught directly through informational text, literary text, and instruction across the subject areas.
Word Work Words with *ear, ir, our, ur*: 259i–259j	**EL.04.WR.15** Spell correctly: syllables (word parts each containing a vowel sound, such as *sur-prise* or *e-col-o-gy*).
Reading **Comprehension** Main Idea: 240–241, 244–255, 258–259, 259b Summarize: 240–241, 244–255 **Vocabulary** Lesson Vocabulary: 242b, 251, 255, 258 Dictionary/Glossary: 242–243, 253, 259c **Fluency** Model Stress/Emphasis: 240l–240m, 259a **Self-Selected Reading:** LR37–45, TR16–17 **Literature** Genre—Expository Nonfiction: 244 Reader Response: 256	**EL.04.RE.01** Read aloud grade-level narrative text and informational text fluently and accurately with effective pacing, intonation, and expression. **EL.04.RE.10** Develop vocabulary by listening to and discussing both familiar and conceptually challenging selections read aloud across the subject areas. **EL.04.RE.17** Locate information in titles, tables of contents, chapter headings, illustrations, captions, glossaries, indexes, graphs, charts, diagrams, and tables to aid understanding of grade-level text. **EL.04.RE.20** Identify and/or summarize sequence of events, main ideas, facts, supporting details, and opinions in informational and practical selections. **EL.04.LI.01** Listen to text and read text to make connections and respond to a wide variety of significant works of literature, including poetry, fiction, non-fiction, and drama, from a variety of cultures and time periods that enhance the study of other subjects.
Language Arts **Writing** Explanation: 259g–259h **Six-Trait Writing Focus/Ideas:** 257, 259g–259h **Grammar, Usage, and Mechanics** Plural Possessive Nouns: 259e–259f **Research/Study** Time Line: 259l **Technology** New Literacies: 259k	**EL.04.WR.25** Write informational reports: develop the topic with simple facts, details, examples, and explanations. **EL.04.WR.31** Understand the organization of almanacs, newspapers, and periodicals and how to use those print materials.
Unit Skills **Writing** How-To Report: WA2–9 **Poetry:** 260–263 **Project/Wrap-Up:** 264–265	**EL.04.WR.25** Write informational reports: ask and then address a central question about an issue or event; include facts and details for focus; develop the topic with simple facts, details, examples, and explanations; use more than one source of information, including speakers, books, newspapers, other media sources, and online information.

This Week's Leveled Readers

Intensive Intervention

SCOTT FORESMAN

SiDEWALKS

Intensive Intervention for Tier 3 Students

Below-Level

A TRIP TO THE CAPITOL

Nonfiction

EL.04.RE.20 Identify and/or summarize sequence of events, main ideas, facts, supporting details, and opinions in informational and practical selections.

EL.04.RE.25 Determine the author's purpose, and relate it to details in the text.

On-Level

Meet the United States Government
by Joshua Nierenberg

Nonfiction

EL.04.RE.20 Identify and/or summarize sequence of events, main ideas, facts, supporting details, and opinions in informational and practical selections.

EL.04.LI.06 Use knowledge of the situation and setting and of a character's traits and motivations to determine the causes for that character's actions.

Advanced

THE POWER OF OUR PEOPLE

Nonfiction

EL.04.RE.20 Identify and/or summarize sequence of events, main ideas, facts, supporting details, and opinions in informational and practical selections.

EL.04.RE.21 Identify key facts and information after reading two passages or articles on the same topic.

Science

SC.05.LS.01.01 Classify a variety of living things into groups using various characteristics. (Previews Grade 5 Benchmark)

SC.05.LS.03.01 Associate specific structures with their functions in the survival of the organism. (Previews Grade 5 Benchmark)

SC.05.LS.05 Describe the relationship between characteristics of specific habitats and the organisms that live there. (Previews Grade 5 Benchmark)

SC.05.SI.04 Summarize, analyze, and interpret data from investigations. (Previews Grade 5 Benchmark)

Social Studies

SS.05.CG.02 Identify the primary functions of federal, state, and local governments. (Previews Grade 5 Benchmark)

SS.05.CG.07 Recognize and give examples of how nations interact with one another through trade, diplomacy, cultural contacts, treaties, and agreements. (Previews Grade 5 Benchmark)

SS.05.HS.05.05 Identify and understand the causes, course, and impact of the American Revolution, including the roles of George Washington, Samuel Adams, and Thomas Jefferson. (Previews Grade 5 Benchmark)

Oregon!

A FAMOUS OREGONIAN
Herbert Hoover

Herbert Hoover (1874–1964) was the thirty-first President of the United States. Although he was born in Iowa, he spent many of his early years with his aunt and uncle in Oregon. Hoover was a member of the first graduating class at Stanford University and worked as a mining engineer. He was highly successful. After twenty years of work, his net worth was about $4 million. Hoover was in China during the Boxer Rebellion and arranged the rescue of trapped foreigners there. He did the same for Americans trapped in Europe at the onset of World War I.

Students can . . .
Design a postage stamp that honors Herbert Hoover.

A SPECIAL OREGON PLACE
Historic Columbia River Highway

Constructed from 1913 to 1922, the Historic Columbia River Highway (HCRH) runs alongside the Columbia River between The Dalles and Troutdale. With its breathtaking views of the Columbia River Gorge, the HCRH is known as the first scenic highway in the country and the first modern highway built in the Pacific Northwest. After the 1950s, portions of the HCRH were destroyed or bypassed as other major roads were built. The Oregon Department of Transportation is currently restoring these ruined and abandoned sections of the HCRH for use as hiking trails and bike paths.

Students can . . .
Highlight the path of the Historic Columbia River Highway on an outline map of the state. Ask students to color code areas that are being restored and areas that are navigable by car.

OREGON FUN FACTS
Did You Know?

- In 2005 the state legislature adopted the pear as the official state fruit. Pears are the best-selling fruit crop in Oregon.

- Oregon was the first state to celebrate Labor Day as an official holiday and to implement a workers' compensation program.

- A majority of Crook County residents voted for the winner in every presidential election from 1859—the year Oregon gained statehood—to 1992.

Students can . . .
Use an almanac or encyclopedia to find all the U.S. Presidents who were elected between 1859 and 1992. Ask students to list each President and the year he was elected.

Unit 2
Work and Play

CONCEPT QUESTION
What is the value of work and play?

Week 1
How can we learn to appreciate the talents of others?

Week 2
How can we work together to achieve a goal?

Week 3
What can we accomplish by using our imaginations?

Week 4
What is the value of a job well done?

Week 5
What is the job of the President of the United States?

EXPAND THE CONCEPT
What is the job of the President of the United States?

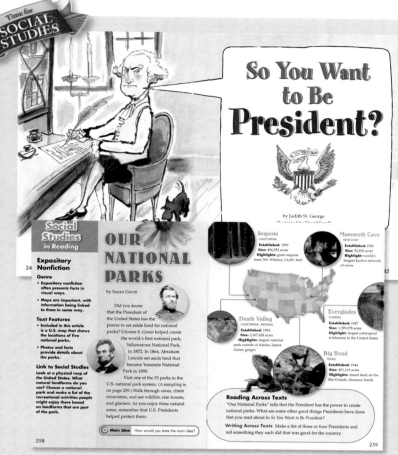

CONNECT THE CONCEPT

▶ **Build Background**
capital, capitol, clerks

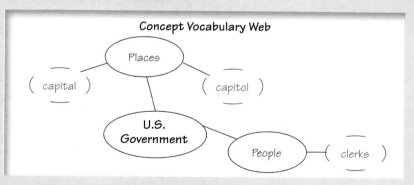

Concept Vocabulary Web

Places
(capital)   (capitol)

U.S. Government
People   (clerks)

▶ **Social Studies Content**
The Secret Service, The Executive Branch, FDR's New Deal, Mount Rushmore

▶ **Writing**
Explanation

▶ **Internet Inquiry**
U.S. Presidency

Preview Your Week

So You Want to Be President?

by Judith St. George
illustrated by David Small

Genre Expository nonfiction gives information about real people and events. As you read, note new or surprising information about our country's Presidents.

What does it take to be President of the United States?

Student Edition pages 244–255

Audio CD

Genre	Expository Nonfiction
Vocabulary Strategy	Dictionary/Glossary
Comprehension Skill	Main Idea
Comprehension Strategy	Summarize

Paired Selection

Reading Across Texts
Describe Good Things Presidents Have Done

Genre
Expository Nonfiction

Text Features
Map
Photos

Social Studies in Reading

OUR NATIONAL PARKS

by Susan Gavin

Expository Nonfiction

Genre
- Expository nonfiction often presents facts and information in visual ways.
- Maps are important, with information being linked to them in some way.

Text Features
- With this brief article, a map of the United States shows the location of five national parks.
- Photos and facts provide details about the parks.

Link to Social Studies
Look at a physical map of the United States. What natural landforms do you see? Choose a national park and make a list of the recreational activities people might enjoy there based on the landforms that are part of the park.

Did you know that the President of the United States has the power to set aside land for national parks? Ulysses S. Grant helped create the world's first national park, Yellowstone National Park, in 1872. In 1864, Abraham Lincoln set aside land that became Yosemite National Park in 1890.

Visit one of the 55 parks in the U.S. national park system. (A sampling is on page 259.) Walk through caves, climb mountains, and see wildlife, rain forests, and glaciers. As you enjoy these natural areas, remember that U.S. Presidents helped protect them.

Sequoia
CALIFORNIA
Established: 1890
Size: 456,552 acres
Highlights: giant sequoia trees; Mt. Whitney (14,491 feet)

Mammoth Cave
KENTUCKY
Established: 1941
Size: 52,830 acres
Highlight: world's longest known network of caves

Death Valley
CALIFORNIA, NEVADA
Established: 1994
Size: 3,367,628 acres
Highlights: largest national park outside of Alaska; desert; dunes, gorges

Everglades
FLORIDA
Established: 1947
Size: 1,399,078 acres
Highlight: world's largest subtropical wilderness in the United States

Big Bend
TEXAS
Established: 1944
Size: 801,163 acres
Highlights: desert land; on the Rio Grande; dinosaur fossils

Reading Across Texts "Our National Parks" tells that the President has the power to create national parks. What are some other good things Presidents have done that you read about in *So You Want to Be President?*

Writing Across Texts Make a list of three or four Presidents and tell something they each did that was good for the country.

Main Idea How would you state the main idea?

258

Student Edition pages 258–259

Audio CD

Read It

ONLINE

PearsonSuccessNet.com

- Student Edition
- Leveled Readers

Leveled Readers

◉ **Skill** Main Idea

◉ **Strategy** Summarize

Lesson Vocabulary

Below-Level

On-Level

Advanced

ELL Reader

- Concept Vocabulary
- Text Support
- Language Enrichment

Time for
SOCIAL STUDIES

Integrate Social Studies Standards

- U.S. History
- U.S. Government
- U.S. Geography

✓ **Read**

So You Want to Be President?, pp. 244–255

"Our National Parks," pp. 258–259

Leveled Readers

Below-Level  On-Level Advanced

- Support Concepts
- Develop Concepts
- Extend Concepts

ELL Reader

✓ **Build Concept Vocabulary**

U.S. Government, pp. 240l–240m

✓ **Teach Social Studies Concepts**

The Secret Service, p. 247
The Executive Branch, p. 249
FDR's New Deal, p. 253
Mount Rushmore, p. 259

✓ **Explore Social Studies Center**

Draw a Diagram, p. 240k

So You Want to Be President? **240c**

Weekly Plan

READING

45–90 minutes

TARGET SKILLS OF THE WEEK

- **Comprehension Skill**
  Main Idea
- **Comprehension Strategy**
  Summarize
- **Vocabulary Strategy**
  Dictionary/Glossary

DAY 1
PAGES 240l–242b, 259a, 259e–259k

Oral Language

QUESTION OF THE WEEK *What is the job of the President of the United States?*

Read Aloud: "Welcome to Washington!" 240m
Build Concepts, 240l

Comprehension/Vocabulary

Comprehension Skill/Strategy Lesson, 240–241
- Main Idea **T**
- Summarize

Build Background, 242a

Introduce Lesson Vocabulary, 242b
Constitution, howling, humble, politics, responsibility, solemnly, vain **T**

Read Leveled Readers

Grouping Options 240f–240g

Fluency

Model Stress/Emphasis, 240l–240m, 259a

DAY 2
PAGES 242–251, 259a, 259e–259k

Oral Language

QUESTION OF THE DAY *Why does the author include so many details about Presidents?*

Comprehension/Vocabulary

Vocabulary Strategy Lesson, 242–243
- Dictionary/Glossary **T**

Read *So You Want to Be President?* 244–251

Grouping Options 240f–240g

- Main Idea **T**
- Summarize
- Dictionary/Glossary **T**
- **REVIEW** Generalize **T**

Develop Vocabulary

Fluency

Choral Reading, 259a

LANGUAGE ARTS

30–60 minutes

Trait of the Week

Organization/Paragraphs

Grammar, 259e
Introduce Plural Possessive Nouns **T**

Writing For Tests, 259g
Introduce Explanation

Model the Trait of the Week: Organization/ Paragraphs

Spelling, 259i
Pretest for Words with *ear, ir, our, ur*

Internet Inquiry, 259k
Identify Questions

Grammar, 259e
Develop Plural Possessive Nouns **T**

Writing For Tests, 259g
Improve Writing with Writing Good Paragraphs

Spelling, 259i
Teach the Generalization

Internet Inquiry, 259k
Navigate/Search

DAILY WRITING ACTIVITIES

Day 1 Write to Read, 240

Day 2 Words to Write, 243
Strategy Response Log, 244, 251

DAILY SOCIAL STUDIES CONNECTIONS

Day 1 U.S. Government Concept Web, 240l

Day 2 Time for Social Studies: The Secret Service, 247; The Executive Branch, 249
Revisit the U.S. Government Concept Web, 251

DAILY SUCCESS PREDICTORS

for Adequate Yearly Progress

Monitor Progress and Corrective Feedback

Vocabulary Check Vocabulary, *240l*

RESOURCES FOR THE WEEK

- Practice Book, *pp. 91–100*
- Word Study and Spelling Practice Book, *pp. 37–40*
- Grammar and Writing Practice Book, *pp. 37–40*
- Selection Test, *pp. 37–40*
- Fresh Reads for Differentiated Test Practice, *pp. 55–60*
- The Grammar and Writing Book, *pp. 104–109*

Grouping Options for Differentiated Instruction

Turn the page for the small group lesson plan.

DAY 3 — PAGES 252–257, 259a, 259e–259k

Oral Language

QUESTION OF THE DAY *If you were the President, what would you like and dislike about your job?*

Comprehension/Vocabulary

Read *So You Want to Be President?* 252–256

Grouping Options 240f–240g

- 🎯 Summarize
- 🎯 Dictionary/Glossary **T**
- Develop Vocabulary

Reader Response

Selection Test

Fluency

Model Stress/Emphasis, 259a

Grammar, 259f
Apply Plural Possessive Nouns in Writing **T**

Writing For Tests, 257, 259h
Write Now
Prewrite and Draft

Spelling, 259j
Connect Spelling to Writing

Internet Inquiry, 259k
Analyze Sources

Day 3 Strategy Response Log, 254
Look Back and Write, 256

Day 3 Time for Social Studies: FDR's New Deal, 253
Revisit the U.S. Government Concept Web, 255

DAY 4 — PAGES 258–259a, 259e–259k

Oral Language

QUESTION OF THE DAY *What are some important qualities that the President of the United States should have? Why?*

Comprehension/Vocabulary

Read "Our National Parks," 258–259

Grouping Options 240f –240g

Expository Nonfiction/Text Features

Reading Across Texts

Content-Area Vocabulary

Fluency

Partner Reading, 259a

Grammar, 259f
Practice Plural Possessive Nouns for Standardized Tests **T**

Writing Workshop, 259h
Draft, Revise, and Publish

Spelling, 259j
Provide a Strategy

Internet Inquiry, 259k
Synthesize Information

Day 4 Writing Across Texts, 259

Day 4 Time for Social Studies: Mount Rushmore, 259

DAY 5 — PAGES 259a–259l

Oral Language

QUESTION OF THE WEEK *To wrap up the week, revisit the Day 1 question.*
Build Concept Vocabulary, 259c

Fluency

Read Leveled Readers

Grouping Options 240f–240g

Assess Reading Rate, 259a

Comprehension/Vocabulary

- 🎯 Reteach Main Idea, 259b **T**
- Expository Nonfiction, 259b
- 🎯 Review Dictionary/Glossary, 259c **T**

Speaking and Viewing, 259d
Press Conference
Analyze a Speech

Grammar, 259f
Cumulative Review

Writing Workshop, 259h
Connect to Unit Writing

Spelling, 259j
Posttest for Words with *ear, ir, our, ur*

Internet Inquiry, 259k
Communicate Results

Research/Study Skills, 259l
Time Line

Day 5 Expository Nonfiction, 259b

Day 5 Revisit the U.S. Government Concept Web, 259c

KEY 🎯 = Target Skill   **T** = Tested Skill

Comprehension — Check Retelling, *256*

Fluency — Check Fluency WCPM, *259a*

Vocabulary — Check Vocabulary, *259c*

SUCCESS PREDICTOR

Small Group Plan for Differentiated Instruction

Daily Plan
AT A GLANCE

Reading
Whole Group
- Oral Language
- Comprehension/Vocabulary

Group Time
Differentiated Instruction

Meet with small groups to provide:
- Skill Support
- Reading Support
- Fluency Practice

Read

This week's lessons for daily group time can be found behind the Differentiated Instruction (DI) tab on pp. DI·42–DI·51.

Whole Group
- Fluency

Language Arts
- Grammar
- Writing
- Spelling
- Research/Inquiry
- Speaking/Listening/Viewing

Use *My Sidewalks on Reading Street* for Tier III intensive reading intervention.

DAY 1

On-Level	Strategic Intervention	Advanced
Teacher-Led *Page DI·43*	**Teacher-Led** *Page DI·42*	**Teacher-Led** *Page DI·43*
• Develop Concept Vocabulary • **Read** On-Level Reader *Meet The United States Government*	• Reinforce Concepts • **Read** Below-Level Reader *A Trip to The Capitol*	• **Read** Advanced Reader *The Power of Our People* • Independent Extension Activity

(i) Independent Activities
While you meet with small groups, have the rest of the class...

- Visit the Reading/Library Center
- Listen to the Background Building Audio
- Finish Write to Read, p. 240
- Complete Practice Book pp. 93–94
- Visit Cross-Curricular Centers

DAY 2

On-Level	Strategic Intervention	Advanced
Teacher-Led *Pages 246–251*	**Teacher-Led** *Page DI·44*	**Teacher-Led** *Page DI·45*
• **Read** *So You Want to Be President?*	• Practice Lesson Vocabulary • Read Multisyllabic Words • **Read** or Listen to *So You Want to Be President?*	• Extend Vocabulary • **Read** *So You Want to Be President?*

(i) Independent Activities
While you meet with small groups, have the rest of the class...

- Visit the Reading/Library Center
- Listen to the AudioText for *So You Want to Be President?*
- Finish Words to Write, p. 243
- Complete Practice Book pp. 95–96
- Write in their Strategy Response Logs, pp. 244, 251
- Visit Cross-Curricular Centers
- Work on inquiry projects

DAY 3

On-Level	Strategic Intervention	Advanced
Teacher-Led *Pages 252–255*	**Teacher-Led** *Page DI·46*	**Teacher-Led** *Page DI·47*
• **Read** *So You Want to Be President?*	• Practice Main Idea and Summarize • **Read** or Listen to *So You Want to Be President?*	• Extend Main Idea and Summarize • **Read** *So You Want to Be President?*

(i) Independent Activities
While you meet with small groups, have the rest of the class...

- Visit the Reading/Library Center
- Listen to the AudioText for *So You Want to Be President?*
- Write in their Strategy Response Logs, p. 254
- Finish Look Back and Write, p. 256
- Complete Practice Book p. 97
- Visit Cross-Curricular Centers
- Work on inquiry projects

① Begin with whole class skill and strategy instruction.

② Meet with small groups to provide differentiated instruction.

③ Gather the whole class back together for fluency and language arts.

DAY 4

On-Level
Teacher-Led
Pages 258–259
- **Read** "Our National Parks"

Strategic Intervention
Teacher-Led
Page DI • 48
- Practice Retelling
- **Read** or Listen to "Our National Parks"

Advanced
Teacher-Led
Page DI • 49
- **Read** "Our National Parks"
- Genre Study

 ## Independent Activities

While you meet with small groups, have the rest of the class...

- Visit the Reading/Library Center
- Listen to the AudioText for "Our National Parks"
- Visit the Writing/Vocabulary Center
- Finish Writing Across Texts, p. 259
- Visit Cross-Curricular Centers
- Work on inquiry projects

DAY 5

On-Level
Teacher-Led
Page DI • 51
- **Reread** Leveled Reader *Meet The United States Government*
- Retell *Meet the United States Government*

Strategic Intervention
Teacher-Led
Page DI • 50
- **Reread** Leveled Reader *A Trip to The Capitol*
- Retell *A Trip to The Capitol*

Advanced
Teacher-Led
Page DI • 51
- **Reread** Leveled Reader *The Power of Our People*
- Share Extension Activity

Independent Activities

While you meet with small groups, have the rest of the class...

- Visit the Reading/Library Center
- Complete Practice Book pp. 98–100
- Visit Cross-Curricular Centers
- Work on inquiry projects

 Grouping Place English language learners in the groups that correspond to their reading abilities in English.

Use the appropriate Leveled Reader or other text at students' instructional level.

TiP Send home the appropriate Multilingual Summary of the main selection on Day 1.

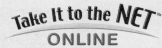
ONLINE
PearsonSuccessNet.com

Donald Leu
For ideas and activities to build new literacies, see the article "The New Literacies" by Scott Foresman author Donald Leu.

TEACHER TALK

New literacies are skills and strategies needed to successfully use information technologies, such as CD-ROMs, the Internet, and e-mail.

Be sure to schedule time for students to work on the unit inquiry project "All in a Day's Work." This week students create classified ads and give brief presentations about their jobs.

 Looking Ahead

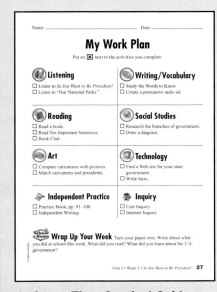

▲ **Group-Time Survival Guide**
p. 27, Weekly Contract

So You Want to Be President? 240g

ORAL LANGUAGE

Concept Development

SOCIAL STUDIES

What is the job of the President of the United States?

CONCEPT VOCABULARY

capital   capitol   clerks

BUILD

☐ **Question of the Week** Introduce and discuss the question of the week. This week students will read a variety of texts and work on projects related to the concept *U.S. Government*. Post the question for students to refer to throughout the week. DAY 1 *240d*

☐ **Read Aloud** Read aloud "Welcome to Washington!" Then begin a web to build concepts and concept vocabulary related to this week's lesson and the unit theme, Work and Play. Introduce the concept words *capital, capitol,* and *clerks* and have students place them on the web. Display the web for use throughout the week. DAY 1 *240l-240m*

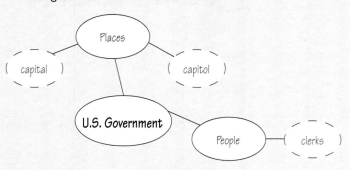

DEVELOP

☐ **Question of the Day** Use the prompts from the Weekly Plan to engage students in conversations related to this week's reading and the unit theme. **EVERY DAY** *240d-240e*

☐ **Concept Vocabulary Web** Revisit the U.S. Government Concept Web and encourage students to add concept words from their reading and life experiences. **DAY 2** *251,* **DAY 3** *255*

CONNECT

☐ **Looking Back** Revisit the U.S. Government Concept Web and discuss how it relates to this week's lesson and the unit theme. **DAY 5** *259c*

CHECK

☐ **Concept Vocabulary Web** Use the U.S. Government Concept Web to check students' understanding of the concept vocabulary words *capital, capitol,* and *clerks*. DAY 1 *240l,* **DAY 5** *259c*

VOCABULARY

☐ **STRATEGY DICTIONARY/ GLOSSARY** When you come across a word whose meaning you don't know, and the words around it don't help, you can use a dictionary or glossary to find the meaning.

LESSON VOCABULARY

Constitution   responsibility
howling   solemnly
humble   vain
politics

TEACH

☐ **Words to Know** Give students the opportunity to tell what they already know about this week's lesson vocabulary words. Then discuss word meaning. DAY 1 *242b*

☐ **Vocabulary Strategy Lesson** Use the vocabulary strategy lesson in the Student Edition to introduce and model this week's strategy, *dictionary/glossary.* **DAY 2** *242-243*

Vocabulary Strategy Lesson

PRACTICE/APPLY

☐ **Leveled Text** Read the lesson vocabulary in the context of leveled text. DAY 1 *LR37-LR45*

Leveled Readers

☐ **Words in Context** Read the lesson vocabulary and apply *dictionary/glossary* in the context of *So You Want to Be President?* **DAY 2** *244-251,* **DAY 3** *252-256*

☐ **Writing/Vocabulary Center** Use Words to Know to create a radio ad persuading others to vote for a President of the United States. **ANY DAY** *240k*

Main Selection—Nonfiction

☐ **Homework** Practice Book pp. 94–95. DAY 1 *242b,* **DAY 2** *243*

☐ **Word Play** Have students skim the selection for adjectives that describe personality traits, and take turns acting out a word for the class to discuss. For a challenge, allow students to use only facial expressions and body movements. **ANY DAY** *259c*

ASSESS

☐ **Selection Test** Use the Selection Test to determine students' understanding of the lesson vocabulary words. **DAY 3**

RETEACH/REVIEW

☐ **Reteach Lesson** If necessary, use this lesson to reteach and review *dictionary/glossary.* **DAY 5** *259c*

❶ Use assessment data to determine your instructional focus.

❷ Preview this week's instruction by strand.

❸ Choose instructional activities that meet the needs of your classroom.

COMPREHENSION

⊙ SKILL MAIN IDEA The main idea is the most important idea about the topic of a paragraph, passage, or article. Small pieces of information, supporting details, tell more about the main idea.

⊙ STRATEGY SUMMARIZE Summarizing is a short retelling of a portion of the text that includes the important information (main ideas).

TEACH

☐ **Skill/Strategy Lesson** Use the skill/strategy lesson in the Student Edition to introduce and model *main idea* and *summarize*. DAY 1 240-241

☐ **Extend Skills** Teach expository nonfiction. ANY DAY 259b

Skill/Strategy Lesson

PRACTICE/APPLY

☐ **Leveled Text** Apply *main idea* and *summarize* to read leveled text. DAY 1 LR37-LR45

☐ **Skills and Strategies in Context** Read *So You Want to Be President?* using the Guiding Comprehension questions to apply *main idea* and *summarize*. DAY 2 244-251, DAY 3 252-256

☐ **Skills and Strategies in Context** Read "Our National Parks," guiding students as they apply *main idea* and *summarize*. Then have students discuss and write across texts. DAY 4 258-259

☐ **Homework** Practice Book pp. 93, 97, 98. DAY 1 241, DAY 3 255, DAY 5 259b

☐ **Fresh Reads for Differentiated Test Practice** Have students practice *main idea* with a new passage. DAY 3

Leveled Readers

Main Selection—Nonfiction

Paired Selection—Nonfiction

ASSESS

☐ **Selection Test** Determine students' understanding of the selection and their use of *main idea*. DAY 3

☐ **Retell** Have students retell *So You Want to Be President?* DAY 3 256-257

RETEACH/REVIEW

☐ **Reteach Lesson** If necessary, reteach and review *main idea*. DAY 5 259b

FLUENCY

SKILL STRESS/EMPHASIS Reading with emotion and stress allows listeners to more easily understand the information in the text. Good readers should stress signal words for effect and sense.

TEACH

☐ **Read Aloud** Model fluent reading by rereading "Welcome to Washington!" Focus on this week's fluency skill, stress/emphasis. DAY 1 240l-240m, 259a

PRACTICE/APPLY

☐ **Choral Reading** Read aloud selected paragraphs from *So You Want to Be President?* Have students specifically listen for words that are being intentionally stressed. As a class, practice adding stress and emotion to their reading by doing three choral readings of the paragraphs. DAY 2 259a, DAY 3 259a

☐ **Partner Reading** Have partners practice reading with emotion and stressing important words. As students reread, they should offer each other feedback and their progress toward their individual fluency goals should be monitored. DAY 4 259a

☐ **Listening Center** Have students follow along with the AudioText for this week's selections. ANY DAY 240j

☐ **Reading/Library Center** Have students reread a selection of their choice. ANY DAY 240j

☐ **Fluency Coach** Have students use Fluency Coach to listen to fluent readings or practice reading on their own. ANY DAY

ASSESS

☐ **Check Fluency** WCPM Do a one-minute timed reading, paying special attention to this week's skill—stress/emphasis. Provide feedback for each student. DAY 5 259a

☑ Customize Your Plan *by Strand*

GRAMMAR

SKILL PLURAL POSSESSIVE NOUNS A possessive noun shows ownership. A plural possessive noun shows that something is owned or shared by more than one person, place, or thing. To form plural possessive nouns add an apostrophe to words that end in *-s, -es, or -ies* or add an apostrophe and *-s* to a plural noun that does not end in *-s, -es, or -ies.*

TEACH

❑ **Grammar Transparency 10** Use Grammar Transparency 10 to teach plural possessive nouns. DAY 1 *259e*

Grammar Transparency 10

PRACTICE/APPLY

❑ **Develop the Concept** Review the concept of plural possessive nouns and provide guided practice. **DAY 2** *259e*

❑ **Apply to Writing** Have students review something they have written and add plural possessive nouns. **DAY 3** *259f*

❑ **Test Preparation** Examine common errors in plural possessive nouns to prepare for standardized tests. **DAY 4** *259f*

❑ **Homework** Grammar and Writing Practice Book pp. 37–39. **DAY 2** *259e,* **DAY 3** *259f,* **DAY 4** *259f*

ASSESS

❑ **Cumulative Review** Use Grammar and Writing Practice Book p. 40. **DAY 5** *259f*

RETEACH/REVIEW

❑ **Daily Fix-It** Have students find and correct errors in grammar, spelling, and punctuation. **EVERY DAY** *259e–259f*

❑ **The Grammar and Writing Book** Use pp. 104–107 of The Grammar and Writing Book to extend instruction for plural possessive nouns. **ANY DAY**

The Grammar and Writing Book

WRITING

Trait of the Week

ORGANIZATION/PARAGRAPHS Good writers organize their writing. They write in an order that will help readers understand what they have to say and show connections among their ideas.

TEACH

❑ **Writing Transparency 10A** Use the model to introduce and discuss the Trait of the Week. DAY 1 *259g*

❑ **Writing Transparency 10B** Use the transparency to show students how writing good paragraphs can improve their writing. **DAY 2** *259g*

Writing Transparency 10A   **Writing Transparency 10B**

PRACTICE/APPLY

❑ **Write Now** Examine the model on Student Edition p. 257. Then have students write their own explanation. **DAY 3** *257, 259h,* **DAY 4** *259h*

> **Prompt** *So You Want to Be President?* explains what it's like to be President of the united States. Think about an activity that you like to do and why you like to do it. Now write two or three paragraphs explaining your interest.

Write Now p. 257

❑ **Writing/Vocabulary Center** Use Words to Know to create a radio ad persuading others to vote for a President of the United States. **ANY DAY** *240k*

ASSESS

❑ **Writing Trait Rubric** Use the rubric to evaluate students' writing. **DAY 4** *259h*

RETEACH/REVIEW

❑ **The Grammar and Writing Book** Use pp. 104–109 of The Grammar and Writing Book to extend instruction for plural possessive nouns, writing good paragraphs, and explanations. **ANY DAY**

The Grammar and Writing Book

SPELLING

GENERALIZATION WORDS WITH *EAR, IR, OUR, UR* The vowel sound in *girl* can be spelled *ear, ir, our,* and *ur: early first, courage, return*. Words with *ear, ir, our,* and *ur* often have the vowel sound heard in *girl*.

TEACH

❑ **Pretest** Give the pretest for words with *ear, ir, our, ur*. Guide students in self-correcting their pretests and correcting any misspellings. **DAY 1** *259i*

❑ **Think and Practice** Connect spelling to the phonics generalization for words with *ear, ir, our, ur*. **DAY 2** *259i*

PRACTICE/APPLY

❑ **Connect to Writing** Have students use spelling words to write a caption for a picture of a handdrawn household machine. The caption should explain the machine's purpose or tell how it works. Then review frequently misspelled words: *heard, our, are*. **DAY 3** *259j*

❑ **Homework** Phonics and Spelling Practice Book pp. 37–40. **EVERY DAY**

RETEACH/REVIEW

❑ **Review** Review spelling words to prepare for the posttest. Then provide students with a spelling strategy—problem parts. **DAY 4** *259j*

ASSESS

❑ **Posttest** Use dictation sentences to give the posttest for words with *ear, ir, our, ur*. **DAY 5** *259j*

Spelling Words

1. return	8. early	15. furniture
2. courage*	9. turtle	16. search
3. surface	10. birthday*	17. curtain
4. purpose	11. journal	18. burrow
5. first*	12. courtesy	19. hamburger
6. turkey	13. nourish	20. survey*
7. heard	14. purse	

Challenge Words

21. turquoise	23. furthermore	25. nourishment
22. absurd	24. flourish	

*Word from the selection

RESEARCH AND INQUIRY

❑ **Internet Inquiry** Have students conduct an Internet inquiry exploring the job of the President of the United States. **EVERY DAY** *259k*

❑ **Time Line** Review what a time line is and what information a time line displays. Have small groups analyze various time lines and answer questions. **DAY 5** *259l*

❑ **Unit Inquiry** Allow time for students to create classified ads and give brief presentations about their jobs. **ANY DAY** *141*

SPEAKING AND VIEWING

❑ **Press Conference** Have students role-play being President of the United States. The President is about to hold a press conference. Students should begin their press conference with a main idea statement that will summarize their plan to make the country better. **DAY 5** *259d*

❑ **Analyze a Speech** Have students view and analyze a taped political speech and answer questions. **DAY 5** *259d*

Resources for
Differentiated Instruction

LEVELED READERS

▶ **Comprehension**
- 🎯 **Skill** Main Idea
- 🎯 **Strategy** Summarize

▶ **Lesson Vocabulary**
- 🎯 Dictionary/Glossary

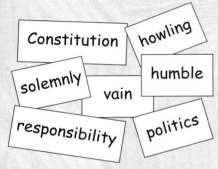

Constitution · howling · solemnly · vain · humble · responsibility · politics

▶ **Social Studies Standards**
- U.S. History
- U.S. Government
- U.S. Geography

ONLINE
PearsonSuccessNet.com

Use the Online Database of over 600 books to

- Download and print additional copies of this week's leveled readers.

- Listen to the readers being read online.

- Search for more titles focused on this week's skills, topic, and content.

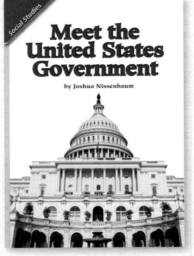

Meet the United States Government
by Joshua Nissenbaum

On-Level Reader

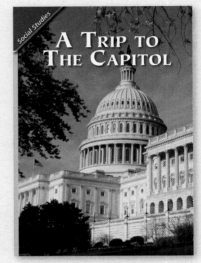

A TRIP TO THE CAPITOL

Below-Level Reader

Name _____ Meet the U.S. Government

Main Idea and Details

- The **main idea** is the most important idea about the topic of a paragraph, passage, or article.
- **Supporting details** are the small pieces of information that tell more about the main idea.

Directions Reread the following passage from *Meet the United States Government*. Then answer the questions about the passage below.

The executive branch of the government is what most people think of when they say "the government." This branch enforces the laws Congress makes and upholds the Constitution. The executive branch is so large that it needs to be divided into departments. The President acts as the head of all these departments. The directors, or secretaries, of each department form a group called the Cabinet.

Maybe you have heard of some of these departments. There is the Department of State, the Department of the Treasury, and the Department of Defense. Over the years these departments have grown, and new departments have been added. Now there are fifteen executive departments.

1. What is the main idea of these two paragraphs? **Possible responses given.**
   The executive branch is large and needs to be divided up.
2. What is one supporting detail in the first paragraph that tells about this main idea?
   The President acts as the head of all the executive departments.
3. What is another supporting detail in the second paragraph that tells more about this main idea?
   The Department of State is one of the executive departments.
4. What is another supporting detail in the second paragraph that tells more about this main idea?
   The Department of the Treasury is one executive department.
5. What is another supporting detail in the second paragraph that tells more about this main idea?
   The Department of Defense is another executive department.

On-Level Practice TE p. LR41

Name _____ A Trip to the Capitol

Main Idea and Details

- The **main idea** is the most important idea about the topic of a paragraph, passage, or article.
- **Supporting details** are the small pieces of information that tell more about the main idea.

Directions Reread the following passage from *A Trip to the Capitol*. Then answer the questions about the passage below.

The Founding Fathers tried to make sure that no one person had too much power. They also knew that a growing nation needed a strong government. They wrote the Constitution to deal with these challenges. In it, they outlined three branches, or parts, of government: legislative, executive, and judicial.

Each branch has responsibility for different jobs. Together, the three branches are designed to make sure the government runs smoothly and protects the rights of its citizens. Each branch has the power to challenge the other two branches. This system of checks and balances prevents any one branch from having too much power.

1. What is the main idea of the first paragraph? **Possible responses given.**
   The Founding Fathers wanted the United States to have a strong government.
2. What is one supporting detail in the first paragraph that tells about this main idea?
   In the Constitution, they outlined three branches of government.
3. What is a detail that supports the supporting detail in question 2?
   The three branches are the legislative, executive, and judicial.
4. What is the main idea of the second paragraph?
   Each branch has different responsibilities; all branches are designed to help the government run smoothly.
5. What is one supporting detail in the second paragraph that tells more about this main idea?
   Each branch has the power to challenge the others.

Below-Level Practice TE p. LR38

Name _____ Meet the U.S. Government

Vocabulary
Directions Fill in the blank with the word from the box that fits the definition.

Check the Words You Know			
__Constitution	__howling	__humble	__politics
__responsibility	__solemnly	__vain	

1. solemnly _____ seriously; earnestly
2. Constitution _____ document that establishes the basic principles of the United States government
3. humble _____ meek; modest
4. politics _____ the art or science of governing or of policies
5. responsibility _____ job; duty; task
6. howling _____ crying; wailing; shrieking
7. vain _____ proud; inflated

Directions Write a brief paragraph about the United States government, using as many vocabulary words as possible.

Responses will vary.

_____
_____
_____
_____

On-Level Practice TE p. LR42

Name _____ A Trip to the Capitol

Vocabulary
Directions Fill in the blank with the word from the box that fits the definition.

Check the Words You Know			
__Constitution	__howling	__humble	__politics
__responsibility	__solemnly	__vain	

1. solemnly _____ seriously; earnestly
2. Constitution _____ document that establishes the basic principles of the U.S. government
3. humble _____ meek; modest
4. politics _____ the art or science of governing
5. responsibility _____ job; duty; task
6. howling _____ crying; wailing; shrieking
7. vain _____ proud; inflated

Directions Write a brief paragraph about a trip to Washington, D.C. Use as many vocabulary words as possible.

Responses will vary.

_____
_____
_____
_____

Below-Level Practice TE p. LR39

Advanced

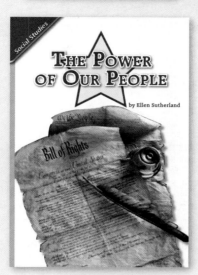

Advanced Reader

ELL Reader

ELL Poster 10

Teacher's Edition Notes

ELL notes throughout this lesson support instruction and reference additional resources at point of use.

Teaching Guide pp. 64–70, 230–231
- Multilingual summaries of the main selection
- Comprehension lesson
- Vocabulary strategies and word cards
- ELL Reader 4.2.5 lesson

ELL and Transition Handbook

Ten Important Sentences
- Key ideas from every selection in the Student Edition
- Activities to build sentence power

Name _____   The Power of Our People

Main Idea and Details

- The **main idea** is the most important idea about the topic of a paragraph, passage, or article.
- **Supporting details** are the small pieces of information that tell more about the main idea.

Directions Reread the following passage adapted from *The Power of Our People*. Then answer the questions below.

In many ways, the Declaration of Independence set the stage for our Constitution. The Constitution is the highest law in the United States. All other laws come from it. The Constitution describes how our government works. It also explains the rights and responsibilities enjoyed by each citizen. If it weren't for our Constitution, we wouldn't have a President,

Congress, or the Supreme Court.
The Constitution is called a "living document." That means that it can be changed to work today as well as in the 1700s. The U.S. Constitution uses simple language to describe our government. It is the oldest written set of governing principles for the United States in use today. It is also short, at about 4,500 words!

1. What is the main idea of the first paragraph?   **Possible responses given.**
   The Constitution is the highest law of the United States.
2. What is one supporting detail in the first paragraph that tells about the main idea?
   All other laws come from it.
3. What is another supporting detail in that paragraph that tells about the main idea?
   The Constitution explains the rights and responsibilities enjoyed by each citizen.
4. What is the main idea of the second paragraph?
   The Constitution is a living document.
5. What is one supporting detail that tells more about this main idea?
   It is written in simple language; it is about 4,500 words long.

Advanced Practice TE p. LR44

Name _____   The Power of Our People

Vocabulary
Directions Fill in the blank with the word from the box that fits the definition.

Check the Words You Know

___amendments	___bicameral
___compromised	___confederation
___politics	___ratified
___representatives	___responsibilities
___sovereignty	___unanimously

1. **sovereignty** ___ supremacy of authority or rule
2. **ratified** ___ approved and given formal sanction to
3. **bicameral** ___ composed of two legislative branches
4. **confederation** ___ a political union of persons, parties, or states
5. **unanimously** ___ in a manner reflecting complete agreement
6. **politics** ___ the art or science of government or governing
7. **amendments** ___ formal revisions to a document
8. **compromised** ___ settled by concessions, or agreements to give in part-way
9. **representatives** ___ delegates or agents acting on behalf of others
10. **responsibilities** ___ things for which one must be accountable

Directions Write a brief paragraph about the U.S. Constitution, using as many vocabulary words as possible.

Responses will vary.

Advanced Practice TE p. LR45

More Reading

Readers' Theater Anthology
- Fluency practice
- Five scripts to build fluency
- Poetry for oral interpretation

Leveled Trade Books

Below-Level
On-Level
Advanced

- Extended reading tied to the unit concept
- Lessons in the Trade Book Library Teaching Guide

School + Home

Homework
- Family Times Newsletter
- ELL Multilingual Selection Summaries

Take-Home Books
- Leveled Readers

Cross-Curricular Centers

Listening

Reading/Library

Art

Listen to the Selections

MATERIALS | SINGLES
CD player, headphones, AudioText CD, student book

LISTEN TO LITERATURE Listen to *So You Want to Be President?* and "Our National Parks" as you follow or read along in your book. As you listen to *So You Want to Be President?*, pay attention to main ideas and supporting details.

If there is anything you don't understand, you can listen again to any section.

Read It Again!

MATERIALS | SINGLES PAIRS GROUPS
Collection of books for self-selected reading, reading logs, student book

Select a book you have already read. Record the title of the book in your reading log. You may want to read with a partner.

Choose from the following:

- **Leveled Readers**
- **ELL Readers**
- **Books or Stories Written by Classmates**
- **Books from the Library**
- ***So You Want to Be President?***

TEN IMPORTANT SENTENCES Read the Ten Important Sentences for *So You Want to Be President?*, and then locate the sentences in the student book.

BOOK CLUB Read another nonfiction book. As a group, tell what you like or didn't like about the book and whether others would enjoy reading it.

Identify Caricatures

MATERIALS | PAIRS GROUPS
Realistic pictures of past Presidents, or social studies book, student book, self-sticking notes, writing and art materials

Compare the caricatures of the Presidents in the selection to real pictures of them.

1. **A caricature is a humorous drawing that exaggerates a person's facial features or body shape. With a partner or group, study the caricatures of the Presidents on pp. 244–255 in the student book.**
2. **Compare the caricatures to real pictures of past Presidents. Use clues from the selection and the real pictures to identify which President each caricature represents.**
3. **Write the name of the President on a self-sticking note and attach it near the caricature in your student book.**

EARLY FINISHERS Draw your own caricature of a President or other famous person. Quiz others to see if they can identify the person you drew.

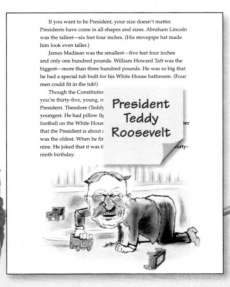

Scott Foresman Reading Street Centers Survival Kit

Use the *So You Want to Be President* materials from the Reading Street Centers Survival Kit to organize this week's centers.

Writing/ Vocabulary

Social Studies

Technology

Create a Political Ad

MATERIALS `GROUPS`
Student book, writing materials, tape recorder

Use Words to Know to create a radio ad persuading others to vote for a President of the United States.

1. Use the Words to Know on p. 242 in the student book in an ad to persuade others to vote for a presidential candidate.
2. Decide how many speaking parts your ad will have. Think about sounds or music you could use.
3. Write the script for a 30-second ad using Words to Know from the selection.

EARLY FINISHERS Act out your ad. Record your ad to share with others. *Drama*

Tina Martin, Radio Ad

(Sound: Marching band music plays softly in background)

NARRATOR: If you want a fresh face in politics today, you want Tina Martin as your next President of the United States. Tina is a woman who knows all about responsibility.

TINA: I am Tina Martin. I own my own business and am raising three children.

Draw a Diagram

MATERIALS `PAIRS` `GROUPS`
Writing materials, reference materials about the branches of the U.S. government

Draw a diagram showing the three branches of the United States government.

1. Find information about the three branches of the United States government.
2. Draw a diagram showing each branch of government.
3. Label your diagram. Name each branch of the government.
4. List the leader for each branch and the role of each branch of government.

EARLY FINISHERS Choose one office or group and explain its responsibilities.

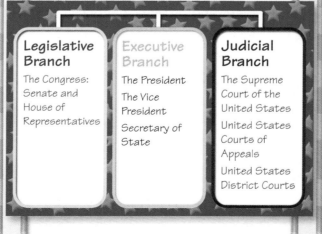

Legislative Branch
The Congress: Senate and House of Representatives

Executive Branch
The President
The Vice President
Secretary of State

Judicial Branch
The Supreme Court of the United States
United States Courts of Appeals
United States District Courts

Visit a Web Site

MATERIALS `SINGLES`
Internet access, writing materials

Visit a Web site to learn more about your state government.

1. Log on to the Internet and search for Web sites that tell about your state government. Use your state name and *government* or the name of your governor for keywords.
2. Read the Web site descriptions to find the site that will be the most helpful or interesting. Visit that Web site and begin gathering information.
3. Write a few facts that you learned about your state government.

EARLY FINISHERS Imagine you are the state governor and you have your own Web site. Tell what kind of information you would put on your Web site.

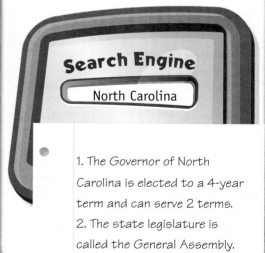

Search Engine

North Carolina

1. The Governor of North Carolina is elected to a 4-year term and can serve 2 terms.
2. The state legislature is called the General Assembly.

ALL CENTERS

OBJECTIVES

- Build vocabulary by finding words related to the lesson concept.
- Listen for main ideas and supporting details.

Concept Vocabulary

capital city where the government of a country, state, or province is located

capitol building in which state or national lawmakers meet

clerks people employed in an office to file papers, type letters, and so on

Monitor Progress

Check Vocabulary

If...	then... review
students are unable to place words on the web,	the lesson concept. Put the words on the web and give more words for practice, such as *Washington, D.C.* and *lawmakers.*

SUCCESS PREDICTOR

DAY 1 **Grouping Options**

Reading
Whole Group
Introduce and discuss the Question of the Week. Then use pp. 240l–242b.

Group Time
Differentiated Instruction
Read this week's Leveled Readers. See pp. 240f–240g for the small group lesson plan.

Whole Group
Use p. 259a.

Language Arts
Use pp. 259e–259k.

Build Concepts

FLUENCY

MODEL STRESS/EMPHASIS As you read the selection, stress important words, such as signal words that indicate contrasts. For example, in the sixth paragraph, emphasize *The CITY where ...* and *The BUILDING where ...* to highlight the difference in meanings of *capital* and *capitol.*

LISTENING COMPREHENSION

After reading "Welcome to Washington!" use the following questions to assess listening comprehension.

1. **What is the main idea of this selection?** *(Possible response: Unlike other cities, the capital city of Washington, D.C., was planned and built from scratch to be a showplace of the nation.)* **Main Idea**

2. **What makes Washington, D.C., a showplace?** *(It includes stately buildings, broad avenues, and the Washington Monument.)* **Details**

BUILD CONCEPT VOCABULARY

Start a web to build concepts and vocabulary related to this week's lesson and the unit theme.

- Draw the U.S. Government Concept Web.
- Read the sentence with the word *capital* again. Ask students to pronounce *capital* and discuss its meaning.
- Place *capital* in an oval attached to *Places*. Explain that a *capital* is the place where a government is located. Read the sentences in which *Capitol* and *clerks* appear. Have students pronounce the words, place them on the Web, and provide reasons.
- Brainstorm additional words and categories for the Web. Keep the Web on display and add words throughout the week.

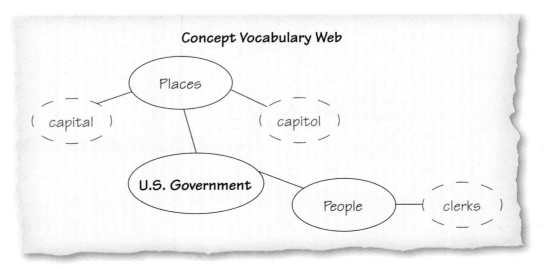

Concept Vocabulary Web

Welcome to Washington!

by Shirley Cimo

Most of America's great cities weren't planned. They just happened. A particular group of people arrived in a particular place, and then, stone by stone, street by street, year after year, a town grew.

Washington was built to order, and the order to build it came from the Congress of the United States. Our nation was the first to create its capital.

In 1790, members of Congress voted to set aside a tract of land along the Potomac River for the federal government. They called this territory the District of Columbia in honor of Christopher Columbus. Not until after the president's death did the capital officially become Washington, D. C. When the capital moved from Philadelphia to Washington in 1800, there were just 126 clerks on the payroll. Now about four hundred thousand people in the Washington area work for the federal government.

Our capital city was built to be the showplace of the nation. Stately buildings are set among green parklands and along broad avenues, but it is the Washington Monument that catches every eye. This four-sided pillar soars up for over 555 feet. It's the tallest masonry structure on earth, and the only skyscraper in Washington. No high-rise buildings are allowed to spoil the scene within the city limits.

By day, sunlight polishes the white dome of the Capitol. At night, floodlights gild the bronze statue *Freedom* on top of the dome. This is the city's most imitated building. Half the capitols of our fifty states are close copies of it.

Although *capital* and *capitol* sound the same, they're spelled differently. The city where a seat of government is located ends with *al*. The building where lawmakers meet ends with *ol*. To distinguish it from others, the nation's Capitol, the house where Congress considers national matters, is written with yet another kind of capital—a capital *C!*

Because the District of Columbia does not belong to any one state, it belongs to all of the people in all the fifty states. You are one of this city's two hundred forty million landlords. Wherever you live in America, this is your hometown.

SKILLS ◆━◆ STRATEGIES IN CONTEXT

Main Idea Summarize

Comprehension

Skill
Main Idea and Details

Strategy
Summarize

OBJECTIVES

- Determine main idea and supporting details.
- Use main ideas and supporting details to summarize.

Skills Trace
Main Idea and Details

Introduce/Teach	**TE: 4.1 112–113; 4.2 240–241; 4.5 582–583**
Practice	TE: 119, 123, 247, 251, 589, 595 PB: 43, 47, 48, 93, 97, 98, 233, 237, 238
Reteach/Review	TE: 4.1 75, 133b, DI·56; 4.2 225, 259b, DI·56; 4.4 475; 4.5 607b, DI·55 PB: 26, 86, 186
Test	Selection Test: 17–20, 37–40, 93–96; Benchmark Test: Unit 2

INTRODUCE

Write the topic "President" and add details: *U.S. Presidents must be born in this country. They must be at least 35 years old.* Ask what might be the main idea in an article with this topic and details. *(Possible response: People must meet certain requirements to become President of the United States.)*

Have students read the information on p. 240. Explain the following:

- Looking for main ideas as you read can help you summarize an article.
- Summarizing can help you recall what you read. A summary should include only important ideas from your reading.

Use Skill Transparency 10 to teach main idea and summarize.

Main Idea and Details

- The focus of a paragraph or an article— what it is all about—is the topic.
- The most important thing the author has to say about the topic is the main idea.
- Small pieces of information that tell more about the main idea are supporting details.

Main Idea

Supporting Detail	Supporting Detail	Supporting Detail

Strategy: Summarize

Good readers summarize as they read. They decide which ideas are important and then put those ideas together into a short statement, or summary. Summarize as you read by pausing to think, "What are the most important ideas so far?"

Write to Read

1. Read "A White House History." Make graphic organizers like the one above to help you find the main ideas of paragraphs two, three, and four.

2. Use your graphic organizers to write a summary of "A White House History."

240

Strategic Intervention

 Main Idea Remind students that a summary includes only the most important ideas; it is not a complete retelling of facts or events. Have students read an article from a newspaper and write three main ideas from the event. Have them use these main ideas to give an oral summary of the article.

ELL

Access Content

Beginning/Intermediate For a Picture It! lesson on main idea and supporting details, see the ELL Teaching Guide, pp. 64–65.

Advanced Before reading "A White House History," have students predict what the article will be about and give reasons why they think so.

A WHITE HOUSE HISTORY

The White House is where the U.S. President lives and works in Washington, D.C. However, our first President, George Washington, never even lived there! The building wasn't finished while he was in office. The building of the White House was not begun until 1792.

Our second President, John Adams, moved into the White House in 1800. Even then, the building wasn't really finished. As a result, it was somewhat uncomfortable for daily life. The President's wife, Abigail, had nowhere to hang the family's laundry, so she used the East Room. Today that room is the biggest and grandest room in the house.

In 1814, while our fourth President, James Madison, was in office, disaster hit the White House. The United States was again at war with England, and the British burned the White House. It had to be rebuilt.

Many people close to the President made their offices in the White House. By 1902, there were so many offices in the White House that our 26th President, Theodore Roosevelt, added more rooms—the West Wing. These rooms served as offices and freed up space in the White House for the President's six lively children and their pets.

Almost every President has made changes to the White House. The house doesn't belong to any one President, though. It belongs to the American people.

1 **Skill** What is the main idea of the first paragraph?
(a) The White House is in Washington, D.C.
(b) The building of the White House started in 1792.
(c) Unlike other Presidents, Washington didn't live in the White House because it wasn't finished.

2 **Strategy** This is a good place to summarize. Tell the main ideas of the first two paragraphs.

3 **Skill** What is the main idea of the third paragraph?

4 **Strategy** Summarize the article to help you remember its main ideas.

241

Available as **Skill Transparency** 10

TEACH

1 **SKILL** Use paragraph 1 to model how to determine the main idea.

Think Aloud **MODEL** From the title, I know the topic of the article is the White House. Most of the paragraph tells about George Washington and why he didn't live in the White House. So the main idea of the paragraph is c.

2 **STRATEGY** Discuss the first two paragraphs of the article.

Think Aloud **MODEL** I know the main idea in the first paragraph is George Washington never lived in the White House because it was being built. The second paragraph tells about President John Adams. The details, like having to hang laundry in the East Room, are about living in a house that is not finished. I think the main idea of this paragraph is: *The family of John Adams lived in the White House while it was still being finished.*

PRACTICE AND ASSESS

3 **SKILL** The White House was burned down in 1814, during the war with England, and was rebuilt.

4 **STRATEGY** Summaries should reflect an understanding of the main ideas of the paragraphs and include the overall main idea of the article.

WRITE Have students complete steps 1 and 2 of the Write to Read activity. You might consider using this as a whole-class activity.

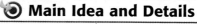

Monitor Progress
Main Idea and Details

If... students are unable to complete **Write to Read** on p. 240,	then... use Practice Book p. 93 to provide additional practice.

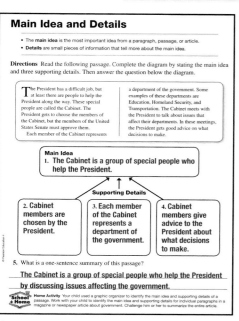

Main Idea and Details

- The **main idea** is the most important idea from a paragraph, passage, or article.
- **Details** are small pieces of information that tell more about the main idea.

Directions Read the following passage. Complete the diagram by stating the main idea and three supporting details. Then answer the question below the diagram.

The President has a difficult job, but at least there are people to help the President along the way. These special people are called the Cabinet. The President gets to choose the members of the Cabinet, but the members of the United States Senate must approve them. Each member of the Cabinet represents a department of the government. Some examples of these departments are Education, Homeland Security, and Transportation. The Cabinet meets with the President to talk about issues that affect their departments. In these meetings, the President gets good advice on what decisions to make.

Main Idea
1. The Cabinet is a group of special people who help the President.

Supporting Details
2. Cabinet members are chosen by the President.
3. Each member of the Cabinet represents a department of the government.
4. Cabinet members give advice to the President about what decisions to make.

5. What is a one-sentence summary of this passage?
The Cabinet is a group of special people who help the President by discussing issues affecting the government.

School + Home Home Activity Your child used a graphic organizer to identify the main idea and supporting details of a passage. Work with your child to identify the main idea and supporting details for individual paragraphs in a magazine or newspaper article about government. Challenge him or her to summarize the entire article.

▲ **Practice Book** p. 93

ONLINE

Students can search the Internet to find biographical information about United States Presidents. Have them use a student-friendly search engine and the keywords *U.S. Presidents* or the name of a specific president.

ELL

Build Background Use ELL Poster 10 to build background and vocabulary for the lesson concept of the United States government.

▲ **ELL Poster** 10

Build Background

ACTIVATE PRIOR KNOWLEDGE

BEGIN A KWL CHART about U.S. Presidents.

- Have students write as many facts as they can about U.S. Presidents. Prompt them with categories from the Concept Web from p. 240l. Record what students know in the first column of a KWL chart.

- Write questions students would like to find answers to about U.S. Presidents. Record their questions in the second column of the KWL chart. Add a question of your own.

- Tell students that, as they read, they should look for the answers to their questions and note any new information to add to the third column of the chart.

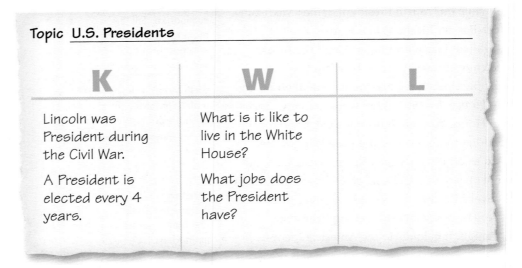

Topic U.S. Presidents

K	W	L
Lincoln was President during the Civil War. A President is elected every 4 years.	What is it like to live in the White House? What jobs does the President have?	

▲ **Graphic Organizer** 4

BACKGROUND BUILDING AUDIO This week's audio explores the history of the White House. After students listen, discuss what they found out and what surprised them most about the White House's history.

Background Building Audio

Introduce Vocabulary

WORD INFORMATION CHART

Create a three-column chart that students can use to provide information about their lesson vocabulary.

Word	Synonym or Short Meaning	Example or Description
Constitution	written laws	judges use the Constitution to make decisions
howling	very great	a howling success
humble	not proud	doesn't brag
politics		
responsibility		
solemnly		
vain		

▲ **Graphic Organizer** 26

Display the lesson vocabulary and have students tell anything they already know about these words. Read aloud each definition, and have students name and list each defined word in the first column. Discuss how to fill the second and third columns for some of the words. Have partners work together to complete the chart. ***Activate Prior Knowledge***

Point out that *vain* and *humble* are antonyms, or words with opposite meanings. Ask students to use both words in a sentence that includes the word *but*. ***Antonyms***

By the end of the week, students should know the lesson vocabulary words. Have them revise their charts and add other examples or information.

Use Multisyllabic Word Routine on p. DI·1 to help students read multisyllabic words.

Lesson Vocabulary

WORDS TO KNOW

T Constitution the written set of fundamental principles by which the United States is governed

T howling very great

T humble not proud; modest

T politics the work of government; management of public business

T responsibility the act or fact of taking care of someone or something; obligation

T solemnly seriously; earnestly; with dignity

T vain having too much pride in your looks, ability, etc.

MORE WORDS TO KNOW

execute to carry out; do

oath a solemn promise

priority something given attention before anything else

T = Tested Word

Vocabulary

Directions Choose a word from the box that best completes each sentence. Write the word on the line shown to the left.

vain ____ 1. A ____ person might look in a mirror all the time.

responsibility ____ 2. The President has much ____.

solemnly ____ 3. He behaved ____ as he took the oath.

Constitution ____ 4. The ____ is an important document.

howling ____ 5. Many people voted, so the election was a ____ success.

Check the Words You Know
____Constitution
____howling
____humble
____politics
____responsibility
____solemnly
____vain

Directions Choose the word from the box that best matches each numbered clue below. Write the letters of the word on the blanks. After you are finished, the boxed letters will spell a secret word.

6. seriously
7. government work
8. the act of taking care of someone
9. having too much pride
10. not proud

6. s o l **e** m n l y
7. p o l i t i **c** s
8. r e s p o n s **i** b i l i t y
9. v **a** i n
10. h u m b **l** e

Write a Speech

Pretend you have just been elected President of the United States. On a separate sheet of paper, write a short speech you would give to the public. In the course of explaining how you will approach your new job, use as many vocabulary words as you can. Speeches should include words from the vocabulary list and details about the job of President.

School + Home Home Activity Your child identified and used vocabulary words from *So You Want to Be President?* Together, read an article about politics or government. Discuss the article, using as many vocabulary words from the selection as you can.

▲ **Practice Book** p. 94

Vocabulary Strategy

◉ Use a dictionary or glossary to determine word meaning.

INTRODUCE

Discuss the strategy for using a dictionary or glossary by following the steps on p. 242.

TEACH

- Have students read "Class Election," paying attention to how the vocabulary is used.
- Model using a dictionary or glossary to determine the meaning of *politics*.

Think Aloud

MODEL I can't tell the meaning of *politics* from the context, so I'll check its meaning and pronunciation in a dictionary or glossary. Since entry words are listed alphabetically, I'll use the guide words at the top of the pages to find words beginning with *P-O*. It says *politics* means "the work of the government."

DAY 2 **Grouping Options**

Reading
Whole Group Discuss the Question of the Day. Then use pp. 242–245.

Group Time Differentiated Instruction
Read *So You Want to Be President?* See pp. 240f–240g for the small group lesson plan.

Whole Group Use p. 259a.

Language Arts
Use pp. 259e–259k.

Words to Know

vain
politics
humble
solemnly
howling
Constitution
responsibility

Vocabulary Strategy
for Unfamiliar Words

Dictionary/Glossary When you are reading, you may come across a word you don't know. If you can't use the context, or words and sentences around the word, to figure out the word's meaning, you can use a dictionary or glossary to help you.

1. Check the back of your book for a glossary. If there is no glossary, look up the word in a dictionary.

2. Find the entry for the word. The entries are in alphabetical order.

3. Read the pronunciation to yourself. Saying the word may help you recognize it.

4. Read all the meanings given for the word.

5. Choose the meaning that makes sense in the sentence.

As you read "Class Election," use a dictionary or glossary to find the meanings of the vocabulary words.

242

Strategic Intervention

◉ **Dictionary/Glossary** Look up vocabulary words in the glossary. Explain that italics show how the word is used in a sentence.

ELL

Access Content Use ELL Poster 10 to preteach vocabulary. Choose from the following to meet language proficiency levels.

Beginning Complete vocabulary frames for unfamiliar words.

Intermediate Ask students if they recognize *Constitution*, *politics*, *responsibility*, and *solemnly* in their home languages. (Spanish cognates: *constitución*, *política*, *responsabilidad*, *solemnemente*.)

Advanced Teach the lesson on pp. 242–243. Revisit the word information chart (p. 242b) and use each word in a sentence.

Resources for home-language words may include parents, bilingual staff members, bilingual dictionaries, or online translation sources.

Class Election

The students in Grade 4 are electing class officers. Four students are running for president.

Steven is vain about his looks. He puts just his name and his face on his signs. He says politics is dull, but winning is fun. Suzanne acts humble about how well she plays sports. Yet all her signs show her making the winning goal in last year's soccer championship. Omar solemnly promises that he will run a clean campaign. Then he makes fun of the other candidates. Still, his speeches are a howling success. Maya says that unlike the President of the United States, the president of Grade 4 does not have to "protect and defend the Constitution of the United States." However, she says the Grade 4 president does have a responsibility to all the students in Grade 4, not just the ones who voted for him or her. Maya was Grade 3 president and is captain of the softball team. If you were a student in Grade 4, whom would you vote for?

Words to Write

Answer the question at the end of the text. Give reasons for your choice. Use words from the Words to Know list.

243

PRACTICE AND ASSESS

- Have students use the glossary to locate the meanings of the remaining vocabulary words and a dictionary to look up any other unfamiliar words. Then have them share how they determined appropriate meanings.

- Point out that if there is more than one possible meaning that might fit, students can use context clues to decide which meaning makes the most sense in the selection.

- If you began a word information chart (p. 242b), have students add new information to their charts.

- Have students complete Practice Book p. 95.

WRITE Writing should include vocabulary words and other words related to candidates' personal qualities or the politics of student government.

Monitor Progress

Dictionary/Glossary

If... students need more practice with the lesson vocabulary,	then... use Tested Vocabulary Cards.

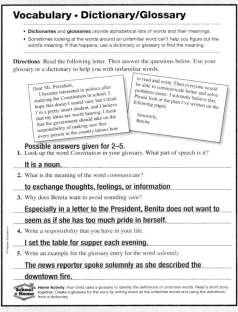

▲ Practice Book p. 95

Prereading Strategies

- Identify main idea and supporting details to improve comprehension.
- Summarize using main ideas and supporting details.

GENRE STUDY

Expository Nonfiction

So You Want to Be President? is expository nonfiction. Explain that expository nonfiction is writing about real people, facts, and events. Its purpose is to explain something.

PREVIEW AND PREDICT

Have students preview the title and illustrations and discuss the topics or ideas they think this selection will cover. Have them predict whether it will use a serious or humorous tone. Encourage students to use lesson vocabulary words as they talk about what they expect to read.

Strategy Response Log

Predict Have students write their predictions in their strategy response logs. Students will confirm their predictions in the Strategy Response Log activity on p. 251.

Genre **Expository nonfiction** gives information about real people and events. As you read, note new or surprising information about our country's Presidents.

244

ELL

Activate Prior Knowledge Point out the words *President of the United States* in the question at the bottom of p. 245. Explain that the leader of the United States is called *the President*. Invite students to name titles used by leaders of their home countries and tell what they know about what the leader of a country does.

Consider having students read the selection summary in English or in students' home languages. See the Multilingual Summaries in the ELL Teaching Guide, pp. 68–70.

So You Want to Be President?

by Judith St. George
illustrated by David Small

What does it take to be President of the United States?

245

SET PURPOSE

Read the first sentence of the selection aloud to students. Ask them to suggest some good things and bad things about being President. Have them tell what they hope to find out as they read.

Remind students to look for main ideas and supporting details as they read.

STRATEGY RECALL

Students have now used these before-reading strategies:

- preview the selection to be aware of its genre, features, and possible content;
- activate prior knowledge about that content and what to expect of that genre;
- make predictions;
- set a purpose for reading.

Remind students to be aware of and flexibly use the during-reading strategies they have learned:

- link prior knowledge to new information;
- summarize text they have read so far;
- ask clarifying questions;
- answer questions they or others pose;
- check their predictions and either refine them or make new predictions;
- recognize the text structure the author is using, and use that knowledge to make predictions and increase comprehension;
- visualize what the author is describing;
- monitor their comprehension and use fix-up strategies.

After reading, students will use these strategies:

- summarize or retell the text;
- answer questions they or others pose;
- reflect to make new information become part of their prior knowledge.

AudioText

Guiding Comprehension

1 🎯 **Main Idea/Details • Inferential**

Reread p. 246. What are the main idea and one supporting detail?

Main idea: There are good things and bad things about being President. Supporting detail: A good thing is that the President doesn't have to eat yucky vegetables.

Monitor Progress

🎯 Main Idea/Details

If... students are unable to determine the main idea and a supporting detail,	**then...** use the skill and strategy instruction on p. 247.

---

2 **Tone • Inferential**

What is the author's tone, her attitude toward her subject? Is it serious or humorous? Explain.

The author's tone is humorous. Mentioning things like not having to take out the garbage or eat broccoli shows that the author is having fun with this subject.

Tech Files
ONLINE

Students can search the Internet to find out more about the Secret Service and its role guarding the President. Have them use a student-friendly search engine and the keywords *Secret Service*. Be sure to follow classroom rules for Internet use.

1 There are good things about being President, and there are bad things about being President. One of the good things is that the President lives in a big white house called the White House.

Another good thing about being President is that the President has a swimming pool, bowling alley, and movie theater.

The President never has to take out the garbage.

2 The President doesn't have to eat yucky vegetables. As a boy, George H. W. Bush had to eat broccoli. When George H. W. Bush grew up, he became President. That was the end of the broccoli!

246

ELL

Understanding Idioms Explain that *to lose one's head* is an idiom which means that one has lost control of a situation. Point out the word play in President Taft's joke (p. 247, paragraph 3) that relies on multiple meanings of *head* (a head of cabbage; a person's head).

One of the bad things about being President is that the President always has to be dressed up. William McKinley wore a frock coat, vest, pin-striped trousers, stiff white shirt, black satin tie, gloves, a top hat, and a red carnation in his buttonhole every day!

The President has to be polite to everyone. The President can't go anywhere alone. The President has lots of homework.

People get mad at the President. Someone once threw a cabbage at William Howard Taft. That didn't bother Taft. He quipped, "I see that one of my adversaries has lost his head."

Lots of people want to be President. If you want to be President, it might help if your name is James. Six Presidents were named James. (President Carter liked to be called Jimmy.) Four Johns, four Williams (President Clinton liked to be called Bill), three Georges, two Andrews, and two Franklins—all became President.

247

The Secret Service

The President doesn't go anywhere alone because he is always protected by the Secret Service. Secret Service agents protect the President, the Vice President, and their immediate families. Agents are constantly checking the President's food and surroundings.

Congress directed the Secret Service to protect the President of the United States in 1901, after the assassination of President William McKinley. Since then, one President has been assassinated (John F. Kennedy), with three other Presidents surviving assassination attempts (Harry Truman, Gerald Ford, and Ronald Reagan).

Time for
SOCIAL STUDIES

  SKILLS ←→ STRATEGIES IN CONTEXT

Main Idea and Details

TEACH

- Remind students that a main idea is an important point about the topic of the article. Sometimes a main idea is given in a sentence that comes at the beginning, middle, or end of the article.
- Supporting details are small pieces of information that tell more about the main idea.
- Model finding the main idea of p. 246.

MODEL I know that sometimes the first sentence of a paragraph or an article gives the main idea. The first sentence of this article seems like it could be a main idea. It says there are good things and bad things about being President. As I read the rest of the page, I see that it gives lots of examples of good things about being President. These are supporting details for the main idea that there are good things about being President. The main idea of this page is that there are good things about being President.

PRACTICE AND ASSESS

Have students reread p. 247, paragraph 2. Ask which of the following is the main idea of this paragraph. *(Choice c)*

a) There are good things and bad things about being President.

b) There are good things about being President.

c) There are bad things about being President.

Guiding Comprehension

3 **Generalize • Inferential**

Have all Presidents been big people?

No. The author says that people of all shapes and sizes have become President.

Monitor Progress

REVIEW Generalize

If... students have difficulty making a generalization about the size of Presidents,	**then...** use the skill and strategy instruction on p. 249.

---

4 **Author's Craft • Inferential**

Question the Author **Why do you think the author includes details such as President Taft's special tub and Teddy Roosevelt's pillow fights?**

Possible response: They are fun to read about and make the Presidents seem more human.

5 **Graphic Sources • Critical**

What idea does the picture on p. 249 illustrate?

It illustrates the idea that it helps to have a President in your family tree. It shows that if someone in your family is President, he can help "pull you up" to the high office.

3 If you want to be President, your size doesn't matter. Presidents have come in all shapes and sizes. Abraham Lincoln was the tallest—six feet four inches. (His stovepipe hat made him look even taller.)

James Madison was the smallest—five feet four inches and only one hundred pounds. William Howard Taft was the biggest—more than three hundred pounds. He was so big that he had a special tub built for his White House bathroom. (Four **4** men could fit in the tub!)

Though the Constitution says you'll have to wait until you're thirty-five, young, old, and in between have become President. Theodore (Teddy) Roosevelt at forty-two was the youngest. He had pillow fights with his children and played football on the White House lawn. "You must always remember that the President is about six," a friend said. Ronald Reagan was the oldest. When he first ran for President, he was sixty-nine. He joked that it was the thirtieth anniversary of his thirty-ninth birthday.

248

ELL

Access Content Students may be unfamiliar with the term *family tree.* Sketch a simple family tree, including parents and siblings. (The illustration on p. 249 may be misleading since it shows only Presidents.)

Do you have pesky brothers and sisters? Every one of our Presidents did. Benjamin Harrison takes the prize—he had eleven! (It's lucky he grew up on a six-hundred-acre farm.) James Polk and James Buchanan both had nine. George Washington, Thomas Jefferson, James Madison, and John Kennedy each had eight. (Two Presidents were orphans, Andrew Jackson and Herbert Hoover.)

A President in your family tree is a plus. John Quincy Adams was John Adams's son. George W. Bush was the son of George H. W. Bush. Theodore Roosevelt and Franklin Roosevelt were fifth cousins. Benjamin Harrison was William Harrison's grandson. James Madison and Zachary Taylor were second cousins.

249

The Executive Branch

Time for SOCIAL STUDIES

The President is the head of the executive branch of the U.S. government. The executive branch enforces the laws of the United States. The President has the power to propose laws to Congress and to sign or veto laws that Congress drafts. The President is the leader of the nation and commander-in-chief of the armed forces. The people who work for and advise the President are members of his Cabinet. The Cabinet consists of the Vice President; the Attorney General, who is in charge of the Justice Department; the 14 Secretaries in charge of other departments; and other government officials chosen by the President.

SKILLS ◆▶ STRATEGIES IN CONTEXT

Generalize REVIEW

TEACH

- Remind students that a generalization is a broad statement that applies to many examples. Words such as *all, none, most, many, always, never,* and *generally* are clues that can signal a generalization.

- A valid generalization is supported by facts.

Think Aloud **MODEL** The text says that "Presidents have come in *all* shapes and sizes." The word *all* is a clue that this is a generalization. Does the author give facts to back it up? I see that she gives three facts— Lincoln was very tall, Madison was small, and Taft was big. A valid generalization is "Presidents can be big or small."

PRACTICE AND ASSESS

- Have students read p. 249, paragraph 1, and find a generalization. Remind them to look for clue words. Have them judge whether the generalization is valid. *(Generalization: Every President has had siblings. Clue word: every. Possible response: I'm not positive the generalization is valid for every President because the author only lists a few Presidents' siblings, but she probably checked her facts.)*

- To assess, use Practice Book p. 96.

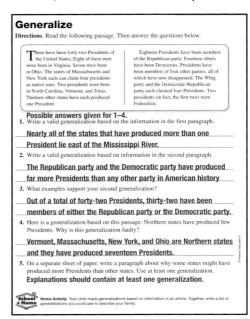

Generalize

Directions Read the following passage. Then answer the questions below.

There have been forty-two Presidents of the United States. Eight of these men were born in Virginia. Seven were born in Ohio. The states of Massachusetts and New York each can claim four presidents as native sons. Two presidents were born in North Carolina, Vermont, and Texas. Thirteen other states have each produced one President.

Eighteen Presidents have been members of the Republican party. Fourteen others have been Democrats. Presidents have been members of four other parties, all of which have now disappeared. The Whig party and the Democratic-Republican party each claimed four Presidents. Two presidents (in fact, the first two) were Federalists.

Possible answers given for 1–4.

1. Write a valid generalization based on the information in the first paragraph.

   Nearly all of the states that have produced more than one President lie east of the Mississippi River.

2. Write a valid generalization based on information in the second paragraph.

   The Republican party and the Democratic party have produced far more Presidents than any other party in American history

3. What examples support your second generalization?

   Out of a total of forty-two Presidents, thirty-two have been members of either the Republican party or the Democratic party.

4. Here is a generalization based on this passage: Northern states have produced few Presidents. Why is this generalization faulty?

   Vermont, Massachusetts, New York, and Ohio are Northern states and they have produced seventeen Presidents.

5. On a separate sheet of paper, write a paragraph about why some states might have produced more Presidents than other states. Use at least one generalization.
   Explanations should contain at least one generalization.

School + Home Home Activity Your child made generalizations based on information in an article. Together, write a list of generalizations you could use to describe your family.

▲ **Practice Book** p. 96

Guiding Comprehension

6 Main Idea/Details • Inferential

Have students determine the main idea and two supporting details on p. 251.

Main idea: Most Presidents were college educated, but some were not. Supporting details: Andrew Johnson didn't learn to write until after he was married. Jefferson was an expert in many fields, founded a university, and wrote the Declaration of Independence.

Monitor Progress

Main Idea and Details

If... students are unable to determine the main idea and supporting details,	**then...** use the skill and strategy instruction on p. 251.

7 Draw Conclusions • Critical

Do you think it is important that the President have a college education? Why or why not?

Responses will vary: No; life experiences are important, too, and some great Presidents did not attend college (Washington, Lincoln). Yes; the world is complex and a college education is essential to fulfill the duties of President.

Do you have a pet? All kinds of pets have lived in the White House, mostly dogs. Herbert Hoover had three dogs: Piney, Snowflake, and Tut. (Tut must have been a Democrat. He and his Republican master never got along.) Franklin Roosevelt's dog, Fala, was almost as famous as his owner.

George H. W. Bush's dog wrote MILLIE'S BOOK: ADVENTURES OF A WHITE HOUSE DOG (as reported to Mrs. Bush!). Ulysses Grant had horses, Benjamin Harrison's goat pulled his grandchildren around in a cart, the Coolidges had a pet raccoon, Jimmy Carter and Bill Clinton preferred cats.

Theodore Roosevelt's children didn't just have pets, they ran a zoo. They had dogs, cats, guinea pigs, mice, rats, badgers, raccoons, parrots, and a Shetland pony called Algonquin. To cheer up his sick brother, young Quentin once took Algonquin upstairs in the White House elevator!

250

ELL

Understanding Idioms Help students see the humor in the expression *whipped up the Declaration of Independence* (p. 251, paragraph 2). When you "whip something up," you do it quickly and easily. The Declaration of Independence is an important document; it announces the separation of the original thirteen colonies from England.

Though most Presidents went to college, nine didn't: George Washington, Andrew Jackson, Martin Van Buren, Zachary Taylor, Millard Fillmore, Abraham Lincoln, Andrew Johnson, Grover Cleveland, and Harry Truman. (Andrew Johnson couldn't read until he was fourteen! He didn't learn to write until after he was married!)

Thomas Jefferson was top-notch in the brains department—he was an expert on agriculture, law, politics, music, geography, surveying, philosophy, and botany. In his spare time he designed his own house (a mansion), founded the University of Virginia, and whipped up the Declaration of Independence. **7**

251

Develop Vocabulary

PRACTICE LESSON VOCABULARY

Students orally respond *yes* or *no* to each question and provide a reason for each answer. Possible reasons are given.

1. Is the city mayor involved in *politics*? *(Yes; local politics is government work.)*

2. Is a *howling* success a disaster? *(No; a howling success is a great success.)*

3. If your teacher says something *solemnly*, is she likely to be joking? *(No; saying something solemnly is saying it seriously.)*

BUILD CONCEPT VOCABULARY

Review previous concept words with students. Ask if students have come across any words today in their reading or elsewhere that they would like to add to their U.S. Government Concept Web such as *expert* or *White House*.

SKILLS ⟷ STRATEGIES IN CONTEXT

Main Idea Summarize

TEACH

Read p. 251. Ask students to identify the important idea that all the facts on this page support. *(Most Presidents were well-educated, but some were not.)* Then model how to summarize the information on this page.

Think Aloud **MODEL** Now that I understand the main idea on this page, I can summarize the information. I'll take the important points and put them in my own words. Most Presidents have been well-educated, but some were not. While many went to college and some, like Jefferson, were very smart, others, including Washington and Lincoln, did not attend college.

PRACTICE AND ASSESS

Have pairs find the main idea on p. 250 and write a short summary using the main idea and two or three supporting details. To assess, make sure summaries express the idea that all kinds of pets have lived in the White House. Summaries should include a few supporting details.

Strategy Response Log

Confirm Predictions Provide the following prompt: Was your prediction accurate? (See p. 244.) Revise your old prediction or make a new prediction about the rest of the selection.

If you want to teach this selection in two sessions, stop here.

Guiding Comprehension

If you are teaching the selection in two days, discuss the main ideas so far and review the vocabulary.

8 **Vocabulary • Dictionary/Glossary**

Ask students to name different ways to determine the meaning of an unfamiliar word. Then have them use a dictionary to determine the meaning of *surveyors.*

Ways: Context clues, word structure, dictionary or glossary. Meaning: People who measure land for size, shape, and boundaries.

Monitor Progress

◎ Dictionary/Glossary

If... students have difficulty using a dictionary to determine meaning,	**then...** use the vocabulary strategy instruction on p. 253.

9 Generalize • Inferential

What generalization can you make about Presidents based on the information on p. 253?

Possible response: All the Presidents have been white men who were either Protestant or Roman Catholic.

DAY 3 Grouping Options

Reading
Whole Group Discuss the Question of the Day.

Group Time Differentiated Instruction
Read *So You Want to Be President?* See pp. 240f–240g for the small group lesson plan.

Whole Group Discuss the Reader Response questions on page 256. Then use p. 259a.

Language Arts
Use pp. 259e–259k.

---

8 Almost any job can lead to the White House. Presidents have been lawyers, teachers, farmers, sailors, engineers, surveyors, mayors, governors, congressmen, senators, and ambassadors. (Harry Truman owned a men's shop. Andrew Johnson was a tailor. Ronald Reagan was a movie actor!)

There they are, a mixed bag of Presidents! What did they think of being head man? George Washington, who became our very first President in 1789, worried about his new line of work. "I greatly fear that my countrymen will expect too much from me," he wrote to a friend. (He was a howling success.) Some loved the job. "No President has ever enjoyed himself as much as I," Theodore Roosevelt said. Others hated it. "The four most miserable years of my life," John Quincy Adams complained.

252

ⓔⓛⓛ

Extend Language Encourage students to think of synonyms for *mixed bag* (p. 252, paragraph 2), which refers to a collection of various items. Examples: *potpourri, hodgepodge, variety, assortment.*

Every President was different from every other and yet no woman has been President. No person of color has been President. No person who wasn't a Protestant or a Roman Catholic has been President. But if you care enough, anything is possible. Thirty-four Presidents came and went before a Roman Catholic—John Kennedy—was elected. Almost two hundred years passed before a woman—Geraldine Ferraro—ran for Vice President. **9**

253

Time for SOCIAL STUDIES

FDR's New Deal

Franklin D. Roosevelt (FDR) became President in 1933, during the Great Depression when one-fourth of American workers were unemployed. Many families lost their homes and stood in bread lines for food. Roosevelt introduced federal programs to help these people. He called his approach a "New Deal" for the "forgotten man."

One of his programs was the Works Progress Administration (WPA), which provided jobs for the unemployed. About two million workers a year got jobs through the WPA from 1935 to 1943. Many important federal programs we have today were begun by FDR. He created the "safety net" of unemployment compensation, disability insurance, and retirement benefits under Social Security.

VOCABULARY STRATEGY
Dictionary/ Glossary

TEACH

Review the main strategies students can use to figure out an unfamiliar word. Then read the first two sentences on p. 252, and model how to use a dictionary to determine the meaning of *surveyors*.

Think Aloud **MODEL** This paragraph gives no clues about the meaning of *surveyors* except to tell me it has to do with a job. The word structure isn't much help because I'm not sure what the base word *survey* means. So I'll look up *surveyors* in a dictionary. I'll use the guide words at the top of the pages and alphabetical order to find the entry word for *surveyors*. The dictionary says a *surveyor* is "a person who surveys land." Right above it, I see that one meaning of *survey* has to do with measuring land. So *surveyors* are people who measure land.

PRACTICE AND ASSESS

Have students use the glossary of their student book to determine an appropriate meaning for an unfamiliar lesson vocabulary word (such as *howling* on p. 252 or *oath* on p. 255). To assess, have them restate the meaning in their own words or use the word in a sentence. Check that the meaning chosen reflects the selection's context.

Guiding Comprehension

10 **Author's Viewpoint • Critical**

What qualities does the author seem to believe make someone a good President? How do you know?

Possible response: The author believes good Presidents should ask a lot of themselves, do what is right, and try to make their country, and the world, a better place. She gives examples of good things past Presidents have done and describes them as "the best."

11 **Summarize • Critical**

Text to World **How can what we've learned about the Presidents help us answer our questions on the KWL chart? Use this information to summarize what we've learned.**

Summaries should include information about Presidents being different kinds of people from different backgrounds, each trying to do his best to serve the country.

Strategy Response Log

Summarize When students finish reading the selection, provide this prompt: Write a one-paragraph summary about what it takes to be President of the United States.

It's said that people who run for President have swelled heads. It's said that people who run for President are greedy. They want power. They want fame.

But being President can be wanting to serve your country— like George Washington, who left the Virginia plantation he loved three times to lead the country he loved even more.

It can be looking toward the future like Thomas Jefferson, who bought the Louisiana Territory and then sent Louis and Clark west to find a route to the Pacific. (They did!)

It can be wanting to turn lives around like Franklin Roosevelt, who provided soup and bread for the hungry, jobs for the jobless, and funds for the elderly to live on.

It can be wanting to make the world a better place like John Kennedy, who sent Peace Corps volunteers around the globe to teach and help others.

ELL

Understanding Idioms Students may be unfamiliar with the expression *That's the bottom line* (p. 255, paragraph 3). Restate as "That's the most important point."

Every single President has taken this oath: "I do solemnly swear (or affirm) that I will faithfully execute the office of President of the United States, and will to the best of my ability, preserve, protect and defend the Constitution of the United States."

Only thirty-five words! But it's a big order when you're President of this country. Abraham Lincoln was tops at filling that order. "I know very well that many others might in this matter as in others, do better than I can," he said. "But . . . I am here. I must do the best I can, and bear the responsibility of taking the course which I feel I ought to take."

That's the bottom line. Tall, short, fat, thin, talkative, quiet, vain, humble, lawyer, teacher, or soldier—this is what most of our Presidents have tried to do, each in his own way. Some succeeded. Some failed. If you want to be President—a good President—pattern yourself after the best. Our best have asked **10** more of themselves than they thought they could give. They have had the courage, spirit, and will to do what they knew was right. Most of all, their first priority has always been the people and the country they served. **11**

255

Develop Vocabulary

PRACTICE LESSON VOCABULARY

Students respond orally to each question and provide a reason.

1. If you tell everyone what a great soccer player you are, are you *vain* or *humble*? (vain; you are overly proud of your skill.)

2. Is the *Constitution* of the United States a set of principles or a history of our country? (a set of principles for government)

3. If it's your *responsibility* to clean your room, is this something you have to do or something you do if you feel like it? (Something you have to do; it's a duty.)

BUILD CONCEPT VOCABULARY

Review previous concept words. Ask if students have come across any words that they would like to add to their U.S. Government Concept Web such as *spirit* or *oath*.

STRATEGY SELF-CHECK

Summarize

Have students identify main ideas from the selection and determine the main idea for the entire selection. Students can use the main ideas to write a summary of the selection. For more practice, use Practice Book p. 97.

SELF-CHECK

Students can ask themselves these questions to assess understanding of the selection.

- Did I accurately identify the main idea for the selection?
- Does my summary include the most important points from the selection?

Monitor Progress
Main Idea

| **If...** students are having difficulty identifying main ideas and writing a summary, | **then...** use the Reteach lesson on p. 259b. |

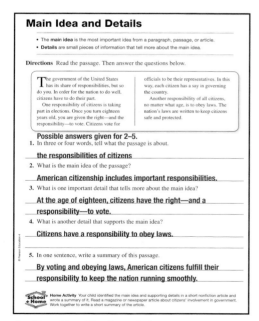

Main Idea and Details

- The **main idea** is the most important idea from a paragraph, passage, or article.
- **Details** are small pieces of information that tell more about the main idea.

Directions Read the passage. Then answer the questions below.

The government of the United States has its share of responsibilities, but so do you. In order for the nation to do well, citizens have to do their part.

One responsibility of citizens is taking part in elections. Once you turn eighteen years old, you are given the right—and the responsibility—to vote. Citizens vote for officials to be their representatives. In this way, each citizen has a say in governing the country.

Another responsibility of all citizens, no matter what age, is to obey laws. The nation's laws are written to keep citizens safe and protected.

Possible answers given for 2–5.
1. In three or four words, tell what the passage is about.
   the responsibilities of citizens
2. What is the main idea of the passage?
   American citizenship includes important responsibilities.
3. What is one important detail that tells more about the main idea?
   At the age of eighteen, citizens have the right—and a responsibility—to vote.
4. What is another detail that supports the main idea?
   Citizens have a responsibility to obey laws.
5. In one sentence, write a summary of this passage.
   By voting and obeying laws, American citizens fulfill their responsibility to keep the nation running smoothly.

School + Home Home Activity Your child identified the main idea and supporting details in a short nonfiction article and wrote a summary of it. Read a magazine or newspaper article about citizens' involvement in government. Work together to write a short summary of the article.

▲ **Practice Book** p. 97

Reader Response

Open for Discussion Personal Response

Think Aloud

MODEL It made me sad to realize that in more than 200 years, no woman has been elected President.

Comprehension Check Critical Response

1. The author's tone is hopeful and positive. For example, she says most Presidents have tried to do the best job possible. **Author's Purpose**

2. Main idea: All kinds of pets have lived in the White House, mostly dogs. Detail: Herbert Hoover had three dogs. ◎ **Main Idea**

3. Responses will vary; students may skim the selection to review its main ideas and find information they can use to encourage a friend. ◎ **Monitor and Fix Up**

4. Responses will vary but should include words such as *election, President, Democrat, Republican.* ◎ **Vocabulary**

Look Back and Write For test practice, assign a 10–15 minute time limit. For assessment, see the Scoring Rubric at the right.

Retell

Have students retell *So You Want to Be President?*

Monitor Progress

Check Retelling [Rubric 4 3 2 1]

If... students have difficulty retelling the selection,	then... use the Retelling Cards and Scoring Rubric for Retelling on p. 257 to assist fluent retelling.

SUCCESS PREDICTOR

Check Retelling Let students listen to other retellings before attempting their own. For more ideas on assessing students' retellings, see the ELL and Transition Handbook.

Reader Response

Open for Discussion "What I enjoyed was. . ." "What made me sad was. . ." "What I learned was. . ." Finish these sentences to give your reaction to *So You Want to Be President?*

1. An author's tone, or manner of writing, shows how the author feels about a topic. What is the author's tone in *So You Want to Be President?* Find parts of the selection that support your answer. Think Like an Author

2. Reread page 250. What sentence states the main idea of this page? What supporting details can you find? Main Idea and Details

3. Suppose a friend announces plans to become President. What will you say to encourage him or her? Summarize

4. *Constitution* and *politics* are Words to Know that relate to government. Identify other words in the selection that relate to government. Vocabulary

Look Back and Write On page 255 find three words that tell what the President is to do with the Constitution of the United States. Write them and tell what they mean.

Meet author **Judith St. George** on page 772 and illustrator **David Small** on page 782.

256

| Scoring Rubric | **Look Back and Write** |

Top-Score Response A top-score response explains the meaning of the words "preserve, protect, and defend" in relation to the Constitution of the United States.

Example of a Top-Score Response *Preserve* means to keep something from changing or disappearing. *Protect* means to keep something from being hurt or damaged. *Defend* means to fight for something to keep it safe. The President must do all of these things with the Constitution of the United States.

For additional rubrics, see p. WA10.

Write Now

Explanation

DURING READING

Prompt

So You Want to Be President? explains what it's like to be President of the United States. Think about an activity that you like to do and why you like to do it.

Now write two or three paragraphs explaining your interest.

Writing Trait

A good explanatory **paragraph** has a topic sentence. Transitions show relationships between ideas and sentences.

Student Model

A strong topic sentence introduces the subject.

> I've always loved the trombone. When I was seven, my grandfather took me to hear a brass band in the park. The trombone looked like so much fun—all that back and forth and up and down. When I got home, I asked my mom if I could take lessons. I've been playing ever since.
>
> The first reason I love playing the trombone is that it's an unusual instrument. For example, lots of kids play the trumpet, violin, or piano, but I don't know anyone else who plays the trombone. If I'm absent from the school band, there's something missing.
>
> Another great thing about the trombone is the music you can play—jazz, classical, even rock and roll. I'm even writing my own songs!

Transitions help organize and connect ideas within paragraphs.

Writer ends the paragraph with an exclamatory sentence.

Use the model to help you write your own explanation.

257

Write Now

Look at the Prompt Explain that each sentence in the prompt has a purpose.

- Sentence 1 presents a topic.
- Sentence 2 suggests students think about the topic.
- Sentence 3 tells what to write—an explanation.

Strategies to Develop Organization/ Paragraphs

Have students

- highlight the main idea of each of their paragraphs.
- brainstorm connector words, such as *however, but,* and *also* and sequence words, such as *first, next,* and *another.*

NO: The cello is hard. You have to practice. It's fun.

YES: The cello is hard, but if you practice you'll soon find it's fun.

For additional suggestions and rubric, see pp. 259g–259h.

Writer's Checklist

☑ **Focus** Do sentences stick to the topic of the activity?

☑ **Organization** Do transitions show connections?

☑ **Support** Do details give information about the activity?

☑ **Conventions** Are grammar and punctuation correct?

Scoring Rubric · Expository Retelling

Rubric 4 3 2 1	4	3	2	1
Connections	Makes connections and generalizes beyond the text	Makes connections to other events, texts, or experiences	Makes a limited connection to another event, text, or experience	Makes no connection to another event, text, or experience
Author's Purpose	Elaborates on author's purpose	Tells author's purpose with some clarity	Makes some connection to author's purpose	Makes no connection to author's purpose
Topic	Describes the main topic	Identifies the main topic with some details early in retelling	Identifies the main topic	Retelling has no sense of topic
Important Ideas	Gives accurate information about events, steps, and ideas using details and key vocabulary	Gives accurate information about events, steps, and ideas with some detail and key vocabulary	Gives limited or inaccurate information about events, steps, and ideas	Gives no information about events, steps, and ideas
Conclusions	Draws conclusions and makes inferences to generalize beyond the text	Draws conclusions about the text	Is able to draw few conclusions about the text	Is unable to draw conclusions or make inferences about the text

Retelling Plan

☑ **Week 1** Assess Strategic Intervention ✓ students.

☑ **Week 2** Assess Advanced students.

☑ **Week 3** Assess Strategic Intervention ✓ students.

☑ **Week 4** Assess On-Level students.

☑ **This week assess any students you have not yet checked during this unit.**

Use the Retelling Chart on p. TR17 to record retelling.

Selection Test To assess with *So You Want to Be President?*, use Selection Tests, pp. 37–40.

Fresh Reads for Differentiated Test Practice For weekly leveled practice use, pp. 55–60.

Retelling

SUCCESS PREDICTOR

Social Studies in Reading

PREVIEW/USE TEXT FEATURES

Preview the article's text features. Then ask:

What can you learn about the parks from the facts listed by each park's name? *(Date established, number of acres, how it is unique.)*

Link to Social Studies

On a physical map, point out features of natural landforms. Have students use these features to draw conclusions about park activities.

EXPOSITORY NONFICTION

Use the sidebar on p. 258 to guide discussion.

- Tell students expository nonfiction provides information about an idea. Have them focus on the photographs or dates.
- Discuss how the photographs, map, and facts on p. 259 help students understand the information on p. 258.

DAY 4 Grouping Options

Reading

Whole Group Discuss the Question of the Day.

Group Time Differentiated Instruction
Read "Our National Parks." See pp. 240f–240g for the small group lesson plan.

Whole Group Use p. 259a.

Language Arts
Use pp. 259e–259k.

Social Studies in Reading

Expository Nonfiction

Genre

- Expository nonfiction often presents facts in visual ways.
- Maps are important, with information being linked to them in some way.

Text Features

- Included in this article is a U.S. map that shows the locations of five national parks.
- Photos and facts provide details about the parks.

Link to Social Studies

Look at a physical map of the United States. What natural landforms do you see? Choose a national park and make a list of the recreational activities people might enjoy there based on landforms that are part of the park.

258

OUR NATIONAL PARKS

by Susan Gavin

Did you know that the President of the United States has the power to set aside land for national parks? Ulysses S. Grant helped create the world's first national park, Yellowstone National Park, in 1872. In 1864, Abraham Lincoln set aside land that became Yosemite National Park in 1890.

Visit one of the 55 parks in the U.S. national park system. (A sampling is on page 259.) Walk through caves, climb mountains, and see wildlife, rain forests, and glaciers. As you enjoy these natural areas, remember that U.S. Presidents helped protect them.

Ⓒ Main Idea How would you state the main idea?

Content-Area Vocabulary	Social Studies
dunes	mounds or ridges of loose sand heaped up by the wind
gorges	deep, narrow valleys, usually steep and rocky, especially ones with a stream
fossils	the hardened remains or traces of things that lived in a former age

AudioText

Sequoia
CALIFORNIA

Established: 1890
Size: 456,552 acres
Highlights: giant sequoia trees; Mt. Whitney (14,491 feet)

Mammoth Cave
KENTUCKY

Established: 1941
Size: 52,830 acres
Highlight: world's longest known network of caves

Death Valley
CALIFORNIA, NEVADA

Established: 1994
Size: 3,367,628 acres
Highlights: largest national park outside of Alaska; desert, dunes, gorges

Everglades
FLORIDA

Established: 1947
Size: 1,399,078 acres
Highlight: largest subtropical wilderness in the United States

Big Bend
TEXAS

Established: 1944
Size: 801,163 acres
Highlights: desert land; on the Rio Grande; dinosaur fossils

Reading Across Texts

"Our National Parks" tells that the President has the power to create national parks. What are some other good things Presidents have done that you read about in *So You Want to Be President?*

Writing Across Texts Make a list of three or four Presidents and tell something they each did that was good for the country.

259

Mount Rushmore

Time for SOCIAL STUDIES

Mount Rushmore National Memorial shows the faces of four U.S. Presidents carved in granite: George Washington, Thomas Jefferson, Abraham Lincoln, and Theodore Roosevelt. The memorial, located in the Black Hills of South Dakota, is part of the National Park System. The memorial was designed by Gutzon Borglum. Work began in 1927 and, with lapses, was completed in 1941. It took about 6.5 years of actual labor, using drills and dynamite to cut into the granite cliff and then shaping and smoothing the surfaces. Today, about 2 million people visit the memorial each year.

Strategies for Nonfiction

USE GRAPHICS Explain to students that they can use graphic sources to help answer test questions. Provide the following strategy.

Use the Strategy
1. Read the test question and locate a key word or phrase.
2. Scan the graphic sources, looking for a picture or detail related to the key word or phrase.

GUIDED PRACTICE Have students discuss how they would use the strategy to answer the following question.

Which of the parks listed on p. 259 was established first?

INDEPENDENT PRACTICE After students answer the following test question, discuss the process they used to find information.

What are the highlights of Big Bend?

Ⓒ Main Idea

Possible response: U.S. Presidents have set aside land for national parks.

CONNECT TEXT TO TEXT

Reading Across Texts
Be sure students can distinguish between the author's humorous examples of being President and the good things Presidents have accomplished.

Writing Across Texts Have students scan the selection for names of specific Presidents they want to write about.

So You Want to Be President? **259**

Fluency Assessment Plan

☑ **Week 1** Assess Advanced students.

☑ **Week 2** Assess Strategic Intervention students.

☑ **Week 3** Assess On-Level students.

☑ **Week 4** Assess Strategic Intervention students.

☑ **This week assess any students you have not yet checked during this unit.**

Set individual goals for students to enable them to reach the year-end goal.

• Current Goal: 100–110 WCPM

• Year-End Goal: 130 WCPM

For English language learners, reading aloud song lyrics, favorite poems, and very short, engaging stories provides good opportunities to increase oral reading fluency.

To develop fluent readers, use Fluency Coach.

DAY 5 Grouping Options

Reading
Whole Group
Revisit the Question of the Week.

Group Time
Differentiated Instruction
Reread this week's Leveled Readers. See pp. 240f–240g for the small group lesson plan.

Whole Group
Use p. 259b–259c.

Language Arts
Use pp. 259d–259l.

STRESS/EMPHASIS
Fluency

DAY 1

Model Reread aloud "Welcome to Washington!" on p. 240m. Explain that you will emphasize certain important words as you read to make it easier for listeners to understand information in the text. Model for students as you read.

DAY 2

Choral Reading Read aloud p. 246, paragraphs 1–3. Have students notice how you stress certain words for effect and sense, such as *good, bad,* and *never.* Read dramatically, so that the emphasis is easy to hear. Have students practice as a class by doing three choral readings of this passage.

DAY 3

Model Read aloud p. 250, paragraph 3. Have students notice which words you stress for emphasis. Practice as a class, doing three choral readings.

DAY 4

Partner Reading Partners practice reading aloud p. 250, paragraph 3, three times. Students should decide in advance which words to stress for sense and humorous effect and offer each other feedback.

Monitor Progress | Check Fluency WCPM

As students reread, monitor their progress toward their individual fluency goals. Current Goal: 100–110 words correct per minute. End-of-Year Goal: 130 words correct per minute.

If... students cannot read fluently at a rate of 100–110 words correct per minute,
then... make sure students practice with text at their independent level. Provide additional fluency practice, pairing nonfluent readers with fluent readers.

If... students already read at 130 words correct per minute,
then... they do not need to reread three times.

SUCCESS PREDICTOR

DAY 5

Assessment
Individual Reading Rate Use the Fluency Assessment Plan and do a one-minute timed reading of either selection from this week to assess students in Week 5. Pay special attention to this week's skill, stress/emphasis. Provide corrective feedback for each student.

RETEACH

Main Idea

TEACH

Review the definitions of *topic, main idea,* and *supporting details* on p. 240. Students can complete Practice Book p. 98 on their own or as a class. Point out that students will need to finish the main idea statement and then fill in the remaining ovals with details that support, or tell more about, the main idea.

ASSESS

Have pairs read p. 249, paragraph 1 and determine the topic *(brothers and sisters of U.S. Presidents),* main idea *(all U.S. Presidents had brothers and sisters),* and supporting details *(Benjamin Harrison had eleven).*

For additional instruction on main idea and supporting details, see DI·56.

EXTEND SKILLS

Expository Nonfiction

TEACH

Expository nonfiction is written to explain something. In expository writing, the author gives information about real people, things, or events.

- When reading nonfiction, you don't always have to read from beginning to end, as you would a story. If you are doing research, for example, you can skim or scan the text and read only the parts you need.
- Text features such as chapter titles, subheads, illustrations, charts, and bold type can help you determine what is covered.

Have students scan *So You Want to Be President?* for information about Jefferson. Discuss whether the selection's organization makes it easy or difficult to find such information.

ASSESS

Have students write an expository paragraph explaining how U.S. Presidents are elected. (You may want to discuss the process first.) Ask:

1. Does your paragraph explain clearly how a President is elected?

2. Is your paragraph well organized?

OBJECTIVES

- Determine topic, main idea, and supporting details.
- Identify traits of expository nonfiction.

Skills Trace

Main Idea and Details

Introduce/Teach	TE: 4.1 112–113; 4.2 240–241; 4.5 582–583
Practice	TE: 119, 123, 247, 251, 589, 595 PB: 43, 47, 48, 93, 97, 98, 233, 237, 238
▶ Reteach/Review	**TE: 4.1 75, 133b, DI•56; 4.2 225, 259b, DI•56; 4.4 475; 4.5 607b, DI•55 PB: 26, 86, 186**
Test	Selection Test: 17–20, 37–40, 93–96; Benchmark Test: Unit 2

ELL

Access Content Reteach the skill by reviewing the Picture It! lesson on main idea and details in the ELL Teaching Guide, pp. 64–65.

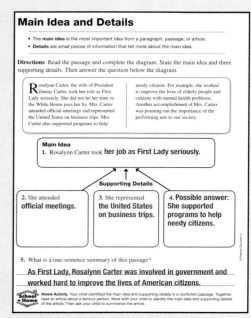

▲ **Practice Book** p. 98

Vocabulary and Word Study

VOCABULARY STRATEGY
Dictionary/ Glossary

UNFAMILIAR WORDS Remind students they can look up unfamiliar words in a glossary or a dictionary. Choose a few challenging words from the selection such as *agriculture, surveying,* or *philosophy.* Ask for volunteers to look up the words in a dictionary and have them describe aloud the steps they follow when using a dictionary. Encourage them to explain to the class how to use guide words, figure out pronunciations, and choose appropriate definitions.

BUILD CONCEPT VOCABULARY
Work and Play

LOOKING BACK Remind students of the Big Idea question: *What is the value of work and play?* Discuss the Big Idea question. Then ask students how the concept vocabulary from each week of this unit relates to the unit theme of work and play and the Big Idea question. Ask students if they have any words or categories to add to this week's concept web. If time permits, create a Unit Concept Web.

Personality Charades

Point out the lesson vocabulary words *humble* and *vain* are adjectives that describe someone's personality. Have students scan the selection and brainstorm other words that describe personality traits. Then have them take turns acting out a word for the class to guess. Encourage students to use facial expressions and body movements to show how someone with that personality might act and speak.

Some Words to Act Out

humble	vain
pesky	greedy
talkative	quiet
polite	miserable

Monitor Progress
Check Vocabulary

If... students suggest words or categories that are not related to the concept,	**then...** review the words and categories on the Concept Web and discuss how they relate to the lesson concept.

SUCCESS PREDICTOR

Speaking and Viewing

SPEAKING

Press Conference

SET-UP Have students imagine that they are each President of the United States announcing a plan to make the country better. Classmates can act as members of the press and ask the "President" questions about the plan.

PLANNING To help students determine a new plan, have them review this week's selections and any research about the powers of the President.

ORGANIZATION Have students open with a main idea statement summarizing their plan. They should explain why the plan is needed and describe how it will help improve people's lives.

AUDIENCE Discuss with the class the role members of the press have during a press conference. If possible, show a televised press conference so students can see how speakers and the press interact with one another.

Speaking Tips
- Each President should speak persuasively and answer each question completely.
- As President, do not comment about the questioner or what you think about the question itself.

VIEWING

Analyze a Speech

Show a political speech. Then have students answer the following questions orally or in writing.

1. **What is the main message in the speech? Does the speaker use anything other than words to get that message across?**
2. **What is the speaker's purpose for giving the speech? How does he or she appeal to listeners' reason and emotions?**
3. **Do you agree with the speaker? Why or why not?**
4. **How might the impact of the speech change if you heard it in person, on the radio, or read about it in a newspaper?**

(Responses will vary but should cite details of the speech and its mode of delivery to support answers.)

Support Vocabulary Use the following to review and extend vocabulary and to explore lesson concepts further:
- ELL Poster 10, Days 3–5 instruction
- Vocabulary Activities and Word Cards in ELL Teaching Guide, pp. 66–67

Assessment For information on assessing students' speaking and viewing, see the ELL and Transition Handbook.

Grammar **Plural Possessive Nouns**

OBJECTIVES

- Define and identify plural possessive nouns.
- Learn how to form plural possessive nouns.
- Use plural possessive nouns correctly in writing.
- Become familiar with plural possessive nouns on high-stakes tests.

Monitor Progress

Grammar

If... students have difficulty identifying plural possessive nouns,	**then...** provide additional instruction and practice in The Grammar and Writing Book pp. 104–107.

DAILY FIX-IT

This week use Daily Fix-It Transparency 10.

Spiral REVIEW

Grammar Support See the Grammar Transition lessons in the ELL and Transition Handbook.

▲ **The Grammar and Writing Book** For more instruction and practice, use pp. 104–107.

DAY 1 Teach and Model

DAILY FIX-IT

1. It would be fun to read an American Presidents' jurnal. *(President's journal)*

2. They're are many interesting activities at the White house. *(There; House)*

READING-GRAMMAR CONNECTION

Write the following sentence on the board:

> Our Presidents' lives are very busy.

Explain that *Presidents'* is a **plural possessive noun.** It is used to show that two or more people, places, or things share or own something. An apostrophe is added to plural nouns that end in *-s, -es,* or *-ies* to make them possessive.

Display Grammar Transparency 10. Read aloud the definitions and sample sentences. Work through the items.

Plural Possessive Nouns

A **plural possessive noun** shows that something is owned or shared by more than one person, place, or thing.
Add an apostrophe (') to a plural noun that ends in *-s, -es,* or *-ies.*
our <u>Presidents'</u> pets   the <u>countries'</u> leaders
Add an apostrophe (') and *-s* to a plural noun that does not end in *-s, -es,* or *-ies.*
the <u>women's</u> dresses   the <u>sheep's</u> fields

Directions Write the possessive form of each underlined plural noun.

1. <u>wives</u> clubs — **wives'**
2. <u>lawyers</u> cases — **lawyers'**
3. <u>children</u> classes — **children's**
4. <u>leaders</u> meetings — **leaders'**
5. <u>guinea pigs</u> teeth — **guinea pigs'**
6. <u>national parks</u> trees — **national parks'**
7. <u>mice</u> tails — **mice's**
8. <u>moose</u> hooves — **moose's**
9. <u>houses</u> doors — **houses'**
10. <u>congressmen</u> offices — **congressmen's**

Directions Write the possessive form of each underlined noun.

11. Our <u>Presidents</u> lives have all been very different. — **Presidents'**
12. These <u>men</u> heights, shapes, and ages have also varied. — **men's**
13. Their <u>families</u> lives are hectic. — **families'**
14. The Roosevelt <u>children</u> pets included guinea pigs, mice, and rats. — **children's**

Unit 2 So You Want to Be President?   Grammar **10**

▲ **Grammar Transparency** 10

DAY 2 Develop the Concept

DAILY FIX-IT

3. Did the childrens' animals ever escape in the White House! *(children's; House?)*

4. Those mices and rats could easily disappear behind a curtin. *(mice; curtain)*

GUIDED PRACTICE

Review the concept of plural possessive nouns.

- A **plural possessive noun** shows that two or more people, places, or things share or own something.

- To make plural nouns that end in *-s, -es,* or *-ies* possessive, add an apostrophe. To make plural nouns that do not end in *-s, -es,* or *-ies* possessive, add an apostrophe and an *s.*

HOMEWORK Grammar and Writing Practice Book p. 37. Work through the first two items with the class.

Plural Possessive Nouns

A **plural possessive noun** shows that something is owned or shared by more than one person, place, or thing.
- Add an apostrophe (') to a plural noun that ends in *-s, -es,* or *-ies.*
our <u>parks'</u> popularity   <u>animals'</u> rights
- Add an apostrophe (') and *-s* to a plural noun that does not end in *-s, -es,* or *-ies.*
the <u>deer's</u> feeding ground   the <u>children's</u> vacation

Directions Write the possessive form of each underlined plural noun.

1. <u>highways</u> roads — **highways'**
2. <u>teeth</u> cavities — **teeth's**
3. <u>states</u> laws — **states'**
4. <u>forests</u> trees — **forests'**
5. <u>raccoons</u> paws — **raccoons'**
6. <u>geese</u> feathers — **geese's**
7. <u>men</u> jackets — **men's**
8. <u>rivers</u> banks — **rivers'**

Directions Choose a plural possessive noun to complete each sentence. Write the word on the line.

9. Our national (parks, parks') landscapes are known around the world. — **parks'**
10. (Automobiles, Automobiles') exhausts can harm the wilderness. — **Automobiles'**
11. The (wolfs', wolves') fangs are very sharp. — **wolves'**
12. Park (rangers', ranger's) jobs are rewarding. — **rangers'**

Home Activity Your child learned about plural possessive nouns. Ask your child to explain the difference between singular and plural possessive nouns. Encourage your child to give examples using the words boys, girls, and children.

▲ **Grammar and Writing Practice Book** p. 37

DAY 3   Apply to Writing

DAILY FIX-IT

5. Which President had a bowling alley builded? *(built?)*

6. If I lived in the White House. Id go to the private movie theater every day. *(House, I'd)*

USE PLURAL POSSESSIVE NOUNS

Point out that possessive nouns can make writing smoother and less wordy.

Wordy: the animals of the children

Not Wordy: the children's animals

- Have students review something they have written to see if they can make it less wordy by using plural possessive nouns.

HOMEWORK Grammar and Writing Practice Book p. 38.

Plural Possessive Nouns

Directions Make each sentence less wordy by replacing the underlined words with a plural possessive noun phrase. Write the new sentences.

1. The wise decisions of our Presidents helped create America's national parks.

   Our Presidents' wise decisions helped create parks.

2. The trees of our forests are for animals as well as for people.

   Our forests' trees are for animals as well as for people.

3. We must protect the creatures of our oceans.

   We must protect our oceans' creatures.

4. People should respect the plants of the deserts.

   People should respect the deserts' plants.

5. All Americans should learn the histories of the states.

   All Americans should learn the states' histories.

Directions Write about a visit to the zoo or a wildlife park. Use at least two plural possessive nouns and underline them.

Possible answer: When I was younger, I went to a children's zoo. I tried to eat the ducks' food, but my mom made me stop. The monkeys' house was very noisy.

School-Home CONNECTION **Home Activity** Your child learned how to use plural possessive nouns in writing. Have your child write a sentence about school using a plural possessive noun. Suggest that he or she use the word *teachers', students', boys',* or *girls'.*

▲ **Grammar and Writing Practice Book** p. 38

DAY 4   Test Preparation

DAILY FIX-IT

7. Our Presidents entertain other countrie's leaders in washington. *(countries'; Washington)*

8. The Presidents wives give dinner partys at the White House. *(Presidents'; parties)*

STANDARDIZED TEST PREP

Test Tip

One way to tell the difference between a possessive noun and a plural noun ending in *-s* is to ask a question beginning with *whose.* For example, if you see the phrase *Presidents' pets,* ask *"Whose pets?"* The answer is *the Presidents'.* If you get an answer to a question starting with *whose,* the word is possessive and requires an apostrophe.

HOMEWORK Grammar and Writing Practice Book p. 39.

Plural Possessive Nouns

Directions Mark the letter of the plural possessive noun that completes each sentence.

1. ___ families live in the White House.
   A President's
   B President
   C Presidents'
   D Presidentes

2. Their ___ lives are different from ours.
   A families
   B familys'
   C famile's
   D familys'

3. Servants take care of all the ___ needs.
   A resident's
   B resident
   C resident's
   D residents'

4. Families bring their ___ toys to the White House.
   A pet
   B pets'
   C petes'
   D pet's

5. The ___ pets have a great life.
   A childrens'
   B children's
   C childs'
   D children'

6. The White House gardens must be ___ playgrounds!
   A cats'
   B cat's
   C cat'
   D cat

7. Do cats hunt for ___ nests in the Rose Garden?
   A birds
   B birds's
   C birds'
   D bird's

8. The Secret Service ___ responsibilities are great.
   A officer's
   B officers
   C officers's
   D officers'

School-Home CONNECTION **Home Activity** Your child prepared for taking tests on plural possessive nouns. Have your child prepare flash cards with a plural noun on one side and its possessive form on the other. Quiz him or her using the flash cards.

▲ **Grammar and Writing Practice Book** p. 39

DAY 5   Cumulative Review

DAILY FIX-IT

9. Every four years americans go to the polls too elect a President. *(Americans; to)*

10. The work is hard but many President's have enjoyed the job. *(hard, but; Presidents)*

ADDITIONAL PRACTICE

Assign pp. 104–107 in The Grammar and Writing Book.

EXTRA PRACTICE Grammar and Writing Practice Book p. 131.

TEST PREPARATION Grammar and Writing Practice Book pp. 153–154.

ASSESSMENT

CUMULATIVE REVIEW Grammar and Writing Practice Book p. 40.

Plural Possessive Nouns

Directions Write the possessive form of each underlined plural noun.

1. cities residents   **cities'**
2. senators speeches   **senators'**
3. streets names   **streets'**
4. shelves ledges   **shelves'**
5. women dresses   **women's**
6. children toys   **children's**
7. feet toes   **feet's**
8. congressmen letters   **congressmen's**

Directions Write the possessive form of each underlined plural noun.

9. Two wolves approached the deer feeding ground.

   deer's

10. The wolves coats were thick and gray.

    wolves'

11. They wanted a deer for their cubs dinners.

    cubs'

12. The deer saw the wolves and vanished into the trees shadows.

    trees'

School-Home CONNECTION **Home Activity** Your child reviewed plural possessive nouns. Have your child find and circle examples of plural possessive nouns in a magazine or newspaper article.

▲ **Grammar and Writing Practice Book** p. 40

Writing For Tests   **Explanation**

Genre Explanation
Writer's Craft Writing Good Paragraphs
Writing Trait Organization/Paragraphs

ELL

Organization/Paragraphs Explain that transition words make order clear in writing. Write *first, next, then, after, before, also,* and *but* on index cards, one to a card, and model their meaning and use. Help language learners use these transition words in their writing.

Writing Traits

FOCUS/IDEAS The writer sticks to her main idea—why soccer is important to her—and a clear purpose—to inform.

ORGANIZATION/PARAGRAPHS The writer uses transition words and phrases to connect paragraphs and ideas (*Another reason, But the best thing*).

VOICE The writer has a friendly, informal voice (*Just put me out on a soccer field*).

WORD CHOICE Vivid images (*soccer fever, the smell of the grass, a big party*) keep the writing lively.

SENTENCES Sentences of varying lengths and kinds make writing interesting.

CONVENTIONS There is excellent control and accuracy.

DAY 1   Model the Trait

READING-WRITING CONNECTION

- When you write a response for tests, remember that good paragraphs are the building blocks of good writing.

- Think about how the writer of *So You Want to Be President?* uses transitions, such as *but, however,* and *although* to link ideas together.

MODEL CONVENTIONS Discuss Writing Transparency 10A. Then discuss the model and the writing trait of organization/paragraphs.

Think Aloud I see that the writer of this explanation has organized it into three paragraphs. Each paragraph clearly explains one reason why the writer loves soccer. The paragraphs are linked using transitions, such as *another reason* and *but.* These words help one paragraph flow into the next.

Writing for Tests

Prompt Think of something you like to do. It may be teaching your dog tricks, playing piano, or helping your mother cook. Think about why you like to do this activity. Write two or three well-organized paragraphs explaining your interest to friends or family members.

Soccer Fever

A strong topic sentence introduces the subject.

Details support the main idea.

I've always loved playing soccer. When the weather grows cool in the fall, I get soccer fever. I love the smell of the grass and the sound of the bouncing ball. I even love getting covered in mud. Just put me out on a soccer field, and I'll be happy.

Transitions connect paragraphs or ideas within a paragraph.

Another reason I have soccer fever is that all my friends play. In fact, soccer practice is like a big party! Everyone I know is running around out there.

But the best thing about soccer is that no one tells me I'm wasting my time. For example, if I watched TV all afternoon, my mom would nag me to do something

An effective final sentence sums up the explanation.

else. Soccer makes everyone happy!

Unit 2 So You Want to Be President?   **Writing Model 10A**

▲ **Writing Transparency** 10A

DAY 2   Improve Writing

WRITER'S CRAFT
Writing Good Paragraphs

Display Writing Transparency 10B. Read the directions and work together to practice writing good paragraphs.

Think Aloud **WRITING GOOD PARAGRAPHS** Tomorrow we will be writing an explanation of why we like a certain activity. I am going to write about riding my mountain bike. My explanation will be stronger if I write good paragraphs explaining my reasons. Each paragraph should start with a strong topic sentence. For example, "Mountain biking is great exercise." Then I can support my reasons by giving specific details. I will end my paragraph with an important idea.

GUIDED WRITING If students have difficulty with transitions, select two or three transitional words or phrases and practice using them with the class.

Writing Good Paragraphs

- A good paragraph often has a topic sentence that clearly states the main idea.
- A good paragraph includes details that support the main idea.
- A good paragraph has transitional words or phrases that show relationships between ideas, sentences, or paragraphs. Here are some common transitions:
  Time *first, then, next, before, finally, at last, later*
  Compare/Contrast *however, but, although, on the other hand, like*
  Example *for example, namely, that is, along with*

Directions Sentences A and B are topic sentences for paragraphs in a how-to report about lighting a fire. Sentences 1 to 8 are supporting details in these paragraphs. Write the letter of the topic sentence that each detail supports.

A The first step in making a campfire is to collect the right fuel.
B The second step is to construct the fire.

1. Put the smallest twigs and bits of bark in the center.	B
2. Collect only dry material.	A
3. Look for birch bark and fallen pine needles.	A
4. Place sticks the size of a pencil on top of the bark.	B
5. Find a flat, clear, dry patch of ground.	B
6. Dead wood that snaps easily is a good choice.	A
7. Dry leaves make excellent kindling.	A
8. Gradually build up the wood into a teepee shape.	B

Directions Write a paragraph using this topic sentence: *My favorite day of the week is* ___ Support your ideas with details and use at least one transition. **Possible answer:**
My favorite day of the week is Monday. My weekends are boring. On the other hand, Monday is always exciting. I eat lunch with my friends and play with them at recess. Sometimes classes are fun too.

Unit 2 So You Want to Be President?   **Writer's Craft 10B**

▲ **Writing Transparency** 10B

DAY 3 Prewrite and Draft

READ THE WRITING PROMPT
on page 257 in the Student Edition.

So You Want to Be President?
*explains what it's like to be President
of the United States.*

*Think about an activity that you like to
do and why you like to do it.*

*Now write two or three paragraphs
explaining your interest.*

Test-Taking Tips

1. **Read the prompt carefully.**
   • Find key words.
   • Consider the purpose and audience.
2. **Develop a plan.** Think about what you
   want to say before writing. Fill out
   a graphic organizer, such as a story
   sequence chart showing beginning,
   middle, and end or a T-chart for a
   comparison/contrast essay.
3. **Support your ideas.** Use facts,
   examples, and details to strengthen
   your response. Avoid making general
   statements that are unsupported.
4. **Use a variety of sentence structures.**
   Include complex and compound
   sentences, varied sentence
   beginnings, and sentences of
   different lengths and types.
5. **Choose clear, precise words.** Use
   concise words that create pictures.
6. **Check your writing.** If this is a
   timed test, neatly add, delete, or
   change words and make corrections
   in spelling, punctuation, or grammar
   instead of recopying. Make sure your
   handwriting is legible. Reread your
   work before handing it in.

DAY 4 Draft and Revise

EDITING/REVISING CHECKLIST

☑ **Focus** Do sentences stick to the
topic of the activity and why you
enjoy it?

☑ **Organization** Is the explanation
developed in a logical order, using
transition words to link paragraphs?

☑ **Support** Do specific words make
the explanation interesting and
engaging? Is the voice enthusiastic?

☑ **Conventions** Have I indented correctly to make my organization
clear? Have I used correct punctuation and capitalization to make the
explanation easy to read?

Revising Tips

Organization/ Paragraphs

• Be sure that main ideas are in an
  order that makes sense.
• Strengthen your writing by
  connecting ideas with transitional
  words and phrases.
• Save your most important idea
  until last.

ASSESSMENT Use the scoring rubric
to evaluate students' work.

DAY 5 Connect to Unit Writing

How-to Report	
Week 1	Poem 161g–161h
Week 2	News Story 187g–187h
Week 3	Play Scene 211g–211h
Week 4	Describe a Job 239g–239h
Week 5	Explanation 259g–259h

PREVIEW THE UNIT PROMPT

*Think of something that you know
how to do well. Write a clear, step-
by-step description of how to do this
task or activity. Make your report
interesting to read and easy to understand.*

APPLY

• A how-to report explains the steps
  for making or doing something.
• The writer of a how-to report
  includes transitions to clearly show
  how ideas are related.

Writing Trait Rubric

	4	3	2	1
Organization/ Paragraphs	Well-organized paragraphs; includes transitions	Organized paragraphs; some transitions	Disorganized paragraphs; few transitions	No organization to paragraphs; no transitions
	Explanation logically developed	Explanation somewhat logically developed	Explanation lacks logical development	Explanation confused or meaningless

Spelling & Phonics Words with *ear, ir, our, ur*

OBJECTIVE

- Spell words with *ear, ir, our,* and *ur.*

Generalization

Connect to Phonics The vowel sound in *girl* can be spelled *ear, ir, our,* and *ur: early, first, courage, return.* Words with *ear, ir, our,* and *ur* often have the vowel sound heard in *girl.*

Spelling Words

1. return
2. courage*
3. surface
4. purpose
5. first*
6. turkey
7. heard
8. early
9. turtle
10. birthday*
11. journal
12. courtesy
13. nourish
14. purse
15. furniture
16. search
17. curtain
18. burrow
19. hamburger
20. survey*

Challenge Words

21. turquoise
22. absurd
23. furthermore
24. flourish
25. nourishment

*Word from the selection

Spelling/Phonics Support See the ELL and Transition Handbook for spelling support.

PRETEST

Use the Dictation Sentences from Day 5 to administer the pretest. Read the word, read the sentence, and then read the word again. Guide students in self-correcting their pretests and correcting any misspellings.

Monitor Progress

Spelling

If... students misspell more than 5 pretest words,	**then**... use words 1–10 for Strategic Intervention.
If... students misspell 1–5 pretest words,	**then**... use words 1–20 for On-Level practice.
If... students correctly spell all pretest words,	**then**... use words 1–25 for Advanced Learners.

HOMEWORK Spelling Practice Book, p. 37.

Words with *ear, ir, our, ur*

Generalization The vowel sound in *girl* can be spelled *ear, ir, our,* and *ur: early, first, courage, return.*

Word Sort Sort the list words by the spelling of the vowel sound in *girl.*

ear
1. heard
2. early
3. search

ir
4. first
5. birthday

our
6. courage
7. journal
8. courtesy
9. nourish

ur
10. return
11. surface
12. purpose
13. turkey
14. turtle
15. purse
16. furniture
17. curtain
18. burrow
19. hamburger
20. survey

Spelling Words
1. return
2. courage
3. surface
4. purpose
5. first
6. turkey
7. heard
8. early
9. turtle
10. birthday
11. journal
12. courtesy
13. nourish
14. purse
15. furniture
16. search
17. curtain
18. burrow
19. hamburger
20. survey

Challenge Words
21. turquoise
22. absurd
23. furthermore
24. flourish
25. nourishment

Challenge Words

our
21. flourish
22. nourishment

ur
23. turquoise
24. absurd
25. furthermore

School + Home Home Activity Your child is learning to spell words with *ear, ir, our,* and *ur.* Read all the words in one spelling category and ask your child which spelling of the vowel sound in *girl* all the words share.

▲ **Spelling Practice Book** p. 37

TEACH

The letter combinations *ear, ir, our,* and *ur* can all stand for the vowel sound found in *girl.* Write *heard.* Underline *ear.* Explain that *ear* stands for the vowel sound in *girl.* Write *first, journal,* and *purse* and help students name the letters that stand for the vowel sound in *girl.*

heard

FILL IN THE BLANK Have students write each word on a note card, replacing the letters that stand for the vowel sound in *girl* with a single line. Then tell them to write the missing letters on the back of the card. Have students use the cards to quiz themselves on the words.

HOMEWORK Spelling Practice Book, p. 38.

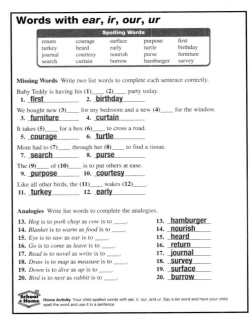

Words with *ear, ir, our, ur*

Spelling Words				
return	courage	surface	purpose	first
turkey	heard	early	turtle	birthday
journal	courtesy	nourish	purse	furniture
search	curtain	burrow	hamburger	survey

Missing Words Write two list words to complete each sentence correctly.

Baby Teddy is having his (1)____ (2)____ party today.
1. **first** 2. **birthday**

We bought new (3)____ for my bedroom and a new (4)____ for the window.
3. **furniture** 4. **curtain**

It takes (5)____ for a box (6)____ to cross a road.
5. **courage** 6. **turtle**

Mom had to (7)____ through her (8)____ to find a tissue.
7. **search** 8. **purse**

The (9)____ of (10)____ is to put others at ease.
9. **purpose** 10. **courtesy**

Like all other birds, the (11)____ wakes (12)____.
11. **turkey** 12. **early**

Analogies Write list words to complete the analogies.

13. *Hog* is to *pork chop* as *cow* is to ____. 13. **hamburger**
14. *Blanket* is to *warm* as *food* is to ____. 14. **nourish**
15. *Eye* is to *saw* as *ear* is to ____. 15. **heard**
16. *Go* is to *come* as *leave* is to ____. 16. **return**
17. *Read* is to *novel* as *write* is to ____. 17. **journal**
18. *Draw* is to *map* as *measure* is to ____. 18. **survey**
19. *Down* is to *dive* as *up* is to ____. 19. **surface**
20. *Bird* is to *nest* as *rabbit* is to ____. 20. **burrow**

School + Home Home Activity Your child spelled words with *ear, ir, our,* and *ur.* Say a list word and have your child spell the word and use it in a sentence.

▲ **Spelling Practice Book** p. 38

DAY 3 — Connect to Writing

WRITE A CAPTION

Have students draw a picture of a household machine. Ask them to use at least three spelling words to write a caption for the picture that explains the machine's purpose or tells how it works.

Frequently Misspelled Words

heard   our

are

These words may seem easy to spell, but they are often misspelled by fourth-graders. Alert students to these frequently misspelled words. Point out the *ear* pattern that stands for the vowel sound in *heard*. Help students compare the pronunciations, spellings, and usage of *our* and *are*.

HOMEWORK Spelling Practice Book, p. 39.

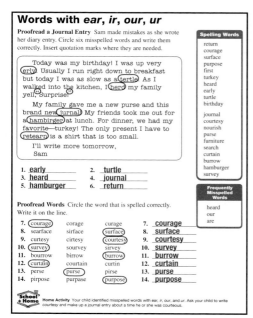

▲ **Spelling Practice Book** p. 39

DAY 4 — Review

REVIEW WORDS WITH *ear, ir, our, ur*

Have students make up a different symbol for each of the letter combinations *ear, ir, our, ur* and write the list words, replacing the letters that stand for the vowel sound with the appropriate symbol. Have students trade papers and figure out which letters each symbol stands for.

Spelling Strategy
Problem Parts

Even short words can be hard to spell until you discover where they come from.

Example: heard

The spelling of *heard* makes sense when you remember that *heard* is the past tense of *hear*. *Hear* is a meaning helper for *heard*.

HOMEWORK Spelling Practice Book, p. 40.

Words with *ear, ir, our, ur*

Spelling Words				
return	courage	surface	purpose	first
turkey	heard	early	turtle	birthday
journal	courtesy	nourish	purse	furniture
search	curtain	burrow	hamburger	survey

Word Parts Draw a line to connect the first part of each list word with its second part. Then write the completed word on the line.

1. sur	day	1.	survey
2. birth	pose	2.	birthday
3. ear	vey	3.	early
4. bur	age	4.	burrow
5. pur	ly	5.	purpose
6. cour	row	6.	courage
7. jour	ish	7.	journal
8. tur	nal	8.	turkey
9. ham	burger	9.	hamburger
10. re	tain	10.	return
11. nour	key	11.	nourish
12. cur	turn	12.	curtain
13. sur	tle	13.	surface
14. tur	face	14.	turtle

Home Activity Your child has learned to read, write, and spell words with *ir, ir,* and *ur.* Have your child read each spelling word and then spell it with eyes closed.

▲ **Spelling Practice Book** p. 40

DAY 5 — Posttest

DICTATION SENTENCES

1. The doctor will <u>return</u> after lunch.
2. Sometimes it takes <u>courage</u> to tell the truth.
3. The water's <u>surface</u> was choppy.
4. What is the <u>purpose</u> of the story?
5. Jan came in <u>first</u> in the race.
6. The <u>turkey</u> sandwich is tasty.
7. We <u>heard</u> a dog barking outside.
8. I woke up <u>early</u> today.
9. A tiny <u>turtle</u> hatched from the egg.
10. The <u>birthday</u> party is on Sunday.
11. Did you write in your <u>journal</u> today?
12. Saying thank you shows <u>courtesy</u>.
13. Plant foods <u>nourish</u> flowers.
14. Jen left her <u>purse</u> in the car.
15. I moved all my bedroom <u>furniture</u>.
16. Tom had to <u>search</u> for his keys.
17. The kitten climbed up the <u>curtain</u>.
18. The chipmunk hid in its <u>burrow</u>.
19. Do you know how to make a <u>hamburger</u>?
20. The <u>survey</u> shows that most people like the color blue.

CHALLENGE

21. The <u>turquoise</u> ring is beautiful.
22. That plan is silly and <u>absurd</u>.
23. <u>Furthermore</u>, I have a few things to add.
24. The ringmaster introduced the act with a <u>flourish</u>.
25. Good <u>nourishment</u> keeps us healthy.

OBJECTIVES

- Formulate an inquiry question that is connected to this week's lesson focus.
- Effectively and efficiently find, evaluate, and communicate information related to an inquiry question using electronic sources.

New Literacies	
Day 1	Identify Questions
Day 2	Navigate/Search
Day 3	Analyze
Day 4	Synthesize
Day 5	Communicate

NEW LITERACIES

Internet Inquiry Activity

EXPLORE THE U. S. PRESIDENCY

Use the following 5-day plan to help students conduct this week's Internet inquiry activity on the job of the President of the United States. Remind students to follow classroom rules when using the Internet.

DAY 1

Identify Questions Discuss the lesson focus question: *What is the job of the President of the United States?* Guide students in determining specific questions to research. For example, some students may want to learn about the President's role in making laws or scheduling a typical workday. Have students write an inquiry question they want to answer.

DAY 2

Navigate/Search Have students determine keywords related to their inquiry questions. Discuss whether Web sites with URLs ending in *.edu* or *.gov* are likely to be more or less reliable than commercial sites ending in *.com*. Have students identify a few sites for further exploration on Day 3.

DAY 3

Analyze Have students explore the Web sites identified on Day 2. Explain how to use the computer's Find feature to locate specific information on each site. Remind students to record source information, such as the name of the Web site, its URL, and the site's owner or any sponsoring organizations.

DAY 4

Synthesize Have students synthesize information from Day 3 by writing main ideas and details in an outline or a main idea chart. Remind students to restate information in their own words, but to keep facts accurate.

DAY 5

Communicate Invite students to share their inquiry results in short reports to the class. They can describe how they found the information as well as sharing the answers to their inquiry questions.

RESEARCH/STUDY SKILLS
Time Line

TEACH

Ask students how they might display information that shows major events in the life of George Washington. Guide discussion to point out that a time line is a good way to display a series of events.

- A **time line** shows information in chronological order. It is divided into sections that represent **periods of time** and is read from left to right or top to bottom.

- The **title** of a time line describes the topic.

- **Labels** give dates and details of events.

- Time lines found on the Internet or on CD-ROMS are often **interactive.** You can click on links, such as a Web site article or video clip, to find additional information about an event.

Provide groups with time lines from textbooks or other reference materials. Have groups share their time lines with their classmates and answer questions such as these:

1. **What is the topic of the time line?**
2. **What time periods does it show?**
3. **What is the longest amount of time that passes between two events?**
4. **Do the labels provide enough useful information? Why or why not?**

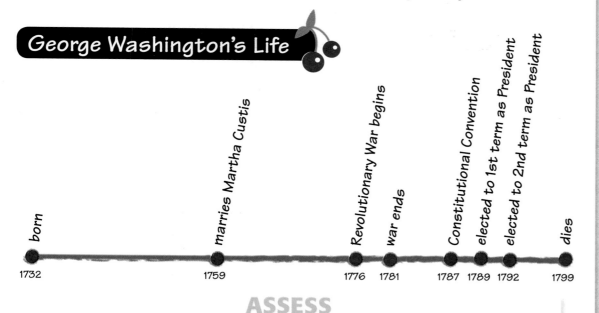

ASSESS

Check students' understanding by asking specific questions about their time lines. For example, ask them to tell when a specific event happened, which event happened during a specific time, how much time elapsed between events, or whether an event happened before or after another event.

For more practice or to assess students, use Practice Book pp. 99–100.

OBJECTIVES

- Review features of a time line.
- Use a time line to locate information.

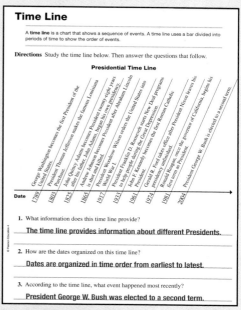

▲ **Practice Book** p. 99

4. When did President Jefferson make the Louisiana Purchase?
   President Jefferson made the Louisiana Purchase in 1803.
5. What happened in 1974 before Gerald R. Ford became President?
   President Nixon left his presidency unfinished.
6. What happened for the first time in 1961?
   A Roman Catholic person became President.
7. How many years passed between the start of George Washington's presidency and President Wilson's decision to enter World War I?
   128 years passed between the two events.
8. Why did Andrew Johnson become President?
   Andrew Johnson became President because President Lincoln had been shot and killed.
9. In what year did John Quincy Adams' father become President? How do you know?
   John Adams became President in 1797, twenty-eight years before his son became president in 1825.
10. How might you use this time line as you do research for a report on American Presidents?
    Possible answer: This time line could provide me with facts about the Presidents, and it could help me organize information by time order.

▲ **Practice Book** p. 100

Assessment Checkpoints *for the Week*

Selection Assessment

Use pp. 37–40 of Selection Tests to check:

 Selection Understanding

  Comprehension Skill *Main Idea*

Selection Vocabulary

Constitution	responsibility
howling	solemnly
humble	vain
politics	

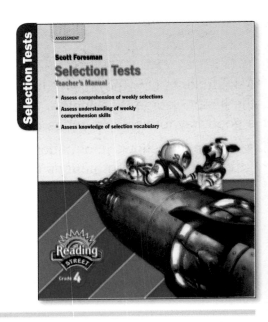

Leveled Assessment

- On-Level
- Strategic Intervention
- Advanced

Use pp. 55–60 of Fresh Reads for Differentiated Test Practice to check:

 Comprehension Skill *Main Idea*

 REVIEW Comprehension Skill *Generalize*

 Fluency *Words Correct Per Minute*

Managing Assessment

Use Assessment Handbook for:

 Observation Checklists

 Record-Keeping Forms

 Portfolio Assessment

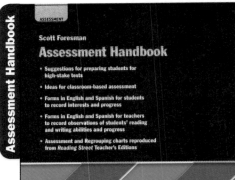

Unit 2
Concept Wrap-Up

CONCEPT QUESTION

What is the value of work and play?

Students are ready to express their understanding of the unit concept question through discussion and wrap-up activities and to take the Unit 2 Benchmark Test.

Unit Poetry

Use the poetry on pp. 260–263 to help students appreciate poetry and further explore their understanding of the unit theme, Work and Play. It is suggested that you

- **read the poems aloud**
- **discuss and interpret the poems with students**
- **have students read the poems for fluency practice**
- **have students write interpretive responses**

Unit Wrap-Up

Use the Unit Wrap-Up on pp. 264–265 to discuss the unit theme, Work and Play, and to have students show their understanding of the theme through cross-curricular activities.

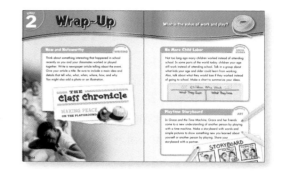

Unit Project

On p. 141, you assigned students a unit-long inquiry project, a classified ad for a job they have researched. Students have investigated, analyzed, and synthesized information during the course of the unit as they prepared their ads. Schedule time for students to present their projects. The project rubric can be found at the right.

Unit Inquiry Project Rubric

4	3	2	1
• Research is accurate and very detailed. Sources are reliable and relevant to inquiry question. • Classified ad describes the job and skills needed for it. It is informative, concise, and clear.	• Research is generally accurate and detailed. Most sources are reliable and relevant. • Ad describes the job and several skills. It is informative and clear but may omit some key information.	• Research includes inaccuracies, irrelevant information, or little detail. Some sources are unreliable. • Ad names the job and lists a few skills, but parts are unclear or missing.	• Research is not accurate, detailed, or relevant. Most sources are unreliable. • Ad does not clearly describe the job or needed skills. Information is incomplete or confusing.

Unit 2
Reading Poetry

Model Fluent Reading

Read "His Hands" aloud. Explain that the poem is told in three sentences, and have students listen to the phrasing, or grouping of words, as you recite it. Emphasize the importance of reading each sentence as a whole.

Discuss the Poem

1 Draw Conclusions • Inferential

How can you tell that the speaker admires the man with the hands she describes?

Possible response: The speaker says the man's "work-proud callouses" are the man's "badges of tough, honest labor."

2 Metaphor • Inferential

Why does the speaker say the man's "hands are strong stories"?

Possible response: The man's hands, with their rough callouses, tell stories of doing hard work on the docks.

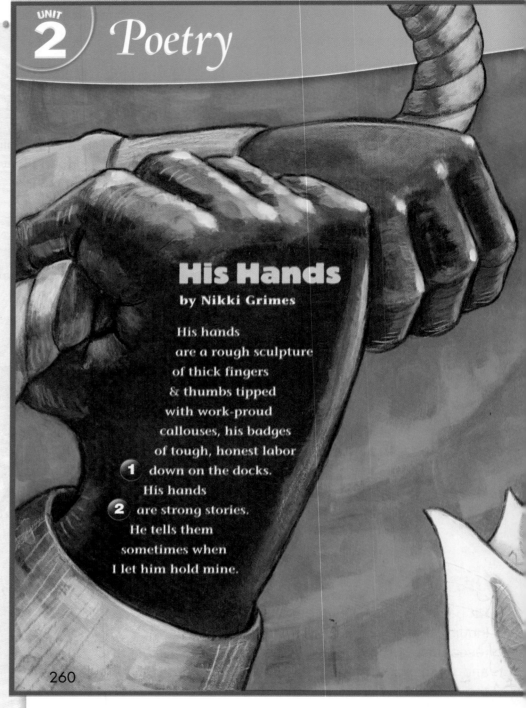

UNIT
2 *Poetry*

His Hands
by Nikki Grimes

His hands
  are a rough sculpture
  of thick fingers
  & thumbs tipped
with work-proud
callouses, his badges
of tough, honest labor
1 down on the docks.
  His hands
2 are strong stories.
He tells them
sometimes when
I let him hold mine.

260

Practice Fluent Reading

Have partners take turns reading "His Hands" aloud. Tell students to pay attention to phrasing, or the way they group words as they read. Suggest that students follow the marks of punctuation to know when to pause. After practice, have students recite the poem to their partners or the class.

Audio CD Audio Text

Homework

by Russell Hoban

Homework sits on top of Sunday, squashing Sunday flat.
Homework has the smell of Monday, homework's very fat.
Heavy books and piles of paper, answers I don't know.
Sunday evening's almost finished, now I'm going to go
Do my homework in the kitchen. Maybe just a snack,
Then I'll sit right down and start as soon as I run back
For some chocolate sandwich cookies. Then I'll really do
All that homework in a minute. First I'll see what new
Show they've got on television in the living room.
Everybody's laughing there, but misery and gloom
And a full refrigerator are where I am at.
I'll just have another sandwich. Homework's very fat. ❷

261

Model Fluent Reading

Read "Homework" aloud. Tell students to listen for how you vary your tone of voice to reflect the emotions of the speaker throughout the poem.

Discuss the Poem

❶ Imagery • Inferential
How does the speaker feel about homework? What images does the poet use to show these feelings?

Possible responses: Images of homework being fat, smelling like Monday, and *squashing Sunday flat* appeal to the senses and show how much the speaker dislikes homework.

❷ Drawing Conclusions • Inferential
Why does the speaker say that "homework's very fat"?

Possible responses: The speaker refers to "heavy books and piles of paper." The speaker also does homework next to a full refrigerator and procrastinates by snacking a lot while working.

WRITING POETRY

Have students write their own poems about a task or chore they dislike. For example, they might write about taking out the trash or doing the dishes. Have students use vivid descriptions, such as those in "Homework," to describe the task and how they try to avoid doing it.

Reading Poetry

Model Fluent Reading

Read "Lem Lonnigan's Leaf Machine" aloud. Tell students to listen for how you vary your rate to match the meaning of the poem.

Discuss the Poem

1 Rhyme • Literal

What end rhymes do you hear in the poem?

Possible responses: Examples of end rhymes include *ease* and *trees, autumn* and *spot'im, get* and *yet,* and *heights* and *kites.*

2 Cause and Effect • Inferential

What things happen as a result of the leaf machine's efficiency?

Possible responses: The machine cleans up autumn leaves, but sometimes it gets a nest, squirrel, or bird by mistake.

EXTEND SKILLS

Mood

The mood of a poem is the feeling it creates in the reader. A writer might create a mood that is scary, sad, or lighthearted. A poet creates mood through the words he or she uses to describe people, objects, or places. Mood often is reflected in word choice when the poet is writing about a character's actions or emotions. In poems about serious topics, writers often use words to describe grim settings or sad emotions.

Lem Lonnigan's Leaf Machine

by Andrea Perry

Lem Lonnigan's Leaf Machine cleans lawns with ease
by vacuuming all that falls down from the trees.
And as you might guess, he's quite busy in autumn.
Just look in a yard full of trees and you'll spot 'im!

He uses a special attachment to get
those few stubborn leaves that have not fallen yet,
extending its claws to reach sky-scraping heights
for snatching up stragglers and sometimes stray kites.

262

Practice Fluent Reading

Have partners take turns reading "Lem Lonnigan's Leaf Machine" aloud. Have students read the poem several times—slowly, quickly, and then at a varying rate to match the emotions of the speaker. Have them discuss which reading best conveys the meaning of the poem.

 **Audio CD** Audio Text

But if by mistake
his machine gets a nest
or a squirrel or bird
in its yard-cleaning zest, **2**
then Lem hits the switch
to discharge it post haste
and carefully sees
that the tenant's replaced.

He's fast and efficient.
He's clean and he's neat
as he rides his machine
tree to tree down the street. **3**
So don't waste time raking
and bagging this fall!
Lem's Leaf Machine's ready,
so give him a call! **4**

263

3 Draw Conclusions • Inferential
What is the speaker's opinion of Lem Lonnigan? How can you tell?

Possible responses: The speaker seems to respect Lem Lonnigan. He or she talks about how hard Lem works collecting leaves, how he reacts when he accidentally picks up a nest or an animal, and how fast, efficient, neat, and clean he is.

4 Mood • Inferential
What is the mood of the poem? How does the poet create this mood?

Possible responses: The mood of the poem is lighthearted. The poet creates this mood by speaking directly to the reader, enthusiastically describing Lem and the work he does with his machine, and ending by telling readers to "give him a call."

Connect Ideas and Themes

Remind students that this unit deals with the value of work and play. Point out that the first two poems describe work, while the third poem describes both work and play. Have students think of how they would describe themselves at work and at play. What value can they see in each type of activity?

WRITING POETRY

Have students imagine a gadget they could use to help them do a difficult task and write a poem about it. They might invent a robot to help them do the dishes or a talking book to help them with homework. Encourage students to add humor to the poem.

Unit 2
Wrap-Up

OBJECTIVES

- Critically analyze unit theme.
- Connect content across selections.
- Combine content and skills in meaningful activities that build literacy.
- Respond to unit selections through a variety of modalities.

WORK AND PLAY

Discuss the Big Idea

What is the value of work and play?

Write the unit theme and Big Idea question on the board. Ask students to think about the selections they have read in the unit. Discuss how each selection and lesson concept can help them answer the Big Idea question from this unit.

Model this for students by choosing a selection and explaining how the selection and lesson concept address the Big Idea.

UNIT 2

Wrap~Up

New and Noteworthy

connect to **WRITING**

Think about something interesting that happened in school recently as you and your classmates worked or played together. Write a newspaper article telling about the event. Give your article a title. Be sure to include a main idea and details that tell *who, what, when, where, how,* and *why.* You might also add a photo or an illustration.

THE
Class Chronicle

MAKING PEACE
ON THE PLAYGROUND

264

What is the value of work and play?

No More Child Labor

connect to SOCIAL STUDIES

Not too long ago many children worked instead of attending school. In some parts of the world today, children your age still work instead of attending school. Talk in a group about what kids your age and older could learn from working. Also, talk about what they would lose if they worked instead of going to school. Make a chart to summarize your ideas.

👥 Children Who Work 📋	
What They Gain	What They Lose

Playtime Storyboard

connect to ART

In *Grace and the Time Machine*, Grace and her friends come to a new understanding of another person by playing with a time machine. Make a storyboard with words and simple pictures to show something new you learned about yourself or another person by playing. Share your storyboard with a partner.

STORYBOARD

Me → | Mom has my baseball. | She gives it to me.
1. | 2. | 3.

ACTIVITIES

New and Noteworthy

Write a News Article Have students examine newspaper articles to see how they are organized. The first sentence, or lead, usually grabs the reader's attention and the rest of the article answers the five *W* and the *H* questions (*Who? What? Where? When? Why?* and *How?*). Point out that a headline gives the main idea of the article in a concise way.

No More Child Labor

Make a Chart Tell groups to begin by discussing different types of work and imagining children doing these jobs. Have them consider the benefits and hardships of having a job and the value of getting an education. Each group should choose one person to take notes during the discussion and another person to record the group's ideas in a T-chart like the one on p. 265.

Playtime Storyboard

Create a Storyboard Tell students to think of times when they have learned something new about themselves or others while playing. Ask: *Did you discover a new talent or interest? Notice a new personality characteristic? Come up with a goal or dream for the future?* Remind students to use both words and pictures in their storyboards.

Glossary

Glossary

How to Use This Glossary

This glossary can help you understand and pronounce some of the words in this book. The entries in this glossary are in alphabetical order. There are guide words at the top of each page to show you the first and last words on the page. A pronunciation key is at the bottom of every other page. Remember, if you can't find the word you are looking for, ask for help or check a dictionary.

The entry word is in dark type. It shows how the word is spelled and how the word is divided into syllables.

The pronunciation is in parentheses. It also shows which syllables are stressed.

Part-of-speech labels show the function or functions of an entry word and any listed form of that word.

an·ces·tor (an′ses′tər), *NOUN.* person from whom you are descended, such as your great-grandparents: *Their ancestors had come to the United States in 1812.* ❏ *PLURAL* **an·ces·tors.**

Sometimes, irregular and other special forms will be shown to help you use the word correctly.

The definition and example sentence show you what the word means and how it is used.

Aa

a·board (ə bôrd′), *ADVERB.* on board; in or on a ship, train, bus, airplane, etc.: *"All aboard!" shouted the conductor, and everyone rushed for the train.*

a·bun·dance (ə bun′dəns), *NOUN.* quantity that is a lot more than enough: *There is an abundance of apples this year.*

af·ford (ə fôrd′), *VERB.* to give as an effect or a result; provide; yield: *Reading a good book affords real pleasure.* ❏ *VERB* **af·ford·ed, af·ford·ing.**

al·ti·tude (al′tə tüd′), *NOUN.* a high place: *At some altitudes, snow never melts.*

a·maze (ə māz′), *VERB.* to surprise greatly; strike with sudden wonder; astound: *He was amazed at how different the strand of hair looked under a microscope.* ❏ *VERB* **a·mazed, a·maz·ing.**

am·phib·i·an (am fib′ē ən), *NOUN.* any of many cold-blooded animals with backbones and moist, scaleless skins. Their young usually have gills and live in water until they develop lungs for living on land. Frogs, toads, newts, and salamanders are amphibians. ❏ *PLURAL* **am·phib·i·ans.**

an·ces·tor (an′ses′tər), *NOUN.* person from whom you are descended, such as your great-grandparents: *Their ancestors had come to the United States in 1812.* ❏ *PLURAL* **an·ces·tors.**

784

an·cient (ān′shənt), *ADJECTIVE.* of times long past: *In Egypt, we saw the ruins of an ancient temple built 6000 years ago.* (*Ancient* comes from the Latin word *ante* meaning "before.")

an·tic·i·pa·tion (an tis′ə pā′shən), *NOUN.* act of anticipating; looking forward to; expectation: *In anticipation of a cold winter, they cut extra firewood.*

ap·pear (ə pir′), *VERB.* to be seen; come in sight: *One by one, the stars appear.* ❏ *VERB* **ap·peared, ap·pear·ing.**

a·quar·i·um (ə kwâr′ē əm), **1.** *NOUN.* tank or glass bowl in which fish or other water animals and water plants are kept in water. **2.** *NOUN.* building used for showing collections of live fish, water animals, and water plants.

as·tro·naut (as′trə nót), *NOUN.* pilot or member of the crew of a spacecraft. ❏ *PLURAL* **as·tro·nauts.**

astronaut

at·las (at′ləs), *NOUN.* book of maps.

a·vi·a·tion (ā′vē ā′shən), *NOUN.* science or art of operating and navigating aircraft.

a·vi·a·tor (av′ē ā′tər), *NOUN.* person who flies an aircraft; pilot.

a·void (ə void′), *VERB.* to keep away from; keep out of the way of: *We avoided driving through large cities on our trip.* ❏ *VERB* **a·void·ed, a·void·ing.**

awk·ward (ók′wərd), *ADJECTIVE.* not easily managed: *This is an awkward corner to turn.*

Bb

back·board (bak′bôrd′), *NOUN.* in basketball, the flat, elevated surface of glass, plastic, or wood, on which the basket is mounted. Bank shots are bounced off the backboard.

bar·gain (bär′gən), *NOUN.* agreement to trade or exchange; deal: *You can't back out on our bargain.*

a in hat	o in open	sh in she	
ā in age	ō in all	th in thin	
â in care	ô in order	ŦH in then	
ä in far	oi in oil	zh in measure	
e in let	ou in out	ə = a in about	
ē in equal	u in cup	ə = e in taken	
ėr in term	u in put	ə = i in pencil	
i in it	ü in rule	ə = o in lemon	
ī in ice	ch in child	ə = u in circus	
o in hot	ng in long		

785

bawl (ból), *VERB.* to shout or cry out in a noisy way: *a lost calf bawling for its mother.* ❏ *VERB* **bawled, bawl·ing.**

be·wil·der (bi wil′dər), *VERB.* to confuse completely; puzzle: *bewildered by the confusing instructions.* ❏ *VERB* **be·wil·dered, be·wil·der·ing.**

bi·ol·o·gist (bī ol′ə jist), *NOUN.* a scientist who studies living things, including their origins, structures, activities, and distribution.

bluff¹ (bluf), *NOUN.* a high, steep slope or cliff.

bluff¹

bluff² (bluf), *VERB.* to fool or mislead, especially by pretending confidence: *She bluffed the robbers by convincing them that the police were on the way.*

board·ing school (bôr′ding skül′), *NOUN.* school with buildings where the pupils live during the school term.

bow¹ (bou), *VERB.* to bend the head or body in greeting, respect, worship, or obedience: *The people bowed before the queen.* ❏ *VERB* **bowed, bow·ing.**

bow² (bō), **1.** *NOUN.* weapon for shooting arrows. A bow usually consists of a strip of flexible wood bent by a string. **2.** *NOUN.* a looped knot: *The gift had a bow on top.*

bow³ (bou), *NOUN.* the forward part of a ship, boat, or aircraft.

bril·liant (bril′yənt), *ADJECTIVE.* shining brightly; sparkling: *brilliant sunshine.*

brisk (brisk), *ADJECTIVE.* keen; sharp: *A brisk wind was blowing from the north.*

bus·tle (bus′əl), *VERB.* to be noisily busy and in a hurry: *The children were bustling to get ready for the party.* ❏ *VERB* **bus·tled, bus·tling.**

Cc

can·o·py (kan′ə pē), *NOUN.* the uppermost layer of branches in forest trees.

ca·pa·ble (kā′pə bəl), *ADJECTIVE.* having fitness, power, or ability; able; efficient; competent: *He was such a capable student that everyone had great hopes for his future.*

cap·sule (kap′səl), *NOUN.* the enclosed front section of a rocket made to carry instruments, astronauts, etc., into space. In flight, the capsule can separate from the rest of the rocket and go into orbit or be directed back to Earth.

786

car·go (kär′gō), *NOUN.* load of goods carried by a ship, plane, or truck: *The freighter had docked to unload a cargo of wheat.*

ce·les·tial (sə les′chəl), *ADJECTIVE.* of the sky or outer space: *The sun, moon, planets, and stars are celestial bodies.*

chant (chant), *VERB.* to call over and over again: *The football fans chanted, "Go, team, go!"* ❏ *VERB* **chant·ed, chant·ing.**

cho·rus (kôr′əs), *NOUN.* anything spoken or sung all at the same time: *The children greeted the teacher with a chorus of "Good morning."*

cock·pit (kok′pit′), *NOUN.* the place where the pilot sits in an airplane.

co·lo·nel (kėr′nl), *NOUN.* a military rank below general.

con·duct (kon′dukt for noun; kən dukt′ for verb), **1.** *NOUN.* way of acting; behavior thought of as good or bad: *Her conduct was admirable.* **2.** *VERB.* to direct; manage: *The teacher conducted our efforts.* ❏ *VERB* **con·duct·ed, con·duct·ing.**

conduct (def. 2)

con·fide (kən fīd′), *VERB.* to tell as a secret: *He confided his troubles to his brother.* ❏ *VERB* **con·fid·ed, con·fid·ing.**

con·front (kən frunt′), *VERB.* to face boldly; oppose: *Once she confronted her problems, she was able to solve them easily.* ❏ *VERB* **con·front·ed, con·front·ing.**

con·scious (kon′shəs), *ADJECTIVE.* aware of what you are doing; awake: *About five minutes after fainting, he became conscious again.*

con·sist (kən sist′), *VERB.* to be made up; be formed: *A week consists of seven days.* ❏ *VERB* **con·sist·ed, con·sist·ing.**

Con·sti·tu·tion (kon′stə tü′shən), *NOUN.* the written set of fundamental principles by which the United States is governed.

con·sult (kən sult′), *VERB.* to seek information or advice from; refer to: *You can consult travelers, books, or maps for help in planning a trip abroad.* ❏ *VERB* **con·sult·ed, con·sult·ing.**

a in hat	o in open	sh in she	
ā in age	ō in all	th in thin	
â in care	ô in order	ŦH in then	
ä in far	oi in oil	zh in measure	
e in let	ou in out	ə = a in about	
ē in equal	u in cup	ə = e in taken	
ėr in term	u in put	ə = i in pencil	
i in it	ü in rule	ə = o in lemon	
ī in ice	ch in child	ə = u in circus	
o in hot	ng in long		

787

Glossary

con·ti·nent (kon′tə nənt), *NOUN.* one of the seven great masses of land on the Earth. The continents are North America, South America, Europe, Africa, Asia, Australia, and Antarctica. (*Continent* comes from two Latin words, *com* meaning "in" or "together" and *tenere* meaning "to hold.")

con·trap·tion (kən trap′shən), *NOUN.* device or gadget.

con·ver·gence (kən vér′jəns), *NOUN.* act or process of meeting at a point. (*Convergence* comes from two Latin words, *com* meaning "in" or "together" and *vergere* meaning "incline.")

cord (kôrd), *NOUN.* measure of quantity for cut wood, equal to 128 cubic feet. A pile of wood 4 feet wide, 4 feet high, and 8 feet long is a cord.

cow·ard (kou′ərd), *NOUN.* person who lacks courage or is easily made afraid; person who runs from danger, trouble, etc.

coy·o·te (ki ō′tē *or* ki′ōt), *NOUN.* a small, wolflike mammal living in many parts of North America. It is noted for loud howling at night.

cra·dle (krā′dl), *NOUN.* a frame to support weight.

crime (krīm), *NOUN.* activity of criminals; violation of law: *Police forces combat crime.*

crum·ble (krum′bəl), *VERB.* to fall to pieces; decay: *The old wall was crumbling away at the edges.* ❏ *VERB* **crum·bled, crum·bling.**

cur·i·os·i·ty (kyúr′ē os′ə tē), *NOUN.* an eager desire to know: *She satisfied her curiosity about animals by visiting the zoo every week.* (*Curiosity* comes from the Latin word *cure* meaning "care.")

Dd

dan·gle (dang′gəl), *VERB.* to hang and swing loosely. ❏ *VERB* **dan·gled, dan·gling.**

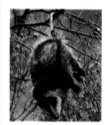

dangle

dap·pled (dap′əld), *ADJECTIVE.* marked with spots; spotted.

dar·ing (dâr′ing), *ADJECTIVE.* bold; fearless; courageous: *Performing on a trapeze high above a crowd is a daring act.*

788

de·ci·pher (di sī′fər), **1.** *VERB.* to make out the meaning of something that is puzzling or not clear: *I can't decipher this poor handwriting.* **2.** *VERB.* to change something in cipher or code to ordinary language; decode. ❏ *VERB* **de·ci·phered, de·ci·pher·ing.**

de·part (di pärt′), *VERB.* to go away; leave: *Your flight departs at 6:15.* ❏ *VERB* **de·part·ed, de·part·ing.** (*Depart* comes from the Latin word *departire* meaning "to divide.")

de·pot (dē′ pō), *NOUN.* a railroad or bus station.

depot

des·ti·na·tion (des′tə nā′shən), *NOUN.* place to which someone or something is going or is being sent.

de·struc·tion (di struk′shən), *NOUN.* great damage; ruin: *The storm left destruction behind it.*

dig·ni·fied (dig′nə fīd), *ADJECTIVE.* having dignity; noble; stately: *The queen has a dignified manner.*

dis·may (dis mā′), *NOUN.* sudden, helpless fear of what is about to happen or what has happened: *I was filled with dismay when the basement began to flood.*

dock (dok), *NOUN.* platform built on the shore or out from the shore; wharf; pier. Ships load and unload beside a dock. ❏ *PLURAL* **docks.**

dol·phin (dol′fən), *NOUN.* any of the numerous sea mammals related to the whale, but smaller. Dolphins have beaklike snouts and remarkable intelligence. ❏ *PLURAL* **dol·phins.**

dor·mi·to·ry (dôr′mə tôr′ē), *NOUN.* a building with many rooms in which people sleep. Many colleges have dormitories for students whose homes are elsewhere.

drab (drab), *ADJECTIVE.* not attractive; dull; monotonous: *the drab houses of the smoky, dingy mining town.*

a in hat	ō in open	sh in she
ā in age	ò in all	th in thin
â in care	ô in order	ŦH in then
ä in far	oi in oil	zh in measure
e in let	ou in out	ə = a in about
ē in equal	u in cup	ə = e in taken
ér in term	ú in put	ə = i in pencil
i in it	ü in rule	ə = o in lemon
ī in ice	ch in child	ə = u in circus
o in hot	ng in long	

789

draft (draft), **1.** *NOUN.* current of air: *I caught cold by sitting in a draft.* **2.** *NOUN.* a rough copy: *She made two drafts of her book report before she handed in the final form.*

drag (drag), **1.** *NOUN.* the force acting on an object in motion, in a direction opposite to the object's motion. It is produced by friction. **2.** *VERB.* to pull or move along heavily or slowly; pull or draw along the ground: *We dragged the heavy crates out of the garage. I dragged along on my sprained ankle.* ❏ *VERB* **dragged, drag·ging.**

drib·ble (drib′əl), *VERB.* to move a ball along by bouncing it or giving it short kicks: *dribble a basketball or soccer ball.* ❏ *VERB* **drib·bled, drib·bling.**

dude (düd), **1.** *NOUN.* in the western parts of the United States and Canada, person raised in the city, especially an easterner who vacations on a ranch. **2.** *NOUN.* guy; fellow (slang). ❏ *PLURAL* **dudes.**

duke (dük), *NOUN.* nobleman of the highest title, ranking just below a prince.

dun·geon (dun′jən), *NOUN.* a dark underground room or cell to keep prisoners in.

dunk (dungk), *VERB.* to shoot a basketball by leaping, so that the hands are above the rim, and throwing the ball down through the netting. ❏ *VERB* **dunked, dunk·ing.**

dwell (dwel), *VERB.* to make your home; live: *He dwells in the city.* ❏ *VERB* **dwelled, dwell·ing.**

Ee

el·e·gant (el′ə gənt), *ADJECTIVE.* having or showing good taste; gracefully and richly refined; beautifully luxurious: *The palace had elegant furnishings.*

em·bar·rass·ment (em bar′əs mənt), *NOUN.* shame; an uneasy feeling: *He blushed in embarrassment at such a silly mistake.*

en·chant (en chant′), *VERB.* to delight greatly; charm: *The music enchanted us all.* ❏ *VERB* **en·chant·ed, en·chant·ing.** ❏ *ADJECTIVE* **en·chant·ing.**

en·coun·ter (en koun′tər), *NOUN.* an unexpected meeting: *The explorers had a surprising encounter with a polar bear.*

encounter

790

en·dur·ance (en dúr′əns), *NOUN.* power to last and to withstand hard wear: *It takes great endurance to run a marathon.*

endurance

en·grave (en grāv′), *VERB.* to cut deeply in; carve in; carve in an artistic way: *The jeweler engraved my initials on the back of the watch.* ❏ *VERB* **en·graved, en·grav·ing.**

es·cape (e skāp′), *VERB.* to get out and away; get free: *The bird escaped from its cage.* ❏ *VERB* **es·caped, es·cap·ing.**

es·cort (e skôrt′), *VERB.* to go with another to give protection, show honor, provide companionship, etc. ❏ *VERB* **es·cort·ed, es·cort·ing.**

etch (ech), **1.** *VERB.* to engrave a drawing or design on a metal plate, glass, etc. **2.** *VERB.* to impress deeply: *Her face was etched in my memory.* ❏ *VERB* **etched, etch·ing.**

ex·e·cute (ek′sə kyüt), *VERB.* to carry out; do: *He executed her instructions.* ❏ *VERB* **ex·e·cut·ed, ex·e·cut·ing.**

ex·hale (eks hāl′), *VERB.* to breathe out: *We exhale air from our lungs.* ❏ *VERB* **ex·haled, ex·hal·ing.**

ex·hib·it (eg zib′it), *NOUN.* display or public showing: *The village art exhibit drew 10,000 visitors.*

ex·ile (eg′zīl *or* ek′sīl), *VERB.* to be forced to leave your country or home, often by law as a punishment; banish: *Napoleon was exiled to Elba.* ❏ *VERB* **ex·iled, ex·il·ing.**

ex·pect (ek spekt′), *VERB.* to think something will probably happen: *They expected the hurricane to change directions.* ❏ *VERB* **ex·pect·ed, ex·pect·ing.**

ex·po·sure (ek spō′zhər), *NOUN.* condition of being without protection; condition of being uncovered.

a in hat	ō in open	sh in she
ā in age	ò in all	th in thin
â in care	ô in order	ŦH in then
ä in far	oi in oil	zh in measure
e in let	ou in out	ə = a in about
ē in equal	u in cup	ə = e in taken
ér in term	ú in put	ə = i in pencil
i in it	ü in rule	ə = o in lemon
ī in ice	ch in child	ə = u in circus
o in hot	ng in long	

791

Glossary

Ff

fas·ci·nate (fas'n āt), *VERB.* to interest greatly; attract very strongly; charm: *She was fascinated by the designs and colors in African art.* ❑ *VERB* **fas·ci·nat·ed, fas·ci·nat·ing.**

fa·vor (fā'vər), *NOUN.* act of kindness: *Will you do me a favor?*

fee·bly (fē'blē), *ADVERB.* weakly; without strength: *She walked feebly when she was first recovering from the flu.*

flex (fleks), *VERB.* to bend: *She flexed her stiff arm slowly.* ❑ *VERB* **flexed, flex·ing.**

flex·i·ble (flek'sə bəl), **1.** *ADJECTIVE.* easily bent; not stiff; bending without breaking: *Leather, rubber, and wire are flexible.* **2.** *ADJECTIVE.* able to change easily to fit different conditions: *My mother works from our home, and her hours are very flexible.*

flexible (def. 1)

for·bid·ding (fər bid'ing), *ADJECTIVE.* causing fear or dislike; looking dangerous or unpleasant: *The coast was rocky and forbidding.*

fore·cast (fôr'kast'), *NOUN.* statement of what is coming; prediction: *What is the weather forecast today?* ❑ *PLURAL* **fore·casts.**

for·ma·tion (fôr mā'shən), *NOUN.* series of layers or deposits of the same kind of rock or mineral. ❑ *PLURAL* **for·ma·tions.**

foul (foul), *VERB.* to make an unfair play against. ❑ *VERB* **fouled, foul·ing.**

fra·grant (frā'grənt), *ADJECTIVE.* having or giving off a pleasing odor; sweet-smelling: *fragrant roses.*

friend·less (frend'les), *ADJECTIVE.* to be without people who know and like you.

frost (frôst), **1.** *NOUN.* a freezing condition; temperature below the point at which water freezes: *Frost came early last winter.* **2.** *NOUN.* moisture frozen on or in a surface; feathery crystals of ice formed when water vapor in the air condenses at a temperature below freezing: *On cold fall mornings, there is frost on the grass.*

frus·tra·tion (fru strā'shən), *NOUN.* a feeling of anger and helplessness, caused by bad luck, failure, or defeat.

fur·i·ous·ly (fyür'ē əs lē), *ADVERB.* with unrestrained energy, speed, etc.

792

Gg

gash (gash), *NOUN.* a long, deep cut or wound.

gen·e·ra·tion (jen'ə rā'shən), **1.** *NOUN.* all people born about the same time. Your parents and their siblings and cousins belong to one generation; you and your siblings and cousins belong to the next generation. **2.** *NOUN.* about thirty years, or the time from the birth of one generation to the birth of the next generation. There are three generations in a century. ❑ *PLURAL* **gen·e·ra·tions.**

gen·ius (jē'nyəs), *NOUN.* person having very great natural power of mind: *Shakespeare was a genius.*

gla·cier (glā'shər), *NOUN.* a great mass of ice moving very slowly down a mountain, along a valley, or over a land area. Glaciers are formed from snow on high ground wherever winter snowfall exceeds summer melting for many years.

gleam (glēm), *VERB.* to flash or beam with light: *The car's headlights gleamed through the rain.* ❑ *VERB* **gleamed, gleam·ing.**

glid·er (gli'dər), *NOUN.* aircraft without an engine. Rising air currents keep it up in the air.

glider

glimpse (glimps), **1.** *NOUN.* a short, quick view or look: *I caught a glimpse of the falls as our train went by.* **2.** *NOUN.* a short, faint appearance: *There was a glimpse of truth in what they said.* ❑ *PLURAL* **glimp·ses.**

glint (glint), *NOUN.* a gleam; flash: *The glint in her eye showed that she was angry.*

glo·ri·ous (glôr'ē əs), *ADJECTIVE.* magnificent; splendid: *a glorious day.* (*Glorious* comes from the Latin word *gloria* meaning "praise.")

grand (grand), *ADJECTIVE.* excellent; very good: *We had a grand time at the party last night.*

gran·ite (gran'it), *ADJECTIVE.* made from a very hard gray or pink rock that is formed when lava cools slowly underground: *a granite countertop.*

griz·zly (griz'lē), **1.** *ADJECTIVE.* grayish; gray. **2.** *NOUN.* grizzly bear; a large, gray or brownish gray bear of western North America.

a in hat	ȯ in open	sh in she
ā in age	ȯ in all	th in thin
ã in care	ô in order	ᴛʜ in then
ä in far	oi in oil	zh in measure
e in let	ou in out	ə = a in about
ē in equal	u in cup	ə = e in taken
ėr in term	ü in put	ə = i in pencil
i in it	ü in rule	ə = o in lemon
ī in ice	ch in child	ə = u in circus
o in hot	ng in long	

793

Hh

hang·ar (hang'ər), *NOUN.* building for storing aircraft. ❑ *PLURAL* **hang·ars.**

hatch¹ (hach), **1.** *VERB.* to come out of an egg: *One of the chickens hatched today.* **2.** *VERB.* to keep an egg or eggs warm until the young come out: *The heat of the sun hatches turtles' eggs.*

hatch² (hach), *NOUN.* a trapdoor covering an opening in an aircraft's or ship's deck.

heave (hēv), **1.** *VERB.* to lift with force or effort: *The heavy cargo plane heaved off the runway.* **2.** *VERB.* to rise and fall alternately: *The waves heaved in the storm.* ❑ *VERB* **heaved, heav·ing.**

her·mit (hèr'mit), *NOUN.* person who goes away from others and lives alone.

hi·er·o·glyph (hī'ər ə glif), *NOUN.* picture, character, or symbol standing for a word, idea, or sound. The ancient Egyptians used hieroglyphics instead of an alphabet like ours. ❑ *PLURAL* **hi·er·o·glyphs.**

home·land (hōm'land'), *NOUN.* country that is your home; your native land.

hoop (hüp *or* hup), *NOUN.* ring; round, flat band: *a hoop for embroidery, a basketball hoop.*

ho·ri·zon (hə rī'zn), *NOUN.* line where the Earth and sky seem to meet; skyline. You cannot see beyond the horizon.

howl·ing (hou'ling), *ADJECTIVE.* very great: *a howling success.*

hum·ble (hum'bəl), *ADJECTIVE.* not proud; modest: *to be humble in spite of success.*

hyp·no·tize (hip'nə tīz), *VERB.* to put someone into a state resembling deep sleep, but more active, in which the person acts according to the suggestions of the person who brought about the condition. ❑ *VERB* **hyp·no·tized, hyp·no·tiz·ing.**

Ii

ice·berg (īs'bėrg'), *NOUN.* a large mass of ice, detached from a glacier and floating in the sea. About 90 percent of its mass is below the surface of the water. ❑ *PLURAL* **ice·bergs.**

iceberg

794

---

im·mense (i mens'), *ADJECTIVE.* very large; huge; vast: *An ocean is an immense body of water.*

im·pact (im'pakt), *NOUN.* action of striking one thing against another; collision: *The impact of the heavy stone against the windowpane shattered the glass.*

im·pres·sive (im pres'iv), *ADJECTIVE.* able to have a strong effect on the mind or feelings; able to influence deeply.

in·con·sol·a·ble (in'kən sō'lə bəl), *ADJECTIVE.* not able to be comforted; brokenhearted: *The girl was inconsolable because her kitten was lost.*

in·fer·i·or (in fir'ē ər), *ADJECTIVE.* not very good; below most others; low in quality: *an inferior grade of coffee.*

in·jus·tice (in jus'tis), *NOUN.* lack of justice, fairness, lawfulness: *We were angry at the injustice of the new rule.*

in·land (in'lənd), *ADVERB.* in or toward the interior: *He traveled inland from New York to Chicago.*

Jj

jer·sey (jèr'zē), *NOUN.* shirt that is pulled over the head, made of soft, knitted cloth: *Members of the hockey team wear red jerseys.*

Ll

la·goon (lə gün'), *NOUN.* pond or small lake, especially one connected with a larger body of water.

land·lord (land'lôrd'), *NOUN.* person who owns buildings or land that is rented to others.

las·so (la' sō), *VERB.* to catch with a long rope with a loop on one end. ❑ *VERB* **las·soed, las·so·ing.**

lei·sure·ly (lē'zhər lē), *ADVERB.* without hurry; taking plenty of time: *He walked leisurely across the bridge.*

link (lingk), *NOUN.* anything that joins or connects, as a loop of a chain does: *a link between his love of art and his career.*

liz·ard (liz'ərd), *NOUN.* any of many reptiles with long bodies and tails, movable eyelids, and usually four legs. Some lizards have no legs and look much like snakes. Iguanas, chameleons, and horned toads are lizards. ❑ *PLURAL* **liz·ards.**

a in hat	ȯ in open	sh in she
ā in age	ȯ in all	th in thin
ã in care	ô in order	ᴛʜ in then
ä in far	oi in oil	zh in measure
e in let	ou in out	ə = a in about
ē in equal	u in cup	ə = e in taken
ėr in term	ü in put	ə = i in pencil
i in it	ü in rule	ə = o in lemon
ī in ice	ch in child	ə = u in circus
o in hot	ng in long	

795

long (lòng), **1.** *ADJECTIVE.* measuring a great distance from end to end: *A year is a long time.* **2.** *VERB.* to wish very much; desire greatly: *long to see a good friend.* ❑ *VERB* **longed, long•ing.**

loom (lüm), *VERB.* to appear dimly or vaguely as a large, threatening shape: *A large iceberg loomed through the thick fog.* ❑ *VERB* **loomed, loom•ing.**

lull (lul), *VERB.* to soothe with sounds or caresses; cause to sleep: *The soft music lulled me to sleep.* ❑ *VERB* **lulled, lull•ing.**

lum•ber•jack (lum′bər jak′), *NOUN.* person whose work is cutting down trees and sending the logs to the sawmill; woodsman; logger.

lu•nar (lü′nər), *ADJECTIVE.* of, like, or about the moon: *a lunar landscape.*

lurk (lėrk), *VERB.* to move about in a secret and sly manner: *Several people were seen lurking near the house before it was robbed.* ❑ *VERB* **lurked, lurk•ing.**

Mm

ma•gi•cian (mə jish′ən), *NOUN.* person who entertains by art or skill of creating illusions, especially a sleight of hand: *The magician pulled not one, but three rabbits out of his hat!*

maj•es•ty (maj′ə stē), *NOUN.* title used in speaking to or of a king, queen, emperor, empress, etc.: *Your Majesty, His Majesty, Her Majesty.*

man•u•al (man′yü əl), **1.** *ADJECTIVE.* done with the hands: *Digging a trench with a shovel is manual labor.* **2.** *NOUN.* a small book that helps its readers understand and use something; handbook: *A manual came with my pocket calculator.*

mar•vel (mär′vəl), *VERB.* to be filled with wonder; be astonished: *She marveled at the beautiful sunset.* ❑ *VERB* **mar•veled, mar•vel•ing.**

mas•sive (mas′iv), *ADJECTIVE.* big and heavy; bulky: *a massive boulder.*

me•chan•i•cal (mə kan′ə kəl), *ADJECTIVE.* like a machine; automatic; without expression: *The performance was very mechanical.*

me•mo•ri•al (mə môr′ē əl), *ADJECTIVE.* helping people to remember some person, thing, or event: *memorial services.*

memorial

796

me•squite (me skēt′), *ADJECTIVE.* any of several trees or bushes common in the southwestern United States and Mexico, which often grow in dense clumps or thickets. Mesquite pods furnish a valuable food for cattle. The wood is used in grilling food.

mi•grate (mī′grāt), *VERB.* to go from one region to another with the change in the seasons: *Most birds migrate to warmer countries in the winter.* ❑ *VERB* **mi•grat•ed, mi•grat•ing.**

migrate

min•i•a•ture (min′ē ə chùr or min′ə chər), *NOUN.* anything represented on a small scale: *In the museum, there is a miniature of the famous ship.* ❑ *PLURAL* **min•i•a•tures.**

min•is•ter (min′ə stər), *NOUN.* member of the clergy; spiritual guide; pastor.

mir•a•cle (mir′ə kəl), *NOUN.* a wonderful happening that is contrary to, or independent of, the known laws of nature: *His family considered his complete recovery from the accident to be a miracle.*

mod•ule (moj′ül), *NOUN.* a self-contained unit or system within a larger system, often designed for a particular function: *The lunar module circled the moon.*

mon•u•ment (mon′yə mənt), *NOUN.* something set up to honor a person or an event. A monument may be a building, pillar, arch, statue, tomb, or stone.

monument

mu•tu•al (myü′chü əl), *ADJECTIVE.* done, said, felt, etc., by each toward the other; both given and received: *They had mutual affection for each other.*

a in hat	ō in open	sh in she
ā in age	ò in all	th in thin
â in care	ô in order	ᴛʜ in then
ä in far	oi in oil	zh in measure
e in let	ou in out	ə = a in about
ē in equal	u in cup	ə = e in taken
ėr in term	ù in put	ə = i in pencil
i in it	ü in rule	ə = o in lemon
ī in ice	ch in child	ə = u in circus
o in hot	ng in long	

797

Nn

nat•ur•al•ist (nach′ər ə list), *NOUN.* person who makes a study of living things.

nau•ti•cal (nô′tə kəl), *ADJECTIVE.* of or about ships, sailors, or navigation.

nav•i•ga•tion (nav′ə gā′shən), *NOUN.* skill or process of finding a ship's or aircraft's position and course.

no•ble (nō′bəl), *ADJECTIVE.* high and great by birth, rank, or title; showing greatness of mind; good: *a noble person.*

nour•ish•ing (nėr′ish ing), **1.** *ADJECTIVE.* keeping well-fed and healthy; producing health and growth: *a nourishing diet.* **2.** *ADJECTIVE.* supporting, encouraging.

nu•mer•ous (nü′mər əs), *ADJECTIVE.* very many: *The child asked numerous questions.*

Oo

oath (ōth), *NOUN.* a solemn promise: *The oath bound him to secrecy.*

of•fend (ə fend′), *VERB.* to hurt the feelings of someone; make angry; displease; pain: *My friend was offended by my laughter.* ❑ *VERB* **of•fend•ed, of•fend•ing.**

out•spo•ken (out′spō′kən), *ADJECTIVE.* not reserved; frank: *an outspoken person.*

Pp

pal•ette (pal′it), **1.** *NOUN.* a thin board, usually oval or oblong, with a thumb hole at one end, used by painters to lay and mix colors on. **2.** *NOUN.* set of colors used by a painter. ❑ *PLURAL* **pal•ettes.**

pan•to•mime (pan′tə mīm), *VERB.* to express by gestures: *They pantomimed being hungry by pointing to their mouths and their stomachs.* ❑ *VERB* **pan•to•mimed, pan•to•mim•ing.**

pantomime

par•lor (pär′lər), **1.** *NOUN.* formerly, a room for receiving or entertaining guests; sitting room. **2.** *NOUN.* room or set of rooms used for various business purposes; shop: *a beauty parlor, an ice cream parlor.*

pay•roll (pā′rōl′), *NOUN.* list of persons to be paid and the amount that each one is to receive.

798

peas•ant (pez′nt), *NOUN.* farmer of the working class in Europe, Asia, and Latin America.

pe•cul•iar (pi kyü′lyər), *ADJECTIVE.* strange; odd; unusual: *It was peculiar that the fish market had no fish last Friday.*

plush (plush), *ADJECTIVE.* luxurious; expensive; stylish: *a plush office.*

pol•i•tics (pol′ə tiks), *NOUN SINGULAR OR PLURAL.* the work of government; management of public business: *Our senior senator has been engaged in politics for many years.*

pol•len (pol′ən), *NOUN.* a fine, yellowish powder released from the anthers of flowers. Grains of pollen carried by insects, wind, etc., to the pistils of flowers fertilize the flowers.

pol•li•nate (pol′ə nāt), *VERB.* to carry pollen from anthers to pistils; bring pollen to. Flowers are pollinated by bees, bats, birds, wind, etc. ❑ *VERB* **pol•li•nat•ed, pol•li•nat•ing.**

por•ridge (pôr′ij), *NOUN.* food made of oatmeal or other grain boiled in water or milk until it thickens.

pos•i•tive (poz′ə tiv), *ADJECTIVE.* permitting no question; without doubt; sure: *We have positive evidence that the Earth moves around the sun.*

po•ten•tial (pə ten′shəl), *NOUN.* something possible: *a potential for danger.*

prair•ie (prâr′ē), **1.** *NOUN.* a large area of level or rolling land with grass but few or no trees, especially such an area making up much of central North America. **2.** *NOUN.* (regional) a wide, open space.

pre•serve (pri zėrv′), *VERB.* to keep from harm or change; keep safe; protect: *Good nutrition helps preserve your health.* ❑ *VERB* **pre•served, pre•serv•ing.**

preserve— fly preserved in amber

pride•ful (prīd′ fəl), *ADJECTIVE.* haughty; having too high an opinion of oneself.

a in hat	ō in open	sh in she
ā in age	ò in all	th in thin
â in care	ô in order	ᴛʜ in then
ä in far	oi in oil	zh in measure
e in let	ou in out	ə = a in about
ē in equal	u in cup	ə = e in taken
ėr in term	ù in put	ə = i in pencil
i in it	ü in rule	ə = o in lemon
ī in ice	ch in child	ə = u in circus
o in hot	ng in long	

799

Glossary

pri•or•i•ty (pri ôr′ə tē) *NOUN.* something given attention before anything else: *The young couple's first priority was to find a pleasant house.*

pro•mote (prə mōt′), *VERB.* to raise in rank, condition, or importance: *Pupils who pass the test will be promoted to the next higher grade.* ❑ *VERB* **pro•mot•ed, pro•mot•ing.**

pul•pit (púl′pit), *NOUN.* platform or raised structure in a church from which the minister preaches.

pulse (puls), **1.** *NOUN.* the regular beating of the arteries caused by the rush of blood into them after each contraction of the heart. By feeling a person's pulse in the artery of the wrist, you can count the number of times the heart beats each minute. **2.** *NOUN.* any regular, measured beat: *the pulse in music.* ❑ *PLURAL* **pul•ses.**

Qq

quaint (kwānt), *ADJECTIVE.* strange or odd in an interesting, pleasing, or amusing way: *Many old photographs seem quaint to us today.*

quar•an•tine (kwôr′ən tēn′ or kwär′ən tēn′), *NOUN.* detention, isolation, and other measures taken to prevent the spread of an infectious disease.

quiv•er (kwiv′ər), *VERB.* to shake; shiver; tremble: *The dog quivered with excitement.* ❑ *VERB* **quiv•ered, quiv•er•ing.**

Rr

re•call (ri kôl′), *VERB.* to call back to mind; remember: *I can recall stories told to me when I was a small child.* ❑ *VERB* **re•called, re•call•ing.**

re•cruit•er (ri krüt′ər), *NOUN.* a person who gets new members, who gets people to join or come: *The college recruiter attended our football game to watch our quarterback.*

ref•er•ence (ref′ər əns), *ADJECTIVE.* used for information or help: *The reference librarian can find the article that you need.*

reign (rān), **1.** *VERB.* to rule: *A king reigns over his kingdom.* **2.** *VERB.* to exist everywhere; prevail: *On a still night, silence reigns.* ❑ *VERB* **reigned, reign•ing.**

re•mote (ri mōt′), *ADJECTIVE.* out of the way; secluded.

rep•tile (rep′til), *NOUN.* any of many cold-blooded animals with backbones and lungs, usually covered with horny plates or scales. Snakes, lizards, turtles, alligators, and crocodiles are reptiles. Dinosaurs were reptiles. ❑ *PLURAL* **rep•tiles.**

re•seat (rē sēt′), *VERB.* to sit again. ❑ *VERB* **re•seat•ed, re•seat•ing.**

re•sem•blance (ri zem′bləns), *NOUN.* similar appearance; likeness: *Twins often show great resemblance.*

res•er•va•tion (rez′ər vā′shən), **1.** *NOUN.* arrangement to have a room, a seat, etc., held in advance for your use later on: *make a reservation for a room in a hotel.* **2.** *NOUN.* land set aside by the government for a special purpose: *an Indian reservation.*

res•er•voir (rez′ər vwär), *NOUN.* place where water is collected and stored for use: *This reservoir supplies the entire city.*

re•sist•ance (ri zis′təns), *NOUN.* thing or act that resists; opposing force; opposition: *Air resistance makes a feather fall more slowly than a pin.*

re•spon•si•bil•i•ty (ri spon′sə bil′ə tē), *NOUN.* the act or fact of taking care of someone or something; obligation: *We agreed to share responsibility for planning the party.*

rift (rift), *NOUN.* a split; break; crack: *The sun shone through a rift in the clouds.*

rille (ril), *NOUN.* a long, narrow valley on the surface of the moon.

rim (rim), *NOUN.* an edge, border, or margin on or around anything: *the rim of a wheel, the rim of a glass.*

riv•er•bed (riv′ər bed′), *NOUN.* channel in which a river flows or used to flow.

round•up (round′up′), *NOUN.* act of driving or bringing cattle together from long distances.

rud•der (rud′ər), *NOUN.* a flat piece of wood or metal hinged vertically to the rear end of an aircraft and used to steer it.

rug•ged (rug′id), *ADJECTIVE.* covered with rough edges; rough and uneven: *rugged ground.*

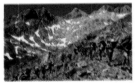

rugged

ruin (rü′ən), *NOUN.* often ruins, *PL.* what is left after a building, wall, etc., has fallen to pieces: *the ruins of an ancient city.* (*Ruin* comes from the Latin word *ruina* meaning "a collapse.")

a in hat	ō in open	sh in she
ā in age	ó in all	th in thin
â in care	ô in order	ᴛʜ in then
ä in far	oi in oil	zh in measure
e in let	ou in out	ə = a in about
ē in equal	u in cup	ə = e in taken
ėr in term	ú in put	ə = i in pencil
i in it	ü in rule	ə = o in lemon
i in ice	ch in child	ə = u in circus
o in hot	ng in long	

rum•ble (rum′bəl), *VERB.* to make a deep, heavy, continuous sound: *Thunder was rumbling in the distance.* ❑ *VERB* **rum•bled, rum•bling.**

runt (runt), *NOUN.* animal, person, or plant that is smaller than the usual size. If used about a person, *runt* is sometimes considered offensive.

Ss

sal•a•man•der (sal′ə man′dər), *NOUN.* any of numerous animals shaped like lizards, but related to frogs and toads. Salamanders have moist, smooth skin and live in water or in damp places. ❑ *PLURAL* **sal•a•man•ders.**

sas•sy (sas′ē), *ADJECTIVE.* lively; spirited: *a sassy attitude.*

scan (skan), *VERB.* to glance at; look over hastily. ❑ *VERB* **scanned, scan•ning.**

scent (sent), *NOUN.* a smell: *The scent of roses filled the air.*

schol•ar (skol′ər), *NOUN.* a learned person; person having much knowledge: *The professor was a famous scholar.* ❑ *PLURAL* **schol•ars.** (*Scholar* comes from the Greek word *schol* meaning "discussion.")

sculp•ture (skulp′chər), **1.** *NOUN.* the art of making figures by carving, modeling, casting, etc. Sculpture includes the cutting of statues from blocks of marble, stone, or wood, casting in bronze, and modeling in clay or wax. **2.** *NOUN.* sculptured work; piece of such work. ❑ *PLURAL* **sculp•tures.**

sculpture (def. 2)

sea•coast (sē′kōst′), *NOUN.* land along the ocean or sea; seaboard: *the seacoast of Maine.*

seek•er (sēk′ər), *NOUN.* one who tries to find; one who searches: *That judge is a seeker of truth.*

se•lect (si lekt′), *VERB.* to pick out; choose: *Select the book you want.* ❑ *VERB* **se•lect•ed, se•lect•ing.**

shat•ter (shat′ər), *VERB.* to break into pieces suddenly: *A stone shattered the window.* ❑ *VERB* **shat•tered, shat•ter•ing.**

shield (shēld), *VERB.* to protect; defend: *They shielded me from unjust punishment.* ❑ *VERB* **shield•ed, shield•ing.**

shim•mer (shim′ər), *VERB.* to gleam or shine faintly: *Both the sea and the sand shimmered in the moonlight.* ❑ *VERB* **shim•mered, shim•mer•ing.** ❑ *ADJECTIVE* **shim•mer•ing.**

shriek (shrēk), *VERB.* to make a loud, sharp, shrill sound. People sometimes shriek because of terror, anger, pain, or amusement. ❑ *VERB* **shrieked, shriek•ing.**

sil•hou•ette (sil′ü et′), *NOUN.* a dark image outlined against a lighter background: *Silhouettes of skyscrapers could be seen against the moonlit sky.*

silhouette

slith•er (slirH′ər), *VERB.* to go with a sliding motion: *The snake slithered into the weeds.* ❑ *VERB* **slith•ered, slith•er•ing.**

slope (slōp), *NOUN.* any line, surface, land, etc., that goes up or down at an angle: *If you roll a ball up a slope, it will roll down again.* ❑ *PLURAL* **slopes.**

so•ci•e•ty (sə sī′ə tē), **1.** *NOUN.* the people of any particular time or place: *twentieth-century society, American society.* **2.** *NOUN.* company; companionship: *I enjoy their society.*

sol•emn•ly (sol′əm lē), *ADVERB.* seriously; earnestly; with dignity.

so•lo (sō′lō), **1.** *ADJECTIVE.* without a partner, teacher, etc.; alone: *The flying student made her first solo flight.* **2.** *ADVERB.* on one's own, alone: *to fly solo.*

spe•cies (spē′shēz), *NOUN.* a set of related living things that all have certain characteristics. Spearmint is a species of mint.

spec•i•men (spes′ə mən), *NOUN.* one of a group or class taken to show what the others are like; sample: *He collects specimens of all kinds of rocks and minerals.*

speech•less (spēch′lis), *ADJECTIVE.* not able to talk: *He was speechless with wonder.*

a in hat	ō in open	sh in she
ā in age	ó in all	th in thin
â in care	ô in order	ᴛʜ in then
ä in far	oi in oil	zh in measure
e in let	ou in out	ə = a in about
ē in equal	u in cup	ə = e in taken
ėr in term	ú in put	ə = i in pencil
i in it	ü in rule	ə = o in lemon
i in ice	ch in child	ə = u in circus
o in hot	ng in long	

Glossary

spell·bound (spel′bound′), *ADJECTIVE*. too interested to move; fascinated: *The children were spellbound by the circus performance.*

sphere (sfir), *NOUN*. ball or globe. The sun, moon, Earth, and stars are spheres.

splen·dor (splen′dər), *NOUN*. magnificent show; glory.

spur (spėr), *NOUN*. a metal point or pointed wheel, worn on a rider's boot heel for urging a horse on. ❑ *PLURAL* **spurs**.

stag·ger (stag′ər), *VERB*. to become unsteady; waver: *The troops staggered because of their exhaustion.* ❑ *VERB* **stag·gered, stag·ger·ing**.

stall (stȯl), *VERB*. to stop or bring to a standstill, usually against your wish: *The engine stalled.* ❑ *VERB* **stalled, stall·ing**.

steam·ship (stēm′ship′), *NOUN*. ship moved by engines that work by the action of steam under pressure.

stern¹ (stėrn), *ADJECTIVE*. harshly firm; hard; strict: *a stern parent.*

stern² (stėrn), *NOUN*. the rear part of a ship or boat.

still (stil), **1.** *ADJECTIVE*. staying in the same position or at rest; without motion; motionless: *to stand or lie still. The lake is still today.* **2.** *VERB*. to make or become calm or quiet: *The father stilled the crying baby.* ❑ *VERB* **stilled, stil·ling**.

stump (stump), *VERB*. to puzzle: *The riddle stumped me.* ❑ *VERB* **stumped, stump·ing**.

sub·merge (səb mėrj′), *VERB*. to put under water; cover with water: *A big wave momentarily submerged us.* ❑ *VERB* **sub·merged, sub·merg·ing**.

sum·mon (sum′ən), *VERB*. to stir to action; rouse: *We were summoning our courage before entering the deserted house.* ❑ *VERB* **sum·moned, sum·mon·ing**.

sur·face (sėr′fis), **1.** *NOUN*. the top of the ground or soil, or of a body of water or other liquid: *The stone sank beneath the surface of the water.* **2.** *NOUN*. the outward appearance: *He seems rough, but you will find him very kind below the surface.* **3.** *VERB*. to rise to the surface: *The submarine surfaced.*

surge (sėrj), *NOUN*. a swelling motion; sweep or rush, especially of waves: *Our boat was upset by a surge.*

sus·pi·cious·ly (sə spish′əs lē), *ADVERB*. without trust; doubtfully.

swat (swät), *VERB*. to hit sharply or violently: *swat a fly.* ❑ *VERB* **swat·ted, swat·ting**.

Tt

taunt (tȯnt), *VERB*. to jeer at; mock; reproach: *My classmates taunted me for being the teacher's pet.* ❑ *VERB* **taunt·ed, taunt·ing**.

teem (tēm), *VERB*. to be full of; abound; swarm: *The swamp teemed with mosquitoes.* ❑ *VERB* **teemed, teem·ing**.

tem·ple (tem′pəl), *NOUN*. building used for the service or worship of God or gods. ❑ *PLURAL* **tem·ples**. (*Temple* comes from the Latin word *templum* meaning "temple.")

ter·race (ter′is), *VERB*. to form into flat, level land with steep sides; terraces are often made in hilly areas to create more space for farming. ❑ *VERB* **ter·raced, ter·rac·ing**. (*Terrace* comes from the Latin word *terra* meaning "earth, land.")

terrace

ter·ror (ter′ər), *NOUN*. great fear: *The dog has a terror of thunder.*

thick·et (thik′it), *NOUN*. bushes or small trees growing close together: *We crawled into the thicket and hid.* ❑ *PLURAL* **thick·ets**.

tim·id (tim′id), *ADJECTIVE*. easily frightened; shy: *The timid child was afraid of the dark.*

tor·rent (tȯr′ənt), *NOUN*. a violent, rushing stream of water: *The mountain torrent dashed over the rock.* (*Torrent* comes from the Latin word *torrentum* meaning "boiling.")

torrent

tow·er·ing (tou′ər ing), **1.** *ADJECTIVE*. very high: *a towering mountain peak.* **2.** *ADJECTIVE*. very great: *Developing a polio vaccine was a towering achievement.*

a in hat	ō in open	sh in she
ā in age	ȯ in all	th in thin
â in care	ô in order	ᴛʜ in then
ä in far	oi in oil	zh in measure
e in let	ou in out	ə = a in about
ē in equal	u in cup	ə = e in taken
ėr in term	ů in put	ə = i in pencil
i in it	ü in rule	ə = o in lemon
ī in ice	ch in child	ə = u in circus
o in hot	ng in long	

trans·late (tran slāt′ or tranz lāt′), *VERB*. to change from one language into another: *translate a book from French into English.* ❑ *VERB* **trans·lat·ed, trans·lat·ing**. (*Translate* comes from the Latin word *trans*, which means "across, through, or behind.")

trans·mis·sion (tran smish′ən or tranz mish′ən), *NOUN*. passage of electromagnetic waves from a transmitter to a receiver: *When transmission is good, even foreign radio stations can be heard.*

treas·ur·y (trezh′ər ē), *NOUN*. money owned; funds: *We voted to pay for the party out of the club treasury.*

trench (trench), *NOUN*. any ditch; deep furrow: *to dig a trench for a pipe.*

tri·umph (trī′umf), *NOUN*. victory; success: *The exploration of outer space is a great triumph of modern science.*

trop·i·cal (trop′ə kəl), *ADJECTIVE*. of or like the regions 23.45 degrees north and south of the equator where the sun can shine directly overhead: *tropical heat.*

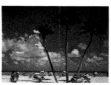

tropical

trudge (truj), *VERB*. to walk wearily or with effort. *We trudged up the hill.* ❑ *VERB* **trudged, trudg·ing**.

twang (twang), *VERB*. to make or cause to make a sharp, ringing sound: *The banjos twanged.* ❑ *VERB* **twanged, twang·ing**.

Uu

un·be·liev·a·ble (un′bi lē′və bəl), *ADJECTIVE*. incredible; hard to think of as true or real: *an unbelievable lie.*

un·cov·er (un kuv′ər), *VERB*. to make known; reveal; expose: *The reporter uncovered a scandal.* ❑ *VERB* **un·cov·ered, un·cov·er·ing**.

un·ex·plain·a·ble (un ek splān′ə bəl), *ADJECTIVE*. not able to be explained; mysterious.

Vv

vain (vān), *ADJECTIVE*. having too much pride in your looks, ability, etc.: *a good-looking but vain person.*

van·ish (van′ish), *VERB*. to disappear, especially suddenly: *The sun vanished behind a cloud.* ❑ *VERB* **van·ished, van·ish·ing**.

ve·hi·cle (vē′ə kəl), *NOUN*. device for carrying people or things, such as a car, bus, airplane, etc. Cars and trucks are motor vehicles. Rockets are space vehicles.

ven·ture (ven′chər), *VERB*. to dare to come or go: *We ventured out on the thin ice and almost fell through.* ❑ *VERB* **ven·tured, ven·tur·ing**.

Ww

wharf (wȯrf), *NOUN*. platform built on the shore or out from the shore, beside which ships can load and unload. ❑ *PLURAL* **wharves**.

wil·der·ness (wil′dər nis), *NOUN*. a wild, uncultivated region with few or no people living in it.

wilderness

with·stand (wiᴛʜ stand′), *VERB*. to stand against; hold out against; resist; endure: *These heavy shoes will withstand much hard wear.* ❑ *VERB* **with·stood, with·stand·ing**.

won·drous (wun′drəs), *ADJECTIVE*. wonderful; marvelous, remarkable.

wreck·age (rek′ij), *NOUN*. what is left behind after the destruction of a motor vehicle, ship, building, train, or aircraft: *The hurricane left behind much wreckage.*

Yy

yearn (yėrn), *VERB*. to feel a longing or desire; desire earnestly: *I yearned for home.* ❑ *VERB* **yearned, yearn·ing**.

a in hat	ō in open	sh in she
ā in age	ȯ in all	th in thin
â in care	ô in order	ᴛʜ in then
ä in far	oi in oil	zh in measure
e in let	ou in out	ə = a in about
ē in equal	u in cup	ə = e in taken
ėr in term	ů in put	ə = i in pencil
i in it	ü in rule	ə = o in lemon
ī in ice	ch in child	ə = u in circus
o in hot	ng in long	

English/Spanish Selection Vocabulary List

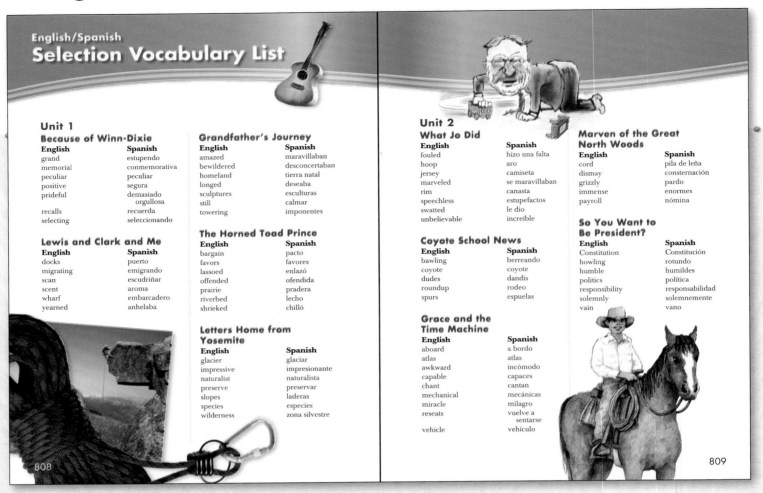

English/Spanish Selection Vocabulary List

Unit 1

Because of Winn-Dixie

English	Spanish
grand	estupendo
memorial	conmemorativa
peculiar	peculiar
positive	segura
prideful	demasiado orgullosa
recalls	recuerda
selecting	seleccionando

Lewis and Clark and Me

English	Spanish
docks	puerto
migrating	emigrando
scan	escudriñar
scent	aroma
wharf	embarcadero
yearned	anhelaba

Grandfather's Journey

English	Spanish
amazed	maravillaban
bewildered	desconcertaban
homeland	tierra natal
longed	deseaba
sculptures	esculturas
still	calmar
towering	imponentes

The Horned Toad Prince

English	Spanish
bargain	pacto
favors	favores
lassoed	enlazó
offended	ofendida
prairie	pradera
riverbed	lecho
shrieked	chilló

Letters Home from Yosemite

English	Spanish
glacier	glaciar
impressive	impresionante
naturalist	naturalista
preserve	preservar
slopes	laderas
species	especies
wilderness	zona silvestre

Unit 2

What Jo Did

English	Spanish
fouled	hizo una falta
hoop	aro
jersey	camiseta
marveled	se maravillaban
rim	canasta
speechless	estupefactos
swatted	le dio
unbelievable	increíble

Coyote School News

English	Spanish
bawling	berreando
coyote	coyote
dudes	dandis
roundup	rodeo
spurs	espuelas

Grace and the Time Machine

English	Spanish
aboard	a bordo
atlas	atlas
awkward	incómodo
capable	capaces
chant	cantan
mechanical	mecánicas
miracle	milagro
reseats	vuelve a sentarse
vehicle	vehículo

Marven of the Great North Woods

English	Spanish
cord	pila de leña
dismay	consternación
grizzly	pardo
immense	enormes
payroll	nómina

So You Want to Be President?

English	Spanish
Constitution	Constitución
howling	rotundo
humble	humildes
politics	política
responsibility	responsabilidad
solemnly	solemnemente
vain	vano

808

809

Unit 3

The Stranger

English	Spanish
draft	corriente de aire
etched	grabadas
fascinated	fascinaba
frost	escarcha
parlor	salón
terror	terror
timid	tímido

Adelina's Whales

English	Spanish
biologist	bióloga
bluff	despeñadero
lagoon	laguna
massive	inmensas
rumbling	retumbante
tropical	tropical

How Night Came from the Sea

English	Spanish
brilliant	brillante
chorus	coro
coward	cobarde
gleamed	relucía
shimmering	centelleante

Eye of the Storm

English	Spanish
destruction	destrucción
expected	esperaba
forecasts	pronósticos
inland	tierra adentro
shatter	hace añicos
surge	oleada

The Great Kapok Tree

English	Spanish
canopy	copas (de los árboles)
dangle	colgar
dappled	salpicada
fragrant	fragante
pollen	polen
pollinate	polimizar
slithered	se deslizó
wondrous	maravilloso

Unit 4

The Houdini Box

English	Spanish
appeared	apareció
bustling	bulliciosa
crumbled	se desintegró
escape	escapar
magician	mago
monument	monumento
vanished	desapareció

Encantado: Pink Dolphin of the Amazon

English	Spanish
aquarium	acuario
dolphins	delfines
enchanted	encantado
flexible	flexibles
glimpses	vistazos fugaces
pulses	impulsos
surface	superficie

The King in the Kitchen

English	Spanish
duke	duque
dungeon	mazmorra
furiously	furiosamente
genius	genio
majesty	majestad
noble	noble
peasant	campesino
porridge	gachas de avena

Seeker of Knowledge

English	Spanish
ancient	antiguo
link	conexión
scholars	eruditos
seeker	buscador
temple	templo
translate	traducir
triumph	triunfo
uncover	descubrir

Encyclopedia Brown and the Case of the Slippery Salamander

English	Spanish
amphibians	anfibios
crime	crimen
exhibit	exposición
lizards	lagartos
reference	referencia
reptiles	reptiles
salamanders	salamandras
stumped	perplejo

810

811

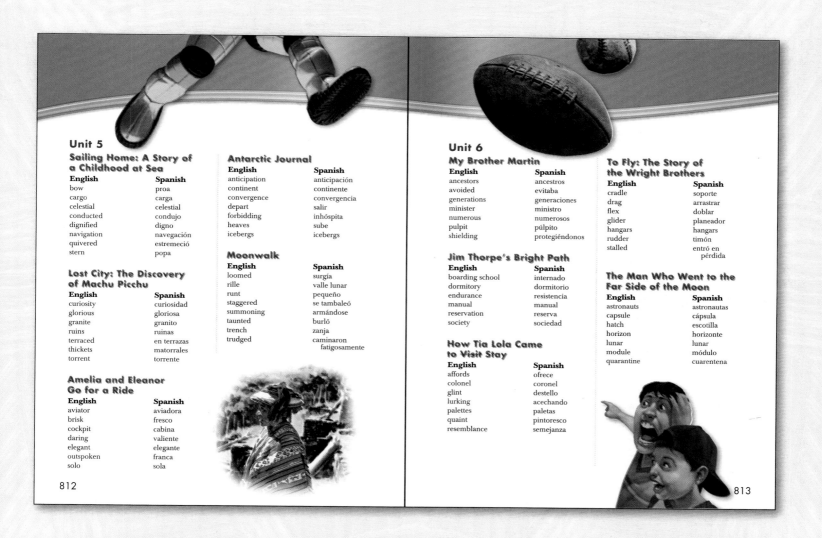

Unit 5

Sailing Home: A Story of a Childhood at Sea

English	Spanish
bow	proa
cargo	carga
celestial	celestial
conducted	condujo
dignified	digno
navigation	navegación
quivered	estremeció
stern	popa

Lost City: The Discovery of Machu Picchu

English	Spanish
curiosity	curiosidad
glorious	gloriosa
granite	granito
ruins	ruinas
terraced	en terrazas
thickets	matorrales
torrent	torrente

Amelia and Eleanor Go for a Ride

English	Spanish
aviator	aviadora
brisk	fresco
cockpit	cabina
daring	valiente
elegant	elegante
outspoken	franca
solo	sola

Antarctic Journal

English	Spanish
anticipation	anticipación
continent	continente
convergence	convergencia
depart	salir
forbidding	inhóspita
heaves	sube
icebergs	icebergs

Moonwalk

English	Spanish
loomed	surgía
rille	valle lunar
runt	pequeño
staggered	se tambaleó
summoning	armándose
taunted	burló
trench	zanja
trudged	caminaron fatigosamente

812

Unit 6

My Brother Martin

English	Spanish
ancestors	ancestros
avoided	evitaba
generations	generaciones
minister	ministro
numerous	numerosos
pulpit	púlpito
shielding	protegiéndonos

Jim Thorpe's Bright Path

English	Spanish
boarding school	internado
dormitory	dormitorio
endurance	resistencia
manual	manual
reservation	reserva
society	sociedad

How Tía Lola Came to Visit Stay

English	Spanish
affords	ofrece
colonel	coronel
glint	destello
lurking	acechando
palettes	paletas
quaint	pintoresco
resemblance	semejanza

To Fly: The Story of the Wright Brothers

English	Spanish
cradle	soporte
drag	arrastrar
flex	doblar
glider	planeador
hangars	hangars
rudder	timón
stalled	entró en pérdida

The Man Who Went to the Far Side of the Moon

English	Spanish
astronauts	astronautas
capsule	cápsula
hatch	escotilla
horizon	horizonte
lunar	lunar
module	módulo
quarantine	cuarentena

813

Acknowledgments

Acknowledgments

Text

22: *Because of Winn-Dixie.* Copyright © 2000 by Kate DiCamillo; Cover Illustration Copyright © 2000 by Chris Sheban. Reprinted by permission of Candlewick Press, Inc., Cambridge, MA; **36:** "Fast Facts: Black Bears" by Kathy Kranking as appeared in *Ranger Rick,* August 1995. © Kathy Kranking. Reprinted with permission of the author; **44:** Text excerpt and selected illustrations from *Lewis and Clark and Me, A Dog's Tale* by Laurie Myers, illustrated by Michael Dooling. Text © 2002 by Laurie Myers, illustrations © 2002 by Michael Dooling. Reprinted by permission of Henry Holt and Company, LLC; **70:** From *Grandfather's Journey* by Allen Say. Copyright © 1993 by Allen Say. Reprinted by permission of Houghton Mifflin Company. All rights reserved; **92:** From *The Horned Toad Prince* by Jackie Mims Hopkins. Illustrated by Michael Austin. Text © 2000 by Jackie Mims Hopkins. Illustrations © 2000 by Michael Austin. Reprinted by permission of Peachtree Publishers; **108:** "Horned Lizards and Harvesting Ants," from *Journey into the Desert* by John Brown, copyright © 2002 by John Brown. Reprinted by permission of Oxford University Press, Inc.; **116:** From *Letters Home from Yosemite* by Lisa Halvorsen, Blackbirch Press. © 2000, Blackbirch Press. Reprinted by permission of The Gale Group; **130:** "This Land Is Your Land." Words and Music by Woody Guthrie. TRO - Copyright 1956 (Renewed), 1958 (Renewed), 1970 (Renewed), 1972 (Renewed), Ludlow Music, Inc., New York, NY. Used by permission; **134:** "We're All in the Telephone Book" from *The Collected Poems of Langston Hughes* by Langston Hughes, copyright © 1994 by The Estate of Langston Hughes. Used by permission of Alfred A. Knopf, a division of Random House, Inc.; **135:** "Speak Up" from *Good Luck Gold And Other Poems* by Janet S. Wong. Copyright © 1994 by Janet S. Wong. Reprinted with permission of Margaret K. McElderry Books, an imprint of Simon & Schuster Children's Publishing Division. All rights reserved; **136:** "City I Love" by Lee Bennett Hopkins. Copyright © 2002 by Lee Bennett Hopkins. First appeared in *Home to Me: Poems Across America,* published by Orchard Books. Reprinted by permission of Curtis Brown, Ltd.; **137:** "Midwest Town" by Ruth De Long Peterson, *The Saturday Evening Post,* Nov. 13, 1954. © 1954 (renewed). Used by permission of The Saturday Evening Post Society; **146:** "What Jo Did," from *Tall Tales: Six Amazing Basketball Dreams* by Charles R. Smith Jr., copyright © 2000 by Charles R. Smith Jr. Used by permission of Dutton Children's Books, A Division of Penguin Young Readers Group, A Member of The Penguin Group (USA) Inc., 345 Hudson Street, New York, NY 10014. All rights reserved; **158:** "Fast Break," from *Rimshots: Basketball Pix, Rolls and Rhythms* by Charles R. Smith Jr., copyright © 1999 by Charles R. Smith Jr. Used by permission of Dutton Children's Books, A Division of Penguin Young Readers Group, A Member of Penguin Group (USA) Inc., 345 Hudson Street, New York, NY 10014. All rights reserved; **160:** "Allow Me to Introduce Myself," from *Short Takes: Fast Break Basketball Poetry* by Charles R. Smith Jr., copyright © 2001 by Charles R. Smith Jr. Used by permission of Dutton Children's Books, A Division of Penguin Young Readers Group, A Member of Penguin Group (USA) Inc., 345 Hudson Street, New York, NY 10014. All rights reserved; **166:** Text and illustrations from *Coyote School News* by Joan Sandin. Copyright © 2003 by Joan Sandin. Reprinted by permission of Henry Holt and Company, LLC; **192:** "Grace and the Time Machine" adapted from *Starring Grace* by Mary Hoffman, Frances Lincoln Books, London. Copyright text © 2000 Mary Hoffman c/o Rogers, Coleridge & White Ltd., 20 Powis Mews, London W11 1JN. Reprinted by permission; **210:** "What's There to Do?" formerly titled "Help an Elderly Neighbor with Yard Work" and "Put on an Outdoor Arts-and-Crafts Show" from *101 Outdoor Adventures* by Samantha Beres, copyright © 2002 by Dutton Children's Books. Used by permission of Dutton Children's Books, A Division of Penguin Young Readers Group, A Member of Penguin Group (USA) Inc., 345 Hudson Street, New York, NY 10014. All rights reserved; **216:** From *Marven of the Great North Woods* by Kathryn Lasky Knight, illustrated by Kevin Hawkes. Text copyright © 1997 by Kathryn Lasky Knight. Illustrations copyright © 1997 by Kevin Hawkes. Reprinted by permission of Harcourt, Inc.; **239:** Adaptation of "Cook Shanty & Bunkhouse" from the Paul Bunyan Logging Camp Web site, paulbunyancamp.org. Reprinted by permission of the Paul Bunyan Logging Camp Museum, Eau Claire, WI; **244:** From *So You Want to Be President?* by Judith St. George, illustrations by David Small, copyright © 2000 by Judith St. George, text, copyright © 2000 by David Small, illustrations. Used by permission of Philomel Books, A Division of Penguin Young Readers Group, A Member of Penguin Group (USA) Inc., 345 Hudson Street, New York, NY 10014. All rights reserved; **260:** "His Hands", from *My Man Blue* by Nikki Grimes, copyright © 1999 by Nikki Grimes. Used by permission of Dial Books for Young Readers, A Division of Penguin Young Readers Group, A Member of Penguin Group (USA) Inc., 345 Hudson Street, New York, NY 10014. All rights reserved; **261:** "Homework" by Russell Hoban from *Egg Thoughts and Other Frances Songs.* Copyright © 1964 by Russell Hoban. Reprinted by permission of David Higham Associates Ltd.; **262:** "Lem Lonnigan's Leaf Machine" from *Here's What You Do When You Can't Find Your Shoe* by Andrea Perry. Text copyright © 2003 by Andrea Perry. Reprinted with the permission of Atheneum Books for Young Readers, an imprint of Simon & Schuster Children's Publishing Division; **272:** From *The Stranger* by Chris Van Allsburg. Copyright © 1986 by Chris Van Allsburg. Reprinted by permission of Houghton Mifflin Company. All rights reserved; **296:** From *Adelina's Whales* by Richard Sobol, copyright © 2003 by Richard Sobol. Used by permission of Dutton Children's Books, A Division of Penguin Young Readers Group, A Member of Penguin Group (USA) Inc., 345 Hudson Street, New York, NY 10014. All rights reserved; **318:** *How Night Came from the Sea* retold by Mary-Joan Gerson, illustrations by Carla Golembe. Text copyright © 1994 by Mary-Joan Gerson. Illustrations copyright © 1994 by Carla Golembe. Reprinted by permission of Goodman Associates Literary Agents as authorized agent for Mary-Joan Gerson and Carla Golembe; **334:** "The Ant and the Bear" from *Spirit of the Cedar People: More Stories and Paintings of Chief Lelooska* edited by Christine Normandin. A DK Ink Book, 1998. Reprinted by permission of the Estate of Don Lelooska Smith, Lelooska Foundation, www.lelooska.org; **342:** From *Eye of the Storm* by Stephen Kramer, photographs by Warren Faidley, copyright © 1997 by Stephen Kramer, text. Used by permission of G. P. Putnam's Sons, A Division of Penguin Young Readers Group, A Member of Penguin Group (USA) Inc., 345 Hudson Street, New York, NY 10014. All rights reserved; **364:** From *The Great Kapok Tree: A Tale of the Amazon Rain Forest,* copyright © 1990 by Lynne Cherry, reprinted by permission of Harcourt, Inc.; **380:** From *Living in a World of Green* by Tanya Lee Stone. Copyright © 2001 Blackbirch Press, Inc. Used by permission of Thomson Learning; **384:** "Autumn" by Charlotte Zolotow from *River Winding* by Charlotte Zolotow. Copyright © 1970 by Carlotte Zolotow. Reprinted by permission of Scott Treimel NY. All rights reserved; **386:** "Early Spring" from *Navajo: Visions and Voices Across the Mesa* by Shonto Begay. Copyright © 1995 by Shonto Begay. Reprinted by permission of Scholastic Inc.; **396:** From *The Houdini Box* by Brian Selznick. Copyright © 1991 by Brian Selznick. Reprinted and edited with the permission of Atheneum Books for Young Readers, Simon & Schuster Children's Publishing Division. All rights reserved; **412:** "So You Want to Be an Illusionist," from *Who Was Harry Houdini?* by Tui T. Sutherland, illustrated by John O'Brien, copyright © 2002 by Tui T. Sutherland, text. Used by permission of Grosset & Dunlap, A Division of Penguin Young Readers Group, A Member of Penguin Group (USA) Inc., 345 Hudson Street, New York, NY 10014. All rights reserved; **420:** Abridged from *Encantado: Pink Dolphin of the Amazon* by Sy Montgomery with photographs by Dianne Taylor-Snow. Text copyright © 2002 by Sy Montgomery. Photographs copyright © 2002 by Dianne Taylor-Snow. Reprinted by permission of Houghton Mifflin Company. All rights reserved; **444:** From "The King in the Kitchen" by Margaret E. Slattery in *30 Plays from Favorite Stories,* edited by Sylvia E. Kamerman. Copyright © 1964, 1997 by Plays/Sterling Partners, Inc. Reprinted by permission; **464:** "A Man for All Seasonings" from *The Spouse in the House* by Richard Armour, 1975, McGraw-Hill Book Company. Reprinted by permission of Geoffrey Armour; **465:** "A Confectioner" from *A Lollygag of Limericks* by Myra Cohn Livingston. Copyright © 1978 by Myra Cohn Livingston. Used by permission of Marian Reiner; **470:** From *Seeker of Knowledge: The Man Who Deciphered Egyptian Hieroglyphs* by James Rumford. Copyright © 2000 by James Rumford. Reprinted by permission of Houghton Mifflin Company. All rights reserved; **486:** "What is Picture Stories?" and "In the Desert" from www.instituteofthefuture.org. Used by permission of Rahul Bhargava, Institute of the Future; **492:** From *Encyclopedia Brown and the Case of the Slippery Salamander* by Donald J. Sobol and illustrated by Warren Chang, copyright © 1999 by Donald J. Sobol. Used by permission of Random House Children's Books, a division of Random House, Inc.; **508:** "Who Knows?" by Fatou Ndiaye Sow, translated by Véronique Tadjo from *Talking Drums:*

814

A Selection of Poems from Africa South of the Sahara edited and illustrated by Véronique Tadjo. © A & C Black Publishers, 2000. Reprinted by permission; **509:** "Poetry" from *Eleanor Farjeon's Poems for Children* by Eleanor Farjeon. Copyright 1938 by Eleanor Farjeon. Copyright renewed 1966 by Gervase Farjeon. Reprinted by permission of Harold Ober Associates Incorporated; **510:** "The Seed" from *Always Wondering* by Aileen Fisher. Copyright © 1991 by Aileen Fisher. Used by permission of Marian Reiner; **511:** "Carolyn's Cat" from *When Whales Exhale and Other Poems* by Constance Levy. Copyright © 1996 by Constance Levy (A Margaret K. McElderry Book). Reprinted by permission of Marian Reiner; **520:** *Sailing Home: A Story of a Childhood at Sea* by Gloria Rand, illustrated by Ted Rand. Text copyright © 2001 by Gloria Rand. Illustrations © 2001 by Ted Rand. Reprinted by arrangement with North-South Books Inc., New York. All rights reserved; **542:** From *Lost City: The Discovery of Machu Picchu* by Ted Lewin, copyright © 2003 by Ted Lewin. Used by permission of Philomel Books, A Division of Penguin Young Readers Group, A Member of Penguin Group (USA) Inc., 345 Hudson Street, New York, NY 10014. All rights reserved; **564:** From *Amelia and Eleanor Go for a Ride* by Pam Munoz Ryan, illustrated by Brian Selznick. Text copyright © 1999 by Pam Munoz Ryan, illustrations copyright © by Brian Selznick. Published by Scholastic Press/Scholastic Inc. Reprinted by permission; **586:** From *Antarctic Journal: Four Months at the Bottom of the World* by Jennifer Owings Dewey. Copyright © 2001 by Jennifer Owings Dewey. Used by permission of HarperCollins Publishers; **612:** "Moonwalk" by Ben Bova. Copyright © 2002 by Ben Bova. Reprinted with permission of Ben Bova and *Boys' Life,* November 2002, published by the Boy Scouts of America; **630:** "The Best Paths," from *Toasting Marshmallows: Camping Poems* by Kristine O'Connell George. Text copyright © 2001 by Kristine O'Connell George. Reprinted by permission of Clarion Books/Houghton Mifflin Company. All rights reserved; **631:** "Roller Coasters" by X. J. Kennedy. First appeared in *The Kite That Braved Old Orchard Beach,* published by Margaret K. McElderry Books. Copyright © 1991 by X. J. Kennedy. Reprinted by permission of Curtis Brown, Ltd.; **632:** "The Door" by Miroslav Holub from *Miroslav Holub: Selected Poems,* translated by Ian Milner and George Theiner. Copyright © 1967 by Miroslav Holub. Translation copyright © 1967 Penguin Books. Reproduced by permission of Penguin Books Ltd.; **642:** From *My Brother Martin* by Christine King Farris, illustrated by Chris Soentpiet. Text copyright © 2003 Christine King Farris. Illustrations copyright © 2003 Chris Soentpiet. Reprinted with the permission of Simon & Schuster Books for Young Readers, an imprint of Simon & Schuster Children's Publishing Division; **658:** "Haiku" by Cristina Beecham, *Skipping Stones,* Sept.-Oct. 2003. Reprinted with permission, Skipping Stones Magazine (www.SkippingStones.org); **659:** "When You Hope, Wish, and Trust" by Ek Ongkar K. Khalsa, *Skipping Stones,* Sept.-Oct. 2003. Reprinted with permission, Skipping Stones Magazine (www.SkippingStones.org); **659:** "My Life Is a Buried Treasure" by Dawn Withrow, *Ten-Second Rainshowers: Poems by Young People,* compiled by Sandford Lyne, Simon & Schuster Books for Young Readers, 1996; **664:** *Jim Thorpe's Bright Path* by Joseph Bruchac. Text copyright © 2004 by Joseph Bruchac, illustrations copyright © 2004 by S. D. Nelson. Permission arranged with Lee & Low Books Inc., New York, NY 10016; **690:** "Two Happy Months in Vermont" from *How Tía Lola Came to ~~Visit~~ Stay.* Copyright © 2001 by Julia Alvarez. Published by Dell Yearling and in hardcover by Alfred A. Knopf Children's Books, a division of Random House, New York. Reprinted by permission of Susan Bergholz Literary Services, New York. All Rights Reserved; **708:** From *Sadaharu Oh: A Zen Way of Baseball* by Sadaharu Oh and David Falkner, copyright © 1984 Sadaharu Oh and David Falkner. Used by permission of Times Books, a division of Random House, Inc.; **716:** Excerpts from *To Fly: The Story of the Wright Brothers* by Wendie C. Old. Text copyright © 2000 by Wendie C. Old. Abridged and reprinted by permission of Houghton Mifflin Company. All rights reserved; **737:** "Clement Ader's Eole" from First Flight Web site, http://firstflight.open.ac.uk. Used by permission of Dr. Peter Whalley; **742:** From *The Man Who Went to the Far Side of the Moon* by Bea Uusma Schyffert. Copyright © 1999 by Bea Uusma Schyffert. Reprinted with the permission of Chronicle Books LLC, San Francisco. www.chroniclebooks.com; **758:** "The Earth and the Moon" (originally titled "Earth", "The Moon" and "Exploring the Moon"), from *Scott Foresman Science,* Grade 4. Copyright © 2006 Pearson Education, Inc.; **762:** "Dream Dust" from *The Collected Poems of Langston Hughes* by Langston Hughes, copyright © 1994 by The Estate of Langston Hughes. Used by permission of Alfred A. Knopf, a division of Random House, Inc.; **762:** "Martin Luther King" from *No Way of Knowing: Dallas Poems* by Myra Cohn Livingston. Copyright © 1980 by Myra Cohn Livingston. Used by permission of Marian Reiner; **763:** "Martin Luther King Day" by X. J. Kennedy. First appeared in *The Kite That Braved Old Orchard Beach,* published by Margaret K. McElderry Books. Copyright © 1991 by X. J. Kennedy. Reprinted by permission of Curtis Brown, Ltd.; **764:** "Fall Football", from *Fearless Fernie: Hanging out with Fernie and Me* by Gary Soto, copyright © 2002 by Gary Soto, text. Used by permission of G. P. Putnam's Sons, A Division of Penguin Young Readers Group, A Member of Penguin Group (USA) Inc., 345 Hudson Street, New York, NY 10014. All rights reserved; **765:** "First Men on the Moon" by J. Patrick Lewis. © J. Patrick Lewis, 1998. Reprinted by permission of the author.

Illustrations

Cover: Tim Jessell; **17, 22-33:** ©Kevin Hawkes; **21, 489:** Barry Gott; **37, 96, 259, 312, 515, 558, 612-622, 812:** Peter Bollinger; **48, 130-132:** Robert Crawford; **70:** Dave Stevenson; **89-91:** Laura Ovresat; **134-136:** Patrick Corrigan; **141, 192-208:** Matt Faulkner; **186:** Sachiko Yoshikawa; **189:** Shelly Hehenberger; **210:** Stephen Kroninger; **215:** Erika Le Barre; **260-262:** Lee White; **361:** Richard Downs; **391, 444, 462, 811:** Matthew Trueman; **391, 492-502:** Brett Helquist; **412-415:** Vitali Konstantinov; **441-443:** Christine Benjamin; **464:** Amy Vangsgard; **508-510, 609:** Joel Nakamura; **517:** Dan Andreasen; **630-632:** Franklin Hammond; **637, 664-680:** S.D. Nelson; **637, 690-706, 813:** Macky Pamintuan; **658:** Stephen Daigle; **662-663:** Gwen Connelly; **709-711:** SuLing Wang; **713:** Mark Neely; **756:** Bea Uusma Schyffert; **762-764:** Rafael Lopez.

Photographs

Every effort has been made to secure permission and provide appropriate credit for photographic material. The publisher deeply regrets any omission and pledges to correct errors called to its attention in subsequent editions.

Unless otherwise acknowledged, all photographs are the property of Scott Foresman, a division of Pearson Education.

Photo locators denoted as follows: Top (T), Center (C), Bottom (B), Left (L), Right (R), Background (Bkgd).

4: ©Laurance B. Aiuppy/Getty Images; **6:** ©Paul King/Getty Images; **8:** ©Stewart Cohen/Getty Images; **10:** (TL, TR) ©ChiselVision/Corbis; **12:** ©Jerry Lofaro/Courtesy of Konica Minolta Business Solutions/American Artists Represents; **14:** ©Jerry Lofaro/Courtesy of Konica Minolta Business Solutions/American Artists Represents; **16:** ©Royalty-Free/Corbis; **17:** Corel; **20:** ©Stockbyte; **36:** ©Steve Kaufman/Corbis; **37:** (BL) ©Art Wolfe/Getty Images, (CR) ©Norbert Rosing/NGS Image Collection; **38:** (TR) ©George D. Lepp/Corbis, (BR) ©Art Wolfe/Photo Researchers, Inc., (Bkgd) ©Tim Davis/Photo Researchers, Inc.; **39:** (TCL) ©George F. Mobley/NGS Image Collection, (TR) ©Joe McDonald; **41:** (T) ©Royalty-Free/Corbis, (TR) Corbis; **42:** Getty Images; **43** ©Bettmann/Corbis; **46**: Getty Images; **48:** Getty Images; **53** Getty Images; **57:** Getty Images; **58:** Getty Images; **62:** ©brt Photo/Mira; **63:** ©Michael Haynes; **64:** (R) ©Michael Haynes, (TR) ©The Newark Museum/Art Resource, NY; **65:** Andreas Von Einsiedel/©DK Images; **67:** (BL) ©Arnold Genthe/Corbis, (TR) ©Bill Varie/Corbis; **69:** (TL) ©Joseph Sohm/Corbis, (TR) Corbis; **82:** ©Royalty-Free/Corbis; **84:** (TR) ©Dallas and John Heaton/Corbis, (BR) ©Roger Ressmeyer/Corbis; **87:** (TL) ©Dex Image, (TR) ©Orion Press/Getty Images, (CL) ©Roger Ressmeyer/Corbis, (CR) ©Ken Biggs/Getty Images; **113:** (B) ©Robert Y. Ono/Corbis, (BC) Getty Images; **114:** ©Royalty-Free/Corbis; **115:** (TL) ©Royalty-Free/Corbis, (TR) Corbis; **116:** (C) ©David Muench/Corbis, (TL, TR, CR) Getty Images; **117:** Getty Images; **118:** Getty Images; **119:** (CR) Getty Images, (BC) Corel, (T) ©Sam Clemens/Getty Images; **120:** (TC, BL) Corel; **121:**(TL) ©Sam Clemens/

815

Getty Images, (TR) Royalty-Free/Corbis, (BR) Corel; **122:** ©Harvey Lloyd/Getty Images; **123:** (CR) ©Royalty-Free/Corbis, (BR, T) Corel; **124:** (TL) ©Boyle & Boyle/Animals Animals/Earth Scenes, (CR) ©Don Mason/Corbis; **125:** (C, BL) Getty Images; **126:** ©Royalty-Free/ Corbis; **127:** (BR, TR) Getty Images, (TC) Corel, (CR) ©Phil Schermeister/Corbis; **128** ©Royalty-Free/Corbis; **138:** ©Laurance B. Aiuppy/Getty Images; **139:** Getty Images; **140:** ©Paul King/Getty Images; **143:** (TR, BC) Getty Images; **145** ©Royalty-Free/Corbis; **156:** (BR, BC) Getty Images; **163:** ©Yann Arthus-Bertrand/Corbis; **164:** Getty Images; **165:** ©Macduff Everton/Corbis; **190:** ©Jim Sugar/Corbis; **191:** ©W. A. Sharman/Corbis; **213:** ©ThinkStock/SuperStock; **232:** (BL, TR) Courtesy the Lasky Family; **236:** ©W. J. Lubken/Corbis; **237:** Corbis; **238:** (BL) ©E. F. Keller/Corbis, (BR) ©Bluford W. Muir/Corbis; **239:** ©Minnesota Historical Society/Corbis; **241:** ©William Manning/Corbis; **258:** Getty Images; **259:** (TL, CL) ©Royalty-Free/Corbis, (CR) ©Jeffrey Greenberg/Photo Researchers, Inc., (BC, BL) Getty Images, (TR) ©David Muench/Corbis; **264:** (BL) ©Paul King/Getty Images, (CR, CC) Getty Images; **266:** ©Stewart Westmoreland/ Corbis; **267:** (BCR) ©Warren Faidley/Weatherstock, (TC) ©Stewart Cohen/ Getty Images; **269** (T, BR) Getty Images; **271:** Getty Images; **288:** ©Royalty-Free/Corbis; **290:** ©ThinkStock/SuperStock; **291:** ©Chase Swift/Corbis; **293:** ©Tom Brakefield/Corbis; **294:** ©Alan Schein Photography/Corbis; **295:** Brand X Pictures; **310:** ©Natalie Fobes/Corbis; **311:** (CR) ©Flip Nicklin/Minden Pictures, (BL) ©Gunter Marx Photography/Corbis, (BC) Alaska Stock; **312:** (TR) ©Royalty-Free/Corbis, (CR) ©Natalie Fobes/Corbis; **313:** (TR) ©Joel W. Rogers/Corbis, (BL) ©Jeffrey L. Rotman/Corbis; **315:** Getty Images; **316:** Getty Images; **317:** (T) ©Carlos Dominguez/Corbis, (B) ©Carl & Ann Purcell/Corbis; **339:** Corbis; **340:** (BC) Getty Images, (BR) ©Space Frontiers/Getty Images; **341:** ©Walter Rawlings/Robert Harding World Imagery; **342:** ©Warren Faidley/Weatherstock; **343:** (TR, BR, BL) Getty Images; **344:** (TR, BL, BC, BR) ©Warren Faidley/Weatherstock, (B) Getty Images; **345:** (B, BR) ©Warren Faidley/Weatherstock, (BR) Getty Images; **346-348:** ©Warren Faidley/Weatherstock; **349:** (T) Warren Faidley/Weatherstock, (TL) Getty Images; **350:** (TC, TL, TCL, CL) ©Warren Faidley/Weatherstock; **351:** (B) ©Warren Faidley/Weatherstock, (CR) Getty Images; **352:** (TR) Getty Images, (T) ©Warren Faidley/Weatherstock; **353:** ©Warren Faidley/Weatherstock; **354:** ©Warren Faidley/Weatherstock; **356:** Corbis; **357:** (T) Getty Images, (CR) ©Ralph Wetmore/Getty Images; **358:** (T, BR, BC) Getty Images, (CR) ©David R. Frazier/The Image Works, Inc.; **359:** Getty Images; **362:** ©Schafer & Hill/Getty Images; **363:** (T) ©Peter Lilja/Getty Images, (BR) ©Chase Swift/Corbis; **380:** (TR) Brand X Pictures, (BC) Digital Vision; **381:** (TC) Corel, (BR) Frank Greenaway/ Courtesy of the Natural History Museum, London/©DK Images; **382:** ©Tom Brakefield/Corbis; **383:** Corel; **386:** ©Todd Gipstein/NGS Image Collection; **388:** ©Stewart Cohen/Getty Images; **389:** (CR) ©Comstock Inc., (CC) Getty Images; **390:** ©ChiselVision/Corbis; **393:** ©Bettmann/Corbis; **394:** Comstock Production Department/©Comstock Inc.; **395:** (TL) Dave King/©DK Images, (TR) ©Royalty-Free/Corbis, (BR) ©Myrleen Ferguson/PhotoEdit; **417:** (TR) Brand X Pictures, (CL) ©Royalty-Free/Corbis; **418:** ©Bob Krist/Corbis; **419:** (TR) ©Royalty-Free/Corbis, (BR) Getty Images; **420:** ©Todd Pusser/Nature Picture Library; **422:** ©Wolfgang Kaehler/Corbis; **423:** Getty Images; **424:** Getty Images; **428:** Brand X Pictures; **429:** ©Andre Baertschi; **430:** ©Royalty-Free/Corbis; **433:** Getty Images; **434:** (TL) ©Buddy Mays/Corbis, (B) ©Hong Kong Dolphinwatch, Ltd.; **436:** (BR) ©Darek Karp/Animals Animals/Earth Scenes, (TR) ©Dr. Morley Read/Photo Researchers, Inc.; **437:** (TR, BR) Getty Images, (CR) Andy Crawford/©DK Images; **438:** ©William Grenfell/Visuals Unlimited; **466:** ©Gianni Dagli Orti/Corbis; **468:** ©Royalty-Free/Corbis; **469:** ©Archivo Iconografico, S.A./Corbis; **472-482:** Getty Images; **484:** ©Royalty-Free/Corbis; **486:** (BL) ©Ralph A. Clevenger/Corbis, (BC, CC, BC, BL) Getty Images, (BL) ©Lisa Henderling/Images, Inc.; **487:** (TL, BL) ©Comstock, Inc., (TC, TCL, TCR, CR) Getty Images, (TR) ©Images/Corbis, (CL) ©Rubberball Productions, (BC) ©Royalty-Free/Corbis; **490:** Getty Images; **491:** Getty Images; **505:** ©Royalty-Free/Corbis; **506:** (TL) ©Becky Shink/Lansing State Journal, (BC) Getty Images; **507:** Getty Images; **512:** ©ChiselVision/Corbis; **513:** (BR) Brand X Pictures, (CR) Getty Images, (TR) ©ChiselVision/Corbis; **514:** (C, Bkgd) ©Royalty-Free/Corbis; **515:** ©Jennifer Owings Dewey; **519:** (TC) Getty Images, (BR) ©Royalty-Free/Corbis; **532:** (BC) San Francisco Maritime National Historical Park, (BR) Jefferson County Historical Society; **533:** (BL) Jefferson County Historical Society, (BC, BR) Ena Marie Sroat; **536:** ©Harry Benson; **537** ©Kevin Horan/Time Life Pictures/Getty Images; **539:** (TL) Corbis, (TR) ©Lowell Georgia/Corbis; **541:** (T) Getty Images, (B) ©Roger Ressmeyer/Corbis; **556:** ©Jim Erickson/Corbis; **558:** (CR) ©Roman Soumar/Corbis, (B) ©Dave Wilhelm/Corbis; **559:** (CL) ©Kevin Schafer/Corbis, (TR) ©Francesco Venturi/Corbis; **561:** Corbis; **562:** Corbis; **563:** (TC) ©National Aviation Museum/Corbis, (CC) Corbis; **575:** National Air and Space Museum/Smithsonian Institution; **578:** (B) Corbis, (TR) Library of Congress; **580:** (CL) Bridgeman Art Library, (TL) Library of Congress; **581:** (TL) Courtesy, Marin History Museum, (T) Digital Vision; **583:** ©Ralph A. Clevenger/Corbis; **584:** Getty Images; **585:** ©Joel W. Rogers/Corbis; **586:** Digital Vision; **590:** ©Jennifer Owings Dewey; **592:** (TR, CL, BC) National Science Foundation, (BR) ©Jennifer Owings Dewey; **594:** (BL, BC) ©Jennifer Owings Dewey; **595-602:** National Science Foundation; **604:** Corbis; **605:** ©Gabriella Miotto; **606:** (TL) ©Gabriella Minotto, (BR) AP/Wide World Photos; **607:** Corbis; **610:** ©1996/Original image courtesy of NASA/Corbis; **611:** (T) ©1996/Original image courtesy of NASA/Corbis, (TL) ©NASA/Roger Ressmeyer/Corbis, (TR, BR) Corbis; **626:** Getty Images; **627:** Getty Images; **628:** (B) ©1996/Original image courtesy of NASA/Corbis, (CL) Getty Images; **629:** (TL) Getty Images, (CR) NASA/Corbis; **634:** ©Jerry Lofaro/Courtesy of Konica Minolta Business Solutions/American Artists Represents; **635:** (BR) Corbis, (TR) ©Jerry Lofaro/Courtesy of Konica Minolta Business Solutions/American Artists Represents; **636:** ©Jerry Lofaro/Courtesy of Konica Minolta Business Solutions/American Artists Represents; **639:** ©Bettmann/Corbis; **640:** ©Comstock, Inc.; **641:** (BR, TR) ©Comstock Inc.; **661:** (T) Corbis, (TC) Getty Images; **678:** (CL, CR, BR) Cumberland County Historical Society/Carlisle, PA, (TL) Getty Images; **679:** (TL, BR, CC) Cumberland County Historical Society/Carlisle, PA, (BC) Getty Images; **682:** (T) ©Joseph Sohm/ChromoSohm, Inc/Corbis, (BC) ©Reuters/Corbis; **683:** ©Stephane Cardinale/Corbis; **684:** (TL) ©Robert W. Ginn/PhotoEdit, (TR) ©Kathleen Kliskey-Geraghty/Index Stock Imagery, (B, BL) ©Jonathan Nourok/PhotoEdit; **685:** (TR) ©The Times/AP/Wide World Photos, (TC) ©The Daily Oakland Press/AP/Wide World Photos; **687:** (TL) Getty Images, (TR) ©Royalty-Free/Corbis; **688:** ©W. Cody/Corbis; **689:** (TL) Getty Images, (TR) ©Bass Museum of Art/Corbis; **715:** (T, B) ©Royalty-Free/Corbis; **734:** (BR) Corbis, (TR) ©Underwood & Underwood/ Corbis; **735:** Getty Images; **736:** (BR, TCL) Corbis, (TL, TCR) ©Bettmann/Corbis, (TC) ©Underwood & Underwood/Corbis; **737:** The Granger Collection, NY; **739:** Getty Images; **741** (T, B, BR) Getty Images; **743-751:** NASA; **752:** NASA; **753:** NASA; **754:** ©Time Life Pictures/Getty Images; **755:** ©Time Life Pictures/Getty Images; **758:** Getty Images; **759:** Getty Images; **760:** Getty Images; **761:** Getty Images; **766:** (CL) ©Hulton-Deutsch Collection/Corbis, (BCL, CR, BCR) Corbis, (BL) ©Jerry Lofaro/Courtesy of Konica Minolta Business Solutions/American Artists Represents; **767:** Getty Images; **773:** ©Ted Lewin; **774:** ©Laurie Myers; **775:** ©Wendy Barry/ Houghton Mifflin Company; **785:** JSC/NASA; **786:** ©E. R. Degginger/Animals Animals/Earth Scenes; **787:** ©Oliver Benn/Getty Images; **788:** ©Stouffer Productions/Animals Animals/Earth Scenes; **791:** ©Robert Amft; **793:** ©Bernard Desestres/Vandystadt/Photo Researchers, Inc.; **794:** SuperStock; **797** (CL) ©Amy and Chuck Wiley/Wales/Index Stock Imagery, (CR) ©Rob Crandall/Stock Connection; **798:** Corbis; **799:** ©H. Taylor/OSF/Animals Animals/Earth Scenes; **801:** ©Robert Frerck/Odyssey/Chicago; **802:** SuperStock; **805:** ©Tim Brown/Index Stock Imagery; **806:** ©Steve Vidler/SuperStock; **807:** ©Michael Fogden/OSF/Animals Animals/Earth Scenes; **808:** (BR) Getty Images, (BL) ©Don Mason/Corbis; **813:** (TL, TC) Getty Images.

Glossary

The contents of this glossary have been adapted from *Thorndike Barnhart Intermediate Dictionary.* Copyright © 1997, Pearson Education, Inc.

816

Writing

Writing Trait of the Week

Writing Traits.. WA1

Writing Workshop

Unit 1 Personal Narrative

Unit 2 How-to Report WA2

Unit 3 Compare and Contrast Essay
Unit 4 Story
Unit 5 Persuasive Essay
Unit 6 Research Report

Writer's Craft:

Include Necessary Information WA4

Elaboration: Vivid Words WA5

Differentiated Instruction with Leveled Prompts and Support WA8

Rubrics

Rubric 4 3 2 1

Look Back and Write Rubrics WA10

Writing Rubrics WA11

Assessment

Assessment

Monitoring Fluency WA15

Assess and Regroup WA17

Student Tips for Making Top Scores in Writing Tests

❶ Use transitions such as those below to relate ideas, sentences, or paragraphs.

in addition	nevertheless	finally	however
then	instead	therefore	as a result
for example	in particular	first	such as

❷ Write a good beginning. Make readers want to continue.
- I shouldn't have opened that green box.
- Imagine being locked in a crate at the bottom of the sea.
- When I was four, I saw a purple dog.
- Have you ever heard of a talking tree?

❸ Focus on the topic.
If a word or detail is off-topic, get rid of it. If a sentence is unrelated or loosely related to the topic, drop it or connect it more closely.

❹ Organize your ideas.
Have a plan in mind before you start writing. Your plan can be a list, bulleted items, or a graphic organizer. Five minutes spent planning your work will make the actual writing go much faster and smoother.

❺ Support your ideas.
- Develop your ideas with fully elaborated examples and details.
- Make ideas clear to readers by choosing vivid words that create pictures. Avoid dull (*get, go, say*), vague (*thing, stuff, lots of*), or overused (*really, very*) words.
- Use a voice that is appropriate to your audience.

❻ Make writing conventions as error-free as possible.
Proofread your work line by line, sentence by sentence. Read for correct punctuation, then again for correct capitalization, and finally for correct spelling.

❼ Write a conclusion that wraps things up but is more than a repeating of ideas or "The end."
- After all, he was my brother, weird or not.
- The Internet has changed our lives for better and for worse.
- It's not the largest planet but the one I'd choose to live on.
- Now tell me you don't believe in a sixth sense.

Writing Traits

Rubric
4 3 2 1

Focus/Ideas

Organization/
Paragraphs

Voice

Word Choice

Sentences

Conventions

- **Focus/Ideas** refers to the main purpose for writing and the details that make the subject clear and interesting. It includes development of ideas through support and elaboration.

- **Organization/Paragraphs** refers to the overall structure of a piece of writing that guides readers. Within that structure, transitions show how ideas, sentences, and paragraphs are connected.

- **Voice** shows the writer's unique personality and establishes a connection between writer and reader. Voice, which contributes to style, should be suited to the audience and the purpose for writing.

- **Word Choice** is the use of precise, vivid words to communicate effectively and naturally. It helps create style through the use of specific nouns, lively verbs and adjectives, and accurate, well-placed modifiers.

- **Sentences** covers strong, well-built sentences that vary in length and type. Skillfully written sentences have pleasing rhythms and flow fluently.

- **Conventions** refers to mechanical correctness and includes grammar, usage, spelling, punctuation, capitalization, and paragraphing.

Writing Workshop

How-to Report

OBJECTIVES

- Develop an understanding of a how-to report.
- Use time-order words to show the steps of a process.
- Describe a familiar task using vivid words.
- Establish criteria for evaluating a how-to report.

Key Features
How-to Report

In a how-to report, a writer gives a step-by-step account of a specific task.

- Explains a task fully
- Uses words like *first* to show the order of the steps
- Provides necessary information and details
- Has clear sentences to guide readers

Connect to Weekly Writing

Week 1	Poem 161g–161h
Week 2	News Story 187g–187h
Week 3	Play Scene 211g–211h
Week 4	Describe a Job 239g–239h
Week 5	Explanation 259g–259h

Strategic Intervention

See Differentiated Instruction p. WA8.

Advanced

See Differentiated Instruction p. WA9.

E L L

See Differentiated Instruction p. WA9.

Additional Resource for Writing
Writing Rubrics and Anchor Papers, pp. 48–54

Writing Prompt: Work and Play

Think of something that you know how to do well. Write a clear, step-by-step description of how to do this task or activity. Make your report interesting to read and easy to understand.

Purpose: Explain how to do a familiar task

Audience: A friend or classmate

READ LIKE A WRITER

Look back at *Marven of the Great North Woods*. Remind students of the scene in which Marven creates a system to record what the lumberjacks earn. Point out that the step-by-step description of how Marven organized his job is similar to a **how-to-report**.

EXAMINE THE MODEL AND RUBRIC

GUIDED WRITING Read the model aloud. Point out time-order words such as *first*, *next*, and *then* that the writer uses to signal the steps of the process. Discuss how the model reflects traits of good writing.

How to Build a House of Cards

When it's a rainy day and there's nothing to do, invite some friends over to build a house. A house of cards!

First, you'll need one or two decks of cards. For a very large house, you may want to use more than two decks. For a more colorful house, find cards with different pictures on them.

Next, find a flat surface. The floor is good, or you can use a large table. Just make sure the table is steady, or your house might collapse before it's finished. Once you have a flat surface and all the cards you'll need, you are ready to begin. The first step is to lean two cards vertically against each other to make an upside-down V. Then repeat this step, adding more pairs of cards in a row.

After you have finished the "ground floor," lay cards flat across the top. This makes a new surface, and you can continue building. Make sure that each level is slightly smaller than the one below it. If you have lots and lots of cards, you might decide to build an apartment building instead of a house.

The last step is the most fun. When the structure is built, stand back and admire it. Then, with a paper ball or a flick of your finger, knock it down!

Unit 2 How-to Report • PREWRITE   Writing Process **8**

▲ **Writing Transparency** WP8

Traits of a Good How-to Report

Focus/Ideas	Body of the how-to report focuses on steps in the process.
Organization/ Paragraphs	Writer wrote steps in paragraphs rather than a numbered list. She also included a brief introduction and a conclusion.
Voice	The voice is conversational. Writer writes as though talking to a friend.
Word Choice	Time-order words such as *first, next, then,* and *last* are used to show order of the steps. Phrases such as *ground floor* and *upside-down V* give precise information.
Sentences	Sentences are varied and of different lengths and structures. A sentence fragment is used to grab the reader's attention at the beginning.
Conventions	Writer has a good control of spelling, grammar, capitalization, and usage.

Unit 2 How-to Report • PREWRITE   Writing Process **9**

▲ **Writing Transparency** WP9

FINDING A TOPIC

- Ask students to list activities they do at home, at school, or for fun. Have them circle the activities they could describe step by step.
- Brainstorm a list of chores students are asked to do. Discuss which chores could be explained in a how-to report.
- Have students think about step-by-step instructions that people use regularly. Ask them to provide some examples, such as directions for a school project, game instructions, or a recipe.

NARROW A TOPIC

How to Make Your Bed   This is too simple.

How to Clean the Kitchen   This may be too complicated.

How to Set the Table   This can be explained in steps.

PREWRITING STRATEGY

GUIDED WRITING Display Writing Transparency WP10. Model how to complete a how-to chart.

Think Aloud

MODEL This student has decided to explain how to set the table. Notice that the steps are numbered, but in a how-to report you may use time-order words to show each step. This student has also planned an introduction and a conclusion.

PREWRITING ACTIVITIES

- Have students use Grammar and Writing Practice Book p. 164 to help them organize information about their chosen topic.
- Students can add details and time-order words for each step in the process they are describing.

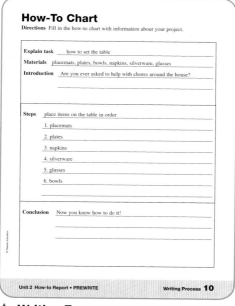

How-To Chart

Directions Fill in the how-to chart with information about your project.

Explain task	how to set the table
Materials	placemats, plates, bowls, napkins, silverware, glasses
Introduction	Are you ever asked to help with chores around the house?

Steps	place items on the table in order
	1. placemats
	2. plates
	3. napkins
	4. silverware
	5. glasses
	6. bowls

| Conclusion | Now you know how to do it! |

Unit 2 How-to Report • PREWRITE   Writing Process **10**

▲ **Writing Transparency** WP10

How-to Chart

Directions Fill in the how-to chart with information about your project.

Explain Task **Answers should include details about the introduction, conclusion, and steps of each student's how-to report.**

Materials

Introduction

Steps

Conclusion

164 Unit 2   Grammar and Writing Practice Book

▲ **Grammar and Writing Practice Book** p. 164

Taking Notes

| 1. Find the items | First, make sure you know where to find the items. |
| 2. Start with placemats | Begin by laying a placemat at each person's place at the table. |

Writing Workshop

1 PREWRITE **2** DRAFT **3** REVISE **4** EDIT **5** PUBLISH

Think Like a Writer

Visualize the Steps Before you write, close your eyes and visualize the steps for your task, from beginning to end. Think of a verb to tell what is done in each step.

ELL

Support Writing Invite students to talk with you about what they plan to write. Record key words and ideas that they mention and help them generate language for other key words and ideas. See the ELL and Transition Handbook for additional strategies that support the writing process.

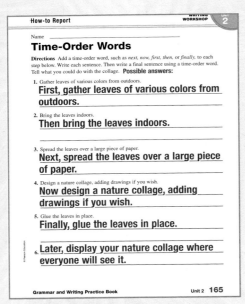

▲ **Grammar and Writing Practice Book** p. 165

WRITING THE FIRST DRAFT

GUIDED WRITING Use Writing Transparency WP11 to practice using time-order words.

- Point out that each sentence begins with a time-order word, which signals its place in the paragraph.
- Discuss the correct order of the sentences. Ask students to share their ideas aloud and explain how the time-order words show the correct sequence of the steps.

Think Aloud

MODEL The sentences here are out of order. Read them to yourself, noticing the time-order words. Let's put these sentences in the correct order, using the time-order words as a guide. Think about how you will use time-order words in your report to show the steps of your task.

Time-Order Words

Time-order words, such as *first*, *next*, *then*, and *finally*, show the order of steps. Look at the time-order words in the sentences below. Use these time-order words to write the sentences in the correct order.

Then fold a napkin and place it on the placemat to the left of the plate.

Second, lay a placemat at each person's place at the table.

First, make sure you know where to find the following: placemats, plates, bowls, napkins, silverware, and glasses.

Next, set a plate on each placemat.

Now you're ready for the silverware.

1. First, make sure you know where to find the following: placemats, plates, bowls, silverware, and glasses.

2. Second, lay a placemat at each person's place at the table.

3. Next, set a plate on each placemat.

4. Then fold a napkin and place it on the placemat to the left of the plate.

5. Now you're ready for the silverware.

Unit 2 How-to Report • DRAFT   Writing Process **11**

▲ **Writing Transparency** WP11

WRITER'S CRAFT Include Necessary Information

Here are some necessary parts of a how-to report:

- Make sure all required materials are listed near the beginning.
- Use time-order words such as *before*, *after*, *first*, *next*, and *finally*.
- Plan a brief introduction and a conclusion for the report.
- Refer to the dates or times of day that events occurred.

DRAFTING STRATEGIES

- Have students review their how-to chart before they write.
- Students should check for time-order words to show the sequence of steps.
- Remind students to keep their audience and purpose in mind.
- Students should make sure they have included all necessary information.
- Have students use Grammar and Writing Practice Book p. 165 to choose time-order words.

WRITER'S CRAFT Elaboration

VIVID WORDS Explain that one way to elaborate is to use vivid, precise words. For example, using specific nouns and verbs is one way to focus ideas and make writing more descriptive.

Vague	<u>Do</u> a picture with <u>paint</u>.
Improved	<u>Create</u> a picture with <u>watercolors or oil pastels</u>.

Use Grammar and Writing Practice Book p. 166 to practice elaboration by using vivid, precise words.

REVISING STRATEGIES

GUIDED WRITING Use Writing Transparency WP12 to model revising. Point out the Revising Marks, which students should use when they revise their work.

Think Aloud **MODEL** This is part of the how-to report on setting a table. In the first sentence, the time-order word *now* has been added to the beginning of the sentence. This signals a new step to the reader. In the second sentence, the writer has changed the vague verb *goes* to the more specific verb *rests* and replaced *next* to with the more specific *on the right side of*. Finally, the words *of the knife* have been deleted at the end of the third sentence to eliminate unnecessary words.

PEER REVISION Write the Revising Checklist on the board or make copies to distribute. Students can use this checklist to revise their how-to reports. Have partners read each other's first drafts. Remind them to be courteous and specific with suggestions.

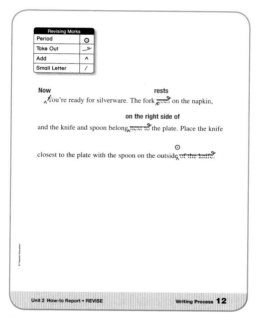

▲ **Writing Transparency** WP12

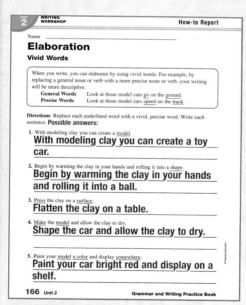

▲ **Grammar and Writing Practice Book** p. 166

Writing Workshop

1 PREWRITE 2 DRAFT 3 REVISE 4 EDIT 5 PUBLISH

Editing Checklist

✔ Did I spell all plural nouns correctly?

✔ Did I use the correct forms for singular and plural possessives?

✔ Did I indent the beginning of each new paragraph?

✔ Did I spell compound words correctly?

Support Writing Invite students to read their drafts aloud to you. Observe whether they seem to note any spelling or grammatical errors by stumbling or self-correcting. Return to those errors and explain how to correct them. Use the appropriate Grammar Transition Lessons in the ELL Resource Handbook to explicitly teach the English conventions.

EDITING STRATEGY

READ YOUR WORK ALOUD Suggest that students read their how-to report aloud to a partner. Partners should consider the following questions as they listen to the reports: *Are there any missing steps? Could I follow the sequence of steps in this report? Do I need more information to perform the task?*

GUIDED WRITING Use Writing Transparency WP13 to model the process of reading work aloud. Indicate the Proofreading Marks, which students should use when they edit their work. Write the Editing Checklist on the board or make copies to distribute. Students can use this checklist to edit their work.

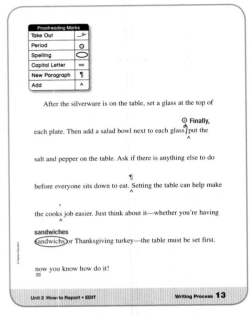

▲ **Writing Transparency** WP13

 MODEL The first sentence of this report is fine, but the second sentence is actually two sentences. The writer has corrected this run-on by adding a period after the word *glass* and beginning the new sentence with the time-order word *Finally.* This shows the reader that the last step of the process is being described. The writer began a new paragraph at the word *Setting* to set off the conclusion. She has added an apostrophe after the *k* in *cook* to show the correct possessive form, capitalized the *n* at the beginning of the final sentence, and corrected the spelling of *sandwiches.*

 **USING TECHNOLOGY** Students who have written or revised their how-to reports on computers should keep these points in mind as they edit:

- Computer grammar checkers are a good start, but sometimes they don't catch mistakes. Double-check your work with a grammar book.

- If your program has a print preview or a page layout feature, you may wish to use this when you are done typing your work. It will show you how your final draft will appear on the page.

- You can determine margins, line lengths, borders, shading, paragraph indents, and other features using the Format menu.

SELF-EVALUATION

Prepare students to fill out a Self-Evaluation Guide. Display Writing Transparency WP14 to model the self-evaluation process.

Think Aloud **MODEL** I would give the how-to report a *4*.

Focus/Ideas This how-to report clearly explains the steps involved in a specific task: setting the table.

Organization/Paragraphs Writer provides an introduction, the steps in paragraphs, and a conclusion.

Voice Tone is conversational as though the process is being described to a friend.

Word Choice Time-order words such as *first, next,* and *then* show sequence of steps.

Sentences Sentences are clear and concise.

Conventions Grammar, capitalization, and spelling are excellent.

EVALUATION Assign Grammar and Writing Practice Book p. 167. Tell students that when they evaluate their own reports, assigning a score of 3, 2, or even 1 does not necessarily indicate a bad paper. The ability to identify areas for improvement in future writing is a valuable skill.

How to Set the Table

Do you help with chores around the house? Well, here's an easy way to pitch in and help at dinnertime. Just follow these steps.

First, make sure you know where to find the following: placemats, plates, bowls, napkins, silverware, and glasses. Second, lay a placemat at each person's place at the table. Next, set a plate on each placemat. Then fold a napkin and place it on the placemat to the left of the plate.

Now you're ready for the silverware. The fork rests on the napkin, and the knife and spoon belong on the right side of the plate. Place the knife closest to the plate with the spoon on the outside.

After the silverware is on the table, set a glass at the top of each plate. Then add a salad bowl next to each glass. Finally, put the salt and pepper on the table. Ask if there is anything else to do before everyone sits down to eat.

Setting the table can help make the cook's job easier. Just think about it—whether you're having sandwiches or Thanksgiving turkey—the table must be set first. Now you know how to do it!

Unit 2 How-to Report • PUBLISH   Writing Process **14**

▲ **Writing Transparency** WP14

Ideas for Publishing

Class Books Create a class book, celebrating everyone's area of expertise. Bind all the reports together under the title *Our How-to Manual.*

Author's Chair Ask volunteers to read their how-to reports aloud to the class. Classmates may ask questions about the reports.

How-to Report | WRITING WORKSHOP | UNIT 2

Name

Self-Evaluation Guide

How-to Report

Directions Think about the final draft of your how-to report. Then rate yourself on a scale from 4 to 1 (4 is the highest) on each writing trait. After you fill out the chart, answer the questions.

Writing Traits	4	3	2	1
Focus/Ideas				
Organization/Paragraphs				
Voice				
Word Choice				
Sentences				
Conventions				

1. What is the best part of your how-to report?
   Answers should show that students have given thought to the how-to reports they have written.

2. Write one thing you would change about this how-to report if you had the chance to write it again.

Grammar and Writing Practice Book   Unit 2 **167**

▲ **Grammar and Writing Practice Book** p. 167

Scoring Rubric | How-to Report

Rubric 4 3 2 1	4	3	2	1
Focus/Ideas	How-to report well focused and developed with complete steps	How-to report generally focused and developed with most steps	How-to report lacking complete explanation of steps	How-to report without focus or sufficient information
Organization/ Paragraphs	Clear sequence of events with time-order words	Reasonably clear sequence with some time-order words	Confused sequence of events, few time-order words	No attempt to put events into sequence
Voice	Conversational, knowledgeable	Engaging but lacks expertise	Voice uncertain	Dull writing with no clear voice
Word Choice	Uses vivid words correctly	Uses some vivid words	Little or no vivid language	No attempt to use vivid words
Sentences	Clear sentences with no run-ons	Mostly clear sentences	Some sentences unclear	Incoherent sentences or short, choppy sentences
Conventions	Few, if any, errors	Several minor errors	Errors that detract from writing and may interfere with understanding	Errors that distract from report

For 6-, 5-, and 3-point Scoring Rubrics, see pp. WA11–WA14.

Writing Workshop

How-to Report
Differentiated Instruction

WRITING PROMPT: Work and Play

Think of something that you know how to do well. Write a clear, step-by-step description of how to do this task or activity. Make your report interesting to read and easy to understand.

Purpose: Explain how to do a familiar task

Audience: A friend or classmate

MODIFY INSTRUCTION

Pick One

ALTERNATIVE PROMPTS

ALTERNATIVE PROMPTS: Expository Writing

Strategic Intervention What is your favorite board game or video game? Think about how you would describe the rules of this game to a friend. List the steps you take to play this game. Write a sentence for each step.

On-Level Think of the simple skills you learned years ago, such as tying your shoes or making your own lunch. Write a how-to report explaining one of these skills to a younger child.

Advanced Think of something you have accomplished that was challenging. It might be participating in a competition or helping an adult or older sibling. Write a how-to report explaining the activity to another student who is attempting this same challenge for the first time. What can you include in your report that will help that person do his or her best?

Strategic Intervention

MODIFY THE PROMPT

Help emerging writers choose a simple task to explain in their how-to report. Pair each emerging writer with an able writer who can listen to an oral explanation of the task and help by listing the steps of the process.

PREWRITING SUPPORT

- Encourage students to write about a familiar task. Initiate a discussion in which students can share their how-to successes: activities, games, or sports at which they excel.
- Remind students to include an attention-getting introduction at the beginning of their report.
- Interview students to determine the steps of their how-to report. Guide their decision-making process by suggesting a task that can be explained in manageable steps.

OPTIONS

- Give students the option of writing a group how-to report under your supervision.

CHECK PROGRESS Segment the assignment into manageable pieces. Check work at intervals, such as graphic organizers and first drafts, to make sure writing is on track.

Advanced

MODIFY THE PROMPT

Expect advanced writers to explain a more complicated task in their how-to report. You may want to set a minimum number of steps they must include. Advanced writers should use vivid, precise words; correct grammar; and good sentence structure throughout their reports.

APPLY SKILLS

- As students revise their work, have them consider some ways to improve it.

  Underline nouns and verbs and consider whether any of these can be replaced with more vivid words.

  Check the time-order words in the report to see that they are used correctly to signal each step.

  Reread the conclusion to make sure the report does not end abruptly at the last step.

OPTIONS

- Students can follow these steps to create their own class rubrics.

  1. Read examples of class how-to reports and rank them 1–4, with 4 the highest.

  2. Discuss how they arrived at each rank.

  3. Isolate the six traits and make a rubric based on them.

CHECK PROGRESS Discuss the students' Self-Evaluation Guides. Work with students to monitor their growth and identify their strengths and weaknesses as writers.

ELL

MODIFY THE PROMPT

Allow beginning speakers to work with a partner, dictating the steps of their how-to report as their partner records them as a list. In the revising step, have students rewrite the list, adding time-order words.

BUILD BACKGROUND

- Display instructions from a board game, a recipe, and an instruction manual to students. Ask them to explain what these items have in common. (They all inform the reader how to do something.) Tell students a how-to report explains how to do something. Discuss the list of Key Features of a how-to report that appears in the left column of p. WA2.

OPTIONS

- As students write their how-to reports, guide them toward books, magazines, or Web sites that provide comprehension support through features such as the following:

  step-by-step instructions

  illustrated game directions

  text in the home-language

- For more suggestions on scaffolding the Writing Workshop, see the ELL and Transition Handbook.

CHECK PROGRESS You may need to explain certain traits and help students fill out their Self-Evaluation Guides. Downplay conventions and focus more on ideas. Recognize examples of vocabulary growth and efforts to use language in more complex ways.

Scoring Rubric | Look Back and Write

2 points The response indicates that the student has a complete understanding of the reading concept embodied in the task. The response is accurate, complete, and fulfills all the requirements of the task. Necessary support and/or examples are included, and the information given is clearly text-based.

1 point The response indicates that the student has a partial understanding of the reading concept embodied in the task. The response includes information that is essentially correct and text-based, but the information is too general or too simplistic. Some of the support and/or examples may be incomplete or omitted.

0 points The response indicates that the student does not demonstrate an understanding of the reading concept embodied in the task. The student has either failed to respond or has provided a response that is inaccurate or has insufficient information.

Scoring Rubric | Look Back and Write

4 points The response indicates that the student has a thorough understanding of the reading concept embodied in the task. The response is accurate, complete, and fulfills all the requirements of the task. Necessary support and/or examples are included, and the information is clearly text-based.

3 points The response indicates that the student has an understanding of the reading concept embodied in the task. The response is accurate and fulfills all the requirements of the task, but the required support and/or details are not complete or clearly text-based.

2 points The response indicates that the student has a partial understanding of the reading concept embodied in the task. The response that includes information is essentially correct and text-based, but the information is too general or too simplistic. Some of the support and/or examples and requirements of the task may be incomplete or omitted.

1 point The response indicates that the student has a very limited understanding of the reading concept embodied in the task. The response is incomplete, may exhibit many flaws, and may not address all requirements of the task.

0 points The response indicates that the student does not demonstrate an understanding of the reading concept embodied in the task. The student has either failed to respond or has provided a response that is inaccurate or has insufficient information.

Scoring Rubric | Narrative Writing

Rubric 4 3 2 1

	6	5	4	3	2	1
Focus/Ideas	Excellent, focused narrative; well elaborated with quality details	Good, focused narrative; elaborated with telling details	Narrative focused; adequate elaboration	Generally focused narrative; some supporting details	Sometimes unfocused narrative; needs more supporting details	Rambling narrative; lacks development and detail
Organization/ Paragraphs	Strong beginning, middle, and end; appropriate order words	Coherent beginning, middle, and end; some order words	Beginning, middle, and end easily identifiable	Recognizable beginning, middle, and end; some order words	Little direction from beginning to end; few order words	Lacks beginning, middle, end; incorrect or no order words
Voice	Writer closely involved; engaging personality	Reveals personality	Pleasant but not compelling voice	Sincere voice but not fully engaged	Little writer involvement, personality	Careless writing with no feeling
Word Choice	Vivid, precise words that bring story to life	Clear words to bring story to life	Some specific word pictures	Language adequate but lacks color	Generally limited or redundant language	Vague, dull, or misused words
Sentences	Excellent variety of sentences; natural rhythm	Varied lengths, styles; generally smooth	Correct sentences with some variations in style	Correctly constructed sentences; some variety	May have simple, awkward, or wordy sentences; little variety	Choppy; many incomplete or run-on sentences
Conventions	Excellent control; few or no errors	No serious errors to affect understanding	General mastery of conventions but some errors	Reasonable control; few distracting errors	Weak control; enough errors to affect understanding	Many errors that prevent understanding

Scoring Rubric | Narrative Writing

Rubric 4 3 2 1

	5	4	3	2	1
Focus/Ideas	Excellent, focused narrative; well elaborated with quality details	Good, focused narrative; elaborated with telling details	Generally focused narrative; some supporting details	Sometimes unfocused narrative; needs more supporting details	Rambling narrative; lacks development and detail
Organization/ Paragraphs	Strong beginning, middle, and end; appropriate order words	Coherent beginning, middle, and end; some order words	Recognizable beginning, middle, and end; some order words	Little direction from beginning to end; few order words	Lacks beginning, middle, end; incorrect or no order words
Voice	Writer closely involved; engaging personality	Reveals personality	Sincere voice but not fully engaged	Little writer involvement, personality	Careless writing with no feeling
Word Choice	Vivid, precise words that bring story to life	Clear words to bring story to life	Language adequate but lacks color	Generally limited or redundant language	Vague, dull, or misused words
Sentences	Excellent variety of sentences; natural rhythm	Varied lengths, styles; generally smooth	Correctly constructed sentences; some variety	May have simple, awkward, or wordy sentences; little variety	Choppy; many incomplete or run-on sentences
Conventions	Excellent control; few or no errors	No serious errors to affect understanding	Reasonable control; few distracting errors	Weak control; enough errors to affect understanding	Many errors that prevent understanding

Scoring Rubric | Narrative Writing

Rubric 4 3 2 1

	3	2	1
Focus/Ideas	Excellent, focused narrative; well elaborated with quality details	Generally focused narrative; some supporting details	Rambling narrative; lacks development and detail
Organization/ Paragraphs	Strong beginning, middle, and end; appropriate order words	Recognizable beginning, middle, and end; some order words	Lacks beginning, middle, end; incorrect or no order words
Voice	Writer closely involved; engaging personality	Sincere voice but not fully engaged	Careless writing with no feeling
Word Choice	Vivid, precise words that bring story to life	Language adequate but lacks color	Vague, dull, or misused words
Sentences	Excellent variety of sentences; natural rhythm	Correctly constructed sentences; some variety	Choppy; many incomplete or run-on sentences
Conventions	Excellent control; few or no errors	Reasonable control; few distracting errors	Many errors that prevent understanding

Scoring Rubric — Descriptive Writing

Rubric 4 3 2 1	6	5	4	3	2	1
Focus/Ideas	Excellent, focused description; well elaborated with quality details	Good, focused description; elaborated with telling details	Description focused; good elaboration	Generally focused description; some supporting details	Sometimes unfocused description; needs more supporting details	Rambling description; lacks development and detail
Organization/ Paragraphs	Compelling ideas enhanced by order, structure, and transitions	Appealing order, structure, and transitions	Structure identifiable and suitable; transitions used	Adequate order, structure, and transitions to guide reader	Little direction from beginning to end; few transitions	Lacks direction and identifiable structure; no transitions
Voice	Writer closely involved; engaging personality	Reveals personality	Pleasant but not compelling voice	Sincere voice but not fully engaged	Little writer involvement, personality	Careless writing with no feeling
Word Choice	Vivid, precise words that create memorable pictures	Clear, interesting words to bring description to life	Some specific word pictures	Language adequate; appeals to senses	Generally limited or redundant language	Vague, dull, or misused words
Sentences	Excellent variety of sentences; natural rhythm	Varied lengths, styles; generally smooth	Correct sentences with variations in style	Correctly constructed sentences; some variety	May have simple, awkward, or wordy sentences; little variety	Choppy; many incomplete run-on sentences
Conventions	Excellent control; few or no errors	No serious errors to affect understanding	General mastery of conventions but some errors	Reasonable control; few distracting errors	Weak control; enough errors to affect understanding	Many errors that prevent understanding

Scoring Rubric — Descriptive Writing

Rubric 4 3 2 1	5	4	3	2	1
Focus/Ideas	Excellent, focused description; well elaborated with quality details	Good, focused description; elaborated with telling details	Generally focused description; some supporting details	Sometimes unfocused description; needs more supporting details	Rambling description; lacks development and detail
Organization/ Paragraphs	Compelling ideas enhanced by order, structure, and transitions	Appealing order, structure, and transitions	Adequate order, structure, and some transitions to guide reader	Little direction from beginning to end; few transitions	Lacks direction and identifiable structure; no transitions
Voice	Writer closely involved; engaging personality	Reveals personality	Sincere voice but not fully engaged	Little writer involvement, personality	Careless writing with no feeling
Word Choice	Vivid, precise words that create memorable pictures	Clear, interesting words to bring description to life	Language adequate; appeals to senses	Generally limited or redundant language	Vague, dull, or misused words
Sentences	Excellent variety of sentences; natural rhythm	Varied lengths, styles; generally smooth	Correctly constructed sentences; some variety	May have simple, awkward, or wordy sentences; little variety	Choppy; many incomplete or run-on sentences
Conventions	Excellent control; few or no errors	No serious errors to affect understanding	Reasonable control; few distracting errors	Weak control; enough errors to affect understanding	Many errors that prevent understanding

Scoring Rubric — Descriptive Writing

Rubric 4 3 2 1	3	2	1
Focus/Ideas	Excellent, focused description; well elaborated with quality details	Generally focused description; some supporting details	Rambling description; lacks development and detail
Organization/ Paragraphs	Compelling ideas enhanced by order, structure, and transitions	Adequate order, structure, and some transitions to guide reader	Lacks direction and identifiable structure; no transitions
Voice	Writer closely involved; engaging personality	Sincere voice but not fully engaged	Careless writing with no feeling
Word Choice	Vivid, precise words that create memorable pictures	Language adequate; appeals to senses	Vague, dull, or misused words
Sentences	Excellent variety of sentences; natural rhythm	Correctly constructed sentences; some variety	Choppy; many incomplete or run-on sentences
Conventions	Excellent control; few or no errors	Reasonable control; few distracting errors	Many errors that prevent understanding

Scoring Rubric — Persuasive Writing

Rubric 4 3 2 1	6	5	4	3	2	1
Focus/Ideas	Persuasive argument carefully built with quality details	Persuasive argument well supported with details	Persuasive argument focused; good elaboration	Persuasive argument with one or two convincing details	Persuasive piece sometimes unfocused; needs more support	Rambling persuasive argument; lacks development and detail
Organization/Paragraphs	Information chosen and arranged for maximum effect	Evident progression of persuasive ideas	Progression and structure evident	Information arranged in a logical way with some lapses	Little structure or direction	No identifiable structure
Voice	Writer closely involved; persuasive but not overbearing	Maintains persuasive tone	Persuasive but not compelling voice	Sometimes uses persuasive voice	Little writer involvement, personality	Shows little conviction
Word Choice	Persuasive words carefully chosen for impact	Argument supported by persuasive language	Uses some persuasive words	Occasional persuasive language	Generally limited or redundant language	Vague, dull, or misused words; no persuasive words
Sentences	Excellent variety of sentences; natural rhythm	Varied lengths, styles; generally smooth	Correct sentences with variations in style	Carefully constructed sentences; some variety	Simple, awkward, or wordy sentences; little variety	Choppy; many incomplete or run-on sentences
Conventions	Excellent control; few or no errors	No serious errors to affect understanding	General mastery of conventions but some errors	Reasonable control; few distracting errors	Weak control; enough errors to affect understanding	Many errors that prevent understanding

Scoring Rubric — Persuasive Writing

Rubric 4 3 2 1	5	4	3	2	1
Focus/Ideas	Persuasive argument carefully built with quality details	Persuasive argument well supported with details	Persuasive argument with one or two convincing details	Persuasive piece sometimes unfocused; needs more support	Rambling persuasive argument; lacks development and detail
Organization/Paragraphs	Information chosen and arranged for maximum effect	Evident progression of persuasive ideas	Information arranged in a logical way with some lapses	Little structure or direction	No identifiable structure
Voice	Writer closely involved; persuasive but not overbearing	Maintains persuasive tone	Sometimes uses persuasive voice	Little writer involvement, personality	Shows little conviction
Word Choice	Persuasive words carefully chosen for impact	Argument supported by persuasive language	Occasional persuasive language	Generally limited or redundant language	Vague, dull, or misused words; no persuasive words
Sentences	Excellent variety of sentences; natural rhythm	Varied lengths, styles; generally smooth	Carefully constructed sentences; some variety	Simple, awkward, or wordy sentences; little variety	Choppy; many incomplete or run-on sentences
Conventions	Excellent control; few or no errors	No serious errors to affect understanding	Reasonable control; few distracting errors	Weak control; enough errors to affect understanding	Many errors that prevent understanding

Scoring Rubric — Persuasive Writing

Rubric 4 3 2 1	3	2	1
Focus/Ideas	Persuasive argument carefully built with quality details	Persuasive argument with one or two convincing details	Rambling persuasive argument; lacks development and detail
Organization/Paragraphs	Information chosen and arranged for maximum effect	Information arranged in a logical way with some lapses	No identifiable structure
Voice	Writer closely involved; persuasive but not overbearing	Sometimes uses persuasive voice	Shows little conviction
Word Choice	Persuasive words carefully chosen for impact	Occasional persuasive language	Vague, dull, or misused words; no persuasive words
Sentences	Excellent variety of sentences; natural rhythm	Carefully constructed sentences; some variety	Choppy; many incomplete or run-on sentences
Conventions	Excellent control; few or no errors	Reasonable control; few distracting errors	Many errors that prevent understanding

Scoring Rubric — Expository Writing

Rubric 4 3 2 1	6	5	4	3	2	1
Focus/Ideas	Insightful, focused exposition; well elaborated with quality details	Informed, focused exposition; elaborated with telling details	Exposition focused, good elaboration	Generally focused exposition; some supporting details	Sometimes unfocused exposition needs more supporting details	Rambling exposition; lacks development and detail
Organization/ Paragraphs	Logical, consistent flow of ideas; good transitions	Logical sequencing of ideas; uses transitions	Ideas sequenced with some transitions	Sequenced ideas with some transitions	Little direction from beginning to end; few order words	Lacks structure and transitions
Voice	Writer closely involved; informative voice well suited to topic	Reveals personality; voice suited to topic	Pleasant but not compelling voice	Sincere voice suited to topic	Little writer involvement, personality	Careless writing with no feeling
Word Choice	Vivid, precise words to express ideas	Clear words to express ideas	Words correct and adequate	Language adequate but may lack precision	Generally limited or redundant language	Vague, dull, or misused words
Sentences	Strong topic sentence; fluent, varied structures	Good topic sentence; smooth sentence structure	Correct sentences that are sometimes fluent	Topic sentence correctly constructed; some sentence variety	Topic sentence unclear or missing; wordy, awkward sentences	No topic sentence; many incomplete or run-on sentences
Conventions	Excellent control; few or no errors	No serious errors to affect understanding	General mastery of conventions but some errors	Reasonable control; few distracting errors	Weak control; enough errors to affect understanding	Many errors that prevent understanding

Scoring Rubric — Expository Writing

Rubric 4 3 2 1	5	4	3	2	1
Focus/Ideas	Insightful, focused exposition; well elaborated with quality details	Informed, focused exposition; elaborated with telling details	Generally focused exposition; some supporting details	Sometimes unfocused exposition needs more supporting details	Rambling exposition; lacks development and detail
Organization/ Paragraphs	Logical, consistent flow of ideas; good transitions	Logical sequencing of ideas; uses transitions	Sequenced ideas with some transitions	Little direction from beginning to end; few order words	Lacks structure and transitions
Voice	Writer closely involved; informative voice well suited to topic	Reveals personality; voice suited to topic	Language adequate but may lack precision	Little writer involvement, personality	Careless writing with no feeling
Word Choice	Vivid, precise words to express ideas	Clear words to express ideas	Topic sentence correctly constructed; some sentence variety	Generally limited or redundant language	Vague, dull, or misused words
Sentences	Strong topic sentence; fluent, varied structures	Good topic sentence; smooth sentence structure	Sincere voice suited to topic	Topic sentence unclear or missing; wordy, awkward sentences	No topic sentence; many incomplete or run-on sentences
Conventions	Excellent control; few or no errors	No serious errors to affect understanding	Reasonable control; few distracting errors	Weak control; enough errors to affect understanding	Many errors that prevent understanding

Scoring Rubric — Expository Writing

Rubric 4 3 2 1	3	2	1
Focus/Ideas	Insightful, focused exposition; well elaborated with quality details	Generally focused exposition; some supporting details	Rambling exposition; lacks development and detail
Organization/ Paragraphs	Logical, consistent flow of ideas; good transitions	Sequenced ideas with some transitions	Lacks structure and transitions
Voice	Writer closely involved; informative voice well suited to topic	Sincere voice suited to topic	Careless writing with no feeling
Word Choice	Vivid, precise words to express ideas	Language adequate but may lack precision	Vague, dull, or misused words
Sentences	Strong topic sentence; fluent, varied structures	Topic sentence correctly constructed; some sentence variety	No topic sentence; many incomplete or run-on sentences
Conventions	Excellent control; few or no errors	Reasonable control; few distracting errors	Many errors that prevent understanding

Unit 2
Monitoring Fluency

Ongoing assessment of student reading fluency is one of the most valuable measures we have of students' reading skills. One of the most effective ways to assess fluency is taking timed samples of students' oral reading and measuring the number of words correct per minute (WCPM).

How to Measure Words Correct Per Minute—WCPM

Choose a Text
Start by choosing a text for the student to read. The text should be:
- narrative
- unfamiliar
- on grade level

Make a copy of the text for yourself and have one for the student.

Timed Reading of the Text
Tell the student: As you read this aloud, I want you to do your best reading and to read as quickly as you can. That doesn't mean it's a race. Just do your best, fast reading. When I say *begin*, start reading.

As the student reads, follow along in your copy. Mark words that are read incorrectly.

Incorrect	Correct
• omissions	• self-corrections within 3 seconds
• substitutions	• repeated words
• mispronunciations	
• reversals	

After One Minute
At the end of one minute, draw a line after the last word that was read. Have the student finish reading but don't count any words beyond one minute. Arrive at the words correct per minute—WCPM—by counting the total number of words that the student read correctly in one minute.

Fluency Goals
Grade 4 End-of-Year Goal = 130 WCPM

Target goals by unit

Unit 1 95 to 105 WCPM	**Unit 4** 110 to 120 WCPM
Unit 2 100 to 110 WCPM	**Unit 5** 115 to 125 WCPM
Unit 3 105 to 115 WCPM	**Unit 6** 120 to 130 WCPM

More Frequent Monitoring
You may want to monitor some students more frequently because they are falling far below grade-level benchmarks or they have a result that doesn't seem to align with their previous performance. Follow the same steps above, but choose 2 or 3 additional texts.

Fluency Progress Chart Copy the chart on the next page. Use it to record each student's progress across the year.

Fluency Progress Chart, Grade 4

Name

Timed Reading

	70	75	80	85	90	95	100	105	110	115	120	125	130	135	140	145	150	155	160	165
1																				
2																				
3																				
4																				
5																				
6																				
7																				
8																				
9																				
10																				
11																				
12																				
13																				
14																				
15																				
16																				
17																				
18																				
19																				
20																				
21																				
22																				
23																				
24																				
25																				
26																				
27																				
28																				
29																				
30																				

See also *Assessment Handbook*, p. 168

Name _____

Date _____

Assessment and Regrouping Chart

Unit 2

	Day 3 Retelling Assessment			Day 5 Fluency Assessment			Reteach	Teacher's Comments	Grouping
	The assessed group is highlighted for each week.	Benchmark Score	Actual Score	The assessed group is highlighted for each week.	Benchmark WCPM	Actual Score	✓		
WEEK 1 — *What Jo Did* Cause/Effect	Strategic	1–2		Strategic	Less than 100				
	On-Level	3		On-Level	100–110				
	Advanced	4		Advanced*	100–110				
WEEK 2 — *Coyote School News* Draw Conclusions	Strategic	1–2		Strategic	Less than 100				
	On-Level	3		On-Level	100–110				
	Advanced	4		Advanced*	100–110				
WEEK 3 — *Grace* Draw Conclusions	Strategic	1–2		Strategic	Less than 100				
	On-Level	3		On-Level	100–110				
	Advanced	4		Advanced*	100–110				
WEEK 4 — *Marven* Fact/Opinion	Strategic	1–2		Strategic	Less than 100				
	On-Level	3		On-Level	100–110				
	Advanced	4		Advanced*	100–110				
WEEK 5 — *Want to Be President?* Main Idea	Strategic	1–2		Strategic	Less than 100				
	On-Level	3		On-Level	100–110				
	Advanced	4		Advanced*	100–110				

Unit 2 Benchmark Test Score

- **RECORD SCORES** Use this chart to record scores for the Day 3 Retelling, Day 5 Fluency, and Unit Benchmark Test Assessments.

*Students in the advanced group should read above-grade-level materials.

- **REGROUPING** Compare the student's actual score to the benchmark score for each group level and review the *Questions to Consider*. Students may move to a higher or lower group level, or they may remain in the same group.

- **RETEACH** If a student is unable to complete any part of the assessment process, use the weekly Reteach lessons for additional support. Record the lesson information in the space provided on the chart. After reteaching, you may want to

Unit 2
Assess and Regroup

FYI In Grade 4 there are opportunities for regrouping every six weeks—at the end of Units 2, 3, 4, and 5. These options offer sensitivity to each student's progress although some teachers may prefer to regroup less frequently.

Regroup for Unit 3

To make regrouping decisions at the end of Unit 2, consider students' end-of-unit scores for

- Unit 2 Retelling
- Fluency (WCPM)
- Unit 2 Benchmark Test

Group Time

On-Level	Strategic Intervention	Advanced
To continue On-Level or to move into the On-Level group, students should	**Students would benefit from Strategic Intervention if they**	**To move to the Advanced group, students should**
• score 3 or better on their cumulative unit rubric scores for Retelling	• score 2 or lower on their cumulative unit rubric scores for Retelling	• score 4 on their cumulative unit rubric scores for Retelling and demonstrate expansive vocabulary and ease of language in their retellings
• meet the current benchmark for fluency (100–110 WCPM), reading On-Level text such as Student Edition selections	• do not meet the current benchmark for fluency (100–110 WCPM)	• score 95% on the Unit 2 Benchmark Test
• score 80% or better on the Unit 2 Benchmark Tests	• score below 60% on the Unit 2 Benchmark Tests	• read above-grade-level material fluently (100–110 WCPM)
• be capable of working in the On-Level group based on teacher judgment	• are struggling to keep up with the On-Level group based on teacher judgment	• be capable of handling the problem solving and investigative work of the Advanced group based on teacher judgment

QUESTIONS TO CONSIDER

- What types of test questions did the student miss? Are they specific to a particular skill or strategy?
- Does the student have adequate background knowledge to understand the test passages or selections for retelling?

- Has the student's performance met expectations for daily lessons and assessments with little or no reteaching?
- Is the student performing more like students in another group?
- Does the student read for enjoyment, different purposes, and varied interests?

Benchmark Fluency Scores

Current Goal: **100–110 WCPM**

End-of-Year Goal: **130 WCPM**

Leveled Readers

Table of Contents

Student Edition Selections

Lesson Plans and Leveled Practice ....Page

What Jo Did

4.2.1 BELOW-LEVEL *Cheers for the Cheetahs* **LR1**

ON-LEVEL *Fabulous Female Athletes* **LR4**

ADVANCED *Equality in American Schools* **LR7**

Coyote School News

4.2.2 BELOW-LEVEL *Home on the Range* **LR10**

ON-LEVEL *On a Ranch*..**LR13**

ADVANCED *The Life of César Chávez*..............................**LR16**

Grace and the Time Machine

4.2.3 BELOW-LEVEL *A World Tour of Cultures*...........................**LR19**

ON-LEVEL *To Market, To Market*....................................**LR22**

ADVANCED *Geography Shapes Our World* **LR25**

Marven of the Great North Woods

4.2.4 BELOW-LEVEL *Lumberjacks* **LR28**

ON-LEVEL *After School Excitement* **LR31**

ADVANCED *Danger! Children at Work* **LR34**

So You Want to Be President?

4.2.5 BELOW-LEVEL *A Trip to the Capitol*..................................**LR37**

ON-LEVEL *Meet the United States Government* **LR40**

ADVANCED *The Power of Our People*..............................**LR43**

Answer Key for Leveled Readers...**LR46**

LR

Leveled Readers

Cheers for the Cheetahs

Cheers for the Cheetahs
by Kim Whiting
illustrated by Aleksey Ivanov

Unit 2 Week 1

◉ **CAUSE AND EFFECT**

◉ **PRIOR KNOWLEDGE**

LESSON VOCABULARY fouled, hoop, jersey, marveled, rim, speechless, swatted, unbelievable

SUMMARY A group of girls tries to convince the male coach that they can play basketball as well as the boys. The story is about standing up for your rights to receive equal treatment.

INTRODUCE THE BOOK

BUILD BACKGROUND Ask students: Have you ever been treated unfairly? What did you do about it?

PREVIEW/USE TEXT FEATURES Encourage students to look at the pictures. After students have done so, discuss what they think the story is about based on the illustrations. Ask: Who are the Cheetahs?

ELL Point out key sports phrases in the text, such as *dribbling* or *fouled,* that may not be familiar to students. Have them write out the meanings and use them in a sentence.

TEACH/REVIEW VOCABULARY Use each vocabulary word in a sentence. Have students use context to determine the word's meaning and part of speech.

TARGET SKILL AND STRATEGY

◉ **CAUSE AND EFFECT** Remind students that *cause* is why something happened and *effect* is what happened. Say: A man is cold and builds a fire to keep warm. Why did the man build the fire? What did the fire do?

◉ **PRIOR KNOWLEDGE** Remind students that prior knowledge is the information about a subject that they already know. Ask: What do you already know about boys' and girls' sports teams? Help students understand that by using their knowledge, they can identify causes and effects of a problem more easily. When causes are not stated clearly in the text, reflecting on their own experience may help them see causes and effects.

READ THE BOOK

Use the following questions to support comprehension.

PAGE 6 Why do you think Hannah was chosen to write the letter? *(Response will vary.)*

PAGE 10 Why was writing a letter a risk? *(The principal could get mad.)*

PAGE 11 Was Mr. Giddings deliberately ignoring the girls? How do you know? *(No, he was speechless when he was told they were upset.)*

PAGE 15 When Mr. Giddings saw the girls play, what effect did that have on him? *(He realized how talented they were and asked them to be on a co-ed team.)*

TALK ABOUT THE BOOK

READER RESPONSE

1. Possible responses: Causes: gym teacher wouldn't give the girls a chance; girls felt they weren't treated equally. Effects: girls formed a team; girls won gym teacher's respect.

2. Possible responses: playing sports takes teamwork; anyone can play if you give that person a chance.

3. *Un-* means "not" or "opposite of." *Unbelievable* means "not believable." Students should list at least two additional words with the prefix *un-*.

4. Possible responses: I would have written a letter because the girls were not being treated fairly. I would have gone to talk directly to the gym teacher.

RESPONSE OPTIONS

WRITING To explore how silly stereotypes can be, invite students to write a commentary about why cats are much smarter, faster, and better than dogs and why no dogs should be allowed in the country.

CONTENT CONNECTIONS

SPORTS Have students research other famous female athletes and present their findings to the class.

Cause and Effect

- A **cause** is *why* something happens. An **effect** is *what* happens.
- Sometimes there is more than one cause of an effect, and sometimes there are multiple effects of a cause.

Directions Answer the questions on the lines provided.

1. Why did Mr. Giddings give the boys more gym time? What was the cause of his actions?

_____

_____

2. Although Hannah was not the best player, she did something important for the team that no one else could do. What was this?

_____

_____

3. What did Hannah and her teammates risk by speaking out for themselves? What was the benefit of speaking out?

_____

_____

4. Based on what you know after having read the story, how do you think the coach will act differently from now on? Why?

_____

_____

5. What lesson do you think this story teaches about standing up for yourself?

_____

_____

© Pearson Education 4

34

Vocabulary

Directions Draw a line from the vocabulary word to its correct definition.

Check the Words You Know

___fouled   ___hoop   ___jersey
___marveled   ___rim   ___speechless
___swatted   ___unbelievable

1. swatted

2. fouled

3. hoop

4. jersey

5. marveled

6. rim

7. speechless

8. unbelievable

a. not able to be believed

b. made an error in the game

c. wondered

d. a ring; a round, flat band

e. the edge

f. unable to speak

g. a shirt

h. hit sharply or violently

Directions Unscramble the vocabulary words and then write a definition for each one.

9. ludefo _____

Definition:_____

10. poho _____

Definition:_____

11. yjrese _____

Definition:_____

12. mir _____

Definition:_____

13. eulvalenebib _____

Definition:_____

35

Fabulous Female Athletes

Biography

Fabulous Female Athletes
by Peggy Rasnick Kendler
Social Studies

🔘 **CAUSE AND EFFECT**

🔘 **PRIOR KNOWLEDGE**

LESSON VOCABULARY amateur, fouled, hoop, jersey, marveled, rim, speechless, swatted, unbelievable

---

SUMMARY This book gives an overview of a few famous women in sports history. It encourages a respect for diversity as it prompts students not to let society limit them.

INTRODUCE THE BOOK

BUILD BACKGROUND Ask students: Has there ever been anything you couldn't do because you were a girl or a boy, or too young or too old? Did you have to prove yourself?

PREVIEW/USE TEXT FEATURES Ask students to look through the captions and illustrations. What do they tell students about the book?

TEACH/REVIEW VOCABULARY Review the meanings of the vocabulary words with students, and then create a sports word wall. Ask: What other sports words can you think of? Post the words on word wall.

ELL Point out key sports phrases in the text that may not be familiar to students. Practice words with partners using pictures or pantomime.

TARGET SKILL AND STRATEGY

🔘 **CAUSE AND EFFECT** Remind students that *cause* refers to why something happened and *effect* pertains to what happened as a result of that cause. Ask students to think of two instances of cause and effect that happened in their own lives.

🔘 **PRIOR KNOWLEDGE** Remind students that *prior knowledge* is the information about a subject that they already know. This knowledge can help them make better sense of what they read. Ask students what they already know about women in sports from reading or watching them on TV.

READ THE BOOK

Use the following questions to support comprehension.

PAGE 5 What do you think the term "great all-around athlete" means? *(Possible response: someone who is good at many different sports.)*

PAGE 17 What was the effect of the law called Title IX? *(The law made it illegal not to give the same opportunities to both men and women in college sports.)*

PAGE 19 Why do you think the author refers to these female athletes as "brave"? *(Possible response: They fought against the odds and wouldn't give up.)*

TALK ABOUT THE BOOK

READER RESPONSE

1. Possible response: *Cause:* Men were at war, and people still wanted to watch baseball games. *Effect:* The All-American Girls Professional Baseball League was created to keep baseball alive during the war years.

2. Possible response: I knew that women weren't allowed in the Olympic games. I want to know more about the All-American Girls Professional Baseball League. I can look online to find out more about women in sports.

3. prefix: *un–*; suffix: *–able*; base word: *believe*

4. The World's Fastest Women

RESPONSE OPTIONS

WRITING Invite students to read sports coverage from their local newspapers. Then ask students to pretend they are sports writers writing about a sports event that one of the women in this book has just completed.

CONTENT CONNECTIONS

SOCIAL STUDIES Ask students to research a famous female athlete such as Olympic star Michelle Kwan. Have students present their reports to the class.

Time for **SOCIAL STUDIES**

Cause and Effect

- A **cause** is *why* something happens. An **effect** is *what* happens.
- Sometimes there is more than one cause of an effect, and sometimes there are multiple effects of a cause.

Directions Answer the questions on the lines provided.

1. Why was the All-American Girls Professional Baseball League started? What was the cause?

_____

_____

2. What were the two causes that ended this baseball league?

_____

_____

3. How was Wilma Rudolf able to conquer her illness? How does what she did help you understand how she was able to win in the Olympics?

_____

_____

4. Choose one female athlete in the story and describe the changes she brought about in women's sports.

_____

_____

_____

5. Because brave women fought for the right to compete in sports, women athletes today have three important benefits. Can you name them?

_____

_____

34

© Pearson Education 4

Vocabulary

Directions Using your vocabulary words, put the correct word in each blank below.

Check the Words You Know

___amateur	___fouled	___hoop
___jersey	___marveled	___rim
___speechless	___swatted	___unbelievable

1–5. Nancy got up early and pulled on her bright yellow _____.
Today was the big game, and she was scared. She was not a good player, and many of

her friends thought it was _____ that she had been chosen to play.

   "Don't worry," her best friend Kim told her. "You're an _____.
No one expects you to play like a professional."

   When Nancy got on the court, the ball came right toward her! She grabbed

it and made a _____ shot! Nancy was so

_____ she couldn't say a word!

Directions The words below are spelled incorrectly. Write the correct spelling for
each. Then write the definition of each word.

   6. foled _____

   Definition: _____

   7. swated _____

   Definition: _____

   8. marvelled _____

   Definition: _____

   9. hop _____

   Definition: _____

35

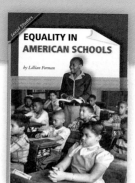

EQUALITY IN AMERICAN SCHOOLS
by Lillian Forman

Unit 2 Week 1

Equality in American Schools

◎ **CAUSE AND EFFECT**

◎ **PRIOR KNOWLEDGE**

LESSON VOCABULARY aspiring, discrimination, diversity, doctrine, integration, jeering, tactics

SUMMARY This book discusses how prejudice led to segregation in our society and our schools. It is a history of the *Brown v. Board of Education* court case and its effect on today's education.

INTRODUCE THE BOOK

BUILD BACKGROUND Ask students if they have ever felt discriminated against. What happened? How did they feel? What were they or their parents able to do about it?

PREVIEW/USE TEXT FEATURES Ask students to go through the text, photographs, and headings. How do they help show you what this book is about?

TEACH/REVIEW VOCABULARY Before teaching the vocabulary words, have students read the sentences where the words appear in the book and predict their meanings.

TARGET SKILL AND STRATEGY

◎ **CAUSE AND EFFECT** Remind students that *cause* refers to why something happened and *effect* is what happened as a result of that cause. Give students three sentences that show cause and effect and ask them to identify the cause and what is the effect in each sentence.

◎ **PRIOR KNOWLEDGE** Remind students that *prior knowledge* is the information about a subject that they already know. Have students recall movies or television shows they have seen or books they have read that have to do with discrimination against African Americans. Ask: What do you already know about prejudice and segregation? What would you like to know more about?

ⒺⓁⓁ Provide books with detailed photographs depicting the Civil Rights Movement and its leaders. Assist students in researching the area of their choice.

READ THE BOOK

Use the following questions to support comprehension.

PAGE 4 What is one cause and effect described on this page? *(Possible response: Cause—The U.S. government sent soldiers to the South to make sure they were allowed to vote; Effect—During this period, many African Americans were elected to become leaders.)*

PAGES 7 AND 10 Why is "separate but equal" not a good idea? *(Segregation is still not right, and the separate schools were never equal.)*

PAGE 18 What were the three ways the *Brown v. Board of Education* decision was fought against? *(People did nothing to help integration along; people refused to obey the laws; people caused violence.)*

PAGE 20 Why was it so important that Thurgood Marshall become a Supreme Court Justice? *(Because he had experienced injustice, he could work against it.)*

TALK ABOUT THE BOOK

READER RESPONSE
1. Possible response: *Cause:* African Americans did not have the same good schools as white people. *Effect:* Supreme Court rules it is illegal to segregate schools.
2. Responses may vary.
3. *Legal* means "of or about the law." prefix: *il–* as in *illegal;* suffix *–ize* as in *legalize*
4. nine years

RESPONSE OPTIONS

WRITING Tell students that there is a new law that prohibits all 4th graders from doing anything fun. Ask them to write an argument for equal treatment.

CONTENT CONNECTIONS

MUSIC Introduce students to some songs about prejudice, such as "If I Had A Hammer." Print out the lyrics and discuss how they call for tolerance.

Cause and Effect

- A **cause** is *why* something happens. An **effect** is *what* happens.
- Sometimes there is more than one cause of an effect, and sometimes there are multiple effects of a cause.

Directions Answer the questions on the lines provided.

1. What was a cause of segregation? What was an effect of segregation?

   _____

   _____

   _____

2. What does "separate but equal" mean? Why didn't separate but equal schools work?

   _____

   _____

   _____

3. What is the NAACP, and why is it so important?

   _____

   _____

   _____

4. Why do people need to fight for their rights? What happened in this book to people when they didn't fight?

   _____

   _____

   _____

5. How does what you know about segregation help you better understand this book?

   _____

   _____

   _____

© Pearson Education 4

34

Vocabulary

Directions Use the vocabulary words in the box to fill in the blanks in the sentences below.

Check the Words You Know
___aspiring   ___discrimination   ___diversity   ___doctrine ___integration   ___jeering   ___tactics

1. Jacob was practicing shooting hoops every day for hours and hours because he was

   an _____ basketball player.

2. "Go home! We don't want anyone here who likes to eat liver and onions!"

   said the crowd of _____ kids.

3. Debby's saying that she will only go to baseball games is

   _____ against football games.

4. People have come from all different countries! Isn't it great that there is so much

   _____ here?

5. When people of all races are able to go to the same schools, this is called

   _____.

6. The _____ of "separate but equal" says that
   it is okay for African Americans and whites to have separate schools as long as the
   schools are equally good.

7. Bill and his team used a variety of _____ to
   gain the lead in the basketball game.

35

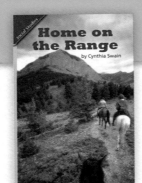

Home on the Range
by Cynthia Swain

Unit 2 Week 2

◎ **DRAW CONCLUSIONS**

◎ **PRIOR KNOWLEDGE**

LESSON VOCABULARY bawling, coyote, dudes, roundup, spurs

Home on the Range

SUMMARY This book explores ranch life in the Southwest. It highlights the changes that have happened in ranch life, including how ranchers began inviting guests to keep the ranches from going out of business.

INTRODUCE THE BOOK

BUILD BACKGROUND Discuss with students what they know about life on a ranch.

PREVIEW/USE TEXT FEATURES Invite students to look at the photographs and ask them what information they learned about ranch life.

TEACH/REVIEW VOCABULARY Review vocabulary with students. Then ask students to write a short paragraph using the words.

ELL Go over the vocabulary words with students. Ask students, "If I saw a *bawling* calf, what would the calf be doing?" Do the same with all other vocabulary words.

TARGET SKILL AND STRATEGY

◎ **DRAW CONCLUSIONS** Remind students that *drawing a conclusion* is arriving at a decision or opinion that makes sense after thinking about some facts and details. Gives students a list of facts about parrots *(parrots can learn tricks; parrots can speak)* and ask them what conclusion they can draw. *(Parrots are smart.)* Suggest that students write down facts as they read and see what kind of conclusions they can draw.

◎ **PRIOR KNOWLEDGE** Remind students that *prior knowledge* is what a reader already knows about a subject based on personal experience or reading. Invite students to look at captions and headings and ask them what they make them think about in relation to their own lives.

READ THE BOOK

Use the following questions to support comprehension.

PAGE 5 Based on what you read on page 5, why are dude ranches a good idea? *(They provide income for ranchers.)*

PAGE 6 How does the poster help you understand why people might want to go to a dude ranch? *(The word* glamour *makes the ranch interesting to some people.)*

PAGES 8–9 What conclusions can you draw about the kind of experience guests on a ranch want? *(Lodging is simple but comfortable. Dudes are not really roughing it.)*

PAGE 11 How is life for a rancher different than life for a guest on the ranch? *(Ranchers and their families live and work on the ranch year-round.)*

TALK ABOUT THE BOOK

READER RESPONSE
1. One conclusion: Grazing damages the environment, so some ranchers might move their cattle more often to limit damage from overgrazing.
2. Responses may include prior knowledge of cowboys but not about all the work it takes to run a ranch.
3. One: to feed on grass and other plants, usually in a meadow. Two: to brush lightly.
4. Sights: branding, roping, separating of calves from their mothers; Sounds: bawling calves, lowing cows, guests roping

RESPONSE OPTIONS

WRITING Suggest students imagine they are guests on a dude ranch. Invite them to write a letter home describing their time.

CONTENT CONNECTION

MUSIC Invite students to research ranch life and make a scrapbook with campfire recipes, songs, and "to do" lists of ranch chores.

Draw Conclusions

- To **draw a conclusion** means to make a decision or form an opinion that makes sense after you think about facts or details.

Directions Below are three conclusions about *Home on the Range*. Go back to the book and find supporting details for each conclusion.

1. **Conclusion:** The U.S. government needed to force ranchers to graze their cattle in different areas.

Supporting Details: _____

_____

_____

2. **Conclusion:** Guests can have a lot of fun at dude ranches.

Supporting Details: _____

_____

_____

3. **Conclusion:** Ranching life is hard.

Supporting Details: _____

_____

_____

4. After reading *Home on the Range*, what conclusions can you draw about how you would like living on a ranch?

_____

_____

_____

_____

© Pearson Education 4

38

Vocabulary

Directions Underline the sentence in which the word is used correctly. Then write a sentence of your own.

Check the Words You Know
___bawling   ___coyote   ___dudes   ___roundup   ___spurs

The coyote was bawling for its mother.
The bawling coyote was so quiet we didn't even know it was there.

1. Your sentence:_____

_____

Wild coyotes live high in the mountains.
My sister had a coyote in her lunchbox.

2. Your sentence:_____

_____

We had a delicious dinner of rice and dudes last night.
Sometimes they call guys "dudes."

3. Your sentence:_____

_____

Please roundup all the beds and then wash the dishes.
At the roundup, all the cattle were put into pens.

4. Your sentence:_____

_____

The cowboy never used his spurs on his horses.
The spurs were not enough to pay for the food.

5. Your sentence:_____

_____

39

Unit 2 Week 2

◉ **DRAW CONCLUSIONS**

◉ **PRIOR KNOWLEDGE**

LESSON VOCABULARY bawling, coyote, dudes, roundup, spurs

On a Ranch

SUMMARY This book informs students about the development of ranches and the work of cowboys.

INTRODUCE THE BOOK

BUILD BACKGROUND Discuss with students what they know about ranch life and cowboys and where their information comes from: books movies, TV, or personal experience. Ask how some of these sources might romanticize cowboy life and emphasize that this book will give them more realistic information.

PREVIEW/USE TEXT FEATURES Ask students what they understand about the book just from looking at the illustrations and photographs and reading the captions.

TEACH/REVIEW VOCABULARY Review vocabulary with students. Then scramble the letters in each word and invite students to unscramble the words and use them in sentences.

ⒺⓁⓁ Go over the vocabulary words with students. Then have them put each word on one side of a flashcard and its definition on the other. Have students quiz themselves and each other.

TARGET SKILL AND STRATEGY

◉ **DRAW CONCLUSIONS** Remind students that to *draw a conclusion* means to come to a decision or opinion that makes sense after thinking about some facts and details along with what they already know. Give students examples of how to draw conclusions and suggest that students come up with conclusions of their own.

◉ **PRIOR KNOWLEDGE** Remind students that *prior knowledge* is when they connect things they already know with what they are currently reading. Suggest that as students read, they look at titles, headings, and captions and ask them what these elements remind them of in their own lives.

READ THE BOOK

Use the following questions to support comprehension.

PAGE 5 What conclusions can you draw about why people did not want to settle in the regions described? *(The land was barren; people wanted to leave the land to the Native Americans already living there because the land was too dry and useless for farming.)*

PAGE 7 Based on your prior knowledge of railroads, why do you think they were so important to ranchers? *(Railroads could transport cattle and feed.)*

PAGES 8–9 What is the main idea and supporting details about cowboys on these pages? *(Cowboys' work was hard and dangerous. Details: they could drown taking cattle across rivers and be injured in stampedes.)*

TALK ABOUT THE BOOK

READER RESPONSE
1. Possible response: Travelers saw the land as dry and useless. They were not right because this land was good for ranching and farming.
2. Possible response: K: Ranches raised cattle, most ranches were in the western United States; W: How can someone become a rancher? L: The history of ranching and what ranching is like today
3. *Dudes* can also mean "guys."
4. Possible response: It isn't an easy thing to do.

RESPONSE OPTIONS

WRITING Have students imagine they are on cattle roundup and write two diary pages about their trip.

CONTENT CONNECTIONS

SOCIAL STUDIES Suggest that students research what family life was like in cow towns. Have them write and illustrate reports to share with the class.

Time for
SOCIAL STUDIES

Draw Conclusions

- **Drawing conclusions** means making a decision or forming an opinion that makes sense after you think about facts or details.

Directions Look back at *On a Ranch*. Take your time and think about the story. Then follow these three steps.

1. First, write down what you already know about life on a ranch.

_____

_____

_____

_____

2. Next, write down three different details that support what you wrote in step 1.

_____

_____

_____

3. Finally, think about any conclusions you can draw about life on a ranch. Try to write about a conclusion that means something to you personally.

_____

_____

_____

© Pearson Education 4

38

Vocabulary

Directions Some of the letters of each vocabulary word have been left out. Fill in the missing letters to make a word. Write a sentence using each vocabulary word.

Check the Words You Know

___bawling	___coyote	___dudes
___roundup	___spurs	

1. _ a w _ _ n g

Your sentence: _____

_____

2. _ _ y _ t e

Your sentence: _____

_____

3. _ _ d e _

Your sentence: _____

_____

4. _ _ u n d _ _

Your sentence: _____

_____

5. _ p _ _ s

Your sentence: _____

_____

39

The Life of César Chávez

Unit 2 Week 2

The Life of César Chávez
by Gretchen McBride

◎ DRAW CONCLUSIONS

◎ PRIOR KNOWLEDGE

LESSON VOCABULARY boycotts, discrimination, fast, grueling, predetermined, strikes

---

SUMMARY This biography of César Chávez includes information about his life as a child on an Arizona ranch, and it describes nonviolent protest.

INTRODUCE THE BOOK

BUILD BACKGROUND Discuss with students what they know about César Chávez and nonviolent protests. Ask: How can organizing people to work together help bring about change?

PREVIEW/USE TEXT FEATURES Remind students how reading the captions can help them understand more about the subject.

TEACH/REVIEW VOCABULARY Review vocabulary words with students. To reinforce the contextual meaning of the word *grueling* on page 8, have students read the sentence and then ask them to describe how the work was *grueling*. Do this with all other vocabulary words.

ELL Review words with students, and then ask them to match definitions with words.

TARGET SKILL AND STRATEGY

◎ DRAW CONCLUSIONS Remind students that to *draw conclusions* means to come to a decision or an opinion that makes sense after thinking about some facts or details along with what they already know. Give students a list of facts and invite them to draw conclusions about them. Ask students to record any conclusions they make as they read, based on facts and supporting details.

◎ PRIOR KNOWLEDGE Remind students that *prior knowledge* is information that a student already knows. Remind students that as they read they should ask themselves what connections they can make between the text and their own lives.

READ THE BOOK

Use the following questions to support comprehension.

PAGE 6 How does knowing about the stock market crash help you understand how the Chávez family suffered? *(It helps me understand how they lost everything.)*

PAGE 8 What conclusion can you draw about César from his decision not to return to school? *(Possible response: His family is very important to him.)*

PAGE 20 How does Chávez's life prove that it is better "to use your mind instead of your fists"? *(His protests organized the workers peacefully so more people were willing to help them gain better lives.)*

TALK ABOUT THE BOOK

READER RESPONSE

1. Responses may include references to Chávez's strong family ties, his happy early years, or his sharing in the experiences of the people he helped.
2. Students may mention the Civil Rights Movement or the anti-war movement.
3. Students should pick out both the italicized words in Spanish and the English words that are closely related to the original Spanish. Possible words include *peones, barrio,* and *hacienda.*
4. Responses may include how the headings show highlights in César Chávez's; life. Information on *La Causa* can be found under *Viva La Causa!*

RESPONSE OPTIONS

LANGUAGE ARTS Suggest that students imagine they are Chávez. Ask them to give a speech to the workers encouraging them to use nonviolent means.

CONTENT CONNECTIONS

SOCIAL STUDIES Suggest that students research and report on other nonviolent leaders such as Dr. Martin Luther King, Jr.

Time for SOCIAL STUDIES

Draw Conclusions

To **draw a conclusion** is to make a decision or form an opinion that makes sense after you think about facts or details.

Directions You've just read about how César Chávez fought injustice and helped his people. Based on what you have read, what conclusions can you draw about what works in solving injustices and what doesn't? Give supporting details for your answers.

1. _____

_____

_____

_____

_____

_____

Directions Imagine there is an injustice in the school. Students are not allowed to eat their lunches at the same time, and because of this, many are going hungry. In the past, students were able to talk to the principal, who would listen to them and try to help. Students have also found that when they work together, they can often get things done faster. What conclusions can you draw about what might work to solve this problem and why?

2. _____

_____

_____

_____

_____

38

Vocabulary

Directions Unscramble each word, match it to its definition, and then make up a sentence of your own.

Check the Words You Know

___boycotts	___discrimination	___fast
___grueling	___predetermined	___strikes

1. cottsyob _____

4. kesirts _____

2. satf _____

5. deterdenimpre _____

3. crimdisination _____

6. elurging _____

7. refusals to buy or use a product or service _____

Your sentence: _____

_____

8. an act of showing an unfair difference in treatment _____

Your sentence: _____

_____

9. to go without food _____

Your sentence: _____

_____

10. very tiring _____

Your sentence: _____

_____

11. determined or decided beforehand _____

Your sentence: _____

_____

© Pearson Education 4

39

A World Tour of Cultures

Unit 2 Week 3

DRAW CONCLUSIONS

ANSWER QUESTIONS

LESSON VOCABULARY aboard, atlas, awkward, capable, chanted, mechanical, miracle, reseats, vehicle

SUMMARY This nonfiction book explores the concept of culture by explaining that every culture has artistic expression, language, food, clothing, and shelter.

INTRODUCE THE BOOK

BUILD BACKGROUND Put the word *culture* at the center of a concept web on the board. Have students brainstorm all the words and ideas that come to mind when they think of the word *culture*. As a class, compare the ideas in the concept web to the ideas presented in the first paragraph on page 3 in the reader.

PREVIEW/USE TEXT FEATURES Read with students the second paragraph on page 3. Use a map to locate the continents mentioned in the paragraph. Then have students skim through the rest of the book, looking at the pictures.

TEACH/REVIEW VOCABULARY Assign each vocabulary word to a group of students. Have each group define its word and identify its part of speech. Then have each group use the word in a sentence describing a visit to another country.

TARGET SKILL AND STRATEGY

DRAW CONCLUSIONS Remind students that to make a decision using the facts in a book and one's prior knowledge is to *draw a conclusion*. Give students some examples of facts and the conclusions that a person can draw from them. As they read, have students draw conclusions about world cultures.

ANSWER QUESTIONS Review with students that when they answer questions about a text, it helps to know what type of question is being asked. Show students that answers to questions may be found in the text, by thinking about what the author means, or by using one's own prior knowledge. Point out that answering questions about a text can help students draw conclusions. Have students look in the text for answers to questions that will help them draw conclusions about world cultures.

READ THE BOOK

Use the following questions to support comprehension.

PAGE 6 What conclusion can you draw from the type of houses described on this page? *(The kinds of homes people live in has a lot to do with where they live.)*

PAGES 8–9 Use the information on these pages to draw a conclusion about clothing around the world. *(Possible response: Many cultures use clothing to tell something about a person.)*

PAGE 11 What question can you ask about the information on page 11? How can you find the answer? *(Answers will vary; students should provide the name of a reference source.)*

TALK ABOUT THE BOOK

READER RESPONSE
1. Possible responses: Stilts: always prepared for floods; junks: land crowded so they live in boats; yurts: people who move from place to place
2. Possible response: by building houses on stilts
3. Answers will vary but should include reference to culture and family or national customs.
4. Answers will vary but should refer to details in photograph.

RESPONSE OPTIONS

WRITING Have students write brief essays on why artistic expression is so important to many cultures.

ELL Have students report on aspects of the cultures of their home countries.

CONTENT CONNECTIONS

SOCIAL STUDIES Instruct each student to pick one aspect of culture and report on how a group of people expresses that part of its culture.

Time for **SOCIAL STUDIES**

Draw Conclusions

- To **draw a conclusion** means to make a decision or form an opinion that makes sense after you think about facts or details.

Directions Read the following passage. Complete the chart by listing facts from the passage. Then draw a conclusion by making a decision that makes sense about the facts.

Paper was invented in China about A.D. 105. At first, it was made from bamboo, hemp, or mulberry plants. Only the rich could afford it. It took another 800 years before all Chinese could afford paper.

Paper is an important part of Chinese culture. During the spring New Year Festival in central China, people hang red paper cuttings to decorate their homes. This is thought to bring good luck.

1. **Fact:** _____

_____

2. **Fact:** _____

_____

3. **Fact:** _____

_____

↓

4. **Conclusion:** In the Chinese culture, _____

_____

Directions Answer the following question about the passage.

5. Why do you think some Chinese people think that paper brings good luck?

_____

_____

© Pearson Education 4

42

Vocabulary

Directions Choose the word from the box that best completes each sentence.
Write the word on the line.

Check the Words You Know
___aboard ___atlas ___awkward ___capable ___chanted
___mechanical ___miracle ___reseats ___vehicle

1. The hat perched on her head at an _____ angle.

2. I used an _____ to find the country of Niger on the continent of Africa.

3. The people danced and _____ to celebrate the new year.

4. A tractor is an important _____ to a farmer.

5. It was a _____ that the falling rocks did not land on the house at the bottom of the cliff.

6. Some people in India use elephants for difficult jobs because they are _____ of pushing and pulling heavy objects.

7. The travelers _____ the ship were excited about sailing to a new land.

8. _____ tools have replaced hand-operated tools in many industries around the world.

Directions The word *reseat* means "to sit back down again." Think about the meaning of the prefix *re-* and use it to define the following words.

9. **revisit** _____

10. **rebuild** _____

43

To Market, To Market

To Market, To Market
by Marianne Lenihan
illustrated by Reggie Holladay

◉ **DRAW CONCLUSIONS**

◉ **ANSWER QUESTIONS**

LESSON VOCABULARY aboard, atlas, awkward, capable, chant, mechanical, miracle, reseats, vehicle

---

SUMMARY This nonfiction book explores some outdoor markets around the world and explains their importance to local people in many countries.

INTRODUCE THE BOOK

BUILD BACKGROUND Invite volunteers to describe any outdoor markets they have been to, especially if they have visited ones away from home. Have students describe the types of goods that were sold and imagine what it would be like to be a vendor at such a market.

ELL Invite students to describe outdoor markets in their home countries.

PREVIEW/USE TEXT FEATURES Have students skim through the book and look at the pictures. Discuss what people are doing and what items are being sold at the various markets depicted.

TEACH/REVIEW VOCABULARY Divide the class into groups. Have each group write a story about a trip, with each student in the group adding one sentence at a time to the story. Each new sentence must use one of the vocabulary words. Groups should continue writing until all of the vocabulary words are used at least once.

TARGET SKILL AND STRATEGY

◉ **DRAW CONCLUSIONS** Remind students that to *draw a conclusion* is to use what they know to make a decision about the facts they read. As they read, have students draw conclusions about outdoor markets.

◉ **ANSWER QUESTIONS** Point out that knowing how to *answer questions* using a text can help students draw conclusions. Ask students specific questions about outdoor markets. Have them tell where they will look for answers to the questions. Guide them to parts of the text which may be helpful and encourage them to use the information to draw conclusions.

READ THE BOOK

Use the following questions to support comprehension.

PAGES 8–9 Draw a conclusion about why vendors might make their crafts at outdoor markets. *(Possible response: People might want to buy the goods if they see how they're made.)*

PAGE 11 What question could you ask that is answered on this page? *(Possible response: What do people sell at Ugandan markets?)*

PAGE 12 What conclusion can you draw about why vendors at the Albert Market use loud and inviting voices? *(Possible response: They want customers to stop and buy their goods.)*

TALK ABOUT THE BOOK

READER RESPONSE
1. Possible responses: They're outside; people sell things; other people buy things.
2. Possible responses: fruits, vegetables, crafts, clothing
3. artist, *-ist*, a person who does or makes; farmer, *-er*, person or thing doing that; governor, *-or*, person or thing doing that; and so on.
4. Possible responses: We might sell tortillas because we make them at home. We might buy sweaters because we don't make those ourselves.

RESPONSE OPTIONS

WRITING Divide students into groups and have each group write up a plan for an outdoor market. Tell groups to think of what types of items to sell, where and when to hold the market, and how to attract shoppers.

CONTENT CONNECTIONS

SOCIAL STUDIES Have students choose one of the markets described in the book and research more about the country where the market is located.

Time for
SOCIAL STUDIES

Draw Conclusions

- **Drawing conclusions** means making a decision or forming an opinion that makes sense after thinking about facts or details.

Directions Reread pages 10–11 in *To Market, To Market*. Then answer the following questions about open-air markets in Uganda.

1. What is the geography like in Uganda?

_____

2. What is the weather like in Uganda?

_____

3. Describe some of the items that people sell at open-air markets in Uganda.

_____

_____

4. How do some vendors display their cooked meats?

_____

5. Look at your answers to the first four questions. Draw a conclusion about open-air markets in Uganda.

_____

_____

_____

_____

_____

42

Vocabulary

Directions Use each of the following words in a sentence about open-air markets.

Check the Words You Know
___aboard   ___atlas   ___awkward
___capable   ___chant   ___mechanical
___miracle   ___reseats   ___vehicle

1. capable

_____

2. awkward

_____

3. chant

_____

4. vehicle

_____

5. mechanical

_____

6. atlas

_____

7. miracle

_____

Directions Use your knowledge of prefixes to answer the following questions.

8. The word *ashore* means "on the shore or on land." What does the prefix *a-* mean? Use your understanding of this prefix to define the word *aboard*.

_____

9. The word *rejoins* means "gets together again." What does the prefix *re-* mean? Use your understanding of this prefix to define the word *reseats*.

_____

10. Use either *aboard* or *reseats* in a sentence.

_____

43

Geography Shapes Our World

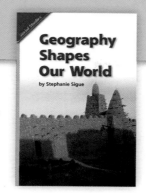

Geography Shapes Our World
by Stephanie Sigue

Unit 2 Week 3

◎ **DRAW CONCLUSIONS**

◎ **ANSWER QUESTIONS**

LESSON VOCABULARY climate, continents, geography, industry, irrigate, native, plantation, products, typhoons

---

SUMMARY *Geography Shapes Our World* explores how geography in different places around the world shapes the cultures of the people who live there.

INTRODUCE THE BOOK

BUILD BACKGROUND Draw a simple cause-and-effect chart on the board. Label the left-hand column *Geography* and the right-hand column *Culture.* Have students list geographical features in the left column. Then have volunteers suggest how each geographical feature might influence the culture of the people who live near it.

PREVIEW/USE TEXT FEATURES Have students skim through the book, looking at the headings and photographs, and reading captions. Discuss with students the different countries presented in the book, and find each on a classroom map or on the map on page 3 in the book.

TEACH/REVIEW VOCABULARY Divide students into groups and assign a vocabulary word to each group. Play charades with the class by having each group act out its word as other students try to guess the answer.

TARGET SKILL AND STRATEGY

◎ **DRAW CONCLUSIONS** Remind students that when they *draw conclusions*, they are making decisions about the facts stated in a text using their prior knowledge, as well. As they read, have students draw conclusions about how geography influences the cultures described in the book.

◎ **ANSWER QUESTIONS** Remind students that *answers to questions* may be found in one or more places in a text, may require them to think about what the author means, or may require them to apply their own prior knowledge. Put the name of each of the four question types on the board: *Right There* (answer in one sentence in text); *Think and Search* (answer in several sentences in text); *Author and You* (answer not in the text, but implied by author; requires prior knowledge); and *On My Own* (answer not in the text; requires prior knowledge). Have students generate questions for each type that will help them draw conclusions about geography and culture.

READ THE BOOK

Use the following questions to support comprehension.

PAGE 8 Why is it so hot in Sao Paolo, Brazil, in February? Where can you find the answer to this question? *(Possible responses: February is a summer month south of the equator; in the text and using my own knowledge of the climate in South America.)*

PAGE 13 What do you learn from the graphic source that is not in the text? *(Jamaican children love to play soccer.)*

PAGES 16–17 Using the graphic sources and text, draw a conclusion about how the geography of Japan has influenced the culture. *(Possible response: The mountainous land has caused most people to live by the coast, so they eat a lot of seafood.)*

TALK ABOUT THE BOOK

READER RESPONSE
1. Possible response: Hurricanes sometimes keep Jamaican children home from school in fall.
2. Answers will vary.
3. Possible responses: farm, hacienda, orchard, manor
4. Possible response: Readers could relate to details.

RESPONSE OPTIONS

WRITING Have students write paragraphs describing how the geography where they live influences their culture.

ELL Have students describe how geography influences culture in their home countries.

CONTENT CONNECTIONS

SOCIAL STUDIES Form student groups. Assign each group a town or city from any place in the world and give them a topographical map of its location. Have groups make predictions about how geography has influenced the culture of the town or city. Have each group use a reference source to check its predictions.

Draw Conclusions

To **draw a conclusion** means to make a decision or form an opinion that makes sense after you think about about facts and details.

Directions Complete the following table with facts or details about each place from the selection *Geography Shapes Our World*. Use them to draw a conclusion about each culture.

Facts About the Geography of Mali	Conclusion About the Culture of Mali
1. _____ _____ 2. _____ _____	3. _____ _____
Facts About the Geography of Brazil	**Conclusion About the Culture of Brazil**
4. _____ _____ 5. _____ _____	6. _____ _____
Facts About the Geography of Jamaica	**Conclusion About the Culture of Jamaica**
7. _____ _____ 8. _____ _____	9. _____ _____

10. Draw a conclusion about how geography can affect the culture of a people.

_____

_____

© Pearson Education 4

42

Vocabulary

Directions Write the word from the box that is a synonym or near synonym for each of the following words.

Check the Words You Know

___climate	___continents	___geography
___industry	___irrigate	___native
___plantation	___products	___typhoons

1. business _____

2. goods _____

3. weather _____

4. farm _____

5. storms _____

Directions Write a definition for each of the following words.

6. continents _____

_____

7. geography _____

_____

8. irrigate _____

_____

9. native _____

_____

10. products _____

_____

11. typhoons _____

_____

12. climate _____

_____

© Pearson Education 4

43

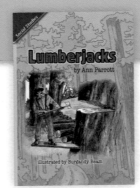

Lumberjacks
by Ann Parrott
Illustrated by Burgandy Beam

◎ **FACT AND OPINION**

◎ **MONITOR AND FIX UP**

LESSON VOCABULARY cord, dismay, grizzly, immense, payroll

Lumberjacks

SUMMARY This book follows the history of logging from the years of the California Gold Rush into the later Industrial Age, when new inventions changed the lives of lumberjacks. It includes a brief look at how Native Americans used forests.

INTRODUCE THE BOOK

BUILD BACKGROUND Ask students if they know what *lumberjack* means. What tools would lumberjacks use to cut trees? Invite students to share any Paul Bunyan tall tales they know.

ELL Ask students to recall and tell any tall tales from their home cultures so that the structure of tall tales can be seen from culture to culture.

PREVIEW/USE TEXT FEATURES Discuss how the headings tell what students are about to read. Ask what additional information the pictures and captions give about the life of a lumberjack.

TEACH/REVIEW VOCABULARY Demonstrate how you can figure out the meaning of a word from its context by reading the second paragraph on page 4. You may point out that if you didn't know what *immense* meant, you can look at the words around it and make a guess. Then show that you can check the meaning in the Glossary on page 16. Invite students to work in pairs to find the remaining words (pages 7, 9, 12, 15), deduce the meanings, and check answers.

TARGET SKILL AND STRATEGY

◎ **FACT AND OPINION** Remind students that a statement of *fact* can be proved true or false and a statement of *opinion* reflects someone's belief. As students read, have them note statements of fact and statements of opinion from the book.

◎ **MONITOR AND FIX UP** As students read, ask them to watch for passages where the text isn't making sense to them. Remind students to use *fix-up strategies* such as, rereading, reading ahead, summarizing, or seeking help from others.

READ THE BOOK

Use the following questions to support comprehension.

PAGE 3 Based on the context, define *tall tale* and explain why a story might have this name. *(Possible response: a legend; It is "taller" or larger than the truth.)*

PAGE 7 Why did it take several days to cut down a large redwood? *(They had to build a platform, plan carefully, and work safely because the trees were large.)*

PAGE 9 Find one statement of fact and one statement of opinion. *(Fact: The logs were pulled along the skid to a nearby river. Opinion: Loggers were eager to reach the sawmill.)*

TALK ABOUT THE BOOK

READER RESPONSE

1. Possible response: Fact: The base of a redwood tree can be fifteen feet wide. Opinion: It wouldn't be very difficult to chop down a small tree.

2. Responses should indicate that students are monitoring their own comprehension.

3. Possible response: The immense redwood trees look as if they touch the sky.

4. Possible response: Paul Bunyan was a giant.

RESPONSE OPTIONS

WRITING Invite students to pretend they are lumberjacks living in northern California during the late 1800s. Have them write a journal entry detailing a typical day.

CONTENT CONNECTIONS

SCIENCE Have students research more about the redwood trees of northern California. Have them locate where they grow, how large they can get, and other facts about them.

TIME FOR Science

Fact and Opinion

- A **statement of fact** can be proved true or false.
- A **statement of opinion** tells someone's judgement, belief, or way of thinking about something.

Directions Tell whether each of the following sentences is a statement of fact, a statement of opinion, or both.

1. _____ Paul Bunyan was not a real man.

2. _____ Even today, lumberjacks work hard in the forests across the United States.

3. _____ Loggers were happy to find the trees since many forests in the eastern United States had been cut down already.

4. _____ This was dangerous work.

5. _____ Water did most of the work at sawmills, which were usually built beside rivers.

6. _____ Loggers would grease the skids with oil or water.

Directions Look through *Lumberjacks*. Record one statement of fact and one statement of opinion from the book.

7. **Statement of Fact:** _____

_____

8. **Statement of Opinion:** _____

_____

46

Name _____

Vocabulary

Directions Answer each question using a word from the box. Write the word on the line.

> ## Check the Words You Know
>
> ___cord   ___dismay   ___grizzly
> ___immense   ___payroll

1. _____ Which word means the opposite of *small*?

2. _____ Which word refers to a type of bear?

3. _____ Which word refers to an amount of wood?

4. _____ Which word refers to a list of people to be paid?

5. _____ Which word refers to a sudden, helpless fear?

Directions Use each word in a sentence.

6. _____

_____

7. _____

_____

8. _____

_____

9. _____

_____

10. _____

_____

47

After School Excitement

SUMMARY This story explores the differences between twin brothers and the consequences of their behavior: Ethan is responsible; Jake is not, but he learns the value of prioritizing.

INTRODUCE THE BOOK

BUILD BACKGROUND Ask students what types of activities they enjoy. What chores do they do to help out at home? Would they rather have fun with their friends or do chores?

PREVIEW/USE ILLUSTRATIONS Ask students to look at the pictures on each page. What do the pictures tell them about the story and the characters?

TEACH/REVIEW VOCABULARY Discuss how some words can have more than one meaning (*cords, grizzly*). Have students look up the vocabulary words in a dictionary and write down the meanings of the words as used in the book.

ELL Have students work in pairs to find vocabulary words and other unfamiliar words in the book. Have them work together to define these words through context clues or by consulting a dictionary.

TARGET SKILL AND STRATEGY

◉ **FACT AND OPINION** Remind students that a statement of *fact* can be proved true or false, and a statement of *opinion* is someone's judgment. Ask: Does fiction contain mostly statements of fact or statements of opinion? Have students explain their answers using examples from the book.

◉ **MONITOR AND FIX UP** As students read, encourage them to ask questions about the text to *monitor* their own comprehension. Who is the story about? What happens in the beginning? What happens in the middle? What is the "problem" in the story? How does the story end? If students have difficulty answering the questions, encourage them to use *fix-up strategies* such as, rereading, skimming and scanning, or summarizing.

READ THE BOOK

Use the following questions to support comprehension.

PAGES 4–5 Compare Ethan and Jake. (*Ethan was strong, he loved bowling, and he helped around the farm. Jake liked to do many things; he had a good time with friends.*)

PAGE 6 Why did the boys' parents give Ethan more chores on the farm? (*Ethan was more responsible. Jake was easily distracted; he didn't finish chores.*)

PAGE 11 What did Jake do when he walked into the fair? Did this confirm what you already thought about him? Explain. (*Possible response: He signed up for lots of activities. Yes. He liked to do lots of things and didn't think much before he acted.*)

TALK ABOUT THE BOOK

READER RESPONSE
1. Possible response: Fact: Bowling goes back over 5,000 years. Each bowling game has ten frames. Opinion: Ethan's size helped him bowl. If Ethan wasn't home, he was bowling.
2. Responses should indicate that students are monitoring comprehension.
3. Possible response: *immense*, huge, *tiny*; *dependable*, reliable, *changeable*; *distracted*, inattentive, *attentive*
4. Responses will vary.

RESPONSE OPTIONS

WRITING/DRAMA Have student pairs write a dialogue between Ethan and Jake in which they express their own points of view of why they behave as they do. Invite students to act out their dialogues.

CONTENT CONNECTIONS

SOCIAL STUDIES Invite students to think about ways they can help out more at home and in their communities. Ask them to list their ideas and describe how they could fit two new volunteer opportunities into their schedules.

Time for **SOCIAL STUDIES**

Fact and Opinion

- A **statement of fact** can be proved true or false.
- A **statement of opinion** tells someone's judgement, belief, or way of thinking about something.

Directions Use the chart below to record five statements of facts about Ethan and Jake. For each statement of fact, write a related statement of opinion.

Statements of Fact	Statements of Opinion
1. _____ _____ _____	2. _____ _____ _____
3. _____ _____ _____	4. _____ _____ _____
5. _____ _____ _____	6. _____ _____ _____
7. _____ _____ _____	8. _____ _____ _____
9. _____ _____	10. _____ _____

© Pearson Education 4

46

Vocabulary

Directions Complete each sentence using one of the vocabulary words.

Check the Words You Know

___cord   ___dismay   ___grizzly
___immense   ___payroll

1. I took one look at the _____ bear and froze.

2. She felt _____ when she learned she had to take the trip all by herself.

3. Mr. Barr was on the _____ and got a check every two weeks.

4. After the pilot had landed the plane safely, he felt as if an _____ weight had been lifted from his shoulders.

5. I bought a _____ of firewood, which lasted me through two winters.

Directions Use each vocabulary word in a sentence.

6. _____

_____

7. _____

_____

8. _____

_____

9. _____

_____

10. _____

_____

47

Danger! Children at Work

Danger!
Children at Work

by Sharon Franklin

FACT AND OPINION

MONITOR AND FIX UP

LESSON VOCABULARY bobbins, breaker boys, child labor, dismay, doffers, payroll, spinners, sweatshops, tenement houses, textile mills

SUMMARY Less than one-hundred years ago, businesses used child labor to keep costs down. Children worked pitifully long hours and even died from dangerous conditions in mines, mills, fields, and other workplaces.

INTRODUCE THE BOOK

BUILD BACKGROUND Ask students what the people they know do for work. How do students help out at home? Should children be allowed to work outside the home? Why or why not?

ELL Invite students to share personal experiences of the ways adults and children help out at home.

PREVIEW/USE TEXT FEATURES As students look through the book, point out the historical photographs. Ask students what these photographs can tell them about child labor. What can they learn from the time line on pages 18–19?

TEACH/REVIEW VOCABULARY Review the vocabulary words with the class. Talk about the compound words and have students look through their books to find the context in which they are used. *(breaker boys, child labor, payroll, sweatshops, tenement houses, textile mills)*

TARGET SKILL AND STRATEGY

FACT AND OPINION Remind students that a statement of *fact* can be proved true or false, and a statement of *opinion* is someone's judgment. Ask: Is this book based on fact or opinion? Do you think the author has an opinion about child labor? What is that opinion?

MONITOR AND FIX UP Point out to students that they may learn a lot of new information in this book. Sometimes it is difficult to keep track of that information. Guide students in strategies to use when reading complex text. Have students read pages 4–7. Suggest they use self-questioning to *monitor* their comprehension. Then encourage students to use *fix-up strategies* such as summarizing, rereading, or asking others for help.

READ THE BOOK

Use the following questions to support comprehension.

PAGE 6 When did child labor begin in the United States? *(in the 1800s)*

PAGE 8 Which children were most likely to work? Why? *(poor immigrant children; little education, needed money to survive)*

PAGE 10 Describe some of the facts you read about what it was like to work in the sweatshops. What is your opinion about children working? *(Responses will vary.)*

TALK ABOUT THE BOOK

READER RESPONSE
1. Possible responses: Fact: Immigrants came from Germany, Italy, Ireland, and other countries. Opinion: Many new immigrants were desperate for education and money.
2. Possible response: I can read on to specific examples of child labor that make difference clearer.
3. Possible response: child labor, sweatshops, textile mills
4. Possible response: tired faces, bare feet, ragged clothes, very young children, dirty conditions

RESPONSE OPTIONS

WRITING Have students reread the "Declaration of Dependence" on page 20. Ask them to write their own declarations about something they feel entitled to, e.g., the right to longer recesses.

CONTENT CONNECTIONS

SOCIAL STUDIES Have groups of students choose a person or topic from the book to research in depth. Invite groups to share their findings with the class.

Time for SOCIAL STUDIES

Fact and Opinion

- A **statement of fact** can be proved true or false.
- A **statement of opinion** tells someone's judgement, belief, or way of thinking about something.

Directions Use the chart below to record five statements of facts that you learned in *Danger! Children at Work*. For each statement of fact, write a related statement of opinion.

Statements of Fact	My Opinions
1. _____	2. _____
_____	_____
_____	_____
3. _____	4. _____
_____	_____
_____	_____
5. _____	6. _____
_____	_____
_____	_____
7. _____	8. _____
_____	_____
_____	_____
9. _____	10. _____
_____	_____
_____	_____

© Pearson Education 4

46

Vocabulary

Directions Write a story using at least five of the words listed in the box.
Circle each vocabulary word you use.

Check the Words You Know

___bobbins	___breaker boys
___child labor	___dismay
___doffers	___payroll
___spinners	___sweatshops
___tenement houses	___textile mills

_____

_____

_____

_____

_____

_____

_____

_____

_____

_____

_____

_____

_____

_____

_____

_____

47

A Trip to the Capitol

SUMMARY This book tells the story of a young student's tour of Washington, D.C. The student learns all about the different branches of the government: executive, legislative, and judicial. The student visits the Capitol Building, the Library of Congress, the House and Senate Office Buildings, and the Botanic Garden Conservatory.

INTRODUCE THE BOOK

BUILD BACKGROUND Discuss with students what they know about the nation's capital. If any of the students have visited there, have them describe what they saw. Did they visit the Capitol building? Which monuments did they see? If they haven't been there before, have them describe what they know about Washington, D.C.

ELL Have students talk about what they know about Washington, D.C.

PREVIEW/USE TEXT FEATURES Encourage students to look at the captions, sidebars, and headings to get a sense of what will be covered in the book.

TEACH/REVIEW VOCABULARY Have students write each vocabulary word and its definition on a note card. Have them draw cards with a partner and use each word they draw in a sentence.

TARGET SKILL AND STRATEGY

◉ **MAIN IDEA AND DETAILS** Remind students that every book is about a topic, and the most important idea about the topic is the *main idea*. Remind students that the main idea will have *supporting details* that give more information about it. As they read this text, have them write down the main idea in a sentence and list supporting details that tell more about it.

◉ **SUMMARIZE** Remind students that in order to find the main ideas, it's a good idea to *summarize* the material as you read along. As they read this text, ask them to try to summarize each section giving its main points.

READ THE BOOK

Use the following questions to support comprehension.

PAGE 4 Why did the Founding Fathers give the government a system of checks and balances? *(to prevent any one branch from having too much power)*

PAGE 5 Which branch of the government is responsible for making laws? *(the legislative branch)*

PAGE 5 How many senators does each state have? *(two)*

TALK ABOUT THE BOOK

READER RESPONSE
1. Responses may vary. The Capitol is an important building, worthy of being home to our nation's legislature.
2. Responses may vary. The executive branch may veto bills passed by Congress and nominate judges and justices to the federal court.
3. *Politics, policy, police,* and *politician* are related words. *Polis* is Greek for "city-state."
4. Responses may vary but they should include a sound explanation.

RESPONSE OPTIONS

WRITING Have students write a letter to their senator or representative. Have them ask questions about or state their opinions on some issue or problem in your country, state, or town.

CONTENT CONNECTIONS

SOCIAL STUDIES Have students research their senator or representative. How long has that person been in office? What did he or she do before taking that position? What are some of that politician's favorite causes? What is his or her schedule in Washington, and when is he or she back home?

Time for SOCIAL STUDIES

Main Idea and Details

- The **main idea** is the most important idea about the topic of a paragraph, passage, or article.
- **Supporting details** are the small pieces of information that tell more about the main idea.

Directions Reread the following passage from *A Trip to the Capitol*. Then answer the questions about the passage below.

> The Founding Fathers tried to make sure that no one person had too much power. They also knew that a growing nation needed a strong government. They wrote the Constitution to deal with these challenges. In it, they outlined three branches, or parts, of government: legislative, executive, and judicial.
>
> Each branch has responsibility for different jobs. Together, the three branches are designed to make sure the government runs smoothly and protects the rights of its citizens. Each branch has the power to challenge the other two branches. This system of checks and balances prevents any one branch from having too much power.

1. What is the main idea of the first paragraph?

_____

_____

2. What is one supporting detail in the first paragraph that tells about this main idea?

_____

3. What is a detail that supports the supporting detail in question 2?

_____

_____

4. What is the main idea of the second paragraph?

_____

_____

5. What is one supporting detail in the second paragraph that tells more about this main idea?

_____

© Pearson Education 4

50

Name _____

Vocabulary

Directions Fill in the blank with the word from the box that fits the definition.

Check the Words You Know			
__Constitution	__howling	__humble	__politics
__responsibility	__solemnly	__vain	

1. _____ seriously; earnestly

2. _____ document that establishes the basic principles of the U.S. government

3. _____ meek; modest

4. _____ the art or science of governing

5. _____ job; duty; task

6. _____ crying; wailing; shrieking

7. _____ proud; inflated

Directions Write a brief paragraph about a trip to Washington, D.C. Use as many vocabulary words as possible.

_____

_____

_____

_____

_____

_____

_____

51

Meet the United States Government

Meet the United States Government
by Joshua Nissenbaum

🎯 **MAIN IDEA AND DETAILS**

🎯 **SUMMARIZE**

LESSON VOCABULARY Constitution, howling, humble, politics, responsibility, solemnly, vain

SUMMARY This book gives students an overview of how the United States government works. It starts by describing the origins of the Constitution. It then describes the functions of the three branches of the government: executive, legislative and judicial.

INTRODUCE THE BOOK

BUILD BACKGROUND Ask students if they have ever watched the President give a speech. Ask them if they ever remember watching political ads on television. What qualities do political leaders and ads tend to show?

PREVIEW/USE TEXT FEATURES Invite students to look at all the illustrations and captions in the book. Ask students how the illustrations give clues as to what is going to happen in the text.

🅔🅛🅛 Have students explain what sort of government they had in their home countries. What similarities and differences have they noticed between the government of their home country and the United States?

TEACH/REVIEW VOCABULARY To reinforce the contextual meanings of the vocabulary words, discuss with students the sentences in the book that surround each word. How do these sentences help convey meaning?

TARGET SKILL AND STRATEGY

🎯 **MAIN IDEA AND DETAILS** Remind students that every book is about a topic and the most important idea about the topic is the *main idea*. Remind students that the main idea is supported by *supporting details* that give more information about it. As they read this text, have them write down the main idea and list supporting details that tell more about the main idea.

🎯 **SUMMARIZE** As they read *Meet the United States Government,* ask students to try to summarize each page giving its main points. Demonstrate how these may be recorded in a simple outline.

READ THE BOOK

Use the following questions to support comprehension.

PAGE 5 Why did it take the colonists eight years to decide on a form of government? *(They were afraid of giving the government too much power.)*

PAGE 6 Which two houses make up the Congress? *(the Senate and the House of Representatives)*

PAGE 9 How long do Supreme Court justices keep their positions? *(for life)*

TALK ABOUT THE BOOK

READER RESPONSE

1. Responses may vary but should include the idea that the three branches create a system of checks and balances, preventing any one branch from becoming too powerful.
2. Responses may vary. The Cabinet makes up all the departments of the executive branch. It deals with important government activities from the military to printing money to keeping food safe.
3. The Constitution establishes how our government is set up.
4. Responses will vary. Accept any answer the student can support.

RESPONSE OPTIONS

WRITING Have students imagine that they are old enough to vote. Have them write a brief essay about how they feel the first time they vote.

CONTENT CONNECTIONS

SOCIAL STUDIES Have students research their state representative. Who is responsible for representing the students' rights in Washington? Have them compare what they find with fellow classmates.

Time for **SOCIAL STUDIES**

Main Idea and Details

- The **main idea** is the most important idea about the topic of a paragraph, passage, or article.
- **Supporting details** are the small pieces of information that tell more about the main idea.

Directions Reread the following passage from *Meet the United States Government*. Then answer the questions about the passage below.

> The executive branch of the government is what most people think of when they say "the government." This branch enforces the laws Congress makes and upholds the Constitution. The executive branch is so large that it needs to be divided into departments. The President acts as the head of all these departments. The directors, or secretaries, of each department form a group called the Cabinet.
>
> Maybe you have heard of some of these departments. There is the Department of State, the Department of the Treasury, and the Department of Defense. Over the years these departments have grown, and new departments have been added. Now there are fifteen executive departments.

1. What is the main idea of these two paragraphs?

_____

2. What is one supporting detail in the first paragraph that tells about this main idea?

_____

3. What is another supporting detail in the second paragraph that tells more about this main idea?

_____

4. What is another supporting detail in the second paragraph that tells more about this main idea?

_____

5. What is another supporting detail in the second paragraph that tells more about this main idea?

_____

© Pearson Education 4

50

Vocabulary

Directions Fill in the blank with the word from the box that fits the definition.

Check the Words You Know

___Constitution   ___howling   ___humble   ___politics
___responsibility   ___solemnly   ___vain
---

1. _____ seriously; earnestly

2. _____ document that establishes the basic principles of the United States government

3. _____ meek; modest

4. _____ the art or science of governing or of policies

5. _____ job; duty; task

6. _____ crying; wailing; shrieking

7. _____ proud; inflated

Directions Write a brief paragraph about the United States government, using as many vocabulary words as possible.

_____

_____

_____

_____

_____

_____

_____

_____

51

The Power of Our People

THE POWER OF OUR PEOPLE
by Ellen Sutherland

◉ **MAIN IDEA AND DETAILS**

◉ **SUMMARIZE**

LESSON VOCABULARY amendments, bicameral, compromised, confederation, politics, ratified, representatives, responsibilities, sovereignty, unanimously

SUMMARY This book is about three founding documents of the United States: The Declaration of Independence, the Constitution, and the Bill of Rights.

INTRODUCE THE BOOK

BUILD BACKGROUND Remind students that the Fourth of July is more than just a time to watch fireworks. Ask students to talk about the Declaration of Independence. Do any of them know what its main idea is?

ELL Ask students to talk about their experience of the Fourth of July. What sights and sounds do they remember?

PREVIEW/USE TEXT FEATURES Invite students to look at all the illustrations and captions in the book. Ask students how the illustrations give clues as to the book's content.

TEACH/REVIEW VOCABULARY To reinforce the contextual meaning of the word *representatives* on page 5, discuss with students how the following phrase "from each of the colonies" helps them understand the meaning of the word. Repeat this exercise with other vocabulary words highlighted throughout the book.

TARGET SKILL AND STRATEGY

◉ **MAIN IDEA AND DETAILS** Remind students that every book is about a topic and the most important idea about the topic is the *main idea*. Remind students that the main idea is supported by *supporting details* that give more information about it. As they read this book, have them think about what the main ideas of each of the three documents are.

◉ **SUMMARIZE** Encourage students to *summarize* sections of material as they read by giving main points. Demonstrate how these may be recorded in a simple outline.

READ THE BOOK

Use the following questions to support comprehension.

PAGE 12 How many times has the Constitution been amended? *(27 times)*

PAGE 20 What is the main idea of the Bill of Rights? *(to guarantee American citizens certain rights and freedoms)*

PAGE 21 Why is our Constitution called a living document? *(It was designed to adapt to new times.)*

TALK ABOUT THE BOOK

READER RESPONSE

1. Responses may vary. Declaration of Independence: Main Idea: declared American independence from England; Details: written on parchment; listed the rights of every man; listed the wrongs committed against the colonists by the king of England; Constitution: Main Idea: the highest law in the U.S.; Details: explains how the government works; explains the rights and responsibilities enjoyed by each citizen; can be amended

2. Responses may vary. Growing dissatisfaction led the colonies to form their own government.

3. Responses may vary. A confederate may be someone who agrees to help you. Confederate soldiers fought the Union in the Civil War.

4. Responses will vary.

RESPONSE OPTION

WRITING Have students imagine themselves back in colonial North America. Have them write a paragraph arguing for American independence from Britain.

CONTENT CONNECTION

SOCIAL STUDIES Have students use the Internet or the library to find a facsimile of the original Declaration of Independence. Who were the signers, and how many of them were there? Have students read the document aloud to the class.

Time for **SOCIAL STUDIES**

Main Idea and Details

- The **main idea** is the most important idea about the topic of a paragraph, passage, or article.
- **Supporting details** are the small pieces of information that tell more about the main idea.

Directions Reread the following passage adapted from *The Power of Our People.* Then answer the questions below.

> In many ways, the Declaration of Independence set the stage for our Constitution. The Constitution is the highest law in the United States. All other laws come from it. The Constitution describes how our government works. It also explains the rights and responsibilities enjoyed by each citizen. If it weren't for our Constitution, we wouldn't have a President, Congress, or the Supreme Court.
>
> The Constitution is called a "living document." That means that it can be changed to work today as well as in the 1700s. The U.S. Constitution uses simple language to describe our government. It is the oldest written set of governing principles for the United States in use today. It is also short, at about 4,500 words!

1. What is the main idea of the first paragraph?

_____

2. What is one supporting detail in the first paragraph that tells about the main idea?

_____

3. What is another supporting detail in that paragraph that tells about the main idea?

_____

_____

4. What is the main idea of the second paragraph?

_____

5. What is one supporting detail that tells more about this main idea?

_____

© Pearson Education 4

50

Vocabulary

Directions Fill in the blank with the word from the box that fits the definition.

> ## Check the Words You Know
>
> ___amendments   ___bicameral
> ___compromised   ___confederation
> ___politics   ___ratified
> ___representatives   ___responsibilities
> ___sovereignty   ___unanimously

1. _____ supremacy of authority or rule

2. _____ approved and given formal sanction to

3. _____ composed of two legislative branches

4. _____ a political union of persons, parties, or states

5. _____ in a manner reflecting complete agreement

6. _____ the art or science of government or governing

7. _____ formal revisions to a document

8. _____ settled by concessions, or agreements to give in part-way

9. _____ delegates or agents acting on behalf of others

10. _____ things for which one must be accountable

Directions Write a brief paragraph about the U.S. Constitution, using as many vocabulary words as possible.

_____

_____

_____

_____

51

Answer Key for Below-Level Reader Practice

Cheers for the Cheetahs LR1

⟳ Cause and Effect, LR2

Possible answers given. **1.** He thought boys were better at sports than girls because he always watched the boys and saw how good they were. **2.** She wrote a letter. **3.** The principal and the coach could get mad. The benefit was that they were able to prove themselves. **4.** The coach will probably be more likely to give all girls a chance at sports now because he has seen that they can play well. **5.** It is important to speak up for yourself. Hannah and her team did, and they got a chance to play that they would not have had otherwise.

Vocabulary, LR3

1. h **2.** b **3.** d **4.** g **5.** c **6.** e **7.** f **8.** a **9.** fouled **10.** hoop **11.** jersey **12.** rim **13.** unbelievable

Home on the Range LR10

⟳ Draw Conclusions, LR11

1. Cattle eat and trample plants. Cattle make waterways dirty. Cattle destroy plant growth, which threatens local plants and the animals that depend on them for food.
2. Guests learn how to rope cattle. They can take tennis or yoga. They are given comfortable quarters and good food.
3. Ranchers must be up before dawn; they aren't done until eight at night; ranching is still done in winter.
4. Answers will vary.

Vocabulary, LR12

Underlined: **1.** The coyote was bawling for its mother. **2.** Wild coyotes live high in the mountains. **3.** Sometimes they call guys "dudes." **4.** At the roundup, all the cattle were put into pens. **5.** The cowboy never used his spurs on his horses.
Sentences will vary.

A World Tour of Cultures LR19

⟳ Draw Conclusions, LR20

Possible responses given. **1.** Paper was invented in China about A.D. 105. **2.** At first, paper was made from bamboo, hemp, or mulberry plants, and only the rich could afford it. **3.** People hang red paper cuttings for good luck during the New Year Festival in central China. **4.** Paper has been important for many years. **5.** Answers will vary.

Vocabulary, LR21

1. awkward **2.** atlas **3.** chanted **4.** vehicle **5.** miracle **6.** capable **7.** aboard **8.** Mechanical **9.** Possible response: to visit something again **10.** Possible response: to build something again

Lumberjacks LR28

⟳ Fact and Opinion, LR29

1. fact **2.** opinion **3.** both **4.** opinion **5.** both **6.** fact **7.** Responses will vary. **8.** Responses will vary.

Vocabulary, LR30

1. immense **2.** grizzly **3.** cord **4.** payroll **5.** dismay **6–10.** Responses will vary.

A Trip to the Capitol LR37

⟳ Main Idea and Details, LR38

Possible responses given. **1.** The Founding Fathers wanted the United States to have a strong government. **2.** In the Constitution, they outlined three branches of government. **3.** The three branches are the legislative, executive, and judicial. **4.** Each branch has different responsibilities; all branches are designed to help the government run smoothly. **5.** Each branch has the power to challenge the others.

Vocabulary, LR39

1. solemnly **2.** Constitution **3.** humble **4.** politics **5.** responsibility **6.** howling **7.** vain
Responses will vary.

Answer Key for On-Level Reader Practice

Fabulous Female Athletes   LR4

 Cause and Effect, LR5

Possible responses given. **1.** Men were away at war, and people wanted to see baseball games. **2.** Men came home from the war; people didn't want to see women playing anymore. **3.** Wilma Rudolf refused to give up. She worked with doctors. She was determined, and this helped her to win in the Olympics. **4.** Billy Jean King got the U.S. Open to award equal prizes to men and women; Althea Gibson made it easier for African American women to compete in sports; Wilma Rudolf made it easier for women to compete in track events. **5.** They earn better pay; they can compete in events that were previously just for men; they get better training.

Vocabulary, LR6

1–5. jersey; unbelievable; amateur; rim; speechless **6.** fouled; made an unfair play **7.** swatted; hit sharply or violently **8.** marveled; filled with wonder **9.** hoop; ring; round, flat band

On a Ranch   LR13

 Draw Conclusions, LR14

1–3. Responses will vary.

Vocabulary, LR15

1. bawling **2.** coyote **3.** dudes **4.** roundup **5.** spurs
Sentences will vary.

To Market, To Market   LR22

 Draw Conclusions, LR23

Possible responses given. **1.** There are mountains, waterfalls, and rain forests. **2.** It is hot and rainy. **3.** They sell bananas, limes, apples, tomatoes, cooked meat, and fish from the local rivers. **4.** on counters made from palm leaves **5.** People sell and use items in Uganda's open-air markets that come from the country's mountains, rivers, and forests.

Vocabulary, LR24

Possible responses given. **1–7.** Sentences will vary. **8.** "on" or "in"; on a ship, airplane, or train **9.** again; takes a seat again **10.** Sentences will vary.

After School Excitement   LR31

 Fact and Opinion, LR32

Possible responses given.
1. Fact: Ethan and Jake are twin brothers. **2.** Opinion: The two boys are as different as could be. **3.** Fact: Ethan loves to bowl. **4.** Opinion: Ethan spends too much time bowling. **5.** Fact: Jake likes to do as many different things as he can. **6.** Opinion: It is silly for Jake to sign up for so many activities. **7.** Fact: Jake and Ethan's parents give Ethan more responsibility. **8.** Opinion: Jake is too easily distracted. **9.** Fact: Miss Sims is Jake's teacher. **10.** Opinion: Miss Sims is a caring teacher.

Vocabulary, LR33

1. grizzly **2.** dismay **3.** payroll **4.** immense **5.** cord
6–10. Responses will vary.

Meet the United States Government   LR32

 Main Idea and Details, LR41

Possible responses given. **1.** The executive branch is large and needs to be divided up. **2.** The President acts as the head of all the executive departments. **3.** The Department of State is one of the executive departments. **4.** The Department of the Treasury is one executive department. **5.** The Department of Defense is another executive department.

Vocabulary, LR42

1. solemnly **2.** Constitution **3.** humble **4.** politics **5.** responsibility
6. howling **7.** vain
Responses will vary.

Equality in Schools — LR7

⊙ Cause and Effect, LR8

Possible answers given. **1.** The doctrine of "separate but equal" caused segregation. One effect was that African Americans had separate and much worse schools than white people. **2.** It means that people can have separate schools or facilities as long as they are the same. The separate but equal schools were not equal. The schools of African Americans were worse. **3.** The National Association for the Advancement of Colored People; it works for the rights of African Americans. **4.** When people didn't continue to fight for integration, the schools began to be segregated again **5.** Answers will vary.

Vocabulary, LR9

Possible answers given. **1.** aspiring **2.** jeering **3.** discrimination **4.** diversity **5.** integration **6.** doctrine **7.** tactics

The Life of César Chávez — LR16

⊙ Draw Conclusions, LR17

1. Answers will vary. **2.** Answers will vary.

Vocabulary, LR18

1. boycotts **2.** fast **3.** discrimination **4.** strikes **5.** predetermined **6.** grueling **7.** boycotts **8.** discrimination **9.** fast **10.** grueling **11.** predetermined
7–11. Sentences will vary.

Geography Shapes Our World — LR25

⊙ Draw Conclusions, LR26

Possible responses given. **1.** The Niger River flows through villages. **2.** There are fish in the river. **3.** People eat fish from the river. **4.** There are beaches. **5.** People hunt and fish along the Amazon River. **6.** People use the water for vacations and food such as fish. **7.** There are colorful flowers and a bright, blue sky. **8.** The land inspires their music. **9.** Jamaica's music, reggae, is loud and bright. **10.** Geography can affect what types of food people eat in a culture.

Vocabulary, LR27

1. industry **2.** products **3.** climate **4.** plantation **5.** typhoons
Possible responses given. **6.** seven large landmasses of Earth **7.** the study of Earth, its people, resources, climate, and physical features **8.** to supply water to crops by artificial means **9.** a person, an animal, or a plant that originally lived or grew in a certain place **10.** things that are manufactured or made by a natural process **11.** violent storms occurring in the western Pacific Ocean **12.** the kind of weather a place has over time

Danger! Children at Work — LR34

⊙ Fact and Opinion, LR35

Possible responses given. **1.** Many immigrant children were sent off to work at a young age. **2.** It was wrong to use child labor. **3.** Many children worked in sweatshops. **4.** The conditions in sweatshops were terrible. **5.** Some newsies were only five years old. **6.** A five-year-old child is too young to work. **7.** In 1929 the stock market crashed. **8.** The stock market crash was the worst thing that had ever happened. **9.** All fifty states now have child-labor laws. **10.** Child-labor laws are important laws.

Vocabulary, LR36

Responses and the words used will vary.

The Power of Our People — LR43

⊙ Main Idea and Details, LR44

Possible responses given. **1.** The Constitution is the highest law of the United States. **2.** All other laws come from it. **3.** The Constitution explains the rights and responsibilities enjoyed by each citizen. **4.** The Constitution is a living document. **5.** It is written in simple language; it is about 4,500 words long.

Vocabulary, LR45

1. sovereignty **2.** ratified **3.** bicameral **4.** confederation **5.** unanimously **6.** politics **7.** amendments **8.** compromised **9.** representatives **10.** responsibilities
Responses will vary.

Differentiated Instruction

Table of Contents

Routine Cards...DI•1

Daily Group Time Lessons

Week 1 **"What Jo Did"**
- Strategic Intervention Days 1–5 .... DI•2, 4, 6, 8, 10
- On-Level Days 1 and 5 ....DI•3, 11
- Advanced Days 1–5 .... DI•3, 5, 7, 9, 11

Week 2 **Coyote School News**
- Strategic Intervention Days 1–5 .... DI•12, 14, 16, 18, 20
- On-Level Days 1 and 5 ....DI•13, 21
- Advanced Days 1–5 .... DI•13, 15, 17, 19, 21

Week 3 **Grace and the Time Machine**
- Strategic Intervention Days 1–5 .... DI•22, 24, 26, 28, 30
- On-Level Days 1 and 5 ....DI•23, 31
- Advanced Days 1–5 .... DI•23, 25, 27, 29, 31

Week 4 **Marven of the Great North Woods**
- Strategic Intervention Days 1–5 .... DI•32, 34, 36, 38, 40
- On-Level Days 1 and 5 ....DI•33, 41
- Advanced Days 1–5 .... DI•33, 35, 37, 39, 41

Week 5 **So You Want to Be President?**
- Strategic Intervention Days 1–5 .... DI•42, 44, 46, 48, 50
- On-Level Days 1 and 5 ....DI•43, 51
- Advanced Days 1–5 .... DI•43, 45, 47, 49, 51

Reteach Lessons...DI•52

Matching Students to Text

Reading Levels ....DI•57

Independent Reading Chart..DI•58

Running Record..DI•59

Routine Cards

Routine Card

Oral Rereading Routine

Use this Routine when students read orally.

1 Read Have students read the entire book orally.

2 Reread For optimal fluency, students should reread the text three or four times.

3 Provide Feedback Listen as students read and provide corrective feedback regarding their oral reading and their use of decoding strategies.

Routine Card

Choral Reading Routine

Use this Routine when students read chorally.

1 Select a Passage Choose an appropriate passage from the selection.

2 Divide into Groups Assign each group a part to read.

3 Model Have students track the print as you read.

4 Read Together Have students read along with you.

5 Independent Reading Have the groups read aloud without you. Monitor progress and provide feedback. For optimal fluency, students should reread three to four times.

Routine Card

Fluent Word Reading Routine

Teach students to read words fluently using this Routine.

1 Connect Write an example word. Isolate the sound-spelling or word structure element you will focus on and ask students to demonstrate their understanding.

2 Model When you come to a new word, look at all the letters in the word and think about its vowel sound. Say the sounds in the word to yourself and then read the word. Model reading the example words in this way. When you come to a new word, what are you going to do?

3 Group Practice Write other similar words. Let's read these words. Look at the letters, think about the vowel sounds, and say the sounds to yourself. When I point to the word, let's read it together. Allow 2-3 seconds previewing time for each word.

Routine Card

Paired Reading Routine

Use this Routine when students read in pairs.

1 Reader 1 Begins Students read the entire book, switching readers at the end of each page.

2 Reader 2 Begins Have partners reread; now the other partner begins.

3 Reread For optimal fluency, students should reread three or four times.

4 Provide Feedback Listen as students read. Provide corrective feedback regarding their oral reading and their use of decoding strategies.

Routine Cards

Routine Card

Multisyllabic Word Routine

Teach students this Routine to read long words with meaningful parts.

1 Teach Tell students to look for meaningful parts and to think about the meaning of each part. They should use the parts to read the word and determine meaning.

2 Model Think aloud to analyze a long word for the base word, ending, prefix, and/or suffix and to identify the word and determine its meaning.

3 Guide Practice Provide examples of long words with endings (-ing, -ed, -s), prefixes (un-, re-, dis-, mis-, non-), and/or suffixes (-ly, -ness, -less, -ful, and so on). Help students analyze base words and parts.

4 Provide Feedback Encourage students to circle parts of the words to help identify parts and determine meaning.

Routine Card

Picture Walk Routine

To build concepts and vocabulary, conduct a structured picture walk before reading.

1 Prepare Preview the selection and list key concepts and vocabulary you wish to develop.

2 Discuss As students look at the pages, discuss illustrations, have students point to pictured items, and/or ask questions that target key concepts and vocabulary.

3 Elaborate Elaborate on students' responses to reinforce correct use of the vocabulary and to provide additional exposure to key concepts.

4 Practice For more practice with key concepts, have each student turn to a partner and do the picture walk using the key concept vocabulary.

Routine Card

Multisyllabic Word Routine

Teach students this Routine to chunk words with no recognizable parts.

1 Teach Tell students to look for chunks in words with no meaningful parts. They should say each chunk slowly and then say the chunks fast to make a whole word.

2 Model Think aloud to demonstrate breaking a word into chunks, saying each chunk slowly, and then saying the chunks fast to make a word.

3 Guide Practice Provide examples of long words with no meaningful parts. Help students chunk the words.

4 Provide Feedback If necessary, reteach by modeling how to break words into chunks.

Routine Card

Concept Vocabulary

Use this Routine to teach concept vocabulary.

1 Introduce the Word Relate the word to the week's concept. Supply a student-friendly definition.

2 Demonstrate Provide several familiar examples to demonstrate meaning.

3 Apply Have students demonstrate understanding with a simple activity.

4 Display the Word Relate the word to the concept by displaying it on a concept web. Have students identify word parts and practice reading the word.

5 Use the Word Often Encourage students to use the word often in their writing and speaking. Ask questions that require students to use the word.

Group Time

ROUTINE

Cheers for the Cheetahs
by Kim Whiting

Illustrated by Aleksey Ivanov

Leveled Reader Database

ONLINE

PearsonSuccessNet.com

1 Build Background

REINFORCE CONCEPTS Display the Developing New Understandings Concept Web. This week's concept is *developing new understandings.* When we develop a new understanding, we learn something new about someone or something. We can develop new understandings at work and at play. Discuss the meaning of each word on the web, using the definitions on p. 142l and the Concept Vocabulary routine on p. DI·1.

CONNECT TO READING This week you will read about ways people react to unexpected events and situations. Some of the situations happen at school. Think about the narrator of "The Circuit." How does he feel as he leaves school? How do you think he will feel about moving? *(happy, excited; unhappy, angry)*

2 Read Leveled Reader *Cheers for the Cheetahs*

BEFORE READING Using the Picture Walk routine on p. DI·1, guide students through the text focusing on key concepts and vocabulary. Ask questions such as:

pp. 4–5 This story tells about girls playing basketball. Does the girl wearing a sweatband seem to be a good player?

pp. 12–15 What are the girls doing on page 12? Right, they are making shirts, or jerseys. What do you think they will use the jerseys for? *(The jerseys are their team uniforms. They will wear them for a basketball game.)*

DURING READING Read pp. 3–4 aloud, while students track the print. Do a choral reading of pp. 5–8. If students are capable, have them read and discuss the remainder of the book with a partner. Ask: What do the girls want to do? Why do they want to do it?

AFTER READING Encourage pairs of students to discuss games and sports that boys and girls play together. We read *Cheers for the Cheetahs* to learn about girls who wanted to play basketball. We will learn about another girl who plays basketball when we read "What Jo Did."

Monitor Progress

Selection Reading and Comprehension

If... students have difficulty reading the selection with a partner,	**then...** have them follow along as they listen to the Online Leveled Reader Audio.
If... students have trouble understanding why the girls are upset,	**then...** reread pp. 6–8 and discuss the girls' plan together.

For alternate Leveled Reader lesson plans that teach

Cause and Effect, **Prior Knowledge,** and **Lesson Vocabulary,** see pp. LR1–LR9.

On-Level

DAY 1

ROUTINE

1 Build Background

DEVELOP VOCABULARY Write the word *nervous* and ask students to define it in their own words. *(When you are nervous, you are a little scared about something.)* Where or when might you feel nervous? *(first day of school, first time to do something)* Repeat this activity with the word *participate* and other words from the Leveled Reader *Fabulous Female Athletes.* Use the Concept Vocabulary routine on p. DI·1 as needed.

2 Read Leveled Reader *Fabulous Female Athletes*

BEFORE READING Have students create time lines titled Women in Sports that start with 1900. This book tells a lot about the history of women playing professional sports. As you read, look for important dates and events, and record them on your time line. Think about how ideas about women and sports have changed over time.

DURING READING Have students follow along as you read pp. 3–7. Then let them complete the book on their own. Remind students to add dates and events to their time lines as they read.

AFTER READING Have students compare their time lines. Point out that knowing how attitudes have changed toward women playing sports will help them as they read tomorrow's story, "What Jo Did."

Advanced

DAY 1

ROUTINE

1 Read Leveled Reader *Equality in American Schools*

BEFORE READING Recall the Read Aloud "The Circuit." How does the narrator feel when Mr. Lema asks him to read? How does Mr. Lema make him feel later in the story? *(nervous, scared; happy, like they are friends, like he is accepted)* Today you will read about the struggle African American students faced in American schools and the ways in which people fought to make sure all students got a good education.

CRITICAL THINKING Have students read the Leveled Reader independently. Encourage them to think critically. For example, ask:

• How do you think African Americans in the early 1900s felt about laws that made them use separate facilities and go to separate schools?

• Why do you think some people believed that the doctrine of "separate but equal" was a good idea?

• Why do you think the author included the chapter "Today"?

AFTER READING Have students review the selection to find five or more unfamiliar words and determine their meanings by using context clues or by consulting a dictionary. Then ask them to write fill-in-the-blank sentences that convey the meanings of the words. Encourage students to meet with you to discuss the selection and the sentences they wrote.

2 Independent Extension Activity

NOW TRY THIS Assign "Now Try This" on pp. 22–23 of *Equality in American Schools* for students to work on throughout the week.

What Jo Did

Group Time

DAY **2**

Audio CD **AudioText**

ROUTINE

1 Word Study/Phonics

LESSON VOCABULARY Use p. 144b to review the meanings of *fouled, hoop, jersey, marveled, rim, speechless, swatted,* and *unbelievable.* Have individuals practice reading the words from word cards.

DECODING MULTISYLLABIC WORDS Write *congratulated,* saying the word as you write it. Then model how to read a word with an ending and no recognizable parts in the base word. *I see the ending -ed on a base word. When I take off the ending, I see a chunk at the beginning of the word: con. I see a chunk in the middle: grat. I see a u, but then I see a chunk at the end: late. I say each chunk slowly and add the ending: con grat u late ed. I say the chunks fast to make a whole word: congratulated. Is it a real word? Yes, I know the word congratulated.*

Use the Multisyllabic Word routine on p. DI·1 to help students read other words from "What Jo Did": *especially, bundled, responded, embarrassment, encouraged,* and *progressed.* Be sure students understand the meanings of words such as *especially* and *progressed.*

Use *Strategies for Word Analysis,* Lesson 6, with students who have difficulty mastering word analysis and need practice with decodable text.

2 Read "What Jo Did," pp. 146–151

BEFORE READING In *Cheers for the Cheetahs,* we read about a group of girls who wanted to play basketball. Think about how the coach treated the girls as you read "What Jo Did."

Using the Picture Walk routine on p. DI·1, guide students through the text, asking questions such as those listed below. Read the question on p. 147 together to set a purpose for reading.

p. 148 Can you tell from the picture whether this is a boy or a girl? Why or why not? *(can't tell; boys and girls wear hats and T-shirts)*

p. 150 What is unusual about this picture? *(It looks like the kid has really long arms. The ball looks like an oval.)* Yes, photographers can use techniques and computers to change or distort photographs.

DURING READING Follow the Guiding Comprehension routine on pp. 148–151. Have students read along with you while tracking the print or do a choral reading of the selection. Stop every two pages to ask what has happened so far. Prompt as necessary.

- What can Jo do that most people can't?
- Why does Jo keep her hat on?

AFTER READING What has happened so far? What do you think will happen next? Reread passages with students as needed.

Monitor Progress

Word and Story Reading

If... students have difficulty reading multisyllabic words in the selection,	**then...** have them look for and read meaningful parts in the words or have them chunk words with no recognizable parts.
If... students need practice reading words fluently,	**then...** use the Fluent Word Reading Routine on the DI tab.
If... students have difficulty reading along with the group,	**then...** have them follow along as they listen to the AudioText.

Advanced

1 Extend Vocabulary

WORD STRUCTURE Choose and read a sentence containing a word with a prefix or suffix, such as this one from p. 7 of *Equality in American Schools:* "A poor school leaves its students at a disadvantage." The prefix *dis-* means "opposite, not." So what does *disadvantage* mean? *(something that is not an advantage; something that causes harm)* How does knowing the meaning of the prefix help you understand the meaning of the word? *(It tells me that a disadvantage is the opposite of an advantage.)* Discuss how recognizing and understanding prefixes and suffixes can be helpful. Remind students to use the strategy as they read "What Jo Did."

2 Read "What Jo Did," pp. 146–151

BEFORE READING Today you will read a story about a girl who uses her skills at basketball to overcome an unfair opinion. As you read, think about other situations you have read about in which people helped others change their minds.

Have students write a list of skills that a good basketball player has in their Strategy Response Logs (p. 146).

CRITICAL THINKING Have students read pp. 146–151 independently. Encourage them to think critically. For example, ask:

- Jo thinks, "They probably think I'm a boy . . . . Might as well enjoy the ride." What does she mean?

AFTER READING Have students review and revise the lists they made in their Strategy Response Logs (p. 151). Then have partners discuss the selection and share their lists. Encourage them to think about any character traits they have listed or that they think Jo has. Have partners list other sports, activities, or jobs in which a person with these traits might be successful.

DAY 2

Audio CD · AudioText

What Jo Did
Group Time

Audio CD AudioText

1 Reinforce Comprehension

◎ SKILL CAUSE AND EFFECT Have students give an example of a cause and an effect *(The light went off because I flipped the switch.)* and list clue words that often signal cause-and-effect relationships *(because, so, cause, since).* If necessary, review the meaning and provide a model. An effect is what happened. A cause is why it happened. The flowers grew because it rained. If I want to find the effect, I ask myself, "What happened?" The flowers grew. If I want to find the cause, I ask myself, "Why did it happen?" Because it rained. I look for clue words like *because* and *so* to help me find the relationship.

Make a chart on the board with *Cause* and *Effect* as the headings. Write example sentences showing cause-and-effect relationships. Ask students to write the cause and the effect in the chart and circle clue words in the sentence.

> **The court was wet, so we did not play.**
> **Because the net was high, Jo learned to jump very high.**
> **Jo was smallest, so she was picked last.**

2 Read "What Jo Did," pp. 152–155

BEFORE READING Have students retell what has happened in the story so far. Ask: How have the boys reacted to playing basketball with Jo? Reread the last two paragraphs of p. 151 and model how to use prior knowledge. As I read I think about what I already know about basketball. I've seen professional players dunk the ball. I wonder if Jo can jump high enough to slam the ball through the net. Remind students to use prior knowledge as they read the rest of "What Jo Did." **◎ STRATEGY Prior Knowledge**

DURING READING Follow the Guiding Comprehension routine on pp. 152–155. Have students read along with you while tracking print or do a choral reading. Stop every two pages to ask students what has happened so far. Prompt as necessary.

- What did Jo try for the first time?
- How did the boys react to Jo's dunk?
- How did the boys react when Jo's hat fell off?

AFTER READING How does this story show people developing new understandings? Reread with students for comprehension as needed. Tell them that tomorrow they will read two poems about playing basketball by the author of "What Jo Did."

DAY **3**

Monitor Progress

Word and Story Reading

If... students have difficulty reading multisyllabic words in the selection,	**then...** have them look for and read meaningful parts in the words or have them chunk words with no recognizable parts.
If... students have difficulty reading along with the group,	**then...** have them follow along as they listen to the AudioText.

Advanced

1 Extend Comprehension

◉ SKILL CAUSE AND EFFECT Have students give simple examples of cause-and-effect relationships. Then have them give examples of cause-effect-cause relationships in which the first effect becomes the cause of another effect. *(Because I was late, I rushed out the door. I tripped over the dog.)*

◉ STRATEGY PRIOR KNOWLEDGE Have students imagine that they know very little about basketball or any sport. Ask:

• How would your lack of prior knowledge affect your understanding of the story?

2 Read "What Jo Did," pp. 152–155

DAY 3

Audio CD   AudioText

BEFORE READING Have students recall what has happened in the selection so far. Remind them to look for cause-and-effect relationships and to use prior knowledge as they read the remainder of "What Jo Did."

CREATIVE THINKING Have students read pp. 152–155 independently. Encourage them to think creatively. For example, ask:

• How would the story change if Jo were a boy and the others were girls?

AFTER READING Have students complete the Strategy Response Log activity (p. 154). Then have them choose a friend of the opposite gender and write a book review/summary of "What Jo Did" for that friend. Discuss with students if and how their reviews changed based on whether the friend was a boy or a girl.

What Jo Did

Group Time

Audio CD AudioText

1 Practice Retelling

REVIEW STORY ELEMENTS Help students identify the main characters and the setting of "What Jo Did." Then guide them in using the Retelling Cards to list story events in sequence. Prompt students to include important details.

RETELL Using the Retelling Cards, have students work in pairs to retell "What Jo Did." Monitor retelling and prompt students as needed. For example, ask:

- Tell me what this story is about in a few sentences.
- What is the author trying to teach us?

If students struggle, model a fluent retelling.

2 Read "Fast Break" and "Allow Me to Introduce Myself"

BEFORE READING Read the genre information on p. 158. Explain to students that poetry is made up of words and lines that sometimes rhyme. Poems are usually very expressive and imaginative even about everyday subjects. These two poems are about playing basketball. As we read them, think about how the poems are different from "What Jo Did."

Point out the words in color and larger print on p. 159 and discuss with students how these words should be read *(with emphasis)*. Then have students read just the bold and colored words on p. 161. What do these words have in common? *(They rhyme.)*

DURING READING Have students read along with you while tracking the print or do a choral reading of the poems. Stop to discuss how to read the poems so that the lines flow together. Remind students not to stop at the end of each line. Have students echo several lines of each poem to demonstrate the rhythm of the lines.

AFTER READING Have students share their reactions to the poems. Then guide them through the Reading Across Texts and Writing Across Texts activities, prompting if necessary.

- What are the poems and the story about?
- In what way are the poems most different from the story?
- How do you feel when you read the story? How do you feel when you read the poems?

Monitor Progress

Word and Poem Reading

If... students have difficulty reading multisyllabic words in the poems,	**then...** have them look for and read meaningful parts in the words or have them chunk words with no recognizable parts.
If... students have difficulty reading along with the group,	**then...** have them follow along as they listen to the AudioText.

Advanced

1 Read "Fast Break" and "Allow Me to Introduce Myself"

CRITICAL THINKING Have students read pp. 158–161 independently. Encourage them to think creatively. For example, ask:

- How are these two poems alike? How are they different?
- What words would you use to describe the poet's style?

AFTER READING Have students meet with you to discuss the poems and Reading Across Texts. Have students do Writing Across Texts independently.

2 Extend Genre Study

RESEARCH Have students use online or print resources to find other poems about their favorite sport or activity. Have them practice reading the poem aloud and then present it to the group. Discuss the different styles of writing shown by different poets.

WRITE Have students write a poem that is opposite in style from Charles R. Smith's poetry. Encourage them to set a slower-paced rhythm and use images that are calm and peaceful instead of active and explosive.

AudioText

Group Time

Leveled Reader
Database
ONLINE

PearsonSuccessNet.com

ROUTINE

1 Reread for Fluency

MODEL Read aloud pp. 3–4 of the Leveled Reader *Cheers for the Cheetahs,* emphasizing the rhythmic patterns of language. Have students note the grouping of your words and the rise and fall of your voice. Point out that the dialogue sounds like people talking to each other. Then read pp. 7–8 word-by-word in a monotone voice or emphasizing the wrong words. Ask students which model sounded better. Discuss how stressing important words creates a more natural rhythm, especially in dialogue.

PRACTICE Have students reread passages from *Cheers for the Cheetahs* with a partner or individually. For optimal fluency, they should reread three or four times. As students read, monitor fluency and provide corrective feedback. Students in this group are assessed in Weeks 2 and 4.

2 Retell Leveled Reader *Cheers for the Cheetahs*

Model how to skim the book, retelling as you skim. Then ask students to retell the book, page-by-page. Prompt them as needed.

- Where does this story take place?
- What is the problem in this story?

Monitor Progress

Fluency

If... students have difficulty reading fluently,	**then...** provide additional fluency practice by pairing nonfluent readers with fluent ones.

For alternate Leveled Reader lesson plans that teach
⊙ Cause and Effect, ⊙ Prior Knowledge, and
Lesson Vocabulary, see pp. LR1–LR9.

On-Level

1 Reread for Fluency ROUTINE

MODEL Read aloud p. 3 of the Leveled Reader *Fabulous Female Athletes,* emphasizing the rhythmic patterns of language. Have students note the grouping of your words into phrases and the rise and fall of your voice. Discuss how reading with a natural rhythm is much more pleasing than reading word-by-word.

PRACTICE Have students reread passages from *Fabulous Female Athletes* with a partner or individually. For optimal fluency, they should reread three or four times. As students read, monitor fluency and provide corrective feedback. Students in this group are assessed in Week 3.

2 Retell Leveled Reader *Fabulous Female Athletes*

Have students use headings and photographs as a guide to summarize important facts they learned from each section of the book. Prompt as needed.

- What is this section mostly about?
- What did you learn from reading this section?
- Why do you think the author wrote this section?

Advanced

1 Reread for Fluency ROUTINE

PRACTICE Have students silently reread passages from the Leveled Reader *Equality in American Schools.* Then have them reread aloud with a partner or individually. As students read, monitor fluency and provide corrective feedback. If students read fluently on the first reading, they do not need to reread three to four times. Assess the fluency of students in this group using p. 161a.

2 Revisit Leveled Reader *Equality in American Schools*

RETELL Have students retell the Leveled Reader *Equality in American Schools.*

NOW TRY THIS Have students complete their projects. You may wish to review their action plans and see if they need additional ideas. Have them share their action plans and tasks with classmates.

Group Time

ONLINE

PearsonSuccessNet.com

Strategic Intervention

ROUTINE

1 Build Background

REINFORCE CONCEPTS Display the Working Together Concept Web. This week's concept is *working together*. Sometimes we play with others, and sometimes we work with them. Think about times when you have worked together with a group. How is working together with others different from working by yourself? Discuss the meaning of each word on the web, using the definitions on p. 162I and the Concept Vocabulary routine on p. DI·1.

CONNECT TO READING This week you will read about people who work and live together on ranches. They work hard, just like Luz in "A Big-City Dream." How do you think Luz might have felt if more people had worked together with her on the lot? *(happy, excited, not so tired)*

2 Read Leveled Reader *Home on the Range*

BEFORE READING Using the Picture Walk routine on p. DI·1, guide students through the text focusing on key concepts and vocabulary. Ask questions such as:

pp. 4–5 This book is about different kinds of ranches. What can you tell about a ranch from these pictures? *(There are cowboys and cattle. Ranches are big areas of land.)* Yes, ranches are large, and people need to work together on them.

pp. 8–9 What are these people learning to do? *(rope a cow)* Sometimes people go to ranches to feel what it is like to be a cowboy or cowgirl.

DURING READING Read pp. 4–6 aloud, while students track the print. Do a choral reading of pp. 7–10. If students are capable, have them read and discuss the remainder of the book with a partner. Ask: What do people do at a dude ranch? What is a working ranch?

AFTER READING Encourage pairs of students to discuss whether they would enjoy working on a ranch. We read *Home on the Range* to learn about some ways people work together on ranches. Understanding what life is like on a ranch will help us as we read *Coyote School News*.

Monitor Progress

Selection Reading and Comprehension

If... students have difficulty reading the selection with a partner,	**then...** have them follow along as they listen to the Online Leveled Reader Audio.
If... students have trouble understanding the purpose of a guest ranch,	**then...** reread p. 10 and discuss how guests help keep the ranch running.

For alternate Leveled Reader lesson plans that teach
⟳ **Draw Conclusions,** ⟳ **Prior Knowledge,** and
Lesson Vocabulary, see pp. LR10–LR18.

On-Level

DAY 1

❶ Build Background ⟋ROUTINE

DEVELOP VOCABULARY Write the word *convince* and ask students to define it in their own words. *(to get someone to do or believe something)* What might you try to convince your parents of? *(that I should be able to stay up later; that I need a certain toy)* Repeat this activity with the word *demonstrate* and other words from the Leveled Reader *On a Ranch.* Use the Concept Vocabulary routine on p. DI·1 as needed.

❷ Read Leveled Reader *On a Ranch*

BEFORE READING Have students create T-charts with the labels *Ranches Then* and *Ranches Now.* This book tells about cattle ranching on the Great Plains. As you read, look for facts about activities that took place on ranches in the 1800s and activities that take place now. Some of the activities might be the same. Record facts in your T-charts.

DURING READING Have students follow along as you read pp. 3–7. Then let them complete the book on their own. Remind students to add facts to their T-charts as they read.

AFTER READING Have students compare their charts. Explain that knowing facts about ranching will help them as they read tomorrow's story, *Coyote School News.*

Advanced

DAY 1

❶ Read Leveled Reader *The Life of César Chávez* ⟋ROUTINE

BEFORE READING Recall the Read Aloud "A Big-City Dream." What was Luz trying to accomplish? *(making a garden out of a trash-covered city lot)* What needed to happen? *(more people needed to help her clean the lot)* Today you will read about one man's efforts to bring people together to make life better for workers.

CRITICAL THINKING Have students read the Leveled Reader independently. Encourage them to think critically. For example, ask:

- In what ways could the NFWA formed by César Chávez help migrant workers better than they could help themselves individually?
- What do you think was Chávez's most important achievement? Why?

AFTER READING Have students review the selection to find five or more unfamiliar words and determine their meanings by consulting a dictionary. Then ask them to write a synonym for each word. Encourage students to meet with you to discuss the selection and the words they listed.

❷ Independent Extension Activity

NOW TRY THIS Assign "Now Try This" on pp. 22–23 of *The Life of César Chávez* for students to work on throughout the week.

Group Time

DAY 2

Audio CD · AudioText

Monitor Progress

Word and Story Reading

If... students have difficulty reading multisyllabic words in the selection,	then... have them look for and read meaningful parts in the words or have them chunk words with no recognizable parts.
If... students need practice reading words fluently,	then... use the Fluent Word Reading Routine on the DI tab.
If... students have difficulty reading along with the group,	then... have them follow along as they listen to the AudioText.

Strategic Intervention

ROUTINE

1 Word Study/Phonics

LESSON VOCABULARY Use p. 164b to review the meanings of *bawling, coyote, dudes, roundup,* and *spurs.* Have individuals practice reading the words from word cards.

DECODING MULTISYLLABIC WORDS Write *attendance,* saying the word as you write it. Then model. This is a three-syllable word formed from the base word *attend* and the suffix *-ance.* First I cover the suffix and read the base word: *attend.* Then I blend the base word and the suffix to read the whole word: *attend ance, attendance.* The suffix *-ance* means "the state of," and *attend* means "to be present." So *attendance* means "the state of attending, or being present."

Use the Multisyllabic Word routine on p. DI·1 to help students read these other words from *Coyote School News: tattletale, patron, rattlesnake, stencil, inspection, lassoes, wrestled, bedrolls, graduate (v.), graduates (n.), promoted,* and *congratulations.* Be sure students understand the meanings of words such as *patron, stencil, bedrolls,* and *promoted.*

Use *Strategies for Word Analysis,* Lesson 7, with students who have difficulty mastering word analysis and need practice with decodable text.

2 Read *Coyote School News,* pp. 166–175

BEFORE READING In *Home on the Range,* we read about people working together on ranches. In *Coyote School News,* we will read about a boy who lives on a ranch and goes to a ranch school in the 1930s.

Using the Picture Walk routine on p. DI·1, guide students through the text, asking questions such as those listed below. Read the question on p. 167. Together set a purpose for reading.

pp. 166–167 This is the Coyote School and the school bus. How are they different from our school and school buses? *(smaller, old-fashioned, some kids riding horses)* Yes, some ranch children rode horses to school.

p. 173 What do you think this is? *(a newspaper or newsletter)* It's a school newspaper printed on a machine before computers.

DURING READING Follow the Guiding Comprehension routine on pp. 168–175. Have students read along with you while tracking the print or do a choral reading. Stop every two pages to ask what has happened so far. Prompt as necessary.

- Where and when did this story take place?
- What did the students at Coyote School work on together?

AFTER READING What has happened in the story so far? What do you think will happen next? Reread passages as needed.

Advanced

1 Extend Vocabulary

🎯 **DICTIONARY/GLOSSARY** Choose and read a sentence containing an unfamiliar word, such as this one from p. 3 of *The Life of César Chávez:* "César met many hardworking people living under difficult circumstances during his lifetime." As you read, you may come across difficult or unfamiliar words such as *circumstances*. If you cannot figure out the word using context clues, you can look up the word in the glossary or dictionary. Ask a student to see whether *circumstances* is in the glossary of the Leveled Reader. *(no)* Have a student look up *circumstances* in a dictionary and read the definition. Ask what steps students should follow to find a word in the dictionary. Remind students to use the strategy as they read *Coyote School News.*

2 Read *Coyote School News,* pp. 166–175

BEFORE READING Today you will read a story about a boy living on a ranch in the late 1930s. The story is fiction, but the setting is very similar to the time and place of César Chávez's boyhood. As you read, think about what you have read about people working on farms and ranches in the Southwest in the 1930s.

Have students record what they know about cowboys, ranching, the Southwest, and the 1930s in their Strategy Response Logs (p. 166). Remind them to think about and revise their ideas as they read.

CRITICAL THINKING/CREATIVE THINKING Have students read pp. 166–175 independently. Encourage them to think critically and creatively. For example, ask:

- Are Monchi's family or classmates anything like yours?
- How do you think Miss Byers feels about her job? What do you think is the hardest part of her job?
- Imagine you live at the time of the story. What job would you want to have?

AFTER READING Have partners discuss the selection and share their Strategy Response Log entries. Encourage them to think about what role they would like to have had on or near a ranch like Monchi's. Would they rather be a teacher, a school bus driver, or one of the vaqueros? Ask students to write a paragraph explaining which role they would choose and why.

Audio CD AudioText

Coyote School News
Group Time

DAY 3

Audio CD AudioText

1 Reinforce Comprehension

◉ **SKILL DRAW CONCLUSIONS** Have students tell what it means to draw a conclusion. *(to make a decision or have an opinion based on facts and details)* If necessary, review the meaning and provide a model. *When I draw a conclusion, I use what I know plus facts and details I've read and seen to make a decision or form an opinion about something. If I look out the window and see people wearing shorts and T-shirts and sunglasses, I can draw the conclusion that it is warm and sunny outside.*

Ask students to draw a conclusion about feeding cattle in winter based on these statements:

> **Cattle need lots of grass to eat. In many places, the ground freezes and is covered by snow in the winter. Ranchers then buy hay.**

(Ranchers feed hay to their cattle in the winter because the grass is frozen or snow covered.)

2 Read *Coyote School News,* pp. 176–183

BEFORE READING Have students retell what has happened in the story so far. Ask: How does Monchi feel about roundup? Reread the first paragraph on p. 174 and model how to use prior knowledge. *As I read, I think about what I already know about big gatherings of family and friends. They are very exciting. Monchi keeps asking his father about roundup. I think he is excited about it.* Remind students to use their prior knowledge as they read the rest of *Coyote School News.* ◉ **STRATEGY Prior Knowledge**

DURING READING Follow the Guiding Comprehension routine on pp. 176–183. Have students read along with you while tracking print or do a choral reading. Stop every two pages to ask students what has happened so far. Prompt as necessary.

- How did Monchi and his family celebrate *Nochebuena,* or Christmas Eve?
- What did Monchi get to do for the first time?
- What happened at the end of the story?

AFTER READING How does this story show people working together? Reread with students for comprehension as needed. Tell them that tomorrow they will read a how-to article about working together to start a school newspaper.

Monitor Progress

Word and Story Reading

If... students have difficulty reading multisyllabic words in the selection,	**then...** have them look for and read meaningful parts in the words or have them chunk words with no recognizable parts.
If... students have difficulty reading along with the group,	**then...** have them follow along as they listen to the AudioText.

ROUTINE

Advanced

DAY 3

① Extend Comprehension

⊙ **SKILL** **DRAW CONCLUSIONS** Read aloud the first two paragraphs on p. 172. Ask students to draw conclusions. *What reaction did Monchi expect Miss Byers to have? (He thought she would be mad.)* *What conclusion can you draw about why Monchi might have expected that reaction? (Other teachers might have scolded the children for speaking in Spanish.)*

⊙ **STRATEGY** **PRIOR KNOWLEDGE** Discuss with students the conclusion they just drew about teachers scolding children for speaking Spanish. Ask:

• *What prior knowledge do you have that helped you draw that conclusion? Why might a teacher have scolded the children for speaking Spanish instead of English?*

② Read *Coyote School News*, pp. 176–183

BEFORE READING Have students recall what has happened in the selection so far. Remind them to draw conclusions and to use prior knowledge as they read the remainder of *Coyote School News.*

CRITICAL THINKING Have students read pp. 176–183 independently. Encourage them to think critically. For example, ask:

• *Do you think Monchi should have gone to school or to roundup? Why?*

AFTER READING Have students complete the Strategy Response Log activity (p. 182). Then have them reread Monchi's article from the newspaper on p. 181. Ask students to rewrite the article from Monchi's point of view *after* he receives his award. Meet with students to review their articles and discuss their reactions to the story.

Audio CD AudioText

Group Time

DAY 4

1 Practice Retelling

REVIEW STORY ELEMENTS Help students identify the main characters and the setting of *Coyote School News.* Then guide them in using the Retelling Cards to list story events in sequence. Prompt students to include important details.

RETELL Using the Retelling Cards, have students work in pairs to retell *Coyote School News.* Monitor retelling and prompt students as needed. For example, ask:

- What is Monchi like?
- Tell me what this story is about in a few sentences.

If students struggle, model a fluent retelling.

2 Read "How to Start a School Newspaper"

BEFORE READING Read the genre information on p. 186. Explain to students that a how-to article is a type of nonfiction that gives directions about how to do or make something. The directions are often listed as numbered steps or as a list. This article is about how to start a school newspaper like the one in *Coyote School News.* As we read, look for the steps that tell you what to do.

Read the rest of the panel on p. 186. Have students scan the article to find keywords that tell the order in which to do things. Then have students scan for bold-faced words in the lists.

DURING READING Have students read along with you while tracking the print or do a choral reading of the article. Stop to discuss content-related vocabulary such as *layout* and *profile.* Make sure students understand the role each person at the paper plays.

AFTER READING Have students share their reactions to the article. Then guide them through the Reading Across Texts and Writing Across Texts activities, prompting if necessary.

- What four newspaper sections are mentioned in the article?
- Which of these sections appear in the newspaper stories in *Coyote School News?* Skim the stories to find out.
- Pick one issue of the newspaper from *Coyote School News.* What kind of writing is each story?

Audio CD AudioText

Monitor Progress

Word and Selection Reading

If... students have difficulty reading multisyllabic words in the selection,	**then...** have them look for and read meaningful parts in the words or have them chunk words with no recognizable parts.
If... students have difficulty reading along with the group,	**then...** have them follow along as they listen to the AudioText.

Advanced

1 Read "How to Start a School Newspaper"

CRITICAL THINKING/CREATIVE THINKING Have students read pp. 186–187 independently. Encourage them to think critically and creatively. For example, ask:

• Which role would you choose on a newspaper? Why?
• What other features would you include in your school newspaper?

AFTER READING Have students meet with you to discuss the article and Reading Across Texts. Have students do Writing Across Texts independently.

2 Extend Genre Study

RESEARCH Have students use online or print resources to find other how-to articles. Have them copy or print an article that tells how to do something they are interested in trying and share it with the class, noting whether the article is in list form or numbered steps.

WRITE Have students choose an activity that they can explain to a younger child in simple steps and write a short how-to article detailing the process. Encourage them to share the information with a student in a lower grade and see whether the child can understand the directions.

Audio CD   AudioText

Group Time

DAY 5

Home on the Range
by Cynthia Swain

Leveled Reader Database
ONLINE
PearsonSuccessNet.com

1 Reread for Fluency

MODEL Read aloud pp. 4–5 of the Leveled Reader *Home on the Range,* emphasizing the correct use of punctuation clues. Have students note that you come to a full stop at periods, pause at commas, and raise your voice with question marks. Then read pp. 6–7 without using punctuation clues. Have students tell you which model sounded better. Discuss how following punctuation clues makes reading understandable.

PRACTICE Have students reread passages from *Home on the Range* with a partner or individually. For optimal fluency, they should reread three or four times. As students read, monitor fluency and provide corrective feedback. Assess the fluency of students in this group using p. 187a.

2 Retell Leveled Reader *Home on the Range*

Model how to skim the book, retelling as you skim. Then ask students to retell the book, one chapter at a time. Prompt them as needed.

- What is this chapter mostly about?
- What did you learn from reading this chapter?

Monitor Progress

Fluency

If... students have difficulty reading fluently,	**then...** provide additional fluency practice by pairing nonfluent readers with fluent ones.

For alternate Leveled Reader lesson plans that teach
Draw Conclusions, Prior Knowledge,
and **Lesson Vocabulary,** see pp. LR10–LR18.

On-Level

1 Reread for Fluency
ROUTINE

MODEL Read aloud p. 3 of the Leveled Reader *On a Ranch,* emphasizing the use of punctuation clues. Have students note your complete stops at periods and pauses at commas. Discuss how using punctuation clues makes your reading more understandable.

PRACTICE Have students reread passages from *On a Ranch* with a partner or individually. For optimal fluency, they should reread three or four times. As students read, monitor fluency and provide corrective feedback. Students in this group are assessed in Week 3.

2 Retell Leveled Reader *On a Ranch*

Have students skim to summarize the important facts they learned from reading the book. Prompt as needed.

- Tell me about the major events from early ranching to today in order.
- What did you learn from reading this book?

Advanced

1 Reread for Fluency
ROUTINE

PRACTICE Have students reread passages from the Leveled Reader *The Life of César Chávez* with a partner or individually. As students read, monitor fluency and provide corrective feedback. If students read fluently on the first reading, they do not need to reread three to four times. Students in this group were assessed in Week 1.

2 Revisit Leveled Reader *The Life of César Chávez*

RETELL Have students retell the Leveled Reader *The Life of César Chávez.*

NOW TRY THIS Have students complete their banners. You may wish to see whether they need any art supplies. Have them explain their banners to you and then present them to the class.

Group Time

Leveled Reader
Database
ONLINE
PearsonSuccessNet.com

Strategic Intervention

ROUTINE

❶ Build Background

REINFORCE CONCEPTS Display the Imagination Concept Web. This week's concept is *imagination*. Think about times when you have used your imagination to play a game and when you have used it to come up with an idea for a project or an essay. Discuss the meaning of each word on the web, using the definitions on p. 188l and the Concept Vocabulary routine on p. DI·1.

CONNECT TO READING This week you will read about people using their imaginations to travel—sometimes to other places, sometimes to other times! Where and how did the narrator of "Journal of a Teenage Genius" travel? *(back in time in a time machine)*

❷ Read Leveled Reader *A World Tour of Cultures*

BEFORE READING Using the Picture Walk routine on p. DI·1, guide students through the text focusing on key concepts and vocabulary. Ask questions such as:

p. 3 Reading this book is like traveling to Africa, Asia, and Europe to see how people there live. What do you think the children in this picture are doing? *(celebrating a holiday with masks, all dressed up)* Celebrating a holiday in this way is part of their culture, or way of life.

p. 6 What do the pictures on this page show? *(different kinds of homes)* Yes, people in different parts of the world live in different kinds of homes. Which of these homes would you like to live in? Why?

DURING READING Read pp. 3–4 aloud, while students track the print. Do a choral reading of pp. 5–8. If students are capable, have them read and discuss the remainder of the book with a partner. Ask: What are some things people around the world use their imaginations to create?

AFTER READING Encourage pairs of students to use their imaginations and discuss what it would be like to take their own trip around the world and what they would see, hear, and do. As we read *A World Tour of Cultures,* we imagined we were traveling to other places to learn how people live. Using your imagination to travel to other places and times will help you as you read *Grace and the Time Machine*.

Monitor Progress

Selection Reading and Comprehension

If... students have difficulty reading the selection with a partner,	**then...** have them follow along as they listen to the Online Leveled Reader Audio.
If... students have trouble understanding the concept of *culture,*	**then...** reread p. 3 and discuss specific examples of language, food, and songs that vary from culture to culture.

For alternate Leveled Reader lesson plans that teach
◉ **Draw Conclusions,** ◉ **Answer Questions,**
and **Lesson Vocabulary,** see pp. LR19–LR27.

On-Level

1 Build Background

DEVELOP VOCABULARY Write the word *excursion* and tell students that it means "a short trip." Ask for personal context: If you could go anywhere on an excursion, where would you go? *(the beach, the mall, my friend's house)* Repeat this activity with the word *culture* and other words from the Leveled Reader *To Market, To Market.* Use the Concept Vocabulary routine on p. DI·1 as needed.

2 **Read** Leveled Reader *To Market, To Market*

BEFORE READING Have students create a web with the label *Open-Air Market* in the center oval. This book tells about outdoor, or open-air, markets around the world. As you read, look for facts about open-air markets. Imagine what those markets look, sound, and smell like. Record these details on your web.

DURING READING Have students follow along as you read pp. 3–9. Then let them complete the book on their own. Remind students to add facts to their webs as they read.

AFTER READING Have students compare their webs. Point out that using their imaginations to picture traveling to an open-air market will help them as they read tomorrow's story, *Grace and the Time Machine.*

Advanced

1 **Read** Leveled Reader *Geography Shapes Our World*

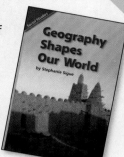

BEFORE READING Recall the Read Aloud "Journal of a Teenage Genius." What role did imagination play in that story? *(Someone had invented a time travel machine.)* If you had a time machine, where and when would you want to go? Would you go to another country? Today you will read about children who live in other parts of world. You can try to imagine what their lives are like.

CRITICAL THINKING Have students read the Leveled Reader independently. Encourage them to think critically. For example, ask:

* How are the lives of these children like your life?
* How are they different?
* Which of these places would you like to visit? Why?

AFTER READING Have students review the selection to find five or more unfamiliar words and determine their meanings by using context clues or consulting a dictionary. Then ask them to write a paragraph about a trip to a country they would like to visit using the words. Encourage students to meet with you to discuss the selection and their paragraphs.

2 Independent Extension Activity

NOW TRY THIS Assign "Now Try This" on pp. 22–23 of *Geography Shapes Our World* for students to work on throughout the week.

Group Time

Audio CD AudioText

Strategic Intervention

DAY 2

1 Word Study/Phonics

LESSON VOCABULARY Use p. 190b to review the meanings of *aboard, atlas, awkward, capable, chant, mechanical, miracle, reseats,* and *vehicle.* Have individuals practice reading from word cards.

DECODING MULTISYLLABIC WORDS Write *existed,* saying the word as you write it. Then model how to use meaningful parts to read longer words. First I look for meaningful parts. If I see a part I know, like *-ed* or *-ing,* I look for a base word. Here I see *-ed* and a base word. I say the base word in chunks: *ex ist.* I know this word: *exist.* It means "to be." I add the ending and say all the parts: *ex ist ed.* Then I say the parts fast to make the whole word: *existed.*

Use the Multisyllabic Word routine on p. DI·1 to help students read these other words from *Grace and the Time Machine: shambles, crutches, favoring, pantomime, overlapping, continual, occasional, imprisoned,* and *contraption.* Be sure students understand the meanings of words such as *favoring* and *pantomime.*

Use *Strategies for Word Analysis,* Lesson 8, with students who have difficulty mastering word analysis and need practice with decodable text.

2 Read *Grace and the Time Machine,* pp. 192–201

BEFORE READING In *A World Tour of Cultures,* we read about real places in the world. In *Grace and the Time Machine,* we will read a play about a group of friends who use their imaginations to travel to places and times in a time machine.

Using the Picture Walk routine on p. DI·1, guide students through the text, asking questions such as those listed below. Read the question on p. 193. Together, set a purpose for reading.

p. 196 What are the children pictured inside the cloudlike bubbles doing? *(relaxing, riding a skateboard, wearing a machine on her head)*

pp. 200–201 To what time have the friends traveled on these pages? *(the time of the dinosaurs)*

DURING READING Follow the Guiding Comprehension routine on pp. 194–201. Have students read along with you while tracking the print or do a choral reading. Stop every two pages to ask what has happened so far. Prompt as necessary.
- What did the characters in the play decide to invent?
- Where did they go first?

AFTER READING What has happened in the play so far? What do you think will happen next? Reread passages as needed.

Monitor Progress

Word and Story Reading

If... students have difficulty reading multisyllabic words in the selection,	then... have them look for and read meaningful parts in the words or have them chunk words with no recognizable parts.
If... students need practice reading words fluently,	then... use the Fluent Word Reading Routine on the DI tab.
If... students have difficulty reading along with the group,	then... have them follow along as they listen to the AudioText.

Advanced

ROUTINE

1 Extend Vocabulary

WORD STRUCTURE Choose and read a sentence or passage containing a word with a prefix, such as this sentence from the Read Aloud "Journal of a Teenage Genius": "And not being able to dial a particular day is very inconvenient." What does the word *inconvenient* mean? *(not convenient, not easy or handy)* How did you determine the word's meaning? *(I saw that the word had the prefix* in- *added to the base word* convenient. In- *means "not," so* inconvenient *means "not convenient.")* Discuss how recognizing and understanding prefixes can be helpful. Remind students to use the strategy as they read *Grace and the Time Machine*.

2 Read *Grace and the Time Machine*, pp. 192–201

DAY
2

BEFORE READING Today you will read another story about time travel. It is a play about a group of friends who "invent" an imaginary time machine. As you read, look for how they use their imaginations to travel to many different times and places around the world.

Have students write two questions about the play in their Strategy Response Logs (p. 192). Tell them to think about the answers to their questions as they read.

CREATIVE THINKING Have students read pp. 192–201 independently. Encourage them to think creatively. For example, ask:
- What else do you think the kids should add to their time machine?
- If you were with Grace and her friends, where would you suggest going?

AFTER READING Have students review their Strategy Response Logs to see whether their questions have been answered. Then have them write a new question about the play. Have partners discuss the selection and share their questions for the rest of the play. Encourage them to think of places they would like to go to in a time machine and why. Have partners choose one time or place and meet with you to explain why they chose that destination.

Audio CD   AudioText

Grace and the Time Machine
Group Time

Audio CD AudioText

Monitor Progress

Word and Selection Reading

If... students have difficulty reading multisyllabic words in the selection,	**then...** have them look for and read meaningful parts in the words or have them chunk words with no recognizable parts.
If... students have difficulty reading along with the group,	**then...** have them follow along as they listen to the AudioText.

Strategic Intervention

ROUTINE

1 Reinforce Comprehension

SKILL DRAW CONCLUSIONS Have students tell what it means to draw a conclusion. *(to use facts and details to form an opinion or decision that makes sense)* If necessary, review the meaning and provide a model. When I draw a conclusion, I use facts and details from what I have read to make a decision or form an opinion about something. Sometimes I also use what I already know to help draw a conclusion. If I hear thunder in the distance and see people outside pulling out their umbrellas, I can draw the conclusion that it is about to rain.

Ask students to draw a conclusion about what happened based on these statements:

> **Maddie pushed the red button. The machine shook and hummed. When she stepped out, Maddie saw covered wagons and a herd of buffalo.**

(Maddie has used a time machine to travel back in time to the Old West.)

2 Read *Grace and the Time Machine*, pp. 202–207

BEFORE READING Have students retell what has happened in the play so far. Ask: Did the children really go into the future? Reread the bottom half of p. 197 and have students look at the picture on p. 198. Model how to answer questions about drawing conclusions. The play doesn't actually tell me if the children traveled into the future. I must draw a conclusion to answer that question. That means I need to use details in the play as well as what I know on my own. Right there on the page it says, "They make time-machine noises." The picture doesn't look like a machine that would work. And I know that time travel is not possible. So I draw the conclusion that the children just made-believe. Remind students to draw conclusions to answer questions as they read the rest of *Grace and the Time Machine*. **STRATEGY Answer Questions**

DURING READING Follow the Guiding Comprehension routine on pp. 202–207. Have students read along with you while tracking print or do a choral reading. Stop every two pages to ask students what has happened so far. Prompt as necessary.
* Where did Nana choose to go in the time machine? Why?
* What happened when Mrs. Myerson came into the yard?

AFTER READING How does this play show people using their imaginations? Reread as needed. Tell them that tomorrow they will read a nonfiction article about other ways to use their imaginations.

Advanced

ROUTINE

1 Extend Comprehension

⊙ SKILL DRAW CONCLUSIONS Have students draw a conclusion about Grace's imagination. Encourage them to use words other than *good*.

⊙ STRATEGY ANSWER QUESTIONS Have students tell how they drew that conclusion.

- What facts and details did you find right there in the play?
- What prior knowledge did you use?

2 Read *Grace and the Time Machine,* pp. 202–207

BEFORE READING Have students recall what has happened in the selection so far. Remind them to draw conclusions to answer questions as they read the remainder of *Grace and the Time Machine*.

PROBLEM SOLVING Have students read pp. 202–207 independently. Encourage them to think in terms of problems and solutions. For example, ask:

- What problem does Mrs. Myerson have? How do Grace and her friends help solve the problem?
- How else might the children help bring Mrs. Myerson "back to life"?

AFTER READING Have students complete the Strategy Response Log activity (p. 206). Have them think about the problems Grace and her friends faced and the problems they solved on their travels. Ask students to choose one problem that they think they could solve by using a time machine and write a paragraph explaining the problem and the solution.

Audio CD · AudioText

Group Time

DAY
4

Audio CD AudioText

1 Practice Retelling

REVIEW PLAY ELEMENTS Help students identify the main characters and the setting of *Grace and the Time Machine*. Then guide them in using the Retelling Cards to list play events in sequence. Prompt students to include important details.

RETELL Using the Retelling Cards, have students work in pairs to retell *Grace and the Time Machine*. Monitor retelling and prompt students as needed. For example, ask:

- Tell me about the major events in order.
- How does this play remind you of other stories?

If students struggle, model a fluent retelling.

PEARSON
Scott Foresman
Retelling Cards
Grade 4

2 Read "What's There to Do?"

BEFORE READING Read the genre information on p. 210. Explain to students that expository nonfiction usually explains an idea. This article is about things you can do with your friends on a summer day. What did Grace and her friends do? *(built a pretend time machine)* As we read "What's There to Do?" think about whether you would like to do the activities described in the article.

Read the rest of the panel on p. 210. Have students scan the article to find subheads. Then have students tell what they think the illustrations show.

DURING READING Have students read along with you while tracking the print or do a choral reading of the article. Stop to discuss content-area vocabulary such as *artistic* and *crocheted*.

AFTER READING Have students share their reactions to the article. Then guide them through the Reading Across Texts and Writing Across Texts activities, prompting if necessary.

- What two activities does the article suggest?
- What kinds of things did Grace and her friends like to do?

Monitor Progress

Word and Selection Reading

If... students have difficulty reading multisyllabic words in the selection,	**then...** have them look for and read meaningful parts in the words or have them chunk words with no recognizable parts.
If... students have difficulty reading along with the group,	**then...** have them follow along as they listen to the AudioText.

ROUTINE

1 **Read** **"What's There to Do?"**

CREATIVE THINKING Have students read pp. 210–211 independently.
Encourage them to think creatively. For example, ask:

- How is helping a neighbor the same as giving a gift?
- What other arts and crafts would you include in your show?

AFTER READING Have students meet with you to discuss the
article and Reading Across Texts. Have students do Writing Across
Texts independently.

2 **Extend Genre Study**

RESEARCH Have students use online or print resources to find other
expository nonfiction that explains imaginative ways to spend one's
time. Ask them to make a list of the titles they find and note what
each article explains.

WRITE Have students write a brief expository article about ways
to earn money—things one can make to sell or services one can
provide. Encourage them to use their imaginations and think of
unusual or creative ideas.

DAY
4

Audio
CD   **AudioText**

Grace and the Time Machine

Group Time

Leveled Reader
Database
ONLINE
PearsonSuccessNet.com

ROUTINE

1 Reread for Fluency

MODEL Read aloud pp. 3–4 of the Leveled Reader *A World Tour of Cultures* with intonation and expression. Have students note that you raise and lower the pitch of your voice and use expression as you read. Then read pp. 5–6 in a monotone. Have students tell you which model sounded better. Discuss how changing the tone of your voice and reading with expression can make nonfiction more interesting and easier to understand.

PRACTICE Have students reread passages from *A World Tour of Cultures* with a partner or individually. For optimal fluency, they should reread three or four times. As students read, monitor fluency and provide corrective feedback. Students in this group are assessed in Weeks 2 and 4.

2 Retell Leveled Reader *A World Tour of Cultures*

Model how to use subheads and photographs to retell the book. Then ask students to retell the book, one section at a time. Prompt them as needed.

- What was this section mostly about?
- What did you learn from reading this section?

Monitor Progress
Fluency

If... students have difficulty reading fluently,	then... provide additional fluency practice by pairing nonfluent readers with fluent ones.

For alternate Leveled Reader lesson plans that teach
Draw Conclusions, Answer Questions,
and **Lesson Vocabulary,** see pp. LR19–LR27.

On-Level

1 Reread for Fluency ROUTINE

MODEL Read aloud p. 3 of the Leveled Reader *To Market, To Market,* emphasizing the use of characterization for the voice of the narrator. Have students note that you read as if you were a person speaking to an audience. Discuss how using an animated voice makes the reading more enjoyable.

PRACTICE Have students reread passages from *To Market, To Market* with a partner or individually. For optimal fluency, they should reread three or four times. As students read, monitor fluency and provide corrective feedback. Assess the fluency of students in this group using p. 211a.

2 Retell Leveled Reader
To Market, To Market

Have students use subheads and illustrations as a guide to summarize important facts they learned from reading the book. Prompt as needed.

• What is this section mostly about?
• What did you learn from reading this section?

Advanced

1 Reread for Fluency ROUTINE

PRACTICE Have students reread passages from the Leveled Reader *Geography Shapes Our World* with a partner or individually. As students read, monitor fluency and provide corrective feedback. If students read fluently on the first reading, they do not need to reread three to four times. Students in this group were assessed in Week 1.

2 Revisit Leveled Reader *Geography Shapes Our World*

RETELL Have students retell the Leveled Reader *Geography Shapes Our World*.

NOW TRY THIS Have students complete their diary pages. Meet with them to discuss and review their work. You may wish to review their sources and see if they need any additional information or visuals. Have them share their diary pages with the class.

Group Time

DAY 1

Leveled Reader
Database
ONLINE
PearsonSuccessNet.com

ROUTINE

1 Build Background

REINFORCE CONCEPTS Display the Citizenship and Responsibility Concept Web. This week's concept is *citizenship and responsibility.* Someone who is a good citizen is a good member of his or her community. Someone who is responsible does what he or she is supposed to do. Discuss the meaning of each word on the web, using the definitions on p. 212l and the Concept Vocabulary routine on p. DI·1.

CONNECT TO READING This week you will read about one kind of worker, lumberjacks, who were responsible for cutting down trees to be used for wood. In "Counting on Johnny," we read about a legendary logging camp. How did Paul Bunyan show he was responsible in that tall tale? *(He started his own logging company. He hired Johnny Inkslinger to help him pay bills.)* In *Lumberjacks,* we will read about real loggers in real camps.

2 Read Leveled Reader *Lumberjacks*

BEFORE READING Using the Picture Walk routine on p. DI·1, guide students through the text focusing on key concepts and vocabulary. Ask questions such as:

pp. 5–6 These drawings show loggers at a logging camp. What can you tell about life in a camp from the pictures? *(Lots of men work and live together.)* Is this camp from today or a long time ago? How can you tell? *(a long time ago; they have fires to heat food; they sit on logs)*

p. 7 What is this lumberjack doing? *(cutting down a tree)* It would be hard work to cut down an immense tree like this one.

DURING READING Read pp. 3–4 aloud, while students track the print. Do a choral reading of pp. 5–8. If students are capable, have them read and discuss the remainder of the book with a partner. Ask: How did lumberjacks work together?

AFTER READING Encourage pairs of students to discuss why it was important for lumberjacks to show responsibility and to be good citizens of their camps. We read *Lumberjacks* to learn about loggers and logging camps. In *Marven of the Great North Woods,* we will read about another job at a logging camp.

Monitor Progress

Selection Reading and Comprehension

If... students have difficulty reading the selection with a partner,	**then...** have them follow along as they listen to the Online Leveled Reader Audio.
If... students have trouble understanding the job done by a logger or lumberjack,	**then...** reread pp. 7–9 and discuss specific steps in the logging process.

For alternate Leveled Reader lesson plans that teach **Fact and Opinion**, **Monitor and Fix Up**, and **Lesson Vocabulary**, see pp. LR28–LR36.

On-Level

ROUTINE

1 Build Background

DEVELOP VOCABULARY Write the word *resourceful* and ask whether students can define it in their own words. *(good at coming up with ideas)* Someone who is resourceful is good at thinking of ways to do things. What might be a good job for someone who is resourceful? *(an inventor or scientist, a builder, an artist)* Repeat this activity with the word *reliable* and other words from the Leveled Reader *After School Excitement.* Use the Concept Vocabulary routine on p. DI·1 as needed.

2 Read Leveled Reader
After School Excitement

BEFORE READING Have students create T-charts with the labels *Ethan* and *Jake*. This story tells about twin brothers who have very different personalities. As you read, look for details that tell about the brothers and how responsibly they do things. Record the details in your charts.

DURING READING Have students follow along as you read pp. 3–9. Then let them complete the book on their own. Remind students to add details to their charts as they read.

AFTER READING Have students compare the details on their T-charts. Explain that understanding what it means to be responsible will help them as they read tomorrow's story, *Marven of the Great North Woods.*

Advanced

ROUTINE

1 Read Leveled Reader
Danger! Children at Work

BEFORE READING Recall the Read Aloud "Counting on Johnny." What job does Johnny get working for Paul Bunyan? *(bookkeeper)* Do you think that being a bookkeeper in a lumber camp is a job for an adult or a child? What jobs should children not be allowed to do? Today you will read about jobs that children in the United States used to do.

CRITICAL THINKING/PROBLEM SOLVING Have students read the Leveled Reader independently. Encourage them to think critically and in terms of problems and solutions. For example, ask:

- What does the author think about child labor?
- How is the children's Declaration of Dependence like our country's Declaration of Independence? How is it different?
- What were the causes of child labor?
- How would you answer the author's question about making a difference in your lifetime?

AFTER READING Have students review the selection to find five or more unfamiliar words and determine their meanings by using context clues or consulting a dictionary. Then ask them to write sentences using each word and including enough context to convey meaning. Encourage students to meet with you to share the sentences they wrote.

2 Independent Extension Activity

NOW TRY THIS Assign "Now Try This" on pp. 22–23 of *Danger! Children at Work* for students to work on throughout the week.

Marven of the Great North Woods

Group Time

DAY 2

Audio CD — AudioText

Strategic Intervention

1 Word Study/Phonics

LESSON VOCABULARY Use p. 214b to review the meanings of *cord*, *dismay*, *grizzly*, *immense*, and *payroll*. Have individuals practice reading the words from word cards.

DECODING MULTISYLLABIC WORDS Write *bunkhouse*, saying the word as you write it. Then model how to read a compound word. First I ask myself if I see any parts that I know. I see *bunk* at the beginning of the word, and I see *house* at the end. I know that a bunk is like a bed or cot that you sleep on, and a house is a building to live in. So I can guess that a bunkhouse is a building with beds where people live and sleep.

Use the Multisyllabic Word routine on p. DI·1 to help students read these other words from *Marven of the Great North Woods*: *bookkeeper*, *frantic*, *cubbyhole*, *blotter*, *inkwell*, *kerosene*, *shuffled*, *skillet*, *equipment*, *thumbprint*, *calculations*, *midday*, *glistened*, *desperately*, and *concentrating*. Be sure students understand the meanings of words such as *kerosene*, *midday*, and *calculations*.

Use *Strategies for Word Analysis*, Lesson 9, with students who have difficulty mastering word analysis and need practice with decodable text.

2 Read *Marven of the Great North Woods*, pp. 216–223

BEFORE READING In *Lumberjacks* we read about men who worked hard together in logging camps. In *Marven of the Great North Woods*, we will read about a real boy who had a great deal of responsibility in a logging camp in the early 1900s.

Using the Picture Walk routine on p. DI·1, guide students through the text, asking questions such as those listed below. Read the question on p. 217. Together, set a purpose for reading.

pp. 218–219 What can you tell about the logging camp from these pictures? *(It is cold and snowy outside. The men are having fun inside.)*

p. 223 Who do you think this is? How would you describe him? *(one of the lumberjacks; big, looks mean, looks kind of scary)*

DURING READING Follow the Guiding Comprehension routine on pp. 218–223. Have students read along with you while tracking the print or do a choral reading. Stop every two pages to ask what has happened so far. Prompt as necessary.

- Where and when did the selection take place?
- What happened the first morning Marven had to wake the men?

AFTER READING What has happened so far? What do you think will happen next? Reread passages with students as needed.

Monitor Progress

Word and Story Reading

If... students have difficulty reading multisyllabic words in the selection,	then... have them look for and read meaningful parts in the words or have them chunk words with no recognizable parts.
If... students need practice reading words fluently,	then... use the Fluent Word Reading Routine on the DI tab.
If... students have difficulty reading along with the group,	then... have them follow along as they listen to the AudioText.

Advanced

ROUTINE

❶ Extend Vocabulary

🔊 **DICTIONARY/GLOSSARY** Choose and write a sentence containing an unfamiliar word, such as this one from p. 21 of the Leveled Reader: "Most states set a <u>minimum</u> wage. . . ." Suppose you don't know the meaning of the underlined word and can't figure it out from the context. What should you do next? *(look it up in a glossary or dictionary)* Ask a student to look up the word in the dictionary, pronounce it, and read the definition. Discuss what steps students should take to look up a word and determine which meaning is appropriate. Remind students to use the strategy as they read *Marven of the Great North Woods.*

❷ **Read** *Marven of the Great North Woods,* pp. 216–223

BEFORE READING Today you will read a biography of a ten-year-old boy who actually worked as a bookkeeper in a logging camp. As you read, think about whether this is a job you think a child should have. Is it a responsibility you would want to have?

Have students create a KWL chart for their Strategy Response Logs (p. 216). Encourage them to add to it as they read.

CREATIVE THINKING Have students read pp. 216–223 independently. Encourage them to think creatively. For example, ask:

- How do you think Marven felt as he went to sleep on his first night at the camp?
- Imagine that Marven wrote a letter home to his parents after his first night and morning at the camp. What might he have told them?

AFTER READING Have students review their Strategy Response Logs and add to their KWL charts (p. 223). Then meet with students to discuss the selection and share their remaining questions. Encourage them to think about how Marven might be feeling about the lumberjacks. Have students write a letter from Marven to his parents telling them about his job and the camp.

DAY 2

Audio CD AudioText

Marven of the Great North Woods

Group Time

ROUTINE

DAY 3

Audio CD AudioText

Monitor Progress

Word and Selection Reading

If... students have difficulty reading multisyllabic words in the selection,	**then...** have them look for and read meaningful parts in the words or have them chunk words with no recognizable parts.
If... students have difficulty reading along with the group,	**then...** have them follow along as they listen to the AudioText.

---

1 Reinforce Comprehension

◎ SKILL FACT AND OPINION Have students give an example of a fact. *(I am wearing a red shirt. We had pizza for lunch.)* Then have them give an example of an opinion. *(That shirt is beautiful. Pizza is the best lunch.)* If necessary, review facts and opinions and provide a model. A statement of fact can be proved true or false. An example is *I am a fourth-grade teacher.* A statement of opinion is a belief or judgment that cannot be proved. An example is *This is the best school in the city.* Some clue words that signal opinions are *best, worst, should,* and *in my opinion.*

Ask students to give statements of fact and opinion or have them choose a fact and an opinion from a group of statements. For example, ask: Which of the following is a fact? *(Loggers cut down trees for wood.)* Which is an opinion? *(Being a logger is the best job in the world.)* How do you know? *(The first one can be proved; the second one is a judgment and uses the word* best.*)*

Loggers cut down trees for wood.
Being a logger is the best job in the world.

2 Read *Marven of the Great North Woods,* pp. 224–231

BEFORE READING Have students retell what happened in the selection so far. Ask: Where did Marven move from? Refer students to p. 220 and model how to use the monitor and fix-up strategy. If I can't recall information, I can scan the text, looking for the name of the place Marven had lived with his family. I see "In Duluth, Marven had to share a bedroom with his two younger sisters." Remind students to monitor and fix up as they read the rest of *Marven of the Great North Woods.* **◎ STRATEGY Monitor and Fix Up**

DURING READING Follow the Guiding Comprehension routine on pp. 224–231. Have students read along with you while tracking print or do a choral reading. Stop every two pages to ask students what has happened so far. Prompt as necessary.

- What problem did Marven have with breakfast? In the office?
- What did Marven do one day after he finished his job early?
- How did Marven feel about Jean-Louis by the end of the selection? Why?

AFTER READING How does Marven show citizenship and responsibility at the logging camp? Reread with students for comprehension as needed. Tell them that tomorrow they will read about using e-mail to find more information about logging camps.

Advanced

1 Extend Comprehension

SKILL FACT AND OPINION Have students give one fact and one opinion based on the selection. Discuss why it might be more difficult to prove some of the facts from this selection compared to expository nonfiction such as *Danger! Children at Work.*

STRATEGY MONITOR AND FIX UP Discuss with students how monitoring their understanding of the selection and using fix-up strategies can be helpful. Ask questions such as:

- What do you look for when you scan for facts? For opinions?
- What can you do if you don't understand something you've just read?

2 Read *Marven of the Great North Woods,* pp. 224–231

BEFORE READING Have students recall what has happened in the selection so far. Remind them to look for facts and opinions and use monitoring and fix-up strategies as they read the remainder of *Marven of the Great North Woods.*

PROBLEM SOLVING Have students read pp. 224–231 independently. Encourage them to think in terms of problems and solutions. For example, ask:

- What problem did Marven have about breakfast? In the office? On the lake in the woods?
- How did he solve each problem?
- Do you agree with how he solved each problem? If not, what would you have done?

AFTER READING Have students complete the final Strategy Response Log activity (p. 230). Meet with them to discuss the selection, the problems Marven faced, and the way he solved them. Have students write a character description of Marven.

DAY 3

AudioText

Group Time

DAY
4

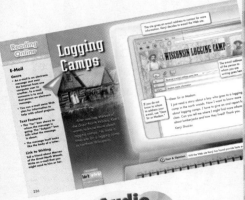

Audio
CD   **AudioText**

ROUTINE

1 Practice Retelling

REVIEW STORY ELEMENTS Help students identify the main characters and the setting of *Marven of the Great North Woods*. Then guide them in using the Retelling Cards to list story events in sequence. Prompt students to include important details.

RETELL Using the Retelling Cards, have students work in pairs to retell *Marven of the Great North Woods*. Monitor retelling and prompt students as needed. For example, ask:

* When does this story take place?
* Tell me what this story is about in a few sentences.
* Tell me about the major events in order.

If students struggle, model a fluent retelling.

2 Read "Logging Camps"

BEFORE READING Read the genre information on p. 236. Explain to students that e-mail can be used to send and receive information over the Internet. This article is about sending e-mail to get more information. What might someone who just read *Marven of the Great North Woods* want to learn more about? *(logging camps)* As we read "Logging Camps," think about what information is being asked for and received.

Read the rest of the panel on p. 236. Have students identify the "To:" and "From:" boxes and the main body of each message.

DURING READING Have students read along with you while tracking the print or do a choral reading of the article. Stop to discuss specific elements of each e-mail. Point out that the text on p. 239 is the actual Web site that Kenji is looking at, not another e-mail.

AFTER READING Have students share their reactions to the selection. Then guide them through the Reading Across Texts and Writing Across Texts activities, prompting if necessary.

* Look at the Web site and *Marven of the Great North Woods*. Where did lumberjacks sleep? What did lumberjacks eat for breakfast?
* Do you think it was easy or hard to be a lumberjack? Why?

Monitor Progress

Word and Selection Reading

If... students have difficulty reading multisyllabic words in the selection,	**then...** have them look for and read meaningful parts in the words or have them chunk words with no recognizable parts.
If... students have difficulty reading along with the group,	**then...** have them follow along as they listen to the AudioText.

Advanced

1 Read "Logging Camps"

CRITICAL THINKING/PROBLEM SOLVING Have students read pp. 236–239 independently. Encourage them to think critically and solve problems. For example, ask:

- Can you assume that every statement of fact listed on a Web site is really true? Why or why not?
- What could Kenji do next if he wanted to find more information about logging camps?

AFTER READING Have students meet with you to discuss the article and Reading Across Texts. Have students do Writing Across Texts independently.

2 Extend Genre Study

RESEARCH Have students use online or print resources to find out more about e-mail. Suggest that they look for facts about the history of e-mail, the volume of e-mails sent every day, or the kinds of e-mail services. If applicable, students may also interview their parents about how they use e-mail and bring in a copy of e-mail.

WRITE Have students write two facts they learned about e-mail from their research. Then ask them to write a statement expressing their opinion about e-mail.

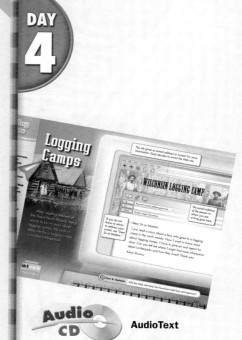

AudioText

Group Time

DAY 5

Leveled Reader Database ONLINE

PearsonSuccessNet.com

ROUTINE

1 Reread for Fluency

MODEL Read aloud pp. 3–4 of the Leveled Reader *Lumberjacks,* using appropriate volume. Have students note that you read in a louder voice for sentences that should show excitement or exaggeration. Then read pp. 5–6 softly and without varying your volume. Have students tell you which model sounded better. Discuss how using the right volume makes a reading more lively and interesting.

PRACTICE Have students reread passages from *Lumberjacks* with a partner or individually. For optimal fluency, they should reread three or four times. As students read, monitor fluency and provide corrective feedback. Assess the fluency of students in this group using p. 239a.

2 Retell Leveled Reader *Lumberjacks*

Model how to use subheads and illustrations to retell the selection. Then ask students to retell the selection, one section at a time. Prompt them as needed.

- What is this section mostly about?
- What did you learn from reading this section?

Monitor Progress

Fluency

If... students have difficulty reading fluently,	**then...** provide additional fluency practice by pairing nonfluent readers with fluent ones.

For alternate Leveled Reader lesson plans that teach
⟳ **Fact and Opinion,** ⟳ **Monitor and Fix Up,**
and **Lesson Vocabulary,** see pp. LR28–LR36.

On-Level

DAY 5

1 Reread for Fluency — ROUTINE

MODEL Read aloud p. 7 of the Leveled Reader *After School Excitement,* using appropriate volume. Have students note changes in the volume of your voice as you read. Point out key words that help you know when to change the volume, for example, *mumbled.* Discuss how varying volume produces a more interesting reading.

PRACTICE Have students reread passages from *After School Excitement* with a partner or individually. For optimal fluency, they should reread three or four times. As students read, monitor fluency and provide corrective feedback. Students in this group were assessed in Week 3.

2 Retell Leveled Reader *After School Excitement*

Have students skim to retell *After School Excitement.* Prompt as needed.

- What are the characters in this story like?
- How was the problem solved?

Advanced

DAY 5

1 Reread for Fluency — ROUTINE

PRACTICE Have students reread passages from the Leveled Reader *Danger! Children at Work* with a partner or individually. As students read, monitor fluency and provide corrective feedback. If students read fluently on the first reading, they do not need to reread three to four times. Students in this group were assessed in Week 1.

2 Revisit Leveled Reader *Danger! Children at Work*

RETELL Have students retell the Leveled Reader *Danger! Children at Work.*

NOW TRY THIS Have students complete their projects about child labor. Meet with them to review and discuss their work. Then invite them to share their writing.

Group Time

DAY 1

Leveled Reader Database ONLINE

PearsonSuccessNet.com

ROUTINE

1 Build Background

REINFORCE CONCEPTS Display the U.S. Government Concept Web. This week's concept is *the U.S. government.* One thing a government does is make laws. Discuss the meaning of each word on the web, using the definitions on p. 240l and the Concept Vocabulary routine on p. DI·1.

CONNECT TO READING This week you will read about the United States Capitol building, where the government makes laws, and other branches of the U.S. government in Washington, D.C. In "Welcome to Washington!" we'll find out how our nation's capital was built. Invite students who have been to Washington to share their experiences with the class.

2 Read Leveled Reader *A Trip to the Capitol*

BEFORE READING Using the Picture Walk routine on p. DI·1, guide students through the text focusing on key concepts and vocabulary. Ask questions such as:

p. 3 Have you seen this building? What words would you use to describe this building? *(really big, important, beautiful)* It is the U.S. Capitol—spelled with an *o*—in Washington, D.C.

p. 5 What is happening here? *(People are meeting.)* Yes, these are legislators, or lawmakers, meeting in the Capitol.

DURING READING Read pp. 3–4 aloud, while students track the print. Do a choral reading of pp. 5–8. If students are capable, have them read and discuss the remainder of the book with a partner. Ask: Who works in the Capitol building?

AFTER READING Encourage pairs of students to discuss the functions of the three branches of government in Washington. We read *A Trip to the Capitol* to learn about all three branches of the U.S. government, especially the legislative branch. Tomorrow we will begin reading *So You Want to Be President?* to learn more about the executive branch.

Monitor Progress

Selection Reading and Comprehension

If... students have difficulty reading the selection with a partner,	then... have them follow along as they listen to the Online Leveled Reader Audio.
If... students have trouble understanding the functions of the government,	then... reread pp. 5–7 and discuss the three branches.

For alternate Leveled Reader lesson plans that teach
Main Idea and Details, **Summarize,** and
Lesson Vocabulary, see pp. LR37–LR45.

On-Level

DAY
1

ROUTINE

1 Build Background

DEVELOP VOCABULARY Write the word
clerks and ask students to define it in
their own words. *(people who work and help
in an office)* What chores do you think a
clerk might do? Repeat this activity with the
word *representative* and other words from
the Leveled Reader *Meet the United States
Government.* Use the Concept Vocabulary
routine on p. DI•1 as needed.

2 **Read** Leveled Reader *Meet the United States Government*

BEFORE READING Have
students create three-column
charts with the headings
Executive, Legislative, and
Judicial. This selection tells
about the three branches,
or parts, of the United
States government. As you
read, look for facts about
each branch and record
them in your chart.

DURING READING Have students follow
along as you read pp. 3–8. Then let them
complete the book on their own. Remind
students to add facts to their charts as
they read.

AFTER READING Have students compare
the facts on their charts. Explain that
understanding facts about each branch
of the government will help them as they
read tomorrow's selection, *So You Want to
Be President?*

Advanced

DAY
1

ROUTINE

1 **Read** Leveled Reader *The Power of Our People*

BEFORE READING Recall
the Read Aloud "Welcome
to Washington!" What
important buildings can you
see in Washington, D.C.?
*(the Capitol, the White
House, the Washington
Monument)* In addition to
these buildings, you can
see the important documents
in Washington, D.C., that helped found our
nation. Today you will read about these
documents—the Declaration of Independence,
the Constitution, and the Bill of Rights.

CRITICAL THINKING/PROBLEM SOLVING
Have students read the Leveled Reader
independently. Encourage them to think
critically and solve problems. For example, ask:

- How does each document show the
power of our people?
- If you could add an amendment to the
Constitution to solve a problem in our
country, what would it say?

AFTER READING Have students review the
selection to find five or more unfamiliar
words and determine their meanings
by using context clues or consulting a
dictionary. Then ask them to write the
words in one column and the definitions in
a different order in a second column. Have
partners trade papers and match words to
definitions. Meet with students to discuss
the selection and the words they chose.

2 Independent Extension Activity

NOW TRY THIS Assign "Now Try This" on
pp. 22–23 of T*he Power of Our People* for
a group of students to work on throughout
the week.

So You Want to Be President?

Group Time

 **AudioText**

DAY 2

ROUTINE

1 Word Study/Phonics

LESSON VOCABULARY Use p. 242b to review the meanings of *Constitution, howling, humble, politics, responsibility, solemnly,* and *vain.* Have individuals practice reading the words from word cards.

DECODING MULTISYLLABIC WORDS Write *adversaries,* saying the word as you write it. Then model how to read a word with no meaningful parts. I see a chunk at the beginning of the word: *ad.* I see a part in the middle: *ver.* I see another part in the middle: *sar.* I see a chunk at the end: *ies.* I say each chunk slowly: *ad ver sar ies.* I say the chunks fast to make a whole word: *adversaries.* An adversary is someone who is against you. *Adversaries* is the plural of *adversary.*

Use the Multisyllabic Word routine on p. DI·1 to help students read these other words from *So You Want to Be President?*: *agriculture, surveying, philosophy, ambassadors, territory, volunteers,* and *priority.* Be sure students understand words such as *surveying* and *priority.*

Use *Strategies for Word Analysis,* Lesson 10, with students who have difficulty mastering word analysis and need practice with decodable text.

2 Read *So You Want to Be President?,* pp. 244–251

BEFORE READING In *A Trip to the Capitol,* we read about Washington, D.C., and the three branches of the U.S. government. Now we're going to read some fun information about the men who have led the executive branch of our government, Presidents of the United States.

Using the Picture Walk routine on p. DI·1, guide students through the text asking questions such as those listed below. Read the question on p. 245. Together, set a purpose for reading.

p. 246 What is the building on this page? *(the White House)* Right, it's the White House, the President's home in Washington.

p. 255 This is a picture of President Abraham Lincoln. How does he look? *(important, serious, deep in thought)* Yes, he looks solemn, as if he's thinking seriously about his responsibilities as President.

DURING READING Follow the Guiding Comprehension routine on pp. 246–251. Have students read along with you while tracking the print or do a choral reading. Stop every two pages to ask what they have learned so far. Prompt as necessary.

- What was page 249 about?
- What did you learn about Theodore Roosevelt?

AFTER READING What have you learned so far? What do you think you will read about next? Reread passages as needed.

Monitor Progress

Word and Story Reading

If... students have difficulty reading multisyllabic words in the selection,	**then...** have them look for and read meaningful parts in the words or have them chunk words with no recognizable parts.
If... students need practice reading words fluently,	**then...** use the Fluent Word Reading Routine on the DI tab.
If... students have difficulty reading along with the group,	**then...** have them follow along as they listen to the AudioText.

Advanced

1 Extend Vocabulary

🔊 **DICTIONARY/GLOSSARY** Write this sentence from p. 16 of the Leveled Reader *The Power of Our People:* "To create the document, they discussed, argued, and <u>compromised</u> for six months." Suppose you don't know the meaning of the underlined word and can't figure it out from the context. What should you do next? *(look it up in a glossary or dictionary)* Ask a student to look up the word in the glossary of the Leveled Reader and read the definition. Where could you look if you wanted to make sure you were pronouncing the word correctly? *(a dictionary)* Ask another student to look up *compromised* in the dictionary. Discuss what steps students should take to look up a word that is in past tense. Remind students to use the strategy as they read *So You Want to Be President?*

2 Read *So You Want to Be President?*, pp. 244–251

BEFORE READING In "Welcome to Washington!" you heard that the city of Washington is the capital of the United States. Today you will read about some of the men who have served as President of the United States. Think about what you already know about being President. You are about to read some surprising and fun information.

Have students write their predictions about the selection in their Strategy Response Logs (p. 244). They will confirm their predictions at the end of the reading.

CREATIVE THINKING Have students read pp. 244–251 independently. Encourage them to think creatively. For example, ask:

- What details does the artist use on p. 247 to help explain and illustrate the text?
- If you were President, what kind of pet would you have in the White House?
- Would you want your father or mother to be President? Why or why not?

AFTER READING Have students review their Strategy Response Log predictions and revise them or write new predictions. Meet with students to discuss the selection and have them share their entries. Encourage students to think about what it might be like to be a child living in the White House. Then have them write a paragraph explaining their ideas.

DAY 2

So You Want to Be President?

by Judith St. George
illustrated by David Small

245

What does it take to be
President of the United States?

Audio CD — AudioText

DAY 3

So You Want to Be President?

Audio CD · AudioText

1 Reinforce Comprehension

SKILL MAIN IDEA AND DETAILS Have students tell what a main idea is. *(the most important thing the author has to say about the topic)* Then have them tell what details are. *(small pieces of information that tell more about the main idea)* If necessary, review main idea and details and provide a model. The main idea of a paragraph or an article is the most important thing the author has to say about the topic. Details give more information about the main idea. Suppose I read this paragraph: "The Capitol is truly beautiful. By day, sunlight polishes the white dome. At night, floodlights bathe the bronze statue Freedom." The main idea is "The Capitol is truly beautiful." The other sentences help explain that statement.

Have students find the main idea *(The President has important responsibilities.)* and details in the paragraph below.

> **The President chooses Cabinet members and can nominate federal judges. The President can also veto bills. As you can see, the President has important responsibilities.**

2 Read *So You Want to Be President?*, pp. 252–255

BEFORE READING Have students retell what they have learned so far. Reread pp. 246–247 and model how to summarize. As I read, I look for the most important ideas and key details. These pages say there are good things and bad things about being President. Those are the most important ideas of all. Next, I'd list the key good things. Then I'd list the key bad things. So my summary would be this: There are good things about being President, including living in the White House, not having to take out the trash, and not having to eat vegetables. There are also bad things about being President, including having to dress up, and having people get mad at you. Remind students to summarize main ideas as they read the rest of *So You Want to Be President?* **STRATEGY Summarize**

DURING READING Follow the Guiding Comprehension routine on pp. 252–255. Have students read along with you while tracking the print or do a choral reading.

- What did you learn about the kinds of jobs Presidents have had?
- What was page 254 about?

AFTER READING How did this selection help you understand more about the U.S. government? Reread as needed. Tell them that tomorrow they will read about one of the powers the President has: creating national parks.

Monitor Progress

Word and Selection Reading

If...	then...
If... students have difficulty reading multisyllabic words in the selection,	**then...** have them look for and read meaningful parts in the words or have them chunk words with no recognizable parts.
If... students have difficulty reading along with the group,	**then...** have them follow along as they listen to the AudioText.

ROUTINE

1 Extend Comprehension

◉ SKILL MAIN IDEA AND DETAILS Have students choose one page they have read from the selection so far and tell the main idea or ideas and two supporting details. Ask students to suggest other kinds of details that could be added.

◉ STRATEGY SUMMARIZE Have a volunteer reread p. 250. Ask students to summarize the page. Ask questions such as:

- What is the main idea of the page?
- What important details should you include in a summary of this page?

DAY 3

2 Read *So You Want to Be President?* **pp. 252–255**

BEFORE READING Have students retell what they have learned so far. Remind them to look for and summarize main ideas as they read the remainder of *So You Want to Be President?*

CRITICAL THINKING Have students read pp. 252–255 independently. Encourage them to think critically. For example, ask:

- How did the type of information—and the author's tone—change in the second half of the selection?
- Do you think it is a problem that no women or people of color have served as President? Why or why not?
- What qualities do you think a President should have?

AFTER READING Have students complete the final Strategy Response Log activity (p. 254). Then have them reread the Oath of Office in the first paragraph on p. 255. Ask students to write their own short oath that they think a President should take after being elected.

AudioText

Group Time

DAY 4

Audio CD   **AudioText**

ROUTINE

1 Practice Retelling

REVIEW MAIN IDEAS Help students identify the main ideas in *So You Want to Be President?* List the ideas students mention. Then ask questions to help students differentiate between essential and nonessential information.

RETELL Using the Retelling Cards, have students work with partners to retell the important ideas. Show partners how to summarize in as few words as possible. Monitor retelling and prompt students as needed. For example, ask:

- What was this selection mainly about?
- What was the author trying to tell us?

If students struggle, model a fluent retelling.

2 Read "Our National Parks"

BEFORE READING Read the genre information on p. 258. Recall the Read Aloud "Welcome to Washington!" Reread portions of the text as necessary. We have read several examples of expository nonfiction this week. What real people and places have we read about? *(Washington, the Capitol, the Presidents)* As we read "Our National Parks," think about what places it tells us about.

Read the rest of the panel on p. 258. Discuss with students how the circle photographs on p. 259 are related to the map of the country.

DURING READING Have students read along with you while tracking the print or do a choral reading of the selection. Stop to discuss difficult content-related vocabulary such as *gorges* and *subtropical*.

AFTER READING Have students share their reactions to the selection. Then guide them through the Reading Across Texts and Writing Across Texts activities, prompting if necessary.

- Skim page 251 and page 254 of *So You Want to Be President?* What good things did some Presidents do?
- Skim page 258. What good things did some Presidents do?

Monitor Progress

Word and Selection Reading

If… students have difficulty reading multisyllabic words in the selection,	**then…** have them look for and read meaningful parts in the words or have them chunk words with no recognizable parts.
If… students have difficulty reading along with the group,	**then…** have them follow along as they listen to the AudioText.

Advanced

ROUTINE

1 Read "Our National Parks"

CRITICAL THINKING/CREATIVE THINKING Have students read pp. 258–259 independently. Encourage them to think critically. For example, ask:

- Do you think it's a good idea that the President has the power to create national parks? Why or why not?
- Which of these parks would you enjoy visiting? Why?
- What would be a good motto for the national parks?

AFTER READING Have students meet with you to discuss the article and Reading Across Texts. Have students do Writing Across Texts independently.

2 Extend Genre Study

RESEARCH Have students use online or print resources to find out more about one of the national parks listed in the article or one that they would like to visit.

WRITE Have students write a short article about the park they researched that would encourage others to visit the park. Encourage them to include interesting facts about the park's history, location, size, and highlights.

AudioText

So You Want to Be President?

Group Time

ONLINE

PearsonSuccessNet.com

1 Reread for Fluency

MODEL Read aloud pp. 3–4 of the Leveled Reader *A Trip to the Capitol,* modeling how to use appropriate stress and emphasis. Stress important words such as *most* and *in person.* Then read pp. 5–6 emphasizing inappropriate words. Have students tell you which model sounded better. Discuss how stressing the right words makes it easier to understand the reading.

PRACTICE Have students reread passages from *A Trip to the Capitol* with a partner or individually. For optimal fluency, they should reread three or four times. As students read, monitor fluency and provide corrective feedback. Assess any students you have not yet checked during this unit.

2 Retell Leveled Reader *A Trip to the Capitol*

Model how to use subheads and illustrations to retell the selection. Then ask students to retell the selection, one section at a time. Prompt them as needed.

- What is this section mostly about?
- Tell me about each place visited.

Monitor Progress	
Fluency	
If... students have difficulty reading fluently,	**then...** provide additional fluency practice by pairing nonfluent readers with fluent ones.

For alternate Leveled Reader lesson plans that teach ⊙**Main Idea and Details,** ⊙**Summarize,** and **Lesson Vocabulary,** see pp. LR37–LR45.

On-Level

1 Reread for Fluency   ROUTINE

MODEL Read aloud p. 3 of the Leveled Reader *Meet the United States Government,* modeling the correct use of stress and emphasis. Have students note how you stress certain words for emphasis. Discuss how emphasizing important words makes it easier to understand a reading.

PRACTICE Have students reread passages from *Meet the United States Government* with a partner or individually. For optimal fluency, they should reread three or four times. As students read, monitor fluency and provide corrective feedback. Assess any students you have not yet checked during this unit.

2 Retell Leveled Reader *Meet the United States Government*

Have students skim the book to summarize the important facts they learned from the selection. Prompt as needed.

- What is this page mostly about?
- What did you learn from reading this page?

Advanced

1 Reread for Fluency   ROUTINE

PRACTICE Have students reread passages from the Leveled Reader *The Power of Our People* with a partner or individually. As students read, monitor fluency and provide corrective feedback. If students read fluently on the first reading, they do not need to reread three to four times. Assess any students you have not yet checked during this unit.

2 Revisit Leveled Reader *The Power of Our People*

RETELL Have students retell the Leveled Reader *The Power of Our People.*

NOW TRY THIS Have students complete their project. Meet with them to review their work and discuss the process they undertook to create it. Did they need to compromise? Have them share their constitution and map with the class.

Cause and Effect

Students who are able to connect what happens in a selection to the reason why it happens can better understand what they read. In fiction, this skill will help them figure out why characters do what they do. In nonfiction, it will give them a better grasp of factual information. Use the following routine to teach cause and effect.

1 DEMONSTRATE CAUSE AND EFFECT

Remind students that an effect is what happens. A cause is why it happened. Demonstrate by turning out the lights. Ask:

What is the effect? (It is dark.)

What is the cause? (You turned off the lights.)

2 IDENTIFY CAUSE AND EFFECT

Write this sentence on the board: *Because it is raining, I took my umbrella to school.* Explain that sometimes a sentence has a clue word such as *because, so,* or *since* that signals a cause-and-effect relationship. Have volunteers circle the cause *(it is raining),* put a box around the effect *(I took my umbrella),* and underline the clue word *(because).*

3 APPLY TO A SELECTION

Read with students a story that has causes and effects. Several causes can lead to one effect: Sunshine <u>and</u> water make flowers grow. One cause can lead to several effects: Leaving a bike in the hallway can cause someone to trip <u>and</u> break an arm.

4 RECORD CAUSES AND EFFECTS

Have students use a cause-effect chart to record the causes and effects in the selection.

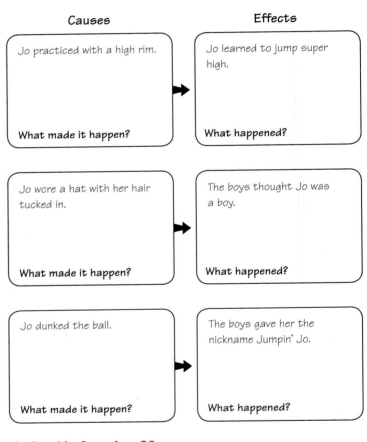

Causes / Effects

Causes	Effects
Jo practiced with a high rim.	Jo learned to jump super high.
What made it happen?	What happened?
Jo wore a hat with her hair tucked in.	The boys thought Jo was a boy.
What made it happen?	What happened?
Jo dunked the ball.	The boys gave her the nickname Jumpin' Jo.
What made it happen?	What happened?

▲ **Graphic Organizer** 20

Research on Cause and Effect

"A great deal of our thought process has to do with cause and effect. To be fully fluent thinkers, children need to learn the logic of cause and effect."

Stanley Greenspan and Serena Weider,
Learning to Think Abstractly

Greenspan, Stanley, and Serena Welder. "Learning to Think Abstractly." *Scholastic Early Childhood Today* (May/June 1998).

Draw Conclusions

When students move beyond the literal meaning of a text to draw conclusions, they get more ideas from what they read and understand better the points an author is trying to make. Use the following routine to guide students in drawing conclusions.

1 DISCUSS DRAWING CONCLUSIONS

Tell students a conclusion is a sensible decision they reach based on details or facts in a story or an article. Explain when they draw conclusions, they think about information in the text and what they already know.

2 MODEL DRAWING A CONCLUSION

Model using your own experiences to draw a conclusion.

 Think Aloud

MODEL The smell of peanuts and cotton candy filled the air. I heard clapping, I even heard loud bellows that sounded like elephants. I knew a circus was going on.

Discuss how you combined what you already knew with details (smell of peanuts and cotton candy, clapping, loud bellows) to draw a conclusion.

3 ASK QUESTIONS

Read aloud a passage and ask questions that foster drawing conclusions. For example: *What kind of person is the main character? How can you tell? Why do you think the character acts this way?*

4 USE A GRAPHIC ORGANIZER

Have partners read both fiction and nonfiction passages. Students can ask each other questions that lead to drawing conclusions. Suggest that they use webs or charts to show the facts or details that support their conclusions.

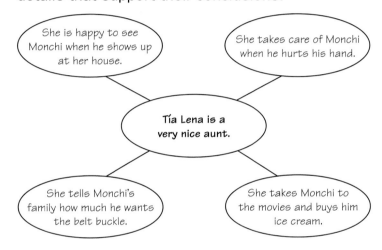

She is happy to see Monchi when he shows up at her house.

She takes care of Monchi when he hurts his hand.

Tía Lena is a very nice aunt.

She tells Monchi's family how much he wants the belt buckle.

She takes Monchi to the movies and buys him ice cream.

▲ **Graphic Organizer** 15

Research on Drawing Conclusions

"Inference is a mosaic, a dazzling constellation of thinking processes, but the tiles available to form each mosaic are limited, circumscribed. There must be a fusion of words on a page—and constraints of meaning they impose—and the experience and knowledge of the reader."

Ellin Oliver Keene and Susan Zimmermann,
Mosaic of Thought

Keene, Ellin Oliver, and Susan Zimmermann. *Mosaic of Thought: Teaching Comprehension in a Reader's Workshop.* Heinemann, 1997, p. 154.

Draw Conclusions

When students move beyond the literal meaning of a text to draw conclusions, they get more ideas from what they read and understand better the points an author is trying to make. Use the following routine to guide students in drawing conclusions.

1 DISCUSS DRAWING CONCLUSIONS

Tell students a conclusion is a sensible decision they reach based on details or facts in a story or an article. Explain when they draw conclusions, they think about information in the text and what they already know.

2 MODEL DRAWING A CONCLUSION

Model using your own experiences to draw a conclusion.

 Think Aloud **MODEL** The smell of peanuts and cotton candy filled the air. I heard clapping, I even heard loud bellows that sounded like elephants. I knew a circus was going on.

Discuss how you combined what you already knew with details (smell of peanuts and cotton candy, clapping, loud bellows) to draw a conclusion.

3 ASK QUESTIONS

Read aloud a passage and ask questions that foster drawing conclusions. For example: *What kind of person is the main character? How can you tell? Why do you think the character acts this way?*

4 USE A GRAPHIC ORGANIZER

Have partners read both fiction and nonfiction passages. Students can ask each other questions that lead to drawing conclusions. Suggest that they use webs or charts to show the facts or details that support their conclusions.

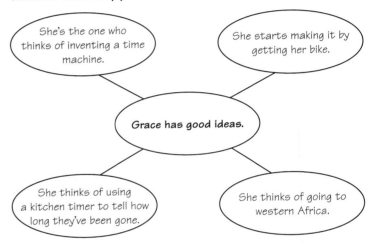

▲ **Graphic Organizer** 15

Research on Drawing Conclusions

"Inference is a mosaic, a dazzling constellation of thinking processes, but the tiles available to form each mosaic are limited, circumscribed. There must be a fusion of words on a page—and constraints of meaning they impose—and the experience and knowledge of the reader."

Ellin Oliver Keene and Susan Zimmermann,
Mosaic of Thought

Keene, Ellin Oliver, and Susan Zimmermann. *Mosaic of Thought: Teaching Comprehension in a Reader's Workshop.* Heinemann, 1997, p. 154.1992, p. 238.

Fact and Opinion

When students can identify statements of fact and opinion, they are able to make critical judgments concerning what they hear, read, and write. Use this routine to help students recognize statements of fact and statements of opinion and distinguish between them.

1 DEFINE FACT AND OPINION

Explain that a statement of fact can be proved true or false. A statement of opinion is someone's judgment, belief, or way of thinking about something. It cannot be proved true or false, but it can be supported or explained.

2 GIVE EXAMPLES

Write three statements on the board:

Charlotte's Web *was published in 1952. E. B. White wrote* Charlotte's Web. *You should read* Charlotte's Web.

Ask: *Which sentences are statements of fact? (the first two) How can you tell?* Elicit ways the facts could be verified, such as looking at the book or asking the school librarian. Talk about other ways to check statements of fact (observing, weighing, measuring, asking an expert).

Ask: *Which sentence is a statement of opinion? (the third one)* Point out the judgment word *should.* Explain opinions often contain judgment words such as *should, I think, cute,* and *best.*

3 PROVIDE PRACTICE

- Partners can read nonfiction selections and use a T-chart to list statements of fact and opinion.

- Have small groups read newspaper editorials. Students can list opinions and their supporting arguments.

Facts	Opinions
1. Marven had a room with a bearskin blanket.	1. Marven's room was awesome.
2. Marven made up a system for keeping track of the jacks' pay.	2. Marven was a whiz at math.
3. Marven thought Jean Louis was a grizzly bear.	3. Jean Louis looked scary.

▲ **Graphic Organizer** 25

Research on Fact and Opinion

"Students will—and should—argue about the difference between fact and opinion . . .; they will often dispute one another about inferences . . . . The point of such discussions is to help student sensitize themselves to the kinds of statements they encounter and make them aware of the inferences of others."

Thomas G. Devine,
Teaching Reading Comprehension

Devine, Thomas G. *Teaching Reading Comprehension.* Allyn and Bacon, Inc., 1986, p. 238.

Main Idea/Details

Determining the main idea in a text helps readers distinguish between important and less important information. When students can correctly identify the main idea, they understand the gist of what they read. Use this routine to teach main idea.

1 EXPLAIN ITS USE

Explain that finding the main idea is an important tool in helping students understand and remember what they read.

2 DEFINE THE TERMS

Explain that the topic is the subject, what the selection is all about. The main idea is the most important idea about the topic. The main idea can be stated in a sentence.

3 MODEL FINDING THE MAIN IDEA

Read a nonfiction paragraph with a stated main idea. Have students identify the topic by asking: *What is this paragraph about?* Then model how you determine the main idea.

4 FINDING SUPPORTING DETAILS

Explain that supporting details are small pieces of information that tell more about the main idea. Model how to identify supporting details.

5 USE A GRAPHIC ORGANIZER

Have students find the main idea and supporting details in a nonfiction selection. Use a main idea chart to help students organize their thoughts.

Choose passages carefully to practice this succession of skills:

- Paragraphs: stated main idea (Grades 2–6); implied main idea (Grades 3–6)

- Articles: stated main idea (Grades 4–6); implied main idea (Grades 4–6)

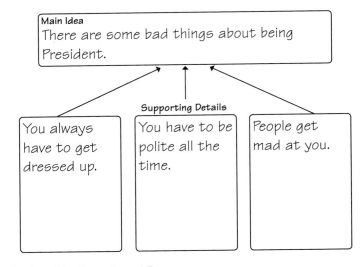

▲ **Graphic Organizer** 17

Research on Main Idea/Details

"When great readers are reading this stuff that has so many ideas in it, they have to listen to that mental voice tell them which words, which sentences or paragraphs, and which ideas are most important. Otherwise they won't get it."

Ellin Oliver Keene and Susan Zimmermann,
Mosaic of Thought

Keene, Ellin Oliver, and Susan Zimmermann. *Mosaic of Thought: Teaching Comprehension in a Reader's Workshop.* Heinemann, 1997, p. 86.

Providing students with reading materials they can and want to read is an important step toward developing fluent readers. A running record allows you to determine each student's instructional and independent reading level. Information on how to take a running record is provided on pp. DI•59–DI•60.

Instructional Reading Level

Only approximately 1 in 10 words will be difficult when reading a selection from the Student Edition for students who are at grade level. (A typical fourth-grader reads approximately 115–130 words correct per minute.)

- Students reading at grade level should read regularly from the Student Edition and On-Level Leveled Readers, with teacher support as suggested in the Teacher's Editions.
- Students reading below grade level can read the Strategic Intervention Leveled Readers. Instructional plans can be found in the Teacher's Edition and the Leveled Reader Teaching Guide.
- Students who are reading above grade level can read the Advanced Leveled Readers. Instructional plans can be found in the Teacher's Edition and the Leveled Reader Teaching Guide.

Independent Reading Level

Students should read regularly in independent-level texts in which no more than approximately 1 in 20 words is difficult for the reader. Other factors that make a book easy to read include the student's interest in the topic, the amount of text on a page, how well illustrations support meaning, and the complexity and familiarity of the concepts. Suggested books for self-selected reading are provided for each lesson on p. TR14 in this Teacher's Edition.

Guide students in learning how to self-select books at their independent reading level. As you talk about a book with students, discuss the challenging concepts in it, list new words students find in sampling the book, and ask students about their familiarity with the topic. A blackline master to help students evaluate books for independent reading is provided on p. DI•58.

Self-Selected/Independent Reading

While oral reading allows you to assess students' reading level and fluency, independent reading is of crucial importance to students' futures as readers and learners. Students need to develop their ability to read independently for increasing amounts of time.

- Schedule a regular time for sustained independent reading in your classroom. During the year, gradually increase the amount of time devoted to independent reading.
- Encourage students to track the amount of time they read independently and the number of pages they read in a given amount of time. Tracking will help motivate them to gradually increase their duration and speed. Blackline masters for tracking independent reading are provided on p. DI•58 and p. TR15.

Choosing a Book for Independent Reading

When choosing a book, story, or article for independent reading, consider these questions:

_____ 1. Do I know something about this topic?

_____ 2. Am I interested in this topic?

_____ 3. Do I like reading this kind of book (fiction, fantasy, biography, or whatever)?

_____ 4. Have I read other things by this author? Do I like this author?

If you say "yes" to at least one of the questions above, continue:

_____ 5. In reading the first page, was only about 1 of every 20 words hard?

If you say "yes," continue:

_____ 6. Does the number of words on a page look about right to me?

If you say "yes," the book or article is probably at the right level for you.

Silent Reading

Record the date, the title of the book or article you read, the amount of time you spent reading, and the number of pages you read during that time.

Date	Title	Minutes	Pages

Taking a Running Record

A running record is an assessment of a student's oral reading accuracy and oral reading fluency. Reading accuracy is based on the number of words read correctly. Reading fluency is based on the reading rate (the number of words correct per minute) and the degree to which a student reads with a "natural flow."

How to Measure Reading Accuracy

1. Choose a grade-level text of about 80 to 120 words that is unfamiliar to the student.
2. Make a copy of the text for yourself. Make a copy for the student or have the student read aloud from a book.
3. Give the student the text and have the student read aloud. (You may wish to record the student's reading for later evaluation.)
4. On your copy of the text, mark any miscues or errors the student makes while reading. See the running record sample on page DI·60, which shows how to identify and mark miscues.
5. Count the total number of words in the text and the total number of errors made by the student. Note: If a student makes the same error more than once, such as mispronouncing the same word multiple times, count it as one error. Self-corrections do not count as actual errors. Use the following formula to calculate the percentage score, or accuracy rate:

$$\frac{\text{Total Number of Words} - \text{Total Number of Errors}}{\text{Total Number of Words}} \times 100 = \text{percentage score}$$

Interpreting the Results

- A student who reads **95–100%** of the words correctly is reading at an **independent level** and may need more challenging text.
- A student who reads **90–94%** of the words correctly is reading at an **instructional level** and will likely benefit from guided instruction.
- A student who reads **89%** or fewer of the words correctly is reading at a **frustrational level** and may benefit most from targeted instruction with lower-level texts and intervention.

How to Measure Reading Rate (wcpm)

1. Follow Steps 1–3 above.
2. Note the exact times when the student begins and finishes reading.
3. Use the following formula to calculate the number of words correct per minute (wcpm):

$$\frac{\text{Total Number of Words Read Correctly}}{\text{Total Number of Seconds}} \times 60 = \text{words correct per minute}$$

Interpreting the Results

An appropriate reading rate for a fourth-grader is 115–130 (wcpm).

Running Record Sample

Running Record Sample

All the maple trees that grow in the northeastern United States and parts of Canada have shaken off their slumber. During the next few months, they put all *of* their energy into growing. Maple trees can live for hundreds of years. During their first hundred years of existence, they grow about *one* a foot each year.

The maple tree's roots anchor the tree to the ground. They burrow */bore/* deep in the soil and push out in every direction. The huge network of roots (has) spread like an *H* enormous open hand with dozens and dozens of outstretched fingers in the ground. The deep roots help keep the tree from toppling over during strong winds. The roots also gather nutrients the *(SC)* tree needs to make sap.

—From *The Maple Tree*
On-Level Reader 4.3.1

Symbols

Accurate Reading
The student reads a word correctly.

Insertion
The student inserts words or parts of words that are not in the text.

Substitution
The student substitutes words or parts of words for the words in the text.

Mispronunciation/Misreading
The student pronounces or reads a word incorrectly.

Omission
The student omits words or word parts.

Hesitation
The student hesitates over a word, and the teacher provides the word. Wait several seconds before telling the student what the word is.

Self-Correction
The student reads a word incorrectly but then corrects the error. Do not count self-corrections as actual errors. However, noting self-corrections will help you identify words the student finds difficult.

Running Record Results ▶
Total Number of Words: **122**
Number of Errors: **5**

Reading Time: **61 seconds**

Reading Accuracy ▶
$\frac{122-5}{122} \times 100 = 95.9 = 96\%$

Accuracy Percentage Score: **96%**

Reading Rate—WCPM
$\frac{117}{61} \times 60 = 115.08 = 115$ words correct per minute

Reading Rate: **115 WCPM**

Teacher Resources

Table of Contents

Word Lists **TR2**

Handwriting.. **TR10**

More Books for Self-Selected Reading **TR14**

Retelling Assessment **TR16**

Scope and Sequence... **TR18**

Index.. **TR26**

Acknowledgments **TR40**

TR

Teacher Resources

Unit 1

	Vocabulary Words	Spelling Words

Because of Winn-Dixie

Vocabulary Words

grand   prideful
memorial   recalls
peculiar   selecting
positive

Spelling Words

Short vowels VCCV

admire	soccer	intend	happen
magnet	engine	fabric	cannon
contest	sudden	flatten	
method	finger	rascal	
custom	accident	gutter	
rally	mitten	mammal	

Lewis and Clark and Me

Vocabulary Words

docks
migrating
scan
scent
wharf
yearned

Spelling Words

Long a and i

sigh	spray	tight	freight
right	braid	raisin	sleigh
weigh	bait	trait	
eight	grain	highway	
detail	slight	frighten	
height	thigh	dismay	

Grandfather's Journey

Vocabulary Words

amazed
bewildered
homeland
longed
sculptures
still
towering

Spelling Words

Long e and o

sweet	throat	croak	seaweed
each	float	shallow	hollow
three	foam	eagle	
least	flown	indeed	
freedom	greet	rainbow	
below	season	grown	

The Horned Toad Prince

Vocabulary Words

bargain
favor
lassoed
offended
prairie
riverbed
shrieked

Spelling Words

Long e

prairie	movie	collie	trolley
calorie	country	breezy	misty
honey	empty	jury	
valley	city	balcony	
money	rookie	steady	
finally	hockey	alley	

Letters Home from Yosemite

Vocabulary Words

glacier
impressive
naturalist
preserve
slopes
species
wilderness

Spelling Words

Long u

usual	scooter	pupil
huge	juice	groove
flute	cruise	confuse
mood	truth	humor
smooth	bruise	duty
threw	cruel	curfew
afternoon	excuse	

Unit 2

	Vocabulary Words	Spelling Words

What Jo Did

Vocabulary Words
fouled
hoop
jersey
marveled
rim
speechless
swatted
unbelievable

Adding -s and -es

monkeys	months	delays	batteries
friends	companies	scratches	donkeys
plays	costumes	counties	
supplies	sandwiches	teammates	
taxes	hobbies	memories	
holidays	daisies	bunches	

Coyote School News

Vocabulary Words
bawling
coyote
dudes
roundup
spurs

Irregular Plurals

videos	cliffs	cuffs	hoofs
teeth	roofs	beliefs	loaves
potatoes	halves	patios	
themselves	moose	banjos	
lives	radios	tornadoes	
leaves	sheep	tomatoes	

Grace and the Time Machine

Vocabulary Words
aboard   reseats
atlas   vehicle
awkward
capable
chant
mechanical
miracle

Words with ar, or

morning	story	Florida	garden
forest	argue	apartment	Arkansas
garbage	backyard	sport	
form	start	force	
alarm	partner	forward	
corner	storm	sharp	

Marven of the Great North Woods

Vocabulary Words
cord
dismay
grizzly
immense
payroll

Digraphs ng, nk, ph, wh

Thanksgiving	wheel	white	chunk
among	nephew	shrink	skunk
think	belong	wharf	
blank	whiskers	trunk	
graph	whisper	strong	
young	elephant	blink	

So You Want to Be President?

Vocabulary Words
Constitution
howling
humble
politics
responsibility
solemnly
vain

Words with ear, ir, our, ur

return	heard	nourish	hamburger
courage	early	purse	survey
surface	turtle	furniture	
purpose	birthday	search	
first	journal	curtain	
turkey	courtesy	burrow	

WORD LIST

Unit 3

Vocabulary Words		Spelling Words			

The Stranger

Vocabulary Words:
draft   parlor
etched   terror
fascinated   timid
frost

Adding -ed and -ing

watched	stopped	noticed	hurried
watching	stopping	noticing	hurrying
danced	dried	robbed	
dancing	drying	robbing	
studied	happened	slipped	
studying	happening	slipping	

Adelina's Whales

Vocabulary Words:
biologist   massive
bluff   rumbling
lagoon   tropical

Homophones

piece	by	aloud	there
peace	bye	allowed	their
break	beat	past	
brake	beet	passed	
threw	thrown	weight	
through	throne	wait	

How Night Came from the Sea: A Story from Brazil

Vocabulary Words:
brilliant
chorus
coward
gleamed
shimmering

Vowel sound in shout

however	towel	browse	eyebrow
mountain	ounce	announce	boundary
mound	coward	hound	
scout	outdoors	trout	
shout	flowerpot	drowsy	
couch	scowl	grouch	

Eye of the Storm

Vocabulary Words:
destruction
expected
forecasts
inland
shatter
surge

Compound words

watermelon	upstairs	touchdown	loud-speaker
homemade	thunder-storm	campfire	laptop
understand	shortcut	skateboard	flashlight
sometimes	doorbell	anyway	
shoelace	jellyfish	fireworks	
highway		haircut	

The Great Kapok Tree

Vocabulary Words:
canopy
dangle
dappled
fragrant
pollen
pollinate
slithered
wondrous

Possessives

its	men's	teacher's
ours	girl's	teachers'
mine	girls'	aunt's
yours	hers	aunts'
family's	theirs	boy's
families'	brother's	boys'
man's	brothers'	

Unit 4

	Vocabulary Words	Spelling Words

The Houdini Box

Vocabulary Words:
appeared
bustling
crumbled
escape
magician
monument
vanished

Contractions

don't	doesn't	where's	when's
won't	I've	hadn't	haven't
wouldn't	here's	aren't	
there's	wasn't	they're	
we're	shouldn't	it's	
you're	couldn't	we've	

Encantado: Pink Dolphin of the Amazon

Vocabulary Words:
aquarium
dolphins
enchanted
flexible
glimpses
pulses
surface

Final -le, -al, -en

chicken	natural	paddle	tangle
eleven	needle	animal	frighten
given	single	spiral	
jungle	citizen	marble	
national	threaten	oval	
several	diagonal	mumble	

The King in the Kitchen

Vocabulary Words:
duke
dungeon
furiously
genius
majesty
noble
peasant
porridge

Words with final -er, -ar

brother	similar	filter	theater
together	regular	hangar	deliver
dinner	summer	never	
popular	clever	shelter	
center	supper	cellar	
calendar	pitcher	caterpillar	

Seeker of Knowledge

Vocabulary Words:
ancient
link
scholars
seeker
temple
translate
triumph
uncover

Consonants /j/, /ks/, and /k/

village	knowledge	Texas	quilt
except	question	fudge	expert
explain	equal	excellent	
quick	queen	exercise	
charge	excited	quart	
bridge	expect	liquid	

Encyclopedia Brown and the Case of the Slippery Salamander

Vocabulary Words:
amphibians
crime
exhibit
lizards
reference
reptiles
salamanders
stumped

Prefixes un-, dis-, in-

distrust	disorder	disrepair
uncertain	discount	inability
incomplete	indirect	disapprove
unlikely	unopened	unsolved
unfair	disrespect	disobey
discontinue	unimportant	unsuspecting
unaware	unlisted	

Unit 5

Unit 5	Vocabulary Words	Spelling Words

Sailing Home: A Story of a Childhood at Sea

Vocabulary Words

bow	dignified
cargo	navigation
celestial	quivered
conducted	stern

Multisyllabic words

reaction	refreshment	unhappily	question-able
prerecorded	unbreakable	watchfully	displace-ment
incorrectly	declaration	gleefully	midship-man
incredibly	retirement	sportsman-ship	
disobedient	misdialed		
disagreeable	undefined	repayment	

Lost City: The Discovery of Machu Picchu

Vocabulary Words

curiosity
glorious
granite
ruins
terraced
thickets
torrent

Syllable patterns V/CV and VC/V

basic	olive	beware	tribute
vacant	tiger	emotion	lizard
secret	spinach	cabin	
honor	second	tripod	
local	donate	dragon	
novel	locust	habit	

Amelia and Eleanor Go for a Ride

Vocabulary Words

aviator
brisk
cockpit
daring
elegant
outspoken
solo

Greek word parts

telephone	barometer	telegraph	periscope
biography	microscope	perimeter	mega-phone
telescope	headphones	paragraph	
photograph	microphone	phonics	
microwave	autograph	symphony	
diameter	microchip	saxophone	

Antarctic Journal: Four Months at the Bottom of the World

Vocabulary Words

anticipation
continent
convergence
depart
forbidding
heaves
icebergs

Words with Latin roots

dictionary	locate	erupt	disrupt
abrupt	portable	passport	dislocate
predict	transport	export	
import	bankrupt	contradict	
locally	dictate	rupture	
verdict	location	interrupt	

Moonwalk

Vocabulary Words

loomed
rille
runt
staggered
summoning
taunted
trench
trudged

Related words

please	production	meter
pleasant	heal	metric
breath	health	compose
breathe	triple	composition
image	triplet	crumb
imagine	relate	crumble
product	relative	

Unit 6

Vocabulary Words	Spelling Words

My Brother Martin

ancestors
avoided
generations
minister
numerous
pulpit
shielding

Schwa

stomach	remember	fortune	cement
memory	forget	giant	yesterday
Canada	suppose	architect	
element	iron	normal	
mystery	gravel	notify	
science	difficult	privilege	

Jim Thorpe's Bright Path

boarding school
dormitory
endurance
manual
reservation
society

Prefixes *mis-, non-, re-*

misplace	mishandle	nonfiction	nonstick
nonsense	nonstop	rebound	misquote
reread	recover	mistreat	
repack	reseal	readjust	
misfortune	misbehavior	misprint	
remove	reunion	nonprofit	

How Tía Lola Came to Visit Stay

affords
colonel
glint
lurking
palettes
quaint
resemblance

Suffixes *-less, -ment, -ness*

countless	statement	tireless	needless
payment	breathless	amazement	painless
goodness	restless	amusement	
fairness	enjoyment	greatness	
hopeless	pavement	punishment	
treatment	flawless	timeless	

To Fly: The Story of the Wright Brothers

cradle
drag
flex
glider
hangars
rudder
stalled

Suffixes *-ful, -ly, -ion*

careful	recently	yearly	correction
tasteful	extremely	successful	eagerly
lonely	certainly	playful	
powerful	wisely	thoughtful	
suggestion	harmful	actually	
peaceful	monthly	pollution	

The Man Who Went to the Far Side of the Moon: The Story of Apollo 11 Astronaut Michael Collins

astronauts
capsule
hatch
horizon
lunar
module
quarantine

Words with silent consonants

island	half	rhyme
column	calf	climber
knee	whistle	limb
often	autumn	plumbing
known	knuckles	ghost
castle	numb	clothes
thumb	Illinois	

Grade 3 Vocabulary

Use this list of third grade tested vocabulary words for review and leveled activities.

A
admire
airport
amount
antlers
anxiously
arranged
attention
attic
average

B
bakery
barrels
batch
bay
beauty
beneath
blade
blizzards
blooming
board
boils
boom
bottom
bows
braided
budding
bulbs
bundles
buried
burro
bursts
business

C
cardboard
carpenter
carpetmaker
celebrate
cellar
channel
cheated
check
chilly
chimney
chipped
chores
clearing
clever
clutched
coins
collection
college
complained
continued
cotton
crops
crown
crystal
cuddles
curious
current
custom
customer

D
dangerously
delicious
depth
described
deserts
dew
dimes
disappeared
discovery
dough
downtown
doze
drifting
drowned

E
earned
earthquakes
echoed
encourages
enormous
errands
excitedly
excitement

expensive
expressive

F
factory
famous
farewell
feast
festival
fetched
fierce
fined
fireflies
fireworks
flights
flippers
flutter
foolish
force
foreign
frozen

G
gardener
giggle
glaring
glassblower
goal
graceful
gully

H
handkerchief
hatch
homesick
humor

I
imagined
ingredients
interest

J
journey
joyful

K
knead
knowledge

L
labeled
languages
laundry
lazy
liberty
local
looping

M
marketplace
medals
melody
memories
mending
mention
merchant
million
mixture
models
motioned

N
narrator
narrow
native
nickels
notepad

O
outrun
overhead
overnight

P
paces
pale
partners
patch
peak

pegs
pecks
perches
pick
pitcher
plenty
poked
popular
preen
public
puffs

Q
quarters

R
raindrops
realize
recipe
recognizing
reeds
reply
rhythm
rich
ruined

S
sadness
scattered
scoop
scrambled
settled
shiny
shivered
shocked
showers
skillet
slammed
snug
snuggles
social
spare
spell
spoil
sprouting
stamps

steady
steep
stirred
stoops
strain
straying
strokes
struggled
supplies
support
surrounded
swooping
symbol
symphony

T
tablet
thousand
thread
tides
torch
treasure
trembles
tune
twist

U
unaware
unforgettable
unveiled
unwrapped

V
valley
value
volcanoes

W
waterfalls
wealth
wobbled
worth

Grade 5 Vocabulary

Use this list of fifth grade tested vocabulary words for leveled activities.

A

abdomen
accomplishments
achieved
acquainted
admiringly
adorn
advice
advised
agreement
algae
appreciate
architect
armor
artificial
assignment
astonished

B

background
barber
bass
behavior
benefactor
bleached
bluish
blunders
branded
bronze

C

cable
cannon
carcasses
cartwheels
caterpillar
cavities
choir
circumstances
civilization
clarinet
cleanse
cocoon
combination
complex

concealed
confidence
conservation
constructed
contribute
cramped
critical
criticizing
cruised

D

daintily
debris
decay
demonstrates
depressed
devastation
diplomat
disrespect
distribution
drenching
driftwood

E

economic
eerie
elbow
emerge
enables
encases
enthusiastic
environment
envy
episode
era
erected
essential
expanded
explosion
extinct

F

fashioned
fastball

fate
fearless
fidgety
fleeing
focus
forgetful
foundations

G

gait
glimmer
gnawed
gratitude
gravity
guaranteed
gymnastics

H

hammocks
handicapped
headland
hesitation
hideous
hustled
hydrogen

I

immigrants
independence
inspired
interior
intersection
investigation
issue

J

jammed

K

kelp

L

lair
lamented

landscape
lifeless
limelight
lingers
lullaby
luxury

M

magnified
midst
migrant
miniature
mocking
mold
monitors
mucus

N

newcomer
nighttime

O

occasion
ooze
outfield
overrun

P

parasites
peddler
permit
philosopher
pitch
plunged
pondered
precious
prehistoric
procedures
procession
profile
proportion

R

ravine
realm

reassembled
recommend
refugees
released
religious
representatives
reputation
resourceful
rival
robotic
role
rustling

S

sacred
scarce
scoundrel
scrawled
scrawny
sea urchins
secondhand
sediment
serpent
severe
shellfish
sinew
sketched
skidded
slavery
somber
somersault
sonar
specialize
specific
spectacles
spoonful
starvation
steed
sterile
sternly
strategy
strict
subject
superiors
suspicions

T

teenager
therapist
thieving
throbbing
tidied
traditions
tundra
tweezers

U

unique
unscrewed

V

vacant
veins
visa

W

weakness
wheelchair
wincing
windup
withered
workshop
worshipped
worthless

Legibility

When handwriting is legible, letters, words and numbers can be read easily. Handwriting that is not legible can cause problems for the reader and make communication difficult. Legibility can be improved if students are able to identify what is causing legibility problems in their handwriting. Focus instruction on the following five elements of legible handwriting.

Size

Letters need to be a consistent size. Students should focus on three things related to size: letters that reach to the top line, letters that reach halfway between the top and bottom line, and letters that extend below the bottom line. Writing letters the correct size can improve legibility. Often the letters that sit halfway between the top and bottom line cause the most problems. When students are writing on notebook paper, there is no middle line to help them size letters such as *m, a, i,* and *r* correctly. If students are having trouble, have them draw middle lines on their notebook paper.

Shape

Some of the most common handwriting problems are caused by forming letters incorrectly. These are the most common types of handwriting problems:

- round letters such as *a, o,* and *g* are not closed
- looped letters such as *i, e,* and *b* have no loops
- letters such as *i, t,* and *d* have loops that shouldn't be there

Have students examine one another's writing to indicate which words are hard to read, and then discuss which letters aren't formed correctly. They can then practice those particular letters.

Spacing

Letters within words should be evenly spaced. Too much or too little space can make writing difficult to read. A consistent amount of space should also be used between words in a sentence and between sentences. Suggest that students use the tip of their pencil to check the spacing between words and the width of their pencil to check the spacing between sentences.

Slant

Correct writing slant can be to the right or to the left, or there may be no slant at all. Slant becomes a legibility problem when letters are slanted in different directions. Suggest that students use a ruler to draw lines to determine if their slant is consistent.

Smoothness

Written letters should be produced with a line weight that is not too dark and not too light. The line should be smooth without any shaky or jagged edges. If students' writing is too dark, they are pressing too hard. If the writing is too light, they are not pressing hard enough. Usually shaky or jagged lines occur if students are unsure of how to form letters or if they are trying to draw letters rather than using a flowing motion.

D'Nealian™ Cursive Alphabet

a b c d e f g
h i j k l m n
o p q r s t u
v w x y z

A B C D E F G
H I J K L M N
O P Q R S T U
V W X Y Z . , ' ?

1 2 3 4 5 6
7 8 9 10

D'Nealian™ Alphabet

a b c d e f g h i

j k l m n o p q r s t

u v w x y z

A B C D E F G

H I J K L M N O

P Q R S T U V

W X Y Z . , ' ?

1 2 3 4 5 6

7 8 9 10

Manuscript Alphabet

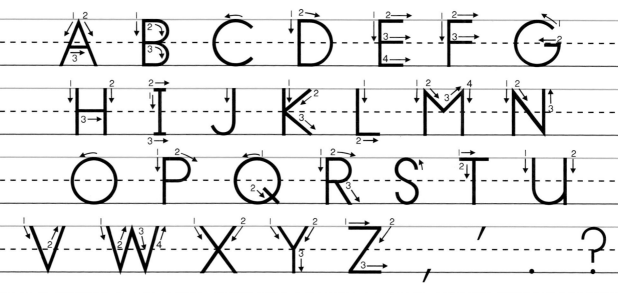

Unit 2 *Work and Play*

	Below-Level	On-Level	Advanced

What Jo Did

To Read Aloud!
Home Run: The Story of Babe Ruth
by Robert Burleigh (Silver Whistle, 1998) Read about the life and baseball talents of the legendary player.

Mama and Me and the Model T
by Faye Gibbons (Morrow, 1999) Mr. Long gets a new Model T but refuses to teach his wife how to drive it, forcing her to show him that cars are not just for men.

First Base, First Place
by Scott Elder (Scholastic, 1993) The Johnson boys are planning to win in summer-league baseball.

Bobby Baseball
by Robert Kimmel Smith (Dell, 1991) Bobby yearns to prove to his father that he is a good baseball player.

Coyote School News

To Read Aloud!
A Handful of Seeds
by Monica Hughes (Orchard, 1996) A young girl named Concepcion moves to the city and helps a group of homeless children plant a garden.

City Green
by DyAnne DiSalvo-Ryan (William Morrow, 1994) When a little girl grows tired of a littered vacant lot by her home, she starts planting there, and the lot becomes a communal garden.

Little House on the Prairie
by Laura Ingalls Wilder (HarperCollins, 1997) Laura and her family journey west in this beloved classic.

My Side of the Mountain
by Jean Craighead George (Penguin, 2000) Sam lives off the land in the Catskill Mountains in this popular modern classic.

Grace and the Time Machine

To Read Aloud!
A Picture Book of Thomas Alva Edison
by David A. Adler (Holiday House, 1996) This informative biography profiles the life of one of America's greatest inventors.

Anansi and the Talking Melon
by Eric A. Kimmel (Holiday House, 1995) Elephant is tricked by a clever spider who hides in a melon and makes it "talk."

The Real McCoy: The Life of An African American Inventor
by Wendy Towle (Scholastic, 1993) A profile of inventor Elijah McCoy, the son of fugitive slaves.

Grandfather's Day
by Ingrid Tomey (Boyds Mills, 1992) When a girl's grandfather grieves after his wife's recent death, the girl tries to help him overcome his sadness.

Marven of the Great North Woods

To Read Aloud!
Alice Ramsey's Grand Adventure
by Don Brown (Houghton Mifflin, 1997) This charming picture book tells the story of Alice, who overcame great odds to become the first woman to motor across the country.

Storm in the Night
by Mary Stolz (HarperCollins, 1988) A boy learns about his grandfather's fear of thunderstorms when he and his grandfather get stuck in one and the lights go out.

When Jessie Came Across the Sea
by Amy Hest (Candlewick, 1997) When Jessie is chosen by the rabbi to travel to America, she and her grandmother are both excited and saddened that they will be parted.

Chester Cricket's New Home
by George Selden (Bantam, 1983) When two ladies sit on and crush Chester's Cricket's home, a worm-eaten stump, his friends help him look for a new place to call home.

So You Want to Be President?

To Read Aloud!
I Am An Artist
by Pat Lowry Collins (Millbrook, 1994) The author and illustrator explains how keen observation is the key to her artwork.

A Picture Book of Benjamin Franklin
by David A. Adler (Holiday House, 1990) This accessible biography surveys Franklin's life, including his work as an inventor.

Snowflake Bentley
by Jacqueline Briggs Martin (Houghton Mifflin, 1998) An enlightening glimpse into the life of artist and scientist Wilson Bentley, whose favorite subject was snow.

I Want To Be a Veterinarian
by Stephanie Maze (Harcourt, 1997) A detailed look at the challenges, requirements, and rewards of being a veterinarian.

Unit 2 Reading Log

Name _____

Dates Read	Title and Author	What is it about?	How would you rate it?	Explain your rating.
From _____ to _____			Great 5 4 3 2 1 Awful	
From _____ to _____			Great 5 4 3 2 1 Awful	
From _____ to _____			Great 5 4 3 2 1 Awful	
From _____ to _____			Great 5 4 3 2 1 Awful	
From _____ to _____			Great 5 4 3 2 1 Awful	

Unit 2 Narrative Retelling Chart

Selection Title _____ Name _____ Date _____

Retelling Criteria/Teacher Prompt	Teacher-Aided Response	Student-Generated Response	Rubric Score (Circle one.)
Connections Has anything like this happened to you? How does this story remind you of other stories?			4 3 2 1
Author's Purpose Why do you think the author wrote this story? What was the author trying to tell us?			4 3 2 1
Characters Describe _____ (character's name) at the beginning and end of the story.			4 3 2 1
Setting Where and when did the story happen?			4 3 2 1
Plot Tell me what the story was about in a few sentences.			4 3 2 1

Summative Retelling Score   4   3   2   1

Comments _____

Unit 2 Expository Retelling Chart

Selection Title _____ **Name** _____ **Date** _____

Retelling Criteria/Teacher Prompt	Teacher-Aided Response	Student-Generated Response	Rubric Score (Circle one.)			
Connections Did this selection make you think about something else you have read? What did you learn about as you read this selection?			4	3	2	1
Author's Purpose Why do you think the author wrote this selection?			4	3	2	1
Topic What was the selection mostly about?			4	3	2	1
Important Ideas What is important for me to know about _____ (topic)?			4	3	2	1
Conclusions What did you learn from reading this selection?			4	3	2	1

Summative Retelling Score 4 3 2 1

Comments _____

Expository Retelling Chart **TR17**

Reading

Concepts of Print and Print Awareness

Concepts of Print and Print Awareness	Pre-K	K	1	2	3	4	5	6
Develop awareness that print represents spoken language and conveys and preserves meaning	•	•	•					
Recognize familiar books by their covers; hold book right side up	•	•						
Identify parts of a book and their functions (front cover, title page/title, back cover, page numbers)	•	•	•					
Understand the concepts of letter, word, sentence, paragraph, and story	•	•	•					
Track print (front to back of book, top to bottom of page, left to right on line, sweep back left for next line)	•	•	•					
Match spoken to printed words	•	•	•					
Know capital and lowercase letter names and match them	•	• T	•					
Know the order of the alphabet	•	•	•					
Recognize first name in print	•	•	•					
Recognize the uses of capitalization and punctuation		•	•					
Value print as a means of gaining information	•	•	•					

Phonological and Phonemic Awareness

Phonological and Phonemic Awareness	Pre-K	K	1	2	3	4	5	6
Phonological Awareness								
Recognize and produce rhyming words	•	•	•					
Track and count each word in a spoken sentence and each syllable in a spoken word	•	•	•					
Segment and blend syllables in spoken words			•					
Segment and blend onset and rime in one-syllable words		•	•					
Recognize and produce words beginning with the same sound	•	•	•					
Identify beginning, middle, and/or ending sounds that are the same or different	•	•	•					
Understand that spoken words are made of sequences of sounds	•	•	•					
Phonemic Awareness								
Identify the position of sounds in words		•	•					
Identify and isolate initial, final, and medial sounds in spoken words	•	•	•					
Blend sounds orally to make words or syllables		•	•					
Segment a word or syllable into sounds; count phonemes in spoken words or syllables		•	•					
Manipulate sounds in words (add, delete, and/or substitute phonemes)	•	•	•					

Phonics and Decoding

Phonics and Decoding	Pre-K	K	1	2	3	4	5	6
Phonics								
Understand and apply the **alphabetic principle** that spoken words are composed of sounds that are represented by letters	•	•	•					
Know letter-sound relationships	•	• T	• T	• T				
Blend sounds of letters to decode		•	• T	• T	• T			
Consonants, consonant blends, and consonant digraphs		•	• T	• T	• T			
Short, long, and r-controlled vowels; vowel digraphs; diphthongs; common vowel patterns			• T	• T	• T			
Phonograms/word families		•	•	•	•			
Word Structure								
Decode words with common word parts		•	• T	• T	• T	•	•	•
Base words and inflected endings			• T	• T	•	•	•	•
Contractions and compound words			• T	• T	• T	•	•	•
Suffixes and prefixes			• T	• T	• T	•	•	•
Greek and Latin roots						•	•	•
Blend syllables to decode words			• T	• T	• T	•	•	•
Decoding Strategies								
Blending strategy: Apply knowledge of letter-sound relationships to decode unfamiliar words		•	•	•	•			
Apply knowledge of word structure to decode unfamiliar words		•	•	•	•	•	•	•
Use context and syntax along with letter-sound relationships and word structure to decode		•	•	•	•	•	•	•
Self-correct			•	•	•	•	•	•

Fluency

Fluency	Pre-K	K	1	2	3	4	5	6
Read aloud fluently with accuracy, comprehension, appropriate pace/rate; with expression/intonation (prosody); with attention to punctuation and appropriate phrasing			• T	• T	• T	• T	• T	• T
Practice fluency in a variety of ways, including choral reading, partner/paired reading, Readers' Theater, repeated oral reading, and tape-assisted reading		•	•	•	•	•	•	•

• instructional opportunity   T tested in standardized test forma

	Pre-K	K	1	2	3	4	5	6
Work toward appropriate fluency goals by the end of each grade			•T	•T	•T	•T	•T	•T
Read regularly in independent-level material			•	•	•	•	•	•
Read silently for increasing periods of time			•	•	•	•	•	•

Vocabulary (Oral and Written)

	Pre-K	K	1	2	3	4	5	6
Word Recognition								
Recognize regular and irregular high-frequency words	•	•	•T	•T				
Recognize and understand selection vocabulary		•	•	•T	•	•	•	•
Understand content-area vocabulary and specialized, technical, or topical words		•	•	•	•	•	•	•
Word Learning Strategies								
Develop vocabulary through direct instruction, concrete experiences, reading, listening to text read aloud	•	•	•	•	•	•	•	•
Use knowledge of word structure to figure out meanings of words		•	•T	•T	•T	•T	•T	•T
Use context clues for meanings of unfamiliar words, multiple-meaning words, homonyms, homographs		•	•T	•T	•T	•T	•T	•T
Use grade-appropriate reference sources to learn word meanings	•	•	•	•	•T	•T	•T	•T
Use picture clues to help determine word meanings	•	•	•	•	•			
Use new words in a variety of contexts	•	•	•	•		•	•	•
Examine word usage and effectiveness		•	•	•	•	•	•	•
Create and use graphic organizers to group, study, and retain vocabulary		•	•	•	•	•	•	•
Extend Concepts and Word Knowledge								
Academic language	•	•	•	•	•	•	•	•
Classify and categorize	•	•	•	•	•	•	•	•
Antonyms and synonyms			•	•T	•T	•T	•T	•T
Homographs, homonyms, and homophones				•	•T	•T	•T	•T
Multiple-meaning words			•	•	•T	•T	•T	•T
Related words and derivations					•	•	•	•
Analogies					•		•	
Connotation/denotation						•	•	•
Figurative language and idioms			•	•	•	•	•	•
Descriptive words (location, size, color, shape, number, ideas, feelings)	•	•	•	•	•	•	•	•
High-utility words (shapes, colors, question words, position/directional words, and so on)	•	•	•	•				
Time and order words	•	•	•	•	•	•	•	•
Transition words						•	•	•
Word origins: Etymologies/word histories; words from other languages, regions, or cultures					•	•	•	•
Shortened forms: abbreviations, acronyms, clipped words			•	•	•	•	•T	

Text Comprehension

	Pre-K	K	1	2	3	4	5	6
Comprehension Strategies								
Preview the text and formulate questions	•	•	•	•	•	•	•	•
Set and monitor purpose for reading and listening	•	•	•	•	•	•	•	•
Activate and use prior knowledge	•	•	•	•	•	•	•	•
Make predictions	•	•	•	•	•	•	•	•
Monitor comprehension and use fix-up strategies to resolve difficulties in meaning: adjust reading rate, reread and read on, seek help from reference sources and/or other people, skim and scan, summarize, use text features			•	•	•	•	•	•
Create and use graphic and semantic organizers		•	•	•	•	•	•	•
Answer questions (text explicit, text implicit, scriptal), including *who, what, when, where, why, what if, how*	•	•	•	•	•	•	•	•
Look back in text for answers			•	•	•	•	•	•
Answer test-like questions			•	•	•	•	•	•
Generate clarifying questions, including *who, what, where, when, how, why, and what if*	•	•	•	•	•	•	•	•
Recognize text structure: story and informational (cause/effect, chronological, compare/contrast, description, problem/solution, propostion/support)	•	•	•	•	•	•	•	•
Summarize text		•	•	•	•	•	•	•
Recall and retell stories	•	•	•	•	•	•	•	•
Identify and retell important/main ideas (nonfiction)	•	•	•	•	•	•	•	•
Identify and retell new information			•	•	•	•	•	•
Visualize; use mental imagery		•	•	•	•	•	•	•
Use strategies flexibly and in combination			•	•	•	•	•	•

Comprehension Skills

	Pre-K	K	1	2	3	4	5	6
Author's purpose			• T	• T	• T	• T	• T	• T
Author's viewpoint/bias/perspective					•	•	•	• T
Categorize and classify	•	•	•	•				
Cause and effect		•	• T	• T	• T	• T	• T	• T
Compare and contrast		•	• T	• T	• T	• T	• T	• T
Details and facts		•	•	•	•	•	•	•
Draw conclusions		•	• T	• T	• T	• T	• T	• T
Fact and opinion				• T	• T	• T	• T	• T
Follow directions/steps in a process	•	•	•	•	•	•	•	•
Generalize					• T	• T	• T	• T
Graphic sources		•	•	•	•	• T	• T	• T
Main idea and supporting details		• T	• T	• T	• T	• T	• T	• T
Paraphrase			•	•	•	•	•	•
Persuasive devices and propaganda				•	•	•	•	•
Realism/fantasy		•	• T	• T	• T			
Sequence of events		• T	• T	• T	• T	• T	• T	• T

Higher Order Thinking Skills

	Pre-K	K	1	2	3	4	5	6
Analyze				•	•	•	•	•
Describe and connect the essential ideas, arguments, and perspectives of a text			•	•	•	•	•	•
Draw inferences, conclusions, or generalizations, support them with textual evidence and prior knowledge	•			•	•	•	•	•
Evaluate and critique ideas and text			•	•	•	•	•	•
Hypothesize						•	•	•
Make judgments about ideas and text			•	•	•	•	•	•
Organize and synthesize ideas and information			•			•	•	•

Literary Analysis, Response, & Appreciation

	Pre-K	K	1	2	3	4	5	6
Genre and Its Characteristics								
Recognize characteristics of a variety of genre	•	•	•	•	•	•	•	•
Distinguish fiction from nonfiction		•	•	•	•	•	•	•
Identify characteristics of literary texts, including drama, fantasy, traditional tales		•	•	•	•	•	•	•
Identify characteristics of nonfiction texts, including biography, interviews, newspaper articles		•	•	•	•	•	•	•
Identify characteristics of poetry and song, including nursery rhymes, limericks, blank verse	•	•	•	•	•	•	•	•
Literary Elements and Story Structure								
Character	•	• T	• T	• T	• T	• T	• T	
Recognize and describe traits, actions, feelings, and motives of characters		•	•	•	•	•	•	•
Analyze characters' relationships, changes, and points of view		•	•	•	•	•	•	•
Analyze characters' conflicts				•	•	•	•	•
Plot and plot structure	•	• T	• T	• T	• T	• T	• T	
Beginning, middle, end	•	•	•	•	•			
Goal and outcome or problem and solution/resolution		•	•	•	•	•	•	•
Rising action, climax, and falling action/denouement; setbacks						•	•	•
Setting	•	• T	• T	• T	• T	• T		
Relate setting to problem/solution						•	•	•
Explain ways setting contributes to mood						•	•	•
Theme		•	• T	• T	•	•	•	•
Use Literary Elements and Story Structure	•	•	•	•	•	•	•	•
Analyze and evaluate author's use of setting, plot, character				•	•	•	•	•
Identify similarities and differences of characters, events, and settings within or across selections/cultures	•	•	•	•	•	•	•	•
Literary Devices								
Allusion								•
Dialect						•	•	•
Dialogue and narration	•	•	•	•	•	•	•	•
Exaggeration/hyperbole						•	•	•
Figurative language: idiom, jargon, metaphor, simile, slang			•	•	•	•	•	•

• instructional opportunity   **T** tested in standardized test form

	Pre-K	K	1	2	3	4	5	6
Flashback						•	•	•
Foreshadowing							•	•
Formal and informal language				•	•	•	•	•
Humor					•	•	•	•
Imagery and sensory words			•	•	•	•	•	•
Mood				•	•		•	•
Personification				•	•		•	•
Point of view (first person, third person, omniscient)					•	•	•	•
Puns and word play				•	•	•	•	•
Sound devices and poetic elements	•	•	•	•	•	•	•	•
Alliteration, assonance, onomatopoeia	•	•	•	•	•	•	•	•
Rhyme, rhythm, repetition, and cadence	•	•	•	•	•	•	•	•
Word choice				•	•	•	•	•
Symbolism				•	•	•	•	•
Tone							•	•

Author's and Illustrator's Craft

	Pre-K	K	1	2	3	4	5	6
Distinguish the roles of author and illustrator		•	•	•				
Recognize/analyze author's and illustrator's craft or style			•	•	•	•	•	•

Literary Response

	Pre-K	K	1	2	3	4	5	6
Recollect, talk, and write about books	•	•	•	•	•	•	•	•
Reflect on reading and respond (through talk, movement, art, and so on)	•	•	•	•	•	•	•	•
Ask and answer questions about text	•	•	•	•	•	•	•	•
Write about what is read	•	•	•	•	•	•	•	•
Use evidence from the text to support opinions, interpretations, or conclusions			•	•	•	•	•	•
Support ideas through reference to other texts and personal knowledge				•	•	•	•	•
Locate materials on related topic, theme, or idea				•	•	•	•	•
Generate alternative endings to plots and identify the reason for, and the impact of, the alternatives	•	•	•	•	•	•	•	•
Synthesize and extend the literary experience through creative responses	•	•	•	•	•	•	•	•
Make connections: text to self, text to text, text to world	•	•	•	•	•	•	•	•
Evaluate and critique the quality of the literary experience				•	•	•	•	•
Offer observations, react, speculate in response to text				•	•	•	•	•

Literary Appreciation/Motivation

	Pre-K	K	1	2	3	4	5	6
Show an interest in books and reading; engage voluntarily in social interaction about books	•	•	•	•	•	•	•	•
Choose text by drawing on personal interests, relying on knowledge of authors and genres, estimating text difficulty, and using recommendations of others	•	•	•	•	•	•	•	•
Read a variety of grade-level appropriate narrative and expository texts		•	•	•	•	•	•	•
Read from a wide variety of genres for a variety of purposes	•	•	•	•	•	•	•	•
Read independently			•	•	•	•	•	•
Establish familiarity with a topic			•	•	•	•	•	•

Cultural Awareness

	Pre-K	K	1	2	3	4	5	6
Develop attitudes and abilities to interact with diverse groups and cultures	•	•	•	•	•	•	•	•
Connect experiences and ideas with those from a variety of languages, cultures, customs, perspectives	•	•	•	•	•	•	•	•
Understand how attitudes and values in a culture or during a period in time affect the writing from that culture or time period						•	•	•
Compare language and oral traditions (family stories) that reflect customs, regions, and cultures		•	•	•	•	•	•	•
Recognize themes that cross cultures and bind them together in their common humanness						•	•	•

Language Arts

Writing	Pre-K	K	1	2	3	4	5	6
Concepts of Print for Writing								
Develop gross and fine motor skills and hand/eye coordination	•	•	•					
Print own name and other important words	•	•	•					
Write using pictures, some letters, and transitional spelling to convey meaning	•	•	•					
Dictate messages or stories for others to write	•	•	•					

	Pre-K	K	1	2	3	4	5	6
Create own written texts for others to read; write left to right on a line and top to bottom on a page	•	•	•					
Participate in shared and interactive writing	•	•	•					

Traits of Writing

Focus/Ideas

	Pre-K	K	1	2	3	4	5	6
Maintain focus and sharpen ideas		•	•	•	•	•	•	•
Use sensory details and concrete examples; elaborate		•	•	•	•	•	•	•
Delete extraneous information			•	•	•	•	•	•
Rearrange words and sentences to improve meaning and focus				•	•	•	•	•
Use strategies, such as tone, style, consistent point of view, to achieve a sense of completeness						•	•	•

Organization/Paragraphs

	Pre-K	K	1	2	3	4	5	6
Use graphic organizers to group ideas		•	•	•	•	•	•	•
Write coherent paragraphs that develop a central idea			•	•	•	•	•	•
Use transitions to connect sentences and paragraphs			•	•	•	•	•	•
Select an organizational structure based on purpose, audience, length						•	•	•
Organize ideas in a logical progression, such as chronological order or by order of importance		•		•	•	•	•	•
Write introductory, supporting, and concluding paragraphs					•	•	•	•
Write a multi-paragraph paper			•	•	•	•	•	•

Voice

	Pre-K	K	1	2	3	4	5	6
Develop personal, identifiable voice and an individual tone/style			•	•	•	•	•	•
Maintain consistent voice and point of view						•	•	•
Use voice appropriate to audience, message, and purpose						•	•	•

Word Choice

	Pre-K	K	1	2	3	4	5	6
Use clear, precise, appropriate language		•	•	•	•	•	•	•
Use figurative language and vivid words			•	•	•	•	•	•
Select effective vocabulary using word walls, dictionary, or thesaurus		•	•	•	•	•	•	•

Sentences

	Pre-K	K	1	2	3	4	5	6
Combine, elaborate, and vary sentences		•	•	•	•	•	•	•
Write topic sentence, supporting sentences with facts and details, and concluding sentence			•	•	•	•	•	•
Use correct word order			•	•	•	•	•	•
Use parallel structure in a sentence							•	•

Conventions

	Pre-K	K	1	2	3	4	5	6
Use correct spelling and grammar; capitalize and punctuate correctly		•	•	•	•	•	•	•
Correct sentence fragments and run-ons					•	•	•	•
Use correct paragraph indention			•	•	•	•	•	•

The Writing Process

	Pre-K	K	1	2	3	4	5	6
Prewrite using various strategies	•	•	•	•	•	•	•	•
Develop first drafts of single- and multiple-paragraph compositions		•	•	•	•	•	•	•
Revise drafts for varied purposes, including to clarify and to achieve purpose, sense of audience, precise word choice, vivid images, and elaboration		•	•	•	•	•	•	•
Edit and proofread for correct spelling, grammar, usage, and mechanics		•	•	•	•	•	•	•
Publish own work	•	•	•	•	•	•	•	•

Types of Writing

	Pre-K	K	1	2	3	4	5	6
Narrative writing (such as personal narratives, stories, biographies, autobiographies)	•	•	• T	• T	• T	• T	• T	• T
Expository writing (such as essays, directions, explanations, news stories, research reports, summaries)		•	• T	• T	• T	• T	• T	• T
Descriptive writing (such as labels, captions, lists, plays, poems, response logs, songs)	•	•	• T	• T	• T	• T	• T	• T
Persuasive writing (such as ads, editorials, essays, letters to the editor, opinions, posters)		•	• T	• T	• T	• T	• T	• T

Writing Habits and Practices

	Pre-K	K	1	2	3	4	5	6
Write on a daily basis	•	•	•	•	•	•	•	•
Use writing as a tool for learning and self-discovery				•	•	•	•	•
Write independently for extended periods of time			•	•	•	•	•	•

ENGLISH LANGUAGE CONVENTIONS in WRITING and SPEAKING

	Pre-K	K	1	2	3	4	5	6

Grammar and Usage in Speaking and Writing

	Pre-K	K	1	2	3	4	5	6
Sentences								
Types (declarative, interrogative, exclamatory, imperative)	•	•	• T	• T	• T	• T	• T	• T
Structure (simple, compound, complex, compound-complex)	•	•	•	•	•	• T	• T	• T

• instructional opportunity   **T** tested in standardized test form

	Pre-K	K	1	2	3	4	5	6
Parts (subjects/predicates: complete, simple, compound; phrases; clauses)				•T	•	•T	•T	•T
Fragments and run-on sentences		•	•	•	•	•	•	•
Combine sentences, elaborate			•	•	•	•	•	•
Parts of speech: nouns, verbs and verb tenses, adjectives, adverbs, pronouns and antecedents, conjunctions, prepositions, interjections		•	•T	•T	•T	•T	•T	•T
Usage								
Subject-verb agreement		•	•T	•	•	•T	•T	•T
Pronoun agreement/referents			•T	•	•	•T	•T	•T
Misplaced modifiers					•	•	•T	•T
Misused words						•	•T	•T
Negatives; avoid double negatives					•	•	•	•

Mechanics in Writing

	Pre-K	K	1	2	3	4	5	6
Capitalization (first word in sentence, proper nouns and adjectives, pronoun *I*, titles, and so on)	•	•	•T	•T	•T	•T	•T	•T
Punctuation (apostrophe, comma, period, question mark, exclamation mark, quotation marks, and so on)		•	•T	•T	•T	•T	•T	•T

Spelling

	Pre-K	K	1	2	3	4	5	6
Spell independently by using pre-phonetic knowledge, knowledge of letter names, sound-letter knowledge	•	•	•	•	•	•	•	•
Use sound-letter knowledge to spell	•	•	•	•	•	•	•	•
Consonants: single, double, blends, digraphs, silent letters, and unusual consonant spellings		•	•	•	•	•	•	•
Vowels: short, long, *r*-controlled, digraphs, diphthongs, less common vowel patterns, schwa	•	•	•	•	•	•	•	•
Use knowledge of word structure to spell								
Base words and affixes (inflections, prefixes, suffixes), possessives, contractions and compound words			•	•	•	•	•	•
Greek and Latin roots, syllable patterns, multisyllabic words			•	•	•	•	•	•
Spell high-frequency, irregular words			•	•	•	•	•	•
Spell frequently misspelled words correctly, including homophones or homonyms		•	•	•	•	•	•	•
Use meaning relationships to spell			•	•	•	•	•	•

Handwriting

	Pre-K	K	1	2	3	4	5	6
Gain increasing control of penmanship, including pencil grip, paper position, posture, stroke	•	•	•	•				
Write legibly, with control over letter size and form; letter slant; and letter, word, and sentence spacing		•	•	•	•	•	•	
Write lowercase and capital letters								
Manuscript	•	•	•	•				
Cursive				•	•	•	•	•
Write numerals	•	•	•					

Listening and Speaking

	Pre-K	K	1	2	3	4	5	6
Listening Skills and Strategies								
Listen to a variety of presentations attentively and politely	•	•	•	•	•	•	•	•
Self-monitor comprehension while listening, using a variety of skills and strategies	•	•	•	•	•	•	•	•
Listen for a purpose								
For enjoyment and appreciation	•	•	•	•	•	•	•	•
To expand vocabulary and concepts	•	•	•	•	•	•	•	•
To obtain information and ideas	•	•	•	•	•	•	•	•
To follow oral directions	•	•	•	•	•	•	•	•
To answer questions and solve problems	•	•	•	•	•	•	•	•
To participate in group discussions	•	•	•	•	•	•	•	•
To identify and analyze the musical elements of literary language	•	•	•	•	•	•	•	•
To gain knowledge of one's own culture, the culture of others, and the common elements of cultures	•	•	•	•	•	•	•	•
Recognize formal and informal language				•	•	•	•	•
Listen critically to distinguish fact from opinion and to analyze and evaluate ideas, information, experiences	•			•	•	•	•	•
Evaluate a speaker's delivery				•	•	•	•	•
Interpret a speaker's purpose, perspective, persuasive techniques, verbal and nonverbal messages, and use of rhetorical devices					•	•	•	•
Speaking Skills and Strategies								
Speak clearly, accurately, and fluently, using appropriate delivery for a variety of audiences, and purposes	•	•	•	•	•	•	•	•
Use proper intonation, volume, pitch, modulation, and phrasing		•	•	•	•	•	•	•
Speak with a command of standard English conventions	•	•	•	•	•	•	•	•
Use appropriate language for formal and informal settings	•	•		•	•	•	•	•

Speaking (continued)

Skill	Pre-K	K	1	2	3	4	5	6
Speak for a purpose	•	•	•	•	•	•	•	•
To ask and answer questions	•	•	•	•	•	•	•	•
To give directions and instructions		•	•	•	•	•	•	•
To retell, paraphrase, or explain information		•	•	•	•	•	•	•
To communicate needs and share ideas and experiences	•	•	•	•	•	•	•	•
To participate in conversations and discussions	•	•	•	•	•	•	•	•
To express an opinion	•	•	•	•	•	•	•	•
To deliver dramatic recitations, interpretations, or performances	•	•	•	•	•	•	•	•
To deliver presentations or oral reports (narrative, descriptive, persuasive, and informational)	•	•	•	•	•	•	•	•
Stay on topic	•	•	•	•	•	•	•	•
Use appropriate verbal and nonverbal elements (such as facial expression, gestures, eye contact, posture)	•	•	•	•	•	•	•	•
Identify and/or demonstrate methods to manage or overcome communication anxiety						•	•	•

Viewing/Media

Skill	Pre-K	K	1	2	3	4	5	6
Interact with and respond to a variety of print and non-print media for a range of purposes	•	•	•	•	•	•	•	•
Compare and contrast print, visual, and electronic media					•	•	•	•
Analyze and evaluate media				•	•	•	•	•
Recognize purpose, bias, propaganda, and persuasive techniques in media messages			•	•	•	•	•	•

Research and Study Skills

Understand and Use Graphic Sources

Skill	Pre-K	K	1	2	3	4	5	6
Advertisement			•	•	•	•	•	•
Chart/table	•	•	•	•	•	•	•	•
Diagram/scale drawing						•	•	•
Graph (bar, circle, line, picture)		•	•	•	•	•	•	•
Illustration, photograph, caption, label	•	•	•	•	•	•	•	•
Map/globe	•	•	•	•	•	•	•	•
Order form/application						•	•	•
Poster/announcement	•	•	•	•	•	•		
Schedule						•	•	•
Sign	•	•	•	•		•		
Time line				•	•	•	•	•

Understand and Use Reference Sources

Skill	Pre-K	K	1	2	3	4	5	6
Know and use parts of a book to locate information	•	•	•	•	•	•	•	•
Use alphabetical order		•	•	•	•	•		
Understand purpose, structure, and organization of reference sources (print, electronic, media, Internet)	•	•	•	•	•	•	•	•
Almanac						•	•	•
Atlas		•		•	•	•	•	•
Card catalog/library database				•	•	•	•	•
Dictionary/glossary		•	•	•	• T	• T	• T	• T
Encyclopedia				•	•	•	•	•
Magazine/periodical				•	•	•	•	•
Newspaper and Newsletter			•	•	•	•	•	•
Readers' Guide to Periodical Literature						•	•	•
Technology (computer and non-computer electronic media)	•	•	•	•	•	•	•	•
Thesaurus				•	•	•	•	•

Study Skills and Strategies

Skill	Pre-K	K	1	2	3	4	5	6
Adjust reading rate			•	•	•	•	•	•
Clarify directions	•	•	•	•	•	•	•	•
Outline				•	•	•	•	•
Skim and scan			•	•	•	•	•	•
SQP3R						•	•	•
Summarize		•	•	•	•	•	•	•
Take notes, paraphrase, and synthesize					•	•	•	•
Use graphic and semantic organizers to organize information		•	•	•	•	•	•	•

• instructional opportunity   **T** tested in standardized test forma[t]

Test-Taking Skills and Strategies

	Pre-K	K	1	2	3	4	5	6
Understand the question, the vocabulary of tests, and key words			•	•	•	•	•	•
Answer the question; use information from the text (stated or inferred)		•	•	•	•	•	•	•
Write across texts			•	•	•	•	•	•
Complete the sentence			•	•	•	•	•	•

Technology/New Literacies

	Pre-K	K	1	2	3	4	5	6
Non-Computer Electronic Media								
Audio tapes/CDs, video tapes/DVDs	•	•	•	•	•	•	•	
Film, television, and radio		•	•	•	•	•	•	•
Computer Programs and Services: Basic Operations and Concepts								
Use accurate computer terminology	•	•	•	•	•	•	•	•
Create, name, locate, open, save, delete, and organize files		•	•	•	•	•	•	•
Use input and output devices (such as mouse, keyboard, monitor, printer, touch screen)	•	•	•	•	•	•	•	•
Use basic keyboarding skills		•	•	•	•	•	•	•
Responsible Use of Technology Systems and Software								
Work cooperatively and collaboratively with others; follow acceptable use policies	•	•	•	•	•	•	•	•
Recognize hazards of Internet searches		•	•	•	•	•	•	•
Respect intellectual property					•	•	•	•
Information and Communication Technologies: Information Acquisition								
Use electronic web (non-linear) navigation, online resources, databases, keyword searches			•	•	•	•	•	•
Use visual and non-textual features of online resources	•	•	•	•	•	•	•	•
Internet inquiry								
Identify questions			•	•	•	•	•	•
Locate, select, and collect information			•	•	•	•	•	•
Analyze information			•	•	•	•	•	•
Evaluate electronic information sources for accuracy, relevance, bias				•	•	•	•	•
Understand bias/subjectivity of electronic content (about this site, author search, date created)					•	•	•	•
Synthesize information					•	•	•	•
Communicate findings					•	•	•	•
Use fix-up strategies (such as clicking *Back, Forward,* or *Undo;* redoing a search; trimming the URL)		•	•	•	•	•	•	•
Communication								
Collaborate, publish, present, and interact with others		•	•	•	•	•	•	•
Use online resources (e-mail, bulletin boards, newsgroups)			•	•	•	•	•	•
Use a variety of multimedia formats			•	•	•	•	•	•
Problem Solving								
Select the appropriate software for the task	•	•	•	•	•	•	•	•
Use technology resources for solving problems and making informed decisions			•	•	•	•	•	•
Determine when technology is useful				•	•	•	•	•

The Research Process

	Pre-K	K	1	2	3	4	5	6
Choose and narrow the topic; frame and revise questions for inquiry		•	•	•	•	•	•	•
Choose and evaluate appropriate reference sources		•	•	•	•	•	•	•
Locate and collect information	•	•	•	•	•	•	•	•
Take notes/record findings				•	•	•	•	•
Combine and compare information				•	•	•	•	•
Evaluate, interpret, and draw conclusions about key information				•	•	•	•	•
Summarize information		•	•	•	•	•	•	•
Make an outline				•	•	•	•	•
Organize content systematically		•	•	•	•	•	•	•
Communicate information		•	•	•	•	•	•	•
Write and present a report			•	•	•	•	•	•
Include citations						•	•	•
Respect intellectual property/plagiarism						•	•	•
Select and organize visual aids		•	•	•	•	•	•	•

A

Abbreviations, 4.6 685e–685f.

Accountability. See **Adequate yearly progress.**

Achieving English proficiency. See **ELL (English Language Learners) suggestions.**

Activate prior knowledge. See **Prereading strategies.**

Adequate yearly progress (AYP), 4.1 16g–16h, 4.2 140g–140h, 4.3 266g–266h, 4.4 390g–390h, 4.5 514g–514h, 4.6 636g–636h

Adjectives, 4.4 537e–537f
   articles, 4.5 537e–537f
   comparative and superlative, 4.5 559e–559f
   proper, 4.4 537e

Advanced learners
   critical thinking, 4.6 654
   group time, 4.1 18f–18g, 40f–40g, 66f–66g, 88f–88g, 112f–112g, DI·3, DI·5, DI·7, DI·9, DI·11, DI·13, DI·15, DI·17, DI·19, DI·21, DI·23, DI·25, DI·27, DI·29, DI·31, DI·33, DI·35, DI·37, DI·39, DI·41, DI·43, DI·45, DI·47, DI·49, DI·51, 4.2 142f–142g, 162f–162g, 188f–188g, 212f–212g, 240f–240g, DI·3, DI·5, DI·7, DI·9, DI·11, DI·13, DI·15, DI·17, DI·19, DI·21, DI·23, DI·25, DI·27, DI·29, DI·31, DI·33, DI·35, DI·37, DI·39, DI·41, DI·43, DI·45, DI·47, DI·49, DI·51, 4.3 268f–268g, 292f–292g, 314f–314g, 338f–338g, 360f–360g, DI·3, DI·5, DI·7, DI·9, DI·11, DI·13, DI·15, DI·17, DI·19, DI·21, DI·23, DI·25, DI·27, DI·29, DI·31, DI·33, DI·35, DI·37, DI·39, DI·41, DI·43, DI·45, DI·47, DI·49, DI·51, 4.4 392f–392g, 416f–416g, 440f–440g, 466f–466g, 488f–488g, DI·3, DI·5, DI·7, DI·9, DI·11, DI·13, DI·15, DI·17, DI·19, DI·21, DI·23, DI·25, DI·27, DI·29, DI·31, DI·33, DI·35, DI·37, DI·39, DI·41, DI·43, DI·45, DI·47, DI·49, DI·51, 4.5 516f–516g, 538f–538g, 560f–560g, 582f–582g, 608f–608g, DI·3, DI·5, DI·7, DI·9, DI·11, DI·13, DI·15, DI·17, DI·19, DI·21, DI·23, DI·25, DI·27, DI·29, DI·31, DI·33, DI·35, DI·37, DI·39, DI·41, DI·43, DI·45, DI·47, DI·49, DI·51, 4.6 638f–638g, 660f–660g, 686f–686g, 712f–712g, 738f–738g, DI·3, DI·5, DI·7, DI·9, DI·11, DI·13, DI·15, DI·17, DI·19, DI·21, DI·23, DI·25, DI·27, DI·29, DI·31, DI·33, DI·35, DI·37, DI·39, DI·41, DI·43, DI·45, DI·47, DI·49, DI·51. See also **Grouping students for instruction.**
   leveled readers, 4.1 LR7–LR9, LR16–LR18, LR25–LR27, LR34–LR36, LR43–LR45, 4.2 LR7–LR9, LR16–LR18, LR25–LR27, LR34–LR36, LR43–LR45, 4.3 LR7–LR9, LR16–LR18, LR25–LR27, LR34–LR36, LR43–LR45, 4.4 LR7–LR9, LR16–LR18, LR25–LR27, LR34–LR36, LR43–LR45, 4.5 LR7–LR9, LR16–LR18, LR25–LR27, LR34–LR36, LR43–LR45, 4.6 LR7–LR9, LR16–LR18, LR25–LR27, LR34–LR36, LR43–LR45
   resources, 4.1 18i, 40i, 66i, 88i, 112i, 4.2 142i, 162i, 188i, 212i, 240i, 4.3 268i, 292i, 314i, 338i, 360i, 4.4 392i, 416i, 440i, 466i, 488i, 4.5 516i, 538i, 560i, 582i, 608i, 4.6 638i, 660i, 686i, 712i, 738i
   writing, 4.1 WA9, 4.2 WA9, 4.3 WA9, 4.4 WA9, 4.5 WA9, 4.6 WA9

Adverbs, 4.5 581e–581f
   comparative and superlative, 4.4 607e–607f

Advertisement. See **Graphic sources.**

Affective domain. See **Habits and attitudes, Literary response and appreciation.**

Affixes. See **Spelling,** word structure; **Word structure,** prefixes, suffixes.

Alliteration. See **Sound devices and poetic elements.**

Almanac. See **Reference sources.**

Alphabetical order, 4.2 253, 4.4 453, 4.6 662b. See also **Vocabulary strategies.**

Analogies. See **Vocabulary strategies.**

Analyzing. See **Reading across texts.** In addition, analytical thinking questions are raised throughout Guiding Comprehension and Reader Response.

Answering questions. See **Questions, answering.**

Antonyms, 4.2 242b, 4.4 394–395, 405, 415c, 490–491, 495, 507c. See also **Vocabulary strategies.**

Application. See **Graphic sources.**

Appropriate word meaning, 4.1 20b, 68–69, 79, 87c, 4.2 231, 4.3 270–271, 277, 291c, 316b, 4.4 418–419, 427, 439c, 457, 4.6 640b, 662–663, 669, 673, 685c, 714b

Art activities. See **Cross-curricular activities.**

Art, interpreting. See **Literary craft,** illustrator's craft/style.

Asking questions. See **Questions, asking.**

Assessment
   classroom-based. "If/then" assessment occurs throughout lessons and Guiding Comprehension.
   fluency, 4.1 39a, 65a, 87a, 111a, 133a, WA15–WA16, DI·57, DI·58, 4.2 161a, 187a, 211a, 239a, 259a, WA15–WA16, DI·57, DI·58, 4.3 291a, 313a, 337a, 359a, 383a, WA15–WA16, DI·57, DI·58, 4.4 415a, 439a, 465a, 487a, 507a, WA15–WA16, DI·57, DI·58, 4.5 537a, 559a, 581a, 607a, 629a, WA15–WA16, DI·57, DI·58, 4.6 659a, 685a, 711a, 737a, 761a, WA15–WA16, DI·57, DI·58
   formal, 4.1 35, 61, 83, 107, 129, 134a, WA7, WA10–WA14, 4.2 157, 185, 209, 235, 257, 260a, WA7, WA10–WA14, 4.3 287, 309, 333, 355, 379, 384a, WA7, WA10–WA14, 4.4 411, 435, 463, 483, 503, 508a, WA7, WA10–WA14, 4.5 535, 555, 577, 603, 625, 630a, WA7, WA10–WA14, 4.6 657, 681, 707, 733, 757, 762a, WA7, WA10–WA11
   scoring guide (rubric), 4.1 34, 35, 60, 61, 82, 83, 106, 107, 128, 129, 134a, WA7, WA10–WA14, 4.2 156, 157, 184, 185, 208, 209, 233, 234, 256, 257, 260a, WA7, WA10–WA14, 4.3 286, 287, 308, 309, 332, 333, 354, 355, 378, 379, 384a, WA7, WA10–WA14, 4.4 410, 411, 434, 435, 462, 463, 482, 483, 501, 502, 508a, WA7, WA10–WA14, 4.5 534, 535, 554, 555, 576, 577, 602, 603, 624, 625, 630a, WA7, WA10–WA14, 4.6 655, 656, 680, 681, 706, 707, 732, 733, 756, 757, 762a, WA7, WA10–WA14
   self-assessment, 4.1 WA7, 4.2 WA7, 4.3 WA7, 4.4 WA7, 4.5 WA7, 4.6 WA7
   spelling, 4.1 39j, 65j, 87j, 111j, 133j, 4.2 161j, 187j, 211j, 239j, 259j, 4.3 291j, 313j, 337j, 359j, 383j, 4.4 415j, 439j, 465j, 487j, 507j, 4.5 537j, 559j, 581j, 607j, 629j, 4.6 659j, 685j, 711j, 737j, 761j
   test-taking strategies, 4.1 34, 38, 60, 64, 82, 106, 110, 128, 133g–133h, 138, 4.2 156, 160, 184, 187, 208, 211, 233, 256, 259, 259g–259h, 4.3 286, 290, 308, 312, 332, 336, 354, 378, 382, 383g–383h, 4.4 410, 414, 434, 438, 462, 482, 501, 506, 507g–507h, 4.5 534, 551, 554, 558, 576, 602, 606, 624, 628, 4.6 655, 659, 680, 684, 706, 710, 732, 756, 760

writing, 4.1 WA7, WA10–WA14, 4.2 WA7, WA10–WA14, 4.3 WA7, WA10–WA14, 4.4 WA7, WA10–WA14, 4.5 WA7, WA10–WA14, 4.6 WA7, WA10–WA11

Atlas. See **Reference sources.**

Attitudes, personal. See **Habits and attitudes.**

Authors (of reading selections)
   Alvarez, Julia, 4.1 139d, 4.6 690–705
   Armour, Richard, 4.4 464
   Beecham, Cristina, 4.6 658
   Begay, Shonto, 4.3 386–387
   Beres, Samantha, 4.2 210–211
   Bova, Ben, 4.1 139l, 4.5 612–623
   Brown, John, 4.1 108–111
   Bruchac, Joseph, 4.1 139j, 4.6 664–679
   Cherry, Lynne, 4.1 139l, 4.3 364–377
   Chief Lelooska, 4.3 334–337
   Daniel, Claire, 4.5 604–607
   Dewey, Jennifer Owings, 4.1 139f, 4.5 586–601
   Díaz, Katacha, 4.5 556–559
   DiCamillo, Kate, 4.1 22–33
   Falkner, David, 4.6 708–711
   Farjeon, Eleanor, 4.4 509
   Farris, Christine King, 4.1 139j, 4.6 642–654
   Fisher, Aileen, 4.4 510
   Gavin, Susan, 4.2 258–259
   George, Kristine O'Connell, 4.5 630
   Gerson, Mary-Joan, 4.3 318–331
   Grimes, Nikki, 4.2 260
   Guthrie, Woody, 4.1 130–133
   Halvorsen, Lisa, 4.1 116–127
   Hoban, Russell, 4.2 261
   Hoffman, Mary, 4.1 139d, 4.2 192–207
   Holub, Miroslav, 4.5 632–633
   Hopkins, Jackie Mims, 4.1 92–105
   Hopkins, Lee Bennett, 4.1 136
   Hughes, Langston, 4.1 134, 4.6 762
   Kennedy, X. J., 4.5 631, 4.6 763
   Kepplinger, Bonnie, 4.4 504–507
   Khalsa, Ek Ongkar K., 4.6 659
   Klobuchar, Lisa, 4.2 186–187
   Kramer, Stephen, 4.1 139f, 4.3 342–353
   Kranking, Kathy, 4.1 36–39
   Lasky, Kathryn, 4.1 139j, 4.2 216–232
   Levy, Constance Kling, 4.4 511
   Lewin, Ted, 4.1 139f, 4.5 542–553
   Lewis, J. Patrick, 4.6 765
   Livingston, Myra Cohn, 4.4 465, 4.6 762
   Massie, Elizabeth, 4.1 62–65
   Montgomery, Sy, 4.4 420–433
   Myers, Laurie, 4.1 44–59
   Nayer, Judy, 4.5 626–629
   Oh, Sadaharu, 4.6 708–711
   Old, Wendie C., 4.6 716–731
   Perez, Marlene, 4.6 682–685
   Perry, Andrea, 4.2 262–263
   Peterson, Ruth De Long, 4.1 137
   Rand, Gloria, 4.5 520–533
   Rumford, James, 4.4 470–481
   Ryan, Pam Muñoz, 4.5 564–575
   Sandin, Joan, 4.1 139h, 4.2 166–183
   St. George, Judith, 4.2 244–255
   Say, Allen, 4.1 70–81, 139h
   Schyffert, Bea Uusma, 4.6 742–755
   Selznick, Brian, 4.4 396–409
   Singer, Marilyn, 4.3 385
   Slattery, Margaret E., 4.4 444–461
   Smith Jr, Charles R., 4.2 146–155, 158–159, 160–161
   Sobol, Donald J., 4.1 139d, 4.4 492–500
   Sobol, Richard, 4.3 296–307
   Soto, Gary, 4.6 764
   Sow, Fatou Ndiaye, 4.4 508
   Stone, Tanya Lee, 4.3 380–383

Strahinich, Helen, 4.3 288–291
Sutherland, Tui T., 4.4 412–415
Van Allsburg, Chris, 4.1 139l, 4.3 272–285
Wachter, Joanne, 4.3 310–313
Washington, Linda, 4.5 536–537
Weil, Ann, 4.4 436–439
Withrow, Dawn, 4.6 659
Wong, Janet S., 4.1 135
Zolotow, Charlotte, 4.3 384

Author's craft/style/language. *See* **Literary craft,** author's craft/style/language.

Author's perspective/viewpoint/bias, 4.1 88l–88m, 4.3 313b, 4.5 537a. *See also* **Literary craft.**

Authors, program, 4.1 xx, 4.2 iv, 4.3 iv, 4.4 iv, 4.5 iv, 4.6 iv
Afflerbach, Peter
Blachowicz, Camille
Boyd, Candy Dawson
Cheyney, Wendy
Juel, Connie
Kame'enui, Edward
Leu, Donald
Paratore, Jeanne
Pearson, P. David
Sebesta, Sam
Simmons, Deborah
Vaughn, Sharon
Watts-Taffe, Susan
Wixson, Karen Kring

Author's purpose, 4.1 31, 40l–40m, 40–41, 47, 57, 63, 65b, 88l–88m, 88–89, 95, 103, 109, 111b, DI·16, DI·17, DI·36, DI·37, DI·53, DI·55, 4.3 369, 4.5 516l–516m, 516–517, 523, 529, 537b, DI·6, DI·7, DI·52, 4.6 695

Author study, 4.1 139b–139l

Autobiography. *See* **Genres.**

B

Background, build. *See* **Concept development; Prereading strategies,** activate prior knowledge.

Base words with and without spelling changes. *See* **Spelling,** word structure; **Word structure.**

Bibliography
self-selected reading, 4.1 DI·59, DI·60, TR14–TR17, 4.2 DI·59, DI·60, TR14–TR17, 4.3 DI·59, DI·60, TR14–TR17, 4.4 DI·59, DI·60, TR14–TR17, 4.5 DI·59, DI·60, TR14–TR17, 4.6 DI·59, DI·60, TR14–TR17
trade book library, 4.1 18i, 40i, 66i, 88i, 112i, 4.2 142i, 162i, 188i, 212i, 240i, 4.3 268i, 292i, 314i, 338i, 360i, 4.4 392i, 416i, 440i, 466i, 488i, 4.5 516i, 538i, 560i, 582i, 608i, 4.6 638i, 660i, 686i, 712i, 738i

Bilingual students. *See* **ELL (English Language Learners) suggestions.**

Biography. *See* **Genres.**

Build background. *See* **Concept development; Prereading strategies,** activate prior knowledge.

C

Capitalization, 4.6 685e–685f
abbreviations, 4.6 685e–685f
adjectives, proper, 4.4 537f
letter conventions, 4.3 313g
nouns, proper, 4.2 161e–161f, 4.6 685e–685f
sentences, 4.6 685e–685f
titles, 4.6 685e–685f, 761e–761f
See also **Writing process,** edit.

Card catalog. *See* **Reference sources.**

Career awareness, 4.2 240j, 4.6 744

Categorizing. *See* **Classifying.**

Cause and effect, 4.1 49, 4.2 142l–142m, 142–143, 149, 161, 161b, DI·6, DI·7, DI·52, 4.3 268l–268m, 268–269, 275, 281, 291, 291b, 323, 338l–338m, 347, DI·52, 4.4 466l–466m, 4.6 638l–638m, 638–639, 645, 653, 659, 659b, 738l–738m, DI·6, DI·7, DI·52

Central message of text. *See* **Main idea, Theme (as a story element).**

Character, 4.4 401, 440l–440m, 440–441, 449, 455, 459, DI·26, DI·27, DI·54, 4.5 DI·54, 4.6 686l–686m, 686–687, 693, 699, 703, 711b, DI·26, DI·27

Character Counts! *See* **Character education.**

Character education (as demonstrated in literature selections)
attentiveness, 4.4 470–481, 492–500, 4.5 586–601, 4.6 716–731, 742–755
caring, 4.1 22–33, 4.2 192–207, 4.5 520–533, 612–623, 4.6 642–654, 664–679
citizenship, 4.1 130–133, 4.2 244–255
fairness, 4.1 92–105, 4.3 334–337, 4.6 642–654, 664–679
initiative, 4.1 70–81, 4.2 192–207, 210–211, 4.4 444–461, 470–481, 4.5 536–537, 542–553, 604–607, 4.6 642–654, 690–705, 716–731
patience, 4.3 296–307, 4.4 420–433, 470–481, 4.6 716–731
respect, 4.1 70–81, 4.3 364–377, 4.5 586–601, 4.6 664–679, 690–705, 708–711
responsibility, 4.2 166–183, 216–232, 244–255, 4.3 364–377, 4.5 612–623, 4.6 742–755
trustworthiness, 4.1 62–65, 92–105, 4.2 216–232, 4.5 612–623

Charts and tables. *See* **Graphic sources.**

Choral reading. *See* **Fluency, reading.**

Chronology. *See* **Sequence.**

Chunking. *See* **Word structure,** chunking.

Classifying
statements of evidence. *See* **Fact and opinion, statements of.**
words into groups, 4.1 20b, 90a, 4.2 144a, 144b, 190a, 242b, 4.3 294b, 4.4 394a, 4.5 518b, 562b, 4.6 662b

Classroom-based assessment. "If/then" assessment occurs throughout lessons and Guiding Comprehension.

Classroom management, 4.1 18d–18e, 18f–18g, 18g-1–18g-4, 40d–40e, 40f–40g, 40g-1–40g-4, 66d–66e, 66f–66g, 66g-1–66g-4, 88d–88e, 88f–88g, 88g-1–88g-4, 112d–112e, 112f–112g, 112g-1–112g-4, 4.2 142d–142e, 142f–142g, 142g-1–142g-4, 162d–162e, 162f–162g, 162g-1–162g-4, 188d–188e, 188f–188g, 188g-1–188g-4, 212d–212e, 212f–212g, 212g-1–212g-4, 240d–240e, 240f–240g, 240g-1–240g-4, 4.3 268d–268e, 268f–268g, 268g-1–268g-4, 292d–292e, 292f–292g, 292g-1–292g-4, 314d–314e, 314f–314g, 314g-1–314g-4, 338d–338e, 338f–338g, 338g-1–338g-4, 360d–360e, 360f–360g, 360g-1–360g-4, 4.4 392d–392e, 392f–392g, 392g-1–392g-4, 416d–416e, 416f–416g, 416g-1–416g-4, 416, 440d–440e, 440f–440g, 440g-1–440g-4, 466d–466e, 466f–466g, 466g-1–466g-4, 488d–488e, 488f–488g, 488g-1–488g-4, 4.5 516d–516e, 516f–516g, 516g-1–516g-4, 538d–538e, 538f–538g, 538g-1–538g-4, 560d–560e, 560f–560g, 560g-1–560g-4, 582d–582e, 582f–582g, 582g-1–582g-4, 608d–608e, 608f–608g, 608g-1–608g-4, 4.6 638d–

638e, 638f–638g, 638g-1–638g-4, 660d–660e, 660f–660g, 660g-1–660g-4, 686d–686e, 686f–686g, 686g-1–686g-4, 712d–712e, 712f–712g, 712g-1–712g-4, 738d–738e, 738f–738g, 738g-1–738g-4

Colon, 4.2 236, 4.3 313h

Comma, 4.6 659e–659f, 711e–711f
appositives, 4.6 711e–711f
compound/complex sentences, 4.1 111e–111f, 133f, 4.6 659e–659f
items in a series, 4.6 711e–711f

Common word parts. *See* **Word structure.**

Communication, effective. *See* **Listening,** tips; **Speaking,** tips.

Community, involvement of. *See* **School-home connection.**

Comparing and contrasting, 4.2 197, 4.4 392l–392m, 392–393, 399, 407, 415, 415b, 416l–416m, 416–417, 423, 431, 439, 439b, 499, DI·6, DI·7, DI·16, DI·17, DI·52, DI·53, 4.5 538l–538m, 538–539, 545, 549, 557, 559b, DI·16, DI·17, DI·53

Composition. *See* **Six-trait writing, Writing forms/ products, Writing Process, Writing purpose.**

Compound words, 4.1 68b, 4.2 214b, 4.6 662b. *See also* **Spelling,** word structure; **Vocabulary strategies.**

Comprehension skills, explicit/implicit instruction. *See* **Author's purpose; Cause and effect; Character; Classifying; Comparing and contrasting; Conclusions, drawing; Fact and opinion, statements of; Graphic sources; Main idea; Plot; Predicting; Sequence; Setting; Summarizing; Theme (as a story element).**

Comprehension strategies. *See* **Graphic and semantic organizers; Monitor and fix up; Questions, answering; Questions, asking; Self-check; Story structure; Text structure; Visualizing.**

Computers, using. *See* **New literacies (for student reading), Technology; Writing with technology.**

Concept development, 4.1 17a, 18a, 18l, 20a, 40a, 40l, 42a, 66a, 66l, 68a, 88a, 88l, 90a, 112a, 112l, 114a, 134a, 4.2 141a, 142a, 142l, 144a, 162a, 162l, 164a, 188a, 188l, 190a, 212a, 212l, 214a, 240a, 240l, 242a, 260a, 4.3 267a, 268a, 268l, 270a, 292a, 292l, 294a, 314a, 314l, 316a, 338a, 338l, 340a, 360a, 360l, 362a, 384a, 4.4 391a, 392a, 392l, 394a, 416a, 416l, 418a, 440a, 440l, 442a, 466a, 466l, 468a, 488a, 488l, 490a, 508a, 4.5 515a, 516a, 516l, 518a, 538a, 538l, 540a, 560a, 560l, 562a, 582a, 582l, 584a, 608a, 608l, 610a, 630a, 4.6 637a, 638a, 638l, 640a, 660a, 660l, 662a, 686a, 686l, 688a, 712a, 712l, 714a, 738a, 738l, 740a, 762a. *See also* **Prereading strategies,** activate prior knowledge.

Conclusions, drawing, 4.2 153, 162l–162m, 162–163, 169, 179, 181, 187b, 188l–188m, 188–189, 195, 203, 205, 211b, DI·16, DI·17, DI·26, DI·27, DI·54, 4.5 569, 591, 608l–608m, 608–609, 615, 619, 627, 629b, DI·46, DI·47, DI·56

Conjunctions, 4.6 659e–659f

Connections, making
text to self, 4.1 32, 46, 74, 98, 148, 4.2 192, 197, 218, 4.3 274, 302, 324, 4.4 400, 422, 460, 472, 4.5 548, 592, 618, 4.6 668, 696, 730, 746
text to text, 4.1 39, 58, 65, 87, 104, 111, 133, 4.2 161, 172, 182, 206, 230, 259, 4.3 291, 313, 330, 337, 368, 383, 4.4 415, 439, 450, 465, 487, 498, 507, 4.5 532, 537, 552, 559, 574, 581, 607, 622, 629, 4.6 646, 659, 678, 685, 737, 761

text to world, 4.1 30, 80, 126, 4.2 154, 254, 4.3 284, 306, 348, 352, 376, 4.4 408, 432, 480, 4.5 566, 600, 4.6 652, 704, 718, 754

Connotation and denotation, 4.4 442b

Content-area texts
  cultures, 4.1 16, 70–81, 84–87, 4.3 364–377, 4.5 542–553, 556–559, 4.6 690–705
  science, 4.1 36–39, 108–111, 130–133, 4.3 288–291, 310–313, 356–359, 380–383, 4.4 412–415, 436–439, 504–507, 4.5 626–629, 4.6 758–761
  social studies, 4.1 65, 4.2 186–187, 210–211, 258–259, 4.5 536–537, 556–559, 604–607, 4.6 682–685, 708–711

Content-area vocabulary, 4.1 36, 62, 108, 130, 4.2 186, 210, 258, 4.3 288, 310, 354, 380, 4.4 412, 436, 464, 504, 4.5 536, 540b, 556, 584b, 604, 626, 4.6 682, 708, 758

Context clues for meaning, 4.1 20b, 90, 101, 111c, 4.2 242b, 4.3 270, 277, 291c, 294, 305, 313c, 316b, 316–317, 325, 337c, 4.4 394–395, 405, 415c, 418–419, 427, 439c, 468b, 490, 495, 507c, 4.5 518–519, 525, 537c, 562–563, 573, 581c, 610b, 610–611, 617, 629c, 4.6 640b, 688–689, 701, 711c, 714b, 714–715, 721, 729, 737c, 740–741, 749, 761c
  antonyms, 4.2 242b, 4.4 394–395, 405, 415c, 490–491, 495, 507c
  appropriate word meaning, 4.1 20b, 4.3 270–271, 277, 291c, 316b, 4.4 418–419, 427, 439c, 4.6 640b, 714b
  definition and explanation, 4.6 714–715
  homographs, 4.5 518–519, 525, 537c, 761c
  homonyms, 4.3 294–295, 305, 315c, 4.5 518–519, 525, 537c, 4.6 740–741, 749, 761c, DI·45
  multiple-meaning words, 4.1 20b, 4.3 270–271, 277, 291c, 316b, 4.4 418–419, 427, 439c, 4.6 640b, 714b
  synonyms, 4.1 90–91, 101, 111c, 4.4 394–395, 405, 415c, 490–491, 495, 507c, 4.5 610b, 610–611, 617, 629c
  unfamiliar words, 4.1 DI·35, 4.3 316–317, 325, 337c, 4.4 486b, DI·5, DI·15, DI·45, 4.5 562–563, 573, 581c, DI·5, DI·25, DI·45, 4.6 688–689, 701, 711c, 714–715, 721, 729, 737c, DI·25, DI·35
  See also **Vocabulary strategies.**

Contractions, 4.4 507e–507f. *See also* **Spelling,** word structure.

Contrasting. See **Comparing and contrasting.**

Conventions of standard language. See **Capitalization, Grammar and usage, Punctuation.**

Creative/dramatic activities, 4.1 39d, 66j, 4.2 188j, 211d, 4.3 268j, 314j, 337d, 4.4 440j, 465d, 4.5 537d, 608j, 4.6 638j. *See also* **Speaking,** activities.

Creative thinking. Creative thinking questions appear throughout Differentiated Instruction Group Time lesson plans for each lesson.

Critical thinking
  analyzing, 4.1 34, 60, 82, 106, 128, 4.2 156, 184, 208, 233, 256, 4.3 286, 308, 332, 354, 378, 4.4 410, 434, 462, 482, 501, 4.5 534, 554, 576, 602, 624, 4.6 655, 680, 706, 732, 756. In addition, analytical thinking questions are raised throughout Guiding Comprehension and Reader Response.
  comparing and contrasting across selections (intertextuality), 4.1 39, 58, 65, 87, 104, 111, 133, 4.2 161, 172, 182, 206, 230, 259, 4.3 291, 313, 330, 337, 368, 383, 4.4 415, 450, 465,

498, 507, 4.5 532, 537, 552, 559, 574, 581, 607, 622, 629, 4.6 646, 659, 678, 685, 737, 761

  comparing and contrasting within a text, 4.2 196, 197, 4.4 392l–392m, 392–393, 398, 399, 407, 415, 415b, 416l–416m, 416–417, 422, 423, 431, 439, 439b, 498, 499, 4.5 538l–538m, 538–539, 545, 548, 549, 557, 559b
  evaluating and critiquing ideas and text, 4.1 34, 60, 82, 106, 128, 4.2 156, 184, 208, 233, 256, 4.3 286, 308, 332, 354, 378, 4.4 410, 434, 462, 482, 501, 4.5 534, 554, 576, 602, 624, 4.6 655, 680, 706, 732, 756
  inferring, 4.1 34, 60, 82, 106, 128, 4.2 156, 184, 208, 233, 256, 4.3 286, 308, 332, 354, 378, 4.4 410, 434, 462, 482, 501, 4.5 534, 554, 576, 602, 624, 4.6 655, 680, 706, 732, 756
  organizing ideas/information, 4.1 20a, 42a, 68a, 90a, 114a, 4.2 144a, 164a, 190a, 214a, 242a, 4.3 270a, 294a, 316a, 340a, 362a, 4.4 394a, 418a, 442a, 468a, 490a, 4.5 518a, 540a, 562a, 584a, 610a, 4.6 640a, 662a, 668a, 714a, 737g–737h, 740a
  synthesizing ideas from different texts and media, 4.1 39k, 58, 65k, 87k, 104, 111k, 133, 133k, 4.2 161k, 187k, 206, 211k, 239k, 259, 259k, 4.3 291, 291k, 313k, 330, 337, 337k, 359k, 383, 383k, 4.4 415k, 439k, 450, 465k, 487k, 498, 507k, 4.5 532, 537, 537k, 552, 559k, 574, 581k, 607, 607k, 622, 629k, 4.6 646, 659, 659k, 678, 685, 711k, 737k, 761k
  synthesizing ideas within a text, 4.2 196, 197, 4.4 392l–392m, 392–393, 398, 399, 407, 415, 415b, 416l–416m, 416–417, 422, 423, 430, 431, 439, 439b, 498, 499, 4.5 538l–538m, 538–539, 545, 548, 549, 557, 559b
  See also **Conclusions, drawing; Generalizations, making; Problems, solving.** In addition, critical thinking questions appear throughout Guiding Comprehension in each lesson and Differentiated Instruction Group Time lesson plans for each lesson.

Cross-curricular activities
  art, 4.1 18j, 40j, 4.2 240j, 4.3 338j, 4.4 416j, 4.5 538j, 4.6 686j
  drama, 4.1 39d, 66j, 4.2 188j, 211d, 4.3 268j, 314j, 337d, 4.4 440j, 465d, 4.5 537d, 608j, 4.6 638j
  health, 4.1 88j, 4.2 212j, 4.4 392j, 4.5 516j, 4.6 738j
  listening, 4.1 18j, 40j, 66j, 88j, 112j, 4.2 142j, 162j, 188j, 212j, 240j, 4.3 268j, 292j, 314j, 338j, 360j, 4.4 392j, 416j, 440j, 466j, 488j, 4.5 516j, 538j, 560j, 582j, 608j, 4.6 638j, 660j, 686j, 712j, 738j
  math, 4.1 112j, 4.2 142j, 4.3 292j, 4.4 466j, 4.5 560j, 4.6 712j
  music, 4.2 162j, 4.3 360j, 4.4 488j, 4.5 582j, 4.6 660j
  science, 4.1 37, 109, 111, 119, 121, 125, 131, 4.2 199, 4.3 268k, 275, 281, 288, 289, 291, 292k, 299, 301, 305, 311, 314k, 321, 329, 335, 338k, 345, 347, 351, 360k, 369, 373, 375, 381, 4.4 392k, 399, 405, 413, 416k, 425, 431, 437, 439, 440k, 457, 459, 465, 466k, 488k, 495, 505, 4.5 516k, 523, 525, 529, 582k, 591, 595, 599, 608k, 615, 617, 621, 4.6 711, 712k, 719, 721, 727, 738k, 745, 747, 753
  social studies, 4.1 18k, 25, 29, 40k, 47, 51, 57, 63, 66k, 73, 75, 79, 88k, 95, 103, 4.2 142k, 149, 153, 159, 162k, 169, 173, 179, 187, 188k, 203, 205, 212k, 219, 225, 227, 229, 240k, 247, 249, 253, 259, 4.4 475, 479, 4.5 536, 538k, 545, 547, 551, 560k, 569, 573, 4.6 638k, 645, 651, 660k, 667, 669, 675, 686k, 693, 695, 701
  technology, 4.1 18k, 40k, 66k, 88k, 112k, 4.2 142k, 162k, 188k, 212k, 240k, 4.3 268k,

292k, 314k, 338k, 360k, 4.4 392k, 416k, 440k, 466k, 488k, 4.5 516k, 538k, 560k, 582k, 608k, 4.6 638k, 660k, 686k, 712k, 738k
  writing/vocabulary, 4.1 18k, 40k, 66k, 88k, 112k, 4.2 142k, 162k, 188k, 212k, 240k, 4.3 268k, 292k, 314k, 338k, 360k, 4.4 392k, 416k, 440k, 466k, 488k, 4.5 516k, 538k, 560k, 582k, 608k, 4.6 638k, 660k, 686k, 712k, 738k

Cross-Curricular Centers, 4.1 18j–18k, 40j–40k, 66j–66k, 88j–88k, 112j–112k, 4.2 142j–142k, 162j–162k, 188j–188k, 212j–212k, 240j–240k, 4.3 268j–268k, 292j–292k, 314j–314k, 338j–338k, 360j–360k, 4.4 392j–392k, 416j–416k, 440j–440k, 466j–466k, 488j–488k, 4.5 516j–516k, 538j–538k, 560j–560k, 582j–582k, 608j–608k, 4.6 638j–638k, 660j–660k, 686j–686k, 712j–712k, 738j–738k

Cross-textual comparisons. *See* **Connections, making; Reading across texts.**

Cultures, appreciating. *See* **Habits and attitudes,** toward other groups and people; **Multicultural connections.**

Cursive. *See* **Handwriting.**

D

Decoding. *See* **Phonics, Word structure.**

Denotation and connotation. *See* **Connotation and denotation.**

Details and facts, 4.1 75, 4.2 247, 4.5 589, 608

Diagram. *See* **Graphic sources.**

Dialogue. *See* **Fluency, reading; Literary devices.**

Dictionary/glossary
  definitions, 4.2 214–215, 221, 253, 4.5 537l, 4.6 711l
  guide words, 4.2 173, 177, 221, 231, 4.4 453, 465c, 4.6 711l
  multiple meaning words, 4.1 68–69, 79, 87c, 231, 4.4 457, DI·25, 4.6 662–663, 669, 673, 685c, DI·15
  pronunciation, 4.2 164–165, 214–215, 221, 239c, 242–243
  spelling, 4.4 WA6, 4.6 711l
  unfamiliar words, 4.2 164–165, 173, 177, 187c, 214–215, 221, 239c, 242–243, 253, 259c, DI·15, DI·35, DI·45, 4.4 442–443, 453, 465c, 468b
  See also **Reference sources,** dictionary/glossary; **Vocabulary strategies.**

Differentiated instruction, 4.1 DI·2–DI·51, 4.2 DI·2–DI·51, 4.3 DI·2–DI·51, 4.4 DI·2–DI·51, 4.5 DI·2–DI·51, 4.6 DI·2–DI·51. *See also* **Advanced learners, Intervention.**

Directions, following
  oral, 4.3 359
  written, 4.3 338k, 4.4 415l, 465l, 4.6 737l

Discussion. *See* **Speaking,** activities.

Drama. *See* **Cross-curricular activities, Genres.**

Dramatic activities, 4.1 39d, 66j, 4.2 188j, 211d, 4.3 268j, 314j, 337d, 4.4 440j, 465d, 4.5 537d, 608j, 4.6 638j. *See also* **Speaking,** activities.

Drawing conclusions. *See* **Conclusions, drawing.**

E

Echo reading. *See* **Fluency,** reading.

Electronic information. *See* **Technology,** skills for using technology.

ELL (English Language Learners) suggestions
access content, 4.1 18m, 18, 20, 22, 36, 39b, 40m, 40, 42, 65b, 66m, 66, 68, 70, 74, 80, 85, 87b, 88m, 88, 90, 92, 94, 100, 109, 111b, 112m, 112, 114, 116, 118, 122, 133b, 4.2 142, 142m, 144, 146, 148, 161b, 162m, 162, 164, 166, 170, 174, 176, 187b, 188m, 188, 190, 196, 200, 211b, 212m, 212, 214, 218, 220, 228, 232, 239b, 240m, 240, 242, 248, 259a, 4.3 268m, 268, 270, 284, 288, 291b, 292m, 292, 294, 302, 313b, 314m, 314, 316, 322, 337b, 338m, 338, 340, 359b, 360m, 360, 362, 364, 374, 383a, 4.4 392m, 392, 394, 398, 412, 415b, 416, 418, 420, 439b, 440m, 440, 442, 444, 450, 465b, 466m, 466, 468, 470, 472, 480, 485, 487b, 488m, 488, 490, 492, 494, 498, 507b, 4.5 516m, 516, 518, 520, 524, 537b, 538m, 538, 540, 544, 550, 556, 559b, 560, 562, 572, 579, 581b, 582m, 582, 584, 590, 596, 604, 607b, 608m, 608, 610, 612, 618, 629b, 4.6 638b, 638, 640, 648, 659b, 660m, 660, 662, 664, 674, 678, 682, 685b, 686m, 686, 688, 711b, 712m, 712, 714, 728, 735, 737b, 738m, 738, 740, 742, 744, 759, 761b
activate prior knowledge, 4.1 48, 104, 4.2 154, 180, 237, 244, 4.3 272, 296, 310, 318, 334, 342, 356, 4.4 396, 504, 4.5 522, 542, 564, 4.5 586, 4.6 642, 676, 690, 754
assessment, 4.2 156, 207, 4.3 354, 4.5 624, 4.6 732
build background, 4.1 20a, 42a, 44, 63, 68a, 72, 90a, 114a, 130, 4.2 144a, 152, 159, 164a, 190a, 192, 214a, 216, 242a, 4.3 270a, 292m, 294a, 316a, 340a, 362a, 368, 381, 4.4 394a, 416m, 418a, 436, 442a, 468a, 474, 490a, 496, 4.5 518a, 526, 540a, 560m, 562a, 574, 584a, 598, 610a, 627, 4.6 640a, 650, 662a, 668, 688a, 692, 700, 709, 714a, 716, 740a, 748, 752
check retelling, 4.1 34, 60, 82, 106, 128, 4.2 184, 233, 256, 4.3 286, 308, 332, 378, 4.4 410, 434, 462, 482, 501, 4.5 534, 554, 576, 602, 4.6 655. 680, 706, 756
context clues, 4.1 28, 54, 78, 96, 124, 4.2 202, 226, 4.3 278, 300, 324, 348, 350, 366, 370, 4.4 422, 430, 446, 458, 4.5 524, 532, 592, 614, 622, 4.6 644, 652, 694
extend language, 4.1 24, 26, 50, 56, 76, 120, 126, 4.2 172, 182, 194, 206, 230, 252, 4.3 276, 298, 304, 320, 330, 346, 4.4 402, 424, 426, 432, 454, 476, 500, 4.5 528, 530, 546, 552, 570, 588, 594, 600, 4.6 666, 672, 696, 702, 718, 720, 724, 726, 730, 746, 750
fluency, 4.1 30, 39a, 65a, 87a, 111a, 133a, 4.3 326, 4.4 406, 452, 4.5 568, 620, 4.6 704
grammar support, 4.1 39e, 65e, 87e, 111e, 133e, 4.2 161a, 161e, 168, 187, 187a, 211a, 211e, 239a, 239e, 259a, 259e, 4.3 282, 291a, 291e, 313a, 313e, 337, 337e, 359a, 359e, 383a, 383e, 4.4 415a, 415e, 439a, 439e, 465a, 465e, 487a, 487e, 507a, 507e, 4.5 537a, 537e, 559a, 559e, 581a, 581e, 607a, 607e, 629a, 629e, 4.6 659a, 659e, 685a, 685e, 711a, 711e, 737a, 737e, 761a, 761e
guided practice, 4.1 38, 86, 132, 4.2 160, 238, 4.3 312, 358, 4.4 438, 486, 4.5 580, 606, 628, 4.6 736
idioms, 4.1 32, 52, 98, 102, 4.2 150, 198, 204, 222, 246, 250, 254, 4.3 274, 280, 306, 328, 344, 352, 4.4 400, 404, 408, 428, 448, 456, 460, 478, 4.5 548, 566, 616, 4.6 646, 670, 698, 722

independent practice, 4.1 64, 110, 4.4 414, 506, 4.6 684
resources, 4.1 18g, 4.2 142g, 162g, 188g, 212g, 240g, 4.3 268g, 292g, 314g, 338g, 360g, 4.4 392g, 416g, 440g, 466g, 488g, 4.5 516g, 538g, 560g, 582g, 608g, 4.6 638g, 660g, 686g, 712g, 738g
spelling/phonics support, 4.1 39i, 65i, 87i, 111i, 133i, 4.2 161i, 187i, 211i, 239i, 259i, 4.3 291i, 313i, 337i, 359i, 383i, 4.4 415i, 439i, 465i, 487i, 507i, 4.5 537i, 559i, 581i, 607i, 629i, 659i, 685i, 711i, 737i, 761i
test practice, 4.3 290, 336, 382, 4.5 606
use the strategy, 4.5 558, 4.6 710, 760
vocabulary support, 4.1 39d, 65d, 87d, 111d, 133d, 4.2 161d, 187d, 211d, 239d, 259d, 4.3 291d, 313d, 337d, 359d, 383d, 4.4 415d, 439d, 465d, 487d, 507d, 4.5 537d, 559d, 581d, 607d, 629d, 4.6 659d, 685d, 711d, 737d, 761d
writing support, 4.1 39g, 65g, 87g, 111g, 133g, WA4, WA6, WA9, 4.2 161g, 187g, 211g, 239g, 259g, WA4, WA6, WA9, 4.3 291g, 313g, 337g, 359g, 383g, 385h, WA4, WA6, WA9, 4.4 415g, 439g, 465g, 487g, 507g, WA4, WA6, WA9, 4.5 537g, 559g, 581g, 607g, 629g, WA4, WA6, WA9, 4.6 659g, 685g, 711g, 737g, 761g, WA4, WA6, WA9

E-mail. *See* **Genres; Technology,** new literacies.

Encyclopedia (as a reference source). *See* **Reference sources.**

Endings. *See* **Spelling,** word structure; **Vocabulary strategies; Word structure.**

End punctuation. *See* **Exclamation mark, Period, Question mark.**

English, conventions of. *See* **Capitalization; Grammar and usage; Punctuation; Writing process,** edit.

ESL (English as a Second Language). *See* **ELL (English Language Learners) suggestions.**

Essential message. *See* **Main idea; Theme (as a story element).**

Etymologies. *See* **Vocabulary development,** etymologies for meaning.

Evaluation. *See* **Assessment.**

Exaggeration. *See* **Literary devices.**

Exclamation mark, 4.1 65e–65f

Expository nonfiction. *See* **Genres.**

F

Fact and fiction. *See* **Fact and opinion, statements of.**

Fact and nonfact. *See* **Fact and opinion, statements of.**

Fact and opinion, statements of, 4.1 125, 4.2 212l–212m, 212–213, 219, 227, 229, 236, 239b, 4.2 DI·36, DI·37, DI·55, 4.3 292l–292m, 292–293, 299, 303, 311, 313b, DI·53, 4.6 651, 660–661, 667, 675, 683, 685b, 747, DI·16, DI·17, DI·53

Family involvement. *See* **School-home connection·**

Fantasy. *See* **Genres.**

Figurative language
idiom, 4.1 39b, 4.4 507b
metaphor, 4.6 685b, 711b
simile, 4.3 359b, 4.6 685b, 761b
slang, 4.1 103

Fix-up strategies. *See* **Monitor and fix up.**

Flashback. *See* **Literary devices.**

Flexible grouping. *See* **Grouping students for instruction.**

Fluency, reading
assessment, 4.1 39a, 65a, 87a, 111a, 133a, WA15–WA16, 4.2 161a, 187a, 211a, 239a, 259a, WA15–WA16, 4.3 291a, 313a, 337a, 359a, 383a, WA15–WA16, 4.4 415a, 439a, 465a, 487a, 507a, WA15–WA16, 4.5 537a, 559a, 581a, 607a, 629a, WA15–WA16, 4.6 659a, 685a, 711a, 737a, 761a, WA15–WA16
characterization, 4.2 188l, 211a, 4.4 488l, 507a
choral reading, 4.1 39a, 87a, 4.2 187a, 259a, 4.3 313a, 337a, 383a, 4.4 465a, 4.5 537a, 581a
dialogue, 4.2 188l, 211a, 4.4 488l, 507a
echo reading, 4.1 65a, 111a, 133a, 4.2 161a, 211a, 239a, 4.3 291a, 359a, 4.4 415a, 439a, 487a, 507a, 4.5 559a, 607a, 629a, 4.6 659a, 685a, 711a, 737a, 761a
emotion, 4.2 162l, 187a, 4.4 392l, 415a, 4.5 582l, 607a, 4.6 686l, 711a
emphasis, 4.2 240l, 259a, 4.4 440l, 465a, 4.6 660l, 685a
modeling by teacher, 4.1 18l, 40l, 66l, 88l, 112l, 4.2 142l, 162l, 188l, 212l, 240l, 4.3 268l, 292l, 314l, 338l, 360l, 4.4 392l, 416l, 440l, 466l, 488l, 4.5 516l, 538l, 560l, 582l, 608l, 4.6 638l, 660l, 686l, 712l, 738l
paired reading, 4.1 39a, 65a, 87a, 111a, 133a, 4.2 161a, 187a, 211a, 239a, 259a, 4.3 291a, 313a, 337a, 359a, 383a, 4.4 415a, 439a, 465a, 487a, 507a, 4.5 537a, 559a, 581a, 607a, 629a, 4.6 659a, 685a, 711a, 737a, 761a
pauses, 4.1 40l, 65a, 4.3 338l, 359a, 4.5 516l, 537a
phrasing, 4.1 112l, 133a, 4.4 439a, 466l, 487a, 4.5 538l, 559a, 4.6 638l, 659a
pitch, 4.3 268l, 291a
punctuation, attention to, 4.3 360l, 383a, 4.6 712l, 737a
rate/pace, 4.1 66l, 87a, 4.5 608l, 629a, 4.6 738l, 761a
rhythmic patterns of language, 4.2 142l, 161a, 4.3 314l, 337a
stress, 4.2 240l, 259a, 4.4 440l, 465a, 4.6 660l, 685a
tempo, 4.1 66l, 87a, 4.5 608l, 629a, 4.6 738l, 761a
tone of voice, 4.1 18l, 39a, 4.3 292l, 313a, 4.5 560l, 581a
volume, 4.1 88l, 111a, 4.2 212l, 239a

Folk tale. *See* **Genres.**

Following directions. *See* **Directions, following.**

Format (of text). *See* **Text structure.**

Free verse. *See* **Literary devices.**

Functional reading, 4.3 356–359, 4.6 708–711

G

Generalizations, making, 4.2 249, 4.3 301, 314l–314m, 314–315, 321, 329, 337, 337b, 360l–360m, 360–361, 367, 373, 383, 383b, DI·54, DI·55, 4.4 425, 4.6 712l–712m, 712–713, 719, 727, 735, 737b, DI·36, DI·37

Generate questions. *See* **Questions, asking.**

Genres
  autobiography, 4.1 139i, 4.6 708–711
  biography, 4.1 139a, 139i, 4.2 216–231, 4.4 470–481, 4.6 642–653, 664–679, 716–731
  drama, 4.2 192–207, 4.4 444–461
  e-mail, 4.2 236–239
  expository nonfiction, 4.1 108–111, 139a, 139e, 4.2 210–211, 244–255, 258–259, 4.3 288–291, 310–313, 342–353, 380–383, 4.4 412–415, 420–433, 436–439, 4.5 626–629, 4.6 682–685
  fable, 4.3 335, 383
  fairy tale, 4.1 139k, 4.4 392l–392m
  fairy tale, modern, 4.1 92–105
  fantasy, 4.1 139a, 139k, 4.3 272–285, 364–377, 383, 4.5 629b
  folk tale, 4.1 139k
  historical fantasy, 4.1 44–59
  historical fiction, 4.1 70–83, 139a, 139g, 4.2 166–183, 4.4 396–409, 4.5 520–533, 564–575
  how-to article, 4.2 186
  humorous fiction, 4.1 92–105
  Internet article, 4.1 84–87, 4.3 356–359, 4.4 484–487, 4.5 578–581, 4.6 734–737
  journal, 4.1 53, 57, 4.5 586–601
  legend, 4.1 139a
  letter, 4.5 592, 594–595
  lyric poetry, 4.1 139a
  mystery, 4.1 139a
  myth, 4.1 139a, 4.3 268m, 4.6 737
  narrative nonfiction, 4.1 62–65, 116–127, 4.5 536–537, 542–553, 604–607, 4.6 742–755
  narrative poetry, 4.1 139a
  new literacies, 4.1 84–87, 4.2 236–241, 4.3 356–359, 4.4 484–487, 4.5 578–581, 4.6 734–737
  newspaper article, 4.4 504–507
  note, 4.4 403
  on-line reading, 4.1 84–87, 4.2 236–241, 4.3 356–359, 4.4 484–487, 4.5 578–581, 4.6 734–737
  personal essay, 4.1 119, 4.5 556–559
  photo essay, 4.3 296–307
  play, 4.2 192–207, 4.4 444–461
  poetry, 4.1 130–133, 134–137, 4.2 158–161, 260–263, 4.3 384–387, 4.4 464–465, 508–511, 4.5 630–633, 4.6 658–659, 762–765
  pourquoi tale, 4.3 318–330, 334–337
  realistic fiction, 4.1 22–33, 4.2 146–155, 4.4 492–500, 4.6 690–704
  science fiction, 4.1 139a, 139k, 4.5 612–623
  short story, 4.2 146–155
  song, 4.1 130–133
  textbook article, 4.6 758–761
  Web site, 4.1 84–87, 139c, 4.3 356–359, 4.4 484–487, 4.5 578–581, 4.6 734–737

Genre study, 4.1 139a–139k, DI·9, DI·19, DI·29, DI·39, DI·49, 4.2 DI·9, DI·19, DI·29, DI·39, DI·49, 4.3 DI·9, DI·19, DI·29, DI·39, DI·49, 4.4 DI·9, DI·19, DI·29, DI·39, DI·49, 4.5 DI·9, DI·19, DI·29, DI·39, DI·49, 4.6 DI·9, DI·19, DI·29, DI·39, DI·49

Gifted students. See **Advanced learners.**

Glossary. See **Dictionary/glossary.**

Goal and outcome. See **Plot, Story structure.**

Grammar and usage. See **Adjectives, Adverbs, Conjunctions, Contractions, Nouns, Prepositions and prepositional phrases, Pronouns, Sentences, Subject/verb agreement, Verbs.**

Graph. See **Graphic sources.**

Graphic and semantic organizers
  as comprehension tool, 4.1 18, 40, 66, 77, 81, 88, 112, DI·26, DI·46, DI·47, 4.2 142, 162, 188, 212, 240, 4.3 268, 292–293, 303, 307, 314, 338–339, 360, 4.4 392, 416, 440, 466, 488,

4.5 516, 538, 560, 582, 608, 4.6 638, 660, 686, 712, 738
  as concept development tool, 4.1 18l, 39c, 40l, 65c, 68l, 87c, 88l, 111c, 112l, 133c, 4.2 142l, 161c, 162l, 187c, 188l, 211c, 212l, 239c, 240l, 259c, 4.3 268l, 291c, 292l, 313c, 314l, 337c, 338l, 359c, 360l, 383c, 4.4 392l, 415c, 416l, 439c, 440l, 465c, 466l, 487c, 488l, 507c, 4.5 516l, 537c, 538l, 559c, 560l, 581c, 582l, 607c, 608l, 629c, 4.6 638l, 659c, 660l, 685c, 686l, 711c, 712l, 737c, 738l, 761c
  as prereading tool, 4.1 20a, 42a, 68a, 90a, 114a, 4.2 144a, 164a, 190a, 214a, 242a, 265b, 4.3 270a, 294a, 316a, 340a, 362a, 4.4 394a, 418a, 442a, 468a, 490a, 4.5 518a, 540a, 562a, 584a, 610a, 4.6 640a, 662a, 688a, 714a, 740a
  as prewriting tool, 4.1 39h, 65h, 87h, 111h, 133h, WA3, 4.2 161h, 187h, 211h, 239h, 259h, WA3, 4.3 291h, 313h, 359h, 383h, WA3, 4.4 415h, 439h, 465h, 487h, 507h, WA3, 4.5 437h, 559h, 581h, 607h, 629h, 635h, WA3, 4.6 659h, 685h, 711h, 761h, WA3
  as vocabulary/word structure tool, 4.1 20b, 39c, 65c, 87c, 90b, 111c, 123, 126, 133c, 4.2 144b, 161c, 187c, 190b, 211c, 214b, 239c, 242b, 4.3 291c, 294b, 313c, 337c, 340b, 359c, 362b, 383c, 4.4 394b, 418b, 439c, 468b, 507c, 4.5 518b, 537c, 562b, 581c, 584b, 4.6 662b, 711c, 714b, 761c
  types
    cause and effect chart, 4.2 142, 268, DI·52, 4.3 DI·52, 4.6 638, DI·52
    column chart, 4.1 40, 65c, 87c, 90a, 111c, 111h, 133c, DI·53, DI·55, 4.2 144a, 144b, 161c, 187c, 187h, 211c, 214b, 242h, 4.3 291c, 294b, 313c, 337c, 359c, 383c, DI·55, 4.4 439c, 439h, 466, 487h, 507c, DI·55, 4.5 516, 518b, 537c, 537h, 559h, 581c, DI·52, DI·55, 4.6 662b, 686, 711c, 711h, 761c, DI·56
    comparison chart, 4.3 337h, 4.4 392, 4.5 538
    fact and opinion chart, 4.2 212, DI·55, 4.3 292–293, 303, 307, DI·53, 4.6 660, DI·53
    facts and details, 4.2 188, 4.5 608
    how-to chart, 4.2 WA3
    KWL chart, 4.1 42a, 114a, 4.2 242a, 4.3 294a, 340a, 4.4 418a, 468a, 4.5 584a, 607h, 610a, 662a, 4.6 714a, WA3, DI·47
    list, 4.1 65g, 4.2 162, 239h, 4.3 313h, 314, 338, 4.4 415h, 4.6 685h, 737h
    main idea chart, 4.1 112, 123, DI·56, 4.2 240, DI·56, 4.5 582, 4.6 712, DI·54
    map, 4.4 466, 4.6 738
    prediction chart, 4.4 442a
    sequence chart, 4.1 39h, 66, DI·52, DI·54, 4.3 359h
    story structure chart, 4.1 88, 4.3 360, 4.4 488, WA3
    T-chart, 4.1 68a, 77, 133h, 4.2 190a, 259h, 4.3 303, 383h, 4.4 394a, 416, 507h, 4.5 562b
    time line, 4.1 81, DI·26, DI·27, 4.5 560, 4.6 659h
    Venn diagram, 4.1 133h, 4.2 214a, 259h, 383h, 416, 4.3 WA3, 4.4 507h, DI·52, 4.5 562a, DI·53, 4.6 688a, 740a, DI·47
    vocabulary frame, 4.1 90b
    web, 4.1 18l, 39c, 40l, 65c, 66l, 87c, 87h, 88l, 111c, 121l, 133c, DI·46, DI·47, 4.2 142l, 161c, 161h, 162l, 164a, 187c, 188l, 211c, 212l, 239c, 240l, 259c, DI·54, 4.3 268l, 270a, 291c, 291h, 292l, 313c, 314l, 316a, 337c, 338l, 359c, 360l, 362a, 383c, DI·54, DI·56, 4.4 392l, 394b, 415c, 416l, 439c, 440l, 440, 465c, 465h, 466l, 487c, 488l, 490a, 507c,

DI·54, 4.5 516l, 518a, 537c, 538l, 540a, 559c, 560l, 581c, 581h, 582l, 607c, 608l, 629c, 629h, DI·54, DI·56, 4.6 638l, 640a, 659c, 660l, 685c, 686l, 711c, 712l, 714b, 737c, 738l, 761c, 761h, DI·55
  word rating chart, 4.2 190b, 4.3 340b, 4.4 418b, 486b, 4.5 584b
  words in context chart, 4.3 362b

Graphic sources, 4.3 338–339, 345, 351, 359b, DI·55, 4.4 447, 466–467, 473, 477, DI·36, DI·55, 4.5 DI·55, 4.6 677, 723, 738–739, 745, 753, 758, DI·46, DI·56
  advertisement, 4.2 211l, 4.6 721
  application, 4.5 629l
  chart/table, 4.2 161l, 4.3 291l, 4.4 466–467, DI·36, 4.5 626, 4.6 753, 758, DI·26, DI·46, DI·47
  diagram/scale drawing, 4.4 412, 4.5 581l, 4.6 738–739, 4.6 DI·26, DI·46, DI·47
  graph, 4.2 239l
  illustration (photograph or art) and/or caption, 4.1 111l, 4.4 473, 477, DI·37, 4.6 745
  map/globe, 4.1 36, 39l, 4.5 556
  order form, 4.5 629l
  poster/announcement, 4.4 439l
  schedule, 4.3 383l
  time line, 4.2 259l

Greek and Latin roots. See **Vocabulary strategies.**

Grouping students for instruction
  advanced learners, 4.1 18f–18g, 40f–40g, 66f–66g, 88f–88g, 112f–112g, DI·3, DI·5, DI·7, DI·9, DI·11, DI·13, DI·15, DI·17, DI·19, DI·21, DI·23, DI·25, DI·27, DI·29, DI·31, DI·33, DI·35, DI·37, DI·39, DI·41, DI·43, DI·45, DI·47, DI·49, DI·51, 4.2 142f–142g, 162f–162g, 188f–188g, 212f–212g, 240f–240g, DI·3, DI·5, DI·7, DI·9, DI·11, DI·13, DI·15, DI·17, DI·19, DI·21, DI·23, DI·25, DI·27, DI·29, DI·31, DI·33, DI·35, DI·37, DI·39, DI·41, DI·43, DI·45, DI·47, DI·49, DI·51, 4.3 268f–268g, 292f–292g, 314f–314g, 338f–338g, 360f–360g, DI·3, DI·5, DI·7, DI·9, DI·11, DI·13, DI·15, DI·17, DI·19, DI·21, DI·23, DI·25, DI·27, DI·29, DI·31, DI·33, DI·35, DI·37, DI·39, DI·41, DI·43, DI·45, DI·47, DI·49, DI·51, 4.4 392f–392g, 416f–416g, 440f–440g, 466f–466g, 488f–488g, DI·3, DI·5, DI·7, DI·9, DI·11, DI·13, DI·15, DI·17, DI·19, DI·21, DI·23, DI·25, DI·27, DI·29, DI·31, DI·33, DI·35, DI·37, DI·39, DI·41, DI·43, DI·45, DI·47, DI·49, DI·51, 4.5 516f–516g, 538f–538g, 560f–560g, 582f–582g, 608f–608g, DI·3, DI·5, DI·7, DI·9, DI·11, DI·13, DI·15, DI·17, DI·19, DI·21, DI·23, DI·25, DI·27, DI·29, DI·31, DI·33, DI·35, DI·37, DI·39, DI·41, DI·43, DI·45, DI·47, DI·49, DI·51, 4.6 638f–638g, 660f–660g, 686f–686g, 712f–712g, 738f–738g, DI·3, DI·5, DI·7, DI·9, DI·11, DI·13, DI·15, DI·17, DI·19, DI·21, DI·23, DI·25, DI·27, DI·29, DI·31, DI·33, DI·35, DI·37, DI·39, DI·41, DI·43, DI·45, DI·47, DI·49, DI·51
  intervention, 4.1 18f–18g, 40f–40g, 66f–66g, 88f–88g, 112f–112g, DI·2, DI·4, DI·6, DI·8, DI·10, DI·12, DI·14, DI·16, DI·18, DI·20, DI·22, DI·24, DI·26, DI·28, DI·30, DI·32, DI·34, DI·36, DI·38, DI·40, DI·42, DI·44, DI·46, DI·48, DI·50, 4.2 142f–142g, 162f–162g, 188f–188g, 212f–212g, 240f–240g, DI·2, DI·4, DI·6, DI·8, DI·10, DI·12, DI·14, DI·16, DI·18, DI·20, DI·22, DI·24, DI·26, DI·28, DI·30, DI·32, DI·34, DI·36, DI·38, DI·40, DI·42, DI·44, DI·46, DI·48, DI·50, 4.3 268f–268g, 292f–292g, 314f–314g, 338f–338g, 360f–360g, DI·2, DI·4, DI·6, DI·8, DI·10, DI·12, DI·14, DI·16, DI·18, DI·20, DI·22, DI·24, DI·26, DI·28, DI·30, DI·32, DI·34, DI·36,

DI·38, DI·40, DI·42, DI·44, DI·46, DI·48, DI·50, **4.4** 392f–392g, 416f–416g, 440f–440g, 466f–466g, 488f–488g, DI·2, DI·4, DI·6, DI·8, DI·10, DI·12, DI·14, DI·16, DI·18, DI·20, DI·22, DI·24, DI·26, DI·28, DI·30, DI·32, DI·34, DI·36, DI·38, DI·40, DI·42, DI·44, DI·46, DI·48, DI·50, **4.5** 516f–516g, 538f–538g, 560f–560g, 582f–582g, 608f–608g, DI·2, DI·4, DI·6, DI·8, DI·10, DI·12, DI·14, DI·16, DI·18, DI·20, DI·22, DI·24, DI·26, DI·28, DI·30, DI·32, DI·34, DI·36, DI·38, DI·40, DI·42, DI·44, DI·46, DI·48, DI·50, **4.6** 638f–638g, 660f–660g, 686f–686g, 712f–712g, 738f–738g, DI·2, DI·4, DI·6, DI·8, DI·10, DI·12, DI·14, DI·16, DI·18, DI·20, DI·22, DI·24, DI·26, DI·28, DI·30, DI·32, DI·34, DI·36, DI·38, DI·40, DI·42, DI·44, DI·46, DI·48, DI·50

Guiding Reading. *See* **Grouping students for instruction.** In addition, Guiding Reading and leveled readers are a part of every lesson plan.

H

Habits and attitudes
  consequences of actions/behaviors/choices (as demonstrated in literature selections). *See* **Character education.**
  humanity and compassion (as demonstrated in literature selections). *See* **Character education.**
  toward other groups and people (multicultural values), **4.1** 16, 44–59, 70–81, 84–87, **4.2** 140, 216–232, **4.3** 266, 318–331, 334–337, 364–377, **4.4** 390, 420–433, 470–481, **4.5** 514, 542–553, 556–559, **4.6** 636, 690–705. *See also* **Multicultural connections.**
  toward reading, writing, listening, speaking, viewing, **4.1** 18l, 20a, 40l, 42a, 66l, 68a, 88l, 90a, 112l, 114a, **4.2** 142l, 144a, 162l, 164a, 188l, 190a, 212l, 214a, 240l, 242a, **4.3** 268l, 270a, 292l, 294a, 314l, 316a, 338l, 340a, 360l, 362a, **4.4** 392l, 394a, 416l, 418a, 440l, 442a, 466l, 468a, 488l, 490a, **4.5** 516l, 518a, 538l, 540a, 560l, 562a, 582l, 584a, 608l, 610a, **4.6** 638l, 640a, 660l, 662a, 686l, 688a, 712l, 714a, 738l, 740a

Handwriting, 4.1 TR10–TR13, **4.2** TR10–TR13, **4.3** TR10–TR13, **4.4** TR10–TR13, **4.5** TR10–TR13, **4.6** TR10–TR13

Health activities. *See* **Cross-curricular activities.**

Higher-order thinking skills. *See* **Critical thinking.**

Historical fantasy. *See* **Genres.**

Historical fiction. *See* **Genres.**

Home-school connection. *See* **School-home connection.**

Homework. *See* **School-home connection.**

Homographs, 4.5 518–519, 525, 537c. *See also* **Vocabulary strategies.**

Homonyms, 4.3 294–295, 305, 313c, **4.5** 518–519, 525, 537c, **4.6** 740–741, 749, 761c. *See also* **Vocabulary strategies.**

Homophones, 4.1 42b, **4.6** 688b. *See also* **Vocabulary strategies.**

How-to article. *See* **Genres.**

Humorous fiction. *See* **Genres.**

Hyperbole. *See* **Literary devices,** exaggeration/hyperbole.

I

Illustrations. *See* **Graphic sources,** illustration and/or caption; **Prereading strategies,** use illustrations.

Illustrator's craft/style. *See* **Literary craft.**

Illustrator study, 4.1 139m–139p

Implied message. *See* **Main idea, Theme (as a story element).**

Independent reading, 4.1 18f–18g, 18j, 40f–40g, 40j, 66f–66g, 66j, 88f–88g, 88j, 112f–112g, 112j, TR14, **4.2** 142f–142g, 142j, 162f–162g, 162j, 188f–188g, 188j, 212f–212g, 212j, 240f–240g, 240j, TR14, **4.3** 268f–268g, 268j, 292f–292g, 292j, 314f–314g, 314j, 338f–338g, 338j, 360f–360g, 360j, TR14, **4.4** 392f–392g, 392j, 416f–416g, 416j, 440f–440g, 440j, 466f–466g, 466j, 488f–488g, 488j, TR14, **4.5** 516f–516g, 516j, 538f–538g, 538j, 560f–560g, 560j, 582f–582g, 582j, 608f–608g, 608j, TR14, **4.6** 638f–638g, 638j, 660f–660g, 660j, 686f–686g, 686j, 712f–712g, 712j, 738f–738g, 738j, TR14. *See also* **Bibliography,** self-selected reading.

Inferences. *See* **Author's purpose; Cause and effect; Comparing and contrasting; Conclusions, drawing; Fact and opinion, statements of; Generalizations, making; Predicting; Summarizing.** In addition, inferential thinking questions appear throughout Guiding Comprehension in each lesson.

Inflected endings. *See* **Spelling,** word structure; **Word structure.**

Informal assessment. *See* **Assessment.**

Integrated curriculum. *See* **Cross-curricular activities.**

Internet (as reference source). *See* **New literacies (for student reading), Reference sources, Technology.**

Internet article. *See* **Genres.**

Intervention
  answer questions, **4.6** 654
  author's purpose, **4.1** 40, 88, **4.5** 516
  cause and effect, **4.2** 142, **4.3** 268, **4.6** 638,
  character, **4.4** 440 **4.6** 686,
  compare and contrast, **4.4** 392, 416, **4.5** 538
  conclusions, draw, **4.2** 162, 188, **4.5** 608,
  context clues, **4.1** 90, **4.2** 224, **4.3** 270, 294, 316, **4.4** 394, 418, 490, **4.5** 518, 562, 610, **4.6** 688, 714, 740
  dictionary/glossary, **4.1** 68, **4.2** 164, 214, 242, **4.4** 442, **4.6** 662
  English language learners. *See* **ELL (English Language Learners) suggestions.**
  fact and opinion, **4.2** 212, **4.3** 292, **4.6** 660,
  generalize, **4.3** 314, 360, **4.6** 712,
  graphic sources, **4.3** 338, **4.4** 466, **4.6** 738,
  group time, **4.1** 18f–18g, 40f–40g, 66f–66g, 88f–88g, 112f–112g, DI·2, DI·4, DI·6, DI·8, DI·10, DI·12, DI·14, DI·16, DI·18, DI·20, DI·22, DI·24, DI·26, DI·28, DI·30, DI·32, DI·34, DI·36, DI·38, DI·40, DI·42, DI·44, DI·46, DI·48, DI·50, **4.2** 142f–142g, 162f–162g, 188f–188g, 212f–212g, 240f–240g, DI·2, DI·4, DI·6, DI·8, DI·10, DI·12, DI·14, DI·16, DI·18, DI·20, DI·22, DI·24, DI·26, DI·28, DI·30, DI·32, DI·34, DI·36, DI·38, DI·40, DI·42, DI·44, DI·46, DI·48, DI·50,

4.3 268f–268g, 292f–292g, 314f–314g, 338f–338g, 360f–360g, DI·2, DI·4, DI·6, DI·8, DI·10, DI·12, DI·14, DI·16, DI·18, DI·20, DI·22, DI·24, DI·26, DI·28, DI·30, DI·32, DI·34, DI·36, DI·38, DI·40, DI·42, DI·44, DI·46, DI·48, DI·50, **4.4** 392f–392g, 416f–416g, 440f–440g, 466f–466g, 488f–488g, DI·2, DI·4, DI·6, DI·8, DI·10, DI·12, DI·14, DI·16, DI·18, DI·20, DI·22, DI·24, DI·26, DI·28, DI·30, DI·32, DI·34, DI·36, DI·38, DI·40, DI·42, DI·44, DI·46, DI·48, DI·50, **4.5** 516f–516g, 538f–538g, 560f–560g, 582f–582g, 608f–608g, DI·2, DI·4, DI·6, DI·8, DI·10, DI·12, DI·14, DI·16, DI·18, DI·20, DI·22, DI·24, DI·26, DI·28, DI·30, DI·32, DI·34, DI·36, DI·38, DI·40, DI·42, DI·44, DI·46, DI·48, DI·50, **4.6** 638f–638g, 660f–660g, 686f–686g, 712f–712g, 738f–738g, DI·2, DI·4, DI·6, DI·8, DI·10, DI·12, DI·14, DI·16, DI·18, DI·20, DI·22, DI·24, DI·26, DI·28, DI·30, DI·32, DI·34, DI·36, DI·38, DI·40, DI·42, DI·44, DI·46, DI·48, DI·50. *See also* **Grouping students for instruction.**
  leveled reader, **4.1** LR1–LR3, LR10–LR12, LR19–LR21, LR28–LR30, LR37–LR39, **4.2** LR1–LR3, LR10–LR12, LR19–LR21, LR28–LR30, LR37–LR39, **4.3** LR1–LR3, LR10–LR12, LR19–LR21, LR28–LR30, LR37–LR39, **4.4** LR1–LR3, LR10–LR12, LR19–LR21, LR28–LR30, LR37–LR39, **4.5** LR1–LR3, LR10–LR12, LR19–LR21, LR28–LR30, LR37–LR39, **4.6** LR1–LR3, LR10–LR12, LR19–LR21, LR28–LR30, LR37–LR39
  main idea, **4.1** 112, **4.2** 240, **4.5** 582
  main idea/details, **4.1** 74, 118
  plot, **4.4** 488
  resources, **4.1** 18h, 40h, 66h, 88h, 112h, **4.2** 142h, 162h, 188h, 212h, 240h, **4.3** 268h, 292h, 314h, 338h, 360h, **4.4** 392h, 440h, 466h, 488h, 616h, **4.5** 516h, 538h, 560h, 582h, 608h, **4.6** 638h, 660h, 686h, 712h, 738h
  sequence, **4.1** 18, 66, **4.5** 560
  setting, **4.4** 440
  theme, **4.6** 686
  word structure, **4.1** 20, 42, 114, **4.2** 144, 190, **4.3** 340, 362, **4.4** 468, **4.5** 540, 584, **4.6** 640
  writing support, **4.1** WA8, **4.2** WA8, **4.3** WA8, **4.4** WA8, **4.5** WA8, **4.6** WA8

Interview. *See* **Speaking,** activities.

Italics, 4.6 761e–761f

J

Journal. *See* **Genres; Logs, strategy response; Writing forms/products.**

Judgments, making. *See* **Author's purpose; Conclusions, drawing; Fact and opinion, statements of; Generalizations, making; Predicting.**

K

KWL reading strategy, 4.1 42a, 114a, 242a, **4.3** 294a, 340a, **4.4** 418a, 468a, **4.5** 584a, 607h, 610a, 662a, **4.6** 714a

L

Language arts. *See* **Capitalization, Creative/dramatic activities, Cross-Curricular Centers, Grammar and usage, Listening, Punctuation, Speaking, Spelling,** *all* **Writing categories.**

Language, oral. *See* **Fluency, reading; Listening; Speaking.**

Latin and Greek roots. See **Vocabulary development,** etymologies for meaning.

Learning Centers. See **Cross-Curricular Centers.**

Legend. See **Genres.**

Less-able readers. See **Intervention.**

Letter. See **Genres.**

Leveled readers, 4.1 18c, 40c, 66c, 88c, 112c, LR1–LR48, 4.2 142c, 162c, 188c, 212c, 240c, LR1–LR48, 4.3 268c, 292c, 314c, 338c, 360c, LR1–LR48, 4.4 392c, 416c, 440c, 466c, 488c, LR1–LR48, 4.5 516c, 538c, 560c, 582c, 608c, LR1–LR48, 4.6 638c, 660c, 686c, 712c, 738c, LR1–LR48

Levels of thinking. See **Critical thinking.**

Limited English proficient students. See **ELL (English Language Learners) suggestions.**

Listening
  activities
    advertisement/commercial, 4.1 87d, 4.4 439d
    announcement, 4.5 559d
    audio products, 4.1 20a, 42a, 68a, 90a, 114a, 4.2 144a, 164a, 190a, 214a, 242a, 4.3 270a, 294a, 316a, 337d, 340a, 362a, 4.4 394a, 418a, 442a, 468a, 490a, 4.5 518a, 540a, 562a, 584a, 610a, 4.6 640a, 662a, 688a, 714a, 740a
    debate, 4.1 133d, 4.6 711d
    demonstration, 4.6 685d
    description, 4.2 239d
    discussion, 4.1 34, 39d, 60, 82, 106, 128, 4.2 156, 184, 208, 233, 256, 4.3 286, 308, 332, 354, 378, 4.4 410, 434, 462, 482, 501, 4.5 534, 554, 576, 602, 624, 4.6 655, 680, 706, 732, 756
    dramatization, 4.1 39d, 4.3 337d
    interview, 4.3 313d, 4.4 415d, 4.5 607d, 4.6 737d
    introductions, 4.1 65d
    media, 4.3 313d, 4.5 537d, 629d
    music, 4.6 737d
    newscast, 4.2 187d, 4.3 359d, 4.4 507d
    opinions, 4.1 133d, 4.3 291d, 4.6 711d
    oral presentation/report, 4.1 111d
    persuasion, 4.1 133d, 4.3 291d, 4.6 711d
    poetry reading, 4.3 291d
    press conference, 4.2 259d
    radio advertisement, 4.1 87d
    read-alouds, 4.1 18m, 40m, 66m, 88m, 112m, 4.2 142m, 162m, 188m, 212m, 240m, 4.3 268m, 292m, 314m, 338m, 360m, 4.4 392m, 416m, 440m, 466m, 488m, 4.5 516m, 538m, 560m, 582m, 608m, 4.6 638m, 660m, 686m, 712m, 738m
    speech, 4.3 383d, 4.5 581d, 4.6 659d
    sportscast, 4.2 161d
    story, 4.1 39d, 4.4 487d
    TV and video, 4.5 629d
    weather broadcast, 4.3 337d
  purposes
    comparison and contrast, 4.3 337d, 4.5 537d
    comprehension, 4.1 18l–18m, 40l–40m, 66l–66m, 88l–88m, 112l–112m, 4.2 142l–142m, 162l–162m, 188l–188m, 212l–212m, 240l–240m, 4.3 268l–268m, 292l–292m, 314l–314m, 338l–338m, 360l–360m, 4.4 392l–392m, 416l–416m, 440l–440m, 466l–466m, 488l–488m, 4.5 516l–516m, 538l–538m, 560l–560m, 582l–582m, 608l–608m, 4.6 668l–638m, 660l–660m, 686l–686m, 712l–712m, 738l–738m
    enjoyment, 4.1 39d, 4.3 291d, 313d, 337d, 4.4 439d, 487d, 4.5 537d, 629d, 4.6 737d
    information, 4.1 87d, 4.2 187d, 239d, 4.3 383d, 4.4 439d, 4.5 581d, 4.6 659d
    persuasion, 4.1 87d, 4.3 383d, 4.4 439d, 4.6 659d
    tips, 4.1 111d, 4.2 161d, 211d, 4.6 685d, 711d, 761d

Literal comprehension. Literal comprehension questions appear in Guiding Comprehension in each lesson.

Literary craft
  author's perspective/viewpoint/bias, 4.1 88l–88m, 139b, 4.3 313b, 4.5 537a
  illustrator's craft/style, 4.1 139m–139p, 4.3 291b, 4.4 487b, 4.5 573, 4.6 669

Literary devices
  dialect, 4.1 111b, 4.2 179
  dialogue, 4.1 29, 4.4 449
  exaggeration/hyperbole, 4.4 405
  flashback, 4.2 211b
  free verse, 4.3 387
  imagery/sensory words, 4.1 65b, 4.3 337b
  mood, 4.2 262
  narration, 4.1 25
  point of view, 4.1 133b, 4.6 659b
  puns and word play, 4.4 497
  simile, 4.3 359b, 4.6 685b, 761b
  slang, 4.1 103
  symbolism, 4.6 753
  tone, 4.3 386, 387
  See also **Figurative language, Sound devices and poetic elements.**

Literary genres. See **Genres.**

Literary response and appreciation, 4.1 34, 60, 82, 106, 128, 139a–139p, 4.2 156, 184, 208, 233, 256, 4.3 286, 308, 332, 354, 378, 4.4 410, 434, 462, 482, 501, 4.5 534, 554, 576, 602, 624, 4.6 655, 680, 706, 732, 756

Literature selections
  "Adelina's Whales," Richard Sobol, 4.3 296–307
  "Amelia and Eleanor Go for a Ride," Pam Muñoz Ryan, 4.5 564–575
  "Ant and the Bear, The," Chief Lelooska, 4.3 334–337
  "Antarctic Journal," Jennifer Owings Dewey, 4.5 586–601
  "Because of Winn Dixie," Kate DiCamillo, 4.1 22–33
  "Coyote School News," Joan Sandin, 4.2 166–183
  "Difficult Art of Hitting, The," Sadaharu Oh and David Falkner, 4.6 708–711
  "Early Flying Machines," Internet article, 4.6 734–737
  "Earth and the Moon, The," from *Scott Foresman Science, Grade 4,* 4.6 758–761
  "Encantado: Pink Dolphin of the Amazon," Sy Montgomery, 4.4 420–433
  "Encyclopedia Brown and the Case of the Slippery Salamander," Donald J. Sobol, 4.4 492–500
  "Eye of the Storm," Stephen Kramer, 4.3 342–353
  "Fast Facts: Black Bears," Kathy Kranking, 4.1 36–39
  "Grace and the Time Machine," Mary Hoffman, 4.2 192–207
  "Grandfather's Journey," Allen Say, 4.1 70–81
  "Great Kapok Tree, The," Lynne Cherry, 4.3 364–377
  "Horned Lizards & Harvesting Ants," John Brown, 4.1 108–111

  "Horned Toad Prince, The," Jackie Mims Hopkins, 4.1 92–105
  "Houdini Box, The," Brian Selznick, 4.4 396–409
  "How Night Came from the Sea," Mary-Joan Gerson, 4.3 318–331
  "How Tía Lola Came to Stay," Julia Alvarez, 4.6 690–705
  "How to Start a School Newspaper," Lisa Klobuchar, 4.2 186–187
  "Jim Thorpe's Bright Path," Joseph Bruchac, 4.6 664–679
  "King in the Kitchen, The," Margaret E. Slattery, 4.4 444–461
  "Letters Home from Yosemite," Lisa Halvorsen, 4.1 116–127
  "Lewis and Clark and Me," Laurie Myers, 4.1 44–59
  "Living in a World of Green," Tanya Lee Stone, 4.3 380–383
  "Logging Camps," Internet article, 4.2 236–239
  "Look at Two Lands, A," Internet article, 4.1 84–87
  "Lost City: The Discovery of Machu Picchu," Ted Lewin, 4.5 542–553
  "Man Who Went to the Far Side of the Moon, The," Bea Uusma Schyffert, 4.6 742–755
  "Marven of the Great North Woods," Kathryn Lasky, 4.2 216–232
  "Moonwalk," Ben Bova, 4.5 612–623
  "My Brother Martin," Christine King Farris, 4.6 642–654
  "Mysterious Animals," Ann Weil, 4.4 436–439
  "Our National Parks," Susan Gavin, 4.2 258–259
  "Riding the Rails to Machu Picchu," Katacha Díaz, 4.5 556–559
  "Sailing Home: A Story of a Childhood at Sea," Gloria Rand, 4.5 520–533
  "Sea Animals on the Move," Joanne Wachter, 4.3 310–313
  "Seeker of Knowledge," James Rumford, 4.4 470–481
  "Severe Weather Safety," Internet article, 4.3 356–359
  "Sharing a Dream," Linda Washington, 4.5 536–537
  "So You Want to Be an Illusionist," Tui T. Sutherland, 4.4 412–415
  "So You Want to Be President?," Judith St. George, 4.2 244–259
  "Special Olympics, Spectacular Athletes," Marlene Perez, 4.6 682–685
  "Stranger, The," Chris Van Allsburg, 4.3 272–285
  "Swimming Towards Ice," Claire Daniel, 4.5 604–607
  "They Traveled with Lewis and Clark," Elizabeth Massie, 4.1 62–65
  "Time for a Change," Helen Strahinich, 4.3 288–291
  "To Fly: The Story of the Wright Brothers," Wendie C. Old, 4.6 716–731
  "Walk on the Moon, A," Judy Nayer, 4.5 626–629
  "What Jo Did," Charles R. Smith Jr., 4.2 146–155
  "What's There to Do?," Samantha Beres, 4.2 210–211
  "Women Explorers," Internet article, 4.5 578–581
  "Word Puzzles," Internet article, 4.4 484–487
  "Young Detectives of Potterville Middle School," Bonnie Kepplinger, 4.4 504–507
  See also **Poetry Selections.**

Logs, strategy response
  activate prior knowledge, 4.1 116, 4.2 146, 166, 4.3 296, 4.4 420, 4.5 520, 4.6 664
  answer questions, 4.1 27, 99, 4.2 201, 4.3 279, 371, 4.4 497, 4.5 549, 593, 4.6 649, 751

ask questions, 4.1 22, 92, 4.2 192, 4.3 272, 364, 4.4 492, 4.5 542, 586, 4.6 642, 742

check predictions, 4.1 53, 4.2 251, 4.3 349, 4.4 403, 451, 4.5 571, 619, 4.6 697, 725

graphic organizer, 4.1 70, 77, 4.2 216, 223, 4.3 318, 327, 4.4 470, 477

monitor comprehension, 4.1 123, 4.2 151, 175, 4.3 303, 4.4 429, 4.5 527, 4.6 671

predict, 4.1 44, 4.2 244, 4.3 342, 4.4 396, 444, 4.5 564, 612, 4.6 690, 716

summarize, 4.1 32, 58, 80, 104, 126, 4.2 154, 182, 206, 230, 254, 4.3 284, 306, 330, 352, 376, 4.4 408, 432, 460, 480, 502, 4.5 532, 552, 574, 600, 622, 4.6 652, 678, 704, 730, 754

M

Magazine (as reference source). See **Reference sources.**

Main idea 4.1 74, 75, 112l–112m, 112–113, 123, 133b, DI·46, DI·47, DI·56, 4.2 225, 240l–240m, 240–241, 247, 251, 259, 259b, DI·46, DI·47, DI·56, 4.4 475, 4.5 582l–582m, 582–583, 589, 595, 607, 607b, DI·36, DI·37

Making connections. See **Connections, making.**

Manual. See **Reference sources.**

Map/globe. See **Graphic sources.**

Mapping selections. See **Graphic and semantic organizers.**

Mass media. See **Viewing.**

Mathematics activities. See **Cross-curricular activities.**

Mechanics (of English grammar and writing). See **Capitalization, Punctuation.**

Media. See **Viewing.**

Metacognition. See **Monitor and fix up; Self-check.**

Modeling. Teacher modeling and think-alouds are presented throughout Skills in Context lessons and After Reading lessons.

Monitor and fix up, 4.2 212–213, 223, 227, 239, DI·37, 4.4 440–441, 451, 455, 461, 465, 4.5 608–609, 619, 623, 629, DI·47, 4.6 738–739, 751, 753, 755, 761
  adjust reading rate, 4.2 212-213, 223, 227, 4.5 608–609, 619
  ask questions, 4.2 DI·37, 4.5 619, DI·47
  read on, 4.5 609, 619
  reread, 4.2 223, 239, 4.4 DI·26, 4.5 608-609, DI·46
  retell, 4.2 DI·36, 4.6 DI·46
  skim/scan, 4.2 212–213, 223, 227
  summarize, 4.4 451, DI·27
  use a graphic organizer, 4.4 451
  use graphic sources, 4.5 629, 4.6 738–739, 751, 753, 755, DI·47
  use a reference source, 4.2 239
  use text features, 4.4 440–441, 451, 455

Monitor comprehension. See **Monitor and fix up, Self-check.**

Mood. See **Literary devices.**

Motivation, 4.1 18l, 20a, 40l, 42a, 66l, 68a, 88l, 90a, 112l, 114a, 4.2 142l, 144a, 162l, 164a, 188l, 190a, 212l, 214a, 240l, 242a, 4.3 268l, 270a, 292l, 294a, 314l, 316a, 338l, 340a, 360l, 362a, 4.4 392l, 394a, 416l, 418a, 440l, 442a, 466l, 468a, 488l, 490a, 4.5 516l, 518a, 538l, 540a, 560l, 562a, 582l,

584a, 608l, 610a, 4.6 638l, 640a, 660l, 662a, 686l, 688a, 712l, 714a, 738l, 740a

Multicultural connections, 4.1 16, 18l, 44–59, 70–81, 84–87, 4.2 140, 216–232, 4.3 266, 318–331, 334–337, 364–377, 4.4 390, 420–433, 470–481, 4.5 514, 542–553, 556–559, 4.6 636, 690–705. See also **Habits and attitudes.**

Multiple-meaning words, 4.1 20b, 68–69, 79, 87c, 4.2 231, 4.3 270–271, 277, 291c, 316b, 4.4 418–419, 427, 439c, 457, 4.6 640b, 662–663, 669, 673, 685c, 714b

Multisyllabic words. See **Spelling,** word structure; **Word structure.**

Music activities. See **Cross-curricular activities.**

N

Narrative nonfiction. See **Genres.**

Narrative poetry. See **Genres.**

New literacies (for student reading), 4.1 84–87, 4.2 236–241, 4.3 356–359, 4.4 484–487, 4.5 578–581, 4.6 734–737. See also **Technology.**

Newspaper (as reference sources). See **Reference sources.**

Newspaper article. See **Genres.**

Nonverbal communication. See **Listening,** tips; **Speaking,** tips.

Note. See **Genres.**

Note-taking, 4.4 403, 4.6 659l, 685g–685h

Nouns
  singular/plural, irregular, 4.2 211e–211f
  singular/plural, regular, 4.2 187e–187f
  possessive, 4.2 239a–239f, 259e–259f, 4.4 439e–439f
  proper, 4.2 161e–161f
  See also **Capitalization.**

O

On-line reading. See **Genres.**

Onomatopoeia. See **Sound devices and poetic elements.**

Opinion and fact. See **Fact and opinion, statements of.**

Oral reading ability
  appropriate phrasing, 4.1 112l, 133a, 4.4 439a, 466l, 487a, 4.5 538l, 559a, 4.6 638l, 659a
  attention to punctuation, 4.3 360l, 383a, 4.6 712l, 737a
  choral reading, 4.1 39a, 87a, 4.2 187a, 259a, 4.3 313a, 337a, 383a, 4.4 465a, 4.5 537a, 581a
  fluency, 4.1 39a, 65a, 87a, 111a, 133a, 4.2 161a, 187a, 211a, 239a, 259a, 4.3 291a, 313a, 337a, 359a, 383a, 4.4 415a, 438a, 465a, 487a, 507a, 4.5 537a, 559a, 581a, 607a, 629a, 4.6 659a, 685a, 711a, 737a, 761a
  paired reading, 4.1 39a, 65a, 87a, 111a, 133a, 4.2 161a, 187a, 211a, 239a, 259a, 4.3 291a, 313a, 337a, 359a, 383a, 4.4 415a, 439a, 465a, 487a, 507a, 4.5 537a, 559a, 581a, 607a, 629a, 4.6 659a, 685a, 711a, 737a, 761a

Order form. See **Graphic sources.**

Organizing information
  classifying, 4.1 20b, 90a, 4.2 144a, 144b, 190a, 242b, 4.3 294b, 4.4 394a, 4.5 518b, 562b, 4.6 662b

outlining, 4.5 559l, 4.6 659h, 737g–737h

summarizing, 4.1 18–19, 26, 27, 32, 33, 39, 65, 4.2 240–241, 251, 254, 255, 4.6 686–687, 697, 699, 705, 711

taking notes, 4.4 403, 4.6 659l, 685g–685h
See also **Graphic and semantic organizers; Logs, strategy response.**

Outlining, 4.5 559l, 4.6 659h, 737g–737h. See also **Graphic and semantic organizers, Organizing information.**

Own life, text's relation to. See **Character education; Connections, making; Habits and attitudes.**

P

Paired reading. See **Fluency, reading.**

Paraphrasing, 4.1 87b. See also **Summarize.**

Parentheses, 4.2 211h

Parents. See **School-home connection.**

Parts of a book
  appendix, 4.5 537l
  bibliography, 4.5 537l
  glossary, 4.5 537l
  index, 4.3 291l, 4.4 415l, 4.5 537l
  table of contents, 4.3 291l, 4.4 415l, 4.5 537l
  title page, 4.5 537l

Penmanship. See **Handwriting.**

Period, 4.1 39e–39f

Personal essay. See **Genres.**

Personal reading programs. See **Bibliography,** self-selected reading.

Persuasion. See **Author's perspective/viewpoint/bias; Persuasive devices; Viewing,** uses of media.

Persuasive devices, 4.2 211l, 4.3 383b, 4.4 439b

Phonics
  chunking. See **Word structure,** chunking.
  consonant digraphs, final, 4.2 239i–239j
  consonants, hard and soft sounds of c and g 4.4 487i–487j
  consonants, silent, 4.6 761i–761j
  strategies. See **Spelling,** phonics, connection to.
  vowels
    common word (vowel) patterns
      VCCV, 4.1 39i–39j
      VCV, 4.5 559i–559j
    in final syllable, 4.4 439i–439j, 465i–465j
    long
      a, 4.1 65i–65j
      e, y, 4.1 87i–87j, 111i–111j
      i, igh, y, 4.1 65i–65j
      o, 4.1 87i–87j
      u, 4.1 133i–133j
    patterns, 4.3 337i–337j
    r-controlled, 4.2 211i–211j, 259i–259j, 4.4 465i–465j
    schwa sound, 4.4 439i–439j, 4.6 659i–659j
    short, 4.1 39i–39j

Photo essay. See **Genres.**

Phrasing. See **Fluency,** reading.

Pictures. See **Graphic sources,** illustration and or caption; **Prereading strategies,** use illustrations.

Pitch. See **Fluency,** reading.

Play. See **Genres.**

Plot, 4.1 88–89, 99, 103, 105, 4.4 401, 488l–488m, 488–489, 497, 507b, DI·46, DI·47, DI·56, 4.5 571, 575, 4.6 660l–660m

Poetic devices. *See* **Sound devices and poetic elements.**

Poetry selections
"**Allow Me to Introduce Myself,**" Charles R. Smith Jr., 4.2 160–161
"**Autumn,**" Charlotte Zolotow, 4.3 384
"**Best Paths, The,**" Kristine O'Connell George, 4.5 630
"**Carolyn's Cat,**" Constance Kling Levy, 4.4 511
"**City I Love,**" Lee Bennett Hopkins, 4.1 136
"**Confectioner, A,**" Myra Cohn Livingston, 4.4 465
"**Door, The,**" Miroslav Holub, 4.5 632–633
"**Dream Dust,**" Langston Hughes, 4.6 762
"**Early Spring,**" Shonto Begay, 4.3 386–387
"**Expert,**" Unknown, 4.4 465
"**Fall Football,**" Gary Soto, 4.6 764
"**Fast Break,**" Charles R. Smith Jr., 4.2 158–159
"**First Men on the Moon,**" J. Patrick Lewis, 4.6 765
"**Haiku,**" Christina Beecham, 4.6 658
"**His Hands,**" Nikki Grimes, 4.2 260
"**Homework,**" Russell Hoban, 4.2 261
"**Lem Lonnigan's Leaf Machine,**" Andrea Perry, 4.2 262–263
"**Man for All Seasonings, A,**" Richard Armour 4.4 464
"**Martin Luther King,**" Myra Cohn Livingston, 4.6 762
"**Martin Luther King Day,**" X. J. Kennedy, 4.6 763
"**Midwest Town,**" Ruth De Long Peterson, 4.1 137
"**My Life Is A Buried Treasure,**" Dawn Withrow, 4.6 659
"**Poetry,**" Eleanor Farjeon, 4.4 509
"**Roller Coasters,**" X. J. Kennedy, 4.5 631
"**Seed, The,**" Aileen Fisher, 4.4 510
"**Speak Up,**" Janet S. Wong, 4.1 135
"**This Land Is Your Land,**" Woody Guthrie, 4.1 130–133
"**We're All in the Telephone Book,**" Langston Hughes, 4.1 134
"**When You Hope, Wish, and Trust,**" Ek Ongkar K. Khalsa, 4.6 659
"**Who Knows?,**" Fatou Ndiaye Sow, 4.4 508
"**Winter Solstice,**" Marilyn Singer, 4.3 385
See also **Genres.**

Point of view. *See* **Literary devices.**

Poster. *See* **Graphic sources.**

Pourquoi tale. *See* **Genres.**

Predicting
confirming predictions, 4.1 53, 4.3 353, 4.4 409, 4.5 533
outcomes, 4.3 338, 4.4 392, 403, 407, 409, 413, DI·6, DI·7, 4.5 516, 527, 529, DI·6, DI·7
previewing and predicting, 4.1 22, 36, 44, 62, 70, 84, 92, 108, 116, 130, 4.2 146, 158, 166, 186, 192, 210, 216, 236, 244, 258, 4.3 272, 288, 296, 310, 318, 334, 342, 356, 364, 380, 4.4 396, 412, 420, 436, 444, 464, 470, 484, 492, 504, 4.5 520, 536, 542, 556, 564, 578, 586, 604, 612, 626, 4.6 642, 658, 664, 682, 690, 708, 716, 734, 742, 758

Prefixes, 4.2 144–145, 151, 161c, 190–191, 199, 211c. *See also* **Spelling,** word structure; **Word structure.**

Prepositions and prepositional phrases, 4.5 629e–629f

Prereading strategies
activate prior knowledge, 4.1 20a, 42a, 68a, 90a, 114a, 4.2 144a, 164a, 190a, 214a, 242a, 4.3 270a, 294a, 316a, 340a, 362a, 4.4 394a,

418a, 442a, 468a, 490a, 4.5 518a, 540a, 562a, 584a, 610a, 4.6 640a, 662a, 688a, 714a, 740a
ask questions, 4.1 42a, 114a, 4.2 242a, 4.3 294a, 340a, 4.4 418a, 468a, 4.5 584a, 610a, 4.6 662a, 714a
graphic organizers
chart, 4.4 442a
column chart, 4.1 90a, 4.2 144a
KWL chart, 4.1 42a, 114a, 4.2 242a, 4.3 294a, 340a, 4.4 418a, 468a, 4.5 584a, 610a, 4.6 662a, 714a
T-chart, 4.1 68a, 4.2 190a, 4.4 394a
Venn diagram, 4.2 214a, 4.5 562a, 4.6 688a, 740a
web, 4.1 20a, 4.2 164a, 4.3 270a, 316a, 362a, 4.4 490a, 4.5 518a, 540a, 4.6 640a
See also **Graphic and semantic organizers.**
preview and predict, 4.1 22, 36, 44, 62, 70, 84, 92, 108, 116, 130, 4.2 146, 158, 166, 186, 192, 210, 216, 236, 244, 258, 4.3 272, 288, 296, 310, 318, 334, 342, 356, 364, 380, 4.4 396, 412, 420, 436, 444, 464, 470, 484, 492, 504, 4.5 520, 536, 542, 556, 564, 578, 586, 604, 612, 626, 4.6 642, 658, 664, 682, 690, 708, 716, 734, 742, 758
set purposes for reading, 4.1 23, 45, 71, 93, 117, 4.2 147, 167, 193, 217, 245, 4.3 273, 297, 319, 343, 365, 4.4 397, 421, 445, 471, 493, 4.5 521, 543, 565, 587, 613, 4.6 643, 665, 691, 717, 743
use illustrations, 4.1 22, 44, 70, 92, 116, 4.2 146, 166, 192, 216, 244, 4.3 272, 296, 318, 342, 364, 4.4 396, 420, 444, 470, 492, 4.5 520, 542, 564, 586, 612, 4.6 642, 665, 690, 716, 742
use reading strategy (KWL, etc.), 4.1 42a, 114a, 4.2 242a, 4.3 294a, 340a, 4.4 418a, 468a, 4.5 584a, 610a, 4.6 662a, 714a
use text features, 4.1 36, 62, 84, 108, 130, 4.2 186, 210, 236, 258, 4.3 288, 310, 334, 356, 380, 4.4 412, 436, 464, 484, 504, 4.5 536, 556, 578, 604, 626, 4.6 682, 708, 734, 758

Previewing. *See* **Prereading strategies.**

Prior knowledge. 4.2 142–143, 155, 159, DI·6, DI·7, 4.4 488–489, 505, DI·46, DI·47. *See also* **Prereading strategies,** activate prior knowledge.

Problems, solving, 4.1 DI·5, 4.2 DI·27, DI·33, DI·37, DI·39, DI·43, 4.4 484–487, DI·5, DI·15, DI·35, 4.5 DI·9, DI·23, DI·27, DI·33, DI·37, 4.6 DI·27. DI·39

Projects, 4.1 16–17, 134a, 138–139, 4.2 140–141, 260a, 264–265, 4.3 266–267, 384a, 388–389, 4.4 390–391, 508a, 512–513, 4.5 514–515, 630a, 634–635, 762a, 4.6 636–637, 766–767

Pronouns
case, 4.4 439e–439f, 487e–487f
pronoun/antecedent agreement, 4.4 465e–465f
singular/plural, 4.4 415e–415f

Proofreading. *See* **Writing process,** edit.

Propaganda, 4.3 383b

Pun. *See* **Literary devices.**

Punctuation. *See* **Apostrophe; Colon; Comma; Exclamation mark; Italics; Parentheses; Period; Question mark; Quotation marks; Semicolon; Writing process,** edit.

Punctuation, attention to. *See* **Fluency, reading.**

Purposes for reading. *See* **Monitor and fix up; Prereading strategies,** set purposes for reading.

Put Reading First text comprehension strategies. *See* **Graphic and semantic organizers; Questions, answering; Questions, asking; Summarizing.**

Question-answer relationship (QAR). *See* **Questions, answering.**

Question mark, 4.1 39e–39f

Questions, answering (QAR), 4.1 40, 41, 52, 53, 56, 57, 58, 59, DI·16, DI·17, 4.2 188–189, 201, 205,207, 211, DI·26, DI·27, 4.6 638–639, 649, 653, 654, DI·6, DI·7

Questions, asking, 4.1 DI·53, DI·55, 4.2 DI·53, 4.3 268–269, 279, 281, 285, 289, 4.4 466–467, 477, 481, 485, 507, DI·36, DI·37, 4.5 DI·52, DI·56, 4.6 712–713, 726, 725, 727, 731, 737, DI·36, DI·37. *See also* **Prereading strategies,** set purposes for reading, **Speaking,** activities.

Quotation marks, 4.6 737e–737f, 761e–761f

Rate. *See* **Fluency, reading; Monitor and fix up.**

Read-aloud, 4.1 18m, 40m, 66m, 88m, 112m, TR14, 4.2 142m, 162m, 188m, 212m, 240m, TR14, 4.3 268m, 292m, 314m, 338m, 360m, TR14, 4.4 392m, 416m, 440m, 466m, 488m, TR14, 4.5 516m, 538m, 560m, 582m, 608m, TR14, 4.6 638m, 660m, 686m, 712m, 738m, TR14

Reader response. *See* **Connections, making; Response to literature.**

Reader's Guide to Periodical Literature. *See* **Reference sources.**

Reading across texts, 4.1 39, 58, 65, 87, 104, 111, 133, 4.2 161, 187, 206, 211, 239, 259, 4.3 291, 313, 330, 337, 359, 383, 4.4 415, 439, 450, 465, 487, 498, 507, 4.5 532, 537, 552, 559, 574, 581, 607, 622, 629, 4.6 646, 659, 678, 685, 711, 737, 761

Reading fluency. *See* **Fluency, reading.**

Reading rate. *See* **Fluency, reading; Monitor and fix up.**

Reading strategies. *See* **Strategies.**

Reading to students. *See* **Read-aloud.**

Realistic fiction. *See* **Genres.**

Recreational reading. *See* **Bibliography,** self-selected reading.

Reference sources
almanac, 4.3 291l
atlas, 4.1 39l
card catalog/library database, 4.4 507l
dictionary/glossary, 4.1 68, 79, 87c, 231, 4.2 164, 173, 177, 187c, 214, 221, 231, 239c, 242, 253, 259c, 4.4 442, 453, 457, 465c, 4.5 537l, 4.6 662, 669, 673, 685c, 711l. *See also* **Dictionary/glossary.**
encyclopedia, 4.1 133l, 4.6 761l
Internet and World Wide Web, 4.1 39k, 65k, 87k, 87l, 111k, 133k, 4.2 161k, 187k, 211k, 239k, 259k, 4.3 291k, 313k, 337k, 359k, 359l, 383k, 4.4 415k, 439k, 465k, 487k, 507k, 4.5 537k, 559k, 581k, 607k, 629k, 4.6 659k, 685k, 711k, 737k, 761k
magazine/periodical, 4.1 133l, 4.2 239l, 4.6 685l
manual, 4.4 415l, 465l, 4.6 737l

media, electronic, 4.1 87l
newspaper/newsletter, 4.1 133l, 4.2 187l, 211l
online manual, 4.6 737l
online telephone directory, 4.3 359l
pamphlets, 4.1 133l
parts of a book, 4.5 537l
Reader's Guide to Periodical Literature, 4.3 313l
technology. See **Technology, new literacies.**
telephone directory, 4.3 359l
textbook, 4.1 133l, 4.3 337l
thesaurus, 4.4 487l
trade book, 4.1 133l, 4.3 337l

Repetition. See **Sound devices and poetic elements.**

Rereading. See **Monitor and fix up.**

Research
activities, 4.1 39l, 65l, 87l, 111l, 133l, 4.2 161l, 187l, 211l, 239l, 259l, 4.3 291l, 313l, 337l, 359l, 383l, 4.4 415l, 439l, 465l, 487l, 507l, 4.5 537l, 559l, 581l, 607l, 629l, 4.6 659l, 685l, 711l, 737l, 761l
process and strategies
citing sources, 4.1 87d, 111d, 4.6 659l, 767b
evaluating, interpreting, and drawing conclusions about key information, 4.1 211l
locating and collecting information, 4.3 359l, 383d, 4.4 507l, 4.5 607l
organizing content, 4.2 187l, 4.5 537l, 559l
outlining, 4.5 559l
pictures and captions, 4.1 211l, 4.2 211l
procedures and instructions, 4.4 415l, 465l, 4.6 737l
skimming/scanning, 4.1 65l
study strategy to find or learn information, 4.1 42a, 114a, 4.2 242a, 4.3 294a, 4.4 418a, 468a, 4.5 584a, 607l, 610a, 4.6 662a, 714a
taking notes/recording findings, 4.6 659l, 676b
using graphic sources, 4.1 39l, 4.2 161l, 239l, 259l, 4.3 383l, DI·55, 4.4 439l, DI·55, 4.5 581l, DI·55, 4.6 DI·56. See also **Graphic sources.**
using reference sources, 4.1 41l, 87l, 133l, 4.3 291l, 313l, 337l, 4.4 487l, 4.6 685l, 711l, 737l, 761l. See also **References sources.**

Research and study skills, 4.1 39l, 65l, 87l, 111l, 133l, 4.2 161l, 187l, 211l, 239l, 259l, 4.3 291l, 313l, 337l, 359l, 383l, 4.4 415l, 439l, 465l, 487l, 507l, 4.5 537l, 559l, 581l, 607l, 629l, 4.6 659l, 685l, 711l, 737l, 761l

Response to literature
oral, 4.1 34, 39, 60, 65, 82, 87, 106, 111, 128, 133, 4.2 156, 161, 184, 187, 208, 211, 233, 239, 256, 259, 4.3 286, 291, 308, 313, 332, 337, 354, 359, 378, 383, 4.4 410, 415, 434, 439, 462, 465, 482, 487, 501, 507, 4.5 534, 537, 554, 559, 576, 581, 602, 607, 624, 629, 4.6 655, 659, 680, 685, 706, 711, 732, 737, 756, 761
written, 4.1 34, 39, 60, 65, 82, 87, 106, 111, 128, 133, 4.2 156, 161, 184, 187, 208, 211, 233, 239, 256, 259, 4.3 286, 291, 308, 313, 332, 337, 354, 359, 378, 383, 4.4 410, 415, 434, 439, 462, 465, 482, 487, 501, 502–503, 507, 4.5 534, 535, 537, 537g–537h, 554, 559, 576, 581, 602, 607, 624, 629, 4.6 655, 659, 680, 685, 706, 707, 711, 711g-711h, 732, 737, 756, 761

Retelling. See **Speaking,** activities.

Rhyme. See **Sound devices and poetic elements.**

Root words. See **Spelling,** word structure; **Word structure,** Greek and Latin roots.

Rubric. See **Assessment,** scoring guide (rubric).

Running record, taking a, 4.1 39a, 65a, 87a, 111a, 133a, DI·57, DI·58, 4.2 161a, 187a, 211a, 239a, 259a, DI·57, DI·58, 4.3 291a, 313a, 337a, 359a, 383a, DI·57, DI·58, 4.4 415a, 439a, 465a, 487a, 507a, DI·57, DI·58, 4.5 537a, 559a, 581a, 607a, 629a, DI·57, DI·58, 4.6 659a, 685a, 711a, 737a, 761a, DI·57, DI·58. See *also* **Fluency, reading.**

S

Safety information. See **Character education.**

Scaffolded instruction, 4.1 19, 25, 41, 67, 73, 89, 95, 101, 113, 119, DI·1, 4.2 143, 163, 169, 179, 189, 195, 213, 241, DI·1, 4.3 269, 275, 277, 293, 305, 315, 325, 339, 361, DI·1, 4.4 393, 399, 405, 417, 423, 427, 441, 449, 467, 473, 489, 495, 497, DI·1, 4.5 517, 523, 525, 539, 545, 561, 567, 573, 583, 589, 609, 615, 617, DI·1, 4.6 639, 645, 661, 687, 701, 713, 721, 739, 745, 749, DI·1

Scale drawing. See **Graphic sources,** diagram/scale drawing.

Schedule. See **Graphic sources.**

School-home connection, 4.1 18i, 18m, 40i, 40m, 66i, 66m, 88i, 88m, 112i, 112m, 4.2 142i, 142m, 162i, 162m, 188i, 188m, 212i, 212m, 240i, 240m, 4.3 268i, 268m, 292i, 292m, 314i, 314m, 338i, 338m, 360i, 360m, 4.4 392i, 392m, 416i, 416m, 440i, 440m, 466i, 466m, 488i, 488m, 4.5 516i, 516m, 538i, 538m, 560i, 560m, 582i, 582m, 608i, 608m, 4.6 638i, 638m, 660i, 660m, 686i, 686m, 712i, 712m, 738i, 738m

Science activities. See **Cross-curricular activities.**

Science fiction. See **Genres.**

Science in reading, 4.1 36–39, 108–111, 130–133, 4.3 288–291, 310–313, 356–359, 380–383, 4.4 412–415, 436–439, 504–507, 4.5 626–629, 4.6 758–761

Self-appraisal and self-correction. See **Monitor and fix up.**

Self-check, 4.1 33, 53, 59, 81, 99, 105, 127, 4.2 155, 175, 183, 201, 207, 223, 255, 4.3 279, 285, 307, 327, 331, 355, 371, 377, 4.4 403, 409, 429, 433, 451, 461, 481, 500, 4.5 527, 533, 553, 575, 593, 601, 623, 4.6 649, 654, 671, 679, 697, 705, 725, 731, 751, 755

Self-monitor and use fix-up strategies. See **Monitor and fix up.**

Self-selected reading, 4.1 DI·59, DI·60, TR14–TR17, 4.2 DI·59, DI·60, TR14–TR17, 4.3 DI·59, DI·60, TR14–TR17, 4.4 DI·59, DI·60, TR14–TR17, 4.5 DI·59, DI·60, TR14–TR17, 4.6 DI·59, DI·60, TR14–TR17

Semicolon, 4.1 111e

Sentences
fragment, 4.1 87e, 4.6 659e
parts of
predicate, 4.1 87e–87f
subject, 4.1 87e–87f
run-on, 4.1 111e, 4.6 659e

structure
complex, 4.1 39e, 133e–133f
compound, 4.1 39e, 111e–111f
types of
declarative, 4.1 39e–39f
exclamatory, 4.1 65e–65f
imperative, 4.1 65e–65f
interrogative, 4.1 39e–39f

Sequence
directions, following, 4.4 415l, 465l, 4.6 737l
sequence of events (time sequence/chronology), 4.1 18l–18m, 18–19, 25, 27, 37, 39, 39b, 66l–66m, 66–67, 73, 77, 85, 87b, 97, DI·6, DI·7, DI·26, DI·27, DI·52, DI·54, 4.5 531, 551, 560l–560m, 560–561, 567, 571, 581, 581b, DI·26, DI·27
steps in a process, 4.4 415b, 4.5 607b

Setting, 4.2 171, 4.4 440l–440m, 440–441, 449, DI·26, DI·27, 4.5 582l–582m

Setting purposes for reading. See **Monitor and fix up, Prereading strategies.**

Simile, 4.3 359b, 4.6 685b, 761b. See *also* **Figurative language.**

Six-trait writing
conventions, 4.1 39g, 65g, 87g, 111g, 129, 133g–133h, WA1, WA2, WA6, 4.2 161g, 187g, 211g, 239g, 259g, WA1, WA2, WA6, 4.3 291g, 313g, 337g, 359g, 379, 383g–383h, WA1, WA2, WA6, 4.4 415g, 439g, 465g, 483, 487g–487h, 507g, WA1, WA2, WA6, 4.5 537g, 559g, 581g, 607g, 629g, WA1, WA2, WA6, 4.6 659g, 685g, 707, 711g–711h, 737g, 761g, WA1, WA2, WA6
focus/ideas, 4.1 39g, 65g, 87g, 107, 111g–111h, 133g, WA1, WA5, WA7, 4.2 161g, 185, 187g–187h, 211g, 234, 239g–239h, 259g, WA1, WA5, WA7, 4.3 291g, 313g, 337g, 359g, 383g, WA1, WA5, WA7, 4.4 415g, 435, 439g–439h, 465g, 487g, 507g, WA1, WA5, WA7, 4.5 535, 537g–537h, 559g, 577, 581g–581h, 607g, 629g, WA1, WA5, WA7, 4.6 659g, 681, 685g–685h, 711g, 737g, 761g, WA1, WA5, WA7
organization/paragraph, 4.1 39g, 65g, 87g, 111g, 133g, WA1, WA3, WA4, WA5, WA7, 4.2 161g, 187g, 209, 211g–211h, 239g, 257, 259g–259h, WA1, WA5, WA7, 4.3 291g, 313g, 337g, 355, 359g–359h, 383g, WA1, WA3, WA4, WA5, WA7, 4.4 415g, 439g, 465g, 487g, 502, 507g–507h, WA1, WA3, WA5, WA7, 4.5 537g, 559g, 581g, 607g, 629g, WA1, WA3, WA5, WA7, 4.6 659g, 685g, 711g, 733, 737g–737h, 761g, WA1, WA3, WA5, WA7
sentences, 4.1 39g, 61, 65g, 65h, 87g, 111g, 133g, WA1, WA5, WA7, 4.2 161g, 187g, 211g, 239g, 259g, WA1, WA5, WA7, 4.3 291g, 309, 313g–313h, 337g, 359g, 383g, WA1, WA5, WA7, 4.4 411, 415g–415h, 439g, 465g, 487g, 507g, WA1, WA5, WA7, 4.5 537g, 559g, 581g, 607g, 629g, WA1, WA5, WA7, 4.6 656, 659g–659h, 685g, 711g, 737g, 757, 761g–761h, WA1, WA5, WA7
voice, 4.1 39g, 65g, 83, 87g–87h, 111g, 133g, WA1, WA5, WA7, 4.2 161g, 187g, 211g, 239g, 259g, WA1, WA5, WA7, 4.3 287, 291g–291h, 313g, 337g, 359g, 383g, WA1, WA5, WA7, 4.4 415g, 439g, 463, 465g–465h, 487g, 507g, WA1, WA5, WA7, 4.5 537g, 559g, 581g, 603, 607g–607h, 629g, WA1, WA5, WA7, 4.6 659g, 685g, 711g, 737g, 761g, WA1, WA5, WA7
word choice, 4.1 35, 39g–39h, 65g, 87g, 111g, 133g, WA1, WA5, WA7, 4.2 157, 161g–161h, 187g, 211g, 239g, 259g, WA1, WA5, WA7, 4.3 291g, 313g, 333, 337g–337h, 359g, 383g, WA1, WA5, WA7, 4.4 415g, 439g, 465g, 487g,

507g, WA1, WA5, WA7, 4.5 537g, 555, 559g–559h, 581g, 607g, 625, 629g–629h, WA1, WA5, WA7, 4.6 659g, 685g, 711g, 737g, 761g, WA1, WA5, WA7

Skimming and scanning, 4.1 65l

Slang. See **Literary devices.**

Social studies activities. See **Cross-curricular activities.**

Social studies in reading, 4.1 65, 4.2 186–187, 210–211, 258–259, 4.5 536–537, 556–559, 604–607, 4.6 682–685, 708–711

Solving problems. See **Problems, solving.**

Song. See **Genres.**

Sound devices and poetic elements
  alliteration, 4.6 763
  free verse, 4.3 387
  onomatopoeia, 4.1 136, 4.2 177, 4.5 631
  repetition, 4.2 260, 4.4 508
  rhyme, 4.4 465, 465b, 4.6 658

Speaking
  activities
    advertisement/commercial, 4.1 87d, 4.4 439d
    announcement, 4.5 559d
    ask questions, 4.3 268–269, 279, 281, 285, 289, 4.4 466–467, 477, 481, 485, 507, 4.6 712, 713, 726, 725, 727, 731, 737
    debate, 4.1 133d, 4.6 711d
    demonstration, 4.6 685d
    description, 4.2 239d
    directions, 4.3 359
    discussion, 4.1 34, 60, 82, 106, 128, 4.2 156, 184, 208, 233, 256, 4.3 286, 308, 322, 354, 378, 4.4 410, 434, 462, 482, 501, 4.5 534, 554, 576, 602, 624, 4.6 655, 659d, 680, 706, 732, 756
    dramatization, 4.1 39d, 4.2 211d, 4.5 537d
    interview, 4.3 313d, 4.4 415d, 4.5 607d, 4.6 737d
    introductions, 4.1 65d
    newscast, 4.2 187d, 4.3 359d, 4.4 507d
    oral presentation/report, 4.1 111d
    oral reading, 4.1 39a, 65a, 87a, 111a, 133a, 4.2 161a, 187a, 211, 239a, 259a, 4.3 291a, 313a, 337a, 359a, 383a, 4.4 415a, 439a, 465a, 487a, 507a, 4.5 537a, 559a, 581a, 607a, 629a, 4.6 659a, 685a, 711a, 737a, 761a
    persuasive, 4.1 133d, 4.3 291d, 383d
    press conference, 4.2 259d
    read aloud poetry, 4.1 134–137, 4.2 260–263, 4.3 384–387, 4.4, 508–511, 4.5 630–633, 4.6 672–675
    Readers' Theater, 4.3 337d, 4.4 465d
    recitation, 4.2 260
    retelling, 4.1 35, 39d, 61, 83, 107, 129, 4.2 157, 185, 209, 234, 257, 4.3 287, 309, 333, 355, 379, 4.4 411, 435, 463, 487d, 502, 4.5 535, 577, 603, 625, 4.6 656, 681, 707, 733, 757
    round-table discussion, 4.6 659d
    speech, 4.1 133d, 4.3 291d, 383d, 4.5 581d, 629d, 4.6 761d
    sportscast, 4.2 161d
    story, 4.4 487d
    weather broadcast, 4.3 359d
  purpose/reasons for speaking
    descriptive, 4.1 65d, 187d, 4.2 239d, 4.5 629d
    expository, 4.1 111d, 4.3 313d, 359d, 4.4 415d, 439d, 507d, 4.5 559d, 581d, 607d, 4.6 685d, 737d, 761d
    expressive, 4.1 39d, 4.3 313d, 4.4 465d, 4.5 537d
    narrative, 4.1 39d, 4.2 161d, 211d, 4.3 313d, 4.4 465d, 487d

persuasive, 4.1 87d, 133d, 4.2 259d, 4.3 291d, 383d, 4.6 711d
  problem solving, 4.6 659d
tips, 4.1 39d, 65d, 87d, 133d, 4.2 239d, 259d, 4.3 291d, 313d, 337d, 359d, 383d, 4.4 439d, 465d, 487d, 507d, 4.5 537d, 581d, 629d, 4.6 659d, 737d

Spelling
  common word (vowel) patterns
    VCCV, 4.1 39i–39j
    VCV, 4.5 559i–559j
  five-step plan for learning words, 4.1 39i–39j, 65i–65j, 87i–87j, 111i–111j, 133i–133j, 4.2 161i–161j, 187i–187j, 211i–211j, 239i–239j, 259i–259j, 4.3 291i–291j, 313i–313j, 337i–337j, 359i–359j, 383i–383j, 4.4 415i–415j, 439i–439j, 465i–465j, 487i–487j, 507i–507j, 4.5 537i–537j, 559i–559j, 581i–581j, 607i–607j, 629i–629j, 4.6 659i–659j, 685i–685j, 711i–711j, 737i–737j, 761i–761j
  meaning relationships
    homophones, 4.3 313i–313j
  phonics, connection to
    consonant digraphs, 4.2 239i–239j
    consonants /j/, /ks/, /kw/, 4.4 487i–487j
    silent consonants, 4.6 761i–761j
    vowels
      diphthongs, 4.3 337i–337j
      in final syllables, 4.4 439i–439j, 465i–465j
      long,
        a, 4.1 65i–65j
        e, y, 4.1 87i–87j, 111i–111j
        i, igh, y, 4.1 65i–65j
        o, 4.1 87i–87j
        u, 4.1 133i–133j
      patterns, 4.3 337i–337j
      r-controlled, 4.2 211i–211j, 259i–259j, 4.4 465i–465j
      schwa sound, 4.4 439i–439j, 4.6 659i–659j
      short, 4.1 39i–39j
  word structure
    affixes, 4.4 507i–507j, 4.6 685i–685j, 711i–711j, 737i–737j
    compound words, 4.3 359i–359j
    contractions, 4.4 415i–415j
    Greek and Latin word parts, 4.5 581i–581j, 607i–607j
    inflected endings, 4.2 161i–161j, 4.3 291i–291j
    plurals, irregular, 4.2 187i–187j
    plurals, regular, 4.2 161i–161j
    possessives, 4.3 383i–383j
    related words (derivatives), 4.5 629i–629j
    roots, 4.5 607i–607j
    syllable constructions, 4.5 537i–537j, 559i–559j

Standard book features. See **Parts of a book.**

Steps in a process, 4.4 415b, 4.5 607b

Stereotypes, analyzing, 4.2 154, 4.5 574

Story elements. See **Character, Plot, Setting, Theme** (as a story element).

Story structure, 4.1 88–89, 99, 103, 105, DI·36, DI·37, 4.3 360–361, 4.5 560–561, 571, 575, DI·26, DI·27

Strategic intervention. See **Intervention.**

Strategies
  comprehension, 4.1 18–19, 40–41, 66–67, 88–89, 112–113, 4.2 142–143, 162–163, 188–189, 212–213, 240–241, 4.3 268–269, 292–293, 314–315, 338–339, 360–361, 4.4 392–393, 416–417, 440–441, 466–467, 488–489, 4.5 516–517, 538–539, 560–561, 582–583, 608–609, 4.6 638–639, 660–661, 686–687, 712–713, 738–739

concept development, 4.1 17a, 18a, 18l, 40a, 40l, 66a, 66l, 88a, 88l, 112a, 112l, 4.2 141a, 142a, 142l, 162a, 162l, 188a, 188l, 212a, 212l, 240a, 240l, 4.3 267a, 268a, 268l, 292a, 292l, 314a, 314l, 338a, 338l, 360a, 360l, 4.4 391a, 392a, 392l, 416a, 416l, 440a, 440l, 466a, 466l, 488a, 488l, 4.5 515a, 516a, 516l, 538a, 538l, 560a, 560l, 582a, 582l, 608a, 608l, 4.6 637a, 638a, 638l, 660a, 660l, 686a, 686l, 712a, 712l, 738a, 738l
context, 4.1 101, 4.3 305, 325, 4.4 405, 427, 495, 4.5 525, 573, 617, 4.6 701, 721, 729, 749
decoding, 4.1 39i–39j, 65i–65j, 87i–87j, 111i–111j, 133i–133j, 4.2 161i–161j, 187i–187j, 211i–211j, 239i–239j, 259i–259j, 4.3 291i–291j, 313i–313j, 337i–337j, 359i–359j, 383i–383j, 4.4 415i–415j, 439i–439j, 465i–465j, 487i–487j, 507i–507j, 4.5 537i–537j, 559i–559j, 581i–581j, 607i–607j, 629i–629j, 4.6 659i–659j, 685i–685j, 711i–711j, 737i–737j, 761i–761j
fluent reading, 4.1 39a, 65a, 87a, 111a, 133a, 4.2 161a, 187a, 211a, 239a, 259a, 4.3 291a, 313a, 337a, 359a, 383a, 4.4 415a, 439a, 465a, 487a, 507a, 4.5 537a, 559a, 581a, 607a, 629a, 4.6 659a, 685a, 711a, 737a, 761a
monitor and fix up, 4.2 212–213, 223, 227, 239, 4.4 440–441, 451, 455, 461, 465, 4.5 608–609, 619, 623, 629, 4.6 738–739, 751, 753, 755, 761
prereading, 4.1 22, 44, 70, 92, 116, 4.2 146, 166, 192, 216, 244, 4.3 272, 296, 318, 342, 364, 4.4 396, 420, 444, 470, 492, 4.5 520, 542, 564, 586, 612, 4.6 642, 664, 690, 716, 742
research, 4.1 39l, 65l, 87l, 111l, 133l, 4.2 161l, 187l, 211l, 239l, 259l, 4.3 291l, 313l, 337l, 359l, 383l, 4.4 415l, 439l, 465l, 487l, 507l, 4.5 537l, 559l, 581l, 607l, 629l, 4.6 659l, 685l, 711l, 737l, 761l
spelling, 4.1 39i–39j, 65i–65j, 87i–87j, 111i–111j, 133i–133j, 4.2 161i–161j, 187i–187j, 211i–211j, 239i–239j, 259i–259j, 4.3 291i–291j, 313i–313j, 337i–337j, 359i–359j, 383i–383j, 4.4 415i–415j, 439i–439j, 465i–465j, 487i–487j, 507i–507j, 4.5 537i–537j, 559i–559j, 581i–581j, 607i–607j, 629i–629j, 4.6 659i–659j, 685i–685j, 711i–711j, 737i–737j, 761i–761j
vocabulary. See **Vocabulary strategies.**

Structural analysis. See **Word structure.**

Study strategies, 4.1 39l, 65l, 87l, 111l, 133l, 4.2 161l, 187l, 211l, 239l, 259l, 4.3 291l, 313l, 337l, 359l, 383l, 4.4 415l, 439l, 465l, 487l, 507l, 4.5 537l, 559l, 581l, 607l, 629l, 4.6 659l, 685l, 711l, 737l, 761l. See also **Assessment,** test-taking practice; **Content-area texts; Graphic sources; Organizing information; Parts of a book; Reference sources; Textbook-reading techniques.**

Style, illustrator's. See **Literary craft.**

Subject-verb agreement, 4.3 337e–337f

Suffixes, 4.1 20–21, 29, 39c, 114–115, 121, 133c, 4.2 144–145, 151, 161c, 4.3 362–363, 375, 383c, 4.4 394b. See **Spelling,** word structure; **Word structure.**

Summarizing, 4.1 18–19, 27, 33, 39, 65, DI·6, DI·7, 4.2 240–241, 251, 255, DI·46, DI·47, 4.6 686–687, 697, 699, 705, 711, DI·26, DI·27

Sustained silent reading. See **Self-selected reading.**

Syllables. See **Spelling,** word structure, syllable constructions; **Word structure,** chunking.

Symbolism. See **Literary devices.**

Synonyms, 4.1 90–91, 101c, 111c, 4.4 394–395, 405, 415c, 490–491, 495, 507c, 4.5 610b, 610–611, 617, 629c. See also **Vocabulary strategies.**

Synthesizing. See **Connections, making; Reading across texts.**

T

Tables. See **Graphic sources,** chart/table.

Taking notes. See **Note-taking.**

Target comprehension skills. See **Comprehension skills, explicit/implicit instruction** for a total listing of these skills.

Target comprehension strategies. See **Comprehension strategies, explicit/implicit instruction** for a total listing of these strategies.

Teaching strategies
informal assessment. See **Assessment.**
modeling. This strategy is part of every lesson.
think-aloud. This strategy is part of every lesson. See also **Graphic and semantic organizers, KWL.**

Technology
e-mail, 4.1 111g–111h, 4.2 236–239
information and communication technologies. See **Technology,** new literacies; **Reference sources,** Internet and World Wide Web.
Internet article, 4.1 84–87, 4.3 356–359, 4.4 484–487, 4.5 578–581, 4.6 734–737
Internet/World Wide Web. See **Technology,** new literacies; **Reference sources,** Internet and World Wide Web.
new literacies
activities, 4.1 39k, 65k, 87k, 111k, 133k, 4.2 161k, 187k, 211k, 239k, 259k, 4.3 291k, 313k, 337k, 359k, 383k, 4.4 415k, 439k, 465k, 487k, 507k, 4.5 537k, 559k, 581k, 607k, 629k, 4.6 659k, 685k, 711k, 737k, 761k
bookmarks, 4.1 85, 161k, 4.2 211k, 4.3 337k, 4.4 415k, 439k, 4.5 537k
documentation of Web site, 4.1 111k
electronic media, 4.1 20a, 26, 39k, 42a, 48, 65k, 68a, 80, 84, 85, 86, 87k, 87l, 90a, 96, 106, 111k, 114a, 118, 133k, 4.2 144a, 148, 161k, 164a, 172, 174, 187k, 190a, 200, 211k, 214a, 220, 228, 236, 237, 238, 239, 239k, 242a, 246, 259k, 4.3 270a, 278, 291k, 294a, 298, 313k, 316a, 320, 337k, 340a, 344, 352, 356, 357, 358, 359, 359k, 359l, 362a, 366, 383k, 4.4 394a, 415k, 418a, 422, 439k, 442a, 463k, 468a, 476, 484, 485, 486, 487k, 490a, 494, 507k, 4.5 518a, 537k, 540a, 546, 559k, 562a, 574, 578, 579, 580, 581k, 584a, 596, 607k, 610a, 614, 629k, 4.6 640a, 648, 659k, 662a, 678, 685k, 688a, 692, 711k, 714a, 724, 734, 735, 736, 737k, 740a, 748, 761k
e-mail, 4.2 236–238
etiquette, 4.1 85, 4.2 237, 4.3 357, 4.4 485, 4.5 579, 4.6 735
evaluating Internet information and sources, 4.1 65k, 111k, 133k, 4.2 161k, 239k, 4.3 359k, 4.4 507k, 4.5 578–581, 629k, 4.6 659k, 734–737
folder, 4.2 238
graphic sources 4.1 86
homepage, 4.1 84, 4.3 356, 357, 4.6 734, 735, 736
Internet article, 4.1 84–87, 4.3 356–359, 4.4 484–487, 4.5 578–581, 4.6 734–737
Internet inquiry, 4.1 20a, 26, 39k, 42a, 48, 65k, 68a, 80, 84, 85, 86, 87k, 87l, 90a, 96, 106, 111k, 114a, 118, 133k, 4.2 144a, 148,161k, 164a, 172, 174, 187k, 190a, 200, 211k, 214a,

220, 228, 236, 237, 238, 239, 239k, 242a, 246, 259k, 4.3 270a, 278, 291k, 294a, 298, 313k, 316a, 320, 337k, 340a, 344, 352, 356, 357, 358, 359, 359k, 359l, 362a, 366, 383k, 4.4 394a, 415k, 418a, 422, 439k, 442a, 463k, 468a, 476, 484, 485, 486, 487k, 490a, 494, 507k, 4.5 518a, 537k, 540a, 546, 559k, 562a, 574, 578, 579, 580, 581k, 584a, 596, 607k, 610a, 614, 629k, 4.6 640a, 648, 659k, 662a, 678, 685k, 688a, 692, 711k, 714a, 724, 734, 735, 736, 737, 740a, 748, 761k
keyword, 4.1 20a, 26, 42a, 48, 65k, 68a, 80, 84, 85, 87k, 90a, 96, 106, 111k, 114a, 118, 133k, 4.2 144a, 148, 161k, 164a, 190a, 200, 211k, 214a, 220, 228, 242a, 246, 259k, 4.3 270a, 278, 291k, 294a, 298, 316a, 320, 340a, 344, 352, 358, 359l, 362a, 366, 383k, 4.4 394a, 418a, 422, 439k, 442a, 465k, 468a, 476, 484, 485, 486, 487k, 490a, 494, 507k, 4.5 537k, 540a, 546, 559k, 562a, 574, 581k, 584a, 596, 607k, 610a, 614, 629k, 4.6 640a, 648, 659k, 662a, 678, 685k, 688a, 692, 714a, 724, 737k, 740a, 748, 761k
links, 4.2 228, 237, 4.3 291k, 356, 4.4 439k, 484, 486, 4.5 559k, 4.6 659k, 734, 735, 736
museum, online, 4.1 65k
navigation 4.2 238
reference sources and directories, online, 4.1 84–87, 111k, 118, 4.2 172, 200, 220, 4.4 422, 465k, 476, 4.5 562a, 578–581, 4.6 640a, 648, 678, 688a, 714a, 734–737, 737k
search engines, 4.1 20a, 26, 42a, 48, 65k, 68a, 80, 87k, 90a, 96, 106, 111k, 114a, 118, 4.2 144a, 148, 164a, 174, 187k, 190a, 200, 214a, 220, 228, 242a, 246, 4.3 270a, 278, 294a, 298, 313k, 316a, 320, 337k, 340a, 344, 352, 359k, 362a, 366, 383k, 4.4 394a, 411, 415k, 418a, 439k, 442a, 465k, 468a, 484, 485, 486, 487k, 490a, 494, 4.5 518a, 537k, 540a, 546, 559k, 562a, 574, 581k, 584a, 596, 607k, 610a, 614, 629k, 4.6 640a, 648, 659k, 678, 685k, 688a, 692, 711k, 714a, 724, 736, 737k, 740a, 748, 761k
search window, 4.1 84, 4.4 484
searching and navigating the Internet, 4.1 20a, 26, 39k, 42a, 48, 65k, 68a, 80, 84, 85, 86, 87k, 87l, 90a, 96, 106, 111k, 114a, 118, 133k, 4.2 144a, 148, 161k, 164a, 172, 174, 187k, 190a, 200, 211k, 214a, 220, 228, 239k, 242a, 246, 4.3 270a, 278, 291k, 294a, 298, 313k, 316a, 320, 337k, 340a, 344, 352, 355, 356, 357, 359k, 359l, 362a, 366, 383k, 4.4 394a, 415k, 418a, 422, 439k, 442a, 465k, 468a, 476, 484, 485, 486, 487k, 490a, 494, 507k, 4.5 518a, 537k, 540a, 546, 559k, 562a, 574, 578, 579, 580, 581k, 584a, 596, 607k, 610a, 614, 629k, 4.6 640a, 648, 659k, 662a, 678, 685k, 688a, 692, 711k, 714a, 724, 734, 736, 737k, 740a, 748, 761k
technology tools, 4.1 84, 4.2 236, 4.3 356, 4.4 484, 4.5 578, 4.6 734
URLs, 4.1 84, 85, 111k, 4.2 161k, 187k, 211k, 239k, 259k, 4.3 291k, 313k, 359k, 4.4 439k, 487k, 4.5 537k, 559k, 578, 629k, 4.6 659k, 711k, 740a
use graphic sources, 4.1 65k, 84, 86, 87k, 4.3 313k, 4.4 465k, 487k, 4.6 734
use website features, 4.1 84, 4.3 356, 4.4 415k, 439k, 465k, 484, 485, 486, 4.6 659k
Web site, 4.1 61, 65k, 68a, 84, 85, 87k, 87l, 111k, 133k, 4.2 161k, 187k, 211k, 237, 239, 239k, 259k, 4.3 291k, 313k, 337k, 355, 356–357, 359k, 383k, 4.4 415k, 439k, 465k, 484–487, 487k, 507k, 4.5 537k, 559k, 578, 579, 580, 581k, 607k, 629k, 4.6 659k, 685k, 711k, 734, 737k, 761k

Scott Foresman Reading Street technology
Background Building Audio CD, 4.1 20a, 42a, 68a, 90a, 114a, 4.2 144a, 164a, 190a, 214a, 242a, 4.3 270a, 294a, 316a, 340a, 362a, 4.4 394a, 418a, 442a, 468a, 490a, 4.5 518a, 540a, 562a, 584a, 610a, 4.6 640a, 662a, 688a, 714a, 740a
Leveled Reader Database, 4.1 18h, 40h, 66h, 88h, 112h, 4.2 142h, 162h, 188h, 212h, 240h, 4.3 268h, 292h, 314h, 338h, 360h, 4.4 392h, 416h, 440h, 466h, 488h, 4.5 516h, 538h, 560h, 582h, 608h, 4.6 638h, 660h, 686h, 712h, 738h
professional development (PearsonSuccessNet. com), 4.1 18i, 40i, 66i, 88i, 112i, 4.2 142i, 162i, 188i, 212i, 240i, 4.3 268i, 292i, 314i, 338i, 360i, 4.4 392i, 416i, 440i, 466i, 488i, 4.5 516i, 538i, 560i, 582i, 608i, 4.6 638i, 660i, 686i, 712i, 738i
Selection AudioText CD (Student Edition), 4.1 23, 45, 71, 93, 117, 4.2 147, 167, 193, 217, 245, 4.3 273, 297, 319, 343, 365, 4.4 397, 421, 445, 471, 493, 4.5 521, 543, 565, 587, 613, 4.6 643, 665, 691, 717, 743
skills for using technology
basic knowledge and skills, 4.1 65k, 84–87, 111k, 4.2 161k, 187k, 236–239, 239k, 259k, 4.3 337k, 356–359, 4.4 439k, 484–487, 4.5 559k, 578–581, 629k, 4.6 734–737
communication, 4.1 111g–111h, 4.2 236–239
compare and contrast, 4.2 211k, 4.5 537k, 574, 4.6 688a
information acquisition, 4.1 39k, 65k, 87k, 111k, 133k, 4.2 161k, 187k, 211k, 239k, 259k, 4.3 291k, 313k, 337k, 359k, 383k, 4.4 415k, 439k, 465k, 487k, 507k, 4.5 537k, 559k, 581k, 607k, 629k, 4.6 659k, 685k, 711k, 737k, 761k
See also **Cross-curricular activities, Reference sources.**

Telephone directory. See **Reference sources.**

Tempo. See **Fluency, reading.**

Testing, formal and informal. See **Assessment.**

Test-taking practice
look back and write, 4.1 34, 60, 82, 106, 128, 4.2 156, 184, 208, 233, 256, 4.3 286, 308, 332, 354, 378, 4.4 410, 434, 462, 482, 501, 4.5 534, 554, 576, 602, 624, 4.6 655, 680, 706, 736, 756
strategies for fiction/poetry
identify theme, 4.1 132
use figurative language, 4.6 659
use plot and characters, 4.3 336
use rhyme, 4.2 160, 4.4 465
nonfiction
use bold-faced words, 4.2 187
use captions, 4.1 110
use charts, 4.5 628, 4.6 760
use diagrams, 4.4 414
use quotations, 4.4 506, 4.6 710
use graphics, 4.2 259, 4.3 312
use illustration, 4.1 64
use maps, 4.1 38
use photographs, 4.5 558, 4.6 684
use sidebars, 4.4 438
use subheads, 4.2 211, 4.3 290, 382
use tables, 4.5 606
writing for tests, 4.1 133g–133h, 4.2 259g–259h, 4.3 383g–383h, 4.4 507g–507h
See also **Assessment.**

Textbook (as reference source). See **Reference sources.**

Textbook article. See **Genres.**

Textbook-reading techniques, 4.3 337l

Text features, 4.1 36, 62, 84, 108, 111l, 4.2 186, 210, 211l, 236, 258, 4.3 288, 310, 334, 356, 380, 4.4 412, 415l, 436, 464, 484, 504, 4.5 536, 537l, 556, 578, 604, 626, 4.6 682, 708, 734, 758

Text structure (method of presenting information), 4.1 66l–66m, 111, 4.5 582–583, 593, 595, 601, DI·36, DI·37, 4.6 660, 661, 671, 675, 679, 685, 709, DI·16, DI·17

Theme (as a story element), 4.5 582l–582m, 621, 4.6 686l–686m, 686–687, 699, 703, 711b, DI·54

Themes for teaching and learning, 4.1 16–17, 17a, 18a, 40a, 66a, 88a, 112a, 138–139, 4.2 140–141, 141a, 142a, 162a, 188a, 212a, 240a, 264–265, 4.3 266–267, 267a, 268a, 292a, 314a, 338a, 360a, 388–389, 4.4 390–391, 391a, 392a, 416a, 440a, 466a, 488a, 512–513, 4.5 514–515, 515a, 516a, 538a, 560a, 582a, 608a, 634–635, 4.6 636–637, 637a, 638a, 660a, 686a, 712a, 738a, 766–767, DI·26, DI·27

Thesaurus. *See* **Reference sources.**

Think-aloud statements. Think-alouds and teacher modeling are demonstrated throughout weekly lessons as a basic teaching strategy.

Thinking strategies. *See* **Critical thinking.**

Time line. *See* **Graphic sources.**

Time sequence. *See* **Sequence.**

Tone. *See* **Fluency, reading; Literacy devices.**

Topic, recognizing. *See* **Main idea.**

Trade books
  as reference source, 4.1 133l, 4.3 337l
  trade book library, 4.1 18i, 40i, 66i, 88i, 112i, 4.2 142i, 162i, 188i, 212i, 240i, 4.3 268i, 292i, 314i, 338i, 360i, 4.4 392i, 416i, 440i, 466i, 488i, 4.5 516i, 538i, 560i, 582i, 608i, 4.6 638i, 660i, 686i, 712i, 738i

Types of literature. *See* **Genres.**

U

Unfamiliar word meaning, 4.1 114b, 4.2 164–165, 173, 177, 187c, 214–215, 239c, 242–243, 253, 259c, 316–317, 325, 337c, 4.4 442–443, 453, 465c, 468b, 4.5 562–563, 573, 581c, 4.6 688–689, 701, 711c, 714–715, 721, 729, 737c

Unit inquiry projects. *See* **Projects.**

Usage. *See* **Adjectives, Adverbs, Conjunctions, Contractions, Nouns, Prepositions and prepositional phrases, Pronouns, Sentences, Subject/verb agreement, Verbs.**

V

Venn diagram. *See* **Graphic and semantic organizers,** types.

Verbs
  action, 4.3 291e–291f
  helping, 4.3 313e–313f
  irregular, 4.3 383e–383f
  linking, 4.3 291e–291f
  main, 4.3 313e–313f
  tense, 4.3 359e–359f
  voice, 4.3 299

Viewing
  kinds of media
    art, 4.1 65d, 4.6 685d, 711d
    illustration, 4.1 65d, 4.6 685d, 711d
    movies/video, 4.2 161d, 211d, 4.4 415d, 465d, 507d
    multimedia, 4.5 607d
    photography, 4.1 62, 111d, 133d, 4.3 359d, 380, 4.5 536, 556, 559d, 626, 4.6 711d, 761d
    print media
      illustration, 4.1 65d, 4.6 685d, 711d
      speech, 4.2 259d
  responding to media
    analyzing, 4.1 65d, 4.2 161d, 211d, 4.4 439d, 465d
    oral, 4.1 65d, 111d, 133d, 4.2 161d, 211d, 259d, 4.3 352d, 4.4 415d, 465d, 507d, 4.5 559d, 607d, 4.6 685d, 711d, 761d
    written, 4.1 111d, 4.2 259d, 4.3 359d, 4.4 465d, 4.5 559d, 607d, 4.6 685d, 761d
  uses of media
    analysis, 4.1 65d, 111d, 133d, 4.3 359d, 4.6 685d, 711d
    enjoyment, 4.2 161d, 4.3 415d, 4.4 465d, 507d
    persuasion, 4.2 259d
    research, 4.5 559d, 607d, 4.6 761d

Visualizing, 4.3 314–315, 327, 329, 331, 4.4 416–417, 429, 431, 433, 437, 4.5 516l–516m, 538–539, 549, 553, 559, DI·16, DI·17

Vocabulary development
  classifying words, 4.1 42b, 4.2 144b, 242b, 4.3 270b, 294b, 4.5 518b, 562b, 610b, 4.6 662b
  concept vocabulary, 4.1 39c, 65c, 87c, 111c, 133c, 4.2 161c, 187c, 211c, 239c, 259c, 4.3 291c, 313c, 337c, 359c, 383c, 4.4 415c, 439c, 465c, 487c, 507c, 4.5 537c, 559c, 581c, 607c, 629c, 4.6 659c, 685c, 711c, 737c, 761c
  connotation and denotation, 4.4 442b
  content-area vocabulary, 4.1 36, 62, 108, 130, 4.2 186, 210, 258, 4.3 288, 310, 340b, 354, 380, 4.4 412, 436, 464, 504, 4.5 536, 540b, 556, 584b, 604, 626, 4.6 682, 708, 758
  etymologies for meaning, 4.2 164b, 4.4 418b, 468, 479, 487c, 490b, 4.5 540–541, 547, 559, 559c, 562b, 584–585, 597, 599, 607c
  graphic organizers for grouping, studying, and retaining, 4.1 20b, 42b, 90b, 4.2 144b, 190b, 214b, 242b, 4.3 294b, 340b, 362b, 4.4 394b, 418b, 442b, 468b, 4.5 518b, 562b, 584b, 4.6 662b, 714b
  introducing selection vocabulary, 4.1 20b, 42b, 68b, 90b, 114b, 4.2 144b, 164b, 190b, 214b, 242b, 4.3 270b, 294b, 316b, 340b, 362b, 4.4 394b, 418b, 442b, 468b, 490b, 4.5 518b, 540b, 562b, 584b, 610b, 4.6 640b, 662b, 688b, 714b, 740b
  listening for vocabulary development, 4.1 18l–18m, 40l–40m, 66l–66m, 88l–88m, 112l–112m, 4.2 142l–142m, 162l–162m, 188l–188m, 212l–212m, 240l–240m, 4.3 268l–268m, 292l–292m, 314l–314m, 338l–338m, 360l–360m, 4.4 392l–392m, 416l–416m, 440l–440m, 466l–466m, 488l–488m, 4.5 516l–516m, 538l–538m, 560l–560m, 582l–582m, 608l–608m, 4.6 638l–638m, 660l–660m, 686l–686m, 712l–712m, 738l–738m
  practice lesson vocabulary, 4.1 27, 33, 53, 59, 77, 81, 99, 105, 123, 127, 4.2 151, 155, 175, 183, 201, 207, 223, 231, 251, 255, 4.3 279, 285, 303, 307, 327, 331, 349, 353, 371, 377, 4.4 403, 409, 429, 433, 451, 461, 477, 481, 497, 499, 4.5 527, 533, 549, 553, 571, 575, 593, 601, 619, 623, 4.6 649, 653, 671, 679, 697, 705, 725, 731, 751, 755

reading for vocabulary development, 4.1 20b, 42b, 68b, 90b, 114b, 4.2 144b, 164b, 190b, 214b, 242b, 4.3 270b, 294b, 316b, 340b, 362b, 4.4 394b, 418b, 442b, 468b, 490b, 4.5 518b, 540b, 562b, 584b, 610b, 4.6 640b, 662b, 688b, 714b, 740b

related words in meaning (derivatives), 4.1 87c, 4.2 190b, 4.6 740b

speaking for vocabulary development, 4.1 18l, 40l, 66l, 88l, 112l, 4.2 142l, 162l, 188l, 212l, 240l, 4.3 268l, 292l, 314l, 338l, 360l, 4.4 392l, 416l, 440l, 466l, 488l, 4.5 516l, 538l, 560l, 582l, 608l, 4.6 638l, 660l, 686l, 712l, 738l

specialized/technical words, 4.2 144b

writing vocabulary, 4.1 39g–39h, 65g, 87g, 111g, 133g, WA7, 4.2 161g–161h, 187g, 211g, 239g, 259g, WA7, 4.3 291g, 313g, 337g–337h, 359g, 383g, WA7, 4.4 415g, 439g, 465g, 487g, 507g, WA7, 4.5 537g, 559g–559h, 581g, 607g, 629g–629h, WA7, 4.6 659g, 685g, 711g, 737g, 761g, WA7

See also **Vocabulary strategies.**

Vocabulary strategies
  alphabetical order, 4.6 662b
  analogies, 4.3 270b
  antonyms, 4.2 242b, 4.4 394–395, 405, 415c, 490–491, 495, 507c
  base words, 4.5 518b
  compound words, 4.1 68b, 4.2 214b, 4.6 662b
  connotation, 4.4 442b
  context clues, 4.1 20b, 90–91, 101, 111c, 4.3 270–271, 277, 291c, 294–295, 305, 313c, 316–317, 325, 337c, 4.4 394–395, 405, 415c, 418–419, 427, 439c, 490–491, 495, 507c, 4.5 518–519, 525, 537c, 562–563, 573, 581c, 610–611, 617, 629c, 4.6 662b, 688–689, 701, 711c, 714–715, 721, 729, 737c, 740–741, 749, 761c
  dictionary/glossary, 4.1 68–69, 79, 87c, 4.2 164–165, 173, 177, 187c, 214–215, 221, 231, 239c, 242–243, 253, 259c, 4.4 442–443, 453, 457, 465c, 4.6 662–663, 669, 673, 685c
  endings, 4.1 42–43, 51, 55, 65c, 68b, 4.3 270b, 340–341, 349, 359c, 362b, 4.4 394b, 4.6 640–641, 647, 659c
  Greek and Latin roots, 4.4 418b, 468, 479, 487c, 4.5 540–541, 547, 559, 559c, 562b, 584–585, 597, 599, 607c
  homographs, 4.5 518–519, 525, 537c
  homonyms, 4.3 294–295, 305, 313c, 4.5 518–519, 525, 537c, 4.6 740–741, 749, 761c
  homophones, 4.1 42b, 4.6 688b
  multiple-meaning words, 4.1 20b, 68–69, 79, 87c, 4.2 231, 4.3 270–271, 277, 291c, 316b, 4.4 418–419, 427, 439c, 457, 4.6 640b, 662–663, 669, 673, 685c, 714b
  noun phrases, 4.3 294b
  nouns and verbs, 4.3 362b
  picture clues, 4.1 90b
  prefixes, 4.2 144–145, 151, 161c, 190–191, 199, 211c
  related words, 4.2 190b, 4.6 740b
  specialized vocabulary, 4.2 144b
  suffixes, 4.1 20–21, 29, 39c, 114–115, 121, 133c, 4.2 144b, 144–145, 151, 161c, 4.3 362–363, 375, 383c, 4.4 394b, 4.6 640b
  synonyms, 4.1 90–91, 101c, 111c, 4.4 394–395, 405, 415c, 490–491, 495, 507c, 4.5 562b, 610b, 610–611, 617, 629c
  unfamiliar words, 4.1 114b, 4.2 164–165, 173, 177, 187c, 214–215, 239c, 242–243, 253, 259c, 316–317, 325, 337c, 4.4 442–443, 453, 465c, 468b, 4.5 562–563, 573, 581c, 4.6 688–689, 701, 711c, 714–715, 721, 729, 737c
  word origins, 4.2 164b, 4.4 490b

word structure, 4.1 29, 39c, 42–43, 51, 55, 65c, 114–115, 121, 133c, 4.2 144–145, 151, 161c, 190–191, 199, 211c, 4.3 340–341, 349, 359c, 362–363, 375, 383c, 4.4 468–469, 479, 487c, 4.5 540–541, 547, 559c, 584–585, 597, 599, 607c, 4.6 640–641, 647, 659c
See also **Context clues for meaning, Vocabulary development.**

Volume. *See* **Fluency, reading.**

Web site. *See* **Genres, Technology.**

Webbing. *See* **Graphic and semantic organizers,** types.

Word attack skills. *See* **Context clues for meaning, Dictionary/glossary, Phonics, Vocabulary strategies, Word structure.**

Word histories. *See* **Vocabulary development,** etymologies for meaning.

Word identification. *See* **Context clues for meaning, Dictionary/glossary, Vocabulary strategies, Word structure.**

Word structure
  base words
    with spelling changes, 4.1 43, 55, DI·15, DI·45, 4.2 DI·4, 4.4 DI·4, 4.5 DI·14, 4.6 641, 647
    without spelling changes, 4.1 DI·14, 4.2 DI·14, DI·24, 4.4 DI·14, 4.5 DI·24, 4.6 DI·4, DI·14
  chunking, 4.1 68b, DI·1, DI·4, 4.2 144b, DI·1, DI·4, DI·44, 4.3 270b, DI·1, 4.4 394b, 419, DI·1, DI·24, DI·34, DI·44, 4.5 518b, DI·1, DI·34, 4.6 640b, DI·1, DI·24, DI·44
  compound words, 4.1 68b, DI·24, DI·34, DI·44, 4.2 214b, DI·34, 4.5 DI·4, DI·44, 4.6 662b, DI·34
  endings, inflected and uninflected, 4.1 42–43, 51, 55, 65c, 4.3 340–341, 349, 359c, 4.6 640–641, 647, 659c, DI·5, DI·14
  Greek and Latin roots, 4.4 418b, 468–469, 479, 487c, DI·35, 4.5 518b, 540–541, 547, 559, 559c, 562b, 584–585, 597, 599, 607c, DI·35
  plurals, 4.6 647
  prefixes, 4.2 144–145, 151, 161c, 190–191, 199, 211c, DI·5, DI·24, 4.6 DI·14
  root words, 4.5 547, 597
  suffixes, 4.1 20–21, 29, 39c, 114–115, 121, 133c, DI·5, DI·14, DI·15, 4.2 144–145, 151, 161c, DI·5, DI·14, 4.3 362–363, 375, 383c, 4.4 394b, DI·4, 4.5 DI·24, 4.6 DI·4
  syllabication, 4.4 419, 4.5 563
  word-learning. *See* **Vocabulary strategies.**
  See also **Spelling, Vocabulary strategies.**

Word study. *See* **Context clues for meaning, Dictionary/glossary, Vocabulary strategies, Word structure.**

Working with words. *See* **Context clues for meaning, Dictionary/Glossary, Vocabulary development, Vocabulary strategies.**

Work stations. *See* **Cross-curricular Centers.**

Writer's craft. *See* **Literary craft,** author's craft/ style/language.

Writing assessment. *See* **Assessment,** scoring guide.

Writing forms/products
  article, 4.6 757, 761g–761h
  biography, 4.6 656–657, 659g–659h
  character sketch, 4.6 707, 711g–711h
  comparison/contrast, 4.3 333, 337g–337h, WA2–WA9

description, 4.2 234–235, 239g–239h, 4.3 287, 291g–291h
editorial, 4.5 555, 559g–559h
e-mail message, 4.1 107, 111g–111h
explanatory paragraph/essay, 4.2 257, 259g–259h
fantasy, 4.3 379, 383g–383h
how-to report, 4.2 WA2–WA9
informational article, 4.6 757, 761g–761h
interview, 4.5 577, 581g–581h
invitation, 4.1 107, 111g–111h
journal, 4.1 61, 65g–65h
letter, business, 4.4 463, 465g–465h, 4.5 603, 607g–607h
letter, friendly, 4.3 309, 313g–313h
memoir, 4.1 35, 39g–39h
narrative writing, 4.1 129, 133g–133h
news article/report/story, 4.2 185, 187g–187h
note/card, 4.1 83, 87g–87h
notes, 4.6 681, 685g–685h
opinion paragraph/essay, 4.5 625, 629g–629h
outline, 4.6 733, 737g–737h
personal narrative, 4.1 WA2–WA9
persuasive argument/essay/paragraph, 4.5 WA2–WA9
play scene, 4.2 209, 11g–211h
plot summary, 4.4 502–503, 507g–507h
poem, 4.1 135, 137, 4.2 157, 161g–161h, 261, 263, 4.3 385, 387, 4.4 508, 511, 4.5 631, 633, 4.6 763, 765
problem/solution, 4.3 355, 359g–359h
research report, 4.6 WA2–WA9
response log. *See* **Logs, strategy response.**
review, 4.5 535, 537g–537h
skit, 4.2 209, 211g–211h
story, 4.4 411, 415g–415h, 483, 487g–487h, WA2–WA9
summary, 4.4 502–503, 507g–507h
travel brochure, 4.4 435, 439g–439h

Writing modes
  descriptive, 4.1 83, 87g–87h, 4.2 234–235, 239g–239h, 4.3 287, 291g–291h, 309, 313g–313h, 4.4 435, 439g–439h, 4.5 535, 537g–537h, 4.6 707, 711g–711h
  expository, 4.1 107, 111g–111h, 4.2 257, 259g–259h, WA2–WA9, 4.3 333, 337g–337h, 355, 359g–359h, WA2–WA9, 4.4 463, 465g–465h, 4.5 577, 581g–581h, 603, 607g–607h, 4.6 681, 685g–685h, 733, 737g–737h, 757, 761g–761h, WA2–WA9
  expressive, 4.1 35, 39g–39h, 61, 65g–65h, WA2–WA9, 4.2 157, 161g–161h, 209, 211g–211h, 4.3 309, 313g–313h
  narrative, 4.1 35, 39g–39h, 61, 65g–65h, WA2–WA9, 4.2 185, 187g–187h, 209, 211g–211h, 4.3 379, 383g–383h, 4.4 411, 415g–415h, 483, 487g–487h, 502–503, 507g–507h, WA2–WA9, 4.6 656–657, 659g–659h
  persuasive, 4.5 535, 537g–537h, 555, 559g–559h, 625, 629g–629h, WA2–WA9

Writing process
  assessing/scoring guide (rubric), 4.1 39h, 65h, 87h, 111h, 133h, WA7, 4.2 161h, 187h, 211h, 239h, 259h, WA7, 4.3 291h, 313h, 337h, 359h, 383h, WA7, 4.4 415h, 439h, 465h, 487h, 507h, WA7, 4.5 537h, 559h, 581h, 607h, 629h, WA7, 4.6 659h, 685h, 711h, 737h, 761h, WA7
  draft, 4.1 39h, 65h, 87h, 111h, 133h, WA4, 4.2 161h, 187h, 211h, 239h, 259h, WA4, 4.3 291h, 313h, 337h, 359h, 383h, WA4, 4.4 415h, 439h, 465h, 487h, 507h, WA4, 4.5 537h, 559h, 581h, 607h, 629h, WA4, 4.6 659h, 685h, 711h, 737h, 761h, WA4
  edit, 4.1 39h, 65h, 87h, 111h, 133h, WA6, 4.2 161h, 187h, 211h, 239h, 259h, WA6, 4.3 291h, 313h, 337h, 359h, 383h, WA6,

4.4 415h, 439h, 465h, 487h, 507h, WA6, 4.5 537h, 559h, 581h, 607h, 629h, WA6, 4.6 659h, 685h, 711h, 737h, 761h, WA6
  prewrite, 4.1 39h, 65h, 87h, 111h, 133h, WA3, 4.2 161h, 187h, 211h, 239h, 259h, WA3, 4.3 291h, 313h, 337h, 359h, 383h, WA3, 4.4 415h, 439h, 465h, 487h, 507h, WA3, 4.5 537h, 559h, 581h, 607h, 629h, WA3, 4.6 659h, 685h, 711h, 737h, 761h, WA3
  publish, 4.1 39h, 65h, 87h, 111h, WA7, 4.2 161h, 187h, 211h, 239h, WA7, 4.3 291h, 313h, 337h, 359h, 4.4 415h, 439h, 465h, 487h, WA7, 4.5 537h, 559h, 581h, 607h, WA7, 4.6 659h, 685h, 711h, 737h, WA7
  revise, 4.1 39h, 65h, 87h, 111h, 133h, WA5, 4.2 161h, 187h, 211h, 239h, 259h, WA5, 4.3 291h, 313h, 337h, 359h, 383h, WA5, 4.4 415h, 439h, 465h, 487h, 507h, WA5, 4.5 537h, 559h, 581h, 607h, 629h, WA5, 4.6 659h, 685h, 711h, 737h, 761h, WA5

Writing purpose
  clarify information, 4.3 333, 337g–337h, WA2–WA9, 4.4 435, 439g–439h, 4.5 577, 581g–581h, 4.6 733, 737g–737h
  express ideas, 4.2 234–235, 239g–239h, 4.4 463, 465g–465h, 4.5 555, 559g–559h, WA2–WA9
  respond to literature, 4.1 34, 39, 60, 65, 82, 87, 106, 111, 128, 133, 4.2 156, 161, 184, 187, 208, 211, 233, 239, 256, 259, 4.3 286, 291, 308, 313, 332, 337, 354, 359, 378, 383, 4.4 410, 415, 434, 439, 462, 465, 482, 487, 501, 502–503, 507, 4.5 534, 535, 537, 537g–537h, 554, 559, 576, 581, 602, 607, 624, 629, 4.6 655, 659, 680, 685, 706, 707, 711, 711g–711h, 732, 737, 756, 761
  share experiences, 4.1 35, 39g–39h, 61, 65g–65h, 83, 87g–87h, 129, 133g–133h, WA2–WA9, 4.3 287, 291g–291h, 309, 313g–313h
  share ideas/information, 4.1 107, 111g–111h, 4.2 185, 187g–187h, 255, 259g–259h, 355, 359g–359h, WA2–WA9, 4.4 502–503, 507g–507h, 4.5 535, 537g–537h, 4.6 681, 685g–685h, 757, 761g–761h, WA2–WA9
  share stories/poems, 4.2 157, 161g–161h, 211, 211g–211h, 4.3 379, 383g–383h, 4.4 411, 415g–415h, 483, 487g–487h, WA2–WA9, 4.6 656–657, 659g–659h, 707, 711g–711h
  specific audience, 4.1 WA2, 4.2 WA2, 4.3 WA2, 4.4 WA2, 4.5 555, 559g–559h, 603, 607g–607h, WA2, 4.6 WA2

Writing, six-trait. *See* **Six-trait writing.**

Writing strategies. *See* **Writing process.**

Writing with technology, 4.1 39h, 65h, 87h, 111h, 133h, WA6, 4.2 161h, 187h, 211h, 239h, 259h, WA6, 4.3 291h, 313h, 337h, 359h, 383h, WA6, WA7, 4.4 415h, 439h, 465h, 487h, 507h, WA6, 4.5 537h, 559h, 581h, 607h, 629h, WA6, WA7, 4.6 659h, 685h, 711h, 737h, 761h, WA6, WA7

Teacher's Edition

Text

KWL Strategy: The KWL Interactive Reading Strategy was developed and is used by permission of Donna Ogle, National-Louis University, Evanston, Illinois, co-author of *Reading Today and Tomorrow*, Holt, Rinehart & Winston Publishers, 1988. (See also *The Reading Teacher*, February 1986, pp. 564–570.)

Page 142m: From *The Circuit: Stories from the Life of a Migrant Child* by Francisco Jiménez. Copyright © 1997 by Francisco Jiménez. Reprinted by permission of the author.

Page 162m: Adapted from "A Big City Dream" (originally titled "Cleanup Day") from *The Big Idea* by Ellen Schecter; illustrated by Bob Dorsey. Copyright © 1996. Reprinted by permission of Hyperion Books for Children.

Page 188m: Adaptation of *Journal of a Teenage Genius* by Helen V. Griffith. Text copyright © 1987 by Helen. V. Griffith. Used by permission of HarperCollins Publishers.

Page 240m: Abridgement of "Welcome to Washington!" from *City! Washington, DC* by Shirley Climo, Macmillan Publishing Company, 1991. Used by permission of the author.

Artists

Tim Jessell: cover, page i

Photographs

Every effort has been made to secure permission and provide appropriate credit for photographic material. The publisher deeply regrets any omission and pledges to correct errors called to its attention in subsequent editions.

Unless otherwise acknowledged, all photographs are the property of Scott Foresman, a division of Pearson Education.

Photo locators denoted as follows: Top (T), Center (C), Bottom (B), Left (L), Right (R), Background (Bkgd)

Page 18j: Mapquest

Page 66k: Digital Wisdom, Inc.

Page 87l: ©Royalty-Free/Corbis

Page 133l: ©Royalty-Free/Corbis

Page 162m: Hemera Technologies

Page 188k: Digital Wisdom, Inc.

Page 268j: Digital Wisdom, Inc.`

Page 268m: Getty Images

Page 338m: Getty Images

Page 516m: Digital Vision

Page 608: Ultimate Symbol, Inc.

Page 685l: Getty Images

Page 712m: Getty Images

TEACHER NOTES